TRANSLATOR AND EDITOR:
Rabbi David Strauss

MANAGING EDITOR:
Baruch Goldberg

ASSOCIATE EDITOR:
Dr. Jeffrey M. Green

COPY EDITOR:
Alec Israel

BOOK DESIGNER:
Ben Gasner

GRAPHIC ARTIST:
Michael Etkin

TECHNICAL STAFF:
Muriel Stein

Random House Staff

PRODUCTION MANAGER:
Richard Elman

ART DIRECTOR:
Bernard Klein

CHIEF COPY EDITOR:
Amy Edelman

THE TALMUD

THE STEINSALTZ EDITION

VOLUME XIX

TRACTATE SANHEDRIN

PART V

VOLUME XIX
TRACTATE SANHEDRIN
PART V

RANDOM HOUSE
NEW YORK

THE TALMUD

תלמוד בבלי

THE STEINSALTZ EDITION

Commentary by Rabbi Adin Steinsaltz (Even Yisrael)

 Published in the United States by
Random House, Inc., New York, and simultaneously in Canada by
Random House of Canada Limited, Toronto.

This is an English translation of a work originally published
in Hebrew by The Israel Institute for Talmudic Publications,
Jerusalem, Israel.

Library of Congress Cataloging-in-Publication Data
(Revised for volume XIX)
The Talmud
English, Hebrew, Aramaic.
Includes bibliographical references.
Contents: v. 1. Tractate Bava metzia—
v. 19. Tractate Sanhedrin, pt. 5
Accompanied by a reference guide.
I. Title.
BM499.5.E4 1989 89-842911
ISBN 0-394-57665-9 (guide)
ISBN 0-394-57666-7 (v. 1)
ISBN 0-375-50248-3 (v. 19)

Random House website address: www.atrandom.com
Printed in the United States of America on acid-free paper

2 4 6 8 9 7 5 3

First Edition

Dedicated
in memory of

יהודה בן צבי והנדה מרל ז״ל
Leo Kaufthal

and
in honor of

תיבדל לחיים
אסתר בת מרדכי הכהן ותשנה
Edith Kahan Kaufthal

by
Linda and Ilan Kaufthal, Joshua, David and Daniel
and
Judy and Uri Kaufthal, Jonathan and Dina, Jeremy and Joshua

״הַעִדֹתִי בָכֶם הַיּוֹם אֶת הַשָּׁמַיִם וְאֶת הָאָרֶץ הַחַיִּים וְהַמָּוֶת נָתַתִּי לְפָנֶיךָ הַבְּרָכָה וְהַקְּלָלָה
וּבָחַרְתָּ בַּחַיִּים״ (דברים ל, יט)

"I call heaven and earth to witness this day that I have set before you life and death, a blessing and a curse, therefore choose life." (Deuteronomy 30:19)

Survivors of the horror of the Shoah, our father ז״ל*, together with our dear mother,* עד מאה ועשרים שנה*, chose to live.*

Our parents chose to build a new life for their families under very trying and difficult circumstances. They made great personal sacrifices, but yet we will always remember our father with a smile on his face and that special twinkle in his eye - especially when he enjoyed the company of his grandchildren.

Our father was a man of few words who, together with our mother, taught us core values of Yiddishkeit through their actions.
We also honor our mother, who selflessly devoted herself to caring for our father.

We miss our father sorely, but his impact, and the continuing influence of our mother, is felt by our entire family, each and every day. We hope to honor our father's memory, and our mother's life, through our own actions and those of our children.

The Steinsaltz Talmud in English

The English edition of the Steinsaltz Talmud is a translation and adaptation of the Hebrew edition. It includes most of the additions and improvements that characterize the Hebrew version, but it has been adapted and expanded especially for the English reader. This edition has been designed to meet the needs of advanced students capable of studying from standard Talmud editions, as well as of beginners, who know little or no Hebrew and have had no prior training in studying the Talmud.

The overall structure of the page is similar to that of the traditional pages in the standard printed editions. The text is placed in the center of the page, and alongside it are the main auxiliary commentaries. At the bottom of the page and in the margins are additions and supplements.

The original Hebrew-Aramaic text, which is framed in the center of each page, is exactly the same as that in the traditional Talmud (although material that was removed by non-Jewish censors has been restored on the basis of manuscripts and old printed editions). The main innovation is that this Hebrew-Aramaic text has been completely vocalized and punctuated, and all the terms usually abbreviated have been fully spelled out. In order to retain the connection with the page numbers of the standard editions, these are indicated at the head of every page.

We have placed a *Literal Translation* on the right-hand side of the page, and its punctuation has been introduced into the Talmud text, further helping the student to orientate himself. The *Literal Translation* is intended to help the student to learn the meaning of specific Hebrew and Aramaic words. By comparing the original text with this translation, the reader develops an understanding of the Talmudic text and can follow the words and sentences in the original. Occasionally, however, it has not been possible to present an exact literal translation of the original text, because it is so different in structure from English. Therefore we have added certain auxiliary words, which are indicated in square brackets. In other cases it would make no sense to offer a literal translation of a Talmudic idiom, so we have provided a close English equivalent of the original meaning, while a note, marked "lit.," explaining the literal meaning of the words, appears in parentheses. Our purpose in presenting this literal translation was to give the student an appreciation of the terse and enigmatic nature of the Talmud itself, before the arguments are opened up by interpretation.

Nevertheless, no one can study the Talmud without the assistance of commentaries. The main aid to understanding the Talmud provided by this edition is the *Translation and Commentary,* appearing on the left side of the page. This is Rabbi Adin Steinsaltz's highly regarded Hebrew interpretation of the Talmud, translated into English, adapted and expanded.

This commentary is not merely an explanation of difficult passages. It is an integrated exposition of the entire text. It includes a full translation of the Talmud text, combined with explanatory remarks. Where the translation in the commentary reflects the literal translation, it has been set off in bold type. It has also been given the same reference numbers that are found both in the original text and in the literal translation. Moreover, each section of the commentary begins with a few words of the Hebrew-Aramaic text. These reference numbers and paragraph headings allow the reader to move from one part of the page to another with ease.

There are some slight variations between the literal translation and the words in bold face appearing in the *Translation and Commentary.* These variations are meant to enhance understanding, for a juxtaposition of the literal translation and the sometimes freer translation in the commentary will give the reader a firmer grasp of the meaning.

The expanded *Translation and Commentary* in the left-hand column is intended to provide a conceptual understanding of the arguments of the Talmud, their form, content, context, and significance. The commentary also brings out the logic of the questions asked by the Sages and the assumptions they made.

Rashi's traditional commentary has been included in the right-hand column, under the *Literal Translation.* We have left this commentary in the traditional "Rashi script," but all quotations of the Talmud text appear in standard square type, the abbreviated expressions have all been printed in full, and Rashi's commentary is fully punctuated.

Since the *Translation and Commentary* cannot remain cogent and still encompass all the complex issues that arise in the Talmudic discussion, we have included a number of other features, which are also found in Rabbi Steinsaltz's Hebrew edition.

At the bottom of the page, under the *Translation and Commentary,* is the *Notes* section, containing additional material on issues raised in the text. These notes deepen understanding of the Talmud in various ways. Some provide a deeper and more profound analysis of the issues discussed in the text, with regard to individual points and to the development of the entire discussion. Others explain Halakhic concepts and the terms of Talmudic discourse.

The *Notes* contain brief summaries of the opinions of many of the major commentators on the Talmud, from the period after the completion of the Talmud to the present. Frequently the *Notes* offer interpretations different from that presented in the commentary, illustrating the richness and depth of Rabbinic thought.

The *Halakhah* section appears below the *Notes.* This provides references to the authoritative legal decisions reached over the centuries by the Rabbis in their discussions of the matters dealt with in the Talmud. It explains what reasons led to these Halakhic decisions and the close connection between the Halakhah today and the Talmud and its various interpreters. It should be noted that the summary of the Halakhah presented here is not meant to serve as a reference source for actual religious practice but to introduce the reader to Halakhic conclusions drawn from the Talmudic text.

English commentary and expanded translation of the text, making it readable and comprehensible

Hebrew/Aramaic text of the Talmud, fully vocalized, and punctuated

Literal translation of the Talmud text into English

TRANSLATION AND COMMENTARY

[1]**and her husband threw her a bill of divorce into her lap or into her basket**, which she was carrying on her head, [2]would you say **here, too,** that **she would not be divorced**? Surely we know that the law is that she *is* divorced in such a case, as the Mishnah (*Gittin* 77a) states explicitly!

אָמַר לֵיהּ [3]Rav Ashi **said** in reply **to** Ravina: The woman's **basket is** considered to be **at rest, and it is she who walks beneath it.** Thus the basket is considered to be a "stationary courtyard," and the woman acquires whatever is thrown into it.

MISHNAH הָיָה רוֹכֵב [4]**If a person was riding on an animal and he saw an ownerless object** lying on the ground, **and he said to another person** standing nearby, **"Give** that object **to me,"** [5]if **the other person took** the ownerless object **and said, "I have acquired it for myself,"** [6]he has **acquired it** by lifting it up, even though he was not the first to see it, and the rider has no claim to it. [7]But **if, after he gave** the object **to** the rider, the person who picked it up **said, "I acquired** the object **first,"** [8]**he** in fact **said nothing.** His words are of no effect, and the rider may keep it. Since the person walking showed no intention of acquiring the object when he originally picked it up, he is not now believed when he claims that he acquired it first. Indeed, even if we maintain that when a person picks up an ownerless object on behalf of someone else, the latter does *not* acquire it automatically, here, by *giving* the object to the rider, he makes a gift of it to the rider.

GEMARA תְּנַן הָתָם [9]**We have learned elsewhere** in a Mishnah in tractate *Pe'ah* (4:9): **"Someone who gathered *pe'ah*** — produce which by Torah law [Leviticus 23:22] is left unharvested in the corner of a field by the owner of the field, to be gleaned by the poor — **and said, 'Behold, this** *pe'ah* which I have gleaned **is** intended **for so-and-so the poor man,'** [10]**Rabbi Eliezer says:** The person who gathered the *pe'ah* **has acquired it**

בִּרְשׁוּת הָרַבִּים [1]וְזָרַק לָהּ גֵּט לְתוֹךְ חֵיקָהּ אוֹ לְתוֹךְ קַלְתָּהּ — [2]הָכָא נַמִי דְּלָא מְגָרְשָׁה? [3]אֲמַר לֵיהּ: קַלְתָּהּ מֵינָח נַיְיחָא, וְאִיהִי דְּקָא מְסַגְּיָא מִתּוּתָהּ.

משנה [4]הָיָה רוֹכֵב עַל גַּבֵּי בְהֵמָה וְרָאָה אֶת הַמְּצִיאָה, וְאָמַר לַחֲבֵירוֹ "תְּנָה לִי", [5]נְטָלָהּ וְאָמַר, "אֲנִי זָכִיתִי בָּהּ", [6]זָכָה בָּהּ. [7]אִם, מִשֶּׁנְּתָנָהּ לוֹ, אָמַר, "אֲנִי זָכִיתִי בָּהּ תְּחִלָּה", [8]לֹא אָמַר כְּלוּם.

גמרא [9]תְּנַן הָתָם: "מִי שֶׁלִּיקֵּט אֶת הַפֵּאָה וְאָמַר, 'הֲרֵי זוֹ לִפְלוֹנִי עָנִי', [10]רַבִּי אֱלִיעֶזֶר

LITERAL TRANSLATION

in a public thoroughfare [1]and [her husband] threw her a bill of divorce into her lap or into her basket, [2]here, too, would she not be divorced?

[3]He said to him: Her basket is at rest, and it is she who walks beneath it.

MISHNAH [4][If a person] was riding on an animal and he saw a found object, and he said to another person, "Give it to me," [5][and the other person] took it and said, "I have acquired it," [6]he has acquired it. [7]If, after he gave it to him, he said, "I acquired it first," [8]he said nothing.

GEMARA [9]We have learned there: "Someone who gathered *pe'ah* and said, 'Behold this is for so-and-so the poor man,' [10]Rabbi Eliezer says:

RASHI

קלתה – סל שעל ראשה, שנותנת בה כלי מלאכתה וטווי שלה. הכי נמי דלא הוי גיטא – והאנן תנן במסכת גיטין (עז,א): זרק לה גיטה לתוך חיקה או לתוך קלתה – הרי זו מגורשת!

משנה לא אמר כלום – דאפילו אמרינן המגביה מציאה לחבירו לא קנה חבירו, כיון דיהבה ליה – קנייה ממה נפשך. אי קנייה קמא דלא מתכוין להקנות לחבירו – הא יהבה ניהליה במתנה. ואי לא קנייה קמא משום דלא היה מתכוין לקנות – הויא ליה הפקר עד דמטא לידיה דהאי, וקנייה האי במאי דעקרה מידיה דקמא לשם קנייה.

גמרא מי שליקט את הפאה – אדם בעלמא שאינו בעל שדה. דאי בבעל שדה – לא אמר רבי אליעזר זכה. דליכא למימר "מגו דזכי לנפשיה", דאפילו הוא עני מוזהר הוא שלא ללקט פאה משדה שלו, כדאמר בשחיטת חולין (קלא,ב): "לא תלקט לעני" – להזהיר עני על שלו.

Hebrew commentary of Rashi, the classic explanation that accompanies all editions of the Talmud

REALIA

קַלְתָּה **Her basket.** The source of this word is the Greek κάλαθος, kalathos, and it means a basket with a narrow base.

Illustration from a Greek drawing depicting such a basket of fruit.

CONCEPTS

פֵּאָה ***Pe'ah.* One of the presents left for the poor (מַתְּנוֹת עֲנִיִּים).** The Torah forbids harvesting "the corners of your field," so that the produce left standing may be harvested and kept by the poor (Leviticus 19:9).
The Torah did not specify a minimum amount of produce to be left as *pe'ah*. But the Sages stipulated that it must be at least one-sixtieth of the crop.
Pe'ah is set aside only from crops that ripen at one time and are harvested at one time. The poor are allowed to use their own initiative to reap the *pe'ah* left in the fields. But the owner of an orchard must see to it that each of the poor gets a fixed share of the *pe'ah* from places that are difficult to reach. The poor come to collect *pe'ah* three times a day. The laws of *pe'ah* are discussed in detail in tractate *Pe'ah*.

Marginal notes provide essential background information

Numbers link the three main sections of the page and allow readers to refer rapidly from one to the other

NOTES

מִי שֶׁלִּיקֵּט אֶת הַפֵּאָה **If a person gathered *pe'ah*.** According to *Rashi*, the Mishnah must be referring to someone other than the owner of the field. By Torah law the owner of a field is required to separate part of his field as *pe'ah*, even if he himself is poor, and he may not take the *pe'ah* for himself. Therefore the "since" (מִגּוֹ) argument

Notes highlight points of interest in the text and expand the discussion by quoting other classical commentaries

HALAKHAH

קַלְתָּה **A woman's basket.** "If a man throws a bill of divorce into a container that his wife is holding, she thereby acquires the bill of divorce and the divorce takes effect." (*Shulḥan Arukh, Even HaEzer* 139:10.)

הַמְלַקֵּט פֵּאָה עֲבוּר אַחֵר **A person who gathered *pe'ah* for someone else.** "If a poor person, who is himself entitled to collect *pe'ah*, gathered *pe'ah* for another poor person, and said, 'This *pe'ah* is for X, the poor person,' he acquires the *pe'ah* on behalf of that other poor person. But if the person who collected the *peah* was wealthy, he does not acquire the *pe'ah* on behalf of the poor person. He must give it instead to the first poor person who appears in the field," following the opinion of the Sages, as explained by Rabbi Yehoshua ben Levi. (*Rambam, Sefer Zeraim, Hilkhot Mattenot Aniyyim* 2:19.)

On the outer margin of the page, factual information clarifying the meaning of the Talmudic discussion is presented. Entries under the heading *Language* explain unusual terms, often borrowed from Greek, Latin, or Persian. *Sages* gives brief biographies of the major figures whose opinions are presented in the Talmud. *Terminology* explains the terms used in the Talmudic discussion. *Concepts* gives information about fundamental Halakhic principles. *Background* provides historical, geographical, and other information needed to understand the text. *Realia* explains the artifacts mentioned in the text. These notes are sometimes accompanied by illustrations.

The best way of studying the Talmud is the way in which the Talmud itself evolved - a combination of frontal teaching and continuous interaction between teacher and pupil, and between pupils themselves.

This edition is meant for a broad spectrum of users, from those who have considerable prior background and who know how to study the Talmud from any standard edition to those who have never studied the Talmud and do not even know Hebrew.

The division of the page into various sections is designed to enable students of every kind to derive the greatest possible benefit from it.

For those who know how to study the Talmud, the book is intended to be a written Gemara lesson, so that, either alone, with partners, or in groups, they can have the sense of studying with a teacher who explains the difficult passages and deepens their understanding both of the development of the dialectic and also of the various approaches that have been taken by the Rabbis over the centuries in interpreting the material. A student of this kind can start with the Hebrew-Aramaic text, examine Rashi's commentary, and pass on from there to the expanded commentary. Afterwards the student can turn to the Notes section. Study of the *Halakhah* section will clarify the conclusions reached in the course of establishing the Halakhah, and the other items in the margins will be helpful whenever the need arises to clarify a concept or a word or to understand the background of the discussion.

For those who do not possess sufficient knowledge to be able to use a standard edition of the Talmud, but who know how to read Hebrew, a different method is proposed. Such students can begin by reading the Hebrew-Aramaic text and comparing it immediately to the *Literal Translation*. They can then move over to the *Translation and Commentary*, which refers both to the original text and to the *Literal Translation*. Such students would also do well to read through the *Notes* and choose those that explain matters at greater length. They will benefit, too, from the terms explained in the side margins.

The beginner who does not know Hebrew well enough to grapple with the original can start with the *Translation and Commentary*. The inclusion of a translation within the commentary permits the student to ignore the *Literal Translation*, since the commentary includes both the Talmudic text and an interpretation of it. The beginner can also benefit from the *Notes*, and it is important for him to go over the marginal notes on the concepts to improve his awareness of the juridical background and the methods of study characteristic of this text.

Apart from its use as study material, this book can also be useful to those well versed in the Talmud, as a source of additional knowledge in various areas, both for understanding the historical and archeological background and also for an explanation of words and concepts. The general reader, too, who might not plan to study the book from beginning to end, can find a great deal of interesting material in it regarding both the spiritual world of Judaism, practical Jewish law, and the life and customs of the Jewish people during the thousand years (500 B.C.E.-500 C.E.) of the Talmudic period.

Contents

THE STEINSALTZ TALMUD IN ENGLISH	IX
INTRODUCTION TO CHAPTER EIGHT	1
CHAPTER EIGHT	3
CONCLUSION TO CHAPTER EIGHT	83
INTRODUCTION TO CHAPTER NINE	85
CHAPTER NINE	87
CONCLUSION TO CHAPTER NINE	183
LIST OF SOURCES	185

THE TALMUD

THE STEINSALTZ EDITION

VOLUME XIX

TRACTATE SANHEDRIN

PART V

Introduction to Chapter Eight

בֵּן סוֹרֵר וּמוֹרֶה

"If a man have a stubborn and rebellious son, who does not obey the voice of his father, or the voice of his mother, and when they have chastened him, will not hearken to them; then shall his father and his mother lay hold on him, and bring him out to the elders of his city, and to the gate of his place; and they shall say to the elders of his city, 'this our son is stubborn and rebellious, he will not obey our voice — he is a glutton and a drunkard.' And all the men of his city shall stone him with stones that he die: so shall you put evil away from among you; and all Israel shall hear and fear." (Deuteronomy 21:18-21.)

"If a thief be found while tunneling, and he be smitten that he die, no blood shall be shed for him. If the sun be risen on him, there shall be blood shed for him; for he shall make full restitution; if he have nothing then he shall be sold for his theft." (Exodus 22:1-2.)

"But if a man find a betrothed damsel in the field, and the man force her and lie with her: then the man only that lay with her shall die. But to the damsel you shall do nothing: there is in the damsel no sin worthy of death: for as when a man rise against his neighbor and slay him, even so is this matter. For he found her in the field, and the betrothed damsel cried, and there was none to save her." (Deuteronomy 22:25-27.)

The disobedient and rebellious son is sentenced to stoning, so this discussion properly belongs to that of transgressors who are stoned in Chapter Seven. However, a special chapter is devoted to this matter because of the great difference between the laws governing the disobedient and rebellious son and other transgressors subject to capital punishment. Ordinarily people are punished for committing some transgression for the sake of either retribution or atonement, and the transgression of the disobedient and rebellious son, according to all opinions, is not so grave as to require the death penalty. The Sages explained that indeed the disobedient and rebellious son is not punished for sins that he has committed, but rather he is executed in his youth because his deeds prove that he is pursuing a course that is becoming ever worse and more flawed, until in the end he will constitute a danger for the entire community. From that point of view, the punishment of the disobedient and rebellious son is preemptive, for the improvement of the society and of himself. According to Rabbinical tradition, the details of the laws governing the disobedient and rebellious son are interpreted in such restrictive fashion that, legally speaking, no one would ever be prosecuted for being a disobedient and rebellious son, or it would be the rarest possible case imaginable. Nevertheless the clarification of these Halakhot are of fundamental importance for their own sake and for other matters: thus we have instruction and interpretation regarding how to relate to these questions, even if such a judgment is never in fact carried out. Moreover, this matter serves as the basis for several other problems, and it shows that there is a place in the Halakhah for extremely severe punishments, not directly proportionate to the gravity of the transgression. Rather these punishments are imposed for the general good, in order to prevent more severe sins.

The Biblical injunction, "and you shall remove the evil from among you," contains the principle that connects the other laws in this chapter with the matter of the disobedient and rebellious son. The Halakhot in this chapter, such as the laws governing a burglar entering in secret, share the assumption that if certain people have proven by their actions that they are liable to endanger the public or to commit severe transgressions, the court, and, with its authority, individuals as well, have the right to see to the extirpation of evil before it is carried out.

Clearly the possibility of preemptive punishment before a sin is committed is liable to be dangerous for society, and it must be exercised with great caution. Indeed, this chapter deals not only with the laws governing various rebellious individuals, but also to a great extent with clarifying and extending the restrictions imposed by the Torah on their punishment.

LITERAL TRANSLATION

MISHNAH [1]A stubborn and rebellious son — [2]from when does he become a stubborn and rebellious son? [3]From the time he produces two hairs, and until a beard grows — [4]the lower one, and not the upper one, [5]for the Sages spoke in modest (lit., "clean") language. [6]As it is stated: "If a man have a [stubborn and rebellious] son." [7]"A son" — and not a daughter, [8]"a son" — and not a man. [9]A minor is exempt, for he has not come within the category of commandments.

GEMARA [10]A minor — from where do we [know] that he is exempt?

[11]From where? [12]As it states the reason: "For he has not come under the category of commandments"! [13]And moreover, where do we find that Scripture punished [a minor],

בֵּן

[1]סוֹרֵר וּמוֹרֶה — [2]מֵאֵימָתַי נַעֲשֶׂה בֵּן סוֹרֵר וּמוֹרֶה? [3]מִשֶּׁיָּבִיא שְׁתֵּי שְׂעָרוֹת, וְעַד שֶׁיַּקִּיף זָקָן — [4]הַתַּחְתּוֹן וְלֹא הָעֶלְיוֹן, [5]אֶלָּא שֶׁדִּבְּרוּ חֲכָמִים בְּלָשׁוֹן נְקִיָּה. [6]שֶׁנֶּאֱמַר: "כִּי יִהְיֶה לְאִישׁ בֵּן". [7]"בֵּן" — וְלֹא בַת, [8]"בֵּן" — וְלֹא אִישׁ. [9]קָטָן פָּטוּר, שֶׁלֹּא בָּא לִכְלַל מִצְוֹת.

גמרא [10]קָטָן מְנָלַן דְּפָטוּר? [11]מְנָלַן? [12]כִּדְקָתָנֵי טַעְמָא: "שֶׁלֹּא בָּא לִכְלַל מִצְוֹת"! [13]וְתוּ: הֵיכָא אַשְׁכַּחַן דְּעָנַשׁ הַכָּתוּב,

TRANSLATION AND COMMENTARY

MISHNAH בֵּן סוֹרֵר [1]We learned in the previous chapter that **a rebellious son** is liable to be punished by stoning. [2]Our Mishnah asks: **From what age** and until when **can** he become liable to receive the punishment of **a rebellious son?** [3]The Mishnah answers: **From the time** he turns thirteen and **produces two** pubic **hairs,** at which time he is considered an adult and subject to punishment, **and until** his **beard grows.** [4]When the Mishnah speaks here of a beard, it refers to **the lower** beard (pubic hair) **and not the upper** beard (facial hair). Why, then, did the Mishnah use the term "beard"? [5]**Because the Sages spoke euphemistically.** [6]The definition of a rebellious son is derived from **the verse** that **states** (Deuteronomy 21:18): **"If a man has a stubborn and rebellious son."** [7]The word **"son"** teaches that only a son is affected by this law, **and not a daughter.** [8]It also teaches that he can only become liable if he is still **"a son," and not** yet **a man;** and once a boy's pubic hair covers the pubic area, he is regarded as a man. [9]**A minor** under the age of thirteen who has not grown two pubic hairs **is exempt** from punishment as a rebellious son, **for he has not** yet **reached** the age of criminal **responsibility.**

GEMARA קָטָן מְנָלַן [10]The Gemara asks: **From where do we know that a minor is exempt** from punishment as a rebellious son?

מְנָלַן [11]The Gemara asks in astonishment: What is meant by the question: **From where** do we know that a minor is exempt from punishment as a rebellious son? [12]Surely the Mishnah itself **states the reason** for this exemption: "A minor is exempt, **because he has not** yet **reached** the age of criminal **responsibility**"! [13]**Moreover, where do we find that Scripture punishes a minor** for

RASHI

משנה בן סורר ומורה וכו׳ — סדר נסקלין דתנים בפרקין דלעיל מסיים הלכותיו ואזיל. משיביא שתי שערות — אבל מקמי הכי לא מיענש, כדמפרש ואזיל שעדיין לא בא לכלל מלות. עד שיקיף זקן — שיהא זקן מוקף שער סביב כולו. התחתון ולא העליון — לא זקן ממש אלא זקן אותו המקום, אלא שדברו חכמים בלשון נקיה. שנאמר בן ולא איש — וזה משהקיף זקן איש הוא — ואף על גב דבן מקטנותו קרוי בן לא מלינן לחיוביה מקמי שיביא שתי שערות דקטן פטור שלא בא לכלל מלות הלכך חיוביה בתר הכי הוא, ואף על גב דמכי מייתי שתי שערות לענין כל התורה איש הוי, מיהו כי מיעטיה קרא לאו בתחלת אישותו קא ממעט כדמפרש בגמרא: בן הסמוך לגבורתו של איש, אלמא בתחלת אישותו חייביה קרא.

גמרא היכא אשכחן — בשאר עונשין דענש הכתוב את הקטן דהכא בעי קרא למיפטריה.

NOTES

שֶׁדִּבְּרוּ חֲכָמִים בְּלָשׁוֹן נְקִיָּה **For the Sages spoke in clean language.** There is an extensive discussion in the beginning of tractate *Pesaḥim* regarding the "clean language" that was used by the Rabbis. It is shown there that the Torah itself used "clean language." The Rabbis referred euphemistically not only to sexual organs and activities, but also to other subjects which that they viewed as undignified, such as pigs and leprosy.

הֵיכָא אַשְׁכַּחַן דְּעָנַשׁ הַכָּתוּב? **Where do we find that Scripture punished a minor?** *Ran* asks: How is this argument

HALAKHAH

מֵאֵימָתַי נַעֲשֶׂה בֵּן סוֹרֵר וּמוֹרֶה? **From when does he become a stubborn and rebellious son?** "The law regarding a rebellious son applies only to a boy who has reached the age of thirteen and produced two pubic hairs, before his pubic beard has sufficiently grown to cover the pubic area," following the Mishnah. (*Ramban, Sefer Shofetim, Hilkhot Mamrim* 7:5.)

"בֵּן" — וְלֹא בַת **"A son" — and not a daughter.** "The Torah decreed that a rebellious son is liable to the punishment of stoning, but a daughter is not governed by this law, for it is not her way to eat and drink gluttonously like a man." (*Ramban, Sefer Shofetim, Hilkhot Mamrim* 7:11.)

[1]דְּהָכָא לִיבָּעֵי קְרָא לְמִיפְטְרֵיהּ? [2]אֲנַן הָכִי קָאָמְרִינַן: [3]אַטּוּ בֵּן סוֹרֵר וּמוֹרֶה עַל חֶטְאוֹ נֶהֱרָג? [4]עַל שֵׁם סוֹפוֹ נֶהֱרָג, [5]וְכֵיוָן דְּעַל שֵׁם סוֹפוֹ נֶהֱרָג — [6]אֲפִילּוּ קָטָן נַמִי. [7]וְעוֹד: ״בֵּן״, וְלֹא אִישׁ, קָטָן מַשְׁמַע.

[8]אָמַר רַב יְהוּדָה אָמַר רַב: [9]דְּאָמַר קְרָא: ״וְכִי יִהְיֶה לְאִישׁ בֵּן״ — [10]״בֵּן״ הַסָּמוּךְ לִגְבוּרָתוֹ שֶׁל אִישׁ.

[11]״וְעַד שֶׁיַּקִּיף זָקָן הַתַּחְתּוֹן כו׳״. [12]תָּנֵי רַבִּי חִיָּיא: ״עַד שֶׁיַּקִּיף עֲטָרָה״.

[13]כִּי אֲתָא רַב דִּימִי אֲמַר:

LITERAL TRANSLATION

[1]so that here a verse is needed to exempt him? [2]We said as follows: [3]Is a stubborn and rebellious son put to death on account of his sin? [4]He is put to death on account of his future. [5]And since he is put to death on account of his future, [6]even a minor as well! [7]And moreover, "A son," and not a man, implies a minor!

[8]Rav Yehudah said in the name of Rav: [9]For the verse states: "If a man has a son" — [10]"a son" who is close to the strength of a man.

[11]"And until a beard grows, the lower one, etc." [12]Rabbi Ḥiyya taught: "Until it encircles like a wreath."

[13]When Rav Dimi came, he said:

TRANSLATION AND COMMENTARY

his wrongdoing, [1]so that we should need a special verse to exempt him here from the punishment prescribed for a rebellious son?

אֲנַן [2]The Gemara responds: When we raised a question, we meant to ask as follows: [3]Is a rebellious son put to death for a sin which he already committed? [4]Rather, he is put to death for what he would do in the future were he allowed to live. His current conduct shows that he will bring his parents to financial ruin and then become a robber and a murderer. [5]And since he is put to death for deeds in the future, [6]there is reason to think that even a minor should be included in the law concerning a rebellious son. [7]Moreover, the restrictive interpretation of the verse, from which we learn that a boy can only become liable for this crime if he is still "a son," and not yet a man, implies that even a minor is included in the law.

אָמַר רַב יְהוּדָה [8]Rav Yehudah said in the name of Rav: [9]A minor is excluded from the law concerning a rebellious son because of the verse that states (Deuteronomy 21:18): "If a man has a son." The Hebrew — וְכִי יִהְיֶה לְאִישׁ בֵּן — can also be understood as: "If a son becomes a man," [10]implying that the law concerning a rebellious son applies only to a boy who is nearly as strong as a full-grown man, meaning that he has reached the age of thirteen and produced two pubic hairs, which would rule out a minor.

וְעַד [11]We have learned in the Mishnah: "A boy can become a rebellious son from when he turns thirteen and produces two pubic hairs, and until the time that his beard grows — his lower beard (his pubic hair)." [12]Rabbi Ḥiyya taught a related Baraita: "A boy can be considered a rebellious son only until his pubic hair encircles his genitals like a wreath."

כִּי אֲתָא [13]When Rav Dimi came to Babylonia from Eretz Israel, he said: When the Baraita speaks about

RASHI

אטו בן סורר ומורה על שם חטאו נהרג — דנבעי בר עונשין, וכי מה חטא שיהרג מפני שאכל תרטימר בשר ושתה חצי לוג יין — ועל שם סופו נהרג כדמפרש בשלהי פרקין סנהדרין (עב,א): סוף שמגמר נכסי אביו ומבקש למודו ואינו מוצא וכו׳ אמרה תורה מוטב ימות זכאי ולא ימות חייב. וכי יהיה לאיש בן סורר ומורה — לכשיגיע לכלל איש הבן הזה קורא לו הכתוב בן סורר ומורה. תני רבי חייא — במתניתיה הכי, משיביא שתי שערות עד שיקיף זקן — עד שיקיף עטרה. כי אתא רב דימי — פרשה, דהא דתנא עד שיקיף עטרה לאשמועינן דהקפת זקן התחתון דקתני מתניתין הקפת גיד קאמר סמוך לביצים, ולא הקפת הכיס של ביצים דהוו לבתר הכי טובא.

SAGES

רַבִּי חִיָּיא Rabbi Ḥiyya. One of the last of the Tannaim and a student and colleague of Rabbi Yehudah HaNasi. See *Sanhedrin*, Part I, pp. 37-9.

רַב דִּימִי Rav Dimi. An Amora of the third and fourth generations. See *Sanhedrin*, Part I, p. 67.

NOTES

different from the first argument? Surely the Torah does not punish a minor for his transgressions since he has not reached the age of criminal responsibility. *Ran* answers that, although a minor is not criminally responsible for his actions, he might be liable to be executed as a rebellious son as a deterrent. Thus, the Gemara argues that we do not find anywhere else that a minor is executed for wrongdoing as a deterrent against others.

כִּי יִהְיֶה לְאִישׁ בֵּן If a man has a son. *Rabbenu Ḥananel* and *Ramah* had a slightly different reading and interpretation of this passage: "That is needed for what Rav Yehudah said in the name of Rav! If so, let the verse state: 'A son who is a man [בֵּן אִישׁ]' — which would imply that the son himself must be a man, thus excluding a minor. What is [meant by]: 'To a man a son [לְאִישׁ בֵּן]' — which implies that the word 'man' refers to the father, thus excluding a son born to a minor? Infer from this according to Rav Ḥisda. If so, let the verse state: 'If there be a son to a man [כִּי יִהְיֶה בֵּן לְאִישׁ]' — for if the word 'man' refers to the father, then the word 'son' should have been written first. This shows that the focus of the passage is on the son, and not on the father. What is [meant by]: 'If a man has a son [כִּי יִהְיֶה לְאִישׁ בֵּן]'? Infer from this two [things]."

TRANSLATION AND COMMENTARY

the boy's pubic hair encircling his genitals, it is referring to a growth of **hair around his penis,** [1]**and not** to a growth of **hair** all **around his scrotum,** which occurs later in his physical development.

אָמַר רַב חִסְדָּא [2]**Rav Ḥisda said:** If it happened that a **minor fathered a son, that son cannot** later **become a rebellious son,** [3]**for the verse states** (Deuteronomy 21:18): **"If a man has a son,"** [4]implying that the law concerning a rebellious son applies to **a son** who was born **to a** full-grown **man, and not** to **a son** who was born **to** someone who was himself still only **a son.**

הַאי מִיבָּעֵי לֵיהּ [5]The Gemara challenges this use of the verse: Surely **that** verse **is needed** to prove that the law regarding a rebellious son does not apply to a minor, **as was argued by Rav Yehudah in the name of Rav.** According to that interpretation the word אִישׁ, "man," refers to the son and not to the father!

אִם כֵּן [6]The Gemara responds: **If** it were **so,** that **the verse** teaches only that a minor is not governed by the law concerning a rebellious son, then it **should have stated: "If there be a son to a man** [כִּי יִהְיֶה בֵּן לְאִישׁ]," which could also have been understood as: "If a son becomes a man," ruling out a minor. [7]**What** did the verse mean when it stated: **"If a man has a son** [כִּי יִהְיֶה לְאִישׁ בֵּן]"? [8]**Infer from this as Rav Ḥisda** said, that the word אִישׁ, "man," refers to the father, and not to the son. Thus if a minor fathered a son, that son cannot later become a rebellious son, even though the man who was a minor when his son was born will be an adult when that son reaches sexual maturity.

וְאֵימָא [9]The Gemara pushes Rav Ḥisda's argument one step further: **But say,** then, **that** the verse **came exclusively** to teach us **that** a son born to a minor cannot later become a rebellious son!

אִם כֵּן [10]The Gemara answers: **If** it were **so,** that **the verse** teaches only that a son born to a minor cannot later become a rebellious son, then it **should have stated: "The son of a man** [בֶּן אִישׁ]," limiting the law to the son born to a full-grown man, to the exclusion of a son born to a minor. [11]**What** did the verse mean when it stated: **"To a man a son** [לְאִישׁ בֵּן]"? Why does the word "man" precede the word "son," thus requiring the insertion of the letter *lamed*? [12]**Infer from this two laws:** A minor is excluded from the law regarding a rebellious son, as was argued by Rav Yehudah in the name of Rav, following the understanding, "If a son becomes a man." And a son born to a minor is excluded from the law regarding a rebellious son, as was argued by Rav Ḥisda, following the understanding of, "If a man has a son."

הַקָּפַת גִּיד, [1]וְלֹא הַקָּפַת בֵּיצִים.

[2]אָמַר רַב חִסְדָּא: קָטָן שֶׁהוֹלִיד — אֵין בְּנוֹ נַעֲשֶׂה בֵּן סוֹרֵר וּמוֹרֶה, [3]שֶׁנֶּאֱמַר: "כִּי יִהְיֶה לְאִישׁ בֵּן", [4]לְאִישׁ בֵּן, וְלֹא לְבֵן בֵּן.

[5]הַאי מִיבָּעֵי לֵיהּ לְכִדְרַב יְהוּדָה אָמַר רַב!

[6]אִם כֵּן לֵימָא קְרָא: "כִּי יִהְיֶה בֵּן לְאִישׁ", [7]מַאי כִּי יִהְיֶה לְאִישׁ בֵּן? [8]שְׁמַע מִינָּהּ לְכִדְרַב חִסְדָּא.

[9]וְאֵימָא כּוּלֵּיהּ לְהָכִי הוּא דַּאֲתָא!

[10]אִם כֵּן נֵימָא קְרָא: "בֵּן אִישׁ", [11]מַאי "לְאִישׁ בֵּן"? [12]שְׁמַע מִינָּהּ תַּרְתֵּי.

LITERAL TRANSLATION

[Hair] around the penis, [1]and not [hair] around the scrotum.

[2]Rav Ḥisda said: If a minor fathered [a son], his son cannot become a stubborn and rebellious son, [3]for it is stated: "If a man has a son" — [4]a son to a man, and not a son to a son.

[5]That is needed for that which Rav Yehudah said in the name of Rav!

[6]If so, let the verse state: "If there be a son to a man." [7]What is [meant by]: "If a man have a son"? [8]Infer from this like that of Rav Ḥisda.

[9]But say that it came entirely for that!

[10]If so, let the verse state: "The son of a man." [11]What is [meant by]: "To a man a son"? [12]Infer from this two [things].

RASHI

רב חסדא — סבר קטן שלא הביא שתי שערות מוליד. לכדרב יהודה — דאמר האי לאיש דבן סורר ומורה עצמו קאי, והכי קאמר: כשיהיה הבן לאיש, כלומר כשיגיע לכלל אישות. הכי גרסינן: אם כן לימא קרא בן לאיש — דמשמע שפיר דהכי קאמר: כי יהיה הבן לכלל איש. מאי כי יהיה לאיש בן — השתא משמע כשיהיה לאיש בן, דהאי איש אאבות קאי, ולמעוטי דבנו של קטן פטור לעולם. ואימא כוליה — האי קרא לכדרב חסדא הוא דאתי למעוטי בנו של קטן אבל קטן עצמו מיחייב דהא בן כתיב, וסמוך לגבורתו של איש מנא לן. הכי גרסינן: אם כן לימא קרא כי יהיה בן איש — אם כן דכוליה אאבות קאי לא לכתוב ביה למ״ד אלא וכי יהיה בן איש סורר ומורה, דמשמע בנו של איש ולא בנו של קטן. מאי — וכי יהיה לאיש למה הקדים לאיש ברישא והוצרך להטיל בו למ״ד. שמע מינה תרתי — משום דהשתא משמע הכי ומשמע הכי, כי יהיה בן לאיש — כשיגיע לגבורתו של איש, ומשתמע נמי אאבוה, כי יהיה לאיש גדול בן, ולא שיהיה לקטן בן.

HALAKHAH

הַקָּפַת גִּיד **Hair around the penis.** "The law regarding a rebellious son no longer applies once the boy's pubic hair surrounds his penis," following Rav Dimi. (*Ramban, Sefer Shofetim, Hilkhot Mamrim* 7:5.)

SAGES

רַב יְהוּדָה **Rav Yehudah (bar Yeḥezkel).** The name Rav Yehudah without any patronymic in the Gemara refers to Rav Yehudah bar Yeḥezkel, one of the greatest Babylonian Amoraim of the second generation. He was the founder of the Pumbedita Yeshivah. According to tradition he was born on the day Rabbi Yehudah died (*Kiddushin* 72b). His father, Rav Yeḥezkel, was an Amora of the first generation, and Rami bar Yeḥezkel was his brother. He studied under Rav and Shmuel, and Shmuel used to call him שִׁינְנָא — "the sharp-witted one." Rav Sheshet was his colleague, and among his students were Rabbah, Rav Yosef, Rabbi Zera and others. Eretz Israel was very dear to him, but he nevertheless strongly opposed the immigration of his students to Eretz Israel. The Hebrew language was very dear to him, and he used it frequently.

רַב **Rav.** This is Rav Abba bar Aivo, the greatest of the first generation of Babylonian Amoraim. Rav was born in Babylonia to a prominent family which had produced many Sages and was descended from King David. He immigrated to Eretz Israel with the family of his uncle, Rabbi Ḥiyya, and studied Torah there, mainly from Rabbi Yehudah HaNasi. Rav was appointed to Rabbi Yehudah's court and remained in Eretz Israel for some time before returning to Babylonia, where he settled. Rav founded the great yeshivah in Sura, raising the level of Torah study in Babylonia to that of Eretz Israel. After some time he was acknowledged as the chief Torah Sage in Eretz Israel as well.

Rav's closest friend and his opponent in Halakhic discussions was Shmuel, and their controversies are recorded throughout the Talmud. In matters of ritual law the Halakhah follows Rav, and in civil matters it follows Shmuel.

רַב חִסְדָּא **Rav Ḥisda.** Considered among the greatest Babylonian Amoraim of the second generation, Rav Ḥisda, a priest, was one of Rav's younger students. After Rav's death he remained a colleague and student of Rav's

¹וּפְלִיגָא דְּרַבָּה, ²דְּאָמַר רַבָּה: קָטָן אֵינוֹ מוֹלִיד, ³שֶׁנֶּאֱמַר: "וְאִם אֵין לָאִישׁ גֹּאֵל", ⁴וְכִי יֵשׁ לְךָ אָדָם בְּיִשְׂרָאֵל שֶׁאֵין לוֹ גּוֹאֵל? ⁵אֶלָּא בְּגֶזֶל הַגֵּר הַכָּתוּב מְדַבֵּר, [69A] ⁶וְאָמַר רַחֲמָנָא: "אִישׁ". ⁷אִישׁ, אַתָּה צָרִיךְ לַחֲזוֹר עָלָיו אִם יֵשׁ לוֹ גּוֹאֲלִין וְאִם לָאו. ⁸קָטָן, אִי אַתָּה צָרִיךְ לַחֲזוֹר עָלָיו, ⁹בְּיָדוּעַ שֶׁאֵין לוֹ גּוֹאֲלִין.

LITERAL TRANSLATION

¹And this is in disagreement with Rabbah, ²for Rabbah said: A minor cannot father [a child], ³for it is stated: "But if a man has no kinsman." ⁴But is there a man in Israel who has no kinsman? ⁵Rather, Scripture refers to the robbery of a convert. [69A] ⁶And the Torah (lit., "the Merciful One") said: "A man." ⁷[Regarding] a man, you are required to investigate him whether he has kinsmen or not. ⁸[But regarding] a minor, you are not required to investigate him, ⁹for it is known that he does not have kinsmen.

TRANSLATION AND COMMENTARY

וּפְלִיגָא ¹Moreover, **this** ruling by Rav Ḥisda **is in disagreement with** the position of **Rabbah, for** it is based on the assumption that a minor can indeed father a child, and **Rabbah said:** ²**A minor cannot father a child.** Rabbah reaches this conclusion from the Torah passage dealing with robbery, which teaches that if a robber denies his crime under oath, and later confesses, he must repay the owner or his heir the value of the stolen article, and also pay him an additional fifth of the article's value, and bring a guilt-offering. ³**A verse** in that passage **states** (Numbers 5:8): **"But if the man has no kinsman** to whom restitution may be made for the trespass, let the trespass which is recompensed to the Lord, be the priest's." ⁴At first glance this verse is problematic, for **is there a man in Israel who has no kinsman** who will succeed to his estate? Since all Jews are related to all other Jews through the Patriarch Jacob, any Jew can inherit from another Jew who is not survived by a closer relative. ⁵**Rather, Scripture** must be **referring** here **to property** that was **robbed from a convert.** According to Torah law, a convert is like a newborn child, with no ties to his natural parents or relatives. This verse teaches that if a person robs a convert and denies the crime under oath, and the convert dies without children, and the robber subsequently confesses to his crime, he must then return the object, or its value, and an additional fifth, to the priests. [69A] ⁶Now **the Torah said:** "But if *the man* has no kinsman," rather than: "But if *he* have no kinsman." The wording here is precise. The stolen property is only given to the priests if the convert has no kinsman. Therefore, an investigation must be held to determine whether, after his conversion, the convert had a child who would now inherit his estate. ⁷The word "man" teaches that it is only **regarding an adult** convert that **you are required to investigate whether or not he has kinsmen.** ⁸**But regarding** a convert who is still **a minor, you are not required to investigate him** whether he has kinsmen. ⁹**For we know that he does not have** any kinsmen, because a minor cannot father a child.

RASHI

ופליגא דרבה — הא דרב חסדא דאמר קטן שמוליד פטור, דאלמא דקטן מוליד פליגא דרבה. **ואם אין לאיש גואל** — גבי גזל ונשבע על שקר דכתיב לעיל מיניה והתודו את חטאתם אשר עשו והשיב את אשמו בראשו והאי אשמו קרן של גזלה. **שאין לו גואלים** — אין לך אדם בישראל שאין לו גואלים, כל זמן שלא כלו בני יעקב, הקרוב קרוב קודם. **בגזל הגר** — ומת לאחר שנשבע לו, ואין לו יורשים. **ואמר רחמנא איש** — ולא כתיב ואם אין לו גואל, מאי טעמא כתיב איש — אלא משום דכתיב ואם דמשמע פעמים שיש לו יורשים ולהכי כתיב איש, ללמדך איש הוא דאיכא לספוקי שמא יוליד בנים משנתגייר ואינך רשאי להפקיע קרן שלו ולתתו לכהן, עד שתדע שאין לו יורשים, אבל קטן גר מסתמא גזל שלו שנשבע עליו ישראל לשקר, לכהן הוא, בידוע שאין לו גואלים.

NOTES

שֶׁאֵין לוֹ גּוֹאֵל **Who has no kinsman.** *Ramah* adds: Surely Israel was promised (Malachi 3:6): "For I am the Lord, I do not change; therefore, you sons of Jacob are not consumed," which implies that no tribe of Israel will ever become totally decimated. Hence every Israelite will always have a fellow tribesman who can inherit from him.

אִישׁ, אַתָּה צָרִיךְ לַחֲזוֹר עָלָיו **Regarding a man, you are required to investigate him.** *Ramah* suggests that Rabbah reads the words אֵין לָאִישׁ as if they were written עַיֵּין לָאִישׁ (as we find that similar expressions are interpreted elsewhere in the Talmud), that is to say, "examine the man to determine whether or not he has a kinsman."

HALAKHAH

אִישׁ, אַתָּה צָרִיךְ לַחֲזוֹר עָלָיו **Regarding a man, you are required to investigate him.** "Why does the Torah use the word 'man' with respect to the robbed property of a convert? Because regarding a man, you are required to investigate and ascertain whether he has heirs. But regarding a minor, you are not required to investigate him, for he is presumed not to have any heirs." (*Rambam, Sefer Kinyan, Hilkhot Gezelah VeAvedah* 8:7.)

student, Rav Huna. Throughout his life Rav Ḥisda showed great affection for Rav's words, and tried to add to his knowledge of Rav's teachings. Though he was poor as a youth, he became wealthy and lived most of his life in comfort.

Rav Ḥisda served as a judge in Sura for many years, together with Rav Huna, and both of them continued the tradition of Rav's school. After Rav Huna's death, Rav Ḥisda took his place as head of the Sura Yeshivah. Much is told of his deeds of charity. He lived to the age of ninety-two. Many of the Sages of the following generation were his students, and he had many sons who became Sages.

רַבָּה **Rabbah.** Rabbah bar Naḥamani the Priest, called Rabbah for short, was one of the greatest Babylonian Amoraim of the third generation. Rabbah studied under Rav Huna, Rav's disciple, and his entire method in the Halakhah followed that of Rav. He also studied Torah with Rav Yehudah and Rav Naḥman, and was a student and colleague of Rav Ḥisda. After Rav Yehudah's death, Rabbah was chosen, despite his youth, to be the head of the Pumbedita Yeshivah, though he did not accept the full appointment until close to the time of his death. Rabbah was involved in Halakhic discussions with all the great Sages of his generation, and the famous controversies between him and his colleague, Rav Yosef (in which the Halakhah follows Rabbah in almost every instance), are an important element of the Babylonian Talmud.

Rabbah trained many students. In fact, all the Sages of the following generation were his students, especially his nephew, Abaye, his outstanding student. His private life was full of suffering, and his sons apparently died in his lifetime. He was very poor, supporting himself with difficulty by agricultural labor. The people of his city also treated him badly. Although Rabbah died relatively young, he established himself as one of the pillars of the Babylonian Talmud.

[1]אֵיתִיבֵיהּ אַבַּיֵי: [2]"'אִישׁ'. אֵין לִי אֶלָּא אִישׁ. [3]בֶּן תֵּשַׁע שָׁנִים וְיוֹם אֶחָד שֶׁרָאוּי לְבִיאָה מִנַּיִין? [4]תַּלְמוּד לוֹמַר: 'וְאִישׁ'". [5]אָמַר לֵיהּ: יֵשׁ לוֹ, וְאֵינוֹ מוֹלִיד. [6]כִּתְבוּאָה שֶׁלֹּא הֵבִיאָה שְׁלִישׁ דָּמֵי.

[7]דְּבֵי חִזְקִיָּה תָּנָא: "'וְכִי יָזִד אִישׁ' — [8]אִישׁ מֵזִיד וּמַזְרִיעַ, וְאֵין קָטָן מֵזִיד וּמַזְרִיעַ".

[9]אָמַר לֵיהּ רַב מָרְדְּכַי לְרַב אַשִׁי: מַאי מַשְׁמַע דְּהַאי מֵזִיד לִישָּׁנָא דְּבוּלֵי הוּא? [10]דִּכְתִיב: "וַיָּזֶד יַעֲקֹב נָזִיד".

[11]וְהָא תָּנָא דְּבֵי רַבִּי יִשְׁמָעֵאל: "'בֵּן' וְלֹא אָב". [12]הֵיכִי דָּמֵי?

LITERAL TRANSLATION

[1]Abaye raised an objection against him: [2]"'A man.' I have only a man. [3]From where [do I know that a boy] nine years and one day old is fit for intercourse? [4]The verse states: 'And a man.'"

[5]He said to him: He has, but he cannot father [a child]. [6]He is like grain that has not grown a third.

[7][A Sage] of the School of Ḥizkiyah taught: "'But if a man come presumptuously.' [8]A man cooks and begets, but a minor does not cook and beget."

[9]Rav Mordekhai said to Rav Ashi: From where [may we] infer that *meizid* is a term of cooking? [10]For it is written: "And Jacob cooked pottage."

[11]But surely [a Sage] of the School of Rabbi Yishmael taught: "'A son' — and not a father." [12]What is it like?

RASHI

איש — גבי שפחה חרופה כתיב (ויקרא יט) ואיש כי ישכב את אשה שכבת זרע וגו׳. **שלא הביאה שליש** — שאם אתה זורעה אינה מצמחת. **וכי יזיד** — מדאפקיה בלשון מזיד ולא כתוב וכי ירשיע איש למימר דרוש ביה נמי האי מזיד מבשל. **בן ולא אב** — לגבי בן סורר ומורה בן ולא אב, וקא סלקא דעתך דממעיט בן שכבר נולד לו בן דשוב אינו נעשה בן סורר ומורה, ואי קטן לא מוליד היכי דמי דאיצטריך למעוטי.

TRANSLATION AND COMMENTARY

אֵיתִיבֵיהּ אַבַּיֵי [1]**Abaye raised an objection against** Rabbah from a Baraita dealing with a designated maidservant, a woman who is half-slave and half-free and who is betrothed to a Hebrew slave. "Regarding such a woman, the verse states (Leviticus 19:20): 'And if a man has carnal relations with a woman, and she is a maidservant designated to a man, and has not been redeemed or given her freedom.' [2]Had the verse stated: 'If **a man,' I would know** that this law applies **only** to **a man,** because he is an adult who is capable of sexual intercourse. [3]**From where do I know that a boy nine years and one day old is** also **capable** of sexual **intercourse?** [4]This I know because **the verse states:** '*And* if **a man.**' The seemingly extraneous *vav* in the word וְאִישׁ extends the law to include a nine-year-old boy, who is capable of sexual intercourse." Now, if a nine-year-old boy is capable of sexual intercourse, it stands to reason that he can also father a child. This contradicts Rabbah!

אָמַר לֵיהּ [5]Rabbah **said to** Abaye: A nine-year-old boy might **have** semen, **but he** still **cannot father a child** before he reaches adulthood. [6]In this regard, **he is like grain that is not** yet **one-third ripe,** which will not grow if planted.

דְּבֵי חִזְקִיָּה תָּנָא [7]**A Sage of the School of Ḥizkiyah taught** the following Baraita: "The verse states (Exodus 21:14): **'But if a man come presumptuously** [יָזִד] upon his neighbor, to slay him with guile.' The verse refers here to 'a man,' and uses the unusual term *yazid* — which is translated here as 'come presumptuously.' However, it may also be understood in the sense of 'cook,' [8]teaching that **a man cooks** (prepares) his semen, **and begets** with it a child, **but a minor does not cook** his semen **and beget** with it a child." Thus the Baraita supports Rabbah, who said that while a nine-year-old boy can engage in sexual intercourse, he cannot father a child.

אָמַר לֵיהּ [9]**Rav Mordekhai said to Rav Ashi: Where do we see that** the word ***meizid* is a term** that can be used in the sense **of cooking?** [10]We see this in **the verse** that **states** (Genesis 25:29): **"And Jacob cooked pottage** [וַיָּזֶד נָזִיד]."

וְהָא תָּנָא [11]The Gemara raises an objection against Rabbah: **But surely a Sage of the School of Rabbi Yishmael taught** the following Baraita: "The verse that states (Deuteronomy 21:18): 'If a man has **a** stubborn and rebellious **son,'** teaches that a boy may become a rebellious son, **but** not if he is already **a father."** This Baraita seems to be saying that a boy who has fathered a child can no longer be considered a rebellious son. Now, if a minor cannot father a child, as was argued by Rabbah, [12]**how** exactly **do you visualize the case?**

NOTES

"אִישׁ" — אֵין לִי אֶלָּא אִישׁ "A man" — I have only a man. According to most Rishonim, the Baraita discusses here whether the law regarding "a maidservant designated to a man" applies to a maidservant who engaged in sexual intercourse with a boy who is nine years and one day old. *Meiri* cites those who understand that the Baraita deals with the question whether the semen ejaculated by a nine-year-old boy is ritually impure.

SAGES

אַבַּיֵי Abaye. One of the greatest Sages of the Talmud. Abaye was a member of the fourth generation of Babylonian Amoraim. He was left an orphan and was raised in the home of his uncle, Rabbah. Abaye was also the student of Rav Yosef, and after Rav Yosef's death Abaye became head of the Pumbedita Yeshivah. Halakhic discussions between him and Rabbah, and even more so between him and Rav Yosef, are found throughout the Talmud. But his most important discussions are with his colleague, Rava.

In Halakhic decision-making the general principle is that in disputes between Abaye and Rava the opinion of Rava is accepted, except in a small number of cases (יע״ל קג״ם). Abaye's son, Bibi bar Abaye, was also a well-known Sage.

חִזְקִיָּה Ḥizkiyah. The son of Rabbi Ḥiyya, Ḥizkiyah was a first-generation Amora. Ḥizkiyah edited collections of Baraitot (as his father Rabbi Ḥiyya had done before him), and the Gemara often cites these as "the School of Ḥizkiyah taught."

רַב מָרְדְּכַי Rav Mordekhai. A Babylonian Amora of the sixth generation, Rav Mordekhai was a pupil of Avimi of Hagrunya, in whose name he transmitted many legal rulings to Rav Ashi. Rav Mordekhai appears several times in the Talmud in the company of Rav Ashi and his colleagues, Amemar and Mar Zutra.

רַב אַשִׁי Rav Ashi. Born in the year that Rava died, he became one of the greatest Amoraim of Babylonia during the sixth generation. He edited the Babylonian Talmud and headed the Mata Meḥasya Yeshivah for sixty years.

רַבִּי יִשְׁמָעֵאל Rabbi Yishmael. One of the leading Tannaim of the fourth generation. Rabbi Yishmael's main colleague and friend was Rabbi Akiva, and the Tannaitic literature contains many examples of their differences of opinion. Rabbi Yishmael developed a comprehensive system of Biblical interpretation based on commonsense understanding of

[1]אִילֵימָא דְּאִיעַבַּר בָּתַר דְּאַיְיתֵי שְׁתֵּי שְׂעָרוֹת [2]וְאוֹלִיד מִקַּמֵּי דְּלַקֵּיף זָקָן, [3]מִי אִיכָּא שָׁהוּת כּוּלֵּי הַאי? [4]וְהָא אָמַר רַבִּי כְּרוּסְפְּדַאי: כָּל יָמָיו שֶׁל בֵּן סוֹרֵר וּמוֹרֶה אֵינוֹ אֶלָּא שְׁלֹשָׁה חֳדָשִׁים בִּלְבַד! [5]אֶלָּא לָאו, דְּאִיעַבַּר מִקַּמֵּי דְּלַיְיתֵי שְׁתֵּי שְׂעָרוֹת וְאוֹלִיד מִקַּמֵּיהּ דְּלַקֵּיף זָקָן? [6]וּשְׁמַע מִינָּהּ: קָטָן מוֹלִיד! [7]לָא. לְעוֹלָם דְּאִיעַבַּר בָּתַר דְּאַיְיתֵי שְׁתֵּי שְׂעָרוֹת, וְאוֹלִיד בָּתַר דְּאַקֵּיף זָקָן. [8]וּדְקָא קַשְׁיָא דְּרַבִּי כְּרוּסְפְּדַאי, [9]כִּי אֲתָא רַב דִּימִי, אֲמַר: [10]אָמְרִי בְּמַעַרְבָא: [11]״בֵּן״, וְלֹא הָרָאוּי לִקְרוֹתוֹ אָב.

LITERAL TRANSLATION

[1]If you say that she conceived after he produced two hairs, [2]and gave birth before [his] beard grew, [3]is there that much time? [4]But surely Rabbi Kruspedai said: All the days of the stubborn and rebellious son are only three months! [5]Rather, is it not that she conceived before he produced two hairs, and gave birth before [his] beard grew around? [6]And infer from this: A minor can father [a child]! [7]No. In fact where she conceived after he produced two hairs, and gave birth after [his] beard grew. [8]And that which is difficult about Rabbi Kruspedai['s ruling], [9]when Rav Dimi came, he said: [10]They say in the West: [11]"A son," and not someone who is fit to be called a father.

TRANSLATION AND COMMENTARY

[1]**If you say that** the boy's wife **conceived** only **after he** reached the age of thirteen and **produced two** pubic **hairs,** thus becoming an adult, [2]**and she gave birth before his** pubic **beard filled out,** and the verse teaches us that he may not be condemned as a rebellious son, although he is the right age, there is a difficulty. [3]**Is there** really **enough time** between when a boy produces two pubic hairs and when his pubic beard grows significantly for a child to be born? [4]**But surely Rabbi Kruspedai said: The entire period** during which a boy can become **a rebellious son is** only **three months.** [5]**Rather, must it not be that** the Baraita is dealing with a boy whose wife **conceived before he produced two** pubic **hairs, and** she **gave birth before his** pubic **beard grew** further? [6]**And** thus it would be legitimate to **infer from this** that **a minor can** indeed **father a child!**

לָא [7]The Gemara rejects this argument: **No,** this inference is invalid, for **in fact** the Baraita is dealing with a boy whose wife **conceived after he** reached the age of thirteen and **produced two** pubic **hairs, and** she was to **give birth** only **after his** pubic **beard** grew further. [8]**And what appears difficult about Rabbi Kruspedai's** ruling is not really difficult. When the Baraita said that a boy can become a rebellious son while he is still only a son, but not after he has become a father, it did not refer to a boy whose wife has given birth, for by then he would be excluded from the law concerning the rebellious son either because his pubic hair had grown significantly, or because three months had passed since he produced his first two pubic hairs. [9]Rather, the Baraita should be understood in accordance with Rav Dimi's ruling. For **when Rav Dimi came** to Babylonia from Eretz Israel, **he said:** [10]**They say in Eretz Israel** that the Baraita is consistent with Rav Kruspedai's ruling that a boy can only become a rebellious son for three months. The verse that states: [11]"If a man has **a** stubborn and rebellious **son,**" teaches that a boy can become a rebellious son, if he is still only a son, **but** not if he is already **fit to be called a father.** If a boy had sexual intercourse with a woman as soon as he reached puberty, and the woman conceived, the pregnancy would be visible three months later. Thus, three months after a boy produces his first two pubic hairs he is fit to be called a father. From then on he can no longer be a rebellious son.

RASHI

אי נימא דאיעברא — אמיה מהאי בתר דאייתי שתי שערות, ושיהיה בו תשעה חדשים להקיף זקן ובתוך כך נולד בן וקא ממעט קרא דאף על גב דראוי הוא לבן סורר ומורה נפטר בשביל שנולד לו בן. **והא אמר רבי כרוספדאי** — כל ימיו של בן סורר ומורה אינן אלא שלשה חדשים בלבד, ואף על גב דלא הקיף זקן אינו נעשה בן סורר ומורה לאחר שלשה חדשים לאחר שהביא שתי שערות, והשתא לא דייק טעמא דרבי כרוספדאי מהיכא ולקמן בעינן ליה מיהו קרא לא צריך למעוטי, דאפילו לא אב הוא יהא מפטר בשלשה חדשים. **אלא לאו** — כי אצטריך למעוטי כגון דאוליד מקמי שלשה חדשים בתר שתי שערות, ועל כרחיך איעברא ששה חדשים מקמי דאייתי שתי שערות, ואוליד מקמי דאקיף זקן, ושלשה חדשים נמי לא עברו עליו, ושמע מינה קטן מוליד. **לא, לעולם דאיעבר בתר דאייתי שתי שערות וכו׳** — והאי דקאמר רבי ישמעאל: בן ולא אב — לא כשילדתו אמו כבר לבנו קא ממעט, דבלאו הכי מפטר מדין בן סורר ומורה או בשלשה חדשים או בהקפת זקן. **אלא כי אתא רב דימי** — פרשה לדתנא דבי רבי ישמעאל דאתא לאשמועינן האי דר׳ כרוספדאי, דמי שעברו עליו שלשה חדשים לאחר שהביא שתי שערות — פטור, והכי קאמר: בן ולא הראוי להיות אב, והיינו לאחר שלשה חדשים אחר שהביא שערות שראוי להיות העובר ניכר אם היה בא על האשה משהביא שתי שערות והיא מתעברת.

the text and established hermeneutic principles. Of the Halakhic Midrashim, the Mekhilta, the Sifrei on Numbers and part of the Sifre on Deuteronomy represent his school of thought, and he is frequently quoted in them. Rabbi Yishmael, like Rabbi Akiva, died as a martyr at the hands of the Romans.

LANGUAGE

כְּרוּסְפְּדַאי Kruspedai. This name derives from a Greek source that is apparently connected with the word κρασπεδον, *kraspedon*, used for ritual fringes (*tzitzit*). Thus כְּרוּסְפְּדַאי would be parallel to a Hebrew expression such as *ben-tzitzit*, which appears in several places.

HALAKHAH

כָּל יָמָיו שֶׁל בֵּן סוֹרֵר וּמוֹרֶה All the days of the stubborn and rebellious son. "The period during which a boy can become a rebellious son is three months from the time that he produces two pubic hairs. If his pubic hair grew in before the three months passed, he can no longer be considered a rebellious son." (*Rambam, Sefer Shofetim, Hilkhot Mamrim* 7:6.)

[1]גּוּפָא, אָמַר רַבִּי כְּרוּסְפְּדַאי אָמַר רַבִּי שַׁבְּתַי: כָּל יָמָיו שֶׁל בֵּן סוֹרֵר וּמוֹרֶה אֵינָן אֶלָּא שְׁלֹשָׁה חֳדָשִׁים בִּלְבַד. [2]וְהָאֲנַן תְּנַן: ״מִשֶּׁיָּבִיא שְׁתֵּי שְׂעָרוֹת וְעַד שֶׁיַּקִּיף זָקָן״! [3]הִקִּיף זָקָן — אַף עַל גַּב דְּלָא מָלוּ שְׁלֹשָׁה חֳדָשִׁים, [4]מָלוּ שְׁלֹשָׁה חֳדָשִׁים — אַף עַל גַּב דְּלָא הִקִּיף.

[5]יָתֵיב רַבִּי יַעֲקֹב מִנְּהַר פְּקוֹד קַמֵּיהּ דְּרָבִינָא וְיָתֵיב וְקָאָמַר מִשְּׁמֵיהּ דְּרַב הוּנָא בְּרֵיהּ דְּרַב יְהוֹשֻׁעַ: [6]שְׁמַע מִינָּהּ מִדְּרַבִּי כְּרוּסְפְּדַאי אָמַר רַבִּי שַׁבְּתַי: [7]יוֹלֶדֶת לְשִׁבְעָה — אֵין עוּבָּרָהּ נִיכָּר לִשְׁלִישׁ יָמֶיהָ. [8]דְּאִי סָלְקָא דַּעֲתָךְ עוּבָּרָהּ נִיכָּר לִשְׁלִישׁ יָמֶיהָ — [9]לָמָּה לִי שְׁלֹשָׁה? [10]בִּתְרֵי וְתִילְתָּא סַגְיָא!

[11]אָמַר לֵיהּ: לְעוֹלָם אֵימָא לָךְ

LITERAL TRANSLATION

[1]The thing itself. Rabbi Kruspedai said in the name of Rabbi Shabetai: All the days of the stubborn and rebellious son are only three months. [2]But surely we have learned: "From when he produces two hairs, and until a beard grows around"!

[3][If] a beard grew, even if three full months did not pass. [4][If] three full months passed, even if [a beard] did not grow around.

[5]Rabbi Ya'akov from Nehar Pekod sat before Ravina, and he sat and said in the name of Rav Huna the son of Rav Yehoshua: [6]Infer from what Rabbi Kruspedai said in the name of Rav Shabetai: [7]A woman who gives birth at seven [months] — her fetus is not recognizable after a third of her time. [8]For if it enters your mind that her fetus is recognizable after a third of her time, [9]why do I need three? [10]Two and a third [months] are enough!

[11]He said to him: In fact, I can say to you [that]

RASHI

והא אנן תנן עד שיקיף – אבל בשלשה חדשים לא מיפטר. הקיף – אשמועינן מתניתין דמפטר אפילו ממהר להקיף מקמי דמלוי, ורבי כרוספדאי אשמעינן מלוי אף על גב דלא הקיף, ונפקא לן מדתנא דבי רבי ישמעאל: בן – ולא הראוי להיות אב. שמע מינה – מדלא קרי ליה ראוי לקרותו אב עד שלשה חדשים שמע מינה אפילו אשתו היתה יולדת לשבעה אינו ניכר בפחות משלשה חדשים, – דאי לשליש ימים ניכר בתרי ירחי ותילתא נפטר כל אדם מדין סורר ומורה דהא ראוי לקרותו אב, ונפקא מינה לאשה שלא שהתה אחר בעלה שלשה חדשים ונשאת ונתעברה ספק מן הראשון ספק מן האחרון, אם הוכר עוברה לשני חדשים ושליש לנשואי האחרון ודאי מן הראשון, דאפילו היא עתידה לילד לשבעה לאחרון לא היה ניכר לשליש ימיה.

TRANSLATION AND COMMENTARY

גּוּפָא [1]**It was taught above: Rabbi Kruspedai said in the name of Rabbi Shabetai: The entire period** during which a boy can become **a rebellious son is** only **three months.** [2]The Gemara asks: **But surely we have learned** in our Mishnah: "A boy can become a rebellious son **from when** he turns thirteen and **produces two** pubic **hairs,** at which time he is subject to punishment as an adult, **and until** his pubic **beard grows** significantly." The Mishnah mentions his physical development and not the passing of a certain period of time.

הִקִּיף זָקָן [3]The Gemara answers: The Mishnah teaches that **if** the boy's pubic **beard has grown significantly**, then **even if three full months have not passed** since he produced his first pubic hairs, he can no longer be a rebellious son. [4]And Rabbi Kruspedai teaches that **if three full months have passed** since the boy produced his first pubic hairs, then **even if his** pubic **beard has not grown** significantly, he can no longer be a rebellious son.

יָתֵיב [5]**Rabbi Ya'akov from Nehar Pekod** once **sat before Ravina, and he said in the name of Rav Huna the son of Rav Yehoshua:** [6]**Infer from what Rabbi Kruspedai said in the name of Rav Shabetai** (that a boy can only become a rebellious son during the three months following puberty, because later he is old enough to become a father) [7]that if **a woman gives birth after seven** months of pregnancy, **her pregnancy is not** yet **visible after a third of her** term (two-and-a-third months), as opposed to a woman who gives birth after nine months of pregnancy, and whose pregnancy is indeed visible after a third of her pregnancy has passed (three months). [8]**For if you think that** in such a case **the pregnancy is** already **visible after a third of her** pregnancy has passed, [9]**why do I need three** full months after the boy reached puberty for him to be regarded as a potential father? [10]**Two-and-a-third** months **should be enough.** If his wife gave birth after seven months of pregnancy, her pregnancy would be recognizable after two-and-a-third months!

אָמַר לֵיהּ [11]Ravina **said to** Rabbi Ya'akov: **In fact, I can say to you** that even in **the** case of a

NOTES

הִקִּיף זָקָן — מָלוּ שְׁלֹשָׁה חֳדָשִׁים **If his pubic beard grew around — if three full months passed.** *Ramah* points out that it cannot be argued that the two measures — three months and until the boy's pubic region is covered with hair — are one and the same, for we see that boys develop at different speeds.

SAGES

רַב יַעֲקֹב מִנְּהַר פְּקוֹד **Rav Ya'akov from Nahar Pekod.** A sixth-generation Babylonian Amora, Rabbi Ya'akov was a disciple and colleague of Ravina.

רָבִינָא **Ravina.** A Babylonian Amora of the fifth and sixth generations, Ravina apparently came from Mata Meḥasya, though some authorities claim that he came from Eretz Israel. He was among Rava's students. Although Ravina was older than Rav Ashi, he accepted him as his teacher and became his student and colleague. Ravina was apparently also actively involved in the editing of the Babylonian Talmud, which was accomplished by Rav Ashi.

BACKGROUND

יוֹלֶדֶת לְשִׁבְעָה **A women who gives birth at seven months.** The Sages write that there are two kinds of full-term pregnancy, of seven and nine months respectively. Since these two kinds of pregnancy were regarded as different from one another, it is not clear whether all the phenomena appearing in one of them also exist in the other.

SAGES

רַב הוּנָא בְּרֵיהּ יְהוֹשֻׁעַ Rav Huna the son of Rav Yehoshua. A fifth-generation Babylonian Amora, Rav Huna the son of Rav Yehoshua was one of the outstanding disciples of Abaye and Rava. He was a close colleague of Rav Pappa from his youth, and these scholars are frequently mentioned together in the Talmud.

TERMINOLOGY

אַף אֲנַן נַמִּי תְּנֵינָא We too have also learned [thus]. This term introduces a quotation from a Mishnah or a Baraita corroborating the previous Amoraic statement.

עוּבָּרָהּ נִיכָּר לִשְׁלִישׁ יָמֶיהָ, [1]זִיל בָּתַר רוּבָּא.

[2]אֲמָרוּהָ קַמֵּיהּ דְּרַב הוּנָא בְּרֵיהּ דְּרַב יְהוֹשֻׁעַ. [3]אָמַר לֵיהּ: וּבְדִינֵי נְפָשׁוֹת מִי אָזְלִינַן בָּתַר רוּבָּא? [4]הַתּוֹרָה אָמְרָה: "וְשָׁפְטוּ הָעֵדָה...וְהִצִּילוּ הָעֵדָה", [5]וְאַתְּ אָמְרַתְּ: זִיל בָּתַר רוּבָּא!

[6]אַהַדְרוּהָ קַמֵּיהּ דְּרָבִינָא. [7]אָמַר לֵיהּ: וּבְדִינֵי נְפָשׁוֹת לָא אָזְלִינַן בָּתַר רוּבָּא? [8]וְהָתְנַן: "אֶחָד אוֹמֵר: 'בִּשְׁנַיִם בַּחֹדֶשׁ', [9]וְאֶחָד אוֹמֵר: 'בִּשְׁלֹשָׁה' — עֵדוּתָן קַיֶּימֶת, [10]שֶׁזֶּה יוֹדֵעַ בְּעִיבּוּרוֹ שֶׁל חֹדֶשׁ [11]וְזֶה אֵינוֹ יוֹדֵעַ." [12]וְאִי סָלְקָא דַּעְתָּךְ לָא אָמְרִינַן זִיל בָּתַר רוּבָּא:

LITERAL TRANSLATION

her fetus is recognizable after a third of her time. [1]Follow the majority.

[2]They said it before Rav Huna the son of Rav Yehoshua. [3]He said to him: But in capital cases do we follow the majority? [4]The Torah said: "And the congregation shall judge....And the congregation shall deliver," [5]and you say: Follow the majority!

[6]They brought it back before Ravina. [7]He said to him: And in capital cases do we not follow the majority? [8]But surely we have learned: "[If] one says: 'On the second of the month,' [9]and one says: 'On the third of the month,' their testimony stands, [10]for this one knows about the intercalation of the month, [11]and this one does not know about the intercalation of the month." [12]And if it enters your mind [that] we do not say: Follow the majority,

TRANSLATION AND COMMENTARY

woman who will give birth after seven months, she **is** already **visibly** pregnant **after a third of her** term. Nevertheless, a boy is subject to the law of a rebellious son for three months after the appearance of his first two pubic hairs, for until that time he is not regarded as a potential father. [1]In this matter we **follow the majority** of women who give birth after nine months, and whose pregnancy is noticeable only after three full months.

אֲמָרוּהָ [2]This discussion **was reported back to Rav Huna the son of Rav Yehoshua,** [3]who **said** in response: **But** is it really true that **in capital cases,** such as one involving a rebellious son, **we follow the majority?** [4]Surely **the Torah said** (Numbers 35:24-25): **"And the congregation shall judge** the slayer....**And the congregation shall deliver** the slayer out of the hand of the blood-avenger." This verse shows that all efforts must be made to find grounds to acquit a person accused of a capital offense. [5]**And** nevertheless, even though there is reason to say that after two-and-one-third months a pubescent boy may be called a father, **you say** that we should **follow the majority** of women who only give birth after nine months of pregnancy, and that we should rule that he may not be called a father until three months after puberty!

אַהַדְרוּהָ קַמֵּיהּ [6]This response **was brought back before Ravina,** and **he countered** as follows: [7]Are you saying that **in capital cases we do not follow the majority?** [8]**But surely we have learned** otherwise in the Mishnah (*Sanhedrin* 40a): **"If one** witness **says:** 'The crime took place **on the second** day **of the month,'** [9]**and the other** witness **says:** 'The offense was committed **on the third** day **of the month,' their testimony stands,** [10]**for** it can be argued that **one** witness **knew that the** previous **month** was a **full** month of thirty days, [11]**and the other** witness **did not know that the** previous **month had been intercalated.** Thus, they were both referring to the same day." [12]Now, **if you think that we do not say** that we **follow the majority** even in capital cases, why should the defendant in a capital case be executed on the basis of such testimony?

RASHI

זיל בתר רובא — להכי לא מפטר כל אדם בתרי ירחי ותילתא לאחר הבאת שתי שערות, — דלא קרינן ביה ראוי, דאזלינן בתר רוב נשים שיולדות לתשעה ואין עוברה ניכר בפחות משלשה חדשים. **והצילו העדה** — לדונו לזכות ואנן מצינן למפטריה משום האי טעמא דראוי להיות אב ביולדת לשבעה, ואת אמרת זיל בתר רובא ולא מפטר עד שראוי לקרותו אב ביולדת לתשעה כרוב נשים. **בעבורו של חדש** — שהיה חדש שעבר מלא וראש חדש ביום שלשים ואחד, וזה שאמר בשלשה סבור שהחדש שעבר חסר וחשב ראש חדש מיום שלשים. **ואי לא אזלינן בתר רובא** — דאינשי דעבידי דטעו בעבורא דירחא, אמאי מצרפין לסהדותייהו וקטלינן ליה להאי, — נימא לא טעה, — אלא האי דוקא שלשה אמר, והאי דוקא אמר שנים ואין עדותן מכוונת ליום אחד.

NOTES

אָזְלִינַן בָּתַר רוּבָּא We follow the majority. The Rishonim discuss at length the source and legal validity of following the majority. The verse that states (Exodus 23:2): "After the many to incline," which applies even to capital cases, shows that we follow the majority even in capital cases. But a distinction may be drawn between a "majority that is before us," such as when we can directly determine the relationship between the majority and the minority, and then follow the majority, as is done when a verdict is issued on the basis of the majority opinion, and a "majority that is not before us," such as a statistical majority (for example, most women give birth after nine months, or most people know that the month has been intercalated). It is the validity of this second type of majority that the Rishonim make efforts to demonstrate (see *Ran, Meiri,* and *Melo HaRo'im*).

[1]נֵימָא הָנֵי דַּוְקָא קָא מְסַהֲדֵי, [2]וְאַכְחוּשֵׁי הוּא דְּקָא מְכַחֲשֵׁי אַהֲדָדֵי. [3]אֶלָּא לָאו — מִשּׁוּם דְּאָמְרִינַן זִיל בָּתַר רוּבָּא, [4]וְרוּבָּא דְּאֶינָשֵׁי עָבְדִי דְּטָעוּ בְּעִיבּוּרָא דְּיַרְחָא.

[5]אָמַר רַבִּי יִרְמְיָה מִדִּפְתִּי: אַף אֲנַן נַמִי תְּנֵינָא: [6]"בַּת שָׁלֹשׁ שָׁנִים וְיוֹם אֶחָד מִתְקַדֶּשֶׁת בְּבִיאָה. [7]וְאִם בָּא עָלֶיהָ יָבָם, קְנָאָהּ. [8]וְחַיָּיבִין עָלֶיהָ מִשּׁוּם אֵשֶׁת אִישׁ, [9]וּמְטַמְּאָה אֶת בּוֹעֲלָהּ לְטַמֵּא מִשְׁכַּב הַתַּחְתּוֹן כָּעֶלְיוֹן. [10]נִישֵּׂאת לְכֹהֵן, אוֹכֶלֶת בִּתְרוּמָה. [11]בָּא עָלֶיהָ אֶחָד מִן הַפְּסוּלִין, פְּסָלָהּ מִן הַכְּהוּנָּה. [12]וְאִם בָּא עָלֶיהָ אֶחָד מִכׇּל הָעֲרָיוֹת הָאֲמוּרוֹת בַּתּוֹרָה, [13]מוּמָתִין עָלֶיהָ, וְהִיא פְּטוּרָה".

LITERAL TRANSLATION

[1]say that these testified precisely, [2]and they contradict each other. [3]Rather, is it not because we say: Follow the majority, [4]and the majority of people are liable to err regarding the intercalation of the month.

[5]Rabbi Yirmeyah of Difti said: We, too, have learned [this]: [6]"A girl three years and one day may be betrothed through intercourse. [7]And if the levir had intercourse with her, he acquires her. [8]And they are liable for her on account of a married woman. [9]And she imparts ritual impurity to the man who has intercourse with her, so that he renders the object upon which he lies impure like the cover over [a man suffering from gonorrhea]. [10][If] she marries a priest, she eats terumah. [11][If] one of those who are disqualified had intercourse with her, she is disqualified from the priesthood. [12]And if one of those forbidden to her who are mentioned in the Torah had intercourse with her, [13]they are put to death on account of her, and she is exempt."

TRANSLATION AND COMMENTARY

[1]Why not **say** here **that** both witnesses knew about the intercalation of the previous month, that they both **testified precisely,** [2]**and** that **they contradict each other?** [3]**Rather, is it not because we say** that even in capital cases we **follow the majority,** even if that will lead to the defendant's execution, [4]**and the majority of people are liable to err regarding the intercalation of the month.**

אָמַר רַבִּי יִרְמְיָה מִדִּפְתִּי [5]**Rabbi Yirmeyah of Difti said: We, too, have learned** the following Baraita, which implies that we follow the majority, even if that will lead to the defendant's execution: "Sexual intercourse with a girl over three years of age is regarded as sexual intercourse for all purposes. [6]Therefore, **a girl** who is **three years and one day** old and is given away in betrothal by her father **may be betrothed by** way of sexual **intercourse** with her bridegroom. [7]**If** her husband dies without children, and **his brother engages in** sexual **intercourse with her, he acquired her** as his levirate wife. If she is given away in betrothal by her father, and a man other than her husband engages in intercourse with her, [8]**he is liable to** the death penalty **for** having had intercourse with **a married woman.** [9]If she is menstruating, **she imparts ritual impurity to the man with whom she has intercourse, so that** he is ritually impure for seven days, and **he renders the object upon which he lies impure,** that object conveying the same level of ritual impurity **as the cover over a man suffering from gonorrhea.** The object upon which he lies has the status of first-degree ritual impurity, and so it renders food and drink ritually impure, but not people or utensils. [10]**If she** is the daughter of an ordinary Israelite and is **married off** by her father to **a priest, she** is permitted to **eat terumah.** [11]**If someone of unfit status has intercourse with her,** such as a non-Jew, or a son born to a priest and a woman whom he was forbidden to marry, **she becomes disqualified from** marrying into **the priesthood,** and if she is the daughter of a priest, she becomes disqualified from eating terumah in her father's house. [12]**And if one of those whom the Torah says is forbidden to her,** such as her father, **has intercourse with her,** [13]**he is put to death because of her, but she is exempt** from punishment, for a minor bears no liability."

RASHI

אף אנן נמי תנינא — דאזלינן בתר רובא וקטלינן. **מתקדשת בביאה** — אם מסרה אביה לאחד לבא עליה לשום קדושין, אבל לא מדעת עצמה דאין מעשה קטנה כלום. **קנאה** — ליורשה וליטמא לה ולאאת בגט ובלא חליצה, ובלבד שיקבל אביה את גיטה. **וחייבין עליה משום אשת איש** — אם קבל אביה קדושיה מאיש אחד ובא עליה איש אחר. **ומטמאה את בועלה** — בנדתה. **לטמא משכב התחתון כעליון** — כבר פירשתיו בפרק ארבע מיתות (נה,ב) שיהא תחתונו כעליונו של זב שמטמא אוכלין ומשקין אפילו לא נגע בו, — מפני ששכב עליו, אבל פחותה מבת שלש הבא עליה בנדותה אינו כבועל נדה אלא כנוגע בנדה, ואין משכבו מטמא אפילו אוכלין ומשקין אפילו נגע בו, דנוגע בנדה אינו אלא ראשון לטומאה ואינו מטמא כלים ואפילו נגע, וכל שכן דאינו מטמא משכב בלא נגיעה. **נשאת לכהן** — על ידי קדושי אביה, ואמרו רבנן: אין האשה אוכלת בתרומה עד שתכנס לחופה, וזו אם נכנסה לחופה אוכלת, אבל פחותה מכן אפילו נכנסה לחופה אינה אוכלת אף על גב דגדולה, כיון שנכנסה לחופה אף על פי שלא נבעלה — אוכלת, אלמא לאו בביאה תליא מילתא אלא בחופה, מיהו ראויה לביאה בעינן, וכל שאין לה ביאה אין לה חופה. **בא עליה אחד מן הפסולין** — כגון נכרי, חלל, נתין, וממזר — עשאה חללה, ופסלה, כדאמרינן ביבמות (סח,א) כי תהיה לאיש זר כיון שנבעלה לפסול לה — פסלה. **והיא פטורה** — מפני שהיא קטנה, ואינה בת עונשין, קתני מיהא חייבין עלה משום אשת איש, וקא סלקא דעתך חייבין מיתה קאמר, ובמזיד.

CONCEPTS

אַיְילוֹנִית **Aylonit.** From the detailed discussions in the Talmud, especially in tractate *Yevamot,* it seems that an *aylonit* is a woman with a genetic flaw preventing her from giving birth. In contrast to a barren woman, who generally suffers from some secondary disability though her physical and sexual development is normal, an *aylonit* is characterized by abnormal physical development (such as the failure to develop secondary sexual traits). From the descriptions in Talmudic literature it seems that there are various kinds of *aylonit,* ranging from those with excess male hormones to those who suffer from Turner's syndrome. In the Halakhah there are many laws relating to the status of the *aylonit,* mainly because she either completely lacks secondary sexual traits or because these appear only at a later age. Consequently various questions arise regarding the age at which an *aylonit* reaches legal majority.

[69B] [1]וְאַמַּאי? [2]אֵימָא אַיְילוֹנִית הִיא, וְאַדַּעְתָּא דְּהָכִי לָא קַדִּישׁ! [3]אֶלָּא לָאו דְּאָמְרִינַן: זִיל בָּתַר רוּבָּא, [4]וְרוֹב נָשִׁים לָאו אַיְילוֹנִית נִינְהוּ.
[5]לֹא, [6]״מַאי חַיָּיב עָלֶיהָ״ דְּקָתָנֵי? [7]קָרְבָּן.
[8]וְהָא ״מוּמָתִין עַל יָדָהּ״ קָתָנֵי!
[9]בְּבָא עָלֶיהָ אָבִיהָ.
[10]וְהָא ״אִם בָּא עָלֶיהָ אֶחָד מִכָּל הָעֲרָיוֹת״ קָתָנֵי!
[11]אֶלָּא: הָכָא בְּמַאי עָסְקִינַן דְּקִבְּלָהּ עִילָּוֵיהּ.

LITERAL TRANSLATION

[69B] [1]But why? [2]Say [that] she is an *aylonit,* and with that in mind he did not betroth her! [3]Rather, is it not that we say: Follow the majority, [4]and most women are not sexually undeveloped women?

[5]No. [6]What is that which is taught: "He is liable on account of her"? [7]A sacrifice.

[8]But surely it was taught: "They are put to death on account of her"!

[9]When her father had intercourse with her.

[10]But surely it was taught: "And if one of all those forbidden to her had intercourse with her"!

[11]Rather, here we are dealing with when he accepted her upon himself.

RASHI

ואמאי דילמא איילונית – תמצא, ונמצא קדושיה קדושי טעות. **דאדעתא דהכי לא קדיש** – ולא אשת איש היא. **קרבן** – ובשוגג דאזלינן בתר רובא, אבל מקטל לא קטלינא משום רובא. **בבא עליה אביה** – קאמר דחיובא לאו משום אישות אלא משום קורבא. **והא אחד מכל עריות קתני** – דמשמע אפילו הנך דאתו לה לחייבה משום קדושין, כגון חמיה וחורגה או כל אדם משום אשת איש. **אלא** – איבעיא לדחויה דלא נילף מינה דנזיל בקטלא בתר רובא אוקמא הכי. **הבא במאי עסקינן דקבלה** – בעלה עלויה, דאפילו תמצא איילונית – חפץ הוא בה וקדושיה קידושין.

TRANSLATION AND COMMENTARY

[69B] [1]Rabbi Yirmeyah of Difti explains how this Baraita shows that even in capital cases we follow the majority: If a girl over the age of three was given in betrothal by her father, and a man other than her husband engaged in intercourse with her, **why** is he liable to the death penalty? [2]**Say** that the girl might grow up to **be an** *aylonit* (a sexually undeveloped woman who is incapable of having children), **and bearing that in mind** her bridegroom **did not marry her!** In such a case, the betrothal would be retroactively annulled, because the bridegroom expected to marry a woman capable of bearing children. Thus, the girl would not be a married woman, and so the man who had intercourse with her should be exempt from the death penalty. [3]**Rather, is it not that we say** that even in capital cases we **follow the majority,** [4]**and** that **most women are not sexually undeveloped women?** The girl's betrothal is valid, so the man who had intercourse with her is liable to the death penalty for having had intercourse with a married woman.

לֹא [5]The Gemara rejects this argument: **No,** this conclusion is unwarranted. [6]**What is** meant by **that which was taught** in the Baraita: "If someone had intercourse with the girl after she was given in betrothal by her father, **he is liable for** having had intercourse with a married woman"? The Baraita means to say that if someone ignorant of her married status had intercourse with the girl, [7]he is liable to the penalty of **a** sin-**offering.** But if he sinned intentionally, he is not put to death, because we do not follow a majority in capital cases.

וְהָא [8]The Gemara raises an objection: **But surely it was taught** in that very same Baraita: "If one of those whom the Torah says is forbidden to her had intercourse with her, **he is put to death on account of her"!**

בְּבָא [9]The Gemara explains: That part of the Baraita refers to **the girl's father** or some other blood relative who **had** sexual **intercourse with her.** The man's liability is not dependent upon the validity of the girl's betrothal, because he is guilty of incest, and the possibility that she will turn out to be a sexually undeveloped woman is irrelevant. But if the man's liability is dependent upon the validity of the girl's betrothal, as in the case of her father-in-law or a total stranger whom we wish to execute for having intercourse with a married woman, he would not be liable to the death penalty, for we do not follow the majority if that will lead to the defendant's execution.

וְהָא [10]The Gemara objects to this answer: **But surely it was taught** in that Baraita: **"If one of those whom** the Torah says **is forbidden to her had intercourse with her,** he is put to death on account of her"! That formulation includes a relative by marriage whose liability to the death penalty is based on the validity of the girl's betrothal. Hence we follow the majority even in capital cases!

אֶלָּא [11]**Rather,** Rabbi Yirmeyah of Difti's argument can be rebutted as follows: **Here** in the Baraita **we are dealing with a** bridegroom who **accepted** the girl **upon himself** as his wife, even if she later turns out to be a sexually undeveloped woman who is incapable of bearing children. In such a case, even a relative by marriage is liable to the death penalty for sexual intercourse with the girl, for even if her sexual development turns out to be abnormal, her betrothal will still be valid.

TRANSLATION AND COMMENTARY

תָּנוּ רַבָּנָן [1]**Our Rabbis taught** the following Baraita: **"If a woman acted lewdly with her minor son,** in the course of which **he engaged with her in the first stage of sexual intercourse,** [2]**the School of Shammai say: He disqualified her from** marrying into the **priesthood.** [3]**And the School of Hillel** disagree and **say that she remains fit** to marry into the priesthood." Regarding most laws involving sexual intercourse, no differentiation is made between the first stage and the completion of the act. (Elsewhere, the Sages disagree about what is considered the first stage of sexual intercourse for these purposes, whether external genital contact suffices, or whether some measure of penetration is required.) If a woman has sexual relations with a man forbidden to her by the Torah and with whom she cannot establish a marriage bond, she falls into the category of a *zonah,* and is forbidden thereafter to marry a priest. The School of Shammai maintain that if a woman engaged in the first stage of sexual intercourse with her minor son, to whom she is forbidden by Torah law, she becomes forbidden to marry into the priesthood, for the sexual intercourse of a minor has legal consequences. The School of Hillel argue that such a woman remains fit to marry into the priesthood, for the sexual intercourse of a minor is not regarded as sexual intercourse.

אָמַר [4]**Rabbi Ḥiyya the son of Rabbah bar Naḥmani said in the name of Rav Ḥisda,** [5]**and some say that Rav Ḥisda said** what he said **in the name of Ze'eiri:** [6]**All agree** — both the School of Shammai and the School of Hillel — **about a boy** who is **nine years and one day old, that his** sexual **intercourse is** regarded as sexual **intercourse** which can disqualify a woman from marrying into the priesthood. [7]And they also all agree about a boy who is **less than eight** years old, that **his** sexual **intercourse is not** regarded as sexual **intercourse** which can disqualify a woman from marrying a priest. [8]**They only disagree about** a boy who is **an eight-year-old.** [9]**For the School of Shammai maintain** that **we can learn from the first generations** that an eight-year-old boy can

LITERAL TRANSLATION

[1]Our Rabbis taught: "[If] a woman acted lewdly with her minor son, and he engaged with her in the first stage of sexual intercourse, [2]the School of Shammai say: He disqualified her from the priesthood. [3]And the School of Hillel say that she is fit."

[4]Rabbi Ḥiyya the son of Rabbah bar Naḥmani said in the name of Rav Ḥisda, [5]and some say [that] Rav Ḥisda said [it] in the name of Ze'eiri: [6]All agree about a boy nine years and one day old, that his intercourse is intercourse. [7]Less than eight — his intercourse is not intercourse. [8]They only disagree about an eight-year-old. [9]For the School of Shammai maintain: We learn from the

[1]תָּנוּ רַבָּנָן: "הַמְסוֹלֶלֶת בִּבְנָהּ קָטָן וְהֶעֱרָה בָּהּ, [2]בֵּית שַׁמַּאי אוֹמְרִים: פְּסָלָהּ מִן הַכְּהוּנָה, [3]וּבֵית הִלֵּל מַכְשִׁירִין". [4]אָמַר רַבִּי חִיָּיא בְּרֵיהּ דְּרַבָּה בַּר נַחְמָנִי אָמַר רַב חִסְדָּא, [5]וְאָמְרִי לָהּ אָמַר רַב חִסְדָּא אָמַר זְעֵירִי: [6]הַכֹּל מוֹדִים בְּבֶן תֵּשַׁע שָׁנִים וְיוֹם אֶחָד שֶׁבִּיאָתוֹ בִּיאָה. [7]פָּחוֹת מִבֶּן שְׁמֹנָה [8]שֶׁאֵין בִּיאָתוֹ בִּיאָה. לֹא נֶחְלְקוּ אֶלָּא בְּבֶן שְׁמֹנָה. [9]דְּבֵית שַׁמַּאי סָבְרֵי: גָּמְרִינַן מְדוֹרוֹת

RASHI

הַמְסוֹלֶלֶת — לְשׁוֹן פְּרִיצוּת. וְהֶעֱרָה בָּהּ — אִיכָּא לְמַאן דְּאָמַר (יבמות נה,ב) הַעֲרָאָה זוֹ נְשִׁיקָה, וְאִיכָּא לְמַאן דְּאָמַר זוֹ הַכְנָסַת עֲטָרָה. פְּסָלָהּ מִן הַכְּהוּנָה — וּמְשַׁוֵּי לָהּ זוֹנָה, דְּהַעֲרָאָה כִּגְמַר בִּיאָה כְּדְאָמְרִינַן בַּגְּמָרָא דִּיבָמוֹת (נד,א) וּפָרְקִינַן דִּלְעֵיל (סנהדרין נה,א), וּמִיהוּ מִיתָה לֹא מְחַיְּיבוּ כְּגוֹן שֶׁלֹּא הָמְרוּ בָּהֶן. וּבֵית הִלֵּל מַכְשִׁירִין — כִּדְמְפָרֵשׁ לְקַמָּן דְּקָטָן לָאו בַּר בִּיאָה הִיא. מְדוֹרוֹת הָרִאשׁוֹנִים — שֶׁהָיוּ מוֹלִידִין בְּנֵי שְׁמוֹנֶה שָׁנָה, כְּדֵילְפִינַן לְקַמָּן.

NOTES

מְסוֹלֶלֶת **Acted lewdly.** Some understand the word מְסוֹלֶלֶת in the sense of "treading, trampling," in which case it is related to the word מְסִלָּה, "road," which is treaded upon by passers-by (*Ramah*). The Jerusalem Talmud has the reading: מְסַלֶּדֶת.

דּוֹרוֹת הָרִאשׁוֹנִים **The early generations.** The Rishonim ask: How can we learn anything from the early generations when we see today that an eight-year-old boy cannot father a child? They respond that if in the early generations an eight-year-old boy could father a child, then today his

sexual intercourse should at least be regarded as sexual intercourse. As for the difference between then and now, *Ramah* suggests that in the past people were stronger than they are today, and so they could father a child at an earlier age. Alternatively, in those days, they enjoyed divine help, and so even an eight-year-old boy could miraculously father a child (*Ramah*). Others argue that even in the days of the early generations, a boy fathering a child at the age of eight was exceptional (see *Ran* and *Meiri*).

HALAKHAH

תֵּשַׁע שָׁנִים וְיוֹם אֶחָד **Nine years and one day old.** "If a boy who is nine years and one day old has sexual intercourse with a woman who is forbidden to him, she is liable to be punished (and becomes a *zonah* so that she is thereafter disqualified from marrying into the priesthood),

and he is exempt. If he is less than nine, both the woman and the boy are exempt, following the School of Hillel." (*Rambam, Sefer Kedushah, Hilkhot Issurei Bi'ah* 1:13; *Shulḥan Arukh, Even HaEzer* 6:9; 167:1.)

BACKGROUND

הוֹלָדָה בְּגִיל צָעִיר Giving birth at an early age. Although the Sages themselves set the age of sexual maturity for girls at twelve and for boys at thirteen, they realized that in exceptional cases younger children could give birth. As a result of certain hormonal disorders such as Cushing's disease, sexual maturity can occur very early, even during the first year of life. Hence it is also possible for young children to impregnate and give birth.

TRANSLATION AND COMMENTARY

indeed father a child, and so his sexual intercourse has legal consequences and can disqualify a woman from marrying into the priesthood. [1] **And the School of Hillel maintain** that **we cannot learn** anything **from the first generations,** and so the sexual intercourse of an eight-year-old boy is of no legal significance and cannot disqualify a woman from marrying into the priesthood.

וְדוֹרוֹת הָרִאשׁוֹנִים [2] The Gemara asks: **From where do we know** that **in the first generations they fathered children** at the age of eight? [3] **You might say** that we know this **from** what the Bible tells us regarding Achitofel, Eli'am, Batsheba, and Solomon. For **the verse states** (II Samuel 11:3): **"Is not this Batsheba, the daughter of Eli'am, the wife of Uriah the Hittite?"** [4] **And** another **verse states** (II Samuel 23:34): **"Eli'am the son of Achitofel the Gilonite,"** and so it follows that Batsheba was Achitofel's granddaughter. [5] **And** regarding the birth of Solomon, the son of Batsheba, **the verse states** (II Samuel 12:25): **"And he sent by the hand of Nathan the Prophet; and he called his name Jedidiah, for the Lord's sake."** [6] **And a verse** in the following chapter **states** (II Samuel 13:23): **"And it came to pass after two full years, that Absalom had sheepshearers,"** and it was then that Absalom had Amnon put to death (verses 23-29), and so it follows that that event took place two years after Solomon's birth. [7] And **a** later **verse states** (II Samuel 13:38): **"And Absalom fled, and went to Gesher, and was there three years,"** until five years after Solomon's birth. [8] **And** later **the verse states** (II Samuel 14:28): **"And Absalom dwelt two years in Jerusalem, and did not see the king's face,"** bringing us to seven years after Solomon was born. [9] It was then that Absalom began his revolt, as **the verse states** (II Samuel 15:7): **"And it came to pass after forty years, that Absalom said to the king, I pray you, let me go and pay my vow, which I have vowed to the Lord, in Hebron."** [10] And it was in the course of that revolt that Achitofel committed suicide, as **the verse states** (II Samuel 17:23): **"And when Achitofel saw that his counsel was not followed, he saddled his ass, and arose, and went to his house, to his city, and put his household in order, and strangled himself."** [11] **And** elsewhere **the verse states** (Psalms 55:24): **"Bloody and**

הָרִאשׁוֹנִים. [1] וּבֵית הִלֵּל סָבְרִי: לָא גָּמְרִינַן מִדּוֹרוֹת הָרִאשׁוֹנִים. [2] וְדוֹרוֹת הָרִאשׁוֹנִים מְנָלַן דְּאוֹלִיד? [3] אִילֵימָא מִדִּכְתִיב: ״הֲלוֹא זֹאת בַּת שֶׁבַע בַּת אֱלִיעָם אֵשֶׁת אוּרִיָּה הַחִתִּי״, [4] וּכְתִיב: ״וֶאֱלִיעָם [אֱלִיעָם] בֶּן אֲחִיתֹפֶל הַגִּלֹנִי״, [5] וּכְתִיב: ״וַיִּשְׁלַח בְּיַד נָתָן הַנָּבִיא וַיִּקְרָא אֶת שְׁמוֹ יְדִידְיָה בַּעֲבוּר (כִּי) ה׳ (אֲהֵבוֹ)״, [6] וּכְתִיב: ״וַיְהִי לִשְׁנָתַיִם יָמִים וַיִּהְיוּ גֹזְזִים לְאַבְשָׁלוֹם״, [7] וּכְתִיב: ״וְאַבְשָׁלוֹם בָּרַח וַיֵּלֶךְ גְּשׁוּרָה וַיְהִי שָׁם שָׁלֹשׁ שָׁנִים״, [8] וּכְתִיב: ״וַיֵּשֶׁב אַבְשָׁלוֹם בִּירוּשָׁלַיִם שְׁנָתַיִם יָמִים וּפְנֵי הַמֶּלֶךְ לֹא רָאָה״, [9] וּכְתִיב: ״וַיְהִי מִקֵּץ אַרְבָּעִים שָׁנָה וַיֹּאמֶר אַבְשָׁלוֹם אֶל הַמֶּלֶךְ אֵלְכָה נָּא (וַאֲשַׁלְּמָה) אֶת נִדְרִי אֲשֶׁר נָדַרְתִּי לַה׳ בְּחֶבְרוֹן, [10] וּכְתִיב: ״וַאֲחִיתֹפֶל רָאָה כִּי לֹא נֶעֶשְׂתָה עֲצָתוֹ וַיַּחֲבֹשׁ אֶת הַחֲמוֹר וַיָּקָם וַיֵּלֶךְ אֶל בֵּיתוֹ (וְאֶל) עִירוֹ וַיְצַו אֶל בֵּיתוֹ וַיֵּחָנַק״, [11] וּכְתִיב: ״אַנְשֵׁי דָמִים וּמִרְמָה לֹא יֶחֱצוּ יְמֵיהֶם״.

LITERAL TRANSLATION

first generations. [1] And the School of Hillel maintain: We do not learn from the first generations.

[2] And [regarding] the first generations, from where [do we know] that they fathered children? [3] You might say from that which is written: "Is not this Batsheba, the daughter of Eli'am, the wife of Uriah the Hittite." [4] And it is written: "Eli'am the son of Achitofel the Gilonite." [5] And it is written: "And he sent by the hand of Nathan the prophet; and he called his name Jedidiah, because the Lord loved him." [6] And it is written: "And it came to pass after two full years, that Absalom had sheepshearers." [7] And it is written: "And Absalom fled, and went to Gesher, and was there three years." [8] And it is written: "And Absalom dwelt two years in Jerusalem, and did not see the king's face." [9] And it is written: "And it came to pass after forty years, that Absalom said to the king, I pray you, let me go and pay my vow, which I have vowed to the Lord, in Hebron." [10] And it is written: "And when Achitofel saw that his counsel was not followed, he saddled his ass, and arose, and went to his house, to his city, and put his household in order, and strangled himself." [11] And it is written: "Bloody and deceitful men shall not live out half their days."

RASHI

אי נימא מדכתיב בת שבע בת אליעם ואליעם בן אחיתופל וכתיב בלדת שלמה בנה ויקרא את שמו ידידיה וסמיך ליה ויהי לשנתים ימים אחר לידתו הרג אבשלום את אמנון וברח לגשור וישב שם שלש שנים — הרי חמש שנים לשלמה, וכששב מגשור שפייס יואב את דוד על ידי התקועית להשיבו ישב בירושלים שנתים ואחר כך מרד דכתיב בתריה ויהי מקץ ארבעים שנה והני ארבעים שנה נקט ליה למנין ששאלו מלך, כדאמרינן בתמורה (יד,ב) שהלך ומרד, ובאותו פרק נחנק אחיתופל כדכתיב ואחיתופל ראה כי לא נעשתה עצתו וילך אל ביתו ויחנק הרי שלמה בן שבע שנים.

[1] וְתַנְיָא: ״כָּל שְׁנוֹתָיו שֶׁל דּוֹאֵג אֵינָן אֶלָּא שְׁלֹשִׁים וְאַרְבַּע, וְשֶׁל אֲחִיתֹפֶל אֵינָן אֶלָּא שְׁלֹשִׁים וְשָׁלֹשׁ״. [2] כַּמָּה הָוְיָא לְהוּ? תְּלָתִין וּתְלָת. [3] דַּל שְׁבַע דַּהֲוָה שְׁלֹמֹה, [4] פָּשׁ לְהוּ עֶשְׂרִים וְשִׁית. [5] דַּל תַּרְתֵּי שְׁנֵי לִתְלָתָא עֲבוּרֵי. [6] אִשְׁתַּכַּח דְּכָל חַד וְחַד בִּתְמָנֵי אוֹלִיד.

[7] מִמַּאי? [8] דִּלְמָא תַּרְוַיְיהוּ בִּתְשַׁע אוֹלִיד, [9] וּבַת שֶׁבַע אוֹלִידָא בְּשִׁית, מִשּׁוּם דְּאִיתְּתָא בָּרְיָא.

[10] תֵּדַע, דְּהָא הָוֵי לָהּ וָלָד מֵעִיקָּרָא!

[11] אֶלָּא מֵהָכָא: [12] ״אֵלֶּה תּוֹלְדֹת

LITERAL TRANSLATION

[1] And it was taught: "All the years of Do'eg were only thirty-four, and of Achitofel were only thirty-three." [2] How many were they? Thirty-three. [3] Deduct seven when Solomon was, [4] [and] twenty-six are left. [5] Deduct two years for three pregnancies. [6] It turns out that each one fathered a child at [the age of] eight.

[7] From what? [8] Perhaps two of them fathered a child at nine, [9] and Batsheba gave birth at six, for a woman is stronger.

[10] Know [that this is true], for she had a child previously!

[11] Rather, from here: [12] "And these are the generations

TRANSLATION AND COMMENTARY

deceitful men shall not live out half their days." [1] **And** based on this verse, **it was taught** in a Baraita: **"All the years of Do'eg were only thirty-four, and** all the days **of Achitofel were only thirty-three."** An average lifetime being seventy years, as the verse states (Psalms 90:10): "The days of our years are seventy," half a lifetime is thirty-five years. Since Do'eg and Achitofel were "bloody and deceitful men," they did not live out half their days, but rather they died at the age of thirty-four and thirty-three, respectively. From all that has been said above, it follows that Solomon was Achitofel's great-grandson — the son of Batsheba, who was the daughter of Eli'am, who was the son of Achitofel — and that Achitofel died at the age of thirty-three, when Solomon was seven. [2] The following calculations may now be made: **How many** years did Achitofel live? **Thirty-three.** [3] **Deduct seven** years of his life which coincided with those of **Solomon,** [4] **and twenty-six** years **are left.** Thus, it follows that in the course of twenty-six years three generations were born — Eli'am, Batsheba, and Solomon. [5] **Deduct two** more **years for the three pregnancies** which ended with the birth of those three generations, and twenty-four years are left. [6] Thus, **it turns out that each one** — Achitofel, Eli'am, and Batsheba — **begot a child at the age of eight.** We see from here that in early generations a boy could father a child at the age of eight, and so his sexual intercourse must surely be regarded as sexual intercourse that has legal consequences.

מִמַּאי [7] The Gemara rejects this line of reasoning: **How** do you know this? [8] **Perhaps** each of **the two** men — Achitofel and his son Eli'am — **fathered a child at** the age of **nine,** [9] **and Batsheba gave birth at** the age of **six, for a woman is stronger** than a man.

תֵּדַע [10] The Gemara adduces proof in support of its argument: **Know that this is true, for** surely before Solomon was born, Batsheba **had** already given birth to another **child** who died in infancy (see II Samuel 11:27, and 12:14 and on)!

אֶלָּא מֵהָכָא [11] The Gemara continues: **Rather,** we learn from the following source that in the early generations, boys begot children at the age of eight: [12] The verse states (Genesis 11:27): **"And these are the**

RASHI

חצי ימיו של אדם שלשים וחמש — דכתיב (תהלים צ) ימי שנותינו בהם שבעים שנה פשו להו עשרין ושית לאחיתופל כשנולד שלמה, ובתוך עשרים ושש שנים נולדו שלשה דורות: אליעם ובת שבע ושלמה. **דל תרתי שנין דתלתא עבורי** — כלומר פחות משמנה חדשים אין שהות לעובר, שבע חדשים להריון וחודש לימי נדות וטהרה. **אשתכח דכל חד וחד בתמני אוליד** — אחיתופל הוליד אליעם לשמנה שנה ושמנה חדשים, ואליעם הוליד בת שבע לשמנה שנה ושמנה חדשים, ובת שבע לשמנה שנה ושמנה חדשים ללידתו של שלמה — הרי עשרים ושש שנים. **דאתתא בריא היא** — אשה דרכה להיות בריאה וממהרת להזריע. **ותדע** — על כרחך דאשה ממהרת, דהא הוה לה לבת שבע ולד מקמי שלמה אותו הולד שמת לדוד שנולד ראשון, דכתיב ביה (שמואל ב׳ יב) וכאשר מת הילד קמת ותאכל לחם.

NOTES

אֲחִיתֹפֶל שְׁלֹשִׁים וְשָׁלֹשׁ Achitofel was thirty-three. An average lifetime is seventy years, and so half a lifetime is thirty-five years. Thus, Do'eg, who did not live out half his days, died at the age of thirty-four, and Achitofel, who committed suicide, died a year earlier at the age of thirty-three (*Ramah*).

תַּרְתֵּי שְׁנֵי לִתְלָתָא עֲבוּרֵי Two years for three pregnancies. *Rashi* accounts for the two years as follows: Each of the three pregnancies required eight months — seven months for the pregnancy itself, and another month for the woman to purify herself following childbirth. The Rishonim point out the difficulty with this explanation: We are dealing here with the pregnancies of three different women, and so the month of purification should be irrelevant. Rather, three pregnancies of seven months each allow for a deduction of twenty-one months (*Ramah, Ri*), or three pregnancies of nine months each allow for a deduction of twenty-seven months (*Rivan, Ḥamre Veḥaye*), and the Gemara approximated those periods of time as two years.

SAGES

רַבִּי יִצְחָק **Rabbi Yitzḥak.** A Palestinian Amora of the second and third generations, Rabbi Yitzḥak's full name is Rabbi Yitzḥak Nappaḥa. See *Sanhedrin*, Part IV, p. 93.

TRANSLATION AND COMMENTARY

generations of Terach: Terach begot Avram, Nahor, and Haran." [1]The order in which Terach's sons are listed in this verse implies that **Abraham was** at least **a year older than Nahor, and** that **Nahor was** at least **a year older than Haran,** and so **it turns out that Abraham was** at least **two years older than Haran.** [2]**And** another **verse states: "And Avram and Nahor took wives for themselves,** the name of Avram's wife was Sarai; and the name of Nahor's wife, Milkah, the daughter of Haran, the father of Milkah, and the father of Yiskah." [3]**And Rabbi Yitzḥak said:** This **Yiskah,** the daughter of Haran, **was** actually **Sarah,** Abraham's wife. [4]**Why was** Sarah **called Yiskah** (יִסְכָּה)? [5]**Because she** was able to **see** (סוֹכָה) into the future **with the holy spirit.** [6]**And this is what is** meant by God's words to Abraham (Genesis 21:12): **"In all that Sarah has said to you, hearken to her voice."** [7]According to **another explanation,** Sarah was called **Yiskah because everybody would gaze** (סָכִים) **at** her on account of **her beauty.** [8]**And** another **verse states** (Genesis 17:17): **"And Abraham fell upon his face, and laughed, and said in his heart,** Shall a child be born to him that is a hundred years old? And shall Sarah, that is ninety years old, give birth?" [9]Now the following calculations may be made: **How much older was Abraham than Sarah?** [10]He was **ten years** older. [11]**And** Abraham **was older than** Sarah's **father,** Haran, **by** at least **two years,** as is evidenced by the fact that Terach's sons were listed in the order: Abraham, Nahor, and Haran. [12]Thus, **it turns out that when Haran fathered Sarah, he was** no more than **eight** years old.

תֶּרַח תֵּרַח הוֹלִיד אֶת אַבְרָם אֶת נָחוֹר וְאֶת הָרָן". [1]וְאַבְרָהָם גָּדוֹל מִנָּחוֹר שָׁנָה, וְנָחוֹר גָּדוֹל מֵהָרָן שָׁנָה, נִמְצָא אַבְרָהָם גָּדוֹל שְׁתֵּי שָׁנִים מֵהָרָן. [2]וּכְתִיב: "וַיִּקַּח אַבְרָם וְנָחוֹר לָהֶם נָשִׁים וגו'". [3]וְאָמַר רַבִּי יִצְחָק: יִסְכָּה זוֹ שָׂרָה, [4]וְלָמָּה נִקְרָא שְׁמָהּ יִסְכָּה? [5]שֶׁסּוֹכָה בְּרוּחַ הַקֹּדֶשׁ. [6]וְהַיְינוּ דִּכְתִיב: "כֹּל אֲשֶׁר תֹּאמַר אֵלֶיךָ שָׂרָה שְׁמַע בְּקֹלָהּ". [7]דָּבָר אַחֵר: יִסְכָּה — שֶׁהַכֹּל סָכִים בְּיוֹפְיָהּ. [8]וּכְתִיב: "וַיִּפֹּל עַל פָּנָיו וַיִּצְחָק וַיֹּאמֶר בְּלִבּוֹ וגו'". [9]כַּמָּה קַשִּׁישׁ אַבְרָהָם מִשָּׂרָה? [10]עֶשֶׂר שְׁנִין. [11]וְקַשִּׁישׁ מֵאֲבוּהּ תַּרְתֵּין שְׁנִין. [12]אִשְׁתַּכַּח כִּי אוֹלְדָהּ הָרָן לְשָׂרָה — בִּתְמָנֵי אוֹלִידָהּ. [13]מִמַּאי? [14]דִּלְמָא אַבְרָהָם זוּטָא דַּאֲחוּהּ הֲוָה, [15]וְדֶרֶךְ חָכְמָתָן קָא חָשֵׁיב לְהוּ. [16]תֵּדַע, דְּקָא חָשֵׁיב לְהוּ קְרָא דֶּרֶךְ חָכְמָתָן, [17]וּכְתִיב: "וַיְהִי נֹחַ בֶּן חֲמֵשׁ מֵאוֹת שָׁנָה וַיּוֹלֶד נֹחַ אֶת שֵׁם אֶת חָם וְאֶת יָפֶת".

LITERAL TRANSLATION

of Terach: Terach begot Avram, Nahor, and Haran." [1]And Abraham was a year older than Nahor, and Nahor was a year older than Haran. It turns out that Abraham was two years older than Haran. [2]And it is written: "And Avram and Nahor took wives for themselves, etc." [3]And Rabbi Yitzḥak said: Yiskah — that is Sarah. [4]And why was her name called Yiskah? [5]Because she sees with the holy spirit. [6]And this is what is stated: "In all that Sarah has said to you, hearken to her voice." [7]Another explanation: Yiskah — because all gaze at her beauty. [8]And it is written: "And Abraham fell upon his face, and laughed, and said in his heart, etc." [9]How much older was Abraham than Sarah? [10]Ten years. [11]And he was older than her father [by] two years. [12]It turns out that when Haran fathered Sarah — he fathered her at [the age of] eight. [13]From what? [14]Perhaps Abraham was the youngest of his brothers. [15]And it lists them in the order of their wisdom. [16]Know [that this is true], that the verse lists them in the order of their wisdom, [17]for it is written: "And Noah was five hundred years old: and Noah begot Shem, Ham, and Yefet."

RASHI

אברהם גדול מנחור שנה — מדקא חשיב ליה קרא ברישא — וכתיב ויקח אברם ונחור להם נשים, שם אשת אברם שרי, ושם אשת נחור מלכה בת הרן אבי מלכה ואבי יסכה — אלמא יסכה בת הרן, יסכה זו שרה. **דילמא זוטר דאחי הוה** — והרן הוא דקשיש מיניה. **ויהי נח בן חמש מאות שנה** — לאחר שהיה בן חמש מאות שנה הוליד את שלשתן, שם בן מאה שנה ויולד את ארפכשד שנתים אחר המבול.

מִמַּאי [13]The Gemara challenges this line of reasoning: **How** do you know this? [14]**Perhaps Abraham was** actually **the youngest of his brothers.** The order in which the brothers are listed in the verse does not prove otherwise, [15]for the verse may **list them in the order of their wisdom.** Abraham may be mentioned first, not because he was the oldest, but because he was the wisest.

תֵּדַע [16]The Gemara introduces a proof in support of this argument: **Know that this is true, that** brothers **are** sometimes **listed** in the Bible **in the order of their wisdom,** and not according to age, [17]**for the verse states** (Genesis 5:32): **"And Noah was five hundred years old: and Noah begot Shem, Ham, and Yefet."**

NOTES

שֵׁם חָם יָפֶת **Shem, Ham, and Yefet.** *Tosafot* asks: If the verse lists the three brothers in the order of their wisdom,

TRANSLATION AND COMMENTARY

[1]Now, if the brothers are listed here in the order of their age, it would follow that **Shem was a year older than Ham, and** that **Ham was a year older than Yefet,** and so **it would turn out that Shem was two years older than Yefet.** [2]And elsewhere, **the verse states** (Genesis 7:6): **"And Noah was six hundred years old when the flood of waters was upon the earth."** [3]**And** another **verse states** (Genesis 11:10): **"These are the generations of Shem: Shem was a hundred years old, and begot Arpachshad two years after the flood."** [4]Now, if the verse cited above lists Noah's three sons according to age, how could Shem have been **a hundred years old** when he begot Arpachshad two years after the flood? Surely, if he was the oldest of the brothers, he must have been born when his father was five hundred years old. And since the flood occurred when Noah was six hundred years old, Shem must have been a hundred years old at the time. If this were the case, two years later, when he begot Arpachshad, [5]**he must have** already **been a hundred and two!** [6]**Rather,** the verse **lists** Noah's three sons **in the order of their wisdom,** and Shem was listed first because he was the wisest. [7]**Here, too,** then, it may be argued, the verse **lists** the three sons of Terach **in the order of their wisdom,** and not according to age.

אָמַר רַב כָּהֲנָא [8]**Rav Kahana said: I reported this discussion before Rav Zevid of Neharde'a,** [9]and **he said to me: You learn** that Shem was not Noah's firstborn from **that verse.** [10]**but we learn that from** this verse (Genesis 10:21): **"To Shem, also, the father of all the children of Ever, the brother of Yefet the elder,"** [11]for this verse implies that **Yefet,** and not Shem, **was the eldest among his brothers.**

אֶלָּא מְנָלַן [12]The Gemara has now rejected two Midrashic demonstrations that eight-year-old boys once could father children, and it tries a third time: **Rather, from where do we learn** that in the early generations, boys fathered children at the age of eight? [13]We learn that **from here** (Exodus 38:22): **"And Betzalel, the son of Uri, the son of Hur, of the tribe of Judah,** made all that the Lord commanded Moses." [14]**And** elsewhere **it is stated** (I Chronicles 2:19-20): **"And when Azuvah, Caleb's wife was dead, Caleb took to him Efrat, who bore him Hur.** And Hur begot Uri, and Uri begot Betzalel," which shows that Betzalel was Caleb's great-grandson.

[1]שֵׁם גָּדוֹל מֵחָם שָׁנָה, וְחָם גָּדוֹל מִיֶּפֶת שָׁנָה נִמְצָא שֵׁם גָּדוֹל מִיֶּפֶת שְׁתֵּי שָׁנִים. [2]וּכְתִיב: ״וְנֹחַ בֶּן שֵׁשׁ מֵאוֹת שָׁנָה וְהַמַּבּוּל הָיָה מַיִם עַל הָאָרֶץ״. [3]וּכְתִיב: ״(וְאֵלֶּה) תּוֹלְדֹת שֵׁם שֵׁם בֶּן מְאַת שָׁנָה וַיּוֹלֶד אֶת אַרְפַּכְשָׁד שְׁנָתַיִם אַחַר הַמַּבּוּל. [4]בֶּן מֵאָה שָׁנָה?״ [5]בַּר מֵאָה וְתַרְתֵּין שְׁנִין הֲוָה! [6]אֶלָּא, דֶּרֶךְ חָכְמָתָן קָא חָשֵׁיב לְהוּ? [7]הָכָא נַמִי, דֶּרֶךְ חָכְמָתָן קָא חָשֵׁיב לְהוּ.

[8]אָמַר רַב כָּהֲנָא: אָמְרִיתָהּ לִשְׁמַעֲתָא קַמֵּיהּ דְּרַב זְבִיד מִנְּהַרְדְּעָא. [9]אֲמַר לִי: אַתּוּן מֵהָכָא מַתְנִיתוּ, [10]וַאֲנַן מֵהָכָא מַתְנֵינַן לָהּ: ״וּלְשֵׁם יֻלַּד גַּם הוּא אֲבִי כָּל בְּנֵי עֵבֶר אֲחִי יֶפֶת הַגָּדוֹל״, [11]יֶפֶת הַגָּדוֹל שֶׁבְּאֶחָיו הֲוָה.

[12]אֶלָּא מְנָלַן? [13]מֵהָכָא: ״וּבְצַלְאֵל בֶּן אוּרִי בֶן חוּר לְמַטֵּה יְהוּדָה״, [14]וּכְתִיב: ״וַתָּמָת עֲזוּבָה (אֵשֶׁת כָּלֵב) וַיִּקַּח לוֹ כָלֵב אֶת אֶפְרָת וַתֵּלֶד

LITERAL TRANSLATION

[1]Shem was a year older than Ham, and Ham was a year older than Yefet. It turns out that Shem was two years older than Yefet. [2]And it is written: "And Noah was six hundred years old when the flood of waters was upon the earth." [3]And it is written: "These are the generations of Shem: Shem was a hundred years old, and begot Arpachshad two years after the flood."

[4]A hundred years old? [5]He was a hundred and two years old! [6]Rather, it lists them in the order of their wisdom. [7]Here too, it listed them in the order of their wisdom.

[8]Rav Kahana said: I said this teaching before Rav Zevid of Neharde'a. [9]He said to me: You learn this from here, [10]but we learn this from here: "To Shem, also, the father of all the children of Ever, the brother of Yefet the elder" — [11]Yefet was the eldest among his brothers.

[12]Rather, from where do we [learn this]? [13]From here: "And Betzalel, the son of Uri, the son of Hur, of the tribe of Judah." [14]And it is written: "And [when] Azuvah the wife of Caleb died, Caleb took to him Efrat, who bore

RASHI

בר מאה ותרתין הוה — הואיל והוא גדול מכולן נמצא שנולד בחמש מאות שנה לנח, וכשירד המבול היה בן מאה שנה, אלא שמע מינה קטן מכולן הוה ובחמש מאות ושתי שנים לאבוה אתילד, ודרך חכמתן חשיב להו. **ותמת עזובה ויקח לו כלב את אפרת ותלד לו את חור** — אלמא חור בר כלב הוה,

NOTES

then Ham, and not Yefet, should have been mentioned last! Some suggest that the Gemara means that Shem was mentioned first because he was the wisest of the brothers, and then once the verse did not list them according to age, it listed them in reverse age order, starting with the youngest — Shem — and ending with the oldest — Yefet (*Rosh*).

לוֹ אֶת חוּר״. [1]וְכִי עֲבַד בְּצַלְאֵל מִשְׁכָּן, בַּר כַּמָּה הֲוֵי? [2]בַּר תְּלֵיסַר, דִּכְתִיב: ״אִישׁ אִישׁ מִמְּלַאכְתּוֹ אֲשֶׁר הֵמָּה עֹשִׂים״. [3]וְתַנְיָא: ״שָׁנָה רִאשׁוֹנָה עָשָׂה מֹשֶׁה מִשְׁכָּן, [4]שְׁנִיָּה הֵקִים מִשְׁכָּן וְשָׁלַח מְרַגְּלִים״. [5]וּכְתִיב: ״בֶּן אַרְבָּעִים שָׁנָה אָנֹכִי בִּשְׁלֹחַ מֹשֶׁה עֶבֶד ה׳ וגו׳ וְעַתָּה הִנֵּה אָנֹכִי הַיּוֹם בֶּן חָמֵשׁ וּשְׁמֹנִים שָׁנָה״. [6]כַּמָּה הָוְיָא לְהוּ? אַרְבְּעִין. [7]דַּל אַרְבֵּיסַר דַּהֲוָה בְּצַלְאֵל — [8]פְּשָׁא לְהוּ עֶשְׂרִים וְשִׁית. [9]דַּל תַּרְתֵּי שְׁנֵי דִּתְלָתָא עִיבּוּרֵי — [10]אִשְׁתַּכַּח דְּכָל חַד וְחַד בִּתְמָנֵי אוֹלִיד.

[11]״׳בֵּן׳ וְלֹא בַּת״. [12]תַּנְיָא: ״אָמַר רַבִּי שִׁמְעוֹן: [13]בְּדִין הוּא שֶׁתְּהֵא בַּת רְאוּיָה לִהְיוֹת כְּבֵן סוֹרֵר

LITERAL TRANSLATION

him Hur." [1]And when Betzalel fashioned the Tabernacle, how old was he? [2]Thirteen, for it is written: "Every man from his work which they did." [3]And it was taught: "The first year Moses made the Tabernacle, [4]the second [year] he erected the Tabernacle and sent the spies." [5]And it is written: "Forty years old was I when Moses the servant of the Lord sent me....And now, lo, I am this day five and eighty years old." [6]How many were they? Forty. [7]Deduct fourteen when Betzalel was, [8][and] twenty-six are left. [9]Deduct two years for three pregnancies. [10]It turns out that each one fathered [a child] at the age of eight.

[11]"'A son' — and not a daughter." [12]It was taught: "Rabbi Shimon said: [13]By right a daughter should have been fit to become a rebellious

TRANSLATION AND COMMENTARY

Now, the following calculations may be made: [1]**When Betzalel fashioned the Tabernacle, how old was he?** [2]He was **thirteen, for the verse states** (Exodus 36:4): "And all the wise men, that carried out all the work of the sanctuary, came **every man from his work which they did,**" the term "man" implying that anybody who worked on the Tabernacle was at least thirteen years old. [3]**And it was taught** in a Baraita: "During **the first year** following the Exodus from Egypt, **Moses made the Tabernacle;** [4]during **the second year** following the Exodus, **he erected the Tabernacle and sent** out **the spies** to scout the land of Canaan." [5]**And it is stated** that Caleb said to Joshua (Joshua 14:7,10): **"Forty years old was I when Moses the servant of the Lord sent me** from Kadesh-Barnea to spy out the land....**And now, lo, I am this day five and eighty years old."** [6]**How old,** then, was Caleb when he was sent out as a spy? **Forty.** And how much older was Caleb than his great-grandson, Betzalel? [7]**Deduct** at least **fourteen** years of Caleb's life which coincided with those of **Betzalel,** for if Betzalel was at least thirteen years old the first year following the Exodus when he made the Tabernacle, then he was fourteen years old the next year when Moses sent out the spies. [8]Thus, it follows that in the course of **twenty-six years** three generations were born — Hur, Uri, and Betzalel. [9]**Deduct two** more **years for the three pregnancies** that ended with the birth of those three generations — Hur, Uri, and Betzalel — and twenty-four years are left. [10]Thus, **it turns out that each one** — Caleb, Hur, and Uri — **fathered a child at the age of eight.** Thus, we see that in the early generations a boy could father a child at the age of eight.

׳בֵּן׳ וְלֹא בַּת [11]We have learned in our Mishnah: "The word **'son'** teaches that only a son is included in the law of a rebellious child, **and not a daughter."** [12]**It was taught** in a related Baraita: **"Rabbi Shimon said:** [13]**By right a** rebellious **daughter should have been treated** just **like a rebellious son,** and punished in the same

RASHI

ובצלאל היה דור שלישי לה. וכי עבד משכן היה בן שלש עשרה — דקרי ליה איש איש ממלאכתו, וכשנשתלחו המרגלים בשנה השנית כבר היה בן ארבע עשרה שנה וכתיב בן ארבעים שנה אנכי היום.

NOTES

בְּדִין הוּא שֶׁתְּהֵא בַּת **By right a daughter.** The Jerusalem Talmud notes that, by right, liability as a rebellious child should have been imposed upon a daughter, and not upon a son, upon an adult, and not upon a child, upon someone who steals from others, and not upon someone who steals from his own parents. And yet the Torah imposes liability upon a son, and not upon a daughter, upon a child, and not upon an adult, upon someone who steals from his own parents, and not upon someone who steals from others, teaching us that the laws regarding a rebellious child are divine decrees. *Rambam* writes that a daughter is not governed by the laws of a rebellious son because girls are not led to more serious transgressions through gluttonous eating and drinking. *Radbaz* understands that this is the rationale of the Rabbis who disagree with Rabbi Shimon. *Leḥem Mishneh* suggests that, since the law of a rebellious son is a divine decree, the distinction between a boy and a girl offered by *Rambam* is sufficient reason to interpret the verse as limiting the law to a boy, to the exclusion of a girl.

TRANSLATION AND COMMENTARY

manner if she committed the same offense, [70A] **for there are many** people **around her** who are ready to **sin** with her. If she eats and drinks gluttonously as a young girl, there is reason to think that when she reaches full maturity, she will continue to sin and cause others to sin. [1]**But** nevertheless **the Torah decrees** that only a **'son'** can be declared rebellious, **and not a daughter."**

MISHNAH מֵאֵימָתַי [2]**From when is** a rebellious son **liable** to the punishment of stoning? [3]**From when he eats a** ***tartemar*** **of meat** at one meal, **and drinks half a log of Italian** or some other fine **wine** at a time. [4]**Rabbi Yose** disagrees and **says:** He is only liable if he eats **a maneh of meat, and** drinks **a** full **log of wine.**

אָכַל [5]If the boy **ate** meat and drank wine **at a meal** celebrating **a mitzvah,** such as a wedding or a circumcision, [6]**or if he partook** of meat and wine **at a meal marking the intercalation of a month** (it was customary for the court to host a special meal after adding an extra day to the month in order to make the decision known), [7]**or if he partook** of meat and wine purchased with **second-tithe** money **in Jerusalem,** [8]**or if he ate animals that were improperly slaughtered or diseased animals or creeping or crawling things,** [9]**or if he ate** ***tevel*** (produce from which the priestly dues and other tithes had not been separated), **or first tithe from which its terumah** (the portion of the first tithe

וּמוֹרֶה, [70A] שֶׁהַכֹּל מְצוּיִין אֶצְלָהּ בַּעֲבֵירָה, [1]אֶלָּא גְּזֵירַת הַכָּתוּב הִיא: ׳בֵּן׳ וְלֹא בַּת״.

משנה [2]מֵאֵימָתַי חַיָּיב? [3]מִשֶּׁיֹּאכַל תַּרְטֵימָר בָּשָׂר וְיִשְׁתֶּה חֲצִי לוֹג יַיִן הָאִיטַלְקִי. [4]רַבִּי יוֹסֵי אוֹמֵר: מָנֶה בָּשָׂר וְלוֹג יַיִן.

[5]אָכַל בַּחֲבוּרַת מִצְוָה, [6]אָכַל בְּעִיבּוּר הַחֹדֶשׁ, [7]אָכַל מַעֲשֵׂר שֵׁנִי בִּירוּשָׁלַיִם, [8]אָכַל נְבֵילוֹת וּטְרֵיפוֹת שְׁקָצִים וּרְמָשִׂים, [9](אָכַל טֶבֶל וּמַעֲשֵׂר רִאשׁוֹן

LITERAL TRANSLATION

son, [70A] for all are found with her in sin. [1]But it is a decree of the verse: 'A son,' and not a daughter."

MISHNAH [2]From when is he liable? [3]From when he eats a *tartemar* of meat, and drinks half a log of Italian wine. [4]Rabbi Yose says: A maneh of meat, and a log of wine.

[5]If he ate in company [to celebrate] a mitzvah, [6][or if] he ate at [a meal marking] the intercalation of the month, [7][or if] he ate second tithe in Jerusalem, [8][or if] he ate improperly slaughtered or diseased animals, or creeping or crawling things, [9][or if] he ate *tevel,* or first tithe

RASHI

שהכל מצויין אצלה בעבירה — וכשהיא זוללה וסובאה בקטנותה סופה כשלא תמצא למודה עומדת בפרשת דרכים ומרגלת הבריות לעבירה בשביל אתנן.

משנה תרטימר — בגמרא מפרש לה. **יין האיטלקי** — טוב ומעולה הוא וממשיך בתריה, אבל בחמרא אחרינא אינו חייב בחצי לוג. **בחבורת מצוה** — בסעודת מצוה אכל לתרטימר זה אפילו גנבו משל אביו, וכן אם אכלו במנין שהיו נקבצין לעבר החדש גם שם היו עושים סעודות.

LANGUAGE

תַּרְטֵימָר ***Tartemar.*** This word derives from the Greek τριτημοριον, *tritymorion,* and meaning a third or equal to a third. This was also the name of a coin during the Talmudic period.

SAGES

רַבִּי יוֹסֵי Rabbi Yose. This is Rabbi Yose ben Ḥalafta, one of the greatest of the Tannaim. See *Sanhedrin,* Part I, pp. 84-5.

BACKGROUND

לוֹג Log. The log was the standard liquid measure, equal to about 250 grams.

מָנֶה Maneh. The maneh was an ancient unit of weight used for thousands of years. Because of changes over time and in different places, its weight varied. There was also a difference between the maneh used to weigh ordinary substances and that used to weigh precious metals. An ordinary maneh was about 400 grams, but there was also a double maneh that weighed approximately twice that. The unit referred to here is probably an ordinary maneh.

NOTES

יַיִן הָאִיטַלְקִי Italian wine. The Rishonim disagree about the significance of the term *"Italian."* Our commentary follows *Rashi* and others who understand that the word *"Italian"* modifies the word *"wine."* Only if the boy drank Italian wine, which is particularly strong, is he liable for drinking half a log of the beverage, but if he drank other wines, he is not liable unless he drank a larger quantity. *Ramah* understands that the word *"Italian"* modifies the word log, and teaches that here we use the larger Italian unit of measure, rather than the usual "wilderness" unit. *Rambam* does not specify "Italian" wine. *Radbaz* explains that the Mishnah mentions Italian wine, because that was a good-quality wine of that day. But the boy is also liable if he drank half a log of similar wine.

אָכַל טֶבֶל וּמַעֲשֵׂר רִאשׁוֹן If he ate ***tevel,*** **or first tithe.** A number of Rishonim note that this line should be erased, for the Mishnah speaks of "eating" *tevel* and first tithe, and they cannot mean meat, but only wine, which is "drunk" (*Ramah, Tosafot Yom Tov,* and others). *Meiri* suggests that the Mishnah is referring to a case where the boy sold *tevel* or first tithe and purchased meat with the proceeds. Others suggest that the Mishnah is in fact referring to wine that is *tevel* or first tithe, and that the term "eating" may be understood as referring to "drinking" (*Tiferet Yisrael, Arukh LeNer*).

HALAKHAH

מֵאֵימָתַי חַיָּיב? From when is he liable? "A rebellious son is only liable to the death penalty if he ate the weight of fifty dinars (a *tartemar*) of meat and drank half a log of wine at one time. (*Radbaz* notes that it is not necessary for the wine to be Italian.)" (*Rambam, Sefer Shofetim, Hilkhot Mamrim* 7:2.)

אָכַל בַּחֲבוּרַת מִצְוָה If he ate a meal to celebrate a mitzvah. "If the rebellious son ate meat and drank wine in a gluttonous manner at a meal celebrating a mitzvah, or if he ate meat and wine purchased with second-tithe money in Jerusalem, or if he ate meat and wine at a meal of consolation served in a house of mourning, he is exempt from the death penalty. Similarly, if he ate forbidden foods, whether they were forbidden by Torah law or only by Rabbinic decree, like eating on a public fast, he is exempt from the death penalty." (*Rambam, Sefer Shofetim, Hilkhot Mamrim* 7:2.)

SAGES

רַבִּי זֵירָא Rabbi Zera. Born in Babylonia, Rabbi Zera became one of the greatest of the third generation of Palestinian Amoraim. See *Sanhedrin,* Part III, p. 66.

רַב הוּנָא Rav Huna. The great Babylonian Amora of the second generation. See *Sanhedrin,* Part I, p. 61.

TRANSLATION AND COMMENTARY

that the Levite must remove and give to a priest) **was not taken,** [1]**or second tithe or consecrated property which was not redeemed,** [2]**or if he ate something that it is a mitzvah to eat,** even if only by Rabbinic enactment, as at a mourner's house, **or** if he ate **something that it is forbidden** to eat, even if only by Rabbinic decree, as on a communal fast, [3]**or if he ate any** other **food, but did not eat meat,** [4]**or if he drank any** other **drink, but did not drink wine** — [5]in all these cases **he does not become a rebellious son.** He is not considered a rebellious son [6]**unless he ate meat and drank wine, for the verse states** (Deuteronomy 21:20): **"He is a glutton** [זוֹלֵל] **and a drunkard** [סֹבֵא]," and those terms refer to eating meat and drinking wine in excess. [7]**Even though there is no** clear **proof** in the Bible that those terms specify meat and wine, [8]**there is an allusion to this in the verse** that **states** (Proverbs 23:20): **"Be not among the swillers of wine** [סֹבְאֵי יָיִן], **among gluttonous eaters of meat** [זֹלְלֵי בָשָׂר]."

GEMARA אָמַר רַבִּי זֵירָא [9]**Rabbi Zera said: I do not know how much a** ***tartemar*** **is, but since Rabbi Yose doubled the standard** amount **of wine** — [10]**it follows that he also doubled the standard** amount **of meat** required by the anonymous first Tanna. Since, according to Rabbi Yose, a boy can only become a rebellious son if he eats a full maneh of meat, [11]**it follows** that according to the anonymous first Tanna, he can become a rebellious son even if he only eats half a maneh of meat. Thus **a** ***tartemar*** **is half a maneh.**

אָמַר [12]**Rav Ḥanan bar Moladah said in the name of Rav Huna:** A rebellious son **is not liable** to be put to death by stoning **unless he purchased meat cheaply and ate it,** [13]**and he purchased wine cheaply and drank it, as the verse states** (Deuteronomy 21:20): **"He is a glutton** [זוֹלֵל] **and a drunkard."** The word זוֹלֵל, translated here as "glutton," contains the word זוֹל, "cheap." A rebellious son is only liable if he stole money from his father to buy food and drink, and a boy has few opportunities to steal enough money for expensive meat and wine. Hence, there is little concern that partaking of expensive comestibles will lead to intemperance and more serious transgressions.

שֶׁלֹּא נִטְּלָה תְּרוּמָתוֹ [1]וּמַעֲשֵׂר שֵׁנִי וְהֶקְדֵּשׁ שֶׁלֹּא נִפְדּוּ). [2]אָכַל דָּבָר שֶׁהוּא מִצְוָה וְדָבָר שֶׁהוּא עֲבֵירָה, [3]אָכַל כָּל מַאֲכָל וְלֹא אָכַל בָּשָׂר, [4]שָׁתָה כָּל מַשְׁקֶה וְלֹא שָׁתָה יַיִן — [5]אֵינוֹ נַעֲשֶׂה בֵּן סוֹרֵר וּמוֹרֶה, [6]עַד שֶׁיֹּאכַל בָּשָׂר וְיִשְׁתֶּה יַיִן, שֶׁנֶּאֱמַר: "זוֹלֵל וְסֹבֵא". [7]וְאַף עַל פִּי שֶׁאֵין רְאָיָה לַדָּבָר, [8]זֵכֶר לַדָּבָר, שֶׁנֶּאֱמַר: "אַל תְּהִי בְסֹבְאֵי יָיִן בְּזֹלְלֵי בָשָׂר לָמוֹ".

גמרא [9]אָמַר רַבִּי זֵירָא: תַּרְטֵימָר זֶה אֵינִי יוֹדֵעַ מַהוּ, אֶלָּא מִתּוֹךְ שֶׁכָּפַל רַבִּי יוֹסֵי בַּיַּיִן, [10]נִמְצָא כּוֹפֵל אַף בַּבָּשָׂר, [11]וְנִמְצָא תַּרְטֵימָר חֲצִי מָנֶה.

[12]אָמַר רַב חָנָן בַּר מוֹלָדָה אָמַר רַב הוּנָא: אֵינוֹ חַיָּיב עַד שֶׁיִּקַּח בָּשָׂר בְּזוֹל וְיֹאכַל, [13]יַיִן בְּזוֹל וְיִשְׁתֶּה, דִּכְתִיב: "זוֹלֵל וְסֹבֵא".

LITERAL TRANSLATION

from which its terumah was not taken, [1]or second tithe or consecrated property which was not redeemed, [2][or if] he ate something that it is a mitzvah [to eat], or something that is a transgression, [3][or if] he ate every food, but did not eat meat, [4][or if] he drank every drink, but did not drink wine — [5]he does not become a rebellious son, [6]unless he eats meat and drinks wine, as it is stated: "He is a glutton and a drunkard." [7]And even though there is no proof to the matter, [8]there is a remembrance of the matter, as it is stated: "Be not among swillers of wine, among gluttonous eaters of meat."

GEMARA [9]Rabbi Zera said: I do not know what this *tartemar* is, but since Rabbi Yose doubled the [standard amount of] wine, [10]it follows that he also doubled the [standard amount of] meat, [11]and it follows that a *tartemar* is half a maneh.

[12]Rav Ḥanan bar Moladah said in the name of Rav Huna: He is not liable unless he purchases meat cheaply and eats [it], [13][and purchases] wine cheaply and drinks [it], for it is written: "He is a glutton and a drunkard."

RASHI

אבל מעשר שני – וכן כולם, אף על פי שגנבו משל אביו – פטור, וטעמא מפרש בגמרא. **ואף על פי שאין ראיה לדבר** – דדילמא מאכל אחרינא נמי קרא ליה זולל, ומיהו שלמה אהא אזהריה דממשיך טפי. **זכר לדבר** – דבבשר מקרי זולל וביין מקרי סובא.

גמרא מתוך שכפל רבי יוסי ביין – דקאמר תנא קמא חצי לוג, והוא אמר: לוג. **כפל נמי בבשר** – והוי מנה דקאמר שני תרטימר. **יין בזול** – אבל ביוקר לא שכיחי ליה מעות לגנוב כולי האי ולא ממשיך. **זולל** – לשון זול, ואסמכתא למילתיה הוא.

HALAKHAH

לֹא אָכַל בָּשָׂר וְלֹא שָׁתָה יַיִן If he did not eat meat and if he did not drink wine. "If a rebellious son ate any other food, but did not eat red meat (even if he ate poultry), or if he drank any other drink, but did not drink wine, he is exempt from the death penalty," following the Mishnah. (*Rambam, Sefer Shofetim, Hilkhot Mamrim* 7:3.)

עַד שֶׁיִּקַּח בָּשָׂר בְּזוֹל Unless he purchases meat cheaply. "A rebellious son is only liable to the death penalty if he himself purchased the meat and wine cheaply." (*Rambam, Sefer Shofetim, Hilkhot Mamrim* 7:2.)

LITERAL TRANSLATION

[1]And Rav Ḥanan bar Moladah said in the name of Rav Huna: [2]He is not liable unless he eats raw meat and drinks unmixed wine.

[3]Is that so? [4]But surely Rabbah and Rav Yosef both said: [If] he ate raw meat and [drank] unmixed wine, [5]he does not become a rebellious son!

[6]Ravina said: Unmixed wine — [7]mixed, but not mixed. [8]Raw meat — [9]cooked, but not cooked, [10]like the roasted meat that thieves eat.

[11]Rabbah and Rav Yosef both said: [If] he ate salted meat, or drank wine from his winepress, [12]he does not become a rebellious son.

[13]We have learned elsewhere: "On the day before the Ninth of Av,

[1]וְאָמַר רַב חָנָן בַּר מוֹלָדָה אָמַר רַב הוּנָא: [2]אֵינוֹ חַיָּיב עַד שֶׁיֹּאכַל בָּשָׂר חַי וְיִשְׁתֶּה יַיִן חַי. [3]אִינִי? [4]וְהָא רַבָּה וְרַב יוֹסֵף דְּאָמְרִי תַּרְוַיְיהוּ: אָכַל בָּשָׂר חַי וְשָׁתָה יַיִן חַי [5]אֵינוֹ נַעֲשֶׂה בֵּן סוֹרֵר וּמוֹרֶה.

[6]אָמַר רָבִינָא: יַיִן חַי — [7]מְזִיג וְלָא מְזִיג. [8]בָּשָׂר חַי — [9]בְּשִׁיל וְלָא בְּשִׁיל, [10]כִּבְשַׂר כִּיבָּא דְּאָכְלִי גַּנָּבֵי.

[11]רַבָּה וְרַב יוֹסֵף דְּאָמְרִי תַּרְוַיְיהוּ: אָכַל בְּשַׂר מָלִיחַ וְשָׁתָה יַיִן מִגִּיתּוֹ, [12]אֵין נַעֲשֶׂה בֵּן סוֹרֵר וּמוֹרֶה.

[13]תְּנַן הָתָם: "עֶרֶב תִּשְׁעָה בְּאָב

TRANSLATION AND COMMENTARY

וְאָמַר [1]**Rav Ḥanan bar Moladah said in the name of Rav Huna:** [2]A rebellious son **is not liable** to the punishment of death by stoning **unless he eats raw meat and drinks unmixed wine.**

אִינִי [3]The Gemara asks: But **is that** really **so?** [4]**Surely Rabbah and Rav Yosef both said** just the opposite: **If** a rebellious son **ate raw meat and unmixed wine,** [5]**he does not become a rebellious son,** for he does derive enjoyment from them.

אָמַר רָבִינָא [6]**Ravina said:** When Rav Huna said that a rebellious son is only liable if he drank **unmixed wine,** he was not referring to wine that was not mixed at all, for if he drank such wine, he would indeed be exempt, as was argued by Rabbah and Rav Yosef. [7]Rather, he was referring to wine that was **mixed** with a certain amount of water, **but not mixed** with the usual amount of water. [8]And when Rav Huna said that a rebellious son is only liable if he ate **raw meat,** he was not referring to meat that was totally raw, for if he ate such meat, he would indeed be exempt, as was argued by Rabbah and Rav Yosef. [9]Rather, he was referring to meat that was partially **cooked, but not** completely **cooked,** [10]**like the roasted meat that thieves eat.** If a rebellious son drank partially diluted wine and ate partially cooked meat, he is liable, but if the wine was thoroughly diluted or the meat was fully cooked, he is not liable, for the boy-thief does not have the time to prepare his food in the proper manner, and so he is not drawn to foods of that kind.

רַבָּה [11]**Rabbah and Rav Yosef both said: If** a rebellious son **ate** heavily **salted meat, or drank wine** straight **from his winepress** before it fully fermented, [12]**he does not become a rebellious son**, for these are not signs of unrestrained gluttony.

תְּנַן הָתָם [13]**We have learned elsewhere** in the Mishnah (*Ta'anit* 26b): **"On the day before the Ninth**

RASHI

מולדה — שם אביו. **יין חי** — ממשיך מפני שמשובח הוא, ולקמיה מוקי לה במזיג ולא מזיג, אבל בתר יין מזיג לא ממשיך. **בשר חי** — כדמפרש לקמן בשיל ולא בשיל, דזו היא מדת גנב למהר, אבל בשיל שפיר לא ממשיך למעבד כי האי גוונא — לפי שמתוך שהוא גנב ועושה בסתר אין לו שהות. **אמר רבינא יין חי** — דקאמר רב הונא מזיג ולא מזיג לאפוקי היכא דנתן בו מים הרבה, ואף על פי שרוב בני אדם שותין כן. **בשר כיבא דאכלי גנבי** — כוויה בגחלים, ודכותה בעירובין (כט,ב) וניכביה וניכול, בזבחים (מו,ב) לאפוקי כבבא דלא. **בשר מליח ויין מגתו** — לא חשיבי ולא ממשיך.

NOTES

כִּבְשַׂר כִּיבָּא Like the roasted meat. *Ramah* understands that this refers to meat which thieves eat in wineshops "between the barrels of wine." The thieves who frequent such shops in order to have easy access to wine bring with them partially cooked meat in order to counteract the intoxicating effects of the wine. (See also *Arukh.*)

HALAKHAH

בָּשָׂר חַי יַיִן חַי Raw meat and unmixed wine. "If the rebellious son ate raw meat, or drank unmixed wine, he is exempt from stoning." (*Rambam, Sefer Shofetim, Hilkhot Mamrim* 7:4.)

בְּשַׂר מָלִיחַ יַיִן מִגִּיתּוֹ Salted meat and wine from his winepress. "If the rebellious son ate salted meat on the third day after it was salted, or if he drank wine straight from his winepress, he is not liable to the death penalty," following Rabbah and Rav Yosef. (*Rambam, Sefer Shofetim, Hilkhot Mamrim* 7:4.)

עֶרֶב תִּשְׁעָה בְּאָב The day before the Ninth of Av. "On the day before the Ninth of Av, during the final meal before the fast, a person may not eat meat or drink wine, nor may he eat two cooked foods." (*Shulḥan Arukh, Oraḥ Ḥayyim* 552:1.)

TRANSLATION AND COMMENTARY

of Av, during the last meal prior to the fast, **a person may not eat two cooked foods, nor may he eat meat or drink wine."** [1]**And a Sage taught** a Baraita which states: **"But he may eat** heavily **salted meat and drink wine** straight **from his winepress."** [2]Regarding **salted meat — how long** does it remain forbidden on the day before the Ninth of Av? [3]**Rabbi Ḥanina bar Kahana said:** For **as long as it** could still be eaten were it **a peace offering,** two days and the intervening night. But by the third day, the salt has altered the taste of the meat, and so it may be eaten even on the day before the Ninth of Av. [4]**And** regarding **wine** straight **from his winepress, how long** does it remain permitted on the day before the Ninth of Av? [5]**As long as it is** still **fermenting.** [6]**And it was taught** in a Baraita: **"Fermenting wine is not governed by the laws regarding uncovered foods.** The Rabbis decreed that wine, water, or other liquids (and certain foods) that were left exposed and unattended may not be consumed, because a poisonous snake may have contaminated them by depositing venom in them. But there is no such concern regarding wine that is still fermenting. [7]**How long does the fermentation** process continue? [8]**Three days."** Now that we have learned the definitions of salted meat and fermenting wine regarding the day before the Ninth of Av, [9]the Gemara asks: **What is the law here** regarding a rebellious son?

הָתָם [10]The Gemara answers: **There,** regarding the day before the Ninth of Av, eating meat and drinking wine are forbidden **because of the joy** that these things bring a person. [11]Even heavily salted meat, **while** it is permitted to be eaten as **a peace-offering,** [12]**brings** a person a certain amount of **joy.** Only after three full days of salting can we say that it is no longer enjoyed as meat. [13]But **here,** regarding a rebellious son, he is liable for eating meat and drinking wine, **because** we are concerned that **he will be led** to graver transgressions. [14]Therefore, if a boy ate heavily salted meat, even **a short time** after it was salted, he does not become a rebellious son, for the meat's taste has already been altered, and there is **no** concern that **he will be led** to more serious offenses. [15]Regarding a rebellious son, **wine** is considered as coming straight from the winepress **for forty days,** for until that time it does not have the full taste of wine. Thus, there is no concern that he will be led to more serious transgressions, if he drinks it.

לֹא יֹאכַל אָדָם שְׁנֵי תַבְשִׁילִין וְלֹא יֹאכַל בָּשָׂר וְלֹא יִשְׁתֶּה יַיִן״. [1]וְתָנָא: ״אֲבָל אוֹכֵל הוּא בְּשַׂר מָלִיחַ וְשׁוֹתֶה יַיִן מִגִּתּוֹ״. [2]בְּשַׂר מָלִיחַ — עַד כַּמָּה? [3]אָמַר רַבִּי חֲנִינָא בַּר כָּהֲנָא: כָּל זְמַן שֶׁהוּא כִּשְׁלָמִים. [4]וְיַיִן מִגִּיתּוֹ — עַד כַּמָּה? [5]כָּל זְמַן שֶׁהוּא תּוֹסֵס. [6]וְהָתַנְיָא: ״יַיִן תּוֹסֵס אֵין בּוֹ מִשּׁוּם גִּילּוּי. [7]וְכַמָּה תְּסִיסָתוֹ? [8]שְׁלֹשָׁה יָמִים״. [9]הָכָא מַאי?
[10]הָתָם, מִשּׁוּם שִׂמְחָה הוּא. [11]כָּל זְמַן שֶׁהוּא כִּשְׁלָמִים, [12]נַמִי אִית בֵּיהּ שִׂמְחָה. [13]הָכָא מִשּׁוּם אִימְשׁוֹכֵי הוּא, [14]וּבְכָל שֶׁהוּא לֹא מִימְשִׁיךְ. [15]וְיַיִן עַד אַרְבָּעִים יוֹם.

LITERAL TRANSLATION

a person may not eat two cooked foods, nor may he eat meat or drink wine." [1]And [a Sage] taught: "But he may eat salted meat and drink wine from his winepress." [2]Salted meat — how long? [3]Rabbi Ḥanina bar Kahana said: As long as it is like a peace offering. [4]And wine from his winepress — for how long? [5]As long as it is fermenting. [6]And it was taught: "Fermenting wine is not governed by [the laws regarding] uncovered foods. [7]And how long is its fermentation? [8]Three days." [9]Here, what [is the law]? [10]There, it is on account of joy. [11]As long as it is like a peace-offering, [12]he has joy. [13]Here it is on account of being led [astray], [14]and with a slight amount he will not be led [astray]. [15]And wine until forty days.

RASHI

כל זמן שהוא כשלמים — שלא עבר עליו זמן אכילת שלמים שני ימים ולילה אחד עדיין בלחלוחותו הוא ולא אקרי מליח ומשמח את הלב, דכתיב (דברים כז) וזבחת שלמים ואכלת שם ושמחת אלמא בר שמחה הוא, אבל בתר הכי הוי מליח ונחלף טעמו במלחו. **כל זמן שהוא תוסס** — שהוא נושך בגרון מחמת שהוא מחמיץ. **הכא** — בבן סורר ומורה. **מאי** — עד כמה לא קרינן מליח למיפטר בן סורר ומורה. **ובבל שהוא לא ממשיך** — משעבר לילה

NOTES

וְיַיִן עַד אַרְבָּעִים יוֹם **And wine until forty days.** Our commentary follows *Rashi* and *Ramah,* who understand that the Gemara

HALAKHAH

אֲבָל אוֹכֵל הוּא בְּשַׂר מָלִיחַ **But he may eat salted meat.** "At the last meal before the Ninth of Av fast, it is customary not even to eat salted meat three days after it has been salted, nor the meat of fowl or fish, nor wine taken from the winepress that has fermented for less than three days." (*Tur,* in the name of *Or Zaru'a.*) (*Shulḥan Arukh, Oraḥ Ḥayyim* 552:2.)

אֵין בּוֹ מִשּׁוּם גִּילּוּי **Is not governed by the laws regarding uncovered foods.** "Fermenting wine during the first three days of the fermentation process is not governed by the laws regarding uncovered foods." (*Tur, Shulḥan Arukh, Yoreh De'ah* 116.)

TRANSLATION AND COMMENTARY

אָמַר רַב חָנָן [1]Having discussed several Halakhic points regarding wine, the Gemara now cites a number of Aggadic statements on the topic. **Rav Hanan said: Wine was only created in the world to comfort mourners and to reward the wicked** in this world for any good deeds they may have performed, so that they may be punished more severely in the World to Come. [2]This is learned from **the verse** that **states** (Proverbs 31:6): **"Give strong drink to him that is ready to perish and wine to those of heavy heart."**

אָמַר רַבִּי יִצְחָק [3]**Rabbi Yitzhak said: What is** the meaning of **the verse that states** (Proverbs 23:31): **"Look not upon wine when it is red"?** [4]**Look not upon wine** and allow yourself to be attracted to it, for it **reddens the faces of the wicked in this world** when they drink of it, **but it whitens their faces** with shame **in the World to Come.**

רָבָא אָמַר [5]**Rava said: "Look not upon wine when it is red"** — [6]**look not upon wine** and allow yourself to be attracted to it, **for it leads to bloodshed.**

רַב כָּהֲנָא רָמֵי [7]**Rav Kahana pointed out** a certain contradiction: The word *tirosh,* "young wine," **is** sometimes **written** in a defective manner (without a *vav*), so that it can be read as ***tirash,*** **and** yet **it is** always **read *tirosh,*** as if it were written plene (with a *vav*). [8]This teaches that **if** a person **merits** and is careful to drink wine in moderation, **he will become a head** (*rosh*), [9]but **if he does not merit** and he drinks excessively, **he will become poor** (*rash*).

רָבָא רָמֵי [10]**Rava pointed out** a different contradiction: The verse states (Psalms 104:15): "And wine that makes glad the heart of man." The word *yesamah* **is written** so that it can also be read as ***yeshamah*** (with a *shin*), **but it is read** as ***yesamah*** (with a *sin*). [11]This teaches that **if** a person **merits** and is careful to drink wine in moderation, the wine **will make him glad** (*yesamah*). [12]But **if he does not merit** and he drinks in an excessive manner, the wine **will** only **ruin him** (*yeshamah*). [13]**And this is what Rava said: Wine and** aromatic **spices** have **made me wise,** showing that drinking wine in moderation can be beneficial.

[1]אָמַר רַב חָנָן: לֹא נִבְרָא יַיִן בָּעוֹלָם אֶלָּא לְנַחֵם אֲבֵלִים וּלְשַׁלֵּם שָׂכָר לָרְשָׁעִים, [2]שֶׁנֶּאֱמַר: "תְּנוּ שֵׁכָר לְאוֹבֵד וְיַיִן לְמָרֵי נָפֶשׁ".

[3]אָמַר רַבִּי יִצְחָק: מַאי דִּכְתִיב: "אַל תֵּרֶא יַיִן כִּי יִתְאַדָּם"? [4]אַל תֵּרֶא יַיִן שֶׁמַּאְדִּים פְּנֵיהֶם שֶׁל רְשָׁעִים בָּעוֹלָם הַזֶּה, וּמַלְבִּין פְּנֵיהֶם לָעוֹלָם הַבָּא.

[5]רָבָא אָמַר: [6]"אַל תֵּרֶא יַיִן כִּי יִתְאַדָּם" — אַל תֵּרֶא יַיִן שֶׁאַחֲרִיתוֹ דָּם.

[7]רַב כָּהֲנָא רָמֵי: כְּתִיב: תִּירָשׁ, וְקָרֵינַן: "תִּירוֹשׁ". [8]זָכָה, נַעֲשֶׂה רֹאשׁ; [9]לֹא זָכָה, נַעֲשֶׂה רָשׁ.

[10]רָבָא רָמֵי: כְּתִיב: "יְשַׁמַּח", וְקָרֵינַן: "יְשַׂמַּח". [11]זָכָה, מְשַׂמְּחוֹ; [12]לֹא זָכָה, מְשַׁמְּמֵהוּ. [13]וְהַיְינוּ דְּאָמַר רָבָא: חַמְרָא וְרֵיחָנֵי פַּקְחִין.

LITERAL TRANSLATION

[1]Rav Hanan said: Wine was only created in the world to comfort mourners and to reward the wicked, [2]as it is stated: "Give strong drink to him that is ready to perish, and wine to those of heavy heart."

[3]Rabbi Yitzhak said: What is that which is written: "Look not upon wine when it is red"? [4]Look not upon wine that reddens the faces of the wicked in this world, and whitens their faces in the World to Come.

[5]Rava said: "Look not upon wine when it is red" — [6]Look not upon wine for its end is blood.

[7]Rav Kahana raised (lit., "cast") [a contradiction]: It is written: *"Tirash,"* and we read: *Tirosh.* [8][If] he merits, he becomes a head; [9][if] he does not merit, he becomes poor.

[10]Rava raised (lit., "cast") [a contradiction]: It is written: *"Yeshamah,"* and we read: *Yesamah.* [11][If] he merits, it makes him glad; [12][if] he does not merit, it confounds him. [13]And this is what Rava said: Wine and spices made me wise.

RASHI

אחת מפיג טעמו ולא חשוב. **לשלם שכר לרשעים** – שמתעדנין בו בעולם הזה ומקבלין בו שכר מצוה שעושין בעולם הזה. **לאובד** – היינו רשע שנטרד והולך לו. **למרי נפש** – לאבלים, לפכוחי צערייהו. **אל תרא יין** – כלומר אל תתן עיניך לימשך אחריו. **שאחריתו דם** – סופו יהרג עליו. **כתיב יין ישמח לבב אנוש** – בשי"ן, דמשמע לשון שומם, שמשממהו ונוטל חכמת לבו. **וקרינן ישמח** – לשון שמחה. **זכה** – כלומר אם זכה וידע להזהר בעצמו מלשתות יותר מדאי – משמחו, שמפקח את הלב. **פקחין** – עשאוני פקח.

NOTES

resolves its problem and distinguishes between the law regarding the Ninth of Av and the law regarding a rebellious son, ruling that a boy does not become a rebellious son if he eats heavily salted meat, even a short time after it is salted, or if he drinks wine within forty days after it is pressed. *Rambam* understands that the Gemara presents this as one possibility, but does not decide the matter. Thus, the boy is only exempt from liability if he eats the meat on the third day after it is salted, or drinks the wine within three days after it is pressed (see *Meiri*).

TRANSLATION AND COMMENTARY

אָמַר [1] **Rav Amram the son of Rabbi Shimon bar Abba said in the name of Rabbi Ḥanina:** [2] **What is the** meaning of **the verses that state** (Proverbs 23:29-30): **"Who cries, 'Woe'? Who cries, 'Alas'? Who has quarrels? Who has complaints? Who has wounds for nothing? Who has redness of eyes? They who tarry long at the wine; they who go to seek mixed wine."?** [3] **When Rav Dimi came** from Eretz Israel to Babylonia, **he said:** [4] **In Eretz Israel they say** as follows: **These verses** can be expounded in either direction. If **someone expounds** the passage **from its beginning to its end,** [5] **it is expounded** well: Who cries, "Woe," or, "Alas"? Who has quarrels or complaints? He who tarries long at the wine. [6] And if someone expounds the passage in the other direction **from its end to its beginning, it is** also **expounded** well: For whom is it fitting to tarry long after the wine? For someone who cries, "Woe," or, "Alas" — a mourner, and for someone who quarrels, complains, and is responsible for pointless wounds — a wicked man.

דָּרֵישׁ [7] **A wayfarer from Galilee expounded: Thirteen** verbs beginning with the letter *vav* **are found in** the Torah passage describing the disastrous results of Noah's drinking **wine** (Genesis 9:20-24), each *vav* alluding to the exclamatory word *vy* ("woe"): **"And Noah began** [וַיָּחֶל] **to be a man of the soil, and he planted** [וַיִּטַּע] **a vineyard; and he drank** [וַיֵּשְׁתְּ] **of the wine, and was drunk** [וַיִּשְׁכָּר]**; and he was uncovered** [וַיִּתְגַּל] **within his tent. And Ham, the father of Canaan, saw** [וַיַּרְא] **the nakedness of his father, and told** [וַיַּגֵּד] **his two brothers outside. And Shem and Japhet took** [וַיִּקַּח] **the garment, and laid** [וַיָּשִׂימוּ] **it upon both their shoulders, and went** [וַיֵּלְכוּ] **backward, and covered** [וַיְכַסּוּ] **the nakedness of their father, and their faces** were turned away, and they saw not their father's nakedness. **And Noah** [וַיִּיקֶץ] **awoke from his wine, and knew** [וַיֵּדַע] **what his younger son had done to him."**

[1] אֲמַר רַב עַמְרָם בְּרֵיהּ דְּרַבִּי שִׁמְעוֹן בַּר אַבָּא אֲמַר רַבִּי חֲנִינָא: [2] מַאי דִּכְתִיב: "לְמִי אוֹי לְמִי אֲבוֹי לְמִי מְדָנִים לְמִי שִׂיחַ לְמִי פְּצָעִים חִנָּם לְמִי חַכְלִלוּת עֵינָיִם (וגו׳) לַמְאַחֲרִים עַל הַיָּיִן לַבָּאִים לַחְקֹר מִמְסָךְ". [3] כִּי אֲתָא רַב דִּימִי אֲמַר: [4] אָמְרִי בְּמַעַרְבָא: הַאי קְרָא מַאן דְּדָרֵישׁ לֵיהּ מֵרֵישֵׁיהּ לְסֵיפֵיהּ — [5] מִדְּרִישׁ. [6] וּמִסֵּיפֵיהּ לְרֵישֵׁיהּ — מִדְּרִישׁ.

[7] דָּרֵישׁ עוֹבֵר גְּלִילָאָה: שְׁלֹשׁ עֶשְׂרֵה וָוִי״ן נֶאֶמַר בַּיַּיִן: "וַיָּחֶל נֹחַ אִישׁ הָאֲדָמָה וַיִּטַּע כָּרֶם וַיֵּשְׁתְּ מִן הַיַּיִן וַיִּשְׁכָּר וַיִּתְגַּל בְּתוֹךְ אָהֳלוֹ וַיַּרְא חָם אֲבִי כְנַעַן אֵת עֶרְוַת אָבִיו וַיַּגֵּד לִשְׁנֵי אֶחָיו בַּחוּץ וַיִּקַּח שֵׁם וָיֶפֶת אֶת הַשִּׂמְלָה וַיָּשִׂימוּ עַל שְׁכֶם שְׁנֵיהֶם וַיֵּלְכוּ אֲחֹרַנִּית וַיְכַסּוּ אֵת עֶרְוַת אֲבִיהֶם וּפְנֵיהֶם וגו׳ וַיִּיקֶץ נֹחַ מִיֵּינוֹ וַיֵּדַע אֵת אֲשֶׁר עָשָׂה לוֹ בְּנוֹ הַקָּטָן".

LITERAL TRANSLATION

[1] Rav Amram the son of Rabbi Shimon bar Abba said in the name of Rabbi Ḥanina: [2] What is that which is written: "Who cries, 'Woe'? Who cries, 'Alas'? Who has quarrels? Who has complaints? Who has wounds for nothing? Who has redness of eyes? They who tarry long at the wine; they who go to seek mixed wine."? [3] When Rav Dimi came, he said: [4] They say in the West: [Regarding] this verse, he who expounds it from its beginning to its end — [5] it is expounded. [6] And from its end to its beginning — it is expounded.

[7] A wayfarer from Galilee expounded: Thirteen *vavs* were stated regarding wine: "And Noah began to be a man of the soil, and he planted a vineyard; and he drank of the wine, and was drunk; and he was uncovered within his tent. And Ham, the father of Canaan, saw the nakedness of his father, and told his two brothers outside. And Shem and Japhet took the garment, and laid it upon both their shoulders, and went backward, and covered the nakedness of their father, and their faces, etc. And Noah awoke from his wine, and knew what his younger son had done to him."

RASHI

אבוי — לשון צעקה בלשון ארמי, כמו בייא בייא (סנהדרין סד,א). **שיחי** — צערי, כמו אריד בשיחי (תהלים נה). **למי כל אלה** — למאחרים על היין. **מרישיה לסיפיה** — מאן דדריש ליה מרישיה לסיפיה. **מדריש** — נדרש משמעותיה יפה, והכי קאמר: למי כל אלה — למאחרים על היין, לבאים לחקור ממסך, שחוקרין להיכן היין הטוב הממוסך בבשמים, כמו מסכה יינה (משלי ט). **ומאן דדריש ליה מסיפיה לרישיה מדריש** — נדרש משמעותו יפה, והכי קאמר: למי שיש לו אוי ואבוי ושיח דהיינו אבלים, ולמי שיש לו מדנים ופצעים חנם, דהיינו רשע הנלחם עם הבריות, ולמי שיש לו חכלילות עינים מרוב שומנו ושקיטתו — להם ראוי להיות מאחרים על היין. **י״ג ווי״ן** — לשון וי וי ויאמר ארור כנען לא חשיב, אלא עד דידע דנגמר לו עונשו של יין.

NOTES

שְׁלֹשׁ עֶשְׂרֵה וָוִי״ן **Thirteen *vavs*.** The Gemara does not count all the words in the passage that begin with a *vav*, but only those words that begin with *vav-yod*. It also does not count the word וָיֶפֶת, "and Japhet," either because it is a name (*Tosafot*), or because the *vav* is vocalized with a *kamatz* (see *Maharsha, Torat Ḥayyim*).

[1]רַב וּשְׁמוּאֵל, חַד אָמַר: סֵרְסוֹ. [2]וְחַד אָמַר: רְבָעוֹ. [3]מַאן דְּאָמַר סֵרְסוֹ — [4]מִתּוֹךְ שֶׁקִּלְקְלוֹ בָּרְבִיעִי קִלְּלוֹ בָּרְבִיעִי. [5]וּמַאן דְּאָמַר רְבָעוֹ — [6]גָּמַר "וַיַּרְא" "וַיַּרְא". [7]כְּתִיב הָכָא: "וַיַּרְא חָם אֲבִי כְנַעַן אֵת עֶרְוַת אָבִיו", [8]וּכְתִיב הָתָם: "וַיַּרְא אוֹתָהּ שְׁכֶם בֶּן חֲמוֹר וגו'". [9]בִּשְׁלָמָא לְמַאן דְּאָמַר סֵרְסוֹ, [10]מִשּׁוּם הָכִי קִלְּלוֹ בָּרְבִיעִי. [11]אֶלָּא לְמַאן דְּאָמַר רְבָעוֹ, מַאי שְׁנָא רְבִיעִי? [12]נִלַטְיֵיהּ בְּהֶדְיָא! [13]הָא וְהָא הֲוַאי. [14]"וַיָּחֶל נֹחַ אִישׁ הָאֲדָמָה וַיִּטַּע כָּרֶם". [15]אָמַר רַב חִסְדָּא אָמַר רַב עוּקְבָא, [16]וְאָמְרִי לַהּ מָר עוּקְבָא אָמַר רַבִּי זַכַּאי: [17]אָמַר לוֹ הַקָּדוֹשׁ בָּרוּךְ הוּא לְנֹחַ:

LITERAL TRANSLATION

[1]Rav and Shmuel [disagreed]. One said: He castrated him. [2]And one said: He sodomized him. [3]The one who said [that] he castrated him — [4]since he injured him with the fourth, he cursed him with the fourth. [5]And the one who said [that] he sodomized him — [6]he learned "And he saw" [from] "And he saw." [7]It is written here: "And Ham, the father of Canaan, saw the nakedness of his father," [8]and it is written there: "And Shechem, the son of Hamor, saw her, etc."

[9]Granted according to the one who said [that] he castrated him, [10]therefore he cursed him with his fourth. [11]But according to the one who said [that] he sodomized him, how is the fourth different? [12]Let him curse him directly.

[13]There was this and that.

[14]"And Noah began to be a man of the soil, and he planted a vineyard." [15]Rav Ḥisda said in the name of Rav Ukva, [16]and some say, Mar Ukva said in the name of Rabbi Zakkai: [17]The Holy One, blessed be He, said to Noah:

TRANSLATION AND COMMENTARY

רַב וּשְׁמוּאֵל [1]**Rav and Shmuel disagreed** about what Ham did to his father. **One said** that Ham **castrated** Noah. [2]**The other one said** that Ham **sodomized him.**

מַאן דְּאָמַר [3]The Amora **who said that** Ham **castrated** Noah refers to the following verse (Genesis 9:25): "Cursed be Canaan; a servant of servants shall he be to his brothers." Now Canaan was Ham's fourth child (see Genesis 10:6: "And the sons of Ham: Kush, and Mitzrayim, and Put, and Canaan"). [4]**Since** Ham **caused** his father **an injury** which prevented him from having his **fourth** child, Noah **cursed** Ham **by way of his fourth** child, Canaan. [5]**And the** Amora **who said that** Ham **sodomized his** father **derived** the significance of the expression, [6]**"And he saw,"** by a *gezerah shavah* **from** another instance of the expression, **"And he saw."** [7]**Here the verse states: "And Ham, the father of Canaan, saw the nakedness of his father,"** [8]**and elsewhere the verse states** (Genesis 34:2): **"And Shechem the son of Hamor** the Hivvite, prince of the country, **saw her,** and he took her, and lay with her, and defiled her." Just as Shechem's seeing led to sexual intercourse, so, too, did Ham's seeing lead to sexual intercourse.

בִּשְׁלָמָא [9]The Gemara asks: **Granted, according to the** Amora **who said that** Ham **castrated his** father, [10]that Noah **therefore cursed** Ham **by way of his fourth** child, Canaan. [11]**But according to the** Amora **who said that** Ham **sodomized him, in what way is** Ham's **fourth** child **different** from his other children? [12]Surely, Noah **should have cursed** Ham **directly!**

הָא וְהָא הֲוַאי [13]The Gemara answers: According to this Amora, Ham was guilty of both **this and that.** Rav and Shmuel agree that Ham castrated his father, but they disagree as to whether he also sodomized him. Thus, according to both of them it was fitting for Noah to curse Ham by way of his fourth child, since he caused his father an injury that prevented him from having a fourth child.

וַיָּחֶל [14]The Torah passage describing Ham's offense opens (Genesis 9:20): **"And Noah began to be a man of the soil, and he planted a vineyard."** [15]**Rav Ḥisda said in the name of Rav Ukva,** [16]**and some say** that it was **Mar Ukva** who **said in the name of Rabbi Zakkai:** Why was Noah called a man of the soil? [17]**The Holy One,**

RASHI

מתוך שקלקלו ברביעי — שמנעו מלהוליד בן רביעי, קלל בן רביעי שלו; כוש ומצרים ופוט וכנען. איש האדמה — אמאי קרי ליה איש האדמה — על ידי שהוכיחו הקדוש ברוך הוא: היה לו ללמוד מאיש האדמה, דהיינו אדם הראשון, שהיין קנס עליו מיתה.

NOTES

סֵרְסוֹ, רְבָעוֹ **He castrated him, he sodomized him.** At first glance, the Rabbinic interpretations of Ham's transgression are quite astounding, for the plain sense of the text does not seem to imply that he was guilty of such serious offenses. It might be suggested that the curse which Noah pronounced upon his son Ham, in contrast to the usual demonstration of compassion between father and son, indicates that Ham must indeed have committed a heinous sin. This is supported by the verse (Genesis 9:24): "And he knew what his younger son had done to him," which implies that not only did Ham "see his father's nakedness" (verse 22), but that he also "did" something to him (*Ramah*). The term וַיַּרְא "and he saw," can also be understood as denoting intercourse, as in the verse (Leviticus 20:17): "And if a man... see [וְרָאָה] her nakedness, and she see [תִרְאֶה] his nakedness" (*Be'er HaGolah*).

[1]״נֹחַ, לֹא הָיָה לְךָ לִלְמוֹד מֵאָדָם הָרִאשׁוֹן, [2]שֶׁלֹּא גָּרַם לוֹ אֶלָּא יַיִן?״

[3]כְּמַאן דְּאָמַר אוֹתוֹ אִילָן שֶׁאָכַל מִמֶּנּוּ אָדָם הָרִאשׁוֹן גֶּפֶן הָיָה. [4]דְּתַנְיָא: ״רַבִּי מֵאִיר אוֹמֵר: [5]אוֹתוֹ אִילָן שֶׁאָכַל אָדָם הָרִאשׁוֹן מִמֶּנּוּ גֶּפֶן הָיָה, [70B] [6]שֶׁאֵין לְךָ דָּבָר שֶׁמֵּבִיא יְלָלָה לָאָדָם אֶלָּא יַיִן. [7]רַבִּי יְהוּדָה אוֹמֵר: חִטָּה הָיָה, שֶׁאֵין הַתִּינוֹק יוֹדֵעַ לִקְרוֹא אַבָּא וְאִימָּא עַד שֶׁיִּטְעוֹם טַעַם דָּגָן. [8]רַבִּי נְחֶמְיָה אוֹמֵר: תְּאֵנָה הָיָה, [9]שֶׁבְּדָבָר שֶׁקִּלְקְלוּ בּוֹ נִתְקְנוּ, [10]שֶׁנֶּאֱמַר: ׳וַיִּתְפְּרוּ עֲלֵה תְאֵנָה׳״.

[11]״דִּבְרֵי לְמוּאֵל מֶלֶךְ מַשָּׂא אֲשֶׁר יִסְּרַתּוּ אִמּוֹ״. [12]אָמַר רַבִּי יוֹחָנָן מִשּׁוּם רַבִּי שִׁמְעוֹן בֶּן יוֹחַי: מְלַמֵּד שֶׁכְּפָאַתּוּ אִמּוֹ עַל הָעַמּוּד, [13]וְאָמְרָה לוֹ: ״׳מַה בְּרִי? וּמַה, בַּר בִּטְנִי? וּמֶה, בַּר נְדָרָי׳? ׳מַה, בְּרִי׳ — [14]הַכֹּל

LITERAL TRANSLATION

[1]"Noah, should you not have learned from the first man, [2]that it was only wine that caused him [to be cast out]?"

[3][This is] in accordance with the one who said that the tree from which the first man ate was a grapevine, [4]for it was taught: "Rabbi Meir said: [5]That tree from which the first man ate was a grapevine, [70B] [6]for there is nothing else that brings lamentation to a person other than wine. [7]Rabbi Yehudah says: It was wheat, for a child does not know how to say 'Father' or 'Mother' until he tastes the taste of wheat. [8]Rabbi Neḥemyah says: It was a fig tree, [9]for by that same thing with which they had sinned, they were restored, [10]as it is stated: 'And they sewed fig leaves together.'"

[11]"The words of king Lemuel, the prophecy, that his mother taught him." [12]Rabbi Yoḥanan said in the name of Rabbi Shimon ben Yoḥai: This teaches that his mother tied him to a column, [13]and said to him: "'What, my son? And what, son of my womb? And what, son of my vows?' 'What, my son?' [14]All

TRANSLATION AND COMMENTARY

blessed be He, said to Noah: [1]**"Noah, should you not have learned from Adam,** the original man fashioned from the earth, [2]**that wine alone caused him to be cast out** of the Garden of Eden?"

כְּמַאן דְּאָמַר [3]The Gemara notes that **this** last statement **is in accordance with the** authority **who said that the "tree** of knowledge" **from** whose fruit Adam ate **was a grapevine,** [4]**as it was taught** in the following Baraita: **"Rabbi Meir said:** [5]**The 'tree** of knowledge' **from whose** fruit Adam **ate was a grapevine,** [70B] [6]**for** even today **there is nothing else that brings lamentation to a person other than wine.** [7]**Rabbi Yehudah says:** The 'tree of knowledge' from which Adam ate **was wheat, for a child does not learn how to say 'Father' or 'Mother' until he experiences the taste of wheat.** [8]**Rabbi Neḥemyah says:** The 'tree of knowledge' from whose fruit Adam and Eve ate **was a fig tree.** [9]God restores people with the same thing with which they sinned, thus **by that same thing with which** Adam and Eve **had sinned, they were restored.** They were restored by way of a fig tree, [10]**as the verse states** (Genesis 3:7): **'And they sewed fig leaves together.'"**

דִּבְרֵי לְמוּאֵל [11]The Gemara continues its discussion about the dangers of wine. The verse (Proverbs 31:1): **"The words of king Lemuel, the prophecy, that his mother taught him,"** alludes to the rebuke which Solomon received from his mother. [12]**Rabbi Yoḥanan said in the name of Rabbi Shimon ben Yoḥai: This** verse **teaches that** when Solomon's **mother,** Batsheba, saw that Solomon was drinking too much, she **tied him to a column** in order to flog him (as is intimated by the word יִסְּרַתּוּ, translated here as "taught him," but which also denotes lashes). [13]She **said to him** as follows (Proverbs 31:2): **"'What, my son? And what, son of my womb? And what, son of my vows?' 'What, my son?'** [14]**Everybody knows that**

RASHI

שאין לך דבר שמביא יללה על אדם אלא יין — הלכך מסתברא דעל ידו נכנסה מיתה ובכיה לעולם. **שאין התינוק יודע וכו׳** — ומדקרי ליה הדעת טוב ורע שמע מינה היינו חטים. **בדבר שנתקלקלו בו נתקנו** — מדת הקדוש ברוך הוא: באיזמל שהוא מכה בו הוא מרפא, גם בתוך גם כמו ויצת אש בציון (איכה ד) וכתיב (זכריה ב) ואני אהיה לה נאום ה׳ חומת אש סביב. **למואל מלך** — שלמה המלך למואל, מעשיו וחכמתו להקדוש ברוך הוא, למואל שכינה הוא, כמו ידי שמתי למו פי (איוב מ). **משא אשר יסרתו אמו** — פרשת תוכחה שהוכחתו אמו. **שכפאתו על העמוד** — להלקותו וייסור לשון מלקות כדאמרינן לקמן (עא,א): ויסרו אותו זה מלקות, ומפני שהיתה רואה שהוא בעל הנאה ומרבה בסעודתו היתה מוכיחתו.

NOTES

חִטָּה הָיָה **It was wheat.** Wheat may legitimately be referred to as a *tree,* for in the future wheat will grow as high as a date palm (*Ein Ya'akov, Hokhmat Mano'aḥ*).

לְמוּאֵל **Lemuel.** *Maharsha* connects this interpretation of the verse with what the Midrash says about Solomon. At first, while he was under the influence of the daughter of Pharaoh, he would drink all night like the other kings of his day and not rise until late in the morning, and then say: לְמוּאֵל, *Lama El,* "Why do I need God?" It was about this behavior that Solomon's mother rebuked him.

SAGES

רַבִּי מֵאִיר **Rabbi Meir.** One of the great Tannaim of the generation preceding the completion of the Mishnah. See *Sanhedrin,* Part I, pp. 54-5.

רַבִּי יְהוּדָה **Rabbi Yehudah.** Where the name Rabbi Yehudah occurs without a patronymic in Talmudic literature, it usually refers to Rabbi Yehudah bar Ilai, one of the great Tannaim of the fourth generation. See *Sanhedrin,* Part I, p. 12.

רַבִּי נְחֶמְיָה **Rabbi Neḥemyah.** A Tanna of the fifth generation. See *Sanhedrin,* Part I, p. 13.

רַבִּי יוֹחָנָן **Rabbi Yoḥanan.** This is Rabbi Yoḥanan bar Nappaḥa, one of the greatest of the Amoraim. See *Sanhedrin,* Part I, p. 46-7.

רַבִּי שִׁמְעוֹן **Rabbi Shimon.** Where the name Rabbi Shimon occurs without a patronymic in Talmudic literature, it usually refers to Rabbi Shimon ben Yoḥai, one of the great Tannaim of the generation preceding the completion of the Mishnah. See *Sanhedrin,* Part I, p. 23.

TRANSLATION AND COMMENTARY

your father feared Heaven, and so you could not have learned to drink from him. [1]**Now people will say:** It could only have been **his mother** who **caused him to sin** in this manner. [2]**'And what, son of my womb?'** [3]**All the** other **women in your father's house, after they conceive, refrain from visiting the king** and abstain from sexual relations. [4]**But I forced** myself **and entered** his chambers, and engaged in sexual intercourse during my pregnancy, **so that I would have a vigorous and fair son,** for sexual intercourse during pregnancy is beneficial to the fetus. [5]**'And what, son of my vows?'** [6]**All the** other **women in your father's house would vow** during their pregnancy: **Let me have a son** who is **fit for royalty.** [7]**But** when I was pregnant, **I vowed and said: Let me have an eager son, full of Torah, and** let him be **fit for prophecy."** [8]Batsheba continued with her rebuke (Proverbs 31:4): **"'It is not for kings, O Lemuel, it is not for kings to drink wine;** nor for princes to say, Where is strong drink?' **'It is not for kings.'** [9]Batsheba **said to** Solomon: **What have** you to do **with the kings** of the nations **who drink wine and become drunk and say: Why do we need God?** [10]**'Nor for princes** [וּלְרוֹזְנִים] **to say, Where is strong drink?'** [11]**Should he to whom all the secrets** [רָזֵי] **of the world are revealed** — Solomon, the wisest of men — **drink wine and become drunk?"** [12]**There are those who say** that this clause should be understood as follows: **"Should he at whose door all the princes of the world appear every morning drink wine and become drunk?"**

אָמַר רַבִּי יִצְחָק [13]**Rabbi Yitzḥak said: From where do we know that Solomon later admitted to his mother** that she was right to rebuke him? [14]**For the verse states** (Proverbs 30:2): **"For I am more brutish than a man,**

יוֹדְעִים שֶׁאָבִיךָ יְרֵא שָׁמַיִם הֲוָה. [1]עַכְשָׁיו יֹאמְרוּ: אִמּוֹ גָּרְמָה לוֹ. [2]'וּמַה, בַּר בִּטְנִי'? [3]כָּל הַנָּשִׁים שֶׁל בֵּית אָבִיךָ כֵּיוָן שֶׁמִּתְעַבְּרוֹת שׁוּב אֵינָן רוֹאוֹת פְּנֵי הַמֶּלֶךְ, [4]וַאֲנִי דָּחַקְתִּי וְנִכְנַסְתִּי, כְּדֵי שֶׁיְּהֵא לִי בֵּן מְזוֹרָז וּמְלוּבָּן. [5]'וּמֶה, בַּר נְדָרָי'? [6]כָּל נָשִׁים שֶׁל בֵּית אָבִיךָ הָיוּ נוֹדְרוֹת: יְהֵא לִי בֵּן הָגוּן לַמַּלְכוּת. [7]וַאֲנִי נָדַרְתִּי וְאָמַרְתִּי: יְהֵא לִי בֵּן זָרִיז וּמְמוּלָּא בַּתּוֹרָה, וְהָגוּן לִנְבִיאוּת. [8]'אַל לַמְּלָכִים לְמוֹאֵל אַל לַמְּלָכִים שְׁתוֹ יָיִן'. 'אַל לַמְּלָכִים'. [9]אָמְרָה לוֹ: מַה לְּךָ אֵצֶל מְלָכִים שׁוֹתִים יַיִן וּמִשְׁתַּכְּרִים וְאוֹמְרִים: לָמָּה לָנוּ אֵל? [10]'וּלְרוֹזְנִים אֵי שֵׁכָר'? [11]מִי שֶׁכָּל רָזֵי עוֹלָם גְּלוּיִים לוֹ יִשְׁתֶּה יַיִן וְיִשְׁתַּכֵּר"? [12]אִיכָּא דְּאָמְרִי: "מִי שֶׁכָּל רוֹזְנֵי עוֹלָם מַשְׁכִּימִין לְפִתְחוֹ יִשְׁתֶּה יַיִן וְיִשְׁתַּכֵּר"?

[13]אָמַר רַבִּי יִצְחָק: מִנַּיִין שֶׁחָזַר שְׁלֹמֹה וְהוֹדָה לְאִמּוֹ? [14]דִּכְתִיב: "כִּי בַעַר אָנֹכִי מֵאִישׁ וְלֹא בִינַת

LITERAL TRANSLATION

know that your father feared Heaven. [1]Now they will say: His mother caused him [to sin]. [2]'And what, son of my womb?' [3]All the women in your father's house, once they conceive no longer see the face of the king, [4]but I forced myself and entered, so that I would have a vigorous and fair son. [5]'And what, son of my vows?' [6]All the women in your father's house would vow: Let me have a son fit for royalty. [7]And I vowed and said: Let me have an eager son, full of Torah, and fit for prophecy. [8]'It is not for kings, O Lemuel, it is not for kings to drink wine.' 'It is not for kings.' [9]She said to him: What have you to do with kings who drink wine and become drunk and say: Why do we need God? [10]'Nor for princes to say, Where is strong drink?' [11]Should he to whom all the secrets of the world are revealed drink wine and become drunk?" [12]There are [those] who say: "Should he at whose door all the princes of the world appear every morning drink wine and become drunk?"

[13]Rabbi Yitzḥak said: From where [do we know] that Solomon later admitted to his mother? [14]For it is written: "For I am more brutish than a man, and have not the understanding

BACKGROUND

מְזוֹרָז וּמְלוּבָּן **Vigorous and fair.** The Sages said that during certain months of pregnancy sexual relations are harmful both to the mother and to her child. In other months, however, they are beneficial to both. To some degree modern doctors concur that abstention from sexual relations during pregnancy is not beneficial to a woman.

RASHI

אמו גרמה לו — להיות רשע, שהרי באביך לא יתלו החובה והיינו מה ברי — למה תגרום לרנן אחריך שאתה בני ולא בן אביך. בר בטני — מעי גרמו לך להיות בעל תורה ובעל כוח, שדחקתי ונכנסתי, שתשמיש יפה לולד ללבנו ולזרזו כדאמרינן במסכת נדה (לא,א): שלשה חדשים האחרונים תשמיש יפה לולד, שמתוך כך יצא הולד מלובן ומזורז. אי שכר — כלומר אל רוזנים לומר איה שכר לא נאה לומר לך. בער אנכי מאיש — בההוא משה כתיב.

NOTES

כִּי בַעַר אָנֹכִי מֵאִישׁ **For I am more brutish than a man.** Solomon was more brutish than a man — Noah — and did not

HALAKHAH

אַל לַמְּלָכִים שְׁתוֹ יָיִן **It is not for kings to drink wine.** "A king is forbidden to drink in a manner that will lead to his intoxication, for the verse states, 'It is not for kings to drink wine.' Rather, he must engage in Torah study and see to the needs of the people of Israel day and night," following the Gemara. (*Rambam, Sefer Shofetim, Hilkhot Melakhim* 3:5.)

SAGES

רַבִּי אַבָּהוּ Rabbi Abbahu. A Palestinian Amora of the third generation. See *Sanhedrin*, Part I, pp. 13-14.

TRANSLATION AND COMMENTARY

and have not the understanding of a man." [1]**"For I am more brutish than a man"** — I, Solomon, am more brutish **than Noah** who was called a man, [2]**as the verse states** (Genesis 9:20): **"And Noah began to be a man of the soil."** [3]**"And have not the understanding of a man"** — **this is** a reference to Adam, **the first man.** Noah and Adam both sinned with wine (following Rabbi Meir, who maintains that the "tree of knowledge" was a grapevine), and I drank more than either of them.

אָכַל [4]We have learned in our Mishnah: **"If the boy ate** meat and drank wine **at a meal** celebrating **a mitzvah,** he does not become a rebellious son." [5]**Rabbi Abbahu said:** A rebellious child **is not liable unless he eats in the company** of men **who are all idlers.** But if even one decent person is present, he is not liable, for he will not be carried away.

וְהָאֲנַן תְּנַן [6]The Gemara objects: **But surely we have learned** in our Mishnah: **"If the** boy **ate** meat and drank wine **at a meal** celebrating **a mitzvah, he does not become a rebellious son."** [7]Now, the Mishnah implies that **the reason** for the exemption **is the mitzvah.** [8]**But if it was not a meal** celebrating **a mitzvah,** he would indeed be liable, **even though** the people he ate with **were not all idlers,** contrary to what Rabbi Abbahu says!

הָא [9]The Gemara responds: There is no contradiction between Rabbi Abbahu's ruling and the Mishnah. **This is what** the Mishnah means to **teach us:** [10]**Even though** the people he ate with **are all idlers, since he was engaged in** a meal celebrating **a mitzvah, he will not be carried away** and does not become a rebellious son.

אָכַל [11]We have learned in our Mishnah: **"If the boy ate** the meat and drank the wine **at a meal marking the intercalation of a month** (it was customary for the court to host a special meal after having added an extra day to the month, in order to make it known that they had intercalated the month), he

אָדָם לִי״. [1]״כִּי בַעַר אָנֹכִי מֵאִישׁ״ — מִנֹּחַ, [2]דִּכְתִיב: ״וַיָּחֶל נֹחַ אִישׁ הָאֲדָמָה״. [3]״וְלֹא בִינַת אָדָם לִי״ — זֶה אָדָם הָרִאשׁוֹן.

[4]״אָכַל בַּחֲבוּרַת מִצְוָה״. [5]אָמַר רַבִּי אַבָּהוּ: אֵינוֹ חַיָּיב עַד שֶׁיֹּאכַל בַּחֲבוּרָה שֶׁכּוּלָּהּ סְרִיקִין.

[6]וְהָאֲנַן תְּנַן: ״אָכַל בַּחֲבוּרַת מִצְוָה אֵינוֹ נַעֲשֶׂה בֵּן סוֹרֵר וּמוֹרֶה״. [7]טַעְמָא — דְּמִצְוָה. [8]הָא לָאו מִצְוָה — אַף עַל גַּב דְּלָאו כּוּלָּהּ סְרִיקִין!

[9]הָא קָא מַשְׁמַע לָן: [10]דְּאַף עַל גַּב דְּכוּלָּהּ סְרִיקִין, כֵּיוָן דִּבְמִצְוָה קָא עָסֵיק, לָא מִימְשִׁיךְ. [11]״אָכַל בְּעִיבּוּר

LITERAL TRANSLATION

of a man." [1]"For I am more brutish than a man" — than Noah, [2]as it is written: "And Noah began to be a man of the soil." [3]"And have not the understanding of a man" — this is the first man.

[4]"If he ate in company [to celebrate] a mitzvah." [5]Rabbi Abbahu said: He is not liable unless he eats in the company [of men] who are all idlers.

[6]But surely we have learned: "If he ate in company [to celebrate] a mitzvah, he does not become a rebellious son." [7]The reason [is that it is a] mitzvah [meal]. [8]But [if it was] not a mitzvah [meal] — even though they are not all idlers!

[9]This is what it teaches us: [10]Even though they are all idlers, since he is engaged in a mitzvah, he will not be carried away.

[11]"[If] he ate at [a meal marking] the intercalation

RASHI

זה אדם הראשון — שנכשל ביין, ואני שתיתי יותר מהן. **שכולה סריקין** — רקים, שירגילוהו בכך, אבל אם יש בחבורה אדם הגון בכי האי גוונא לא ממשיך ואינו נעשה בן סורר ומורה, ובחבורה דלאו מצוה קאמר. **הא קא משמע לן** — מתניתין דאפילו כולה סריקין, כיון דאיחבור השתא למצוה — פטור, ולעולם דינו דבן סורר ומורה אינו אלא בחבורת סריקין. **אבל בעיבור החדש** — כדמפרש לקמן שהן נקבצין עשרה או יותר ועולין בעלייה, ואין אסיפה זו אלא לפרסם הדבר שעברוהו ולא לעיין — דהא אין עולין אלא לאור עיבורו, דהיינו ליל מוצאי שלשים, וכבר מעובר הוא, דהא לא קדשו היום את החדש, וקדוש אין שם ביום מחרת דהיינו יום שלשים ואחד למנות על כך כדאמרינן (ראש השנה כד,א): שלא בזמנו אין מקדשין אותו, ועוד: דאי לקודשי — בשלשה סגי.

NOTES

have the understanding of a man (Adam), for he should have learned from the mistakes of Adam and Noah and taken greater care to drink wine in moderation (*Maharsha*).

HALAKHAH

עַד שֶׁיֹּאכַל בַּחֲבוּרָה שֶׁכּוּלָּהּ סְרִיקִין Unless he eats in the company of men who are all idlers. "A rebellious son is not liable unless he eats in the company of men who are idlers." (*Rambam, Sefer Shofetim, Hilkhot Mamrim* 7:2.)

עִיבּוּר הַחוֹדֶשׁ Intercalation of the month. "When the court intercalated the month because witnesses did not come to testify that they saw the New Moon on the thirtieth of the old month, the judges would go up to a chamber designated for that purpose and partake of a meal on the thirty-first of the old month, which was Rosh Ḥodesh. They

הַחוֹדֶשׁ״. [1] לְמֵימְרָא דְּבָשָׂר וְיַיִן מַסְּקוּ? [2] וְהָתַנְיָא: ״אֵין עוֹלִין לָהּ אֶלָּא בְּפַת דָּגָן וְקִטְנִית בִּלְבַד״!

[3] הָא קָא מַשְׁמַע לָן: אַף עַל גַּב דְּאֵין עוֹלִין לָהּ אֶלָּא בְּפַת וְקִטְנִית, וְאִיהוּ אַסֵּיק בָּשָׂר וְיַיִן וְאָכַל, [4] כֵּיוָן דִּבְמִצְוָה קָא עָסֵיק, לָא מִמְשִׁיךְ.

[5] תָּנוּ רַבָּנַן: ״אֵין עוֹלִין בְּעִיבּוּר הַחוֹדֶשׁ פָּחוֹת מֵעֲשָׂרָה בְּנֵי אָדָם, וְאֵין עוֹלִין לָהּ אֶלָּא בְּפַת דָּגָן וְקִטְנִית, [6] וְאֵין עוֹלִין לָהּ אֶלָּא לְאוֹר עִיבּוּרוֹ, וְאֵין עוֹלִין לָהּ בַּיּוֹם אֶלָּא בַּלַּיְלָה.

[7] וְהָתַנְיָא: ״אֵין עוֹלִין לָהּ בַּלַּיְלָה אֶלָּא בַּיּוֹם״!

[8] כְּדַאֲמַר רַבִּי חִיָּיא בַּר אַבָּא לִבְנֵיהּ: [9] ״אַחְרִיפוּ וְעוּלוּ,

TRANSLATION AND COMMENTARY

does not become a rebellious son." [1] The Gemara asks: **Is this to say that** the judges would **bring meat and wine up** to their chamber on the second story, where they convened to intercalate the month? [2] **But was it not taught** otherwise in a Baraita: **"They** would **go up** to their chamber **with only grain bread and legumes;** this measure prevented excessive eating and drinking, which might interfere with their discussion of the intercalation"?

הָא [3] The Gemara answers: **This is what** the Mishnah means to **teach us: Even though** the judges **go up with only bread and legumes, and** the boy **brought up** with him **meat and wine and** he **ate** them, [4] **since he was engaged in** a meal celebrating **a mitzvah, he will not be carried away** and become a rebellious son.

תָּנוּ רַבָּנַן [5] **Our Rabbis taught** the following Baraita: "The judges **do not go up** to their second-story chamber **for the intercalation of the month with fewer than ten people, and they only go up with grain bread and legumes,** [6] **and they only go up on the night of its intercalation, and they do not go up during the day, but rather at night."**

וְהָתַנְיָא [7] The Gemara asks: **But surely it was taught** otherwise in another Baraita: **"They do not go up at night, but rather during the day."**

כִּדַאֲמַר [8] The Gemara answers: **As Rabbi Ḥiyya bar Abba said to his sons:** [9] "When you go to intercalate

LITERAL TRANSLATION

of the month." [1] Is this to say that they bring up meat and wine? [2] But surely it was taught: "They go up with only grain bread and legumes"!

[3] This is what it teaches us: Even though they go up with only bread and legumes, and he brought up meat and wine and ate, [4] since he was engaged in a mitzvah, he will not be carried away.

[5] Our Rabbis taught: "They do not go up for the intercalation of the month with fewer than ten people, and they only go up for it with grain bread and legumes, [6] and they go up for it only on the night of its intercalation, and they do not go up during the day, but rather at night."

[7] But surely it was taught: "They do not go up at night, but rather during the day!"

[8] As Rabbi Ḥiyya bar Abba said to his sons: [9] "Go early and enter,

SAGES

רַב חִיָּיא בַּר אַבָּא **Rav Ḥiyya bar Abba.** An Amora of the third generation. See *Sanhedrin*, Part I, p. 66.

RASHI

בפת דגן – ולא ידענא משום מאי נקט פת דגן, ומשמע למעוטי פת אורז ודוחן קא אתי. יום עבורו – הוא יום שלשים שנעשה ממנו חדש היוצא מעובר. אור יום עבורו – מוצאי שלשים, ולהודיע שעברוהו. אחריפו – אקדימו, כמו חרפי ואפלי (עבודה זרה עה,א) אחריפו ועולו בלילה, היו יושבין שם ועושין הומה להשמיע קול, וקאמר להו רבי חייא להקדים ולעלות מבעוד יום מעט כדי שיראו אותם עוברי דרכים כשהן עולין ויפרסמו, והיינו דקתני אין עולין לה בלילה אלא ביום, והאי דקתני אין עולין לה ביום אעיקר מילתא קאי – שהסעודה ומשאו ומתנו של דבר בלילה הוא.

NOTES

בְּפַת דָּגָן וְקִטְנִית **With grain bread and legumes.** The Baraita mentions "grain bread" (and not simply "bread"; see *Rashi*), because the expression פַּת וְקִטְנִית, "bread and legumes," might have been understood to mean "legume bread" (*Ramah, Rosh*).

As for the rule that the judges were only to bring grain bread and legumes to the chamber where they convened to intercalate the month, some suggest that the judges were barred from bringing meat and wine, lest they become intoxicated and not decide the matter properly. Alternatively, they were limited in what they could bring so that their entry into the chamber could only be for the sake of intercalating the month, and not for the sake of a feast. Another explanation is that they were only permitted to bring plain and simple foods, so as not to embarrass those who could not afford to bring more lavish dishes (*Ramah*).

לְאוֹר עִיבּוּרוֹ **The night of its intercalation.** The Rishonim disagree about the meaning of the term "the night of its intercalation." According to *Rashi* and *Rambam*, this refers to the night of the thirty-first — that is to say, the intercalation feast was only celebrated if witnesses did not arrive on the thirtieth of the month to testify that they had seen the New Moon, so that the month was automatically intercalated. According to *Rabbenu Ḥananel* (see *Ramah*), this refers to the night of the thirtieth, when the judges would already assemble and intercalate the month if according to their calculations the New Moon could not possibly be seen that night.

אַחְרִיפוּ וְעוּלוּ **Go early and enter.** According to *Rashi*, the judges would spend the entire night in the second-story

HALAKHAH

would not go up at night, but rather shortly before sunrise. At least ten people would be invited to participate in this meal. At the meal they would eat only grain bread and legumes." These rulings follow the Baraita and Rabbi Ḥiyya bar Abba. (*Rambam, Sefer Zemanim, Hilkhot Kiddush HaḤodesh* 3:7.)

TRANSLATION AND COMMENTARY

the month, **enter early and come out early, so that people will hear you** and know that you have assembled to intercalate the month." The judges used to enter their second-story chamber early in the morning while it was still night and come out shortly after daybreak. Hence, one Baraita says that they went up at night, and the other says that they went up during the day.

אָכַל [1]We have learned in our Mishnah: **"If the boy ate** meat and wine purchased with **second-tithe** money **in Jerusalem,** he does not become a rebellious son." [2]The Gemara explains: **Since** the boy **consumes** the meat and wine **in the ordinary manner** that foods purchased with second-tithe money are consumed, **he will not be carried away** and become a rebellious son.

אָכַל [3]Our Mishnah continues: **"If the boy ate** the meat of animals that were forbidden to him, such as carcasses of **animals that** died of natural causes or **were improperly slaughtered, or** the meat of **animals afflicted with an organic disease** or congenital defect that would cause them to die within twelve months, **or creeping or crawling things,** he does not become a rebellious son." [4]**Rava said: If** the boy **ate the meat of fowl, he does not become a rebellious son.**

וְהָא [5]The Gemara argues: **But surely we have learned** in our Mishnah: **"If he ate** the meat of **improperly slaughtered or diseased animals, or creeping or crawling things, he does not become a rebellious son."** [6]**But** this implies that if he ate the meat **of clean animals,** even that of fowl, **he** does indeed **become a rebellious son,** contrary to what Rava says!

אַחְרִיפוּ וּפוּקוּ, כִּי הֵיכִי דְּלִישְׁמְעוּ בְּכוּ אֱינָשֵׁי״.

[1]״אָכַל מַעֲשֵׂר שֵׁנִי בִּירוּשָׁלַיִם״.

[2]כֵּיוָן דִּכְּי אוֹרְחֵיהּ הוּא קָא אָכֵיל לֵיהּ, לָא מַמְשִׁיךְ.

[3]״אָכַל נְבֵילוֹת וּטְרֵיפוֹת שְׁקָצִים וּרְמָשִׂים״. [4]אָמַר רָבָא: אָכַל בְּשַׂר עוֹף, אֵינוֹ נַעֲשֶׂה בֵּן סוֹרֵר וּמוֹרֶה.

[5]וְהָא אֲנַן תְּנַן: ״אָכַל נְבֵילוֹת וּטְרֵיפוֹת שְׁקָצִים וּרְמָשִׂים אֵינוֹ נַעֲשֶׂה בֵּן סוֹרֵר וּמוֹרֶה״. [6]הָא טְהוֹרִין, נַעֲשֶׂה בֵּן סוֹרֵר וּמוֹרֶה!

LITERAL TRANSLATION

go early and come out, for thus people will hear you."

[1]"[If] he ate second tithe in Jerusalem." [2]Since he eats it in its ordinary manner, he will not be carried away.

[3]"[If] he ate improperly slaughtered or diseased animals, or creeping or crawling things." [4]Rava said: [If] he ate the meat of fowl, he does not become a rebellious son.

[5]But surely we have learned: "If he ate improperly slaughtered or diseased animals, or creeping or crawling things, he does not become a rebellious son." [6]But of clean animals, he becomes a rebellious son!

RASHI

אחריפו ופוקו בבקר — אל תאחרו לירד, שהרואה אתכם יורדין בהשכמה מבין שישבו שם כל הלילה ומתפרסם הדבר, אבל הרואה אותם יורדין שלא בהשכמה סבור שעכשיו עלו ואין מבין הדבר. **אבל מעשר שני** — גנב ממעות מעשר שני וקנה בשר ויין — ואכל, דאי גנב בשר ויין עצמו אפילו דחולין נמי לא, כדאמר עד שיקח בשר בזול ויאכל, ויין בזול וישתה (ומן התנוני). **דכי אורחיה** — כדרך מצותו נאמר בבקר ובצאן וביין ובשכר במעשר שני. **אבל נבלות וטריפות** — לקמן יליף לפטורא. **אבל בשר עוף טהור** — פטור, דלא חשיב דלא ממשיך בתריה. **סתם שקצים** — היינו עופות טמאים דכתיב בהם שקץ הם (ויקרא יא) רמשים הן שרצים וטעמא משום דאיננו שומע בקולנו בעינן, ולא זה שאף בקולו של מקום אינו שומע. **הא טהורים חייב** — כדתנן במתניתין דאיצטריך לאשמועינן דפטור אשקצים.

NOTES

chamber. They would enter shortly before nightfall and leave early in the morning, all in order to publicize the matter that they had spent the entire night considering the matter. It would appear from *Rambam* that the judges would enter the chamber early in the morning, while it was still dark, and come out shortly after daybreak. According to *Ramah,* the word אַחְרִיפוּ does not mean "go early," but rather "go sharply," in such a manner that everybody will know that the judges have entered their chamber.

אָכַל בְּשַׂר עוֹף, אֵינוֹ נַעֲשֶׂה בֵּן סוֹרֵר וּמוֹרֶה If he ate the meat of fowl, he does not become a rebellious son. Several explanations have been offered regarding this regulation. A boy does not become a rebellious son if he ate the meat of fowl, for such meat is considered light food that is not favored by robbers. Or else he is exempt because fowl's meat is expensive, and it is therefore not likely that the boy will come to eat such meat on a regular basis (*Ramah*). Others suggest that the boy does not become liable, because eating the fowl's meat cannot provide the same joy as the eating of the meat of cattle (*Riva*).

HALAKHAH

אָכַל בְּשַׂר עוֹף If he ate the meat of fowl. "If the boy ate the meat of fowl, he does not become a rebellious son. But if he ate mostly cattle meat, and completed the minimum *tartemar* of meat with the meat of fowl, he is liable," following the Gemara. (*Rambam, Sefer Shofetim, Hilkhot Mamrim* 7:3.)

[1] כִּי תְּנַן נַמִי מַתְנִיתִין — לְהַשְׁלִים.
[2] ״אָכַל דָּבָר שֶׁהוּא מִצְוָה וּדְבַר עֲבֵירָה״. [3] ״דְּבַר מִצְוָה״ — תַּנְחוּמֵי אֲבֵלִים. [4] ״דְּבַר עֲבֵירָה״ — תַּעֲנִית צִיבּוּר.
[5] וְטַעְמָא מַאי? [6] אָמַר קְרָא: ״אֵינֶנּוּ שֹׁמֵעַ בְּקֹלֵנוּ״ — [7] בְּקוֹלֵנוּ וְלֹא בְּקוֹלוֹ שֶׁל מָקוֹם.
[8] ״אָכַל כָּל מַאֲכָל וְלֹא אָכַל בָּשָׂר, שָׁתָה כָּל מַשְׁקֶה וְלֹא שָׁתָה יַיִן וכו׳״. [9] ״אָכַל כָּל מַאֲכָל וְלֹא אָכַל בָּשָׂר״ — לְאִיתּוּיֵי דְּבֵילָה קְעִילִית. [10] ״שָׁתָה כָּל מַשְׁקֶה וְלֹא שָׁתָה יַיִן״ — לְאִיתּוּיֵי דְּבַשׁ וְחָלָב. [11] דְּתַנְיָא: ״אָכַל דְּבֵילָה קְעִילִית, וְשָׁתָה דְּבַשׁ וְחָלָב, וְנִכְנַס

LITERAL TRANSLATION

[1] When our Mishnah was also taught — to complete. [2] "[If] he ate something that [it] is a mitzvah [to eat], or something that [constitutes] a transgression." [3] "Something that [it] is a mitzvah" — the consolation of mourners. [4] "Something that [constitutes] a transgression" — a communal fast.

[5] And what is the reason? [6] The verse says: "He will not obey our voice" — our voice, [7] but not the voice of God.

[8] "[If] he ate every food, but did not eat meat, [or if] he drank every drink, but did not drink wine, etc." [9] "If he ate every food, but did not eat meat" — to include preserved figs from Ke'ilah. [10] "If he drank every drink, but did not drink wine" — to include honey and milk. [11] As it was taught: "[If] he ate preserved figs from Ke'ilah, or drank honey and milk, and entered

RASHI

להשלים — שאפילו אכל תרטימר בשר חסר כזית מבהמה טהורה, והשלימה לתרטימר מבשר עופות טמאים — פטור, משום דאינו שומע בקולו של מקום, דכוותה בטהורים — מיחייב. **לאיתויי תנחומי אבלים** — דאף על גב דתקנתא דרבנן בעלמא הוא דאי מרישא הוה אמינא חבורת מצוה היינו כהנים שאוכלין קדשים או פסחים. **תענית צבור** — אף על גב דלא עבר אלא אדרבנן. **וטעמא מאי** — מפטר אדבר עבירה. **איננו שומע בקולנו** — מיעוטא הוא, ולאפוקי האי דאף בקולו של מקום אינו שומע. **דבילה קעילית** — מאותו מקום, ואף

TRANSLATION AND COMMENTARY

כִּי תְּנַן [1] The Gemara answers: **When our Mishnah taught** that if the boy ate the meat of creeping or crawling things, he does not become a rebellious son, it was talking about a boy who ate such things **to complete** the minimum measure of meat that he had to eat in order to become liable. If the boy ate slightly less than a *tartemar* of permitted red meat, and he completed the measure with creeping or crawling things, he does not become a rebellious son. But if he completed the measure with the meat of fowl, he does indeed become a rebellious son. When Rava said that if the boy ate the meat of fowl, he does not become a rebellious son, he was referring to a boy who ate the entire *tartemar* of fowl.

אָכַל [2] Our Mishnah continues: **"If the boy ate something that it is a mitzvah to eat, or something that is forbidden,** he does not become a rebellious son." [3] The Gemara explains: This rule concerning **"something that it is a mitzvah** to eat" adds that even if the boy ate something that one is commanded to eat only by Rabbinic enactment, such as the meal of **consolation** offered **to mourners,** he does not become a rebellious son. [4] And this rule concerning **"something that is forbidden"** adds that even if the boy ate something that is forbidden to eat only by Rabbinic decree, for example, if he ate meat and drank wine on a communal fast, he does not become a rebellious son.

וְטַעְמָא מַאי [5] The Gemara asks: **What is the reason** that the boy does not become a rebellious son if he ate something that is forbidden? [6] The Gemara explains: **The verse states** (Deuteronomy 21:20): **"He will not obey our voice,"** teaching that the boy becomes a rebellious son only if he does not obey **"our voice,"** that is, the voice of his parents. [7] **But** if he eats forbidden foods, and does **not** obey **the voice of God,** he is not a rebellious son.

אָכַל [8] We have learned in our Mishnah: "If the boy **ate any** other **food, but did not eat meat, or if he drank any** other **drink, but did not drink wine, he does not become a rebellious son."** [9] The Gemara explains: **"If the** boy **ate any** other **food, but did not eat meat" — includes preserved figs from Ke'ilah.** [10] **"If he drank any** other **drink, but did not drink wine" — this includes honey and milk.** Even though Ke'ilan figs, honey, and milk are somewhat intoxicating, partaking of them does not make a boy a rebellious son. Ke'ilan figs, milk, and honey can be intoxicating [11] **as it was taught** in a Baraita: **"If someone ate preserved figs from Ke'ilah, or**

HALAKHAH

דָּבָר שֶׁהוּא מִצְוָה וּדְבַר עֲבֵירָה **Something that is a mitzvah, and something that is a transgression.** "If the boy ate something that it is a mitzvah to eat, even if it is a mitzvah only by Rabbinic enactment (such as, if he partook of the meal of consolation offered to mourners), or if the boy ate something that it is forbidden to eat, even if it is forbidden only by Rabbinic decree (such as, if he ate on a communal fast day), he does not become a rebellious son." (*Rambam, Sefer Shofetim, Hilkhot Mamrim* 7:2.)

אָכַל דְּבֵילָה קְעִילִית, וְשָׁתָה דְּבַשׁ **If he ate preserved figs from Ke'ilah, or drank honey.** "If a priest, becomes intoxicated from beverages other than wine, he is forbidden to enter the Temple. If he entered the Temple and participated in the service while intoxicated by other

לַמִּקְדָּשׁ — [71A] חַיָּיב״.
[1]״אֵינוֹ נַעֲשֶׂה בֵּן סוֹרֵר וּמוֹרֶה עַד שֶׁיֹּאכַל בָּשָׂר וְיִשְׁתֶּה יַיִן״. [2]תָּנוּ רַבָּנַן: ״אָכַל כָּל מַאֲכָל וְלֹא אָכַל בָּשָׂר, שָׁתָה כָּל מַשְׁקֶה וְלֹא שָׁתָה יַיִן, [3]אֵינוֹ נַעֲשֶׂה בֵּן סוֹרֵר וּמוֹרֶה עַד שֶׁיֹּאכַל בָּשָׂר וְיִשְׁתֶּה יַיִן, [4]שֶׁנֶּאֱמַר: ׳זוֹלֵל וְסֹבֵא׳. [5]וְאַף עַל פִּי שֶׁאֵין רְאָיָה לַדָּבָר — [6]זֵכֶר לַדָּבָר, שֶׁנֶּאֱמַר: ׳אַל תְּהִי בְסֹבְאֵי יָיִן בְּזֹלְלֵי בָשָׂר לָמוֹ׳, [7]וְאוֹמֵר: ׳כִּי סֹבֵא וְזוֹלֵל יִוָּרֵשׁ וּקְרָעִים תַּלְבִּישׁ נוּמָה׳״.
[8]אָמַר רַבִּי זֵירָא: כָּל הַיָּשֵׁן בְּבֵית הַמִּדְרָשׁ, תּוֹרָתוֹ נַעֲשֵׂית לוֹ קְרָעִים, [9]שֶׁנֶּאֱמַר: ״וּקְרָעִים תַּלְבִּישׁ נוּמָה״.
משנה [10]גָּנַב מִשֶּׁל אָבִיו

LITERAL TRANSLATION

the Temple, [71A] he is liable."
[1]"He does not become a rebellious son, unless he ate meat and drank wine." [2]Our Rabbis taught: "[If] he ate every food, but did not eat meat, [or if] he drank every drink, but did not drink wine — [3]he does not become a rebellious son, unless he ate meat and drank wine, [4]as it is stated: 'He is a glutton and a drunkard.' [5]And even though there is no proof of the matter, [6]there is a remembrance of the matter, as it is stated: 'Be not among wine drinkers, among gluttonous eaters of meat.' [7]And it states: 'For the drunkard and the glutton shall come to poverty; and drowsiness shall clothe a man with rags.'"
[8]Rabbi Zera said: Whoever sleeps in a house of study, his Torah becomes full of tears, [9]as it is stated, "And drowsiness shall clothe a man with rags."
MISHNAH [10][If] he stole from what belongs to his father,

TRANSLATION AND COMMENTARY

drank honey and milk, and entered the Temple, [71A] **he is liable** to be punished for having entered the Temple while intoxicated."

אֵינוֹ נַעֲשֶׂה [1]Our Mishnah continues: "A boy **does not become a rebellious son unless he ate meat and drank wine** excessively." [2]**Our Rabbis taught** a related Baraita: **"If a** boy **ate any** other **food, but did not eat meat, or if he drank any** other **drink, but did not drink wine,** [3]**he is not considered a rebellious son unless he ate meat and drank wine,** [4]**as the verse states** (Deuteronomy 21:21): **'He is a glutton** [זוֹלֵל] **and a drunkard** [סֹבֵא]**'** — and those terms refer to eating meat and drinking wine to excess. [5]**Even though there is no** clear **proof** in the Bible that those terms imply meat and wine, [6]**there is an allusion to it** in **the verse** that **states** (Proverbs 23:20): **"Be not among wine drinkers** [סֹבְאֵי יָיִן], **among gluttonous eaters of meat** [זֹלְלֵי בָשָׂר]." [7]**And** the next verse **states** (Proverbs 23:21): **'For the drunkard** [סֹבֵא] **and the glutton** [זוֹלֵל] **shall come to poverty; and drowsiness shall clothe a man with rags.'** The first verse teaches that the word זוֹלֵל refers to eating meat, and the word סֹבֵא refers to drinking wine. And the second verse teaches that the passage is alluding to the rebellious son, whom the Torah foresees will continue to eat and drink excessively until he ruins his parents and becomes a robber and a murderer."

אָמַר רַבִּי זֵירָא [8]**Rabbi Zera expounded** this last verse in the following manner: **Whoever sleeps in a house** designated **for the study** of Torah, **his Torah becomes torn to pieces,** [9]**as the verse states** (Proverbs 23:21): **"And drowsiness shall clothe a man with rags."**

MISHNAH גָּנַב [10]**If** a boy **stole** meat and wine **from his father, and** then **ate** the meat and drank the wine

RASHI

על גב דמשכרא לא מיחייב עליה דלא ממשיך. **חייב משום יין ושכר אל תשת וגו׳** — וככהן עסקינן. **כי סובא וזולל יורש** — בתר קרא קמא כתיב, להכי אתייה להכא. **יורש** — סופו להיות עני ומבקש למודו ואינו מוצא. **וקרעים תלביש נומה** — נומה שאדם מתגרה בה תלביש קרעים, כלומר: סוף כל בעל הנאות לבא לידי עניות. **נעשה לו קרעים** — משכח למודו ואינו נזכר אלא בסירוגין.

NOTES

תּוֹרָתוֹ נַעֲשֵׂית לוֹ קְרָעִים **His Torah becomes full of tears.** If a Rabbinic student dozes off, he will sometimes remember the question that was raised, but not the answer, or he will learn an answer without having heard the question, and he will combine questions and answers that are not connected to each other (*Ḥayyim Shenayim Yeshalem*). Moreover, even if he makes up what he missed while he was asleep, his studies will still resemble a torn garment that was mended with a patch (*Iyyun Ya'akov*).

HALAKHAH

beverages, even if he was only intoxicated by milk or preserved figs, he is liable to the punishment of lashes, but his service is valid. According to Rambam, the priest is liable to the punishment of lashes, and not the death penalty," following Rabbi Yehudah in *Keritut* (see *Kesef Mishneh*). (*Rambam, Sefer Avodah, Hilkhot Bi'at Mikdash* 1:2.)

הַיָּשֵׁן בְּבֵית הַמִּדְרָשׁ **Whoever sleeps in a house of study.** "It is forbidden to sleep in a house designated for Torah study. Whoever falls asleep in a house of study, his Torah becomes a torn garment." (*Shulḥan Arukh, Oraḥ Ḥayyim* 151:3; *Yoreh De'ah* 246:16.)

TRANSLATION AND COMMENTARY

in his father's domain, [1]or if he stole **from others, and** then **ate in the domain of others,** [2]or if he stole **from others, and** then **ate in his father's domain** — [3]in all these cases **he is not considered a rebellious son.** [4]A boy does not become a rebellious son **unless he steals** meat and wine **from his father, and** then **eats** the meat and drinks the wine **in the domain of others**.

רַבִּי יוֹסֵי [5]**Rabbi Yose the son of Rabbi Yehudah says:** A boy is not considered a rebellious son **unless he steals** meat and wine **from his father and his mother.**

GEMARA גָּנַב [6]We learned in the Mishnah: **"If** a boy **stole** meat and wine **from his father, and** then **ate** the meat and drank the wine **in his father's domain,** he is not considered a rebellious son." [7]The Gemara explains: **Even though** his father's property **is at hand** and easy **for him** to steal, **he is afraid** of his father, and so we are not concerned that he will continue in his immoral behavior. [8]The Mishnah continues: **"If** the boy **stole from others, and** then **ate in the domain of others,** he is not considered a rebellious son." [9]The Gemara explains: **Even though he is not afraid** of other people, other people's property **is not** usually **at hand** and easy **for him** to steal, and so we are not concerned that his offense will lead him to more serious transgressions. [10]**And all the more so if** the boy **stole from others, and** then **ate in his father's domain** — he is not considered a rebellious son, [11]**for** other people's property **is not** usually **at hand** and easy **for him** to steal, **and he is afraid** of his father, and so there is even less likelihood that he will become a murderous robber. [12]"A boy does not become a rebellious son **unless he steals from his father and eats in the domain of others."** [13]**For** his father's property is **at hand** and easy **for him** to steal, **and he is not afraid** of other people. Thus he is likely to become an inveterate thief.

רַבִּי [14]We learned in our Mishnah: **"Rabbi Yose the son of Rabbi Yehudah says:** A boy is not considered

וְאָכַל בִּרְשׁוּת אָבִיו, [1]מִשֶּׁל אֲחֵרִים וְאָכַל בִּרְשׁוּת אֲחֵרִים, [2]מִשֶּׁל אֲחֵרִים וְאָכַל בִּרְשׁוּת אָבִיו — [3]אֵינוֹ נַעֲשֶׂה בֵּן סוֹרֵר וּמוֹרֶה, [4]עַד שֶׁיִּגְנוֹב מִשֶּׁל אָבִיו וְיֹאכַל בִּרְשׁוּת אֲחֵרִים.

[5]רַבִּי יוֹסֵי בְּרַבִּי יְהוּדָה אוֹמֵר: עַד שֶׁיִּגְנוֹב מִשֶּׁל אָבִיו וּמִשֶּׁל אִמּוֹ.

גמרא [6]״גָּנַב מִשֶּׁל אָבִיו וְאָכַל בִּרְשׁוּת אָבִיו״. [7]אַף עַל גַּב דִּשְׁכִיחַ לֵיהּ, בְּעִית. [8]״מִשֶּׁל אֲחֵרִים וְאָכַל בִּרְשׁוּת אֲחֵרִים״. [9]אַף עַל גַּב דְּלָא בְּעִית, לָא שְׁכִיחַ לֵיהּ. [10]וְכָל שֶׁכֵּן, מִשֶּׁל אֲחֵרִים וְאָכַל בִּרְשׁוּת אָבִיו, [11]דְּלָא שְׁכִיחַ לֵיהּ, וּבְעִית. [12]״עַד שֶׁיִּגְנוֹב מִשֶּׁל אָבִיו וְיֹאכַל בִּרְשׁוּת אֲחֵרִים״ — [13]דִּשְׁכִיחַ לֵיהּ וְלָא בְּעִית.

[14]״רַבִּי יוֹסֵי בְּרַבִּי יְהוּדָה אוֹמֵר: עַד שֶׁיִּגְנוֹב מִשֶּׁל אָבִיו וּמִשֶּׁל

LITERAL TRANSLATION

and ate in his father's domain, [1]from what belongs to others, and ate in the domain of others, [2]from what belongs to others, and ate in his father's domain — [3]he does not become a rebellious son, [4]unless he steals from what belongs to his father, and eats in the domain of others.

[5]Rabbi Yose the son of Rabbi Yehudah says: Unless he steals from what belongs to his father and what belongs to his mother.

GEMARA [6]"[If] he stole from what belongs to his father, and ate in his father's domain." [7]Even though it is at hand for him, he is afraid. [8]"[If he stole] from what belongs to others, and ate in the domain of others." [9]Even though he is not afraid, it is not at hand for him. [10]And all the more so, [if he stole] from what belongs to others, and ate in his father's domain, [11]for it is not at hand for him, and he is afraid. [12]"Until he steals what belongs to his father and eats in the domain of others" — [13]for it is at hand for him and he is not afraid.

[14]"Rabbi Yose the son of Rabbi Yehudah says: Unless he steals from what belongs to his father and what belongs

RASHI

משנה **משל אחרים ואכל ברשות אחרים** — ואפילו לא אכלן ברשות בעלים עצמן, וטעמא מפרש בגמרא.

גמרא **בעית** — מתפחד מאביו שלא יבין, הלכך לא ממשיך. **עד שיגנוב משל אביו** — דשכיח ליה לגנוב תמיד ואכל ברשות אחרים, דלא בעית שלא יראהו אביו וכי האי גוונא ממשיך.

NOTES

עַד שֶׁיִּגְנוֹב מִשֶּׁל אָבִיו וְיֹאכַל בִּרְשׁוּת אֲחֵרִים Unless he steals from his father, and eats in the domain of others. *Sefer Ḥasidim* adds in explanation that if the boy steals from his father, and then eats in somebody else's domain the foods purchased with the stolen money, not only does he himself sin, but he causes others to sin as well.

HALAKHAH

עַד שֶׁיִּגְנוֹב מִשֶּׁל אָבִיו Unless he steals from that of his father. "A rebellious son is only considered such if he stole money from his father, and purchased meat and wine cheaply, and ate the meat and drank the wine in someone else's domain," following the Mishnah. (*Rambam, Sefer Shofetim, Hilkhot Mamrim* 7:2.)

אִמּוֹ״. [1]אִמּוֹ, מְנָא לָהּ? [2]מַה שֶּׁקָּנְתָה אִשָּׁה קָנָה בַּעְלָהּ!
[3]אָמַר רַבִּי יוֹסֵי בְּרַבִּי חֲנִינָא: מִסְּעוּדָה הַמּוּכֶנֶת לְאָבִיו וּלְאִמּוֹ.
[4]וְהָאָמַר רַבִּי חָנָן בַּר מוֹלָדָה אָמַר רַב הוּנָא: [5]אֵינוֹ חַיָּיב עַד שֶׁיִּקְנֶה בָּשָׂר בְּזוֹל וְיֹאכַל, יַיִן בְּזוֹל וְיִשְׁתֶּה!
[6]אֶלָּא אֵימָא: מִדְּמֵי סְעוּדָה הַמּוּכֶנֶת לְאָבִיו וּלְאִמּוֹ.
[7]אִיבָּעֵית אֵימָא: דְּאַקְנֵי לָהּ אַחֵר, [8]וְאָמַר לָהּ: עַל מְנָת שֶׁאֵין לְבַעֲלִיךְ רְשׁוּת בָּהֶן.
משנה [9]הָיָה אָבִיו רוֹצֶה וְאִמּוֹ אֵינָהּ רוֹצָה, [10]אָבִיו אֵינוֹ רוֹצֶה וְאִמּוֹ רוֹצָה — [11]אֵינוֹ

LITERAL TRANSLATION

to his mother." [1]His mother, from where does she have? [2]Whatever a woman acquires is acquired by her husband!

[3]Rabbi Yose the son of Rabbi Ḥanina said: From a meal prepared for his father and his mother.

[4]But surely Rabbi Ḥanan bar Moladah said in the name of Rav Huna: [5]He is not liable unless he purchases meat cheaply and eats [it], [and purchases] wine cheaply and drinks [it]!

[6]Rather, say: From money set aside for a meal for his father and his mother.

[7]If you wish, say: If someone else transferred [it] to her, [8]and said to her: On condition that your husband has no right to it.

MISHNAH [9][If] his father wanted, but his mother did not want, [10][or if] his father did not want, but his mother wanted, [11]he does not

TRANSLATION AND COMMENTARY

a rebellious son **unless he steals from his father and his mother."** [1]The Gemara asks: **From where does his mother have** property that her son can steal from her? [2]Surely there is a general rule that **whatever** property **a woman acquires is** automatically **acquired by her husband!**

אָמַר [3]**Rabbi Yose the son of Rabbi Ḥanina said:** This ruling refers to **a meal that was prepared for his father and his mother,** since the father gives the mother the food that she eats.

וְהָאָמַר [4]The Gemara raises an objection: **But surely Rabbi Ḥanan bar Moladah said in the name of Rav Huna:** [5]A rebellious son **is not liable** to death by stoning **unless he** stole money from his parents, and then **purchased meat cheaply and ate it, and purchased wine cheaply and drank it.** But if he stole the meat and wine from his parents, he is not liable.

אֶלָּא אֵימָא [6]The Gemara answers: **Rather, say** that Rabbi Yose the son of Rabbi Yehudah meant to say as follows: A boy does not become a rebellious son unless he steals **money** that was **set aside for a meal for his father and his mother.**

אִיבָּעֵית [7]The Gemara suggests an alternative answer: **If you wish,** you can **say** as follows: Rabbi Yose the son of Rabbi Yehudah is referring to when **someone else transferred** money **to** the boy's mother, [8]**and said to her:** I give you this money **on condition that your husband have no right to it.** In such a case, the money remains in the woman's possession, and is not acquired by her husband, and the son can indeed steal from both his father and his mother.

MISHNAH הָיָה [9]**If** the boy's **father wanted** to bring his son to court for punishment as a rebellious son, **but his mother** condoned his offense and **did not want** him to be prosecuted, [10]**or if** the boy's **father** condoned his offense and **did not want** to bring him to court, **but his mother wanted** him to be prosecuted, [11]the boy

RASHI

עד שיקח בשר בזול – אבל אם גנב בשר ויין עצמן – לא. **מדמי סעודה המוכנת** – שהיו מעות מוכנים לקנות מהם סעודה לאביו ולאמו, דכיון דלכך נזדמנו משל אמו קרינן בהו, דאיהי נמי שייכא בהם מדינא דבעלה חייב במזונותיה. **על מנת שאין לבעליך רשות בהן** – דאי לא אמר לה הכי זכה בהן בעל, דלא עדיף ממציאתה.

NOTES

שֶׁיִּקְנֶה בָּשָׂר **Unless he purchases meat.** If the boy steals the meat and the wine, we are not concerned that this in itself means he will live a life of crime, for meat and wine are not always available for him to steal. But if he steals money, we are concerned that his offense will lead him to even more serious transgressions, for money is often at hand and easy to steal (*Rabbenu Yehonatan, Ramah*).

דְּאַקְנֵי לָהּ אַחֵר **If someone else transferred it to her.** It has been pointed out that it is possible to construct additional cases in which a married woman has property of her own. For example, if she agreed to maintain herself in exchange for her keeping the profits of her handiwork (*Ḥayyim Shenayim Yeshalem*); or else, if the husband waived his rights to his wife's *milog* property (see *Margoliyot HaYam*).

HALAKHAH

מַה שֶּׁקָּנְתָה אִשָּׁה קָנָה בַּעְלָהּ **Whatever a woman acquires is acquired by her husband.** "If someone gave a woman a gift on condition that her husband have no right to it, the property itself belongs to the woman, but the husband may enjoy the usufruct (like any other *milog* property), unless the donor stipulated that he was giving the woman the gift to use for a specific purpose or to do with as she pleases." (*Shulḥan Arukh, Even HaEzer* 85:11.)

הָיָה אָבִיו רוֹצֶה **If his father wanted.** "If the boy's father wanted to bring his son to court, but his mother did not

TRANSLATION AND COMMENTARY

does not become a rebellious son unless both his father and his mother **want** to bring him to trial, for the verse states (Deuteronomy 21:19): "Then shall his father and his mother lay hold of him, and bring him out to the elders of the city."

רַבִּי יְהוּדָה [1]**Rabbi Yehudah says: If** the boy's **mother was not fit for his father he does not become a rebellious son.**

GEMARA מַאי [2]**What** did Rabbi Yehudah mean when he spoke of the boy's mother being **"not fit"** for his father? [3]The Gemara suggests an interpretation which it immediately rejects: **If you say** that Rabbi Yehudah refers to a boy whose mother and father are forbidden to each other, and that their union is **punishable by excision or judicial execution,** so that their marriage is not valid, there is a problem. [4]Even if their marriage has no legal validity, the boy's **father is nevertheless** still **his father,** [5]**and his mother is** still **his mother.** [6]**Rather,** Rabbi Yehudah meant to **say** that the boy's mother must be **equal to his father** in voice, appearance, and height.

תַּנְיָא [7]The Gemara notes that **the same thing was** also **taught in the** following **Baraita:** [8]**"Rabbi Yehudah says: If** the boy's **mother was not equal to his father in voice, appearance, and height, he does not become a rebellious son."** [9]**What is the reason** that the boy is exempt from liability when there is a physical disparity between his parents? [10]The Gemara explains: **Because the verse states** (Deuteronomy 21:20): **"He will not obey our voice,"** implying that the father and the mother must speak with one voice. [11]**Since** we see that the parents **must be equal** regarding **their voices,** it stands to reason that they **must also be equal in appearance and height.**

כְּמַאן [12]The Gemara asks: **In accordance with** the position of **which** Tanna **was** the following Baraita **taught:** [13]**"There never was a rebellious son, nor will there ever be** one. [14]**Then why was** the law regarding a

LITERAL TRANSLATION

become a rebellious son, unless they both want.

[1]Rabbi Yehudah says: If his mother was not fit for his father, he does not become a rebellious son.

GEMARA [2]What is "not fit"? [3]If you say those who are liable to [the punishment of] excision and those who are liable to [be punished by] judicial execution, [4]in the end, his father is his father, [5]and his mother is his mother. [6]Rather, he said where [she is] equal to his father.

[7]It was also taught as follows: [8]"Rabbi Yehudah says: If his mother was not equal to his father in voice, and in appearance, and in height, he does not become a rebellious son." [9]What is the reason? [10]Because the verse states: "He will not obey our voice." [11]Since, regarding [the] voice, we need them to be equal, so, too, regarding appearance and height, we need them to be equal.

[12]In accordance with whom is that which was taught: [13]"There never was a rebellious son, nor will there ever be. [14]Then why was it written?

נַעֲשֶׂה בֵּן סוֹרֵר וּמוֹרֶה עַד שֶׁיְּהוּ שְׁנֵיהֶם רוֹצִין.

[1]רַבִּי יְהוּדָה אוֹמֵר: אִם לֹא הָיְתָה אִמּוֹ רְאוּיָה לְאָבִיו, אֵינוֹ נַעֲשֶׂה בֵּן סוֹרֵר וּמוֹרֶה.

גמרא [2]מַאי "אֵינָהּ רְאוּיָה"? [3]אִילֵימָא חַיָּיבֵי כְּרִיתוֹת וְחַיָּיבֵי מִיתוֹת בֵּית דִּין, [4]סוֹף סוֹף אֲבוּהּ — אֲבוּהּ נִינְהוּ, [5]וְאִמֵּיהּ — אִמֵּיהּ נִינְהוּ! [6]אֶלָּא: בְּשָׁוָה לְאָבִיו קָאָמַר.

[7]תַּנְיָא נַמִי הָכִי: [8]"רַבִּי יְהוּדָה אוֹמֵר: אִם לֹא הָיְתָה אִמּוֹ שָׁוָה לְאָבִיו בְּקוֹל וּבְמַרְאֶה וּבְקוֹמָה אֵינוֹ נַעֲשֶׂה בֵּן סוֹרֵר וּמוֹרֶה". [9]מַאי טַעְמָא? [10]דְּאָמַר קְרָא: "אֵינֶנּוּ שֹׁמֵעַ בְּקֹלֵנוּ", [11]מִדְּקוֹל בָּעֵינַן שָׁוִין — מַרְאֶה וְקוֹמָה נַמִי בָּעֵינַן שָׁוִין.

[12]כְּמַאן אָזְלָא הָא דְּתַנְיָא: [13]"בֵּן סוֹרֵר וּמוֹרֶה לֹא הָיָה וְלֹא עָתִיד לִהְיוֹת, [14]וְלָמָּה נִכְתַּב?

RASHI

אי נימא חייבי כריתות — שהיתה אמו על אביו בכרת כגון אחותו דלאו בת קדושין. **סוף סוף אביו ואמו נינהו** — דהא בקרא לא כתוב אישות באמו אלא אביו. **בשוה לאביו** — בקול ובמראה וקומה, וטעמא מפרש לקמן. **בקולנו** — חד קול משמע, מדלא כתוב בקולותינו או בקולינו ביו"ד.

NOTES

בְּקֹלֵנוּ **Our voice.** The Rishonim explain that Rabbi Yehudah's position, that a rebellious son is only liable if his parents have similar voices, is based on the fact that the possessive suffix of the word קֹלֵנוּ, "our voice," is written in a defective manner (without a *yod*). *R. I. Pik* adds that, even though the word קֹלֵנוּ is always written in that manner, this spelling is appropriate when it refers to the voices of many people that blend into a single voice. But here we are dealing with two entirely different voices — the voice of a man and the voice of a woman — and so one might have expected that the word be spelled plene as קוֹלֵינוּ.

HALAKHAH

want to do so, or if his mother wanted to bring him to court, but his father did not want to do so, the boy does not become liable as a rebellious son," following the Mishnah. (*Rambam, Sefer Shofetim, Hilkhot Mamrim* 7:10.)

TRANSLATION AND COMMENTARY

rebellious son **written** in the Torah? [1]So that people might **study** it, **and receive reward** for their efforts."

כְּמַאן [2]The Gemara answers: **In accordance with whose** position was this Baraita taught? [3]It was taught **in accordance with** the position of **Rabbi Yehudah** in our Mishnah that a boy cannot become a rebellious son unless his parents are equal in voice, appearance, and height. This condition deprives the law of any practical consequences.

אִיבָּעֵית [4]The Gemara suggests an alternative answer: **If you wish,** you can **say** that the Baraita follows the position of **Rabbi Shimon.** [5]**For it was taught** in a Baraita: **"Rabbi Shimon said:** Is it really possible that merely **because** a boy **ate a** ***tartemar*** **of meat and drank a half log of Italian wine, his father and mother would take him** to court **to have him** prosecuted as a rebellious son and **stoned?** [6]**Rather, there never was** a rebellious son, **nor will there ever be** one. [7]**Then why was** the law regarding a rebellious son **written** in the Torah? [8]The law was taught so that people might **study** it, **and receive reward** for their efforts. [9]**Rabbi Yonatan said:** This is not so, for I myself once **saw** a rebellious son being tried, **and I** later **sat on his grave** after he had been executed."

כְּמַאן [10]The Gemara now raises a similar question: **In accordance with** the position of **which** Tanna **was** the following Baraita regarding a condemned city **taught:** "The Torah teaches (Deuteronomy 13:13-19) that if the majority of a city's inhabitants committed idolatry, the city is judged by the Great Sanhedrin. Those found guilty are beheaded, and all the property of the city (including that of the righteous) is destroyed, and all its buildings are razed to the ground. [11]But the Halakhic limitations are so severe that **there never was** in fact **a condemned city, nor will there ever be** one. [12]**Then why was** the law regarding a condemned city **written** in the Torah? [13]So that people might **study** it, **and receive reward** for their efforts"?

כְּמַאן [14]The Gemara answers: **In accordance with whose** position was this Baraita taught? It was taught **in accordance with** the position of **Rabbi Eliezer.** [15]**For it was taught** in a Baraita: [16]**"Rabbi Eliezer says: Any city which has at least one mezuzah** or any other holy scroll **does not become a condemned city."**

מַאי טַעְמָא [17]The Gemara asks: **What is the reason** that a city cannot be declared a condemned city if it has even a single mezuzah? [18]The Gemara explains: This is learned from **the verse** that **states** (Deuteronomy 13:17): **"And you shall gather all the spoil of it into the midst of the street, and shall burn**

[1]דְּרוֹשׁ וְקַבֵּל שָׂכָר״. [2]כְּמַאן? [3]כְּרַבִּי יְהוּדָה. [4]אִיבָּעֵית אֵימָא: רַבִּי שִׁמְעוֹן הִיא, [5]דְּתַנְיָא: ״אָמַר רַבִּי שִׁמְעוֹן: וְכִי מִפְּנֵי שֶׁאָכַל זֶה תַּרְטֵימָר בָּשָׂר וְשָׁתָה חֲצִי לוֹג יַיִן הָאִיטַלְקִי אָבִיו וְאִמּוֹ מוֹצִיאִין אוֹתוֹ לְסָקְלוֹ? [6]אֶלָּא לֹא הָיָה וְלֹא עָתִיד לִהְיוֹת. [7]וְלָמָּה נִכְתַּב? [8]דְּרוֹשׁ וְקַבֵּל שָׂכָר. [9]אָמַר רַבִּי יוֹנָתָן: אֲנִי רְאִיתִיו, וְיָשַׁבְתִּי עַל קִבְרוֹ״. [10]כְּמַאן אָזְלָא הָא דְּתַנְיָא: [11]״עִיר הַנִּדַּחַת לֹא הָיְתָה וְלֹא עֲתִידָה לִהְיוֹת, [12]וְלָמָּה נִכְתְּבָה? [13]דְּרוֹשׁ וְקַבֵּל שָׂכָר״. [14]כְּמַאן? כְּרַבִּי אֱלִיעֶזֶר, [15]דְּתַנְיָא: [16]״רַבִּי אֱלִיעֶזֶר אוֹמֵר: כָּל עִיר שֶׁיֵּשׁ בָּהּ אֲפִילּוּ מְזוּזָה אַחַת, אֵינָהּ נַעֲשֵׂית עִיר הַנִּדַּחַת״. [17]מַאי טַעְמָא? [18]אָמַר קְרָא: ״וְאֶת כָּל שְׁלָלָהּ תִּקְבֹּץ אֶל תּוֹךְ

LITERAL TRANSLATION

[1]Learn, and receive reward."

[2]In accordance with whom? [3]In accordance with Rabbi Yehudah.

[4]If you wish, say: It is Rabbi Shimon. [5]For it was taught: "Rabbi Shimon said: And because that one ate a *tartemar* of meat and drank a half log of Italian wine, his father and his mother take him out to stone him? [6]Rather, there never was, nor will there ever be. [7]Then why was it written? [8]Learn, and receive reward. [9]Rabbi Yonatan said: I saw him, and I sat on his grave."

[10]In accordance with whom is that which was taught: [11]"There never was a condemned city, nor will there ever be. [12]Then why was it written? [13]Learn, and receive reward."

[14]In accordance with whom? In accordance with Rabbi Eliezer. [15]For it was taught: [16]"Rabbi Eliezer says: Any city which has at least one mezuzah does not become a condemned city."

[17]What is the reason? [18]The verse states: "And you shall gather all the spoil of it into the midst of

RASHI

ואפילו מזוזה אחת – וכל שכן אחד מן החומשין, או ספר מכל הנביאים, שאזכרת השם כתובה שם ולא קרינא ביה "את כל שללה ושרפת".

NOTES

דְּרוֹשׁ וְקַבֵּל שָׂכָר Learn, and receive reward. Studying the laws governing a rebellious son has practical value, for they teach us how important it is for parents to invest in their children's education so that they not stray from the proper path (*Sefer Ḥasidim, Maharsha*). Studying the laws governing a condemned city also has practical value, for they teach us the severity of idol worship. There is also a practical side to studying the laws relating to a leprous house, for they teach us the seriousness of the vice of miserliness (*HaBoneh*).

TRANSLATION AND COMMENTARY

with fire both the city and the entire plunder taken in it." [1]**And if there is a mezuzah** in the city, **it is not possible** to execute this penalty, [2]**for the Torah states** (Deuteronomy 12:3-4): "And you shall overthrow their altars, and break their pillars, and burn their asherim with fire...and destroy the name of them out of that place. **You shall not do this to the Lord your God,"** from which it follows that it is forbidden to burn a mezuzah which contains the Divine Name. Thus, the penalty imposed upon a condemned city cannot be imposed if the city has even a single mezuzah.

אָמַר רַבִּי יוֹנָתָן [3]The Gemara cites testimony which contradicts the Baraita's dictum that there never was in fact a condemned city: **"Rabbi Yonatan said: I** once **saw** a city declared a condemned city, **and I sat on** the **mound** which remained after its buildings had been razed to the ground."

כְּמַאן [4]The Gemara continues with a similar discussion: **In accordance with** the position **of which** Tanna **was** the following Baraita **taught:** "The Torah teaches that if a leprous blemish is detected within a house, the house is quarantined for a certain period of time. If the blemish spreads, the blemished stones are removed. If the blemish returns, the entire house has to be destroyed. [5]But the Halakhic limitations are so severe that **there never was** in fact **a leprous house, nor will there ever be** one. [6]**Then why was** the law regarding a leprous house **written** in the Torah? [7]So that people might **study** it, **and receive reward** for their efforts."

כְּמַאן [8]The Gemara answers: **In accordance with whose** position was this Baraita taught? [9]It was taught **in accordance with** the position of **Rabbi Elazar the son of Rabbi Shimon.** [10]**For we have learned** in the Mishnah (*Nega'im* 12:3): **"Rabbi Elazar the son of Rabbi Shimon says: A house does not become defiled unless a leprous spot the size of two barleycorns is seen on two** adjacent **stones, on two** different **walls** that come together **in the corner** of the house, that spot being **two barleycorns long, and one barleycorn wide."** Since this condition is impossible the law regarding a leprous house has no practical application.

מַאי טַעְמָא [11]The Gemara asks: **What is the reasoning of Rabbi Elazar the son of Rabbi Shimon?** [12]The Gemara explains: **The verse states** (Leviticus 14:37): "Which in sight are lower than the **wall," and that** same **verse states:** "And, behold, if the plague be in the **walls** of the houses." [13]**Which wall** (singular) **is like walls** (plural)? [14]**Say that** the Torah is referring to a leprous spot found in **the corner** of a house, half on one wall and half on the adjacent wall.

רְחֹבָהּ וְשָׂרַפְתָּ בָאֵשׁ". [1]וְכֵיוָן דְּאִי אִיכָּא מְזוּזָה לֹא אֶפְשָׁר, [2]דִּכְתִיב: "לֹא תַעֲשׂוּן כֵּן לַה' אֱלֹהֵיכֶם".

[3]"אָמַר רַבִּי יוֹנָתָן: אֲנִי רְאִיתִיהָ, וְיָשַׁבְתִּי עַל תִּילָּהּ".

[4]כְּמַאן אָזְלָא הָא דְּתַנְיָא: [5]"בַּיִת הַמְנוּגָּע לֹא הָיָה וְלָא עָתִיד לִהְיוֹת. [6]וְלָמָּה נִכְתַּב? [7]דְּרוֹשׁ וְקַבֵּל שָׂכָר".

[8]כְּמַאן? [9]כְּרַבִּי אֶלְעָזָר בְּרַבִּי שִׁמְעוֹן. [10]דִּתְנַן: "רַבִּי אֶלְעָזָר בְּרַבִּי שִׁמְעוֹן אוֹמֵר: לְעוֹלָם אֵין הַבַּיִת טָמֵא עַד שֶׁיֵּרָאֶה כִּשְׁתֵּי גְרִיסִין עַל שְׁתֵּי אֲבָנִים, בִּשְׁתֵּי כְתָלִים, בְּקֶרֶן זָוִית, אָרְכּוֹ כִּשְׁנֵי גְרִיסִין וְרָחְבּוֹ כִּגְרִיס".

[11]מַאי טַעְמָא דְּרַבִּי אֶלְעָזָר בְּרַבִּי שִׁמְעוֹן? [12]כְּתִיב "קִיר", וּכְתִיב "קִירֹת", [13]אֵיזֶהוּ קִיר שֶׁהוּא כְּקִירוֹת? [14]הֱוֵי אוֹמֵר זֶה קֶרֶן זָוִית.

LITERAL TRANSLATION

the street, and shall burn with fire." [1]And if there is a mezuzah, it is not possible, [2]for it is written: "You shall not do this to the Lord your God."

[3]"Rabbi Yonatan said: I saw it, and I sat on its mound."

[4]In accordance with whom is that which was taught: [5]"There never was a leprous house, nor will there ever be. [6]Then why was it written? [7]Learn, and receive reward."

[8]In accordance with whom? [9]In accordance with Rabbi Elazar the son of Rabbi Shimon. [10]For we have learned: "Rabbi Elazar the son of Rabbi Shimon says: A house does not become defiled unless [a leprous spot] is seen the size of two barleycorns on two stones, on two walls in a corner, its length two barleycorns and its width one barleycorn."

[11]What is the reason of Rabbi Elazar the son of Rabbi Shimon? [12]It is written "wall," and it is written "walls." [13]Which wall is like walls? [14]Say that is a corner.

RASHI

לא תעשון כן לה' אלהיכם — בתר "ואבדתם את שמם" כתיב. גריס — זה שיעור נגעים, ושתי גריסין על שתי אבנים דכתיב (ויקרא יד) "וחלצו את האבנים" תרתי משמע, ובכל אחת שיעור נגע. בקרן זוית — ואותן שתי אבנים יהיו בקרן זוית, אחד בכותל זה ואחד בכותל זה, והנגע משוך בשתיהן ארכו שני גריסין ורחבו כגריס, שיהא בכל אבן כגריס על גריס.

BACKGROUND

גְּרִיס **Barleycorn.** The bean referred to here is a split fava bean. In modern terms this refers to a circle of 19-21 millimeters in diameter.

HALAKHAH

בַּיִת הַמְנוּגָּע **A leprous house.** "A house does not become defiled on account of leprous signs that were detected therein unless a leprous spot the size of two barleycorns is seen on two stones," following Rabbi Akiva, and against Rabbi Elazar the son of Rabbi Shimon. (*Rambam, Sefer Taharah, Hilkhot Tum'at Tzara'at* 14:7.)

[1]תַּנְיָא: ״אָמַר רַבִּי אֱלִיעֶזֶר בְּרַבִּי צָדוֹק: [2]מָקוֹם הָיָה בִּתְחוּם עַזָּה וְהָיוּ קוֹרִין אוֹתוֹ חוּרְבָתָא סְגִירְתָא. [3]אָמַר רַבִּי שִׁמְעוֹן אִישׁ כְּפַר עַכּוֹ: פַּעַם אַחַת הָלַכְתִּי לַגָּלִיל וְרָאִיתִי מְקוֹם שֶׁמְּצַיְּינִין אוֹתוֹ, [4]וְאָמְרוּ: אֲבָנִים מְנוּגָּעוֹת פִּינּוּ לְשָׁם״.

מִשְׁנָה [5]הָיָה אֶחָד מֵהֶם גִּידֵּם אוֹ חִיגֵּר אוֹ אִלֵּם אוֹ סוּמָא אוֹ חֵרֵשׁ — אֵינוֹ נַעֲשֶׂה בֵּן סוֹרֵר וּמוֹרֶה, [6]שֶׁנֶּאֱמַר: ״וְתָפְשׂוּ בוֹ אָבִיו וְאִמּוֹ״ — וְלֹא גִּדְמִין, [7]״וְהוֹצִיאוּ אֹתוֹ״ — וְלֹא חִגְּרִין, [8]״וְאָמְרוּ״ — וְלֹא אִלְּמִין, [9]״בְּנֵנוּ זֶה״ — וְלֹא סוּמִין, [10]״אֵינֶנּוּ שֹׁמֵעַ בְּקֹלֵנוּ״ — וְלֹא חֵרְשִׁין. [11]מַתְרִין בּוֹ בִּפְנֵי

LITERAL TRANSLATION

[1]It was taught: "Rabbi Elazar the son of Rabbi Tzaddok said: [2]There was a place in the district of Gaza, and they called it Leprous Ruins. [3]Rabbi Shimon of Kefar Akko said: Once I went to Galilee, and I saw a place which they marked off, [4]and they said: They cleared leprous stones to there."

MISHNAH [5][If] one of them was an amputee, or crippled, or dumb, or blind, or deaf, he does not become a rebellious son, [6]for it is stated: "Then shall his father and his mother lay hold of him" — and not the amputee. [7]"And bring him out" — and not the crippled. [8]"And they shall say" — and not the dumb. [9]"This our son" — and not the blind. [10]"He will not obey our voice" — and not the deaf. [11]They warn him in the presence of

TRANSLATION AND COMMENTARY

תַּנְיָא [1]The Gemara notes that **it was taught** otherwise in a Baraita: **"Rabbi Elazar the son of Rabbi Tzaddok said: [2]There was a place in the district of Gaza, and it was called Leprous Ruins** because the stones of a leprous house had been deposited there. [3]**Rabbi Shimon of Kefar Akko said: Once I visited the Galilee, and I saw a place which was marked off** as a ritually unclean area, [4]**and** the locals **said: Leprous stones** from a leprous house **were cleared away to there."** The testimony of Rabbi Elazar the son of Rabbi Tzaddok and that of Rabbi Shimon of Kefar Akko contradict the Baraita's dictum that the law regarding a leprous house is a purely theoretical matter, and that there never was in fact a leprous house.

MISHNAH הָיָה [5]**If one of the** boy's parents **had an amputated arm, or** he or she **was crippled, or dumb, or blind, or deaf,** the boy **does not become a rebellious son,** [6]**for the verse states** (Deuteronomy 21:19): "Then shall his father and his mother lay hold of him, and bring him out to the elders of his city, and to the gate of his place; and they shall say to the elders of his city, This our son is stubborn and rebellious, he will not obey our voice." **"Then shall his father and his mother lay hold of him"** — **and not** someone whose **arm is amputated,** and cannot lay hold of the boy. [7]**"And bring him out to the elders of his city"** — **and not** someone who is **crippled,** and cannot walk. [8]**"And they shall say"** — **and not** someone who is **dumb,** and cannot speak. [9]**"This our son"** — **and not** someone who is **blind,** and cannot point out another person. [10]**"He will not obey our voice"** — **and not** someone who is **deaf,** and cannot hear whether the boy accepted his reproach. If the boy's parents see that their son is carousing, [11]**they must** first **warn him before three** witnesses

RASHI

מאי טעמא דרבי אלעזר — דבעי קרן זוית. כתיב קיר — ״ומראיהן שפל מן הקיר״ (שם). **חורבתא סגירתא** — חורבה מצורע. מתרגמינן סגירתא, שנותץ משם בית המנוגע. **מציינין אותו** — שלא יאהילו עליו, דאבן מנוגעת מטמאה באהל דמצורע הוקש למת: ״אל נא תהי כמת״.

משנה גידם — ידו קטועה. **בננו זה** — משמע שרואים אותו. **חרשין** — אין יודעין אם קבל דבריהם אם לאו, שאם אמר להם ״איני מקבל״ — אין שומעין לו ואף על פי שרואין שאין מקיים מצותן, מיהו ״איננו שומע בקולנו״ — כתיב ואיכא לאפוכי בזכותיה ולמדרש דבשעת הקול קאמרי דלא שמע, דהאי קרא יתירא הוא כוליה כדאמר בגמרא. **מתרין בו** — לאו משום התראה גמורה כשאר עבירות שאין לוקין אלא בהתראה — דהא התראת עדים בעי, ועוד זו ספק התראה הוא אם עובר הוא אם לאו שלא מיד בפניהם הוא עובר אלא בסתר ולאחר זמן הוא עושה, אלא מוכיחין אותו, דבעינן ״ויסרו אותו״ שלא ירגיל, ואם לא שמע — מלקין אותו בבית דין, ויליף לה מ״ויסרו אותו״.

NOTES

גִּידֵּם אוֹ חִיגֵּר **An amputee, or crippled.** If one of the boy's parents suffered from one of the deformities or limitations mentioned in the Mishnah, the boy does not become a rebellious son, for a handicapped person might have developed a cruel streak on account of his condition (*Meiri*).

לֹא חֵרְשִׁין **And not the deaf.** *Ramah* explains that the word קֹלֵנוּ, "our voice," implies that the father must hear the mother's rebuke, and the mother must hear the father's rebuke, in which case neither of the two can be deaf.

HALAKHAH

הָיָה אֶחָד מֵהֶם גִּידֵּם **If one of them was an amputee.** "If one of the boy's parents had an amputated arm, or he or she was crippled, or dumb, or blind, or deaf, the boy does not become a rebellious son," following the Mishnah. (*Rambam, Sefer Shofetim, Hilkhot Mamrim* 7:10.)

מַתְרִין בּוֹ בִּפְנֵי שְׁלֹשָׁה **They warn him in the presence of three.** "What is the judicial procedure in the case of a rebellious son? The boy's father and mother first bring their son before a court of three judges, and say: This our son is stubborn and rebellious. They bring two witnesses who

שְׁלֹשָׁה, [1] וּמַלְקִין אוֹתוֹ. [2] חָזַר וְקִלְקֵל — נִדּוֹן בְּעֶשְׂרִים וּשְׁלֹשָׁה. [3] וְאֵינוֹ נִסְקָל עַד שֶׁיְּהוּ שָׁם שְׁלֹשָׁה הָרִאשׁוֹנִים, [4] שֶׁנֶּאֱמַר: ״בְּנֵנוּ זֶה״ זֶהוּ שֶׁלָּקָה בִּפְנֵיכֶם.

גמרא [5] שָׁמְעַתְּ מִינָּהּ בָּעֵינַן קְרָא כְּדִכְתִיב!

[6] שָׁאנֵי הָכָא, [71B] דְּכוּלֵּיהּ קְרָא יְתֵירָא הוּא.

[7] ״וּמַתְרִין בִּפְנֵי שְׁלֹשָׁה״. [8] לָמָּה לִי? [9] בִּתְרֵי סַגְיָא!

[10] אָמַר אַבַּיֵּי: הָכִי קָאָמַר: מַתְרִין בּוֹ בִּפְנֵי שְׁנַיִם, [11] וּמַלְקִין אוֹתוֹ בִּפְנֵי שְׁלֹשָׁה.

LITERAL TRANSLATION

three, [1] and flog him. [2] [If] he sinned again, he is judged by [a court of] twenty-three. [3] He is not stoned unless the first three are there, [4] as it is stated: "This our son" — he who was flogged before you.

GEMARA [5] Infer from this that we need the verse as it is written!

[6] It is different here, [71B] for the entire verse is extraneous.

[7] "And they warn him in the presence of three." [8] Why do I need [three]? [9] Two are enough!

[10] Abaye said: He said as follows: They warn him in the presence of two, [11] and they flog him in the presence of three.

TRANSLATION AND COMMENTARY

that if he does not desist from such behavior, they will bring him before a court. If he ignores their reproach and persists in his behavior, his parents may bring him before a court, produce the witnesses who saw that the boy had been warned, and the witnesses who saw him stealing and eating meat and drinking wine excessively, [1] **and** the boy is **flogged.** [2] **If** the boy **sins again, he is brought before a court of twenty-three** judges, and if he is found guilty, he is taken out for execution. [3] **He is not stoned unless** the twenty-three-man court **includes the first three** judges who had sentenced him to flogging, [4] **for the verse states** (Deuteronomy 21:19): **"This our son" — he who had** already **been** sentenced to **flogging before you.**

GEMARA שָׁמְעַתְּ מִינָּהּ [5] The Gemara suggests the following inference from our Mishnah: As we have seen, the Mishnah interprets the verse regarding a rebellious son in a strict manner, and rules that to condemn a son as rebellious, neither parent may be an amputee, crippled, dumb, blind, or deaf. **Infer from this** Mishnah **that we need** to carry out the particulars of **a verse** precisely **as they were written,** as is argued elsewhere by Shmuel (see *Sanhedrin* 45b). That is to say, every detail mentioned in a verse is an indispensable condition for administering punishment.

שָׁאנֵי הָכָא [6] The Gemara rejects this argument: The law **here is different,** [71B] **for the entire verse is extraneous.** The Torah could simply have stated: "And they shall bring him out to the gate of the place, and all the men of his city shall stone him with stones," as we find regarding other people who are executed by stoning. The detailed description of what the parents must say and do teach that the particulars of the verse are indispensable conditions for administering punishment.

וּמַתְרִין [7] We have learned in the Mishnah: "If the boy's parents see that their son is rebellious, **they must** first **warn him before three** witnesses that if he does not desist, they will bring him before a court." [8] The Gemara asks: **Why must** the parents warn their son in the presence of three witnesses? [9] Surely **two** witnesses **should be enough,** as is ordinarily the case!

אָמַר אַבַּיֵּי [10] **Abaye said:** The Mishnah **meant as follows:** If the parents see that their son is rebellious, **they must** first **warn him before two** witnesses that if he continues, they will bring him before a court. [11] If the boy persists, his parents may bring him **before** a court of **three** judges, and if he is found guilty, he is taken out **to be flogged.**

RASHI

גמרא שמעת מינה בעינן קרא כדכתיב – וסייעתא דשמואל בפרק ״נגמר הדין״ (מה,ב). **כוליה קרא יתירא** – דמצי למכתב והוצאתם אותו אל שער העיר ההוא וסקלתם. **בפני שנים** – דבעינן עדים שהוכיחוהו ועבר, שאין אביו ואמו נאמנין עליו להרגו דכתיב (דברים יז) על פי שנים עדים יומת המת. **ומלקין אותו בפני שלשה** – כלומר יביאוהו בפני שלשה דיינין והדיינין יחייבוהו מלקות, וילקוהו שליח בית דין כשאר הלוקין דמלקות בפני שלשה בפרקא קמא (י,א).

HALAKHAH

testify that the boy stole money from his father, purchased meat and wine, and ate the meat and drank the wine in a gluttonous manner after having been warned not to do so. The boy is then flogged, like any other offender who is liable to be punished with lashes. If the boy steals from his father again and eats and drinks in a gluttonous manner, his parents bring him before a court of twenty-three judges, and they bring two witnesses who testify that he committed those offenses after having been duly warned. He is not liable to the punishment of stoning unless the twenty-three-man court includes the first set of three judges," following the Mishnah. (*Rambam, Sefer Shofetim, Hilkhot Mamrim* 7:7.)

מַתְרִין בִּפְנֵי שְׁלֹשָׁה **And they warn him in the presence of three.** "The boy's parents must first warn him before two witnesses, and if he persists in his wanton behavior, they bring him before a court of three judges, who can sentence the boy to flogging." (*Rambam, Sefer Shofetim, Hilkhot Mamrim* 7:7.)

¹מַלְקוּת בְּבֵן סוֹרֵר וּמוֹרֶה, הֵיכָא כְּתִיבָא? ²כִּדְרַבִּי אֲבָהוּ, דְּאָמַר רַבִּי אֲבָהוּ: ³לָמַדְנוּ "וְיִסְּרוּ" מִ"וְיִסְּרוּ", ⁴"וְיִסְּרוּ" מִ"בֵּן", ⁵וּ"בֵן" מִ"בֵּן" — ⁶"וְהָיָה אִם בִּן הַכּוֹת הָרָשָׁע".

⁷"חָזַר וְקִלְקֵל נִידּוֹן בְּעֶשְׂרִים וּשְׁלֹשָׁה, [וכו']". ⁸הַאי מִיבָּעֵי לֵיהּ "זֶה", ⁹וְלֹא סוּמִין!

¹⁰אִם כֵּן, לִכְתּוֹב: "בְּנֵנוּ הוּא". ¹¹מַאי "בְּנֵנוּ זֶה"? ¹²שְׁמַע מִינָּהּ תַּרְתֵּי.

TRANSLATION AND COMMENTARY

מַלְקוּת [1] The Gemara asks: **Where does** the Torah **say** that **a rebellious son is flogged?** Surely that penalty is not stated anywhere explicitly!

כִּדְרַבִּי אֲבָהוּ [2] The Gemara answers: It is **according to what Rabbi Abbahu** stated elsewhere regarding a slanderer, **for Rabbi Abbahu said:** Regarding the slanderer, the Torah states (Deuteronomy 22:18): "And they shall chastise him." We learn that this expression refers to the penalty of flogging as follows: [3] **We learn** the meaning of the expression **"they shall chastise** him" stated with respect to the slanderer **from** the expression **"they shall chastise** him" (Deuteronomy 21:18) stated with respect to the rebellious son. [4] **And** the expression **"they shall chastise** him" stated with respect to the rebellious son is clarified **by** the word **"son"** mentioned in the same verse ("If a man has a stubborn and rebellious son, who will not obey the voice of his father, or the voice of his mother, and they shall chastise him"). Having established that the slanderer can be compared to the rebellious son, we can infer that the chastisement of the slanderer is associated with the word "son." Now that we have associated the chastisement of the slanderer with the word "son," [5] the meaning of that word **"son"** (בֵּן) as it relates to the slanderer is clarified **by** the same word, used to mean **"worthy,"** [6] that appears in the verse (Deuteronomy 25:2): **"And it shall be, if the wicked man is worthy** [בִּן] **to be flogged."** Just as that wicked man is sentenced to be flogged, so is the slanderer. The expression, "they shall chastise him," regarding the slanderer, refers to the penalty of flogging. So, too, the expression "they shall chastise him," regarding the rebellious son, refers to the penalty of flogging.

חָזַר וְקִלְקֵל [7] We have learned in the Mishnah: **"If the** boy **sinned again, he is brought before a court of twenty-three** judges, and if he is found guilty, he is executed. He is not stoned unless the twenty-three-man court includes the first three judges who had sentenced him to flogging, for the verse states (Deuteronomy 21:19): 'This our son' — he who was already sentenced to flogging before you." The Gemara asks: But surely the words "this our son" [8] **are needed for** a different matter, as we learned earlier in the very same Mishnah: **"This our son"** — [9] **and not** someone who is **blind,** and cannot point out another person!

אִם כֵּן [10] The Gemara answers: **If** it were **so,** that the words "this our son" only teach that the twenty-three-man court must include the first three judges who had earlier sentenced the boy to flogging, then **it should have been written: "He our son,"** which would imply: He who had already been sentenced to flogging before you. [11] **Why,** then, does the verse state: **"This our son,"** which implies that the parents must be able to point to their son? [12] **Infer from this two things:** First, that the twenty-three-man court must include the first three judges who had sentenced the boy to flogging. And second, that if one of the boy's parents is blind, he cannot be declared a rebellious son.

LITERAL TRANSLATION

[1] Flogging regarding a rebellious son, where is it written?

[2] Like that of Rabbi Abbahu, for Rabbi Abbahu said: [3] We have learned "they shall chastise" from "they shall chastise," [4] and "they shall chastise" from "son," [5] and "son [בֵּן]" from "worthy [בִּן]" (lit., "son of") — [6] "And it shall be, if the wicked man is worthy [בִּן] to be flogged."

[7] "[If] he sinned again, he is judged by [a court of] twenty-three, [etc.]" [8] This is needed for: "This," [9] and not the blind!

[10] If so, let it be written: "He our son." [11] What is "This our son"? [12] Infer from this two [things].

RASHI

כדרבי אבהו — בכתובות (מו,א) גבי מוציא שם רע, מנא לן דלקי, דכתיב ולקחו זקני העיר את האיש ויסרו אותו. למדנו ויסרו — דמוציא שם רע מויסרו אותו דבן סורר ומורה, וההוא דיסרו דבן סורר ומורה למדנו מבן דכתיב שם אם בן וההוא בן למדנו מבן (דברים כה) והיה אם בן הכות הרשע. אם כן — דלהך מלתא לחודא אתא ולא למעוטי סומין. לכתוב בננו הוא — סורר ומורה, ומשמע הוא שלקה בפניכם, ומדכתיב זה שמראין באצבעו עליו ולא סומין.

NOTES

מַלְקוּת בְּבֵן סוֹרֵר וּמוֹרֶה **Flogging regarding a rebellious son.** The question has been raised: Why does the Gemara search for a Biblical source that a rebellious son is liable to the punishment of flogging? Surely we learned earlier in the tractate (63a) that a rebellious son violates the Biblical prohibition (Leviticus 19:26): "You shall not eat anything with its blood"! *Kesef Mishnah* answers: That prohibition is stated in general terms, including several particular prohibitions of different kinds, and lashes are not administered for the violation of such a prohibition.

SAGES

רַבִּי חֲנִינָא Rabbi Ḥanina (bar Ḥama). A first-generation Amora from Eretz Israel. See *Sanhedrin*, Part I, p. 16.

מִשְׁנָה [1]בָּרַח עַד שֶׁלֹּא נִגְמַר דִּינוֹ, וְאַחַר כָּךְ הִקִּיף זָקָן הַתַּחְתּוֹן, פָּטוּר. [2]וְאִם מִשֶּׁנִּגְמַר דִּינוֹ בָּרַח, וְאַחַר כָּךְ הִקִּיף זָקָן הַתַּחְתּוֹן, חַיָּיב.

גְּמָרָא [3]אָמַר רַבִּי חֲנִינָא: בֶּן נֹחַ שֶׁבֵּירֵךְ אֶת הַשֵּׁם וְאַחַר כָּךְ נִתְגַּיֵּיר — פָּטוּר, [4]הוֹאִיל וְנִשְׁתַּנָּה דִּינוֹ, [5]נִשְׁתַּנָּה מִיתָתוֹ. [6]נֵימָא מְסַיְּיעָא לֵיהּ: [7]״בָּרַח עַד שֶׁלֹּא נִגְמַר דִּינוֹ, וְאַחַר כָּךְ הִקִּיף זָקָן הַתַּחְתּוֹן, פָּטוּר״. [8]מַאי טַעְמָא? [9]לָאו מִשּׁוּם דְּאָמְרִינַן: הוֹאִיל וְאִישְׁתַּנֵּי, אִישְׁתַּנֵּי? [10]לָא, שָׁאנֵי הָכָא, דְּאִי עָבֵד הַשְׁתָּא, [11]לָאו בַּר קְטָלָא הוּא.

LITERAL TRANSLATION

MISHNAH [1][If] he fled before his judgment was concluded, and afterward his pubic hair (lit., "lower beard") grew, he is exempt. [2]But if he fled after his judgment was concluded, and afterward his pubic hair grew, he is liable.

GEMARA [3]Rabbi Ḥanina said: A non-Jew (lit., "descendant of Noah") who cursed (lit., "blessed") the Divine Name, and later converted, is exempt, [4]since his law changed, [5][and] his execution changed.

[6]Shall we say that it supports him: [7]"[If] he escaped before his judgment was concluded, and afterward his pubic hair grew, he is exempt"? [8]What is the reason? [9]Is it not because we say: "Since it changed, it changed"?

[10]No, it is different here, for if he did it now, [11]he is not liable to be executed.

TRANSLATION AND COMMENTARY

MISHNAH בָּרַח [1]**If** the boy **fled** any time **before his** death **sentence was passed, and** before he was recaptured **his pubic hair grew significantly, he is** now **exempt** from liability as a rebellious son, for after a boy's pubic hair grows significantly, he can no longer be condemned as a rebellious son. [2]**But if he fled after his** death **sentence was passed, and** before he was recaptured **his pubic hair grew, he remains liable,** so that if he is caught he is put to death.

GEMARA אָמַר רַבִּי חֲנִינָא [3]**Rabbi Ḥanina said:** If a **non-Jew cursed the Divine Name,** thus violating one of the seven Noachide laws that are punishable by execution, **and afterward he converted** to Judaism, he **is exempt** from liability for his offense. [4]**Since the laws** governing his trial **changed,** [5]**his** mode of **execution changed.** When he was a non-Jew, he could be tried by a single judge, on the basis of testimony given by a single witness, and without having been warned prior to the commission of his offense; but were he to commit the same crime as a Jew, he could only be tried by a court of twenty-three judges, on the basis of testimony given by two witnesses, and after having received a proper warning. Further, when he was a non-Jew, he was liable to death by decapitation, but were he to commit the same crime as a Jew, he would be liable to death by stoning. Therefore he is exempt from all liability, for a person can only be found liable if at the time of his verdict he is governed by the same laws that applied to him at the time of his offense.

נֵימָא [6]The Gemara asks: **Shall we say that** our Mishnah **supports** Rabbi Ḥanina's ruling? For we have learned in our Mishnah: [7]**"If the boy fled** any time **before his** death **sentence was passed, and** before he was recaptured **his pubic hair covered his pubic area, he is** now **exempt** from liability as a rebellious son." [8]**What is the reason** that the boy is exempt from liability? [9]**Is it not because we say: "Since** his personal status **changed,** the laws by which he is governed also **changed"?**

לָא [10]The Gemara rejects the comparison: **No, it is different here** in the case of the rebellious son, **for if he committed** the same offense **now,** after his pubic hair already grew, [11]**he would not be liable to execution.** And so he is exempt for the offense he committed while subject to his previous legal status. But regarding the non-Jew who cursed God and then converted to Judaism, if he committed the same offense after his conversion, he would be liable to execution. Thus, he should be tried for the offense committed as a non-Jew according to the laws that would apply now were he to commit the same offense as a Jew.

RASHI

משנה ברח עד שלא נגמר דינו ואחר כך הקיף זקן פטור — דהא לא דייניגן ליה, כיון דאילו עבד השתא לאו בר קטלא הוא. ואם משנגמר דינו ברח — משעת גמר דין הוי כגברא קטילא, ושוב אין לנו לחפש בזכותו ולהצילו.

גמרא הואיל ונשתנה דינו (נשתנה מיתתו) — דאילו מעיקרא נידון בעד אחד ובדיין אחד ובלא התראה, ואילו עביד השתא בעינן התראה וסנהדרין של עשרים ושלשה ועדים. ונשתנית מיתתו — דכל מיתת בני נח סייף, ואילו עביד השתא בעו למדייניה בסקילה והוא לא איחייב בהא מיתה — הלכך פטור. שאני הכא דאילו עביד השתא לאו בר קטלא הוא — אבל הכא אילו עביד השתא — בר קטלא הוא אף על גב דנשתנה דינו ומיתתו

HALAKHAH

בָּרַח וְאַחַר כָּךְ הִקִּיף זָקָן הַתַּחְתּוֹן If he fled, and afterward his pubic beard grew. "If the boy fled before his death sentence was issued, and in the meantime his pubic hair grew significantly, he is now exempt from liability. But if he fled after his death sentence was issued, then whenever he is caught, even years later, he is put to death by stoning." (*Rambam, Sefer Shofetim, Hilkhot Mamrim* 7:9.)

בֶּן נֹחַ שֶׁבֵּירֵךְ אֶת הַשֵּׁם וְאַחַר כָּךְ נִתְגַּיֵּיר A non-Jew who cursed the Divine Name, and afterward converted. "If a non-Jew cursed God, or committed idolatry, or had

[1]תָּא שְׁמַע: ״אִם מִשֶּׁנִּגְמַר דִּינוֹ בָּרַח, וְאַחַר כָּךְ הִקִּיף זָקָן הַתַּחְתּוֹן, חַיָּיב״.
[2]״נִגְמַר דִּינוֹ״ קָאָמְרַתְּ? [3]נִגְמַר דִּינוֹ, גַּבְרָא קְטִילָא הוּא.
[4]תָּא שְׁמַע: ״בֶּן נֹחַ שֶׁהִכָּה אֶת חֲבֵירוֹ וּבָא עַל אֵשֶׁת חֲבֵירוֹ, [5]וְנִתְגַּיֵּיר, פָּטוּר. [6]עָשָׂה כֵּן בְּיִשְׂרָאֵל וְנִתְגַּיֵּיר״, חַיָּיב. [7]וְאַמַּאי? [8]נֵימָא: הוֹאִיל וְאִישְׁתַּנֵּי, אִישְׁתַּנֵּי!
[9]דִּינוֹ וּמִיתָתוֹ בָּעֵינַן. [10]וְהַאי — דִּינוֹ אִישְׁתַּנֵּי, [11]מִיתָתוֹ לָא אִישְׁתַּנֵּי.
[12]בִּשְׁלָמָא רוֹצֵחַ, מֵעִיקָּרָא סַיִיף וְהָשְׁתָּא סַיִיף. [13]אֶלָּא אֵשֶׁת

LITERAL TRANSLATION

[1]Come [and] hear: "If he escaped after his judgment was concluded, and afterward his pubic hair grew, he is liable."

[2]Did you say "his judgment was concluded"? [3]If his judgment was concluded, he is a dead man.

[4]Come [and] hear: "A non-Jew (lit., 'descendant of Noah') who struck his fellow, or had intercourse with his fellow's wife, [5]and converted, is exempt. [6][If] he did it to a Jew, and converted, he is liable." [7]But why? [8]Say: Since it changed, it changed!

[9]We need his law and his execution. [10]But this one — his law changed, [11][but] his execution did not change.

[12]Granted the murderer, at first the sword, and now the sword. [13]But [someone who had intercourse with] a married

RASHI

לא מיפטר ודיינינן ליה בדינא דהשתא.
תא שמע — מסיפא תיובתא. **חייב** — אלמא אף על גב דאשתני לא אפטר. **שהכה את חבירו** — הרג דהוי בסייף, וכן בא על אשת חבירו פטור משום דאילו עביד השתא לאו בר קטלא הוא. **עשה כן** — בהיותו בגויותו. **לישראל** — כגון שהרג את ישראל או בא על אשת איש ישראל ונתגייר — חייב, דאי עבד השתא — בר קטלא הוא, ואף על גב דנשתנה דינו לדון בעדה ועדים והתראה אי הוה עביד השתא מיתתו לא אישתני, דרוצח נמי השתא בסייף.

TRANSLATION AND COMMENTARY

תָּא שְׁמַע [1]**Come and hear** what we have learned in our Mishnah, which disproves Rabbi Ḥanina's position: **"If** the rebellious son **fled after his** death **sentence was passed, and** before he was recaptured **his pubic hair grew, he remains liable,** so that if he is caught, he is put to death." Even though the boy's personal status and the laws by which he is governed have now changed, he is still liable to execution. Hence a non-Jew who cursed God and then converted to Judaism should still be liable to execution.

נִגְמַר [2]The Gemara rejects this argument: **Did you say "his** death **sentence was passed"?** [3]**If his** death **sentence was passed, he is** viewed **as a dead man.** Once a verdict is issued, it remains in force no matter what changes the condemned criminal undergoes. But this ruling has no bearing on the case discussed by Rabbi Ḥanina, where the non-Jew converted to Judaism before he was convicted for cursing God.

תָּא שְׁמַע [4]**Come and hear** the following Baraita, which contradicts the position of Rabbi Ḥanina: "If **a non-Jew struck a fellow** non-Jew, killing him with a fatal blow, **or had** sexual **intercourse with the wife of a fellow** non-Jew, [5]**and** then he **converted,** he **is exempt** from liability. Were he now to kill a non-Jew, or have intercourse with a non-Jew's wife, he would not be liable to execution, and so he is exempt from liability for the offenses that he committed prior to his conversion. [6]But **if** the non-Jew **committed** those offenses **against a Jew,** and then converted, **he is** still **liable** to the death penalty." [7]According to Rabbi Ḥanina, the question may be raised: **Why,** in the second case, is the convert **liable** for the crimes that he committed prior to his conversion? [8]**Say** that, **since** his personal status **changed,** the laws by which he is governed also **changed.**

דִּינוֹ [9]The Gemara rejects this argument: In order to release the offender from liability, **we need** a change in **the laws** governing his trial, **and** also a change regarding the mode of **his execution.** [10]**But in this** case, **the laws** governing the convert's trial **changed** — for as a non-Jew he could be tried by a single judge, on the basis of the testimony of a single witness, and without a warning, but as a Jew, he can only be tried by a court of twenty-three judges, on the basis of the testimony of two witnesses, and after having received a proper warning. [11]But the mode of **execution** to which he is liable **did not change** with his conversion (as will be explained below), and so his liability for the offenses committed prior to his conversion remains in force.

בִּשְׁלָמָא [12]The Gemara raises an objection: **Granted** that we understand this answer with respect to **the murderer,** for **at first** when he was a non-Jew, his offense was punishable by execution by **decapitation, and now** that he has converted, the same crime is also punishable by execution by **decapitation.** [13]**But** regarding the **one who had intercourse with a married woman — at first,** when he was a non-Jew, his offense was

HALAKHAH

intercourse with the wife of a fellow non-Jew, or killed a fellow non-Jew, and then converted, he is exempt. But if he killed a Jew, or had intercourse with the wife of a Jew, and then converted, he is liable to execution by the mode of execution that would apply to a Jew." (*Rambam, Sefer Shofetim, Hilkhot Melakhim* 10:4.)

אִישׁ, מֵעִיקָּרָא סַיִיף וְהָשְׁתָּא חֶנֶק!

1 בְּנַעֲרָה הַמְאוֹרָסָה, דְּאִידִי וְאִידִי בִּסְקִילָה.

2 וְהָא "עָשָׂה כֵּן בְּיִשְׂרָאֵל" דּוּמְיָא דְּאֵשֶׁת חֲבֵירוֹ קָתָנֵי!

3 אֶלָּא: קַלָּה בַּחֲמוּרָה מֵישַׁךְ שַׁיְיכָא.

4 הָנִיחָא לְרַבָּנַן דְּאָמְרִי: סַיִיף חָמוּר. 5 אֶלָּא לְרַבִּי שִׁמְעוֹן דְּאָמַר: חֶנֶק חָמוּר, 6 מַאי אִיכָּא לְמֵימַר?

7 רַבִּי שִׁמְעוֹן סָבַר לָהּ כְּתַנָּא דְּבֵי מְנַשֶּׁה, דְּאָמַר: 8 "כָּל מִיתָה

LITERAL TRANSLATION

woman — at first the sword and now by strangulation!

1 [If he had intercourse with] a betrothed girl, for this and that are by stoning.

2 But surely it teaches: "[If] he did it to a Jew" — similar to his fellow's wife!

3 Rather: The more lenient [mode of execution] is included in the more severe [mode].

4 This is well according to the Rabbis who say: The sword is more severe. 5 But according to Rabbi Shimon, who says: Strangulation is more severe, 6 what is there to say?

7 Rabbi Shimon agrees with the Tanna of the academy of Menashe, who said: 8 "Every execution

TRANSLATION AND COMMENTARY

punishable by execution by **decapitation, and now** that he has converted the same crime is punishable **by strangulation!** Thus, the laws governing the convert's trial changed, as did the mode of execution. Nevertheless, you claim that he is liable for the offense that he committed prior to his conversion!

בְּנַעֲרָה 1 The Gemara answers: The Baraita refers to a non-Jew who **had intercourse with a betrothed** Jewish **girl, for** which, **in any event** he is liable to execution **by stoning.**

וְהָא 2 The Gemara objects: **But surely** the Baraita **teaches: "If** the non-Jew **committed** those offenses **against a Jew,** he is still liable to the death penalty," which implies that the crime that the non-Jew committed with the Jew's wife **is similar to** the crime mentioned in the first half of Baraita, which he committed against **the wife of a fellow** non-Jew. Since non-Jews do not practice betrothal in the Halakhic sense, the first half of the Baraita must be referring to a non-Jew who had intercourse with a woman who was married to a fellow non-Jew. Thus the second half of the Baraita must be dealing with a non-Jew who had intercourse with a woman who was married — and not only betrothed — to a Jew. So the question remains: Why does the convert remain liable for the offense that he committed prior to his conversion, when the laws regarding both his trial and the mode of execution have changed after his conversion?

אֶלָּא 3 The Gemara answers: **Rather,** the matter should be understood as follows: In fact, the Baraita is dealing with a non-Jew who had intercourse with a woman who was married to a Jew. He remains liable for that offense even after his conversion to Judaism, because the mode of execution for which he is liable did not really change with his conversion, for **the more lenient mode of execution is included in the more severe mode** of execution. When he was a non-Jew, his crime was punishable by the more severe mode of execution, decapitation, and now that he is a Jew that same crime would be punishable by the more lenient mode of execution, strangulation. Since strangulation is included in decapitation, he is put to death now by way of strangulation. The case of blasphemy is different, for if a non-Jew curses God, he is liable to the more lenient mode of execution, decapitation. But a Jew who curses God is liable to the more severe mode of execution, stoning. Thus, if a non-Jew cursed God and then converted, his conversion ends his liability for the mode of execution for which he would be liable changed with his conversion.

הָנִיחָא 4 The Gemara asks: **This conforms with the views of the Rabbis who say** that **decapitation is a more severe** mode of execution than strangulation. 5 **But according to Rabbi Shimon, who** disagrees with the Rabbis and **says** that **strangulation is a more severe** mode of execution than decapitation, 6 **what is there to say?**

רַבִּי שִׁמְעוֹן 7 The Gemara explains: **Rabbi Shimon agrees with the Tanna of the academy of Menashe, who said:** 8 **"Every execution stated** in the Torah **with regard to a non-Jew is** death by **strangulation."** And so, a

RASHI

דאידי ואידי בסקילה — אם לא נתגייר נמי נדון בסקילה כדאמרינן נמי בפרקין דלעיל (סנהדרין נז,א), דבא על ערות ישראל, שאין להם לבן נח, נדון בדיני ישראל, ואוקימנא בנערה המאורסה דלדידהו לית להו ודיינינן להו בדינא דידן. **והא עשה כן בישראל דומיא דאשת חברו קתני** — אלמא בישראל בעולת בעל עסקינן, דאילו באשת חבירו ליכא נערה המאורסה כדאמרינן: בעולת בעל יש להן, נערה המאורסה אין להם. **אלא קלה בחמורה מישך שייכא** — כלומר לעולם באשת איש, ודקא קשיא לך: אמאי חייב, הרי נשתנה דינו ומיתתו — אין כאן שינוי מיתה, דיש בכלל מיתה חמורה מיתה קלה, וכיון דמעיקרא הוי סייף דחמירא והשתא מיתת חנק קלה בכלל מיתה זו הוה ויותר היה ראוי לו מתחלה, אבל ברכת השם מעיקרא הוה סייף קל והשתא סקילה דחמירא. **מאי איכא למימר** — הרי נשתנה מיתתו, דבמיתה חמורה זו לא היה ראוי.

הָאֲמוּרָה לִבְנֵי נֹחַ אֵינָהּ אֶלָּא חֶנֶק״.

[1]״בִּשְׁלָמָא אֵשֶׁת אִישׁ, [2]מֵעִיקָּרָא חֶנֶק וְהָשְׁתָּא חֶנֶק. [3]אֶלָּא רוֹצֵחַ, מֵעִיקָּרָא חֶנֶק וְהָשְׁתָּא סַיִיף!

[4]קַלָּה בַּחֲמוּרָה מֵישַׁךְ שַׁיְיכָא.

[5]לֵימָא מְסַיְּיעָא לֵיהּ: ״סָרְחָה וְאַחַר כָּךְ בָּגְרָה — [6]תִּידּוֹן בְּחֶנֶק״. [7]בִּסְקִילָה מַאי טַעְמָא לָא? [8]לָאו מִשּׁוּם דְּהוֹאִיל וְאִישְׁתַּנֵּי, אִישְׁתַּנֵּי, [9]וְכָל שֶׁכֵּן הָכָא דְּאִישְׁתַּנֵּי לְגַמְרֵי?

[10]הָאָמַר לֵיהּ רַבִּי יוֹחָנָן לְתַנָּא:

LITERAL TRANSLATION

stated about non-Jews is only strangulation."

[1]Granted [someone who had intercourse with] a married woman, [2]at first strangulation, and now strangulation. [3]But the murderer — at first strangulation, and now the sword!

[4]The more lenient [mode of execution] is included in the more severe [mode].

[5]Shall we say that it supports him: "If she sinned, and afterward she came of age, [6]she is sentenced [to death] by strangulation"? [7]What is the reason that she is not [sentenced to death] by stoning? [8]Is it not that, since it changed, it changed, [9]and all the more so here where it changed entirely?

[10]Surely Rabbi Yoḥanan said to the Tanna:

TRANSLATION AND COMMENTARY

non-Jew who had intercourse with the wife of a Jew remains liable to execution, even if he converts to Judaism, for the mode of execution is unchanged.

בִּשְׁלָמָא [1]The Gemara raises an objection: **Granted** that we understand this answer with respect to a non-Jew **who had intercourse with the wife** of a Jew, [2]for **at first,** when he was a non-Jew, his offense was punishable by execution by **strangulation, and now** that he has converted, the same crime is also punishable by execution by **strangulation.** [3]**But** regarding **the murderer — at first,** when he was a non-Jew, his offense was punishable by **strangulation, and now** that he has converted the same crime is punishable by **decapitation!** Since the mode of execution changed after his conversion, he should be exempt.

קַלָּה [4]The Gemara answers: The mode of execution did not really change with his conversion, for **the more lenient mode of execution is included in the more severe mode.** Since decapitation is included in strangulation, he is put to death now by way of decapitation.

לֵימָא [5]The Gemara asks: **Shall we say that** the following Baraita **supports** Rabbi Ḥanina's ruling: **"If a** *na'arah* (a young girl between the ages of twelve and twelve-and-a-half) **sins,** and commits adultery while betrothed, **but** the witnesses testify against her only **afterward,** when she has already reached the age of twelve-and-a-half, [6]**she is sentenced to death by strangulation,** just as if she had committed the offense after coming of age"? Adultery is only punishable by stoning if the female partner was a betrothed virgin between twelve and twelve-and-a-half years of age. But if she was an adult, she and the man are both subject to the penalty of strangulation. [7]**What is the reason that she is not sentenced to death by stoning,** the punishment to which she was liable at the time of her offense? [8]**Is it not that** we say that **since** her personal status **changed,** the execution to which she is liable has also **changed?** Even though she is not exempt, for the more lenient mode of execution, strangulation, is included in the more severe mode of execution, stoning, [9]does it not follow **all the more so here** that, regarding a non-Jew who cursed God and then converted to Judaism, since his personal status **changed entirely,** he should now be exempt from all liability, as argued by Rabbi Ḥanina?

הָאָמַר לֵיהּ [10]The Gemara rejects this argument, suggesting that this Baraita should be emended: **Surely Rabbi Yoḥanan corrected the Tanna** (the reciter of Baraitot) who recited this Baraita in his presence: **State** the rule of the Baraita as follows: "If the *na'arah* sins and commits adultery during the period of her betrothal, but the witnesses come and testify against her only afterward, when she has already come of age, **she is sentenced to death by stoning.**" Thus, according to the Baraita, as emended by Rabbi Yoḥanan, the death penalty to which the girl is subject does not change, even if she has changed. Although she would be subject to death by strangulation if she committed adultery now, she is still subject to death by stoning for

RASHI

לימא מסייע ליה — לרבי חנינא, דאמר: כדינא דהשתא בעי למדייניה. **סרחה** — נערה המאורסה בימי נערות שהיא בסקילה, **ולבסוף בגרה** — משעמדה בדין. **תדון בחנק** — כדינא דהשתא. **בסקילה מאי טעמא לא** — מתדנה, משום דכיון דאישתני גופה אישתני קטלא, ונהי דלגמרי לא מיפטרא משום דקלה בחמורה מישך שייכא, כל שכן הכא דאישתני לגמרי בין בדינו בין במיתתו, וכיון דלא מחייב בהא מיתה — פטור לגמרי.

HALAKHAH

סָרְחָה וְאַחַר כָּךְ בָּגְרָה If she sinned, and afterward she came of age. "If, after a young girl came of age, witnesses testified that she committed adultery while still a *na'arah*, she is liable to death by stoning" (see also *Ra'avad* and *Maggid Mishneh*). (*Rambam, Sefer Kedushah, Hilkhot Issurei Bi'ah* 3:10.)

תְּנֵי: ״תִּידּוֹן בִּסְקִילָה״.

מִשְׁנָה [1] בֵּן סוֹרֵר וּמוֹרֶה נִידּוֹן עַל שֵׁם סוֹפוֹ. [2] יָמוּת זַכַּאי, וְאַל יָמוּת חַיָּיב, [3] שֶׁמִּיתָתָן שֶׁל רְשָׁעִים הֲנָאָה לָהֶן וַהֲנָאָה לָעוֹלָם. [4] לַצַּדִּיקִים — רַע לָהֶן וְרַע לָעוֹלָם. [5] יַיִן וְשֵׁינָה לָרְשָׁעִים — הֲנָאָה לָהֶן וַהֲנָאָה לָעוֹלָם. [6] וְלַצַּדִּיקִים — רַע לָהֶן וְרַע לָעוֹלָם. [7] פִּיזּוּר לָרְשָׁעִים — הֲנָאָה לָהֶן וַהֲנָאָה לָעוֹלָם. [8] וְלַצַּדִּיקִים — רַע לָהֶן וְרַע לָעוֹלָם. [9] כִּנּוּס לָרְשָׁעִים — רַע לָהֶן וְרַע לָעוֹלָם. [10] וְלַצַּדִּיקִים — הֲנָאָה לָהֶן וַהֲנָאָה לָעוֹלָם.

LITERAL TRANSLATION

Teach: "She is sentenced [to death] by stoning."

MISHNAH [1] A rebellious son is judged on account of his future. [2] Let him die innocent, and let him not die guilty, [3] for the death of the wicked is beneficial to them and beneficial to the world. [4] [But the death] of the righteous is bad for them, and bad for the world.

[5] Wine and sleep for the wicked, it is beneficial to them and beneficial to the world. [6] But for the righteous, it is bad for them, and bad for the world.

[7] The dispersion of the wicked is beneficial to them, and beneficial to the world. [8] But [the dispersion] of the righteous is bad for them, and bad for the world.

[9] The gathering of the wicked is bad for them, and bad for the world. [10] But [the gathering] of the righteous is beneficial to them and beneficial to the world.

TRANSLATION AND COMMENTARY

the adultery she committed before she came of age. Consequently, the non-Jew who cursed God, and then converted, should still be liable to decapitation, the death penalty to which he was liable at the time of his offense.

MISHNAH בֵּן סוֹרֵר וּמוֹרֶה [1] **A rebellious son is judged,** not on account of what he has actually done, but **on account of** what he will do in **the future** were he allowed to live. His current conduct shows that he will bring his parents to financial ruin, [2] and then become a robber and a murderer, and the Torah said that **it is better for him to die** now while he is still **innocent** of bloodshed **than to die** later when he is **guilty.** [3] **The death of the wicked is beneficial to them,** for once they are dead, they can no longer sin, **and** their death is also **beneficial to the world.** [4] **But the death of the righteous is bad for them,** for they can no longer fulfill the Torah's commandments, **and** their death is also **bad for the world,** for during their lifetime the righteous shield their generation from punishment.

יַיִן וְשֵׁינָה [5] When **the wicked** drink **wine or** go to **sleep, it is beneficial to** the wicked **themselves, and to the world,** for while they are drunk or asleep they cannot sin. [6] **But** when **the righteous** drink wine or go to sleep, **it is bad for** the righteous **themselves, and for the world,** for while they are drunk or asleep they cannot engage in Torah study or fulfill the commandments, nor can they protect the world.

פִּיזּוּר [7] **The dispersion of the wicked is beneficial to them and to the world,** for when the wicked are disunited, they cannot perpetrate their evil designs against the righteous. [8] **But the dispersion of the righteous is bad for them and for the world,** for when the righteous are disunited, they cannot improve the social order.

כִּנּוּס [9] **The gathering of the wicked is bad for them and for the world,** for when the wicked are united, they can impose their evil upon the world. [10] **But the gathering of the righteous is beneficial to them and to the world,** for when the righteous stand together as one, the force of good is strengthened in the world.

RASHI

תדון בסקילה — דמעיקרא אף על גב דאישתני גופה לא אישתני קטלא, הכא נמי נדייניה כדמעיקרא במיתתו הקלה.

משנה הנייה להם — שאין מוסיפין לחטוא. **והנייה לעולם** — ששקטה כל הארץ. **רע להם** — שהיו מוסיפין זכיות. **רע לעולם** — שהיו מגינין על דורם ומוכיחין את הדורות. **יין ושינה לרשעים הנייה להם והנייה לעולם** — כל זמן ששותין וישנין אינן חוטאין ואינן מריעין לבריות. **לצדיקים רע להם** — שאין עוסקין בתורה. **ורע לעולם** — שהתורה שהן עוסקין בה מגינה על הדור, וכשהן מתבטלין פורענות בא לעולם. **פיזור** — שנפרדין זה מזה ואין יכולין להועץ עלה רעה ולסייע זה את זה.

NOTES

נִידּוֹן עַל שֵׁם סוֹפוֹ **He is judged on account of his future.** This idea explains why, when other sinners are properly warned against sinning, and they violate that warning, they are punished immediately, but a rebellious son is only punished after two warnings. As stated here in the Mishnah, the rebellious son is not punished for what he actually did, but for the evil path upon which he has embarked. Thus, he is only punished if he demonstrates that he is committed to that evil path (*Torat Ḥayyim*).

יָמוּת זַכַּאי, וְאַל יָמוּת חַיָּיב **Let him die innocent, and let him not die guilty.** This argument does not contradict the rule that a person is only punished for the sins that he has actually committed, for the rebellious son is a sinner, deserving of punishment. The Mishnah does not state: "Let him die a righteous person," but rather it states: "Let him die innocent" — guilty of the offenses that he has committed, but innocent of the more serious future offenses. A truly righteous person would surely not be punished for the sins that he might commit in the future (*Ḥayyim Shenayim Yeshalem*).

כִּנּוּס לַצַּדִּיקִים **The gathering of the righteous.** A gathering of righteous people strengthens and encourages each

SAGES

רַבִּי יוֹסֵי הַגְּלִילִי Rabbi Yose the Galilean. He was a Tanna of the generation following the destruction of the Second Temple, and is not to be confused with Rabbi Yose ben Ḥalafta, a distinguished scholar of the following generation. We do not know who the teachers of Rabbi Yose the Galilean were, but when he arrived at Yavneh he was already an important Sage. We find him in the company of Rabbi Akiva, Rabbi Tarfon, and Rabbi Elazar ben Azaryah. On several occasions he disagrees with Rabbi Akiva, who treated him with great respect. Rabbi Yose the Galilean applied special exegetical methods to the study of Halakhah. These methods were not unanimously accepted, but his views were followed where he lived. The Talmud, in several places, speaks of his virtues, especially in relationships with his fellow man, and also of his great righteousness.

Two of sons, Rabbi Elazar and Rabbi Ḥanina, were important Sages in the following generation.

TRANSLATION AND COMMENTARY

שֶׁקֶט [1] **The tranquility of the wicked is bad for them and for the world,** for when the wicked are at peace they have more opportunity to devise evil plots against others. [2] **But the ease and peace of the righteous is beneficial to them and to the world,** for when the righteous are at peace they have more time to engage in the Torah and the commandments, and teach others how to lead a more righteous life.

[72A] **GEMARA** תַּנְיָא [3] **It was taught** in a related Baraita: **"Rabbi Yose the Galilean says:** [4] Is it really possible that **because** a young lad **ate a** *tartemar* **of meat and drank a half log of Italian wine,** [5] **the Torah says that he should be brought before a court to be** convicted as a rebellious son and **stoned?** Is what he did a capital offense? [6] **Rather, the Torah foresaw the behavior of the rebellious son,** [7] **that in the end** he would **consume** all of **his father's assets and seek** the pleasures **to which he had become accustomed and not find them, and** then **go out to the crossroads and rob** and murder **people** in order to satisfy his desires. [8] **The Torah said** that **it is better for** the rebellious son **to die** now, while he is still **innocent** of bloodshed, **than to die** later, when he is already **guilty,** [9] **for the death of the wicked is beneficial to them,** for they can no longer sin, **and** their death is also **beneficial to the world,** for the righteous no longer suffer at their hands. [10] **But the death of the righteous is bad for them,** for they can no longer fulfill the Torah's commandments, **and** their death is also **bad for the world,** for the righteous shield their generation from punishment."

שֵׁינָה וְיַיִן [11] "When **the wicked** drink **wine or** go to **sleep, it is beneficial to** the wicked **themselves, and to the world,** for while they are drunk or asleep they cannot sin, or cause damage to others. [12] **But** when **the righteous** drink wine or go to sleep, **it is bad for** the righteous **themselves, and for the world,** for while they are drunk or asleep, they cannot engage in Torah study or fulfill the commandments, nor can they protect the world from impending calamities."

[1] שֶׁקֶט לָרְשָׁעִים — רַע לָהֶן וְרַע לָעוֹלָם. [2] לַצַּדִּיקִים — הֲנָאָה לָהֶן וַהֲנָאָה לָעוֹלָם.

[72A] **גמרא** [3] תַּנְיָא: "רַבִּי יוֹסֵי הַגְּלִילִי אוֹמֵר: [4] וְכִי מִפְּנֵי שֶׁאָכַל זֶה תַּרְטֵימָר בָּשָׂר וְשָׁתָה חֲצִי לוֹג יַיִן הָאִיטַלְקִי, [5] אָמְרָה תּוֹרָה יֵצֵא לְבֵית דִּין לִיסָּקֵל? [6] אֶלָּא, הִגִּיעָה תּוֹרָה לְסוֹף דַּעְתּוֹ שֶׁל בֵּן סוֹרֵר וּמוֹרֶה, [7] שֶׁסּוֹף מְגַמֵּר נִכְסֵי אָבִיו וּמְבַקֵּשׁ לְמוּדוֹ וְאֵינוֹ מוֹצֵא, וְיוֹצֵא לְפָרָשַׁת דְּרָכִים וּמְלַסְטֵם אֶת הַבְּרִיּוֹת. [8] אָמְרָה תּוֹרָה: יָמוּת זַכַּאי וְאַל יָמוּת חַיָּיב, [9] שֶׁמִּיתָתָן שֶׁל רְשָׁעִים הֲנָאָה לָהֶם וַהֲנָאָה לָעוֹלָם. [10] וְלַצַּדִּיקִים רַע לָהֶם וְרַע לָעוֹלָם".

[11] "שֵׁינָה וְיַיִן לָרְשָׁעִים, הֲנָאָה לָהֶם וַהֲנָאָה לָעוֹלָם. [12] לַצַּדִּיקִים, רַע לָהֶם וְרַע לָעוֹלָם".

LITERAL TRANSLATION

[1] The tranquility of the wicked is bad for them, and bad for the world. [2] [But the ease] of the righteous is beneficial to them, and beneficial to the world.

[72A] **GEMARA** [3] It was taught: "Rabbi Yose the Galilean says: [4] And because that one ate a *tartemar* of meat and drank a half log of Italian wine, [5] the Torah said that he goes out to the court to be stoned? [6] Rather, the Torah reached the bottom of the mind of the rebellious son, [7] that in the end he would consume his father's assets and seek that to which he is accustomed and not find [it], and go out to the crossroads and rob people. [8] The Torah said: Let him die innocent, and let him not die guilty, [9] for the death of the wicked is beneficial to them and beneficial to the world. [10] [But the death] of the righteous is bad for them, and bad for the world."

[11] "Wine and sleep for the wicked, it is beneficial to them and beneficial to the world. [12] [But] for the righteous, it is bad for them, and bad for the world."

RASHI

גמרא מגמר — מכלה. למודו — מה שהורגל בבשר ויין.

NOTES

individual righteous person, when he sees that others are walking along the same path. Similarly a gathering of wicked people reinforces each individual wicked person (*Ramah*).

וּמְלַסְטֵם אֶת הַבְּרִיּוֹת And rob people. The Rishonim ask (see *Tosafot's Commentary to the Torah*): Granted that the rebellious son is judged on account of his future, and that his future as a murderer is foreseen. But why is he liable to the more severe penalty of death by stoning, when a convicted murderer is only liable to the less severe penalty of death by decapitation? According to *Ramah,* we assume that were the rebellious son allowed to live, he would also desecrate Shabbat and commit other transgressions punishable by death by stoning. Others suggest that we are more stringent with the rebellious son than with the murderer, because the rebellious son is likely to commit many murders (*Be'er HaGolah*). Yet others argue that, since the rebellious son treats his parents with scorn and disrespect, he is put to death by stoning, the punishment imposed upon a child who curses his parents (*Iyyun Ya'akov*).

¹״שֶׁקֶט לָרְשָׁעִים רַע לָהֶם וְרַע לָעוֹלָם, ²וְלַצַּדִּיקִים, הֲנָאָה לָהֶם וַהֲנָאָה לָעוֹלָם״.
³״פִּיזּוּר, לָרְשָׁעִים — הֲנָאָה לָהֶם וַהֲנָאָה לָעוֹלָם, ⁴וְלַצַּדִּיקִים, רַע לָהֶם וְרַע לָעוֹלָם״.

משנה ⁵הַבָּא בַּמַּחְתֶּרֶת נִידּוֹן עַל שֵׁם סוֹפוֹ. ⁶הָיָה בָּא בַּמַּחְתֶּרֶת וְשָׁבַר אֶת הֶחָבִית, ⁷אִם יֵשׁ לוֹ דָּמִים — חַיָּיב, ⁸אִם

LITERAL TRANSLATION

[1]"The tranquility of the wicked is bad for them, and bad for the world. [2][But the tranquility] of the righteous is beneficial to them, and beneficial to the world."

[3]"The dispersion of the wicked is beneficial to them, and beneficial to the world. [4]But [the dispersion] of the righteous is bad for them, and bad for the world."

MISHNAH [5]Someone who burrows [his way in] is judged on account of his future. [6][If] he burrowed [his way in] and broke a barrel — [7]if one is forbidden to kill him (lit., "he has blood"), he is liable. [8]If

TRANSLATION AND COMMENTARY

שֶׁקֶט [1]**"The tranquility of the wicked is bad for them and for the world,** for when the wicked are at peace they have more opportunity to devise evil plots against others. [2]**But the tranquility of the righteous is beneficial to them and to the world,** for when the righteous are at peace they have more time to engage in the Torah and the commandments, and to teach others how to lead a more righteous life."

פִּיזּוּר [3]**"The dispersion of the wicked is beneficial to them and to the world,** for when the wicked are disunited they cannot perpetrate their evil designs against the righteous. [4]**But the dispersion of the righteous is bad for them and for the world,** for when the righteous are disunited they cannot improve the social order."

MISHNAH הַבָּא בַּמַּחְתֶּרֶת [5]The previous Mishnah taught that the rebellious son is judged on account of his future, and the next Mishnah teaches that the same principle applies to a thief who breaks into a person's house. Regarding such a person, the Torah states (Exodus 22:1-2): "If a thief is found breaking in, and is beaten to death, there shall be no blood shed on his account. If the sun has risen on him, there shall be blood shed on his account." These verses teach that if the owner thinks that the thief might harm him, he is permitted not only to defend himself but even to kill the thief. But if he is sure that the thief came only to steal, and not to harm him, the owner is forbidden to kill the thief, and if he kills him, he is liable to be charged for murder. Our Mishnah explains that a thief **who breaks into** a person's house **is judged on account of his future,** for he is viewed as a potential murderer whom one is permitted to kill. [6]**If** a thief **broke into** a house, **and damaged a barrel** or some other utensil, the following distinction applies: [7]**If** the owner **is forbidden to kill** the thief, as was explained above, the thief **is liable** to pay for the damage like anyone else. [8]But **if** the owner **is permitted to kill** the thief, the thief is regarded as subject to a death sentence. He **is** therefore **exempt** from liability for the damage that he caused while breaking into the house. For there is a rule that if a person committed an act entailing both the death penalty and the payment of monetary compensation, the more severe penalty is imposed, and

RASHI

שקט לצדיקים הנייה להם והנייה לעולם — שיש להם פנאי לעסוק בתורה ובמצות.

משנה הבא במחתרת — שאמרה תורה יהרג. **נידון על שם סופו** — דהא לא קטל, ומקטיל משום דסופו להרוג בעל הבית כשיעמוד כנגדו להציל ממונו. **יש לו דמים חייב** — אם אינו ראוי ליהרג, כגון אב על הבן, דתניא לקמן דאין הבן רשאי להרוג את אביו הבא עליו במחתרת משום דרחמי האב על הבן, ולא בא על עסקי נפשות, ואי הוה קאי בריה לאפיה להציל ממונו, אין בדעתו של אביו להורגו. **חייב** — לשלם החבית כשאר מזיק.

NOTES

נִידּוֹן עַל שֵׁם סוֹפוֹ **Is judged on account of his future.** *Rabbenu Yehonatan* understands this as follows: By right, a thief who breaks into a house is treated as a pursuer, and any means may be used to prevent him from committing the violent crime that he threatens to commit. If, however, it is possible to stop the pursuer without killing him, he may not be killed. But the law regarding a thief who breaks into a house is different. Even if the owner could have stopped the burglar in some other way, he is exempt from all liability even if he killed him, for break-ins are usually conducted at night when it is not possible to avoid inflicting a lethal injury.

אִם יֵשׁ לוֹ דָּמִים **If one is forbidden to kill him.** According to *Rambam* in his *Commentary to the Mishnah,* if witnesses are present during the burglary, the owner is forbidden to kill the thief, and if he kills him he is liable for murder.

HALAKHAH

הַבָּא בַּמַּחְתֶּרֶת **Someone who breaks in.** "Why did the Torah permit a person to kill a thief who broke into his house? Because the thief is viewed as a potential killer, so that any means may be used to stop him," following the Mishnah and the Gemara's clarification. (*Rambam, Sefer Nezikin, Hilkhot Genevah* 9:9.)

אֵין לוֹ דָּמִים — פָּטוּר.
גמרא [1]אָמַר רָבָא: מַאי טַעְמָא דְּמַחְתֶּרֶת? [2]חֲזָקָה אֵין אָדָם מַעֲמִיד עַצְמוֹ עַל מָמוֹנוֹ. [3]וְהַאי מֵימַר אָמַר: אִי אָזִילְנָא, [4]קָאֵי לְאַפַּאי וְלָא שָׁבֵיק לִי. [5]וְאִי קָאֵי לְאַפַּאי, קָטְלִינָא לֵיהּ. [6]וְהַתּוֹרָה אָמְרָה: אִם בָּא לְהוֹרְגְךָ, הַשְׁכֵּם לְהוֹרְגוֹ.
[7]אָמַר רַב: הַבָּא בַּמַּחְתֶּרֶת וְנָטַל כֵּלִים וְיָצָא, פָּטוּר. [8]מַאי טַעְמָא? [9]בְּדָמִים קָנְנְהוּ.
[10]אָמַר רָבָא: מִסְתַּבְּרָא מִילְּתֵיהּ

LITERAL TRANSLATION

one is permitted to kill him (lit., "he does not have blood"), he is exempt.

GEMARA [1]Rava said: What is the reason regarding someone who burrows [his way in]? [2]There is a presumption that a person will not restrain himself regarding his property. [3]And that one says: If I go, [4]he will stand up against me and not leave me. [5]And if he stands up against me, I will kill him. [6]And the Torah says: If someone comes to kill you, kill him first.

[7]Rav said: [If] someone burrowed [his way in] and took utensils and went out, he is exempt. [8]What is the reason? [9]He acquired them with his blood.

[10]Rava said: The words of

TRANSLATION AND COMMENTARY

he is exempt from the monetary compensation. Even if the owner did not kill the thief, the thief is exempt from paying, since this rule applies even when the more severe penalty of execution is not administered.

GEMARA אָמַר רָבָא [1]**Rava said: What is the reasoning** that underlies the law **regarding** a thief **who breaks into** a house? [2]The law **is** based on **the presumption that a person will not restrain himself** when he sees someone coming to take **his property,** and that he will do whatever he can to protect it. [3]The thief **says** to himself: **If I go** and break into someone else's house, and the owner sees me, [4]surely **he will stand up against me, and not allow** me to rob him. [5]**And if he stands up against me,** and prevents me from robbing him, **I will** be forced to **kill him.** [6]Regarding such a situation, **the Torah says:** "There shall be no blood shed on his account." If the owner kills the thief, he is not guilty of murder, for **if someone comes to kill you,** you are permitted to defend yourself and **kill him first.**

אָמַר רַב [7]**Rav said: If** a thief **broke into** a house, **took utensils, and left,** and was subsequently caught, **he is exempt** from returning the stolen utensils. [8]**What is the reason** for the thief's exemption? [9]**He acquired them when he risked his life** during the burglary. When the thief broke into the house, the owner was permitted to kill him, and so the thief was regarded as subject to the death sentence and thus exempt from any other — less severe — penalty, including returning the stolen property.

אָמַר רָבָא [10]**Rava said: Rav's view stands to reason** if the thief **broke** the utensils that he stole, for they

RASHI

אין לו דמים — כגון שאר כל האדם שניתן רשות לבעל הבית להורגו — פטור מלשלם, דחיוב מיתה וחיוב תשלומין באין כאחד, ואף על פי שניצל — פטור מן התשלומין, דקיימא לן (כתובות לה,א) חייבי מיתות שוגגין כגון שלא התרו בהן — אין משלמין ממון שעם המיתה, אף על פי שאין נהרגין.

גמרא מאי טעמא דמחתרת — שאמרה תורה אין לו דמים כלומר, הרי הוא לך כמי שאין לו דם ונשמה ומותר להורגו. **חזקה אין אדם מעמיד עצמו על ממונו** — שרואה שאחר נוטלו ושותק, הלכך יודע הגנב הזה שבעל הבית עומד על ממונו להצילו, ומימר אמר הגנב: אי אזילנא לגביה קאי באפאי, ואי קאי — קטילנא ליה, ואמרה לך תורה: "אין לו דמים" ומלמדך מאחר שהוא בא להרגך השכם אתה להרגו. **הבא במחתרת** — חתר את הבית ממש. **פטור** — מלהחזירם אף על פי שהם קיימין. **בדמים קננהו** — בדמי נפשו קנאן, הואיל ונתחייב מיתה בלקיחתם. **מסתברא** — מילתא דרב דפטור בששבר בין עכשיו בין לאחר זמן, דליתנהו, ותשלומין מדידיה לא מצינן לחיוביה במקום מיתה.

NOTES

הַתּוֹרָה אָמְרָה: אִם בָּא לְהוֹרְגְךָ **The Torah said: If someone comes to kill you.** Where is this principle stated in the Torah? *Midrash Tanhuma* argues that this is derived from the verses (Numbers 25:17-18): "Assail the Midianites, and smite them. For they assailed you by the trickery they practiced against you in the matter of Peor." This verse teaches that, because the Midianites continually devised evil plots to assail the Israelites, the Israelites were permitted to go out and strike them first (see *Meiri*).

אִם בָּא לְהוֹרְגְךָ, הַשְׁכֵּם לְהוֹרְגוֹ **If someone comes to kill you, kill him first.** *Ramah* asks: If the owner is prepared to kill the thief in order to protect his property, why, then, do we not treat him as a pursuer and allow the thief to kill him? He explains that the owner does not initiate the confrontation. Rather, the thief breaks into his house, knowing that he will have to kill the owner if he puts up a fight to protect his property. Therefore it is the thief who is regarded as the pursuer, and not the owner. *Ran* adds that the Torah penalized the thief, proclaiming him the pursuer, and not the owner.

HALAKHAH

אִם בָּא לְהוֹרְגְךָ, הַשְׁכֵּם לְהוֹרְגוֹ **If someone comes to kill you, kill him first.** "A person who is being pursued by another person who wishes to kill him may defend himself and kill the pursuer." (*Shulḥan Arukh, Ḥoshen Mishpat* 425:1.)

TRANSLATION AND COMMENTARY

are no longer intact. In such a case, the thief's being subject to the more severe penalty of death exempts him from the less severe penalty of monetary compensation. [1]**But if** the thief **took** the utensils, and they are still intact, he should **not** be exempt from returning them, for as long as the stolen utensils are still intact they are regarded as a deposit which must be returned to the rightful owner. [2]**But by God, Rav** indeed **said:** The thief is exempt from returning the stolen utensils, **even if he took them,** and they are still intact. What is the reason? [3]**For** if the utensils were taken by a thief whom **one is forbidden to kill,** the thief is surely obligated to return the utensils to their rightful owner, for he was never liable to the more severe penalty of death. [4]And **if** the utensils **broke by accident** before he returned them, **he is liable** to pay for them. [5]Now **this implies** that the utensils are not regarded as a deposit, the accidental loss of which would fall upon the owner, and for which the thief would not be liable. Rather the utensils are regarded as **standing in** the thief's **possession,** so that their accidental loss falls upon the thief. [6]**Here, too,** if the utensils were taken by a thief whom one is permitted to kill, we should say that the stolen utensils are not regarded as a deposit, but rather are regarded as **standing in** the thief's **possession.** Since the thief was liable to the death penalty, he is exempt now from making any monetary compensation from goods in his possession.

וְלָא הִיא [7]Rava rejects this argument: **But this is not so.** Even if we say that if the utensils were taken by a thief whom one is forbidden to kill, the thief is liable to pay for the utensils that he broke, it is not because the stolen utensils belong to him in the same way that the rest of his property belongs to him. [8]For **when the Torah put** the stolen property **in** the thief's **possession,** it was only to make him liable to pay monetary compensation should it be lost or broken through an unavoidable **accident.** [9]**But as for acquiring** the stolen property that remains intact, which the thief might want to keep and return money in its place, **it remains in the possession of its** original **owner** and must be returned to him. [10]This is **similar to** the law applying to **a borrower,** who has to pay monetary compensation if the borrowed property was lost or broken through an unavoidable accident, but nevertheless must return the property as is to its rightful owner as long as it remains intact. The thief's being subject to the more severe penalty of death should not exempt him from the obligation to return the owner's property that is still intact.

דְּרַב בְּשֶׁשִּׁיבֵּר, דְּלֵיתַנְהוּ. [1]אֲבָל נָטַל, לֹא. [2]וְהָאֱלֹהִים! אָמַר רַב: אֲפִילּוּ נָטַל. [3]דְּהָא יֵשׁ לוֹ דָּמִים, [4]וְנֶאֶנְסוּ, חַיָּיב, [5]אַלְמָא: בִּרְשׁוּתֵיהּ קָיְימִי. [6]הָכָא נַמִי בִּרְשׁוּתֵיהּ קָיְימִי.

[7]וְלָא הִיא. [8]כִּי אוֹקְמִינָא רַחֲמָנָא בִּרְשׁוּתֵיהּ — לְעִנְיַן אוֹנָסִין, [9]אֲבָל לְעִנְיַן מִקְנָא — בִּרְשׁוּתֵיהּ דְּמָרַיְיהוּ קָיְימִי, [10]מִידֵּי דַּהֲוָה אַשּׁוֹאֵל.

LITERAL TRANSLATION

Rav stand to reason if he broke [them], so that they are no more. [1]But if he took [them], no. [2]But by God, Rav said: Even [if] he took [them]. [3]For if one is forbidden to kill him, [4]and they broke by accident, he is liable. [5]This implies: They stand in his possession. [6]Here, too, they stand in his possession.

[7]But it is not so. [8]When the Torah (lit., "the Merciful One") put it in his possession — regarding accidents. [9]But regarding acquisition — it stands in the possession of its owner, [10]as it is regarding a borrower.

RASHI

אבל נטל לא — מסתברא בהא מילתא דרב דפטר בה, דכיון דקיימין הן כל היכא דאיתנהו דמרייהו נינהו, ואין זה חייב בתשלומין דפקדון בעלמא נינהו גביה. **והאלהים** — שבועה, אמר רב דפטור ואפילו איתנהו, וטעמא מהכא דהאי "אם יש לו דמים" כגון אב על הבן דמודה בהו רב דלא קנה וחייב להחזיר, אחרי כן אמרינן דאפילו נאנסו מיניה משבאו לרשותו חייב להחזיר דמיהן, אלמא לא אמרינן פקדון הוו גביה ואבדו לבעלים, אלא אמרינן: ברשותו הן ואבדו לו, הכא נמי לענין אין לו דמים, אף על פי דאיתנהו אמרינן לאו פקדון נינהו — אלא ברשותו ובאחריותו קיימי, וכי גבו להו בי דינא מיניה יש כאן תשלומין עם חיוב מיתה כאילו גובין מאחר נכסים. **ולא היא** — מסקנא דמילתא דרבא הוא, ולא היא — לא מסתברא טעמא דרב בהא, דאף על גב דהיכא דיש לו דמים חייבין באחריותו לאו קנין הן לו להיות כשאר נכסיו, דכי אוקמיה רחמנא ברשותיה וחייב את הגזלנין לשלם הני מילי לענין שלומי, דלא מצי למימר ליה: נאנסו, דאשכחן בשומרין דחייבן הכתוב לישבע "אם לא שלח יד במלאכת רעהו" — הא שלח אף על גב דטעין מת או נשבר, דהיינו אונס — חייב, דנעשה עליה גזלן בשליחות יד. **אבל לענין מקנא לא קני** — אם קיימין הן אצלו והוא היה בא לעכבו ולומר דמים אני מחזיר לך — לא קני ומהדר להו בעינייהו, דכתיב (ויקרא ה) "והשיב את הגזילה", והאי דכי נאנסו מחזיר דמים ולא מצי אמר ליה נאנסו ומיפטר — משום דלא גרע גזלן משואל, דמשום דכל הנאה שלו אוקמינהו רחמנא ברשותו לשלומי אם נאנס, דכל כמה דקיימא הדרא בעינא, הא נמי כל הנאה שלו ומיחייב לשלומי.

HALAKHAH

שִׁיבֵּר וְנָטַל **If he broke it, if he took it.** "If a thief broke into a house, and damaged utensils in the process, he is exempt from liability for the utensils. If he broke them on the way out, it would appear (from *Rambam's Commentary to the Mishnah*) that he is liable. If he stole the utensils, and they remained intact, he must return them to their rightful owner." (*Rambam, Sefer Nezikin, Hilkhot Genevah* 9:13, in *Maggid Mishneh; Tur, Ḥoshen Mishpat* 351.)

[1] תְּנַן: ״בָּא בַּמַּחְתֶּרֶת וְשִׁיבֵּר אֶת הֶחָבִית, יֵשׁ לוֹ דָּמִים — חַיָּיב. [2] אֵין לוֹ דָּמִים, פָּטוּר״. [3] טַעְמָא דְשִׁיבֵּר, [4] דְּכִי אֵין לוֹ דָּמִים, פָּטוּר. [5] הָא נָטַל, לֹא! [6] הוּא הַדִּין דַּאֲפִילּוּ נָטַל נַמִי. [7] וְהָא דְּקָא תָּנֵי: ״שִׁבֵּר אֶת הֶחָבִית״, [8] קָא מַשְׁמַע לָן דְּכִי יֵשׁ לוֹ דָּמִים, [9] אַף עַל גַּב דְשִׁיבֵּר נַמִי, חַיָּיב.

[10] פְּשִׁיטָא, מַזִּיק הוּא!

[11] הָא קָא מַשְׁמַע לָן דַּאֲפִילּוּ שֶׁלֹּא בְּכַוָּונָה.

[12] מַאי קָא מַשְׁמַע לָן? אָדָם מוּעָד לְעוֹלָם. [13] תָּנֵינָא: ״אָדָם מוּעָד לְעוֹלָם, בֵּין בְּשׁוֹגֵג בֵּין בְּמֵזִיד [14] בֵּין בְּאוֹנֶס בֵּין בְּרָצוֹן״!

[15] קַשְׁיָא.

[16] מְתִיב רַב בִּיבִי בַּר אַבַּיֵי: [17] ״הַגּוֹנֵב כִּיס בַּשַּׁבָּת, חַיָּיב,

LITERAL TRANSLATION

[1] We have learned: "[If] he burrowed [his way in] and broke a barrel — if one is forbidden to kill him, he is liable. [2] If one is permitted to kill him, he is exempt." [3] The reason is that he broke [it], [4] so that if one is permitted to kill him, he is exempt. [5] But if he took [it], no!

[6] The same law applies even if he took [it]. [7] And that which it taught: "[If] he broke a barrel," [8] teaches us that when one is forbidden to kill him, [9] even if he broke [it], he is also liable.

[10] This is obvious, [for] he caused damage!

[11] It teaches us that even without intention.

[12] What does it teach us? A man is always regarded as forewarned. [13] We have learned: "A man is always regarded as forewarned, whether he acted inadvertently or intentionally, [14] whether by accident or willfully."

[15] It is difficult.

[16] Rav Bivi bar Abaye objected: [17] "[If] someone steals a wallet on Shabbat, he is liable,

TRANSLATION AND COMMENTARY

תְּנַן [1] The Gemara raises another objection against Rav from what **we have learned** in our Mishnah: **"If** a thief **broke into** a house, **and damaged a barrel** or some other utensil, and the owner **was forbidden to kill** him, the thief **is liable** to pay for the damage. [2] But **if** the owner **was permitted to kill** the thief, the thief **is exempt** from liability for the damage that he caused." A careful reading of our Mishnah leads us to the following conclusion: [3] Its rulings apply only if the thief **broke** the utensil. [4] In such a case, if the owner **was permitted to kill** the thief, the thief **is exempt** from liability for the damage that he caused. [5] **But** it follows from this that **if** the thief **took** the stolen property, and it is still intact, he would **not** be exempt. Rather he would be obligated to return the stolen property to its rightful owner, against Rav.

הוּא הַדִּין [6] The Gemara answers: In fact, **the same law applies even** if the thief **took** the utensil, and it is still intact. The thief does not have to return the stolen property, as was argued by Rav. [7] **And** the reason that the Mishnah **was formulated** as it was — **"If** the thief **broke a barrel,"** rather than: "If the thief took a barrel" — [8] is that it wanted to **teach us that** if the owner **was forbidden to kill** the thief, [9] then **even if** the thief **broke** the barrel, **he is obliged** to pay monetary compensation, just like anyone else.

פְּשִׁיטָא [10] The Gemara asks: What does the Mishnah teach us? Surely **it is obvious** that the thief is obliged to pay monetary compensation, **for** he did indeed **cause damage!**

הָא קָא מַשְׁמַע לָן [11] The Gemara answers: The Mishnah **teaches us that** the thief is obliged to pay monetary compensation, **even** if he broke the utensil **unintentionally.**

מַאי קָא מַשְׁמַע לָן [12] The Gemara asks again: **What does** the Mishnah **teach us** with this ruling? If you say that the Mishnah teaches us that **a man is** regarded as **always forewarned,** and therefore liable for the consequences of his actions, even those performed inadvertently, there is a difficulty, [13] for surely **we have already learned** this elsewhere (see *Bava Kamma* 33b): **"A man is** regarded as **always forewarned,** and therefore liable for any damage that he caused, **whether he acted inadvertently or intentionally,** [14] **whether** he caused the damage **by** unavoidable **accident or willingly."**

קַשְׁיָא [15] The Gemara responds: Our Mishnah does indeed present **a difficulty** when applied to the position of Rav.

מְתִיב [16] **Rav Bivi bar Abaye raised an objection** against Rava from the following Baraita: [17] **"If someone steals a wallet on Shabbat,** picking it up and removing it from its owner's house, **he is liable** for

SAGES

רַב בִּיבִי בַּר אַבַּיֵי **Rav Bivi bar Abaye.** A Babylonian Amora of the fifth generation, Rav Bivi was the son of Abaye, Rava's colleague. His teachers were Rav Yosef and his own father. His contemporaries were Rav Pappi and Rav Huna the son of Rav Yehoshua. His Halakhic and Aggadic teachings are found in many places in the Talmud.

RASHI

מועד לעולם – אפילו שלא בכוונה. **קשיא** – קשיא מתניתין לתרוצה אליבא דרב, ומכל מקום תיובתא לא הוי, דלאו בהדיא קתני לה נטל חייב, ואיכא לשנויי בדוחקא כדשנין: דמשום רישא נקט שבר, והיינו דאיכא בין קושיא לתיובתא. **מתיב רב ביבי** – לרבא פריך, דאמר: נטל, דאיתניהו – חייב. **הגונב כיס בשבת** – שהגביהו

HALAKHAH

אָדָם מוּעָד לְעוֹלָם **A man is always forewarned.** "A man is regarded as always forewarned, so that he is responsible for any damage he causes, whether intentional or not, whether he was awake or asleep." (*Shulḥan Arukh, Ḥoshen Mishpat* 421:3.)

הַגּוֹנֵב כִּיס בַּשַּׁבָּת **If someone steals a wallet on Shabbat.** "If a thief stole a wallet on Shabbat, dragging it out from the owner's private domain to the public domain, and the

TRANSLATION AND COMMENTARY

the theft, even though he is also subject to the death penalty for violating Shabbat. [1]**For he became liable** to be punished **for theft** the moment he picked up the wallet in its owner's house, **before he transgressed the prohibition against violating the Sabbath.** [2]**If,** on the other hand, the thief **drags** the wallet **out** of its owner's house without picking it up, **he is exempt** from culpability for the theft, [3]**for** in this case **the violation of theft and the violation** of the Shabbat prohibition which is **punishable by stoning were committed simultaneously.** A thief who drags an object along the ground without picking it up is liable to be punished for the theft only when the object leaves its owner's domain. Likewise, a person who drags an object from a private domain into the public domain on Shabbat becomes liable when the object leaves the private domain. This contradicts Rava's ruling that if a thief broke into a house and took utensils, he is obligated to return those utensils that are still intact, even though he became liable to the death sentence when he broke into the house.

וְהִלְכְתָא [4]The Gemara concludes: **The law is** that the thief who dragged the wallet out of its owner's house on Shabbat is only exempt from culpability for the theft if the wallet is no longer intact, as when **he cast** it **into a river.** The thief's liability to the more severe penalty of death for his violation of Shabbat exempts him from the less severe penalty of monetary compensation. But if the wallet is still intact, the thief is indeed obligated to return it to its rightful owner, as was argued by Rava.

רָבָא אִיגַּנְבוּ לֵיהּ [5]It was related that **rams were** once **stolen from Rava** by thieves who **broke into** his house. [6]The thieves were later apprehended, and **they** wished to **return** the rams to Rava, **but he would not accept them.** [7]**He said:** I myself maintain that a thief who broke into a house is obligated to return the stolen property that is still intact. But I will not take my rams back, **for Rav ruled** that a thief is exempt from returning the property that he stole during a break-in.

תָּנוּ רַבָּנַן [8]**Our Rabbis taught** the following Baraita: "The verse states (Exodus 22:1): **'There shall be no blood shed on his account.'** [9]And the next verse (Exodus 22:2) states: **'If the sun be risen upon him.'** [10]It

[1]שֶׁהֲרֵי נִתְחַיֵּיב בִּגְנֵיבָה קוֹדֶם שֶׁיָּבֹא לִידֵי אִיסּוּר שַׁבָּת. [2]הָיָה מְגָרֵר וְיוֹצֵא, פָּטוּר, [3]שֶׁהֲרֵי אִיסּוּר גְּנֵבָה וְאִיסּוּר סְקִילָה בָּאִין כְּאֶחָד".

[4]וְהִלְכְתָא: דִּשְׁדַנְהוּ בְּנַהֲרָא.

[5]רָבָא אִיגַּנְבוּ לֵיהּ דִּיכְרֵי בְּמַחְתַּרְתָּא. [6]אַהַדְרִינְהוּ נִיהֲלֵיהּ וְלָא קַבְּלִינְהוּ, [7]אֲמַר: הוֹאִיל וּנְפַק מִפּוּמֵיהּ דְּרַב.

[8]תָּנוּ רַבָּנַן: "'אֵין לוֹ דָּמִים אִם [9]זָרְחָה הַשֶּׁמֶשׁ עָלָיו'. [10]וְכִי

LITERAL TRANSLATION

[1]for he became liable for theft before he transgressed the prohibition against [violating] the Sabbath. [2][If] he was dragging it out, he is exempt, [3]for the prohibition of theft and the prohibition [punishable] by stoning come as one."

[4]And the law is: Where he cast it into the river.

[5]Rams were stolen from Rava during a break-in. [6]They returned them, but he would not accept them. [7]He said: Since it issued forth from the mouth of Rav.

[8]Our Rabbis taught: "'There shall be no blood on his account. [9]If the sun be risen upon him.' [10]But

RASHI

וקנאו בהגבהה – חייב להחזיר, ואף על גב שהוציאו אחר כך לרשות הרבים ונתחייב בהוצאתו מיתה. שהרי נתחייב בגניבה קודם שיבא לידי איסור שבת – ובשביל חיוב מיתה הבא עליו לאחר מכן אינו נפטר מן התשלומין. היה מגרר ויוצא – שלא הגביהו ולא קנאו בתוך הבית אבל כשיוצא לרשות הרבים קנאו בשנוי רשות שהוציאו מרשות הבעלים, ויריך ידו למטה משלשה וקבלה בידו, דידו חשובה לו כארבעה על ארבעה, והרי הוא לו כחצרו, ואף על פי שאין כאן הגבהה, והכי מוקים לה בכתובות. פטור מתשלומין – אלמא אף על פי שהכלים והמעות קיימין אמרינן בדמי קנינהו, ולא מפקינן ליה מיניה, ותיובתא דרבא דאמר: נטל – לא. והלכתא – הא דקתני פטור כגון דשדינהו בנהרא דליתנהו. דכרי – אילים. אהדרינהו ניהליה – הגנבים. הכי גרסינן: תנו רבנן אין לו דמים אם זרחה וגו' אלא אם

NOTES

הוֹאִיל וּנְפַק מִפּוּמֵיהּ **Since it issued forth from his mouth.** In several places we find Rabbinic authorities taking care to follow rulings that were issued by their teachers, even when they believed that those rulings were not Halakhically binding.

אִם זָרְחָה הַשֶּׁמֶשׁ **If the sun be risen upon him.** Several authorities have noted that even if we accept the metaphoric interpretation of the verse offered here in the Gemara, the verse may still be understood according to its plain sense. According to its plain meaning, the verse teaches that if a thief breaks into a house during the day, the owner may not kill him. A burglar who breaks into a

HALAKHAH

wallet was lost, he is exempt from liability to pay for it, for the crime of theft and the desecration of Shabbat were committed simultaneously. But if he stole the wallet, and picked it up in the private domain, and then took it out to the public domain, and threw it into a river, he is liable for payment, for he became liable for theft before he became liable for Shabbat desecration." (*Rambam, Sefer Nezikin, Hilkhot Genevah* 3:2; *Shulḥan Arukh, Ḥoshen Mishpat* 351:1.)

הַשֶּׁמֶשׁ עָלָיו בִּלְבַד זָרְחָה? [1]אֶלָּא: אִם בָּרוּר לְךָ הַדָּבָר כַּשֶּׁמֶשׁ שֶׁאֵין לוֹ שָׁלוֹם עִמְּךָ, הָרְגֵהוּ. [2]וְאִם לָאו, אַל תַּהַרְגֵהוּ״.

[3]תַּנְיָא אִידָךְ: ״׳אִם זָרְחָה הַשֶּׁמֶשׁ עָלָיו דָּמִים לוֹ׳. [4]וְכִי הַשֶּׁמֶשׁ עָלָיו בִּלְבַד זָרְחָה? [5]אֶלָּא: אִם בָּרוּר לְךָ כַּשֶּׁמֶשׁ שֶׁיֵּשׁ לוֹ שָׁלוֹם עִמְּךָ, אַל תַּהַרְגֵהוּ. [6]וְאִם לָאו, — הָרְגֵהוּ״.

[7]קַשְׁיָא סְתָמָא אַסְּתָמָא!

[8]לָא קַשְׁיָא, [72B] [9]כָּאן, בְּאָב עַל הַבֵּן; [10]כָּאן, בְּבֵן עַל הָאָב.

LITERAL TRANSLATION

does the sun rise for him alone? [1]Rather: If the matter is as clear to you as the sun that he has no peace with you, kill him. [2]But if not, do not kill him."

[3]It was taught in another [Baraita]: "'If the sun be risen upon him, there shall be blood shed on his account.' [4]But does the sun rise for him alone? [5]Rather: If it is as clear to you as the sun that he has peace with you, do not kill him. [6]But if not, kill him."

[7][The law regarding] the unclear case contradicts [the law regarding] the unclear case!

[8]It is not difficult. [72B] [9]Here, when the father [breaks in] on the son; [10]here, when the son [breaks in] on the father.

TRANSLATION AND COMMENTARY

may be asked: **Does the sun rise for** the thief **alone?** [1]**Rather,** these verses should be understood as a metaphor. When shall there be no blood shed on his account? When the sun rises upon him. **If the matter is as clear to you as the sun that** the thief **has not come to you in peace,** so that if you resist him, he will try to kill you, you are permitted to **kill him,** and you will not be held accountable for his murder. [2]**But if** it is **not** clear to you that the thief will harm you, **you may not kill him."**

תַּנְיָא אִידָךְ [3]**It was taught** in a slightly different manner **in another Baraita:** "The verse states: **'If the sun be risen upon him, there shall be blood shed on his account.'** It may be asked: [4]**Does the sun rise for** the thief **alone?** [5]**Rather,** this verse should be understood as a metaphor. When shall there be blood shed on his account? When the sun rises upon him. **If it is as clear to you as the sun that** the thief **has come to you in peace, you may not kill him.** [6]**But if** his intentions are **not** clear to you, you are permitted to **kill him,** and you will not be guilty of murder."

קַשְׁיָא [7]The Gemara notes: **The law regarding the unclear case** that emerges from the first Baraita **contradicts the law regarding the unclear case** that emerges from the second Baraita, for the first Baraita implies that if the owner is not sure that the thief is ready to kill him, he may not kill the thief, whereas the second Baraita implies that unless the owner is certain that the thief has no intention of killing him, he is permitted to kill him.

לָא קַשְׁיָא [8]The Gemara responds: **There is** really **no difficulty.** [72B] [9]**Here,** in the first Baraita, we are dealing with **a father who breaks into** the house of **his son.** The son may only kill his father if it is as clear as day to him that his father hates him, and is ready to kill him. [10]And **here,** in the second Baraita, we are dealing with **a son who breaks into** the house of **his father,** and all the more so with a case where the thief is a total stranger. There is no presumption that the son's filial feelings will stop him from killing his father. The father is only forbidden to kill his son, if it is as clear as day to him that his son loves him the way a father loves a son.

RASHI

ברור לך הדבר כשמש שאין לו שלום עמך הרגהו וכו׳ אין לו דמים וסמיך ליה אם זרחה השמש, ודרשינן סמוכין: אימתי מותר להורגו — בזמן שהשמש זרחה עליו, כלומר: שברור לך שלהרגך בא אם תעמוד כנגדו, אבל מספק — אל תהרגהו. **ותניא אידך: אם זרחה השמש עליו דמים לו** — אימתי אסור להרגהו — בזמן שזרחה השמש עליו, כלומר: שברור הדבר לך כאור שהוא רחמני עליך, ואפילו אתה עומד כנגדו להציל ממונך מידו — לא יהרגך, ואם לאו, שספקא הוא לך — הרגהו, קשיין אהדדי. **אב הבא על הבן** — במחתרת, מספק אל יהרגהו בנו, דודאי רחמי האב על בנו ואפילו הוא מציל ממונו לא יהרגהו, הלכך דמים לו עד שיודע לך כשמש שהוא אכזרי עליך ושונאך. **בן על האב** — וכל שכן איניש דעלמא — הרגהו מספק, דודאי אדעתא דהכי אתא, דאי קיימת ליה לאפיה קטיל לך, עד שיודע לך כשמש שהוא רחמני עליך כאב על הבן.

NOTES

house at night when people are usually at home comes prepared to kill the home owner, and so he is regarded as a pursuer whom the home owner may kill. But a burglar who breaks into a house during the day thinks that nobody is home. Since he comes only to steal, and not to kill, he is not regarded as a pursuer, and so the owner may not kill him (*Ra'avad, Rabbi Abraham the son of Rambam; Rabbenu Beḥayah*).

בָּאָב עַל הַבֵּן **When the father breaks in on the son.** The Sages maintained that the closest human relationship, as

HALAKHAH

אִם בָּרוּר לְךָ הַדָּבָר כַּשֶּׁמֶשׁ **If the matter is as clear to you as the sun.** "If it is as clear as day that the burglar has no intention of killing, the owner of the home is forbidden to kill him, and if he kills him, he is liable for murder, for the verse states: 'If the sun be risen upon him, there shall be blood shed on his account.'" (*Rambam, Sefer Nezikin, Hilkhot Genevah* 9:10; *Shulḥan Arukh, Ḥoshen Mishpat* 425:1, in *Rema*.)

אָב עַל הַבֵּן **When the father breaks in on the son.** "If a father breaks into his son's house, the son may not kill

TRANSLATION AND COMMENTARY

אָמַר רַב [1]**Rav said: I** would **kill any** thief **who breaks into my** house, even if I recognized him, [2]**with the exception of Rav Ḥanina bar Shela.** [3]The Gemara asks: **What is the reason?** [4]**If you say** that Rav would spare Rav Ḥanina bar Shela **because** he knew **him to be a righteous man,** that is difficult, [5]for in this hypothetical situation Rav Ḥanina bar Shela **broke into** Rav's house, indicating that he was not so righteous. [6]**Rather,** Rav argued as follows: I would not kill Rav Ḥanina bar Shela, **because I am sure that he would have compassion upon me the way a father would have compassion upon his** own **son.**

תָּנוּ רַבָּנַן [7]**Our Rabbis taught** a related Baraita: "The verse that states: 'If the sun be risen upon him, **there shall be blood shed on his account,'** [8]teaches that **both during the week and on Shabbat,** one is forbidden to kill a thief who breaks into one's house if it is as clear as day that the thief has come only to steal. [9]The verse that states: 'If a thief be found breaking in, and be smitten that he die, **there shall be no blood shed on his account'** — [10]teaches that **both during the week and on Shabbat** one is permitted to kill a thief who breaks into one's house."

בִּשְׁלָמָא [11]The Gemara asks: Granted that **it was necessary** for the Baraita to state that the verse, "If a thief be found breaking in, and be smitten that he die, **there shall be no blood shed on his account,"** teaches that both **during the week and on Shabbat** a home owner is permitted to kill a thief who he is not sure will not kill him. [12]For without the Baraita **you might have thought** that the law applying to a burglar is **similar to** the law applying to criminals **who are subject to judicial execution.** [13]Just as **we do not execute** a condemned criminal **on Shabbat** — as is learned from the verse (Exodus 35:3): "You shall kindle no fire in all of your habitations," which teaches that we do not execute a condemned criminal on the Sabbath by burning, or by any other form of capital punishment — so, too, a home owner may not kill a burglar who breaks into his house on Shabbat. [14]Therefore, the Baraita **teaches us** that one may indeed **kill**

[1]אָמַר רַב: כָּל דְּאָתֵי עִלָּאֵי בְּמַחְתַּרְתָּא — קָטֵילְנָא לֵיהּ, [2]לְבַר מֵרַב חֲנִינָא בַּר שֵׁילָא. [3]מַאי טַעְמָא? [4]אִילֵימָא: מִשּׁוּם דְּצַדִּיק הוּא — [5]הָא קָאָתֵי בְּמַחְתַּרְתָּא! [6]אֶלָּא מִשּׁוּם דְּקִים לִי בְּגַוֵּויהּ דִּמְרַחֵם עֲלַי כְּרַחֵם אָב עַל הַבֵּן.

[7]תָּנוּ רַבָּנַן: "'דָּמִים לוֹ', [8]בֵּין בַּחוֹל בֵּין בַּשַּׁבָּת. [9]'אֵין לוֹ דָּמִים' — [10]בֵּין בַּחוֹל בֵּין בַּשַּׁבָּת".

[11]בִּשְׁלָמָא "אֵין לוֹ דָּמִים בֵּין בַּחוֹל בֵּין בַּשַּׁבָּת" — אִיצְטְרִיךְ, [12]סָלְקָא דַּעֲתָךְ אָמִינָא: מִידֵּי דַּהֲוָה אַהֲרוּגֵי בֵּית דִּין, [13]דִּבְשַׁבָּת לָא קָטְלִינַן. [14]קָא

LITERAL TRANSLATION

[1]Rav said: Whoever breaks in on me, I will kill him, [2]except for Rav Ḥanina bar Shela. [3]What is the reason? [4]If you say: Because he is a righteous man [5]surely he broke in. [6]Rather, because I am sure about him that he has compassion for me the way a father has compassion for a son.

[7]Our Rabbis taught: "'There shall be blood shed on his account' — [8]both during the week and on Shabbat. [9]'There shall be no blood shed on his account' — [10]both during the week and on Shabbat.'"

[11]Granted that it was necessary [to say], "'There shall be no blood shed on his account' — both during the week and on Shabbat." [12][For] it might have entered your mind to say: Just like those executed by the court, [13]whom we do not kill on Shabbat. [14]It

RASHI

דמים לו — לשון רביה הוא להכי אתא לומר לך: דבין בחול בין בשבת אסור לבן להרוג את אביו במחתרת, שהרי לא בא על עסקי נפשות. אין לו דמים — לשון רביה דכתיב גבי אינש דעלמא להכי אתא, לומר לך: אין לו דמים לא בחול ולא בשבת והרגהו. הרוגי בית דין בשבת לא קטלינן — כדאמרינן בפרק "אחד דיני ממונות" (סנהדרין לה,ב) מ"לא תבערו אש בכל מושבותיכם".

NOTES

regards one person showing mercy and compassion to another, is that which exists between a father and his child, as it is stated in the verse (Psalms 103:13): "As a father pities his children." So the Rabbis said (*Yalkut Shimoni*): "It is the way of a mother to offer comfort, and the way of a father to show compassion." Various Scriptural proofs support the thesis that a father's mercy upon his child is greater than a child's mercy upon his father.

HALAKHAH

him, for it is clear that the father would not kill his son. But if a son breaks into his father's house, the father may kill him." (*Rambam, Sefer Nezikin, Hilkhot Genevah* 9:10.)

אֵין לוֹ דָּמִים בֵּין בַּחוֹל בֵּין בַּשַּׁבָּת **There shall be no blood shed on his account — both during the week and on Shabbat.** "If a thief breaks into a house, whether by day or at night, whether during the week or on Shabbat, anybody is permitted to kill him," following the Gemara. (*Rambam, Sefer Nezikin, Hilkhot Genevah* 9:7.)

TRANSLATION AND COMMENTARY

a thief who breaks into one's house, even on Shabbat, for the permission to kill the thief is based on the principle of self-defense that applies at all times. [1]**But** there is a difficulty with the first part of the Baraita which states that the verse, **"there shall be blood shed on his account,"** [2]teaches that **both during the week and on Shabbat,** a home owner is forbidden to kill a thief if it is as clear as day that the thief has come only to steal, and not to kill him. [3]**If** one is **not** permitted **to kill** the burglar **during the week, was it necessary to mention** that he is forbidden to kill him on **Shabbat?**

אָמַר רַב שֵׁשֶׁת [4]**Rav Sheshet said:** That part of the Baraita **was necessary** in order to teach us that if a wall collapsed upon a thief who came only to steal, and not to kill the home owner, there is an obligation to **remove the heap of debris from on top of him** and save his life, even on Shabbat. You might have thought that, while one may not kill such a burglar, there is no obligation to desecrate Shabbat in order to save him.

תָּנוּ רַבָּנַן [5]**Our Rabbis taught** the following Baraita: "The verse states: 'If a thief is found breaking in, and be smitten that he die, there shall be no blood shed on his account.' [6]The words, **'and be smitten,'** teach that not only may the home owner himself kill the intruder, but **any person** may do so, for otherwise the verse should have read, 'And *he* smite him.' [7]The words, **'that he die,'** teach that the home owner may kill the intruder, not only by smiting him, but **by any possible mode of killing."** [8]The Gemara asks: **Granted that** it **was necessary** for the Baraita to state that the words, **"and be smitten,"** [9]teach that **any person** may kill the intruder. [10]For otherwise **you might have thought** that only the home owner himself is permitted to kill the burglar, because the burglar **knows that the home owner** will protect his property, for **a person is unable to restrain himself** when he sees someone coming to take **his property.** We assume that a thief is prepared to kill the home owner, and so the home owner may kill him first. [11]**But** regarding **another person,** the burglar does **not** know that he will try to stop the robbery. Thus, there are no grounds to assume that the burglar is prepared to kill that other person, and so that other person ought to be forbidden to kill him. [12]Therefore, the Baraita **teaches us that** the burglar **is** viewed as **a pursuer,**

מַשְׁמַע לָן דְּקָטְלִינַן. [1]אֶלָּא: "'דָּמִים לוֹ' — [2]בֵּין בַּחוֹל בֵּין בַּשַּׁבָּת". [3]הָשְׁתָּא בַּחוֹל לָא קָטְלִינַן לֵיהּ, בַּשַּׁבָּת מִבָּעֲיָא? [4]אָמַר רַב שֵׁשֶׁת: לֹא נִצְרְכָא אֶלָּא לְפַקֵּחַ עָלָיו אֶת הַגַּל. [5]תָּנוּ רַבָּנַן: [6]"'וְהֻכָּה' — בְּכָל אָדָם. [7]'וָמֵת' — בְּכָל מִיתָה שֶׁאַתָּה יָכוֹל לַהֲמִיתוֹ". [8]בִּשְׁלָמָא, "'וְהֻכָּה' — [9]בְּכָל אָדָם" אִיצְטְרִיךְ. [10]סָלְקָא דַּעֲתָךְ אָמִינָא: בַּעַל הַבַּיִת הוּא דְּקִים לְהוּ דְּאֵין אָדָם מַעֲמִיד עַצְמוֹ עַל מָמוֹנוֹ. [11]אֲבָל אַחֵר, לֹא. [12]קָא מַשְׁמַע לָן, דְּרוֹדֵף הוּא,

LITERAL TRANSLATION

teaches us that we kill [them]. [1]Rather: "'There shall be blood shed on his account' — [2]both during the week and on Shabbat." [3]Now if during the week we do not kill him, was it necessary [to mention] Shabbat?

[4]Rav Sheshet said: It was only necessary as regards removing a heap [of debris] for his sake.

[5]Our Rabbis taught: [6]"'And be smitten' — by any person. [7]'That he die' — with any way of killing that you can kill him." [8]Granted [that] "'And be smitten' — [9]by any person" was necessary. [10]It might have entered your mind to say: It is the owner about whom he is sure, for a person will not restrain himself regarding his property. [11]But another person, no. [12]It teaches us that he is a pursuer,

RASHI

קא משמע לן — דקטלינן משום פקוח נפש דהאיך. **לפקח עליו את הגל** — אם כשהיה חותר נפל עליו (את) הגל — מפקחין עליו היכא דלא בא על עסקי נפשות, אבל אם בא על עסקי נפשות כיון דניתן להרגו בלא התראה — גברא קטילא הוא משעת (חתירה). **והוכה** — בכל אדם, אפילו אינו בעל הממון מותר להרגו מדלא כתיב "והכהו". **בעל הבית** — הוא דמותר להרגו, משום דלהאי גנב קים ליה בגוויה דבעל הבית אינו מעמיד עצמו על ממונו, הלכך אדעתיה דלמקטליה אתא. **אבל שאר כל אדם** — **לא** — שהרי גנב זה לא בא אלא על עסקי נפשות של זה. **קא משמע לן** — דכיון דעל עסקי נפשות ישראל אתא — רודף הוא וניתן להצילו לבעל הבית בנפשו של זה.

NOTES

לְפַקֵּחַ עָלָיו אֶת הַגַּל **For removing a heap of debris for his sake.** If a wall collapsed upon a thief whom the home owner is forbidden to kill, he must remove the heap of debris and save his life. But if the wall collapsed upon a thief whom the home owner is permitted to kill, he may not remove the debris on Shabbat. *Meiri* argues that this

HALAKHAH

לְפַקֵּחַ עָלָיו אֶת הַגַּל **As regards removing a heap of debris for his sake.** "If a wall collapsed upon a thief whom one is not permitted to kill, one is required to remove the heap of debris from on top of him and save his life, even on Shabbat. But as for a thief whom one is permitted to kill, one may not violate the Shabbat law in order to save him." (*Rambam, Sefer Nezikin, Hilkhot Genevah* 9:13; *Shulḥan Arukh HaRav, Ḥoshen Mishpat* 329:5.)

בְּכָל אָדָם — בְּכָל מִיתָה **By any person, and with any means of killing.** "Anybody is permitted to kill a thief who

TRANSLATION AND COMMENTARY

for he is prepared to kill the home owner, **and even another person** may kill him to save the home owner's life. [1]**But why do I need** the next part of the Baraita, which states that the words, **"that I die,"** teach that the home owner may kill the intruder **any way he can?** [2]Surely **this may be learned from** the law applying to **a** convicted **murderer,** [3]**for it was taught** in a Baraita: "The verse states (Numbers 35:21): **'He that smote him shall surely be put to death; he is a murderer.'** Had the verse stated merely, 'he shall be put to death [יוּמַת], [4]**I would only know** that the murderer may be put to death by **the mode of execution that is** specifically **written in his regard,** decapitation. [5]**From where do I know that if** for some reason **he cannot be put to death by the mode of execution that is** specifically **written in his regard,** [6]**he may be put to death by way of any possible mode of execution?** [7]That is derived from **the verse** that **states: 'He shall surely be put to death** [מוֹת יוּמַת],' [8]the double-verb form teaching that, when necessary, **any mode** of execution may be employed." Similarly, a burglar may be put to death in any possible manner!

שָׁאנֵי הָתָם [9]The Gemara objects: The law regarding a burglar does not necessarily follow from the law regarding a murderer. **There** the law might **be different, for the verse states** explicitly: [10]**"He shall surely be put to death,"** but here regarding a burglar there is no similar verse.

וְנִיגְמַר מִינֵּיהּ [11]The Gemara asks: **But** why not **learn** the law applying to a burglar **from** the law applying to a murderer by way of the principle of *binyan av,* generalizing from one case where details are specified to other similar cases where such details are not specified?

מִשּׁוּם [12]The Gemara answers: This law applying to a murderer cannot be extended by a *binyan av* to other cases, **because** the law applying to **a murderer and** the law applying to **a blood avenger** — a relative of a person who was killed, who takes it upon himself to avenge his relative's death — constitute **"two verses that come together."** [13]The rule governing such cases is that **"whenever two verses come together they do not teach,"** meaning that a *binyan av* may not be derived from two analogous cases. This is because a law that had to be mentioned in two different places cannot be a general rule. The law that capital punishment need not necessarily be imposed in accordance with the instructions stipulated by the Torah is taught in two cases — that of a murderer and that of a blood avenger. We find such a law regarding a murderer, as we said above, that where it is not possible to execute the killer by way of decapitation, he may be put to death in any other possible manner. Regarding the blood avenger, the law is as follows: A person who unintentionally but negligently killed another person is exiled to a city of refuge, and has to remain there until the death of the High Priest. If the killer leaves the city of refuge, a relative of the victim, known as the blood avenger, is

וַאֲפִילּוּ אַחֵר נַמִי. [1]אֶלָּא ״׳וָמֵת׳ — בְּכָל מִיתָה שֶׁאַתָּה יָכוֹל לַהֲמִיתוֹ״ — לָמָּה לִי? [2]מֵרוֹצֵחַ נָפְקָא, [3]דְּתַנְיָא: ״׳מוֹת יוּמַת הַמַּכֶּה רֹצֵחַ הוּא׳. [4]אֵין לִי אֶלָּא בְּמִיתָה הָאֲמוּרָה בּוֹ. [5]וּמִנַּיִן שֶׁאִם אִי אַתָּה יָכוֹל לַהֲמִיתוֹ בְּמִיתָה הַכְּתוּבָה בּוֹ, [6]שֶׁאַתָּה רַשַּׁאי לַהֲמִיתוֹ בְּכָל מִיתָה שֶׁאַתָּה, יָכוֹל לַהֲמִיתוֹ? [7]תַּלְמוּד לוֹמַר: ׳מוֹת יוּמַת׳ — [8]מִכָּל מָקוֹם״.

[9]שָׁאנֵי הָתָם, דְּאָמַר קְרָא: [10]״מוֹת יוּמַת״.

[11]וְנִיגְמַר מִינֵּיהּ!

[12]מִשּׁוּם דַּהֲוָה רוֹצֵחַ וְגוֹאֵל הַדָּם שְׁנֵי כְתוּבִין הַבָּאִין כְּאֶחָד, [13]וְכָל שְׁנֵי כְתוּבִין הַבָּאִין כְּאֶחָד

LITERAL TRANSLATION

and even another person also. [1]But "'That he die' — with any way of killing that you can kill him" — why do I [need it]? [2]This is learned from the murderer, [3]for it was taught: "'He that smote him shall surely be put to death; he is a murderer.' [4]I have only the [mode of] execution that is said regarding him. [5]From where [do I know] that if you cannot kill him with the [mode of] execution that is written regarding him, [6]you kill him with any [mode of] execution with which you can kill him? [7]The verse states: 'He shall surely be put to death' — [8]any [mode]."

[9]It is different there, because the verse states: [10]"He shall surely be put to death."

[11]And let us learn from there!

[12]Because a murderer and a blood avenger are two verses that come together. [13]And whenever two verses come together

RASHI

שאם אי אתה יכול להרגו בסייף — כגון שהיה מכשף או שהיה לו נהר מפסיק ואתה יכול לירות בו חץ או אבן. **שני כתובין הבאין כאחד** — בפרק ״נגמר הדין״, דלא בעינן בהו קרא כדכתיב, הלכך אי לא רבייה הוה אמינא ליבעי

NOTES

second ruling applies only if we think the thief is dead. But if we are certain that the thief is still alive, the debris must be removed, for he is like any other Jew whose rescue supersedes all the commandments of the Torah. Other Rishonim seem to disagree (see *Rashi*).

HALAKHAH

breaks into a house, and any means may be used to kill him." (*Rambam, Sefer Nezikin, Hilkhot Genevah* 9:7.)

אֵין מְלַמְּדִין.

[1]תָּנוּ רַבָּנַן: "'מַחְתֶּרֶת'. [2]אֵין לִי אֶלָּא מַחְתֶּרֶת. [3]גַּגּוֹ חֲצֵירוֹ וְקַרְפֵּיפוֹ מִנַּיִן? [4]תַּלְמוּד לוֹמַר: 'יִמָּצֵא הַגַּנָּב' — מִכָּל מָקוֹם. [5]אִם כֵּן מַה תַּלְמוּד לוֹמַר 'מַחְתֶּרֶת'? [6]מִפְּנֵי שֶׁרוֹב גַּנָּבִים מְצוּיִין בַּמַּחְתֶּרֶת."

[7]תַּנְיָא אִידָךְ: "'מַחְתֶּרֶת'. [8]אֵין לִי אֶלָּא מַחְתֶּרֶת. [9]גַּגּוֹ חֲצֵירוֹ וְקַרְפֵּיפוֹ מִנַּיִן? [10]תַּלְמוּד לוֹמַר: 'יִמָּצֵא הַגַּנָּב' — מִכָּל מָקוֹם. [11]אִם כֵּן מַה תַּלְמוּד לוֹמַר 'מַחְתֶּרֶת'? [12]מַחְתַּרְתּוֹ זוֹ הִיא הַתְרָאָתוֹ".

LITERAL TRANSLATION

they do not teach.

[1]Our Rabbis taught: "'Breaking in.' [2]I only have a breach. [3]From where [do I know about] his roof, his court, and his enclosure? [4]The verse states: 'If a thief be found' — anywhere. [5]If so, why does the verse state 'breaking in'? [6]Because most thieves are found in a breach."

[7]It was taught in another [Baraita]: "'Breaking in.' [8]I only have a breach. [9]From where [do I know about] his roof, his court, and his enclosure? [10]The verse states: 'If a thief be found' — anywhere. [11]If so, why does the verse state 'breaking in'? [12]His breach is his warning."

TRANSLATION AND COMMENTARY

permitted to kill him (see Numbers 35). Regarding the blood avenger, it was taught in a Baraita as follows: "The verse states (35:21): 'The blood avenger shall slay the murderer' — the mitzvah of killing the unintentional killer who left the city of refuge falls upon the blood avenger. Moreover, if the deceased has no blood avenger, the court appoints someone else to serve for him in that capacity as his avenger. This is derived from the continuation of that very same verse which states: 'The blood avenger shall slay the murderer when he encounters him,' in any case, whether he is a blood relative or an avenger appointed by the court." The law that capital punishment is not necessarily imposed in accordance with the instructions stipulated by the Torah is taught with regard to two different cases. Therefore, it cannot be generalized. Thus, it was necessary for the Baraita to state that the words, 'that he die,' teach that the home owner may kill the intruder, not only by smiting him, but any way he can."

תָּנוּ רַבָּנַן [1]**Our Rabbis taught** the following Baraita: "The verse states: 'If a thief is found **breaking in,** and is smitten so that he dies, there shall be no blood shed on his account.' [2]From here **I only know** that a thief who was found **breaking into** a house may be killed by the home owner. [3]**From where do I know** that the same law applies to a thief found on the home owner's **roof,** in **his court, or** in **his enclosure?** [4]This is derived from **the verse** that **states: 'If a thief be found'** — which implies that the thief may be killed **anywhere** that he is found. [5]**If so, why does the verse state:** 'If the thief be found **breaking in'?** [6]**Because** the Torah was formulated in reference to ordinary situations, and **most thieves break into** other people's houses."

תַּנְיָא אִידָךְ [7]**It was taught in another Baraita:** "The verse states: 'If a thief is found **breaking in,** and is smitten so that he dies, there shall be no blood shed on his account.' [8]From here **I only know** that a thief who was found **breaking into** a house may be killed by the owner. [9]**From where do I know** that the same law applies to a thief found on the **roof,** in **his court, or** in **his enclosure?** [10]This is derived from **the verse** that **states: 'If a thief is found'** — which implies that the thief may be killed **anywhere** that he is found. [11]**If so, why does the verse state:** 'If the thief is found **breaking in'?** [12]This teaches that the thief's **breaking into** the house **stands in place of a warning.** The owner does not have to forewarn the thief, because he is regarded as a pursuer, who may be killed without warning. But if the owner found the thief on his roof, in his court, or in his enclosure, he may not kill him without a proper warning, for the thief may have found a door open and come in only to steal, and such a thief is not prepared to kill."

RASHI

מיתה הכתובה בו — כגון הכאה, אבל לא לחונקו, להטביעו במים. **ואין לי אלא מחתרת** — שחתר כותל. **גגו** — ועלה לו בסולם. **חצרו וקרפיפו** — ונכנס בו דרך הפתח שמצאו פתוח מנין? **תלמוד לומר ימצא הגנב** — מדלא כתיב: "אם במחתרת ימצאנו" וכתיב "הגנב" יתירה — משמע בכל לדדין שיהא נראה לך גנב. **מצויין במחתרת** — כלומר מצויין ורגילין לחתור. **זו היא התראתו** — שאין צריך התראה אחרת אלא הורגו מיד, דכיון דטרח ומסר נפשיה לחתור אדעתא דהכי אתא, דאי קאי לאפאי קטילנא ליה, ואמרה תורה כיון דרודף הוא אין צריך התראה אלא מצילין אותו בנפשו, אבל נכנס לחצרו וגגו דרך הפתח אינו הורגו עד שיתרו בו בעדים: חזי דקאימנא באפך וקטילנא לך, וזה יקבל עליו התראה ויאמר: יודע אני, ועל מנת כן אני עושה שאם תעמוד לנגדי אהרוג אותך, אבל בלא התראה — לא, דדילמא לאו אדעתא דנפשות קא אתי אלא דאשכח פתחא להדיא ועל אדעתא דאי קאי באפאי — ליפוק.

HALAKHAH

גַּגּוֹ חֲצֵירוֹ וְקַרְפֵּיפוֹ **His roof, his court, and his enclosure.** "The same law that applies to a thief who breaks into a house applies to a thief found on the home owner's roof, in his court, or in his enclosure. But if a thief breaks into a place where people are not ordinarily found, one is forbidden to kill him." (*Rambam, Sefer Nezikin, Hilkhot Genevah* 9:8; *Shulḥan Arukh HaRav, Ḥoshen Mishpat* 329:2.)

מַחְתַּרְתּוֹ זוֹ הִיא הַתְרָאָתוֹ **His breach is his warning.** "Some say that we say that his breaking into a house stands as a warning only regarding a thief who actually breaks

TRANSLATION AND COMMENTARY

אָמַר רַב הוּנָא [1]Rav Huna said: If a minor was pursuing someone with the manifest intention to kill him, one is permitted to save the victim with the pursuer's life, even though the pursuer is only a minor. [2]This implies that Rav Huna maintains that a pursuer need not be given a warning, whether he is an adult or a minor. Were it necessary to warn the pursuer, the law of a pursuer would not apply to a minor, for a minor lacks the understanding to receive a warning.

אֵיתִיבֵיהּ [3]Rav Ḥisda raised an objection against Rav Huna from a Mishnah which states (*Ohalot* 7:6): "If a fetus in its mother's womb is endangering its mother's life, we kill it in order to save the mother. [4]But if the delivery has begun, and the baby's head has emerged, we may not harm the baby in any way in order to save the mother, [5]for we may not set aside the baby's life on account of the life of the mother." [6]But according to you, one is permitted to kill a minor who is threatening another person's life; so why may we not kill the baby in order to save his mother? [7]Surely, the baby should be regarded as a pursuer, who may be killed in order to save his victim!

שָׁאנֵי הָתָם [8]The Gemara answers: There it is different, for it is Heaven that is pursuing her. The baby is not acting willfully, and we may not give preference to the mother's life over that of the baby.

[1]אָמַר רַב הוּנָא: קָטָן הָרוֹדֵף נִיתָּן לְהַצִּילוֹ בְּנַפְשׁוֹ. [2]קָסָבַר: רוֹדֵף אֵינוֹ צָרִיךְ הַתְרָאָה, לָא שְׁנָא גָּדוֹל וְלָא שְׁנָא קָטָן.
[3]אֵיתִיבֵיהּ רַב חִסְדָּא לְרַב הוּנָא: [4]"יָצָא רֹאשׁוֹ, אֵין נוֹגְעִין בּוֹ, [5]לְפִי שֶׁאֵין דּוֹחִין נֶפֶשׁ מִפְּנֵי נֶפֶשׁ." [6]וְאַמַּאי? [7]רוֹדֵף הוּא!
[8]שָׁאנֵי הָתָם, דְּמִשְּׁמַיָּא קָא רַדְפִי לָהּ.

LITERAL TRANSLATION

[1]Rav Huna said: [In the case of] a minor who is a pursuer, one may save [the pursued] with his life. [2]He maintains: A pursuer does not need a warning, no distinction being made between an adult and a minor.

[3]Rav Ḥisda objected to Rav Huna: [4]"[If] his head emerged, we do not touch him, [5]for we do not set aside [one] life on account of [another] life." [6]But why? [7]He is a pursuer!

[8]There it is different, for it is from Heaven that they pursue her.

RASHI

קטן הרודף — את קטן אחר להרגו. ניתן להצילו בנפשו — כדילפינן לקמן (עג,א) רוצח נתן להצילו בנפשו, והאי אף על גב דקטן הוא ולאו בר קבולי התראה הוא לגבי רדיפה דינו כגדול. קסבר — רב הונא רודף אין צריך התראה לענין להצילו בנפשו, דלא ניתנה התראה אלא לענין בית דין דלא מצי למקטליה אם הרג בלא התראה. יצא ראשו — באשה המקשה לילד ומסוכנת, וקתני רישא: החיה פושטת ידה וחותכתו ומוציאתו לאברים, דכל זמן שלא יצא לאויר העולם לאו נפש הוא וניתן להורגו ולהציל את אמו, אבל יצא ראשו — אין נוגעים בו להורגו, דהוה ליה כילוד ואין דוחין נפש מפני נפש, ואם תאמר מעשה דשבע בן בכרי (שמואל ב,כ) הנה ראשו מושלך אליך דדחו נפש מפני נפש! התם משום דאפילו לא מסרוהו לו היה נהרג בעיר כשיתפסנה יואב והן נהרגין עמו, אבל אם היה הוא ניצול אף על פי שהן נהרגין לא היו רשאין למסרו כדי להציל עצמן, אי נמי: משום דמורד במלכות הוה, והכי מפרש לה בתוספתא (דתמורה). משמיא קא רדפי לה — לאמיה.

NOTES

אֵיתִיבֵיהּ רַב חִסְדָּא **Rav Ḥisda objected.** An objection was raised against Rav Ḥisda's position that a pursuer may not be killed without prior warning: As the Gemara argues with regard to false, conspiring witnesses, since the pursuer does not warn his intended victim, it would be unjust to require the victim to warn his pursuer before killing him in self-defense (*Rosh*).

יָצָא רֹאשׁוֹ, אֵין נוֹגְעִין בּוֹ **If his head emerged, we do not touch him.** As long as the fetus is still inside its mother's womb, it is not regarded as a person, whose killing is a capital offense. This follows from the law regarding a person who struck a woman, causing her to miscarry (see Exodus 21:22). The offender is required to pay a monetary penalty, but he is not liable to capital punishment as a murderer (*Ramah*).

דְּמִשְּׁמַיָּא קָא רַדְפִי לָהּ **For it is from Heaven that they pursue her.** *Rambam* reformulates this ruling as follows (*Sefer Nezikin, Hilkhot Rotze'aḥ* 1:9): "For we do not sacrifice

HALAKHAH

into a house. But if the thief was found on the home owner's roof, in his court, or in his enclosure, he may not be killed without prior warning (*Maggid Mishneh*). So, too, some say that one is forbidden to kill a thief who breaks into a house during the day (*Ra'avad*). So, too, one may not kill the thief if he is on the way out of the house, or if there are people who will defend the home owner should the thief attack him, or if there are witnesses who saw the thief enter, and he saw them." (*Maggid Mishneh and Ra'avad, Sefer Nezikin, Hilkhot Genevah* 9:8; *Shulḥan Arukh HaRav, Ḥoshen Mishpat* 329:2)

קָטָן הָרוֹדֵף **A minor who is a pursuer.** "If someone was pursuing another person with the manifest intent to kill him, even if the pursuer was a minor, the obligation falls upon all those present to save the victim by injuring the pursuer, and, when necessary, by killing him." (*Shulḥan Arukh, Ḥoshen Mishpat* 425:1.)

יָצָא רֹאשׁוֹ, אֵין נוֹגְעִין בּוֹ **If his head emerged, we do not touch him.** "If a fetus in its mother's womb endangers its mother's life, one is permitted to kill it to save the mother. But if the baby's head has emerged, one may not harm the baby in any way in order to save the mother, for one may

[1]נֵימָא מְסַיַּיע לֵיהּ: [2]״רוֹדֵף שֶׁהָיָה רוֹדֵף אַחַר חֲבֵירוֹ לְהוֹרְגוֹ, אוֹמֵר לוֹ: [3]׳רְאֵה שֶׁיִּשְׂרָאֵל הוּא, וּבֶן בְּרִית הוּא, [4]וְהַתּוֹרָה אָמְרָה: ״שֹׁפֵךְ דַּם הָאָדָם בָּאָדָם דָּמוֹ יִשָּׁפֵךְ״. [5]אָמְרָה תּוֹרָה: הַצֵּל דָּמוֹ שֶׁל זֶה בְּדָמוֹ שֶׁל זֶה׳״.

[6]הַהִיא רַבִּי יוֹסֵי בְּרַבִּי יְהוּדָה הִיא. [7]דְּתַנְיָא: ״רַבִּי יוֹסֵי בְּרַבִּי יְהוּדָה אוֹמֵר: [8]חָבֵר אֵין צָרִיךְ הַתְרָאָה, [9]לְפִי שֶׁלֹּא נִיתְּנָה

TRANSLATION AND COMMENTARY

נֵימָא [1]The Gemara tries to adduce support for Rav Huna's ruling: **Shall we say that** the following Baraita **supports** Rav Huna: [2]**"If a pursuer was pursuing someone to kill him,** whoever sees him **says to him:** [3]**'See that** the person whose life you are threatening **is a Jew,** and he has not become an apostate, **and** so **he remains a member of the Covenant.** Regarding such a person, [4]**the Torah said** (Genesis 9:6): **"Whoever sheds man's blood by man shall his blood be shed."** [5]**The Torah** means to **say:** If someone threatens to shed another man's blood, his blood shall be shed for the sake of that other man, for you are to **save this one's blood** — that of the intended victim — **with that one's blood** — that of the pursuer.'" Now, elsewhere (*Sanhedrin* 40b) it was taught that an offender is only liable if he was warned before the transgression, and he accepted the warning, stating that he understood the consequences of his actions. Since the Baraita does not mention that the pursuer must accept the warning, it follows that the obligation to rescue a potential victim from his pursuer applies even where the pursuer has not been warned, as was argued by Rav Huna.

הַהִיא [6]The Gemara rejects this argument: A pursuer might in fact require a warning, Rav Huna's argument notwithstanding. And **this** Baraita, which does not mention that the pursuer must acknowledge the warning, follows the position of **Rabbi Yose the son of Rabbi Yehudah,** who says that an offender who was properly warned is liable to be punished, even if he did not acknowledge the warning. [7]**For it was taught** in another Baraita: **"Rabbi Yose the son of Rabbi Yehudah says:** [8]**A scholar need not** receive **a warning** prior to a transgression so as to be liable to punishment, [9]**for** the obligation to **warn** the offender **was only imposed in order to** enable the court to **distinguish between the unintentional** offender, who is ignorant of the law,

LITERAL TRANSLATION

[1]Shall we say that this supports him: [2]"[If] a pursuer was pursuing another person to kill him, he says to him: [3]'See that he is a Jew, and he is a member of the Covenant, [4]and the Torah said: "Whoever sheds a man's blood, by man shall his blood be shed." [5]The Torah said: Save this one's blood with that one's blood.'"

[6]That is Rabbi Yose the son of Rabbi Yehudah, [7]for it was taught: "Rabbi Yose the son of Rabbi Yehudah says: [8]A scholar does not need a warning, [9]for a warning was only

RASHI

והתורה אמרה שופך דם האדם באדם דמו ישפך – כל הרואה אותו ישפוך דמו בשביל אותו אדם שהוא רודף דהיינו "באדם" – בשביל הצלת אדם הנרדף, והא הכא דלא קתני "יודע אני ועל מנת כן אני עושה" ואין כאן קבלת התראה – ואפילו הכי מיחייב. **ההוא רבי יוסי בר יהודה היא** – דאפילו בהרוגי בית דין לא בעי התראה אלא להבחין, הלכך חבר לא בעי התראה ולא הבחנה, ועם הארץ בעי לאיתרויי דלא נימא: שוגג הייתי, אבל קבלת התראה אפילו בעם הארץ לא בעי.

NOTES

one life on account of another life, and this is the way of the world." *Rambam* means to say that the baby does not mean to threaten its mother, but rather it is part of the natural order that childbirth involves risk to the mother. The Jerusalem Talmud explains that if the baby's head has emerged, we may not harm the baby in order to save the mother, for we can no longer determine who is the pursuer and who is the victim, whether the baby is threatening the mother, or the mother is threatening the baby.

וְהַתּוֹרָה אָמְרָה: שֹׁפֵךְ דַּם **And the Torah said: Whoever sheds a man's blood.** It may be asked: Why should the pursuer be warned with the verse that refers to the universal prohibition applying both to Jews and non-Jews, rather than with the prohibition given specifically to the Jewish people, "You shall not kill"? *Rabbi Tzvi Ḥayyot* explains that this verse was chosen because it refers explicitly to the law regarding a pursuer.

מַחְתַּרְתּוֹ זוֹ הִיא הַתְרָאָתוֹ **His breach is his warning.** The Gemara means to say that the law regarding a thief who breaks into a house teaches us that whenever it is manifestly clear that someone is pursuing someone else in order to kill him, it is no longer necessary to forewarn the pursuer, but rather he may be killed right away (*Ramah*).

HALAKHAH

not sacrifice the baby's life on account of the life of the mother." (*Shulḥan Arukh, Ḥoshen Mishpat* 425:2.)

רוֹדֵף שֶׁהָיָה רוֹדֵף אַחַר חֲבֵירוֹ לְהוֹרְגוֹ **If a pursuer was pursuing another person to kill him.** "If someone was pursuing another person to kill him, and he was warned to stop, but he continued to pursue him, someone who is present may kill him, even if the pursuer did not acknowledge the warning. When necessary, the pursuer may be killed even without a warning." (*Shulḥan Arukh, Ḥoshen Mishpat* 425:1.)

TRANSLATION AND COMMENTARY

and the intentional offender. The Halakhah recognizes ignorance of the law as a valid defense. Thus, unless a person is warned immediately prior to committing his transgression, he can later claim that he had acted under the mistaken belief that his behavior was permitted. But a Torah scholar cannot present such a claim. Now, according to Rabbi Yose the son of Rabbi Yehudah, the obligation to warn the offender was only imposed in order to enable the court to distinguish between the unintentional offender and the intentional offender, and so the offender is liable for punishment even if he did not acknowledge the warning. The Baraita regarding a pursuer refers to an ordinary person, and follows the position of Rabbi Yose the son of Rabbi Yehudah. Thus, the pursuer must be given a warning, but he may be killed even if he did not acknowledge the warning.

תָּא שְׁמַע [1]**Come and hear** the following Baraita, which implies that a pursuer must indeed be warned, and that he must also acknowledge the warning, against the position of Rav Huna: [2]**"If a pursuer was pursuing someone** with the intention **to kill him,** whoever sees him **says to him:** [3]**'Know that** the person whose life you are threatening **is a Jew, and a member of the Covenant.** Regarding such a person, [4]**the Torah said: "Whoever sheds a man's blood, by man shall his blood be shed."'** [5]If the pursuer **says: 'I know that it is so,' he is exempt,** and may not be killed. [6]But if he says: **'Therefore I do it,' he is liable,** and may be killed."

לָא צְרִיכָא [7]The Gemara rejects this argument: This Baraita refers to the pursuer's liability for judicial execution. **It was needed** to teach the law **when** the person issuing the warning and the pursuer **were standing on** opposite **sides of a river,** [8]**so that it was not possible for** the person issuing the warning **to save** the pursuer's victim by killing the pursuer. [9]**What is there** for that other person to do? [10]**He must** do whatever must be done **to bring** the murderer **to court.** Thus, he must warn the pursuer against committing his transgression, [11]for in order for a **court** to impose punishment, **it is necessary** for the pursuer to have been **warned.**

אִיבָּעֵית אֵימָא [12]The Gemara suggests another answer: **If you wish,** you can **say: Rav Huna can say to you:** When I said that one is permitted to kill a minor who threatens the life of another person, which implies that a pursuer may be killed even if he has not been forewarned, [13]**I said** it **in accordance with the Tanna** who said regarding a thief who **breaks into** a house: The thief's **breaking into** the house **stands in place of a warning.** Similarly, any pursuer may be killed without forewarning, for his pursuit stands in place of a warning.

[73A] **MISHNAH** וְאֵלּוּ הֵן [14]**The following** offenders **we may kill** in order to **save them** from committing crimes:

הַתְרָאָה אֶלָּא לְהַבְחִין בֵּין שׁוֹגֵג לְמֵזִיד.״

[1]תָּא שְׁמַע: [2]״רוֹדֵף שֶׁהָיָה רוֹדֵף אַחַר חֲבֵירוֹ לְהוֹרְגוֹ, אָמַר לוֹ: [3]׳רְאֵה שֶׁיִּשְׂרָאֵל הוּא, וּבֶן בְּרִית הוּא, [4]וְהַתּוֹרָה אָמְרָה: ״שֹׁפֵךְ דַּם הָאָדָם בָּאָדָם דָּמוֹ יִשָּׁפֵךְ״׳. [5]אִם אָמַר: ׳יוֹדֵעַ אֲנִי שֶׁהוּא כֵּן׳, פָּטוּר. [6]׳עַל מְנָת כֵּן אֲנִי עוֹשֶׂה׳, חַיָּיב״.

[7]לָא צְרִיכָא דְּקָאֵי בִּתְרֵי עִיבְרֵי דְּנַהֲרָא, [8]דְּלָא מָצֵי אַצּוּלֵיהּ. [9]מַאי אִיכָּא — [10]דְּבָעֵי אִיתּוּיֵי לְבֵי דִינָא, [11]בֵּי דִינָא בָּעֵי הַתְרָאָה.

[12]אִיבָּעֵית אֵימָא: אָמַר לָךְ רַב הוּנָא: [13]אֲנָא דְּאָמְרִי כְּתַנָּא דְּמַחְתֶּרֶת, דְּאָמַר: מַחְתַּרְתּוֹ זוֹ הִיא הַתְרָאָתוֹ.

[73A] **מִשְׁנָה** [14]וְאֵלּוּ הֵן

LITERAL TRANSLATION

given to distinguish between the unintentional and the intentional [offender]."

[1]Come [and] hear: [2]"[If] a pursuer was pursuing another person to kill him, he says to him: [3]'See that he is a Jew, and he is a member of the Covenant, [4]and the Torah said: "Whoever sheds man's blood, by man shall his blood be shed."' [5]If he says: 'I know that it is so,' he is exempt. [6]'Therefore I do it,' he is liable."

[7]It was only necessary where they were standing on the two sides of a river, [8]so that he was unable to save him. [9]What is there? [10]He must bring him to court, [11][and] a court requires a warning.

[12]If you wish, say: Rav Huna can say to you: [13]I said [it in accordance with] the Tanna regarding a breach, who said: His breach is his warning.

[73A] **MISHNAH** [14]And these

RASHI

פטור — כל כמה דלא אמר "על מנת כן אני עושה שאהרג עליו", כדילפינן ב"היו בודקין" (סנהדרין מא,א): "יומת המת" — עד שיתיר עצמו למיתה, קא תני הכי גבי רודף דבעי התראה ואם לאו אין מצילין אותו בנפשו. **דקאי בתרי עברי נהרא** — המתרה מצד זה והרודף והנרדף מצד אחר. **דאצולי לא מצי** — והאי פטור וחייב דקאמר — אמיתת בית דין קאי, ולאחר שהרגו לנרדף. **מאי איכא** — כלומר מאי קא רמי עלייהו דהנך רואין למעבד. **דבעי לאיתויי לבי דינא ומקטליה** — דכתיב (דברים כב) "ובערת הרע מקרבך" הלכך בעי התראה, דבלאו הכי לא מקטלי ליה. **זו היא התראתו** — אלמא משום דמחזקינן ליה רודף לא בעי התראה.

משנה ואלו שמצילין אותן — מן העבירה.

TRANSLATION AND COMMENTARY

[1]**Someone who is pursuing another person** with the manifest intent **to kill him;** [2]someone who is pursuing **a male** in order to sodomize him; [3]**and** someone who is pursuing **a betrothed girl** in order to rape her. [4]**But someone who is pursuing an animal** in order to commit bestiality with it, [5]someone who is **desecrating Shabbat,** [6]**and** someone who is **worshiping an idol** — [7]**we may not kill** in order to **save** any of these people from completing their offenses.

GEMARA תָּנוּ רַבָּנַן [8]**Our Rabbis taught** a Baraita which offers a Biblical source for the law recorded in our Mishnah: **"From where do I know** that if **someone is pursuing another person** with the manifest intent **to kill him, one has the right** and the duty **to save** the victim, even **by killing** the pursuer? [9]This is derived from **the verse** that **states** (Leviticus 19:16): **'You shall not stand idly by the blood of your neighbor.'"**

וְהָא [10]The Gemara asks: **But does this** verse **come** to teach us **this** law? [11]Surely **this** verse **is needed for that which was taught** in the following Baraita: [12]**"From where do I know that** if **someone sees**

[1]שֶׁמַּצִּילִין אוֹתָן בְּנַפְשָׁן: הָרוֹדֵף אַחַר חֲבֵירוֹ לְהָרְגוֹ, [2]וְאַחַר הַזָּכָר, [3]וְאַחַר הַנַּעֲרָה הַמְאוֹרָסָה. [4]אֲבָל הָרוֹדֵף אַחַר בְּהֵמָה, [5]וְהַמְחַלֵּל אֶת הַשַּׁבָּת, [6]וְעוֹבֵד עֲבוֹדָה זָרָה — [7]אֵין מַצִּילִין אוֹתָן בְּנַפְשָׁן.

גמרא [8]תָּנוּ רַבָּנַן: ״מִנַּיִין לְרוֹדֵף אַחַר חֲבֵירוֹ לְהָרְגוֹ שֶׁנִּיתָּן לְהַצִּילוֹ בְּנַפְשׁוֹ? [9]תַּלְמוּד לוֹמַר: ׳לֹא תַעֲמֹד עַל דַּם רֵעֶךָ׳״.

[10]וְהָא לְהָכִי הוּא דַּאֲתָא? [11]הַאי מִיבָּעֵי לֵיהּ לְכִדְתַנְיָא: [12]״מִנַּיִין לְרוֹאֶה אֶת חֲבֵירוֹ

LITERAL TRANSLATION

we save them [at the cost] of their lives: [1]Someone who pursues another person to kill him, [2]or a male, [3]or a betrothed girl. [4]But someone who pursues an animal, [5]or desecrates Shabbat, [6]or worships an idol — [7]we do not save them [at the cost] of their lives.

GEMARA [8]Our Rabbis taught: "From where [do I know] about someone who pursues another person to kill him that one may save him with his life? [9]The verse states: 'You shall not stand idly by the blood of your neighbor.'"

[10]But does this come for this? [11]This is needed for that which was taught: [12]"From where [do I know] that someone who sees another person

RASHI

בנפשן — ניתנו ליהרג לכל אדם כדי להצילן מן העבירה, ומקראי נפקי. **אבל הרודף אחר בהמה** — לרבעה, והרוצה לעבוד עבודה זרה, ולחלל שבת, וכל שכן שאר כריתות ומיתות בית דין שאינן עריות, דלא ניתן להצילו בנפשו אלא מדבר שהוא ערוה ויש בה קלון ופגם לנרדף, כגון זכר ונערה המאורסה, ומיהו רוצח בהדיא כתיב ביה, והאי דנקט בהמה משום דדמיא לעריות, ונקט נמי עבודה זרה משום דסלקא דעתך אמינא תיתי בקל וחומר כדלקמן, ושבת נמי תיתי בגזירה שוה.

גמרא לא תעמוד — לא תעמוד עלמך על דמו — אלא הצילהו.

NOTES

מַצִּילִין אוֹתָן בְּנַפְשָׁן **We save them at the cost of their lives.** The Rishonim disagree about the precise meaning of this expression. According to *Rashi,* this means that we save the offenders from their transgressions at the cost of their lives. Others understand that we save the victims from their pursuers at the cost of their pursuers' lives (*Arukh, Rabbenu Yehonatan*). *Ran* points out the difficulty with each explanation, and suggests that the same expression might be used in different senses in the course of the passage.

לֹא תַעֲמֹד עַל דַּם רֵעֶךָ **You shall not stand idly by the blood of your neighbor.** It may be asked: After the Torah stated, "You shall not stand idly by the blood of your neighbor," what still is learned from the verse, "And you shall restore it to him," regarding the obligation to save another person who is threatened by bodily loss? *Talmidei Rabbenu Peretz* explain that the verse, "You shall not stand idly by the blood of your neighbor," imposes an obligation to save a person when he is in mortal danger. The verse, "And you shall restore it to him," teaches that one must come to another person's aid, even if he is not in mortal danger.

HALAKHAH

הָרוֹדֵף אַחַר חֲבֵירוֹ לְהָרְגוֹ **Someone who pursues another person to kill him.** "If someone was pursuing another person with the manifest intent to kill him, everybody is obligated to save the pursued party, even by taking the pursuer's life." (*Rambam, Sefer Nezikin, Hilkhot Rotze'aḥ* 1:6; *Shulḥan Arukh, Ḥoshen Mishpat* 425:1-3.)

הָרוֹדֵף אַחַר הַנַּעֲרָה הַמְאוֹרָסָה **Someone who pursues a betrothed girl.** "If someone was pursuing a woman who was forbidden to him — because relations with her would constitute adultery or incest — in order to rape her, or if he was pursuing a man in order to sodomize him, everybody is obligated to save the pursued party, even by taking the pursuer's life." (*Rambam, Sefer Nezikin, Hilkhot Rotze'aḥ* 1:10-11; *Shulḥan Arukh, Ḥoshen Mishpat* 425:1-3.)

אֲבָל הָרוֹדֵף אַחַר בְּהֵמָה **But someone who pursues an animal.** "If someone sees a person about to commit bestiality, or about to desecrate Shabbat, or about to worship an idol, he may not kill him. Rather, after the person commits the crime, he is apprehended and brought to trial." (*Rambam, Sefer Nezikin, Hilkhot Rotze'aḥ* 1:10-11; *Shulḥan Arukh, Ḥoshen Mishpat* 425:1-3.)

לְרוֹאֶה אֶת חֲבֵירוֹ שֶׁהוּא טוֹבֵעַ בַּנָּהָר **Someone who sees another person drowning in a river.** "If someone is able to save another person from his pursuer, but fails to do so, or if he sees another person drowning or being attacked by bandits, and he is able to save him, whether on his own, or by hiring rescuers, but he fails to do so, he violates the prohibition, 'You shall not stand idly by the blood of your neighbor.'" (*Rambam, Sefer Nezikin, Hilkhot Rotze'aḥ* 1:14; *Shulḥan Arukh, Ḥoshen Mishpat* 426:1.)

TRANSLATION AND COMMENTARY

another person drowning in a river, or being dragged away **by a** wild **beast, or being attacked by bandits,** [1]**he is obligated to save him?** [2]This is derived from **the verse** that **states. 'You shall not stand idly by the blood of your neighbor.'"** Since the verse is needed to teach us the basic obligation to rescue a person whose life is in danger, it cannot also teach us that one is permitted to kill someone who is pursuing another person with the intent to kill him!

אִין [3]The Gemara answers: **Indeed, it is so,** that this verse comes to teach that one is obligated to rescue a person whose life is in mortal danger. [4]**From where,** then, **do I know that one may save** the intended victim **by killing** his pursuer? [5]**This is learned by way of a *kal vaḥomer*** argument **from a betrothed girl** who is threatened with rape. [6]**If, regarding** the rape of **a betrothed girl,** the rapist **comes only to damage her** by violating her virginity, [7]and **the Torah said that one may save her** from violation **by killing** the rapist, [8]then **all the more so** does it follow that regarding **someone who is pursuing another person** with the intent **to kill him,** one may save the victim by killing his pursuer.

וְכִי עוֹנְשִׁין [9]The Gemara raises an objection: **But** is it possible to **inflict punishment on the basis of** a law that was inferred through **a *kal vaḥomer*** argument but not explicitly stated in the Torah?

דְּבֵי רַבִּי [10]The Gemara answers: **A Tanna of the School of Rabbi** Yehudah HaNasi **taught** a Baraita which derives this law by way of **an analogy,** and laws derived that way may indeed serve as the basis for punishment: "The verse dealing with the rape of a betrothed girl states (Deuteronomy 22:26): 'But to the girl you shall do nothing; she has no sin worthy of death: [11]**for as when a man rises against his neighbor, and slays him,** even so is this matter.' The law regarding a betrothed girl is explicitly compared to the law regarding a murderer. [12]**What** new law **do we learn from** this comparison between **a murderer** and a betrothed girl? [13]**Although** the formulation of the verse suggests that the law regarding a murderer **comes to teach** the law regarding a betrothed girl, **the inference is** actually **to be drawn** in the opposite direction, from the rape of a betrothed girl to murder. [14]The verse **compares a murderer to** the rapist of a

שֶׁהוּא טוֹבֵעַ בַּנָּהָר, אוֹ חַיָּה גּוֹרַרְתּוֹ, אוֹ לִסְטִין בָּאִין עָלָיו, [1]שֶׁהוּא חַיָּיב לְהַצִּילוֹ? [2]תַּלְמוּד לוֹמַר: 'לֹא תַעֲמֹד עַל דַּם רֵעֶךָ'".

[3]אִין הָכִי נַמִי. [4]וְאֶלָּא נִיתַּן לְהַצִּילוֹ בְּנַפְשׁוֹ מְנָלַן? [5]אָתְיָא בְּקַל וָחוֹמֶר מִנַּעֲרָה הַמְאוֹרָסָה. [6]מַה נַּעֲרָה הַמְאוֹרָסָה, שֶׁלֹּא בָּא אֶלָּא לְפוֹגְמָהּ, [7]אָמְרָה תּוֹרָה נִיתַּן לְהַצִּילָהּ בְּנַפְשׁוֹ, [8]רוֹדֵף אַחַר חֲבֵירוֹ לְהׇרְגוֹ, עַל אַחַת כַּמָּה וְכַמָּה.

[9]וְכִי עוֹנְשִׁין מִן הַדִּין?

[10]דְּבֵי רַבִּי תָּנָא: הֶקֵּישָׁא הוּא, [11]"'כִּי כַּאֲשֶׁר יָקוּם אִישׁ עַל רֵעֵהוּ וּרְצָחוֹ נֶפֶשׁ', [12]וְכִי מַה לָּמַדְנוּ מֵרוֹצֵחַ? [13]מֵעַתָּה, הֲרֵי זֶה בָּא לְלַמֵּד וְנִמְצָא לָמֵד. [14]מַקִּישׁ רוֹצֵחַ לְנַעֲרָה

LITERAL TRANSLATION

drowning in a river, or a beast dragging him, or bandits coming upon him, [1]that he is obligated to save him? [2]The verse states: 'You shall not stand idly by the blood of your neighbor.'"

[3]Indeed, it is so. [4]But from where [do I know] that one may save him with his life? [5]This is learned by a *kal vahomer* from a betrothed girl. [6]If, regarding a betrothed girl, where he comes only to damage her, [7]the Torah said that one may save her with his life, [8]someone who pursues another person to kill him, all the more so.

[9]But do we punish on the basis of a *kal vahomer*?

[10][A Tanna] of the School of Rabbi taught [that] it is an analogy: [11]"'For as when a man rises against his neighbor, and slays him.' [12]What do we learn from a murderer? [13]Now, it came to teach and was ultimately inferred. [14]It compares a murderer to

RASHI

לפגמה — לביישה ולזלזלה, אמרה תורה נתנה להצילה בנפשו, כדילפינן לקמן מואין מושיע לה. מן הדין — קל וחומר. הקישא הוא — שהוקש רוצח לנערה המאורסה, וכל היקש וגזירה שוה המופנת הרי הוא כמפורש במקרא ועונשין ממנו לפי שלא ניתנה למדרש מעצמו, אבל מקל וחומר שאדם דן קל וחומר מעצמו אף על פי שלא קבלו מרבו — אין עונשין ממנו, כדילפינן במכות (יד,א). וכי מה למדנו מרוצח — כאן לפטור את האונס דקאמר ליה קרא אין לנערה חטא מות כי כאשר יקום איש דמשמע כי היכי דהתם אונס פטור הכי נמי פטורה, אלא משמע שזה בא ללמד על הנערה, ונמצא שנכתב כאן ללמד הימנה כלומר נמצא אף למד, דמשום מילי אחריני איתקוש ותרוייהו ילפי מהדדי.

NOTES

וְכִי מַה לָּמַדְנוּ מֵרוֹצֵחַ? **What do we learn from a murderer?** We do not need the comparison that the verse makes between a murderer and a betrothed girl to teach us that we are dealing with a girl who was raped, for the next verse states explicitly: "But there was none to save her." *Ran* adds that when the Gemara says, "It came to teach and was ultimately inferred," it means "it was also ultimately inferred." For we do in fact learn (see 74a) from this comparison that, just as a person who is forced to commit murder must suffer death rather than violate the prohibition against bloodshed, so, too, a person who is forced to engage in sexual intercourse with a betrothed girl

TRANSLATION AND COMMENTARY

betrothed girl. [1]**Just as** in a sexual attack against a **betrothed girl, one may save her** from violation **by killing** her rapist, [2]**so, too,** in the case of **a murderer, one may save** his victim from death **by killing** the murderer."

וְנַעֲרָה [3]The Gemara asks: **From where do I know** the law applying to **the betrothed girl herself** that one may kill the rapist in order to save her?

כִּדְתָנָא [4]The Gemara explains: **As it was taught by the Tanna of the School of Rabbi Yishmael.** [5]**For the Tanna of the School of Rabbi Yishmael taught** the following Baraita: "The verse states (Deuteronomy 22:27): 'For he found her in the field, and the betrothed girl cried out, **but there was none to save her.**' [6]**But if there is someone** who can **save** the girl, [7]he must save her **by any means,** even by killing the rapist."

גּוּפָא [8]**It was stated above,** in the Baraita: **"From where do I know that** if **someone sees another person drowning in a river, or being dragged** away **by** a wild **beast, or being attacked by bandits, he is obligated to save him?** [9]This is derived from **the verse** that **states: 'You shall not stand idly by the blood of your neighbor.'"** [10]The Gemara asks: **Is this** law **learned from here?** [11]But surely **it is learned from** a different verse, as it was taught in another Baraita: "The verse (Deuteronomy 22:1): 'You shall surely bring them back to your brother,' teaches that one is obligated to restore lost property to its rightful owner. [12]**From where do I know** that one must also rescue someone who is threatened by **bodily loss?** [13]This extension of the concept of loss is derived from the apparently superfluous addition to **the verse** that **states** (Deuteronomy 22:2): **'And you shall restore it to him.'"**

אִי מֵהָתָם [14]The Gemara answers: **If** it were only **from there** that I derive the obligation to save another person's life, **I might have said that rule** applies only if one can save the other person **by himself.** [15]**But as** for having **to make an effort and hire workers** to assist in the rescue, **I might have said** that one is **not**

הַמְּאוֹרָסָה: [1]מַה נַּעֲרָה הַמְּאוֹרָסָה נִיתָּן לְהַצִּילָהּ בְּנַפְשׁוֹ, [2]אַף רוֹצֵחַ נִיתָּן לְהַצִּילוֹ בְּנַפְשׁוֹ".

[3]וְנַעֲרָה מְאוֹרָסָה גּוּפָהּ מְנָלַן? [4]כִּדְתָנָא דְּבֵי רַבִּי יִשְׁמָעֵאל. [5]דְּתָנָא דְּבֵי רַבִּי יִשְׁמָעֵאל: "'וְאֵין מוֹשִׁיעַ לָהּ'. [6]הָא יֵשׁ מוֹשִׁיעַ לָהּ — [7]בְּכָל דָּבָר שֶׁיָּכוֹל לְהוֹשִׁיעַ".

[8]גּוּפָא. "מִנַּיִן לְרוֹאֶה אֶת חֲבֵרוֹ שֶׁהוּא טוֹבֵעַ בַּנָּהָר, אוֹ חַיָּה גּוֹרַרְתּוֹ, אוֹ לִסְטִין בָּאִין עָלָיו, שֶׁהוּא חַיָּיב לְהַצִּילוֹ? [9]תַּלְמוּד לוֹמַר: 'לֹא תַעֲמֹד עַל דַּם רֵעֶךָ'". [10]וְהָא מֵהָכָא נָפְקָא? [11]מֵהָתָם נָפְקָא: [12]"אֲבֵדַת גּוּפוֹ מִנַּיִין? [13]תַּלְמוּד לוֹמַר: 'וַהֲשֵׁבֹתוֹ לוֹ'"!

[14]אִי מֵהָתָם הֲוָה אָמִינָא: הָנֵי מִילֵּי — בְּנַפְשֵׁיהּ. [15]אֲבָל מִיטְרַח

LITERAL TRANSLATION

a betrothed girl. [1]Just as with a betrothed girl, one may save her with his life, [2]so, too, a murderer, one may save him with his life."

[3]And from where [do I know] about the betrothed girl herself?

[4]As [the Tanna] of the School of Rabbi Yishmael taught. [5]For [the Tanna] of the School of Rabbi Yishmael taught: "'But there was none to save her.' [6]But if there is someone to save her — [7]by any means that he can save her."

[8]The thing itself: "From where [do I know] that someone who sees another person drowning in a river, or a beast dragging him, or bandits coming upon him, that he is obligated to save him? [9]The verse states: 'You shall not stand idly by the blood of your neighbor.'" [10]Is this learned from here? [11]It is learned from there: [12]"From where [do I know about] the loss of his body? [13]The verse states: 'And you shall restore it to him.'"

[14]If from there, I might have said: These words — by himself. [15]But to make an effort

RASHI

מה נערה המאורסה ניתן להצילה — מן העבירה בנפשו, אף רוצח וכו׳, ואכתי ילפא נערה מרוצח שתהרג ואל תעבור, כדלקמן, ומיהו הכא לא אסיקנא במילתיה דרבי, דאגב גררא אתיא. **ומדקאמר אין מושיע** — מכלל דבעיא תשועה. **אבדת גופו** — כגון נטבע בנהר מניין שאתה מצווה על השבתו. **תלמוד לומר והשבותו לו** — קרא יתירה הוא למדרש: השב את גופו לעצמו. **הני מילי בנפשו** — אם זה הרואהו יכול להצילהו יצילהו.

NOTES

must suffer death rather than violate the prohibition against relations of that kind.

בְּכָל דָּבָר שֶׁיָּכוֹל לְהוֹשִׁיעַ **By any means that he can save her.** *Rambam* (based on *Sifrei; Ra'avad*) learns that one is permitted to save the pursued party by any means, even by killing the pursuer, from the verse (Deuteronomy 25:12): "Then you shall cut off her hand, your eye shall not pity her."

וַהֲשֵׁבֹתוֹ לוֹ **And you shall restore it to him.** The verse could have stated "And you shall restore to him [וַהֲשֵׁבֹת לוֹ]," and we would have understood that it is referring to lost property. But the verse states: וַהֲשֵׁבֹתוֹ לוֹ, "And you shall restore it to him," which can also be understood as: "And you shall restore *him* to him." That is to say, if he himself is lost, return him to himself. Thus we learn that if someone sees that another person's life or well-being is in danger, he must save him (*Rashi, Ramah*).

TRANSLATION AND COMMENTARY

obligated to do so. Therefore, the verse, "You shall not stand idly by the blood of your neighbor," [1]**teaches us** that a person must do whatever is in his power to save his neighbor's life.

תָּנוּ רַבָּנַן [2]**Our Rabbis taught** a related Baraita: **"Whether the pursuer is pursuing another person** with the manifest intent **to kill him, or** he is pursuing **a male** in order to sodomize him, **or** he is pursuing **a betrothed girl** in order to rape her, [3]**or** he is pursuing another woman who is forbidden to him by a prohibition that is **punishable by judicial execution or excision** — in all these cases, [4]**we may kill** the offender in order to **save** his victim. [5]But if we see **a widow** being pursued by **a High Priest,** or **a divorcee or a** ***halutzah*** being pursued by **an ordinary priest — we may not kill** the offender in order to **save** the victim, for these sexual offenses are only punishable by lashes. [6]**If the transgression has** already **been committed against** the woman, **we may no** longer **kill** the offender in order to **save** her, for the damage has been done. Now the court must try him, and if he is convicted, impose punishment. [7]**If** the victim **can be saved by some other means, we may not save** the victim **by killing** the pursuer. [8]**Rabbi Yehudah says: So, too,** if the attacked woman **says** to those coming to her rescue: **'Leave** my attacker **alone,** and do not interfere.' We may not kill the attacker, [9]even if she said what she said **so that he would not kill her."**

מְנָא [10]The Gemara asks: **From where are these laws** derived? [11]The Gemara explains: **The verse states** (Deuteronomy 22:26): **"But to the girl you shall do nothing; the girl has no sin worthy of death."** The word translated here as "the girl" is spelled נַעַר, *"na'ar,"* "boy," but according to the traditional Masoretic reading it is read as נַעֲרָה, *"na'arah,"* "girl." [12]The written form of the word, ***"na'ar,"***

וּמֵיגַר אָגוֹרֵי, אֵימָא לָא. [1]קָא מַשְׁמַע לָן.

[2]תָּנוּ רַבָּנַן: "אֶחָד הָרוֹדֵף אַחַר חֲבֵירוֹ לְהׇרְגוֹ, וְאַחַר הַזָּכָר, וְאַחַר נַעֲרָה הַמְאוֹרָסָה, [3]וְאַחַר חַיָּיבֵי מִיתוֹת בֵּית דִּין, וְאַחַר חַיָּיבֵי כְּרִיתוֹת — [4]מַצִּילִין אוֹתָן בְּנַפְשׁוֹ. [5]אַלְמָנָה לְכֹהֵן גָּדוֹל, גְּרוּשָׁה וַחֲלוּצָה לְכֹהֵן הֶדְיוֹט — אֵין מַצִּילִין אוֹתָן בְּנַפְשׁוֹ. [6]נֶעֶבְדָה בָּהּ עֲבֵירָה, אֵין מַצִּילִין אוֹתָהּ בְּנַפְשׁוֹ. [7]יֵשׁ לָהּ מוֹשִׁיעַ, אֵין מַצִּילִין אוֹתָהּ בְּנַפְשׁוֹ. [8]רַבִּי יְהוּדָה אוֹמֵר: אַף הָאוֹמֶרֶת: 'הַנִּיחוּ לוֹ', [9]שֶׁלֹּא יַהַרְגֶנָּה".

[10]מְנָא הָנֵי מִילֵּי? [11]אָמַר קְרָא: "וְלַנַּעֲרָה לֹא תַעֲשֶׂה דָבָר; אֵין לַנַּעֲרָה חֵטְא מָוֶת." [12]"נַעַר" —

LITERAL TRANSLATION

and hire workers, I might have said no. [1]It teaches us.

[2]Our Rabbis taught: "Whether he pursues another person to kill him, or a male, or a betrothed girl, [3]or those liable to judicial execution, or those liable to excision — [4]we save them with his life. [5]A widow [pursued by] a High Priest, a divorcee or a *halutzah* [pursued by] an ordinary priest — we do not save them with his life. [6][If] the transgression was perpetrated against her, we do not save her with his life. [7][If] there is someone to save her, we do not save her with his life. [8]Rabbi Yehudah says: So, too, one who says: 'Leave him,' [9]so that he not kill her."

[10]From where are these things [derived]? [11]The verse states: "But to the girl you shall do nothing; the girl has no sin worthy of death." [12]*"Na'ar"* —

RASHI

קא משמע לן — לא תעמוד על דם רעך — לא תעמוד על עצמך משמע אלא חזור על כל צדדין שלא יאבד דם רעך. חייבי כריתות וחייבי מיתות בית דין דעריות — קאמר, דאיכא עבירה ופגם, ותנא דמתניתין נמי הכי סבירא ליה מדלא קא מרמינן סתמא אסתמא ותנא הני והוא הדין לכל עריות. אלמנה לכהן גדול — כהן גדול הרודף אלמנה לאונסה אף על פי שיש שם פגם דקא משוי לה חללה — אין מצילין אותה בנפשו, כדמפרש לקמן דחייבי לאוין אין ניתנין להציל בנפשם. נעבדה בה עבירה — כבר. אין מצילין — דהא אפגימה לה, וקרא אפגימה קפיד מדגלי בהני ולא בעבירות אחרות. יש מושיע לה — על ידי דבר אחר בלא הריגה — אין הורגין אותו ברדיפתו, שהרי כשישיגוהו יהיה לה מושיע. האומרת — למצילין הרודפין אחריו: הניחו לו ואל תרדפו אחריו שלא יהרגנה קודם שתשיגוהו — אף על פי דאנוסה היא ומיראה היא דקאמרה אין מצילין אותו, וטעמא מפרש לקמן. לנערה חטא מות — אכולהו קאי אין מושיע לה וקרא יתירא הוא ולדרשה, דהא כתיב ולנערה לא

NOTES

אֵין לַנַּעֲרָה חֵטְא מָוֶת **The girl has no sin worthy of death.** This part of the verse is totally extraneous, for the verse already stated: "But to the girl you shall do nothing." Therefore, each word may be understood as teaching another case in which one is permitted to kill a pursuer in order to save his victim (*Rashi, Ramah*).

HALAKHAH

נֶעֶבְדָה בָּהּ עֲבֵירָה **If the transgression was committed.** "If someone has seized a woman and already begun to rape her, even if he has not yet completed the sexual act, we may no longer kill him. Rather he is brought to court for trial." (*Rambam, Sefer Nezikin, Hilkhot Rotze'ah* 1:12; *Shulhan Arukh, Hoshen Mishpat* 425:3.)

זֶה זְכוּר. [1]נְעֲרָה — זוֹ נַעֲרָה הַמְאוֹרָסָה. [2]"חֵטְא" — אֵלּוּ חַיָּיבֵי כְּרִיתוֹת. [3]"מָוֶת" — אֵלּוּ חַיָּיבֵי מִיתוֹת בֵּית דִּין.

[4]כָּל הָנֵי לָמָּה לִי? [5]צְרִיכִי, [6]דְּאִי כָּתַב רַחֲמָנָא "נַעַר" — [7]מִשּׁוּם דְּלָאו אוֹרְחֵיהּ, [8]אֲבָל נַעֲרָה — דְּאוֹרְחָהּ, אֵימָא לָא. [9]וְאִי כָּתַב רַחֲמָנָא "נַעֲרָה" — [10]מִשּׁוּם דְּקָא פָּגֵים לָהּ. [11]אֲבָל נַעַר — דְּלָא קָא פָּגֵים לֵיהּ, אֵימָא לָא. [12]וְאִי כָּתַב רַחֲמָנָא הָנֵי — [73B] [13]מִשּׁוּם דְּהַאי לָאו אוֹרְחֵיהּ הוּא, [14]וְהָא קָא פָּגֵים לָהּ. [15]אֲבָל שְׁאָר עֲרָיוֹת, דְּאוֹרְחַיְיהוּ, [16]וְלָא נָפֵישׁ פִּיגְמַיְיהוּ, [17]אֵימָא לָא. [18]כָּתַב רַחֲמָנָא: "חֵטְא". [19]וְאִי כָּתַב רַחֲמָנָא "חֵטְא", הֲוָה אָמִינָא: [20]אֲפִילּוּ חַיָּיבֵי לָאוִין. [21]כָּתַב רַחֲמָנָא:

LITERAL TRANSLATION

this is homosexual intercourse. [1]"*Na'arah*" — this is a betrothed girl. [2]"Sin" — these are those who are liable to excision. [3]"Death" — these are those who are liable to judicial execution.

[4]Why do I need all these? [5]They are needed. [6]For if the Torah (lit., "the Merciful One") wrote "*na'ar*" — [7]because it is not his way. [8]But a *na'arah* — where it is her way, I might have said no. [9]And if the Torah wrote "*na'arah*" — [10]because he damages her. [11]But a *na'ar* — whom he does not impair, I might have said no. [12]And if the Torah wrote those — [73B] [13]because [regarding] this one it is not his way, [14]and [regarding] that one he damages her. [15]But other forbidden sexual relationships, when it is their way, [16]and their damage is not great, [17]I might have said no. [18]The Torah wrote: "Sin." [19]And if the Torah wrote "sin," I might have said: [20]Even those who are liable for prohibitions [punishable by lashes]. [21]The Torah wrote:

TRANSLATION AND COMMENTARY

alludes to **homosexual intercourse.** [1]The vocalized form of the word **"*na'arah*"** may be understood as referring to sexual intercourse with **a betrothed girl.** [2]The word **"sin,"** alludes to forbidden sexual relationships that are **punishable by excision.** [3]The word **"death,"** alludes to forbidden sexual relationships that are **punishable by judicial execution.** Regarding all these cases, the verse states: "But to the girl you shall do nothing," teaching that the victim of rape is exempt from punishment. And regarding all these cases, the next verse states (Deuteronomy 22:27): "But there was none to save her," implying that if there is someone who can save the victim, he has the right and duty to do so, even by killing the pursuer.

כָּל [4]The Gemara asks: **Why was it necessary** for the Torah to refer to **all these** cases? [5]The Gemara explains: **It was,** in fact, **necessary** to mention all the cases. [6]**For had the Torah** only **written *"na'ar,"*** I might have said that one is only permitted to kill the pursuer in order to save a victim from sodomy, [7]because **it is not the way** of the world for one man to engage in homosexual intercourse with another man. Consequently the pain and humiliation suffered by the victim of homosexual rape are particularly great. [8]**But** as for **a *na'arah,* whose way it is** to engage in sexual intercourse with a man, **I might have said** that one is **not** permitted to kill her attacker in order to save her from the ignominy of rape. Therefore, the Torah had to mention *na'arah.* [9]**And had the Torah** only **written *"na'arah,"*** I might have said that one is only permitted to kill the pursuer in order to save a betrothed girl from rape. [10]The pursuer may be killed **because he damages** his victim by violating her virginity, and thus detracts from her value in the eyes of her husband. [11]**But** as for **a *na'ar,* who is not damaged** by homosexual rape, **I might have said** that one is **not** permitted to kill his attacker in order to save him. Therefore, the Torah had to mention *na'ar.* [12]**And had the** Torah only **written those** two — *"na'ar"* and *"na'arah"* — [73B] I might have thought that it is only to prevent homosexual rape and the rape of a betrothed girl that one is permitted to kill the pursuer to save his victim. [13]In the first case, the pursuer may be killed **because** homosexual intercourse **is not the way** of the world. Thus the victim's pain and humiliation are particularly great. [14]In the second case, he may be killed because **he damages** his victim by violating her virginity. [15]**But** as for rape involving **other forbidden sexual relationships,** since **it is the way** of women to engage in sexual intercourse with men, [16]**and the damage** that they suffer **is not** as **great** as that of a betrothed girl, [17]**I might have said** that one is **not** permitted to kill the assailant in order to save a woman from rape. [18]Therefore, **the Torah wrote "sin,"** teaching that one is permitted to kill the assailant to prevent rape involving other forbidden sexual relationships. [19]**And had the Torah** only **written "sin," I might have said** that one is permitted to kill the rapist, [20]**even** in cases involving forbidden sexual relationships **that are** only **punishable by lashes.** [21]Therefore, **the Torah wrote "death,"**

RASHI

מעשה דבר. נער כתיב וקרינן נערה, נדרש מקרא ונדרש מסורת: נער — להביא את הזכור, נערה — כמשמעו. דלאו אורחה — ליבעל, ואיכא בזיון ובשת גדול. פגים לה — בבתולין, ומגנה על בעלה. דאורחייהו — בבעילות. ולא נפיש פגמייהו — כארוסה שחביבה ויעלת חן על הארוס ועכשיו מתגנה עליו, אבל שאר עריות פנויות בתולות לא מפגמי כולי האי, וכן נשואות בעולות לא מפגמי

"מָוֶת". [1]וְאִי כָּתַב רַחֲמָנָא "מָוֶת", הֲוָה אָמִינָא: [2]חַיָּיבֵי מִיתוֹת בֵּית דִּין, אִין; [3]חַיָּיבֵי כְּרִיתוֹת, לָא. [4]כָּתַב רַחֲמָנָא "חֵטְא".

[5]וְלִכְתּוֹב רַחֲמָנָא: "חֵטְא מָוֶת", [6]וְלָא בָּעֵי "נַעַר" וְ"נַעֲרָה"! [7]אִין הָכִי נַמִי. [8]וְאֶלָּא "נַעַר" "נַעֲרָה", [9]חַד לְמַעוּטֵי עוֹבֵד עֲבוֹדָה זָרָה, [10]וְחַד לְמַעוּטֵי בְּהֵמָה וְשַׁבָּת.

[11]וּלְרַבִּי שִׁמְעוֹן בֶּן יוֹחַי דְּאָמַר: עוֹבֵד עֲבוֹדָה זָרָה נִיתָּן לְהַצִּילוֹ בְּנַפְשׁוֹ, [12]לָמָּה לִי?

LITERAL TRANSLATION

"Death." [1]And if the Torah wrote "death," I might have said: [2]Those who are liable for judicial execution, yes; [3]those who are liable for excision, no. [4]The Torah wrote: "Sin."

[5]But let the Torah write: "Sin worthy of death," [6]and it would not need *"na'ar"* and *"na'arah"*! [7]Indeed, it is so. [8]Rather *"na'ar"* and *"na'arah"* — [9]one to exclude an idol worshiper, [10]and one to exclude [a person who pursues] an animal and a Shabbat [desecrator].

[11]And according to Rabbi Shimon ben Yoḥai, who said: "An idol worshiper one may save [at the cost] of his life," [12]why do I [need it]?

TRANSLATION AND COMMENTARY

teaching that the right and the duty to kill the pursuer applies only in cases involving a capital offense. [1]**And had the Torah** only **written "death,"** I **might have said** that to prevent rape involving forbidden sexual relationships [2]**that are punishable by judicial execution,** one is **indeed** permitted to kill the attacker. [3]But as for forbidden sexual relationships **that are** only **punishable by** the less severe penalty of **excision,** one is **not** permitted to kill the pursuer in order to save the woman. [4]Therefore, **the Torah wrote "sin,"** teaching that the pursuer may be killed to prevent rape involving forbidden sexual relationships that are only punishable by excision.

וְלִכְתּוֹב [5]The Gemara objects: **But** if so, **the Torah should have** only **written "sin worthy of death,"** [6]**and** then **it would not have been necessary** to write ***"na'ar"*** **or** ***"na'arah,"*** for homosexual intercourse and intercourse with a betrothed girl are both capital offenses!

אִין [7]The Gemara answers: **Indeed, it is so,** that we would have known the law regarding homosexual rape and the rape of a betrothed girl from the words "sin worthy of death." [8]**Rather** than including those transgressions, the words ***"na'ar"*** **and** ***"na'arah"*** exclude other transgressions from the permission to kill the pursuer. [9]**One** term **excludes an idol worshiper** [10]**and the other** term **excludes** someone who is pursuing **an animal** in order to commit bestiality with it (a transgression similar to forbidden sexual relationships), **and a Shabbat desecrator.** The two extra words teach that in none of these other cases may the transgressor be killed in order to save him from his transgression.

וּלְרַבִּי שִׁמְעוֹן בֶּן יוֹחַי [11]The Gemara asks: **According to Rabbi Shimon ben Yoḥai, who said** (74a) that indeed **one may** even **kill an idol worshiper** in order to **save him** from committing his offense, [12]**why do I need** the words *"na'ar"* and *"na'arah"*?

RASHI

כולי האי כמו ארוסה. ונכתב חטא מות – דאתרבו לה כריתות ומיתות בית דין ולא בעי נער ונערה שהרי הן בכלל. חד למעוטי עבודה זרה – דסלקא דעתך אמינא תיתי בקל וחומר כדלקמן. וחד למעוטי בהמה – משום דדמי לעריות, ושבת כדי נקטיה ואגב גררא איידי דתנן במתניתין, מיהו קרא לא בעי למעוטי – דכיון דאמעיטא עבודה זרה מהיכא תיתי שבת – הא לא סלקא דעתין לאתויי אלא בחילול חילול מעבודה זרה כדלקמן, דרבי שמעון לקמן הוא (סנהדרין עד,ב).

NOTES

לְמַעוּטֵי עוֹבֵד עֲבוֹדָה זָרָה **To exclude an idol worshiper.** It has been suggested that one is not permitted to kill an idol worshiper in order to save him from sin, for an idolater becomes liable to divine punishment as soon as he entertains idolatrous thoughts, even before he actually worships the idol. Hence, killing the idolater as he is about to serve the idol will not save him from his transgression (*Rabbenu Yehonatan*).

לְמַעוּטֵי שַׁבָּת **To exclude a Shabbat desecrator.** *Tosafot* and others ask: Why is a verse necessary to teach us that one may not kill a Shabbat desecrator in order to prevent him from sinning? Killing involves a desecration of Shabbat. Why would I think that I may desecrate Shabbat in order to save someone from desecrating Shabbat? The Aḥaronim suggest various answers: According to *Rashi,* killing the Shabbat desecrator would fall into the category of "work that is not necessary for its own sake," which is not forbidden by Torah law (*Sho'el U'Meshiv*). Alternatively, killing a person in order to save him from sinning is not considered "constructive" work. Unlike judicial execution following the commission of an offense, killing someone in order to prevent him from sinning does not offer him any atonement. Thus, saving a sinner with his life is "destructive" work, which bears no liability by Torah law (*Tzofnat Pa'ane'aḥ*).

חַד לְמַעוּטֵי בְּהֵמָה וְשַׁבָּת **One to exclude someone who pursues an animal and a Shabbat desecrator.** It has been asked: Is there any similarity between someone who pursues an animal and a Shabbat desecrator, so that they should be excluded by the same verse? Some suggest that the Gemara should be emended to read: "One to exclude an idol worshiper and a Shabbat [desecrator]" — the two offenses being similar in that they both involve profanation — "and one to exclude [one who pursues] an animal" (*Talmidei Rabbenu Peretz*).

[1]חַד לְמַעוּטֵי בְּהֵמָה, וְחַד לְמַעוּטֵי שַׁבָּת. [2]סָלְקָא דַּעְתָּךְ אָמִינָא: תֵּיתֵי שַׁבָּת [3]מֵ״חִילּוּל״ ״חִילּוּל״ מֵעֲבוֹדָה זָרָה. [4]וּלְרַבִּי אֶלְעָזָר בְּרַבִּי שִׁמְעוֹן דְּאָמַר: מְחַלֵּל אֶת הַשַּׁבָּת נִיתָּן לְהַצִּילוֹ בְּנַפְשׁוֹ, [5]דְּאָתְיָא שַׁבָּת מֵ״חִילּוּל״ ״חִילּוּל״ מֵעֲבוֹדָה זָרָה, [6]מַאי אִיכָּא לְמֵימַר?

[7]חַד מִיעוּט — לְמַעוּטֵי בְּהֵמָה. [8]וְאִידָךְ — אַיְּידֵי דְּכָתַב רַחֲמָנָא ״נַעַר״, [9]כָּתַב נַמִי ״נַעֲרָה״.

[10]״רַבִּי יְהוּדָה אוֹמֵר: [11]אַף הָאוֹמֶרֶת: ׳הַנִּיחוּ לוֹ׳, [12]שֶׁלֹּא יַהַרְגֶנָּה״. [13]בְּמַאי קָמִיפַּלְגִי? [14]אָמַר רָבָא: בִּמְקַפֶּדֶת עַל פִּיגְמָהּ, [15]וּמַנִּיחָתוֹ, שֶׁלֹּא

LITERAL TRANSLATION

[1]One to exclude [someone who pursues] an animal, and one to exclude a Shabbat [desecrator]. [2]It might have entered your mind to say: Learn about Shabbat by way of [3]"profanation" [and] "profanation" from idol worship.

[4]And according to Rabbi Elazar the son of Rabbi Shimon who said: A Shabbat desecrator one may save with his life, [5]for Shabbat is learned by way of "profanation" [and] "profanation" from idol worship, [6]what is there to say?

[7]One exclusion — to exclude [one who pursues] an animal. [8]And the other — since the Torah wrote *"na'ar,"* [9]it also wrote *"na'arah."*

[10]"Rabbi Yehudah says: [11]So, too, one who says: 'Leave him,' [12]so that he will not kill her." [13]About what do they disagree? [14]Rava said: About someone who is particular about her damage, [15]but allows him, so that he not

TRANSLATION AND COMMENTARY

חַד [1]The Gemara answers: **One** term **excludes** someone pursuing **an animal** for the purpose of bestiality, **and the other** term **excludes a Shabbat desecrator.** [2]**You might have thought of saying** that we may **learn** the law **regarding the Shabbat** desecrator by way of a *gezerah shavah* drawn between the word [3]**"profanation"** regarding Shabbat and the word **"profanation" regarding idol worship.** Regarding Shabbat, the verse states (Exodus 31:14): "Everyone who profanes it shall surely be put to death," and regarding idol worship, the verse states (Leviticus 18:21): "And you shall not let any of your seed pass through the fire to Molekh, neither shall you profane the name of your God." The similarity in the language used in the two verses might lead us to rule that just as one is permitted to kill an idolater in order to save him from his transgression, so, too, should one be permitted to kill a Shabbat desecrator in order to save him from his offense. Therefore, the Torah comes and teaches that an idol worshiper may indeed be killed in order to save him from committing his crime, but a Sabbath desecrator may not.

וּלְרַבִּי אֶלְעָזָר בְּרַבִּי שִׁמְעוֹן [4]The Gemara asks: **According to Rabbi Elazar the son of Rabbi Shimon, who said** (74a) that **one may** even **kill a Shabbat desecrator** in order **to save him** from his transgression, [5]**for** we do indeed **learn** the law regarding the **Shabbat** desecrator by way of a *gezerah shavah* drawn between the word **"profanation"** regarding Shabbat and the word **"profanation" regarding idol worship,** [6]**what is there to say?** Why do I need the words *"na'ar"* and *"na'arah"*?

חַד [7]The Gemara answers: **One exclusion** is needed **to exclude someone pursuing an animal** for the purpose of bestiality. [8]**And the other** term does not exclude anything, but rather we say that **since the Torah wrote *"na'ar,"*** [9]**it also wrote *"na'arah."*** The written form of the word and the vocalized form do not come to teach us two separate laws.

רַבִּי יְהוּדָה [10]The end of the Baraita reads: **"Rabbi Yehudah says:** [11]**So, too,** if the attacked woman **says** to those coming to her rescue: **'Leave** my attacker alone, and do not interfere,' we may not kill the attacker, [12]even if it is clear that she said what she said **so that he would not kill her."** [13]The Gemara asks: **About what do** Rabbi Yehudah and the Rabbis **disagree?**

אָמַר רָבָא [14]**Rava said:** The Tannaim disagree **about** a woman **who is** indeed **particular** and distressed **about the injury to her,** [15]**but** nevertheless **allows** her attacker to violate her, **so that he will not kill her.**

RASHI

איידי דכתב נער — להביא את הזכור, כתב נערה, כלומר כפשטיה דקרא, דעל כרחיה נערה קרינא ביה, דהא בנערה משתעי ולנערה לא תעשה דבר. **במקפדת על פגמה** דאי — בשאינה מקפדת לא קאמרי רבנן למקטליה משום עבירה, דלא חמיר מעבודה זרה ושבת.

HALAKHAH

הָאוֹמֶרֶת: ׳הַנִּיחוּ לוֹ׳ One who says: Leave him. "If a man was attempting to rape a woman, and others were trying to save her, and she told them to leave her attacker be, so that he would not kill her, we do not listen to her, but rather we save her, even by taking the rapist's life." (*Rambam, Sefer Nezikin, Hilkhot Rotze'aḥ* 1:12; *Shulḥan Arukh, Ḥoshen Mishpat* 425:4.)

TRANSLATION AND COMMENTARY

[1]**The Rabbis** who disagree with Rabbi Yehudah **maintain** that **the Torah** said that one must save a betrothed girl from rape, even by killing the rapist, because it **was concerned about damage** to the girl. [2]Here, too, then, since the woman **is particular about injury to her,** one must kill her attacker, and save her from rape. [3]**Rabbi Yehudah** disagrees and **maintains that the Torah said kill** the rapist, [4]**because** some women would rather **suffer death** than be raped. [5]But **this** woman's life is not in jeopardy, for she **is not ready to suffer death** in order to avoid rape, and so one may not kill her attacker.

אֲמַר לֵיהּ [6]**Rav Pappa said to Abaye:** If, indeed, the Torah was concerned about the injury to the woman, as was argued by the Rabbis, then why do we say that if **a widow** was pursued by **a High Priest,** we may not kill the offender? [7]Surely, **he too injures** the woman, for he disqualifies her from marrying into the priesthood!

אֲמַר לֵיהּ [8]Abaye **said to** Rav Pappa: **The Torah was concerned about great damage,** as when the woman is pursued by a man forbidden to her by a prohibition that is punishable by excision, in which case the product of their union is a mamzer. [9]But **the Torah was not concerned about** relatively **small damage,** as when she is pursued by a man forbidden to her only by a prohibition punishable by lashes.

חֵטְא [10]It was stated above that the word **"sin"** alludes to forbidden sexual relationships **punishable by excision,** teaching that we may kill any person attempting to rape a woman who is forbidden to him by a prohibition that is punishable by excision. [11]The Gemara **points out a contradiction** between what is stated here and that which was taught elsewhere in the Mishnah (*Ketubot* 29a): **"These are the girls who are entitled to the fine** paid by the seducer or rapist. [12]**If a man has intercourse with his sister,** she is entitled to the fine paid by the seducer or rapist. The offender is liable to excision for having committed incest, nevertheless the fine is imposed." Now, if it is true that one may kill a man who is attempting to rape a woman forbidden to him by a prohibition punishable by excision, why is a man who raped his sister liable to the fine? Surely,

יַהַרְגֶנָּה. [1]רַבָּנַן סָבְרִי: אַפִּיגְמָהּ קָפֵיד רַחֲמָנָא, [2]וַהֲרֵי מַקְפֶּדֶת עַל פִּיגְמָהּ. [3]וְרַבִּי יְהוּדָה: הַאי דְּקָאָמַר רַחֲמָנָא: קַטְלֵיהּ, [4]מִשּׁוּם דְּמָסְרָה נַפְשָׁהּ לִקְטָלָא. [5]הָא לֹא מָסְרָה נַפְשָׁהּ לִקְטָלָא. [6]אֲמַר לֵיהּ רַב פַּפָּא לְאַבַּיֵי: אַלְמָנָה לְכֹהֵן גָּדוֹל נַמִי, [7]קָא פָּגֵים לָהּ!

[8]אֲמַר לֵיהּ: אַפִּיגְמָה רַבָּה — קָפֵיד רַחֲמָנָא. [9]אַפִּיגְמָה זוּטָא — לָא קָפֵיד רַחֲמָנָא.

[10]״חֵטְא״ — אֵלּוּ חַיָּיבֵי כְּרִיתוּת. [11]וּרְמִינְהוּ: ״וְאֵלּוּ נְעָרוֹת שֶׁיֵּשׁ לָהֶן קְנָס: [12]הַבָּא

LITERAL TRANSLATION

kill her. [1]The Rabbis maintain: The Torah was concerned about her damage, [2]and she is particular about her damage. [3]And Rabbi Yehudah maintains: That which the Torah said: Kill him, [4]because she delivers herself to death. [5]This [woman] does not deliver herself to death.

[6]Rav Pappa said to Abaye: A widow to a High Priest, [7]he too damages her.

[8]He said to him: Regarding great damage — the Torah was concerned. [9]Regarding small damage — the Torah was not concerned.

[10]"Sin" — these are those who are liable for excision. [11]Cast them together: "These are the girls who have a fine: [12][If] someone has intercourse

RASHI

אפגמה קפיד רחמנא — מדלא כתיב בהאי קרא אלא מידי דפגמה, שמע מינה אפגמה קפיד. **דמסרה נפשה לקטלא** — שיש צנועות שמוסרין עצמן למות שיהרגנה ולא תבעל לו, ואמרה תורה הציל דמה ודמו. **הא קא פגים לה** — ואי טעמא דקרא משום פגימה היא — אמאי אמעיטו חייבי לאוין, ואדרבנן קא פריך דאמרי טעמא משום פגמה הוא. **אפגמה רבה** — כגון עריות דכריתות שהן אסורות והויא חרפתה מרובה — שהולד ממזר ונעשית זונה בבעילתו, אבל כהן גדול באלמנה אינה נעשית זונה אלא חללה. **הבא על אחותו** — כלומר אפילו בא על אחותו דלא קרינא בה ולו תהיה לאשה — אפילו הכי קרינא בה ונתן האיש השוכב עמה דאתרבי מקראי בכתובות (כט,ב), ואף על גב דחייב כרת לא מפטר מתשלומין, ואי

NOTES

וְאֵלּוּ נְעָרוֹת שֶׁיֵּשׁ לָהֶן קְנָס These are the girls who have a fine. The laws regarding the rape of a virgin are discussed in Deuteronomy 22:28-29, and at greater length in tractate *Ketubot*. The rapist is obligated to pay a fine of fifty shekels to the girl's father, in addition to the damages that a court may impose upon him according to the laws of personal injury. Such damages may be imposed in all cases of rape, whether the victim was a virgin or not. But the fine of fifty shekels is a special penalty that is only paid if the victim was a virgin. The discussion in our Gemara relates to the issue at what point of sexual intercourse does a girl lose her virginity so that the rapist must pay a fine.

HALAKHAH

וְאֵלּוּ נְעָרוֹת שֶׁיֵּשׁ לָהֶן קְנָס These are the girls who have a fine. "If someone rapes or seduces a virgin *na'arah* whom he is forbidden to marry, whether by a prohibition punishable by lashes, or by a prohibition punishable by excision — if witnesses failed to warn him, so that he is not subject to lashes, he pays the fine." (*Rambam, Sefer Nashim, Hilkhot Na'arah Betulah* 1:11; *Shulḥan Arukh, Even HaEzer* 177.)

TRANSLATION AND COMMENTARY

he is like someone subject to the death penalty, and therefore exempt from all monetary penalties, for a person cannot become subject to the death penalty and a monetary penalty for the same offense!

אֲמַרוּהָ [1] **The Rabbis proposed** the following solution **before Rav Ḥisda:** A man who rapes his sister is liable to the fine, because when he became liable to the fine he was no longer subject to the death penalty, that is to say, it was no longer permissible to kill him. How so? [2] **When** the rapist engaged **in the first stage of sexual intercourse** with his sister, **he injured her** by depriving her of her virginity. Until that point, it would have been permissible to kill the rapist in order to save her from rape. But from then on, [3] **he is no** longer **subject to the death penalty,** for as it was taught earlier in the Baraita, once the transgression has been committed, we may no longer kill the offender. [4] But **he does not** become liable to **pay the fine** for violating the girl's virginity **until the end of sexual intercourse,** when he has ruptured her hymen.

הָנִיחָא [5] Rav Ḥisda raised an objection: **This is well according to the** authority **who says that the first stage of sexual intercourse is** external **genital contact.** At that point the girl has been damaged so that it is no longer permissible to kill the rapist, but she is not yet entitled to the fine, for her hymen is still intact. And so when the rapist completes the sexual act, he becomes liable to the fine. [6] **But according to the** authority **who says that the first stage of sexual intercourse is insertion of the glans, what is there to say?** Surely that involves the rupturing of the girl's hymen! Thus, the rapist should not be subject to the fine, for when he would have become liable to the fine, he was still subject to the death penalty.

אֶלָּא [7] **Rather, Rav Ḥisda said:** When the Mishnah states that a man who raped his sister is liable to a fine, it refers to a case where **he** (or someone else) already **had intercourse with** the girl **in an unnatural manner** (anal intercourse), so that she was damaged, but he left her hymen intact. [8] **Then** he **had intercourse with her in a natural manner** (vaginal intercourse). The rapist is liable to the fine, because when he violated his sister's virginity he was not subject to the death penalty, for she had already been damaged.

רָבָא אָמַר [9] **Rava said:** The Mishnah that states that a man who raped his sister is liable to a fine refers to a girl who **allowed him** to have intercourse with her, and asked her rescuers not to interfere, saying what

עַל אֲחוֹתוֹ״!

[1] אֲמַרוּהָ רַבָּנַן קַמֵּיהּ דְּרַב חִסְדָּא: [2] מִשְּׁעַת הָעֲרָאָה דִּפְגָמָהּ, [3] אִיפְּטַר לֵהּ מִקְּטָלָא. [4] מָמוֹנָא לָא מְשַׁלֵּם עַד גְּמַר בִּיאָה.

[5] הָנִיחָא לְמַאן דַּאֲמַר הָעֲרָאָה זוֹ נְשִׁיקָה. [6] אֶלָּא לְמַאן דַּאֲמַר הָעֲרָאָה זוֹ הַכְנָסַת עֲטָרָה, מַאי אִיכָּא לְמֵימַר?

[7] אֶלָּא, אָמַר רַב חִסְדָּא: כְּגוֹן שֶׁבָּא עָלֶיהָ שֶׁלֹּא כְּדַרְכָּהּ, [8] וְחָזַר וּבָא עָלֶיהָ כְּדַרְכָּהּ.

[9] רָבָא אָמַר: בִּמְנִיחָתוֹ שֶׁלֹּא

LITERAL TRANSLATION

with his sister!"

[1] The Rabbis said this before Rav Ḥisda: [2] From the time of the first stage of sexual intercourse, when he damaged her, [3] he became exempt from the death penalty. [4] He does not pay money until the end of sexual intercourse.

[5] This is well according to the one who says that the first stage of sexual intercourse is genital contact. [6] But according to the one who says that the first stage of sexual intercourse is insertion of the glans, what is there to say?

[7] Rather, Rav Ḥisda said: As when he had intercourse with her in an unnatural manner, [8] and then had intercourse with her in a natural manner.

[9] Rava said: When she allows him, so that he will not

RASHI

ניתן להצילה בנפשו אמאי משלם — הרי מיתה ותשלומים יש כאן ואף על גב דלא אקטול פטור מתשלומין, כדקיימא לן (כתובות לה,א) בכל חייבי מיתות בית דין שוגגין דנפקא לן מדתניא דבי חזקיה מה מכה בהמה לא חלקת בה כו׳ אף מכה אדם לא תחלוק בו וכו׳. **משעת הערה** — קרי ליה נבעלה, ואפגימה במקצת ושוב אין מצילין אותה מגמר ביאה בנפשו, וקנסא לא מיחייבי אלא משום גמר ביאה שהוא מוציא בתוליה, והאי גמר ביאה לאו דווקא ביאת המירוק שהיא מזריע, דקרא אבתולים קפיד דכתיב (דברים כב) נערה בתולה אשר לא אורשה, אלא גמר ביאה דהכא — הכנסת עטרה היא. **הניחא למאן דאמר** — ביבמות (נה,ב) הערה דהויא כבעילה היינו נשיקת אבר איכא לאוקומה דפגימה היא, דמיקרי בעולה ועדיין בתוליה לא יצאו לאיחיוביה קנסא דחמשים. **אלא למאן דאמר הערה** — שעשה הכתוב בכל התורה כבעילה, זו הכנסת עטרה, וגמר ביאה כגון דשפחה חרופה דכתיב בה שכבת זרע (ויקרא יט) היינו ביאת המירוק אין כאן הערה פגם בלא הוצאת בתולים, ונמצאו מיתה דניתן להציל ותשלומין באין כאחד. **שבא עליה** — הוא או אחר כבר שלא כדרכה, וחזר ובא עליה כדרכה, דלא ניתן בביאה זו להצילה בנפשו שכבר נפגמה.

HALAKHAH

הָעֲרָאָה **The first stage of sexual intercourse.** "When the Torah speaks of sexual intercourse, no distinction is made between the first stage of sexual intercourse and the completion of the sexual act. The first stage of sexual intercourse is insertion of the glans," following Rabbi Yoḥanan, against Shmuel. (*Shulḥan Arukh, Even HaEzer* 20:1.)

יַהַרְגֶנָּה. [1]וְרַבִּי יְהוּדָה הִיא. [74A] [2]רַב פַּפָּא אָמַר: בִּמְפוּתָּה, [3]וְדִבְרֵי הַכֹּל.

[4]אַבַּיֵי אָמַר: בְּיָכוֹל לְהַצִּיל בְּאֶחָד מֵאֵבָרָיו, [5]וְרַבִּי יוֹנָתָן בֶּן שָׁאוּל הִיא. [6]דְּתַנְיָא: ״רַבִּי יוֹנָתָן בֶּן שָׁאוּל אוֹמֵר: [7]רוֹדֵף שֶׁהָיָה רוֹדֵף אַחַר חֲבֵירוֹ לְהוֹרְגוֹ, [8]וְיָכוֹל לְהַצִּילוֹ בְּאֶחָד מֵאֵבָרָיו וְלֹא הִצִּיל, [9]נֶהֱרָג עָלָיו״.

[10]מַאי טַעְמָא דְּרַבִּי יוֹנָתָן בֶּן שָׁאוּל? [11]דִּכְתִיב: ״וְכִי יִנָּצוּ אֲנָשִׁים (יַחְדָּו)״ וגו׳. [12]וְאָמַר רַבִּי אֶלְעָזָר: בְּמַצּוּת שֶׁבְּמִיתָה הַכָּתוּב מְדַבֵּר, [13]דִּכְתִיב: ״וְאִם אָסוֹן יִהְיֶה וְנָתַתָּה נֶפֶשׁ תַּחַת נָפֶשׁ״. [14]וַאֲפִילּוּ הָכִי, אָמַר רַחֲמָנָא: ״וְלֹא יִהְיֶה אָסוֹן עָנוֹשׁ

LITERAL TRANSLATION

kill her. [1]And it is Rabbi Yehudah. [74A] [2]Rav Pappa said: With a seduced girl, [3]and according to everybody.

[4]Abaye said: When he can save her with one of his limbs, [5]and it is Rabbi Yonatan ben Shaul. [6]For it was taught: "Rabbi Yonatan ben Shaul says: [7][If] a pursuer was pursuing another person to kill him, [8]and he could save [him] with one of his limbs, but he did not save him, [9]he is put to death on his account."

[10]What is the reasoning of Rabbi Yonatan ben Shaul? [11]For it is written: "If men fight, etc." [12]And Rabbi Elazar said: Scripture refers to fighting with [the intention] of killing, [13]for it is written: "But if any harm ensue, then you shall give life for life." [14]And even so, the Torah (lit., "the Merciful One") said: "And yet no further harm ensue, he shall surely

TRANSLATION AND COMMENTARY

she said **so that** the rapist would **not kill her.** [1]**And** the Mishnah **follows** the position of **Rabbi Yehudah,** who says that in such a situation we may not kill the rapist. [74A] [2]**Rav Pappa said:** The Mishnah stating that a man who had intercourse with his sister is liable to a fine does not refer to rape, but rather to **a girl who was seduced** by her brother. [3]**And** the Mishnah follows the opinion of **all the Tannaim** who agree that we may not save a girl from seduction by killing the seducer, since no violence is involved.

אַבַּיֵי אָמַר [4]**Abaye said:** In fact, the Mishnah in *Ketubot* refers to a case where the brother raped his sister. But killing the rapist could be avoided, for the girl **could be saved with** a blow to **one of** the rapist's **limbs.** [5]**And** the Mishnah **follows** the position of **Rabbi Yonatan ben Shaul,** who maintains that in such a case killing the rapist is forbidden. [6]**For it was taught** in a Baraita: **"Rabbi Yonatan ben Shaul says:** [7]**If someone was pursuing another person** with the manifest intent **to kill him, and** the pursued person **can be saved** by a blow to **one of** the pursuer's **limbs,** [8]**but the rescuer did not save him** in that manner but rather killed him, [9]the killer **is liable to the death penalty** like any other murderer." According to Abaye, the same principle applies to rape.

מַאי טַעְמָא [10]The Gemara asks: **What is the reasoning of Rabbi Yonatan ben Shaul?** [11]The Gemara explains: **For the verse states** (Exodus 21:22): **"If men fight,** and one of them pushes a pregnant woman and a miscarriage results, but no further harm ensues; he shall surely be punished, according as the woman's husband may exact from him, and he shall give as the judges determine." [12]**And Rabbi Elazar said: Scripture refers** here **to** men **fighting with the intention of killing** one another, [13]**for the** next **verse states** (Exodus 21:23): **"But if any harm ensues, then you shall give life for life."** Rabbi Elazar understands that this second verse teaches that if the woman dies, the one who struck her must pay with his life. Now, the killer must have intended to kill his rival, otherwise he would not be liable to capital punishment. [14]**And even so, the Torah said** in the first verse: **"And yet no further harm ensue, he shall surely be punished,"** teaching that the one who struck the woman must pay her husband for the loss of her unborn fetus. Now, if a man who intends to kill someone is regarded as a pursuer, who may be killed in order to save the victim, he is already subject to the death penalty. How, then, can he become liable to monetary compensation

RASHI

רבי יהודה היא — דאמר לא ניתן להצילו בנפשו. **רב פפא אמר** — הא דקתני אחותו יש לה קנס — במפותה קאמר, דבת קנסא נמי היא, ולהצילה לא ניתן — דהא אינה מקפדת. **אביי אמר** — לעולם באנוסה, וכגון דיכול המציל להציל באחד מאבריו של זה שלא ניתן להורגו מעתה, ורבי יונתן בן שאול היא. **ויכול** — הנרדף או הרואהו להציל באחד מאבריו, ולא הציל אלא בנפשו — נהרג עליו. **במצות שבמיתה** — שהוא מתכוין להרוג את חבירו והכה את האשה הכתוב מדבר. **דכתיב ואם אסון יהיה** — ואי לא מתכוין להרוג, דשוגג הוא, — אמאי מקטיל? אלא לאו שמע מינה במתכוין, וסתם רוצח ניתן להצילו בנפשו כדאמרינן לעיל, וזה רודף היה, שהיה מתכוין, ואפילו הכי כתיב דאם לא יהיה אסון — שאין כאן חיוב מיתה, ענוש יענש דמי ולדות.

HALAKHAH

רוֹדֵף שֶׁיָּכוֹל לְהַצִּיל בְּאֶחָד מֵאֵבָרָיו **A pursuer, and he can save him with one of his limbs.** "If someone was pursuing another person with the manifest intent to kill him, and it was possible to save the intended victim by inflicting a blow to one of the pursuer's limbs, but the rescuer killed the pursuer without making any effort to stop him with less force, the killer is regarded as a murderer, but he is not subject to judicial execution (because he did not receive a warning; *Bet Yosef*)." (*Rambam, Sefer Nezikin, Hilkhot Rotze'aḥ* 1:7, 13.)

יֵעָנֵשׁ״. ¹אִי אָמְרַתְּ בִּשְׁלָמָא יָכוֹל לְהַצִּיל בְּאֶחָד מֵאֵבָרָיו לֹא נִיתָּן לְהַצִּילוֹ בְּנַפְשׁוֹ, ²הַיְינוּ דְּמַשְׁכַּחַתְּ לָהּ דְּיֵעָנֵשׁ, ³כְּגוֹן שֶׁיָּכוֹל לְהַצִּיל בְּאֶחָד מֵאֵבָרָיו. ⁴אֶלָּא אִי אָמְרַתְּ יָכוֹל לְהַצִּיל בְּאֶחָד מֵאֵבָרָיו, ⁵נַמִי נִיתָּן לְהַצִּילוֹ בְּנַפְשׁוֹ, ⁶הֵיכִי מַשְׁכַּחַתְּ לָהּ דְּיֵעָנֵשׁ?

⁷דִּילְמָא שָׁאנֵי הָכָא, ⁸דְּמִיתָה לָזֶה, ⁹וְתַשְׁלוּמִין לָזֶה.

¹⁰לָא שְׁנָא, ¹¹דְּאָמַר רָבָא: רוֹדֵף שֶׁהָיָה רוֹדֵף אַחַר חֲבֵירוֹ, ¹²וְשִׁיבֵּר אֶת הַכֵּלִים, בֵּין שֶׁל נִרְדָּף וּבֵין שֶׁל כָּל אָדָם, ¹³פָּטוּר. ¹⁴מַאי טַעְמָא? ¹⁵מִתְחַיֵּיב

LITERAL TRANSLATION

be punished." [1]Granted, if you say that if he can save [him] with one of his limbs, he may not save him with his life, [2]that is when you find that he is punished, [3]as when he could save [him] with one of his limbs. [4]But if you say that if he can save [him] with one of his limbs, [5]he may also save him with his life, [6]how do you find that he is punished? [7]Perhaps it is different here, [8]because death is for this one, [9]and payment is for that one. [10]It is not different, [11]for Rava said: [If] a pursuer was pursuing another person, and he broke utensils, [12]whether belonging to the pursued person or belonging to any person, [13]he is exempt. [14]What is the reason? [15]He is subject to

RASHI

אי אמרת בשלמא וכו׳ — כגון שיכול הרואה להציל באחד מאבריו, דהוא לא ניתן להורגו, הלכך אין כאן מיתה — ויענש. **אלא אי אמרת וכו׳** — אמאי יענש, הא רודף הוא וניתן להציל בנפשו. **דילמא שאני הכא** — להכי משלם, ואף על גב (דליכא) [דאיכא] לך מיתה משום דמיתה לזה ותשלומין לזה, המיתה והתשלומין אינן באין לו על ידי אדם אחד, שהמיתה באה עליו בשביל חבירו שהיה מריב עמו, והתשלומין דבעל האשה הן דאיניש דעלמא הוא, הלכך לא מיפטר מתשלומין דהאי משום חיוב מיתה דמיחייב אאידך. **לא שנא** — אם היה כאן חיוב מיתה אין חילוק להתחייב תשלומין, בין שהמיתה באה עליו בשביל בעל התשלומין, בין שבאה עליו בשביל אחר — פטור. **מתחייב**

TRANSLATION AND COMMENTARY

for the loss of the woman's unborn fetus? [1]**Granted, if you say that if** the rescuer **can save** the victim **with** a blow to **one of** the pursuer's **limbs, he may not save** the victim **with** the pursuer's **life** — [2]**that is** how you can construct a case in **which** the man who struck the woman, killing her unborn fetus, **is subject to** a monetary **punishment.** [3]The man whose life was threatened **could have been saved by** a blow to **one of** the assailant's **limbs.** Thus the assailant was not subject to the death penalty, and he can become liable to monetary compensation. [4]**But if you say that** even **if** the rescuer **can save** the victim **with** a blow to **one of** the pursuer's **limbs,** [5]**he may** still **save** the victim **with** the pursuer's **life,** [6]**how can you** justify the Torah's ruling that the man who struck the woman **is subject to** monetary **punishment?** Since he was subject to the death penalty, he cannot become liable to monetary compensation! Thus one may not save the potential victim by taking the pursuer's life, if the pursuer can be stopped with less drastic measures, as was argued by Rabbi Yonatan ben Shaul.

דִּילְמָא [7]The Gemara tries to rebut this argument: **Perhaps** the Torah refers here to a potential victim who could not be saved with a blow to one of the pursuer's limbs, and so the pursuer was in fact subject to the death penalty. Nevertheless, the pursuer can become liable to a monetary punishment, for **it is different here,** [8]**because** he became liable to the **death** penalty **on account of this one** — the man with whom he was fighting — [9]**and** he becomes liable to **monetary compensation on account of that one** — the husband of the woman whom he struck and whose unborn child he killed. Thus, we cannot infer anything about the case where the victim could have been saved with a blow inflicted to one of the pursuer's non-vital organs.

לָא שְׁנָא [10]The Gemara rejects this possibility: If the pursuer was subject to the death penalty, he cannot become liable to pay monetary compensation, and **it makes no difference** whether those two liabilities are on account of the same person or of two different people. [11]**For Rava said: If someone was pursuing another person** with the manifest intent to kill him, **and** while he was pursuing him **he broke utensils,** [12]**whether** those utensils **belonged to the pursued person or** they **belonged to some other person** not involved in the pursuit, [13]**he is exempt** from liability for the damage that he caused. [14]**What is the reason** that he is exempt? [15]While he was pursuing the other person, **he was subject to the death penalty,** for everybody was permitted to kill him in order to save the victim. A person cannot become subject to the death penalty and liable to pay monetary compensation for the same offense, even if those liabilities are on account of two different

HALAKHAH

רוֹדֵף שֶׁשִּׁיבֵּר אֶת הַכֵּלִים **If a pursuer broke utensils.** "If someone was pursuing another person with the manifest intent to kill (or rape) him, and while he was pursuing him, he broke utensils, he is exempt from liability for the damage, because he was subject to the death penalty while in pursuit. If the pursued person broke utensils belonging to his pursuer while he was fleeing from him, he is exempt, but if he broke utensils belonging to someone else, he is liable, for a person may not save himself with someone else's money, and then not compensate him for

בְּנַפְשׁוֹ הוּא. [1]וְנִרְדָּף שִׁיבֵּר אֶת הַכֵּלִים, [2]שֶׁל רוֹדֵף, פָּטוּר; [3]שֶׁל כָּל אָדָם, חַיָּיב. [4]שֶׁל רוֹדֵף, פָּטוּר, [5]שֶׁלֹּא יְהֵא מָמוֹנוֹ חָבִיב עָלָיו מִגּוּפוֹ. [6]שֶׁל כָּל אָדָם, חַיָּיב, שֶׁמַּצִּיל עַצְמוֹ בְּמָמוֹן חֲבֵירוֹ. [7]וְרוֹדֵף שֶׁהָיָה רוֹדֵף אַחַר רוֹדֵף לְהַצִּילוֹ, וְשִׁיבֵּר אֶת הַכֵּלִים, [8]בֵּין שֶׁל רוֹדֵף בֵּין שֶׁל נִרְדָּף, [9]בֵּין שֶׁל כָּל אָדָם, פָּטוּר. [10]וְלֹא מִן הַדִּין, [11]שֶׁאִם אִי אַתָּה אוֹמֵר כֵּן, נִמְצָא אֵין לְךָ כָּל אָדָם שֶׁמַּצִּיל אֶת חֲבֵירוֹ מִיַּד הָרוֹדֵף.

[12]״אֲבָל הָרוֹדֵף אַחַר בְּהֵמָה״. [13]תַּנְיָא: ״רַבִּי שִׁמְעוֹן בֶּן יוֹחַי אוֹמֵר: הָעוֹבֵד עֲבוֹדָה זָרָה נִיתָּן לְהַצִּילוֹ בְּנַפְשׁוֹ, [14]מִקַּל וָחוֹמֶר: [15]וּמַה פְּגָם הֶדְיוֹט, נִיתָּן לְהַצִּילוֹ בְּנַפְשׁוֹ, [16]פְּגָם גָּבוֹהַּ לֹא כָּל שֶׁכֵּן״?

LITERAL TRANSLATION

the death penalty (lit., "liable for his life"). [1][If] the pursued person broke the utensils, [2]those belonging to the pursuer, he is exempt; [3]those belonging to any person, he is liable. [4]Those belonging to the pursuer, he is exempt, [5]so that his money not be dearer to him than his life. [6]Those belonging to any person, he is liable, for he saves himself with someone else's money. [7]And if a pursuer was pursuing a pursuer to save him, and he broke utensils, [8]whether belonging to the pursuer or belonging to the pursued person, [9]or belonging to any person, he is exempt. [10]And this is not by right, [11]for if you do not say this, we will find that no one will save his fellow from a pursuer.

[12]"But someone who pursues an animal." [13]It was taught: "Rabbi Shimon ben Yoḥai says: An idol worshiper one may save with his life, [14]because of a *kal vaḥomer*: [15]If, for the damage to an ordinary person, one is permitted to save him with his life, [16]for damage to the Most High, all the more so!"

TRANSLATION AND COMMENTARY

people. [1]**If the pursued person broke the utensils** as he was fleeing, the following distinction applies: [2]If he broke utensils **belonging to the pursuer, he is exempt** from liability, [3]but if he broke utensils **belonging to some other person** not involved in the pursuit, **he is liable.** [4]If the pursued party broke utensils **belonging to the pursuer, he is exempt** from liability, [5]**so that** the pursuer's **money will not be dearer to** the pursued party **than** the pursuer's **life.** Had the pursued person killed his pursuer, he would be exempt from all liability. Surely, then, he must be exempt from liability if he merely caused him monetary damage. [6]But if the pursued person broke utensils **belonging to some other person, he is liable** for the damage, **for he saved himself with someone else's money,** and that other person is not required to suffer the loss. [7]**And if someone was pursuing a pursuer** in order **to save** the pursuer's intended victim, **and** while he was coming to the victim's rescue **he broke utensils,** [8]**whether** those utensils **belonged to the pursuer or to the pursued party,** [9]**or** they **belonged to some other person** not involved in the pursuit, **he is exempt** from all liability for the damage that he caused. [10]**This is not by right,** for there is no Halakhic basis to exempt the rescuer from liability. But the Rabbis said that he is exempt, [11]arguing that **if you do not say this, nobody will save his fellow from a pursuer,** for people will refrain from coming to another person's rescue lest they cause damage and incur monetary liability.

אֲבָל [12]We have learned in our Mishnah: **"But someone who is pursuing an animal** in order to commit bestiality with it, someone who is desecrating Shabbat, and someone who is worshiping an idol — we may not kill in order to save them from completing their offenses." [13]**It was taught** in a Baraita that this ruling was not accepted by all: **"Rabbi Shimon ben Yoḥai says: One may kill an idol worshiper** in order to **save him** from his offense. [14]This is **based on a *kal vaḥomer*** argument: [15]**If, for injury to an ordinary person,** such as a woman threatened with rape, **one is permitted to kill** the rapist and thus **save him** from his offense, [16]then **for injury to God,** whose name is profaned through idol worship, **all the more so** should one be permitted to kill the idol worshiper, and thus save him from his crime!"

RASHI

בנפשו הוא — ברדיפה זו, שהרי ניתן להציל בנפשו, ואף על גב דכלים הללו של שאר כל אדם הן דמיתה לזה ותשלומין לזה — פטור. ורודף שהיה רודף — אחר חבירו להורגו, וזה רודף אחריו להצילו ושיבר את הכלים וכו׳.

NOTES

מַצִּיל עַצְמוֹ בְּמָמוֹן חֲבֵירוֹ **He saves himself with someone else's money.** *Ramah* writes that a person is forbidden to save himself with someone else's money, if he has any other way to save himself. But if he has no other way of saving himself, he can surely save himself with the other person's money, for saving a human life supersedes all the

HALAKHAH

his loss. If someone was running to save another person from his pursuer, and he broke utensils that were in his way, he is exempt. The Rabbis exempted him, so that a person would not hesitate to come to someone else's rescue," following the Gemara. (*Shulḥan Arukh, Ḥoshen Mishpat* 380:3.)

[1] וְכִי עוֹנְשִׁין מִן הַדִּין? [2] קָא סָבַר: עוֹנְשִׁין מִן הַדִּין. [3] תַּנְיָא: "רַבִּי אֶלְעָזָר בְּרַבִּי שִׁמְעוֹן אוֹמֵר: [4] הַמְחַלֵּל אֶת הַשַּׁבָּת נִיתָּן לְהַצִּילוֹ בְּנַפְשׁוֹ". [5] סָבַר לָהּ כַּאֲבוּהּ דְּאָמַר: [6] עוֹנְשִׁין מִן הַדִּין, [7] וְאָתְיָא שַׁבָּת בְּ"חִילּוּל" "חִילּוּל" מֵעֲבוֹדָה זָרָה.

[8] אָמַר רַבִּי יוֹחָנָן מִשּׁוּם רַבִּי שִׁמְעוֹן בֶּן יְהוֹצָדָק: [9] נִימְנוּ וְגָמְרוּ בַּעֲלִיַּת בֵּית נִתְזָה בְּלוֹד: [10] כָּל עֲבֵירוֹת שֶׁבַּתּוֹרָה, אִם אוֹמְרִין לָאָדָם: "עֲבוֹר וְאַל תֵּהָרֵג", [11] יַעֲבוֹר וְאַל יֵהָרֵג, [12] חוּץ מֵעֲבוֹדָה זָרָה וְגִילּוּי

TRANSLATION AND COMMENTARY

וְכִי [1] The Gemara asks: **But** is it possible to **inflict punishment on the basis of** a law that was inferred through **a *kal vaḥomer*** argument, but not explicitly stated in the Torah?

קָא סָבַר [2] The Gemara explains: Rabbi Shimon ben Yoḥai **maintains** that it is indeed possible to **inflict punishment on the basis of** a law that was inferred through **a *kal vaḥomer*** argument.

תַּנְיָא [3] **It was taught** in a related Baraita: **"Rabbi Elazar the son of Rabbi Shimon says: [4] A Shabbat desecrator one may kill** in order to **save** him from his offense." [5] The Gemara explains Rabbi Elazar's reasoning: Rabbi Elazar **agrees with his father,** Rabbi Shimon, **who said** that we may kill an idol worshiper in order to save him from completing his offense, [6] because it is possible to **inflict punishment on the basis of a *kal vaḥomer*** argument. [7] And the law regarding a **Shabbat** desecrator **is learned by way of** a *gezerah shavah* drawn between the word **"profanation"** regarding Shabbat and the word **"profanation" regarding idol worship.** Regarding Shabbat, the verse states (Exodus 31:14): "Everyone who profanes it shall surely be put to death," and regarding idol worship, the verse states (Leviticus 18:21): "And you shall not let any of your seed pass through the fire to Molekh, neither shall you profane the name of your God."

אָמַר [8] Having completed its discussion regarding sinners who may be killed to prevent them from sinning, the Gemara now discusses the obligation to die rather than violate certain prohibitions. **Rabbi Yoḥanan said in the name of Rabbi Shimon ben Yehotzadak:** [9] The Rabbis met **in the attic of the house of Natzah in Lydda; they had a vote, and it was resolved** as follows: [10] **Regarding all the Torah's commandments, if a person was told: "Violate** this prohibition, **or else you will be killed,"** [11] **he should violate** the prohibition, for the obligation to preserve life supersedes all other commandments. This rule applies to all the Torah's commandments, [12] **except**

LITERAL TRANSLATION

[1] But do we punish on the basis of a *kal vaḥomer*?

[2] He maintains: We punish on the basis of a *kal vaḥomer*.

[3] It was taught: "Rabbi Elazar the son of Rabbi Shimon says: [4] Someone who desecrates Shabbat, one may save with his life." [5] He agrees with his father, who said: [6] We punish on the basis of a *kal vaḥomer*, [7] and Shabbat is learned by way of "profanation" [and] "profanation" from idol worship.

[8] Rabbi Yoḥanan said in the name of Rabbi Shimon ben Yehotzadak: [9] They were counted, and they resolved in the attic of the house of Natzah in Lydda: [10] [Regarding] all the transgressions in the Torah, if they say to a person: "Transgress, and do not be killed," [11] he should transgress, and not be killed, [12] except for idolatry, prohibited

RASHI

סבר לה כאבוה – בעבודה זרה דעונשים מן הדין, והדר יליף שבת ב"חלול" "חלול" מעבודה זרה "מחלליה מות יומת" (שמות לא) "ומזרעך לא תתן להעביר למולך ולא תחלל" (ויקרא יח). נתזה – שם האיש. יעבור ואל יהרג – "וחי בהם" – ולא שימות בהם. חוץ מעבודה זרה וכו' – לקמן יליף לה.

SAGES

רַבִּי שִׁמְעוֹן בֶּן יְהוֹצָדָק **Rabbi Shimon ben Yehotzadak.** A first generation Palestinian Amora, Rabbi Shimon ben Yehotzadak was a teacher of Rabbi Yoḥanan. Most of his teachings — some of which were given the status of Baraitot — are transmitted by Rabbi Yoḥanan. He was a priest and died in Lod (Lydda).

NOTES

commandments of the Torah, with the exception of idolatry, murder, and forbidden sexual relations. Naturally, he must compensate the other person for the loss that he caused him.

אֵין עוֹנְשִׁין מִן הַדִּין **We do not punish on the basis of a *kal vaḥomer*.** *Rashba* explains that we cannot inflict irrevocable punishment on the basis of a *kal vaḥomer*, because a *kal vaḥomer* is based on a logical argument, and is therefore always open to possible refutation.

חוּץ מֵעֲבוֹדָה זָרָה וְגִילּוּי עֲרָיוֹת וּשְׁפִיכוּת דָּמִים **Except for idolatry, prohibited sexual relations, and bloodshed.** The reason for stringency is different regarding each prohibition.

HALAKHAH

כָּל עֲבֵירוֹת שֶׁבַּתּוֹרָה **All the transgressions in the Torah.** "If a Jew was told to violate a Torah prohibition (with the exception of idolatry, prohibited sexual relationships, and bloodshed), or else be killed, he may violate the prohibition, rather than be killed. If a non-Jew was coercing a Jew to violate a prohibition in order to demonstrate his apostasy, and the Jew wished to be stringent with himself, and suffer death, he would be permitted to do so" (against *Rambam,* who forbids a person to suffer death in such a case). (*Shulḥan Arukh, Yoreh De'ah* 157:1.)

חוּץ מֵעֲבוֹדָה זָרָה וְגִילּוּי עֲרָיוֹת וּשְׁפִיכוּת דָּמִים **Except for idolatry, prohibited sexual relations, and bloodshed.** "If a Jew was being coerced to violate one of the three following prohibitions — idolatry, prohibited sexual relations,

TRANSLATION AND COMMENTARY

for idolatry, prohibited sexual relations (incest and adultery), **and bloodshed."**

וַעֲבוֹדָה זָרָה [1]The Gemara asks: **But** is it really true that one may **not** violate the prohibition against **idolatry,** even when threatened with death? [2]**But surely it was taught** otherwise in a Baraita: **"Rabbi Yishmael said:** [3]**From where do we know that, if a person was told: 'Worship an idol, or else you will be killed,'** [4]**he should** indeed **worship the idol in order not to be killed?** [5]This is learned from **the verse** that **states** (Leviticus 18:5): 'You shall therefore keep My statutes, and my judgments, which if a man does, **he shall live in them'** [6]**and not die because of them.** [7]Had I only had this verse, **I might have thought** that a person may commit idolatry rather than be killed, **even** if he was being coerced to violate the prohibition **in public.** [8]Therefore, **the verse states** (Leviticus 22:32): **'You shall not profane My holy name; but I will be hallowed** among the Children of Israel; I am the Lord who makes you holy.' The public violation of God's commandments causes God's name to be profaned, and so in order to sanctify God's name one must suffer death rather than transgress His laws." Now, this Baraita implies that one may commit idolatry in private rather than be killed, against the decision taken by the Rabbinic council that met at Lydda!

אִינְהוּ [9]The Gemara explains: Those Rabbis **agree with Rabbi Eliezer,** whose position **was taught** in another Baraita: [10]**"Rabbi Eliezer says:** The verse states (Deuteronomy 6:5): **'And you shall love the Lord your God'** — and not exchange Him for an idol — **'with all your heart, and with all your soul, and with all your might.'** [11]**If** the verse **states: 'With all your heart,'** [12]then **why does it** also **state: 'With all your might,'** meaning your money? [13]**And if** the verse **states: 'With all your might,'** [14]then **why does it** also **state: 'With all your heart'?** This apparent superfluity comes to teach that a person must love God with all that is most dear to him. [15]**A person whose** own life and **self are dearer to him than his money** must be ready to sacrifice his life for God,

עֲרָיוֹת וּשְׁפִיכוּת דָּמִים.
[1]וַעֲבוֹדָה זָרָה, לֹא? [2]וְהָא תַּנְיָא: [3]"אָמַר רַבִּי יִשְׁמָעֵאל: [4]מִנַּיִן שֶׁאִם אָמְרוּ לוֹ לָאָדָם: 'עֲבוֹד עֲבוֹדָה זָרָה וְאַל תֵּהָרֵג', מִנַּיִן שֶׁיַּעֲבוֹד וְאַל יֵהָרֵג? [5]תַּלְמוּד לוֹמַר: 'וָחַי בָּהֶם' — [6]וְלֹא שֶׁיָּמוּת בָּהֶם. [7]יָכוֹל אֲפִילּוּ בְּפַרְהֶסְיָא. [8]תַּלְמוּד לוֹמַר: 'וְלֹא תְחַלְּלוּ אֶת שֵׁם קָדְשִׁי; וְנִקְדַּשְׁתִּי'".
[9]אִינְהוּ דַּאֲמוּר כְּרַבִּי אֱלִיעֶזֶר, דְּתַנְיָא: [10]"רַבִּי אֱלִיעֶזֶר אוֹמֵר: 'וְאָהַבְתָּ אֵת ה' אֱלֹהֶיךָ בְּכָל לְבָבְךָ וּבְכָל נַפְשְׁךָ וּבְכָל מְאֹדֶךָ'. [11]אִם נֶאֱמַר: 'בְּכָל נַפְשְׁךָ', [12]לָמָּה נֶאֱמַר: 'בְּכָל מְאֹדֶךָ'? [13]וְאִם נֶאֱמַר: 'בְּכָל מְאֹדֶךָ', [14]לָמָּה נֶאֱמַר: 'בְּכָל נַפְשְׁךָ'? [15]אִם יֵשׁ לְךָ אָדָם שֶׁגּוּפוֹ חָבִיב

LITERAL TRANSLATION

sexual relations, and bloodshed.

[1]But idolatry, not? [2]But surely it was taught: "Rabbi Yishmael said: [3]From where [do we know] that if they said to a person: 'Worship an idol, and do not be killed,' [4]that he should worship the idol, and not be killed? [5]The verse states: 'He shall live in them' — [6]and not die because of them. [7]I might have thought even in public. [8]The verse states: 'You shall not profane My holy name; but I will be hallowed.'"

[9]They said in accordance with Rabbi Eliezer, as it was taught: [10]"Rabbi Eliezer says: 'And you shall love the Lord your God with all your heart, and with all your soul, and with all your might.' [11]If it was stated: 'With all your soul,' [12]why was it stated: 'With all your might'? [13]And if it was stated: 'With all your might,' [14]why was it stated: 'With all your soul'? [15]If there is a person whose self is dearer

RASHI

בפרהסיא – לקמן מפרש כמה פרהסיא. לא תחללו – בפרהסיא איכא חלול השם וצריך לקדש את השם וזהו "ונקדשתי" שמוסר נפשו על אהבת יוצרו. ואהבת את ה' אלהיך – משמע שלא תמירנו בעבודה זרה.

NOTES

A person must suffer death rather than worship an idol, because idolatry involves a rejection of the most fundamental tenets of Judaism. A person much choose death rather than commit murder, because of the logical argument that the murderer's blood is no redder than that of the victim. And a person must suffer death rather than engage in prohibited sexual relations, because of an analogy drawn between murder and the rape of a betrothed girl. Although there are other prohibitions that are just as stringent regarding other matters, one is not required to surrender one's life for them.

HALAKHAH

and bloodshed — then even if he was being coerced to commit the transgression in private, and in a normal period that was not characterized by religious persecution, and even if the non-Jew was forcing the Jew to violate the prohibition for the non-Jew's own enjoyment, the Jew must suffer death rather than violate the prohibition," (following Rabbi Yishmael and Rabbi Yoḥanan, and the Gemara's conclusion). (*Shulḥan Arukh, Yoreh De'ah* 157:1.)

עָלָיו מִמָּמוֹנוֹ, ¹לְכָךְ נֶאֱמַר: ׳בְּכָל נַפְשְׁךָ׳. ²וְאִם יֵשׁ לְךָ אָדָם שֶׁמָּמוֹנוֹ חָבִיב עָלָיו מִגּוּפוֹ ³לְכָךְ נֶאֱמַר: ׳בְּכָל מְאֹדֶךָ׳״.

⁴גִּילּוּי עֲרָיוֹת וּשְׁפִיכוּת דָּמִים, ⁵כִּדְרַבִּי, ⁶דְּתַנְיָא: ״רַבִּי אוֹמֵר: ׳כִּי כַּאֲשֶׁר יָקוּם אִישׁ עַל רֵעֵהוּ, וּרְצָחוֹ נֶפֶשׁ, כֵּן הַדָּבָר הַזֶּה׳. ⁷וְכִי מַה לָּמַדְנוּ מֵרוֹצֵחַ? ⁸מֵעַתָּה, הֲרֵי זֶה בָּא לְלַמֵּד וְנִמְצָא לָמֵד. ⁹מַקִּישׁ רוֹצֵחַ לְנַעֲרָה הַמְאוֹרָסָה. ¹⁰מַה נַּעֲרָה הַמְאוֹרָסָה, נִיתָּן לְהַצִּילוֹ בְּנַפְשׁוֹ, ¹¹אַף רוֹצֵחַ, נִיתָּן לְהַצִּילוֹ בְּנַפְשׁוֹ. ¹²וּמַקִּישׁ נַעֲרָה הַמְאוֹרָסָה לְרוֹצֵחַ. ¹³מָה רוֹצֵחַ, יֵהָרֵג וְאַל יַעֲבוֹר, ¹⁴אַף נַעֲרָה הַמְאוֹרָסָה, תֵּהָרֵג וְאַל תַּעֲבוֹר״.

¹⁵רוֹצֵחַ גּוּפֵיהּ מְנָא לָן? ¹⁶סְבָרָא

LITERAL TRANSLATION

to him than his money, ¹therefore it was stated: 'With all your soul.' ²And if there is a person whose money is dearer to him than his self, ³therefore it was stated: 'With all your might.'"

⁴Prohibited sexual relations and bloodshed, ⁵in accordance with Rabbi, as it was taught: ⁶"Rabbi says: 'For as when a man rises against his neighbor, and slays him, even so is this matter.' ⁷What do we learn from a murderer? ⁸Now, it came to teach and was ultimately inferred. ⁹It compares a murderer to a betrothed girl. ¹⁰Just as with a betrothed girl, one may save him with his life, ¹¹so, too, a murderer, one may save him with his life. ¹²And it compares a betrothed girl to a murderer. ¹³Just as a murderer, he must be killed, and not transgress, ¹⁴so, too, a betrothed girl, she must be killed, and not transgress."

¹⁵From where [do we know about] the murderer himself? ¹⁶It is a common-sense

TRANSLATION AND COMMENTARY

¹**as the verse states: 'With all your soul.'** ²**And a person whose money is dearer to him than his** own life and **self** must be ready to sacrifice his money for Him, ³**as the verse states: 'With all your might.'"** Thus, we see that for the love of God, a person must surrender his own life, rather than worship another god, as was decided by the Rabbis at Lydda.

גילוי ⁴The Gemara continues: From where do we know that one must suffer death rather than engage in **prohibited sexual relations or** commit **murder?** ⁵This is **in accordance with** the view of **Rabbi** Yehudah HaNasi, **as it was taught** in the following Baraita: ⁶**"Rabbi** Yehudah HaNasi **says:** 'The verse dealing with the rape of a betrothed girl states (Deuteronomy 22:26): "But to the girl you shall do nothing; the girl has no sin worthy of death: **for as when a man rises against his neighbor, and slays him, even so is this matter,"** comparing the law regarding a betrothed girl to the law regarding a murderer.' ⁷**What** new law **do we learn from** this comparison between **a murderer** and a betrothed girl? ⁸**Rather,** although the formulation of the verse suggests that the law regarding a murderer is meant **to teach** the law regarding a betrothed girl, **the inference is** actually **to be drawn** in both directions. ⁹The verse **compares a murderer to** the rapist of **a betrothed girl.** ¹⁰**Just as** one **may save the betrothed girl** from violation **by killing** her rapist, ¹¹**so, too, one may save** a potential victim **by killing** the murderer. ¹²**And** the verse **compares** the rapist of **a betrothed girl to a murderer.** ¹³**Just as** a person who is coerced to commit **murder must suffer death rather than violate** the prohibition against bloodshed, ¹⁴**so, too,** a person who is coerced to engage in sexual intercourse with **a betrothed girl must suffer death rather than violate** the prohibition against relations of that kind."

רוֹצֵחַ ¹⁵The Gemara asks: **From where do we know about** the person **himself** who is coerced to commit **murder,** that he must surrender his own life rather than violate the prohibition? ¹⁶This **is** based on **the common-sense argument** that the obligation to preserve one's own life should not take precedence over the

RASHI

לכך נאמר וכו׳ — כלומר תהא אהבתו חביבה לך יותר מכל החביב לך. **מה רוצח יהרג ואל יעבור** — ואם אמר לו: הוי רוצח והרוג את הנפש ואם לאו הריני הורגך — יהרג ואל יעבור. **סברא הוא** — שלא תדחה נפש חבירו, דאיכא תרתי, אבוד נשמה ועבירה מפני נפשו דליכא אלא חדא אבוד נשמה והוא לא יעבור, דכי אמר רחמנא לעבור על המצות משום וחי בהם משום דיקרה בעיניו נשמה של ישראל, והכא גבי רוצח כיון דסוף סוף איכא איבוד נשמה למה יהא מותר לעבור? — מי יודע שנפשו חביבה ליוצרו יותר מנפש חבירו — הלכך דבר המקום לא ניתן לדחות.

NOTES

נַעֲרָה הַמְאוֹרָסָה, תֵּהָרֵג וְאַל תַּעֲבוֹר **A betrothed girl, she must suffer death, and not transgress.** Many Rishonim argue that we must read here: "A betrothed girl, *he* must suffer death, and not transgress," that is to say, a man who was coerced to engage in sexual relations with a betrothed girl must suffer death rather than transgress. But the betrothed girl is not required to suffer death, for as is taught below (74b), the obligation to choose death rather than engage in a prohibited sexual relationship falls only upon a man who is the active partner in the relationship. A woman may passively acquiesce in a forbidden relationship and need not suffer death in order to avoid being raped (*Ramah, Rabbenu Yehonatan*).

TRANSLATION AND COMMENTARY

prohibition against taking the life of another person. [1]The Gemara illustrates this principle with the following anecdote: **A certain person** once **came before Rabbah and said to him:** "What shall I do? [2]**The** non-Jewish **master of my village said to me: 'Go, kill So-and-so, or else I will kill you.'** Must I surrender my life, or should I save my life by killing that other person?" [3]Rabbah **said to him: "Let him kill you, rather than allow yourself to** go out and **kill** that other person. [4]**Who says that your blood is** any **redder than the other person's?** [5]**Perhaps that man's blood is redder than yours!"**

כִּי אֲתָא [6]The Gemara continues: **When Rav Dimi came** from Eretz Israel to Babylonia, **he said in the name of Rabbi Yoḥanan:** [7]**This law,** that one should violate all the other commandments (besides idolatry, prohibited sexual relationships, and bloodshed) rather than suffer death, **applies only in** normal **times that are not** periods **of** religious **persecution** of the entire community. [8]**But in times** of religious **persecution** of the entire community, **even for a minor commandment,** a person **must be killed rather than violate** the commandment.

כִּי אֲתָא [9]The Gemara now reports another tradition in the name of Rabbi Yoḥanan. **When Ravin came** from Eretz Israel to Babylonia, **he said in the name of Rabbi Yoḥanan:** [10]**Even in times that are not** characterized by religious **persecution, this law,** that one should violate all the other commandments rather than suffer death, **applies only in private.** [11]**But in public, even** if he is being threatened with death unless he violates **a minor commandment, he must be killed rather than allow himself to violate** the commandment.

הוּא. [1]דְּהַהוּא דַּאֲתָא לְקַמֵּיהּ דְּרַבָּה, וַאֲמַר לֵיהּ: [2]״אֲמַר לִי מָרִי דוּרָאִי: ׳זִיל קַטְלֵיהּ לִפְלָנְיָא, וְאִי לָא, קָטְלִינָא לָךְ׳״. [3]אֲמַר לֵיהּ: ״לִקְטְלוּךְ, וְלָא תִּיקְטוֹל. [4]מִי יֵימַר דִּדְמָא דִּידָךְ סוּמָּק טְפֵי? [5]דִּילְמָא דָּמָא דְּהוּא גַּבְרָא סוּמָּק טְפֵי״!

[6]כִּי אֲתָא רַב דִּימִי, אֲמַר רַבִּי יוֹחָנָן: [7]לֹא שָׁנוּ אֶלָּא שֶׁלֹּא בִּשְׁעַת הַשְּׁמָד. [8]אֲבָל בִּשְׁעַת הַשְּׁמָד, אֲפִילּוּ מִצְוָה קַלָּה יֵהָרֵג וְאַל יַעֲבוֹר.

[9]כִּי אֲתָא רָבִין אֲמַר רַבִּי יוֹחָנָן: [10]אֲפִילּוּ שֶׁלֹּא בִּשְׁעַת הַשְּׁמָד, לֹא אָמְרוּ אֶלָּא בְּצִינְעָא, [11]אֲבָל בְּפַרְהֶסְיָא, אֲפִילּוּ מִצְוָה קַלָּה יֵהָרֵג וְאַל יַעֲבוֹר.

LITERAL TRANSLATION

argument. [1]For a certain person came before Rabbah and said to him: [2]"The master of my village said to me: 'Go, kill So-and-so, and if not, I will kill you.'" [3]He said to him: "Let him kill you, and do not kill. [4]Who says that your blood is redder [than the other person's]? [5]Perhaps that man's blood is redder [than yours]!"

[6]When Rav Dimi came, he said in the name of Rabbi Yoḥanan: [7]They only taught this not in times of persecution. [8]But in times of persecution, even for a minor commandment he must be killed and not transgress.

[9]When Ravin came, he said in the name of Rabbi Yoḥanan: [10]Even not in times of persecution, they only said [this] in private, [11]but in public, even for a minor commandment, he must be killed, and not transgress.

LANGUAGE

דּוּרָא **Village.** "Dura" was apparently the Babylonian name for a place or village. This word serves as a general term and also in combination with other words, as in place names like "Dura Eiropos" and "Dura Darauta."

RASHI

מרי דוראי — אדון עירי, ונכרי הוה. מאי חזית דדמא דידך סומק טפי — מי יודע שיהא דמך חביב ונאה ליוצרך יותר מדם חבירך? הלכך אין כאן לומר וחי בהם ולא שימות בהם. שלא התיר הכתוב אלא משום חביבות נפשם של ישראל להקדוש ברוך הוא, וכאן שיש אבוד נפש חבירו לא ניתן דבר המלך לדחות שצוה על הרציחה. ואפילו מצוה קלה יהרג ואל יעבור — שלא ירגילו הגויים להמריך את הלבבות לכך.

NOTES

בִּשְׁעַת הַשְּׁמָד **In times of persecution.** In times of religious persecution directed against the entire Jewish community, one must suffer death even for a minor commandment, because suffering martyrdom in such a situation involves a sanctification of God's name. Alternatively, one must choose death rather than violate even a minor commandment, lest the non-Jewish authorities become accustomed to persecute the Jewish community, and the Jewish community become accustomed to not observing the commandments (*Ramah*). *Ran* adds that when the non-Jewish authorities persecute the Jews and try to bring them to abrogate the entire Torah, Jews must not concede even one letter of the Torah. They must suffer death, rather than violate even a minor commandment.

HALAKHAH

אֲבָל בִּשְׁעַת הַשְּׁמָד **But in times of persecution.** "In times of religious persecution (which is directed against the Jewish people alone; *Rema*), a Jew must suffer death rather than violate even a minor custom that is distinctively Jewish, such as make a change regarding his shoe-strap (according to *Rambam,* only when the change involves some violation of an actual prohibition). *Rema* adds that this applies only to negative commandments, but if a decree was issued that the Jews not fulfill a certain positive commandment, a Jew is not obligated to suffer death rather than abstain from fulfilling the commandment. He may, however, choose to fulfill the commandment and risk death." (*Shulḥan Arukh, Yoreh De'ah* 157:1.)

BACKGROUND

עַרְקָתָא דִּמְסָאנָא **Strap of a shoe.**

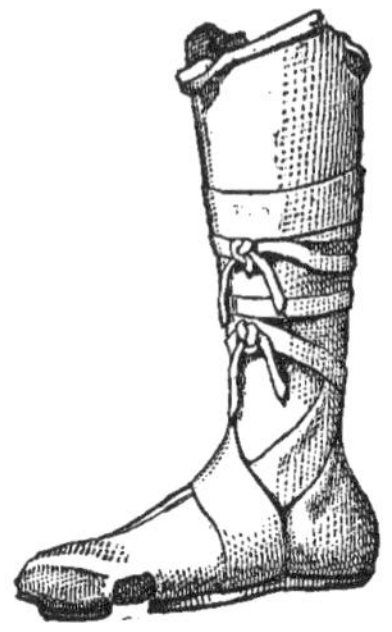

The shoe of men of senatorial rank in Rome.

Shoes were generally constructed in this way, though there were differences in the number of straps and their color, and each type belonged to a different social class. There appears to have been a difference between shoes used by Jews and those used by non-Jews.

LANGUAGE

פַּרְהֶסְיָא **Public.** This word is derived from the Greek.

TRANSLATION AND COMMENTARY

מַאי מִצְוָה קַלָּה [1]The Gemara asks: **What is** considered **a minor commandment** in this context? [2]**Rava bar Rav Yitzḥak said in the name of Rav:** [74B] In times of religious persecution, or even in normal times, if a Jew was coerced to commit a transgression in public, he must choose to die rather than violate any commandment, including minor customs that are distinctively Jewish. For example, if Jews were accustomed to tie their shoes with straps of a distinctive color, or in a particular way, [3]and a Jew was coerced by a non-Jew **to change the** color of his **shoe-strap,** or the way he ties it, to follow the non-Jewish custom, the Jew must suffer death, and thus sanctify God's name, rather than violate the Jewish custom.

וְכַמָּה [4]The Gemara asks: **How many** people must be present in order to call a person's violation of a commandment **a public** act? [5]**Rabbi Ya'akov said in the name of Rabbi Yoḥanan: A public** act **is** one that is performed in the presence of **not fewer than ten people.**

פְּשִׁיטָא [6]The Gemara notes: **It is obvious that** the ten people **must be Jews,** [7]**for the verse** from which we learn the obligation to choose death in order to sanctify God's name **states** (Leviticus 22:32): **"But I will be hallowed among the Children of Israel."**

בָּעֵי [8]**Rabbi Yirmeyah raised** the following **question: What is the law** when a Jew was coerced to commit a transgression in the presence of **nine** other **Jews and one non-Jew?**

תָּא שְׁמַע [9]The Gemara answers: **Come and hear** an answer to this question, **for Rabbi Yannai the brother of Rabbi Ḥiyya bar Abba taught** the following Baraita: [10]"The meaning of the word **'among'** in the verse relating to the obligation to sanctify God's name **is learned** by a *gezerah shavah* **from** the word **'among'** in the passage dealing with the congregation of Korah's followers. [11]**Here,** regarding the sanctification of God's name, **the verse states** (Leviticus 22:32): **'But I will be hallowed among the Children of Israel,'**

[1]מַאי מִצְוָה קַלָּה? [2]אָמַר רָבָא בַּר יִצְחָק אָמַר רַב: [74B] [3]אֲפִילּוּ לְשַׁנּוּיֵי עַרְקְתָא דִּמְסָאנָא.

[4]וְכַמָּה פַּרְהֶסְיָא? [5]אָמַר רַבִּי יַעֲקֹב אָמַר רַבִּי יוֹחָנָן: אֵין פַּרְהֶסְיָא פְּחוּתָה מֵעֲשָׂרָה בְּנֵי אָדָם.

[6]פְּשִׁיטָא, יִשְׂרְאֵלִים בָּעֵינַן, [7]דִּכְתִיב: "וְנִקְדַּשְׁתִּי בְּתוֹךְ בְּנֵי יִשְׂרָאֵל".

[8]בָּעֵי רַבִּי יִרְמְיָה: תִּשְׁעָה יִשְׂרָאֵל וְנָכְרִי אֶחָד, מַהוּ?

[9]תָּא שְׁמַע, דְּתָנֵי רַב יַנַּאי אֲחוּהּ דְּרַבִּי חִיָּיא בַּר אַבָּא: [10]"אָתְיָא 'תּוֹךְ' 'תּוֹךְ', [11]כְּתִיב הָכָא: 'וְנִקְדַּשְׁתִּי בְּתוֹךְ בְּנֵי יִשְׂרָאֵל',

LITERAL TRANSLATION

[1]What is a minor commandment? [2]Rava bar Rav Yitzḥak said in the name of Rav: [74B] [3]Even to change the strap of a shoe.

[4]And how many is "in public"? [5]Rabbi Ya'akov said in the name of Rabbi Yoḥanan: A public is not fewer than ten people.

[6]It is obvious that we need Jews, [7]for it is written: "But I will be hallowed among the Children of Israel."

[8]Rabbi Yirmeyah asked: Nine Jews and one non-Jew, what [is the law]?

[9]Come [and] hear, for Rabbi Yannai the brother of Rabbi Ḥiyya bar Abba taught: [10]"'Among' is learned from 'among.' [11]Here it is written: 'But I will be hallowed among the Children of Israel,'

RASHI

ערקתא דמסאנא — שרוך הנעל, שאם דרך הנכרים לקשור כך ודרך ישראל בענין אחר, כגון שיש צד יהדות בדבר ודרך ישראל להיות צנועים אפילו שנוי זה שאין כאן מצוה אלא מנהג בעלמא יקדש את השם בפני חביריו ישראל, והאי פרהסיא מדבר בישראל. אתיא תוך תוך — דעשרה בעינן וכולהו ישראל.

NOTES

עַרְקָתָא דִּמְסָאנָא **The strap of a shoe.** The Rishonim had a tradition that non-Jews tied their shoes with red straps, while Jews used black straps (*Geonim, Rif, Ramah*). It has been suggested that Jews tied their shoes with black straps as a sign of mourning over the destruction of the Temple (*Arukh*). This fits in with what *Rashi* says, that in times of religious persecution, or even in normal times, if a Jew is coerced to commit a transgression in public, he must choose to die, and not even violate a custom that is distinctively Jewish. According to *Meiri,* non-Jews were accustomed to tie their shoes with string, whereas Jews tied their shoes in a more modest manner with straps. *She'iltot* brings an entirely different explanation: We are dealing here with a case where Jews are being coerced to bow down before an idol. Even if a Jew is told to tie his shoe strap, and make it appear as if he were bowing down before the idol, he is required to suffer death rather than give others the impression that he is committing idolatry.

HALAKHAH

כַּמָּה ״פַּרְהֶסְיָא״? **How many is "in public"?** "If a person is being forced to violate a prohibition in public, he must suffer death rather than commit the transgression. His transgression is regarded as a public act if it is performed in the presence of no fewer than ten men." (*Shulḥan Arukh, Yoreh De'ah* 157:1.)

וּכְתִיב הָתָם: ׳הִבָּדְלוּ מִתּוֹךְ הָעֵדָה הַזֹּאת׳. [2]מַה לְּהַלָּן עֲשָׂרָה וְכוּלְּהוּ יִשְׂרָאֵל, [3]אַף כָּאן עֲשָׂרָה וְכוּלְּהוּ יִשְׂרָאֵל״. [4]וְהָא אֶסְתֵּר פַּרְהֶסְיָא הֲוַאי! [5]אָמַר אַבַּיֵי: אֶסְתֵּר קַרְקַע עוֹלָם הָיְתָה. [6]רָבָא אָמַר: הֲנָאַת עַצְמָן שָׁאנֵי. [7]דְּאִי לָא תֵּימָא הָכִי,

LITERAL TRANSLATION

[1]and there it is written: 'Separate yourselves from among this congregation.' [2]Just as there, there are ten, and all are Jews, [3]so too here, there must be ten and all must be Jews."

[4]But surely Esther was in public!

[5]Abaye said: Esther was like natural ground.

[6]Rava said: Their own enjoyment is different. [7]For if you do not say this,

RASHI

להלן – במרגלים. והא אסתר פרהסיא הואי – ונבעלה לנכרי ולא מסרה נפשה לקטלא. קרקע עולם היא – אינה עושה מעשה, הוא עושה בה מעשה. הנאת עצמו – שאין הנכרי מתכוין להעבירו מירא‍תו אלא להנאת עצמו מתכוין – שאני ואין כאן חלול השם ליהרג על כך.

TRANSLATION AND COMMENTARY

[1]**and there,** regarding the congregation of Korah's followers **the verse states** (Numbers 16:21): **'Separate yourselves from among this congregation.'** And we learn the meaning of the word 'congregation' used in connection with Korah's followers from the word 'congregation' used in connection with the spies sent by Moses to scout the Land of Israel (Numbers 14:27): 'How long shall I bear with this evil congregation?' [2]**Just as there,** the congregation of spies who spoke ill of the Land of Israel consisted of **ten** people, **and all were Jews,** [3]**so, too, here ten** people **must be** present before we can call a person's violation of a commandment a public act, **and all must be Jews."**

וְהָא [4]The Gemara raises an objection: **But surely** Queen **Esther's** marriage to King Ahasuerus **was a public act!** Why, then, did she not choose to suffer death, rather than engage in sexual intercourse with a non-Jew?

אָמַר אַבַּיֵי [5]**Abaye said: Esther was like natural ground** that is plowed. In submitting to Ahasuerus, Esther did not perform any act, but rather she possibly allowed Ahasuerus to perform an act upon her. The obligation to choose death rather than engage in a prohibited sexual relationship falls only upon a man, who is the active partner in the relationship.

רָבָא אָמַר [6]**Rava suggested** an alternative answer: The law in a case where a non-Jew coerces a Jew to commit a transgression, not in order to demonstrate his apostasy, but rather for the non-Jew's **own enjoyment, is different,** for in such a case there is no profanation of God's name for which the Jew must give up his life. [7]This distinction must be true, **for if you do not say this, how dare we give** the Persian priests **the coal-pans** that they demand, rather than refuse to contribute and suffer death? The Persian priests collected coal-pans from every household, and used them to heat up their temples on their holidays. Even Jews were coerced to contribute. Thus, the Jews were forced to assist the Persians in their idolatrous practices, and nowhere do we

NOTES

וְהָא אֶסְתֵּר **But surely Esther.** The Rishonim raise the question: Surely, we learned, above, that a person must suffer death rather than engage in prohibited sexual relations; why, then, did the Gemara only ask about the public nature of Esther's marriage to Ahasuerus, and not about her engaging in prohibited sexual intercourse with a non-Jew? The Rishonim suggest that, while indeed it is forbidden, sexual intercourse with a non-Jew is not included among the prohibited acts of sexual intercourse for which a person must suffer death rather than transgress. Alternatively, it was clear to the Gemara that the obligation to choose death rather than engage in a prohibited sexual relationship did not apply to Esther, who passively acquiesced in the transgression, and therefore only asked why she did not suffer death rather than engage in a public profanation of God's name (see *Tosafot, Ran, Rabbi Zeraḥyah HaLevi*).

אֶסְתֵּר פַּרְהֶסְיָא הֲוַאי **Esther was in public.** Even though ten Jews were not present while Esther engaged in sexual intercourse with Aḥasuerus, ten Jews did see her being taken away to the king's palace (*Ran*). Some argue that, for an act to be considered public, it is not necessary for ten people actually to witness it, but rather it suffices if ten people know about it (*Meiri*). Others maintain that when a man and woman live together as a couple, their sexual relationship is regarded as a public act (*Shakh* and others).

קַרְקַע עוֹלָם **Natural ground.** The Gemara compares a woman to ground, because ground is plowed and sown without any active participation on its part (*She'iltot*). According to this, if a woman was ordered to go elsewhere

HALAKHAH

קַרְקַע עוֹלָם **Natural ground.** "A woman is not required to suffer death rather than engage in forbidden sexual relations, if she plays a purely passive role in the transgression (*Rema*)." (This ruling follows the assumption that Rava and Abaye do not disagree, and that both of their resolutions to the Gemara's difficulty are valid. According to *Rambam*, the two Amoraim disagree, and the law follows the view of Rava.) (*Shulḥan Arukh, Yoreh De'ah* 157:1; *Rambam, Sefer Mada, Hilkhot Yesodei HaTorah* 5:2.)

הֲנָאַת עַצְמָן שָׁאנֵי **Their own enjoyment is different.** "If a Jew is coerced to commit a transgression in public, he is required to suffer death, provided he is being coerced to commit the transgression in order to demonstrate his apostasy. But if the non-Jew is forcing him to break the law for the non-Jew's own enjoyment, the Jew may violate the prohibition rather than suffer death." (*Shulḥan Arukh, Yoreh De'ah* 157:1; *Rambam, Sefer Mada, Hilkhot Yesodei HaTorah* 5:2.)

TRANSLATION AND COMMENTARY

find that the Jews chose death rather than hand over the coal-pans. [1]Their behavior is only understandable if we assume that a transgression for the non-Jew's **own enjoyment is different.** [2]**So, too, here,** Esther was permitted to submit to Ahasuerus because a transgression for the non-Jew's **own enjoyment is different.**

וְאָזְדָא [3]The Gemara notes that **Rava follows his own opinion, for Rava said:** [4]**If a non-Jew said to a Jew:** "Go and **cut grass on Shabbat, and** then **throw it before the animals, or else I will kill you,"** [5]the Jew **should cut the grass, and not be killed.** But if the non-Jew said to the Jew: "Go and cut grass on Shabbat, [6]and then **throw it into the river,** or else I will kill you," [7]the Jew **must be killed rather than cut the grass.** [8]**What is the reason** for this distinction? In the first case, the non-Jew forced the Jew to violate the Shabbat for his own personal needs, so the Jew's desecration of Shabbat does not involve a profanation of God's name. [9]But in the second case, the non-Jew **wanted to make** the Jew **commit a transgression** entirely for the sake of violating the Torah's commandments. In such a case, the Jew must suffer death, if it was a period of religious persecution, or if he was being coerced to commit the transgression in public.

בָּעוּ מִינֵּיהּ [10]**The following question was posed to Rabbi Ammi: Is a non-Jew required to sanctify God's Name** and suffer death if he was being forced to violate one of the Noachide laws, [11]**or is he not commanded to sanctify God's Name?**

הָנֵי קְוואקֵי וְדִימוֹנִיקֵי הֵיכִי יָהֲבִינַן לְהוּ? [1]אֶלָּא, הֲנָאַת עַצְמָן שָׁאנֵי. [2]הָכָא נַמִי: הֲנָאַת עַצְמָן שָׁאנֵי.

[3]וְאָזְדָא רָבָא לְטַעְמֵיהּ, דְּאָמַר רָבָא: [4]נָכְרִי דְּאָמַר לֵיהּ לְהַאי יִשְׂרָאֵל: "קְטוֹל אַסְפַּסְתָּא בְּשַׁבְּתָא וּשְׁדֵי לְחֵיוָתָא, וְאִי לָא קָטֵילְנָא לָךְ", [5]לִיקְטֵיל וְלָא לִקְטְלֵיהּ. [6]"שְׁדֵי לְנַהֲרָא", [7]לִיקְטְלֵיהּ, וְלָא לִיקְטוֹל. [8]מַאי טַעְמָא? [9]לְעַבּוֹרֵי מִילְּתָא קָא בָּעֵי.

[10]בָּעוּ מִינֵּיהּ מֵרַבִּי אַמִּי: בֶּן נֹחַ מְצוּוֶּה עַל קְדוּשַּׁת הַשֵּׁם, [11]אוֹ אֵין מְצוּוֶּה עַל קְדוּשַּׁת הַשֵּׁם?

LITERAL TRANSLATION

how do we give them coal-pans? [1]Rather, their own enjoyment is different. [2]So, too, here, their own enjoyment is different.

[3]And Rava follows his own opinion, for Rava said: [4][If] a non-Jew said to a Jew: "Cut grass on Shabbat, and throw it before the animals, and if not, I will kill you," [5]he must cut [the grass], and not be killed. [6]"Throw [it] into the river," [7]he must be killed, and not cut [the grass]. [8]What is the reason? [9]He wishes to make him commit a transgression.

[10]They asked Rabbi Ammi: Is a non-Jew (lit., "a descendant of Noah") commanded about the sanctification of [God's] Name, [11]or is he not commanded about the sanctification of [God's] Name?

RASHI

הני קוואקי ודימוניקי — כלי נחשת שנותנין בהם גחלים גבוהין הן ועומדין לפני שולחן מלכים להתחמם כנגדן. **היכי יהבינן להו** — יום אחד היה לפרסיים שנוטלין כומרי עבודה זרה אור מכל בית ובית ומעמידין בבית עבודה זרה שלהם ומתחממין העם כנגדן, והיו נוטלין אף מבית ישראל בעל כרחם, היכי יהבינן להו ולא מסרי נפשייהו אקדושת השם הלא חק עבודה זרה הוא. **אלא** — הואיל והנכרי אינו מתכוין להעבירו אלא להנאת עצמו מתכוין שצריך לאותו הכלי — אין כאן קידוש השם ליהרג עליו, ואף על פי שהנכרי אינו צריך לו אלא לחוק עבודה זרה הנאת עצמו הוא, שצריך לאותו כלי ואינו אומר לי שאעבוד אני. **קטיל אספסתא** — קצור עשב מאכל בהמה. **לקטול** — האספסתא, ולא נקטליה הנכרי דכיון דאינו מתכוין להעבירו אלא לצורכי עצמו — אין כאן חילול השם. **שדי לנהרא** — להעבירו הוא מתכוין, ואי פרהסיא הוא או שעת גזרת המלכות נקטליה ולא ליקטול אספסתא, בן נח מוזהר על עבודה זרה כדאמר ב"ארבע מיתות" (נו,א). ואם אמר עבור ואל תהרג מצוה היא לקדש את השם או לא?

LANGUAGE

קְוואקֵי וְדִימוֹנִיקֵי Braziers. The origin of these words is not clear. Some authorities believe they are Persian, while others derive קְוואקֵי from the Greek καυκιον, *kaukion*, meaning "a small cup."

אַסְפַּסְתָּא Grass. This word derives from the Persian *aspast*, meaning "fodder for horses."

LANGUAGE (RASHI)

לו"ד אפרטנמנ"ט* Apparently it should be written לו"ר אפרטנמנ"ץ, the Old French *lor apartenemanz*, meaning, "belonging to them."

NOTES

and engage in an act of prohibited sexual intercourse, or else be killed, she is obligated to choose death, for then she is regarded as an active participant in the transgression (*Rabbi Yehonatan, Meiri*).

בֶּן נֹחַ מְצוּוֶּה עַל קְדוּשַּׁת הַשֵּׁם? Is a non-Jew commanded about the sanctification of God's Name? *Tosafot* asked: What reason is there to say that a non-Jew should be permitted to transgress one of the Noachide laws rather than be killed? *Minḥat Ḥinnukh* suggests that we learn that one may violate a prohibition rather than suffer death from the verse that states (Leviticus 18:5): "You shall therefore keep My statutes, and My judgments, which if a man [הָאָדָם] do, he shall live in them," and the term "a man [הָאָדָם]" includes non-Jews. Moreover, the rule that one may violate a prohibition rather than suffer death is based on the notion that it is preferable to violate the prohibition now, so that one may be able to fulfill many more commandments in the future, and that argument applies to non-Jews as well (see *Margoliyot HaYam*).

HALAKHAH

בֶּן נֹחַ אֵין מְצוּוֶּה עַל קְדוּשַּׁת הַשֵּׁם A non-Jew is not commanded about the sanctification of God's Name. "If a non-Jew is coerced to violate one of the Noachide laws, even if he was being forced to commit idolatry, he may commit the transgression rather than suffer death, for he is not obligated to sanctify God's Name." (*Rambam* understands that this is the Gemara's conclusion, but it would appear from *Tosafot* that the matter remains unresolved.) (*Rambam, Sefer Shofetim, Hilkhot Melakhim* 10:2.)

[1]אָמַר אַבַּיֵי: תָּא שְׁמַע: [2]"שֶׁבַע מִצְוֹת נִצְטַוּוּ בְּנֵי נֹחַ". [3]וְאִם אִיתָא, תְּמָנֵי הָוְיָין!
[4]אֲמַר לֵיהּ רָבָא: [5]אִינְהוּ וְכָל אַבְזָרַיְיהוּ.
[6]מַאי הָוֵי עֲלָהּ? [7]אָמַר רַב אַדָּא בַּר אַהֲבָה, אָמְרִי בֵּי רַב: [8]כְּתִיב: "לַדָּבָר הַזֶּה יִסְלַח ה' לְעַבְדֶּךָ בְּבוֹא אֲדֹנִי בֵית רִמּוֹן לְהִשְׁתַּחֲוֹת שָׁמָּה וְהוּא נִשְׁעָן עַל יָדִי וְהִשְׁתַּחֲוֵיתִי". [9]וּכְתִיב: "וַיֹּאמֶר, לוֹ לֵךְ לְשָׁלוֹם". [75A] [10]וְאִם אִיתָא, לָא לֵימָא לֵיהּ! [11]הָא, בִּצְנְעָה; [12]הָא, בְּפַרְהֶסְיָא.

LITERAL TRANSLATION

[1]Abaye said: Come [and] hear: [2]"Non-Jews were commanded [to obey] seven commandments." [3]And if there is, there are eight!

[4]Rava said to him: [5]They and all that appertains to them.

[6]What was there about it? [7]Rav Adda bar Ahavah said that they said in the School of Rav: [8]It is written: "In this thing the Lord pardon Your servant, that when my master goes into the house of Rimmon to bow down there, and he leans on my hand, and I bow myself." [9]And it is written: "And he said to him, Go in peace." [75A] [10]And if there is, he should not say to him!

[11]This, in private; [12]this, in public.

TRANSLATION AND COMMENTARY

אָמַר אַבַּיֵי [1]**Abaye said: Come and hear** what was taught in a Baraita: [2]**"Non-Jews were given seven commandments** that apply universally to all men." [3]Now, **if** a non-Jew **is** also required to sanctify God's name, and choose death rather than violate a commandment that it is incumbent upon him to fulfill, the Baraita should have stated that **there are eight** Noachide laws!

אֲמַר לֵיהּ [4]**Rava said to** Abaye: That Baraita does not prove anything, for when it states that non-Jews were given seven commandments, [5]it was referring to the commandments **themselves and all that appertains to them.** The obligation to choose death rather than commit idolatry, is included in the Noachide law forbidding idolatry.

מַאי הָוֵי עֲלָהּ [6]Since the issue was not resolved, the Gemara asks: **What is the** final Halakhic **ruling** on this matter? [7]**Rav Ada bar Ahavah said that they said in the School of Rav:** After Naaman the Aramean resolved to stop practicing idolatry, he asked to be forgiven for bowing down before an idol under duress, [8]as **the verse states** (II Kings 5:18): **"In this thing the Lord pardon Your servant, that when my master goes into the house of Rimmon to bow down there, and he leans on my hand, and I bow myself."** [9]And the Prophet Elisha answered him (II Kings 5:19): **"And he said to him, Go in peace."** [75A] [10]Now, **if** a non-Jew **is** also required to sanctify God's name, and choose death rather than violate a commandment, Elisha **should not have said to him,** "Go in peace," implying that he sanctioned his conduct.

הָא [11]The Gemara rejects this argument: The incident involving Naaman does not prove anything, for Naaman violated the prohibition against idolatry **in private.** Ten Jews were not present in Rimmon's home when he bowed down before the idol. Even if a non-Jew is required to sanctify God's name and suffer death rather than violate one of the Noachide laws, [12]this applies only when he was coerced to commit the transgression **in public** in the presence of ten Jews. Thus, the question posed to Rabbi Ammi remains unresolved.

RASHI

אבזרייהו — כל מידי דשייך בהו קדושת השם שייכא בהו, דאם אומר לו לעבור על אותן מצות או יהרג ואם לא יקדש את השם יעבור עליהם, הלכך האי נמי בכללן הוא. **אבזרייהו** — לוד אפרטנמנ"ט*, ודוגמתו במנחות (עג,ב) עולה וכל אביזרהא. **לדבר הזה** — מאחר שקבל עליו נעמן שלא לעבוד עבודה זרה אמר לו לאלישע "לדבר הזה יסלח ה' לעבדך" שאני אנוס בדבר שאדוני נשען על ידי, וכתיב "ויאמר לו לך לשלום" — אלמא הודה לו. **ואם איתא** — דבן נח מוזהר על קדושת השם לא נימא ליה "לך לשלום", דמשמע דהודה לו, נהי דלהוכיחו לא היה מצווה ד"הוכח תוכיח את עמיתך" כתיב (ויקרא יט) ולא גר תושב, מיהו אודויי לדבר איסור לא לודוי. **בצנעה** — נעמן בצנעה הוה ולא היו ישראל בבית רמון שהוא משתחוה לשם, וגבי קדושת השם "בתוך בני ישראל" כתיב, ואפילו נצטוו בני נח עליה לא נצטוו לקדשו בתוך הנכרים אלא בתוך ישראל.

LANGUAGE

אַבְזָרַיְיהוּ Appertains. This word is derived from the Persian *afzar* or *awzar*, the basic meaning of which was an auxilliary utensil, a utensil used in conjunction with some other utensil.

NOTES

וְאִם אִיתָא And if there is. Our commentary follows the reading and explanation of *Rashi,* according to which the question posed to Rabbi Ammi remains unresolved. *Tosafot* had the reading: "And if there is, he should have said to him: This, in private; this in public," according to which the Gemara concludes that a non-Jew is not required to suffer death rather than violate one of the Noachide laws. So, too, the Jerusalem Talmud concludes that a non-Jew is not bound by the obligation to sanctify God's name (see *Ramah*).

בִּצְנְעָה In private. The objection has been made: Surely, idol worship is one of the three severe prohibitions regarding which one must die rather than commit the transgression even in private! *Ramban* answers that since the obligation to choose death rather than commit idolatry even in private is derived from the verse (Deuteronomy 6:5): "And you shall love the Lord your God with all your heart, and with all your soul, and with all your might," that obligation is limited to Jews.

בְּפַרְהֶסְיָא In public. *Ran* argues that we see from here that even though "in public" usually means in the presence of ten Jews, regarding idol worship, since non-Jews are also bound by the prohibition, an act of idolatry committed in the presence of ten non-Jews who observe the prohibition is also considered a public act.

BACKGROUND

הֶעֱלָה לִיבּוֹ טִינָא **His heart was seized with passion.** Ancient medical books such as that of Galen describe love-sickness, and these guided the action of the physicians referred to here.

TRANSLATION AND COMMENTARY

אָמַר רַב יְהוּדָה [1]Having mentioned the obligation to die rather than engage in prohibited sexual relations, the Gemara continues: **Rav Yehudah said in the name of Rav: It once happened that a certain man set his eyes on a certain woman,** and he fell madly in love with in her. [2]**His heart was seized with** such vehement **passion** that he became dangerously ill. [3]**Doctors were consulted and they said: "Nothing will help** the man **until** the woman of his desire allows him to **have sexual intercourse with her."** [4]**The Sages** were then asked for their opinion, and they **said: "Let** the man **die, but** the woman **must not** allow him to **have sexual intercourse with her."** The doctors suggested a compromise: [5]"Then **let her** at least **stand naked before him."** The Sages rejected that idea as well: [6]**"Let** the man **die, but** the woman **must not stand naked before him."** The doctors made a third proposal: [7]"Then **let her** at least **speak with him** while they are alone together **behind the fence."** [8]The Sages insisted: **"Let** the man **die, but** the woman **must not speak with him** while they are alone together **behind the fence."**

פְּלִיגִי בָהּ [9]**Rabbi Ya'akov bar Idi and Rabbi Shmuel bar Naḥmani disagreed.** [10]**One** of the Amoraim **said** that the desired woman **was a married woman.** [11]**The other** Amora **said** that **she was an unmarried woman.**

בִּשְׁלָמָא [12]The Gemara considers these two opinions: **Granted that, according to the** authority **who said that the woman was married,** we **can** understand why the Sages prohibited any intimacy between her and the ailing man, for sexual relations with another man's wife are severely prohibited and punishable by death. [13]**But according to the** authority **who said that the woman was not married, why** did the Sages say **all this,** that the man must die rather be intimate with the woman? She is not forbidden to him!

רַב פַּפָּא [14]**Rav Pappa said:** The Sages forbade the woman from even talking to the man while they were alone together behind a fence, **because** such scandalous behavior would place **a blemish on her** entire **family.**

רַב אַחָא [15]**Rav Aḥa the son of Rav Ika said:** The Sages forbade the woman from engaging in any type of intimacy with the man, **so that the daughters of Israel not act unchastely in sexual matters.**

[1]אָמַר רַב יְהוּדָה אָמַר רַב: מַעֲשֶׂה בְּאָדָם אֶחָד שֶׁנָּתַן עֵינָיו בְּאִשָּׁה אַחַת, [2]וְהֶעֱלָה לִבּוֹ טִינָא. [3]וּבָאוּ וְשָׁאֲלוּ לְרוֹפְאִים, וְאָמְרוּ: "אֵין לוֹ תַּקָּנָה עַד שֶׁתִּבָּעֵל". [4]אָמְרוּ חֲכָמִים: "יָמוּת, וְאַל תִּבָּעֵל לוֹ". [5]"תַּעֲמוֹד לְפָנָיו עֲרוּמָּה"? [6]"יָמוּת וְאַל תַּעֲמוֹד לְפָנָיו עֲרוּמָּה". [7]"תְּסַפֵּר עִמּוֹ מֵאֲחוֹרֵי הַגָּדֵר"? [8]יָמוּת וְלֹא תְּסַפֵּר עִמּוֹ מֵאֲחוֹרֵי הַגָּדֵר.

[9]פְּלִיגִי בָּהּ רַבִּי יַעֲקֹב בַּר אִידִי וְרַבִּי שְׁמוּאֵל בַּר נַחְמָנִי. [10]חַד אָמַר: אֵשֶׁת אִישׁ הָיְתָה, [11]וְחַד אָמַר: פְּנוּיָה הָיְתָה.

[12]בִּשְׁלָמָא לְמַאן דְּאָמַר אֵשֶׁת אִישׁ הָיְתָה — שַׁפִּיר. [13]אֶלָּא לְמַאן דְּאָמַר פְּנוּיָה הָיְתָה מַאי כּוּלֵּי הַאי?

[14]רַב פַּפָּא אָמַר: מִשּׁוּם פְּגַם מִשְׁפָּחָה.

[15]רַב אַחָא בְּרֵיהּ דְּרַב אִיקָא אָמַר: כְּדֵי שֶׁלֹּא יְהוּ בְּנוֹת יִשְׂרָאֵל פְּרוּצוֹת בַּעֲרָיוֹת.

LITERAL TRANSLATION

[1]Rav Yehudah said in the name of Rav: It once happened that a certain man set his eyes on a certain woman, [2]and his heart was seized with passion. [3]They came and asked the doctors, and they said: "He will have no remedy until she has sexual intercourse with him." [4]The Sages said: "Let him die, but she must not have sexual intercourse with him." [5]"Let her stand naked before him?" [6]"Let him die, but she must not stand naked before him." [7]"Let her speak with him behind the fence?" [8]"Let him die, but she must not speak with him behind the fence."

[9]Rabbi Ya'akov bar Idi and Rabbi Shmuel bar Naḥmani disagreed. [10]One said: She was a married woman. [11]And one said: She was an unmarried woman.

[12]Granted, according to the one who said [that] she was a married woman — it is well. [13]But according to the one who said [that] she was an unmarried woman, why all this?

[14]Rav Pappa said: Because of the blemish to the family.

[15]Rav Aḥa the son of Rav Ika said: So that the daughters of Israel not be unchaste regarding sexual matters.

RASHI

העלה לבו טינא — נימוק, מרוב אהבה נטמטם לבו והעלה חולי. **משום פגם משפחה** — האשה שהיו בושין בדבר. **שלא יהו בנות ישראל פרוצות בעריות** — לעמוד בפני האנשים לתת בהם עיניהם וימסרום להם לביאה.

HALAKHAH

מַעֲשֶׂה בְּאָדָם אֶחָד שֶׁנָּתַן עֵינָיו בְּאִשָּׁה אַחַת **It once happened that a certain man set his eyes on a certain woman.** "If a man set his eyes on a certain woman, and he fell mortally ill, and the doctors said that his only hope for recovery was to engage in sexual intercourse with that woman, he must suffer death rather than engage in sexual

TRANSLATION AND COMMENTARY

וְלִינְסְבָהּ מִינְסָב [1]The Gemara objects: **But** if the woman was not married, the love-sick man **should have married her!**

לָא [2]The Gemara answers: If he had married her, **his mind would not have been set at ease, because of** what **Rabbi Yitzhak** said, [3]**for Rabbi Yitzhak said: From the day that the Temple was destroyed, the taste** and enjoyment **of** marital **intercourse was taken** away **and given to those who engage in sinful acts** of intercourse, [4]**as the verse states** (Proverbs 9:17): **"Stolen waters are sweet, and bread eaten in secret is pleasant."**

LITERAL TRANSLATION

[1]But let him marry her!

[2]His mind would not have been set at ease, in accordance with Rabbi Yitzhak, [3]for Rabbi Yitzhak said: From the day that the Temple was destroyed, the taste of intercourse was taken and given to those who commit transgressions, [4]as it is stated: "Stolen waters are sweet, and bread eaten in secret is pleasant."

[1]וְלִינְסְבָהּ מִינְסָב! [2]לָא מִיַּיתְבָה דַּעְתֵּיהּ, כְּדְרַבִּי יִצְחָק, [3]דְּאָמַר רַבִּי יִצְחָק: מִיּוֹם שֶׁחָרַב בֵּית הַמִּקְדָּשׁ נִיטְּלָה טַעַם בִּיאָה וְנִיתְּנָה לְעוֹבְרֵי עֲבֵירָה, [4]שֶׁנֶּאֱמַר: "מַיִם גְּנוּבִים יִמְתָּקוּ וְלֶחֶם סְתָרִים יִנְעָם".

הדרן עלך בן סורר ומורה

RASHI

ולינסבה מינסב – דאין כאן פרוצות בעריות, דכולהו ליעבדן הכי ולינסבן ואין כאן עבירה אלא מצוה. **לא מיתבא דעתיה** – ולא ירפא בכך. **מיום שחרב בית המקדש** – כשל הכח מדאגות רבות ואין רוח קמה באיש להיות תאב לאשתו, לפיכך ניטל טעם ביאה. **וניתן לעוברי עבירה** – שיצר הרע תוקפן ומרבה תאותן. **דכתיב ולחם סתרים ינעם** – לישנא מעליא נקט כמו "כי אם הלחם אשר הוא אוכל" (בראשית לט).

הדרן עלך בן סורר ומורה

NOTES

מִיּוֹם שֶׁחָרַב בֵּית הַמִּקְדָּשׁ **From the day that the Temple was destroyed.** *Rashi* writes that the joy of permitted sexual intercourse diminished after the Temple was destroyed. Worries and anxiety destroyed sexual desire. Others explain that this is one of the divine punishments that accompanied the destruction of the Temple (*Ramah;* see *Maharsha*). *Talmidei Rabbenu Peretz* suggest that the enjoyment of sexual intercourse in the context of marriage diminished after the Temple was destroyed because the sacrifices brought by a woman after childbirth could no longer be offered.

HALAKHAH

intercourse with her, even if she was not married. We may not even tell the man that he may speak with the woman while they are alone together behind a fence, lest this lead to licentiousness among Jewish women." (*Rambam, Sefer Mada, Hilkhot Yesodei HaTorah* 5:9.)

Conclusion to Chapter Eight

An ancient Rabbinical tradition, both in the Mishnah and in the teachings of the Amoraim, interpret the verses concerning the disobedient and rebellious son in the most literal fashion, and, consequently, as restrictively as possible. Thus the possibility that a disobedient and rebellious son could actually be prosecuted is extremely slim. The Sages summarized the discussion by saying, "There has never been a disobedient and rebellious son, and there will never be one. And why was it written? — interpret and receive the reward" (*Sanhedrin* 71a). Indeed, the age of the disobedient and rebellious son is limited, and an extremely short time (three months) is set during which the entire affair must take place: the disobedient and rebellious son is executed only after he has stolen from his father and mother, been caught and flogged by a court, and has repeated his transgression. Moreover, the things that he must eat and drink gluttonously are extremely specific. All of these limitations, in addition to the psychological difficulty of bringing him to trial, make the law governing the disobedient and rebellious son solely theoretical.

However, investigation of the matter is meaningful and has its reward, for it provides instruction concerning education and other areas. Regarding education, it constitutes a very severe injunction against excessive forgiveness, which leads to the son's utter downfall, such that he cannot reform, and which brings disaster upon the entire society. Generally speaking, this law has other ramifications: a Halakhic basis is provided for instances in which one may harm or even kill someone not necessarily as punishment for a sin that he has committed, but to prevent him from committing an intended sin.

Thus the law of the disobedient and rebellious son provides a general ethical lesson regarding the importance of preventing the possibility for transgression, and therefore it is connected to the law governing a burglar who comes in secret. For he, too, like the disobedient and rebellious son, is not killed for a sin that he has committed by stealing, but rather because of the serious suspicion that he will commit murder. Hence we have a general rule, which is not explicitly stated in the Torah, but only alluded to: someone pursued by people who intend to kill him, or of a girl who is about to be raped may be saved by killing the pursuer. Thus, the greater and more self-evident the danger of the effort to commit the crime, the more the need to act and prevent it is emphasized. In the matter of a disobedient and rebellious son, only his parents may initiate the prosecution, but the process of judgment and punishment are the province of the court. However, in laws concerning a burglar who enters in secret, and more so regarding a pursuer, the court does not intervene in the matter. Rather judgment is passed by the community itself, by the people who will be injured (the householder), or by the person who wishes to defend the victim of pursuit and save him from his pursuers.

The relative importance of the various commandments is discussed regarding some of the problems in principle discussed in this chapter. From the question of which transgressions the public has the right to intervene and forestall a straight line of thought leads to the clarification of other questions such as which commandments must a person die rather than violate? Indeed, in this chapter the Halakhic principle is stated that a person is permitted (and some say, even commanded) to violate most commandments for the purpose of saving life, either for medical reasons or because of coercion. Three are, however, three severe exceptions: idolatry, forbidden sexual relations, and bloodshed. All of these apply when the act is ordered by an individual. However, when laws of religious persecution have been passed, the purpose of which is to prevent the Jews from observing the Torah, a Jew must die rather than disobeying any commandment, even if it is merely a rabbinical ordinance or a Jewish custom.

Introduction to Chapter Nine

וְאֵלּוּ הֵן הַנִּשְׂרָפִין

"You shall not uncover the nakedness of a woman and her daughter, neither shall you take her son's daughter or her daughter's daughter to uncover her nakedness; for they are her near kinswomen; it is wickedness." (Leviticus 18:17.)

"The nakedness of your son's daughter, or of your daughter's daughter, even their nakedness you shall not uncover: for theirs is your own nakedness." (Leviticus 18:10.)

"And if he smite him with an instrument of iron so that he die, he is a murderer: the murderer shall surely be put to death. And if he smite him with a stone in the hand, wherewith he may die, and he die, he is a murderer: the murderer shall surely be put to death. Or if he smite him with a hand weapon of wood, wherewith he may die, he is a murderer: the murderer shall surely be put to death. The avenger of blood himself shall slay the murderer: when he meet him, he shall slay him. So, too, if he thrust him in hate or hurled something at him on purpose, that he die; or in enmity smite him with his hand, that he die: he that smote him shall surely he put to death; for he is a murderer: the avenger of blood shall slay the murderer, when he meet him." (Numbers 35:16-21.)

"And if men strive together, and one smite another with a stone, or with his fist, and he does not die, but keep his bed: if he rise again, and walks abroad on his staff, then shall he that smote him be quit: except that he shall pay for the loss of his time, and shall cause him to be thoroughly healed." (Exodus 21:18-19.)

"So shall you put away the guilt of innocent blood from among you, when you shall do that which is right in the sight of the Lord." (Deuteronomy 21:9.)

Continuing the discussion of earlier chapters, this one discusses serious transgressions, in order of their gravity, for which one is executed by burning or by decapitation.

Those punishable by decapitation are the murderer and the residents of a city that has been incited to idol worship. The laws regarding such a city are mainly discussed in the last chapter of this tractate, and the laws here refer mainly to murderers. These severe laws are elaborated in part here in this chapter and in part in tractate *Makkot*.

The Torah states that if someone kills another person without premeditation, only by criminal negligence, he is sentenced to exile. Only premeditated murder is punishable by death. On this matter a great many practical problems arise, with which all systems of criminal in the world must deal, in defining murder caused by direct action, indirectly causing death, and so on.

The example given in the Torah, describing a man who attacks his fellow intentionally and with animosity and wounds him mortally is an extreme and simple one. In reality things take place in many and various ways, and not all of the aspects described in the Torah are evident and clear in every instance. First, it must be clarified how one determines that a certain blow was indeed an act of murder, for the evil intention of the killer is not sufficient, and it must be known whether indeed there was a reasonable possibility of killing a person with such a blow.

Another problem relates to the relation between killing by direct action and indirectly causing death. The boundary between the two is not always clear, and it must be decided when a person's action is to be viewed as an act of murder and when it is regarded as an indirect cause of death, for which the killer is not punished as severely as a murderer. Another question is, how one determines the necessary connection between the act of the killer and its result: whether the death of the injured person was the direct outcome of the act of the accused or whether the victim died for another reason, which is not connected with the action of the person who struck him.

As we have seen in earlier chapters, the laws of evidence, interrogation of the witnesses, and the legal procedures in the court mean that only very rarely is it possible to sentence someone to death for a transgression he has committed. Therefore, there is a need to protect society from criminals who cannot be punished for some formal reason, and this chapter discusses the administrative and other means of punishment available to the court, which were meant to protect society and the general public from criminals. The details of such punishment, as well as the discussion of transgressions which are punished in unusual ways are discussed at length in this chapter.

TRANSLATION AND COMMENTARY

MISHNAH **וְאֵלּוּ** [1]The two previous chapters of tractate *Sanhedrin* discussed offenses that are punishable by stoning. This chapter opens with a discussion of offenses punishable by burning. **These are** the transgressors **who are liable to** be punished by **burning:** [2]**A man who has** sexual **intercourse with a woman and her daughter,** as the verse states (Leviticus 20:14): "And if a man takes a woman and her mother, it is wickedness; they shall be burnt with fire, both he and they, that there be no wickedness among you"; [3]**and the daughter of a priest who commits adultery,** as the verse states (Leviticus 21:9): "And the daughter of any priest, if she profanes herself by playing the harlot, she profanes her father; she shall be burnt with fire." [4]The penalty of burning that is imposed upon a person who has intercourse with **a woman and her daughter** is stated explicitly in the Torah, and is extended by a *gezerah shavah* to **include** the following offenders: Someone who has intercourse with **his daughter,** [5]or **his daughter's daughter,** [6]or **his son's daughter,** even if he was never married to his daughter's or his son's mother; [7]someone who has intercourse with **his wife's daughter,** [8]or **her daughter's daughter,** [9]or **her son's daughter,** even if his wife's daughter or son were from another man; [10]and someone who has intercourse with **his mother-in-law,** [11]or **his mother-in-law's mother,** [12]or **his father-in-law's mother.**

GEMARA **הַבָּא** [13]The Gemara notes that the Mishnah **does not state: A man who has** sexual **intercourse with a woman whose daughter he had married.** That formulation would have implied that the man is liable to death by burning for having intercourse with his mother-in-law. [14]**Rather,** the Mishnah **states: "A man who has intercourse with a**

וְאֵלּוּ

[1]הֵן הַנִּשְׂרָפִין: [2]הַבָּא עַל אִשָּׁה וּבִתָּהּ, [3]וּבַת כֹּהֵן שֶׁזָּנְתָה. [4]יֵשׁ בִּכְלָל אִשָּׁה וּבִתָּהּ בִּתּוֹ, [5]וּבַת בִּתּוֹ, [6]וּבַת בְּנוֹ, [7]וּבַת אִשְׁתּוֹ, [8]וּבַת בִּתָּהּ, [9]וּבַת בְּנָהּ, [10]חֲמוֹתוֹ, [11]וְאֵם חֲמוֹתוֹ, [12]וְאֵם חָמִיו.

גמרא [13]הַבָּא עַל אִשָּׁה שֶׁנָּשָׂא בִּתָּהּ — לָא קָתָנֵי. [14]אֶלָּא: ״הַבָּא עַל אִשָּׁה וּבִתָּהּ״,

LITERAL TRANSLATION

MISHNAH [1]These are those who are burned: [2]Someone who has intercourse with a woman and her daughter, [3]and the daughter of a priest who commits adultery. [4]Included under "a woman and her daughter" are his daughter, [5]and his daughter's daughter, [6]and his son's daughter, [7]and his wife's daughter, [8]and her daughter's daughter, [9]and her son's daughter, [10]his mother-in-law, [11]and his mother-in-law's mother, [12]and his father-in-law's mother.

GEMARA [13]It does not teach: Someone who has intercourse with a woman whose daughter he married. [14]Rather, [it teaches]: "Someone who has intercourse with a woman and her daughter,"

RASHI

משנה אלו הן הנשרפין הבא על אשה ובתה — בגמרא מפרש לה. ובת כהן — כלומר וכן בת כהן שזינתה היא בשריפה, אבל בועלה לאו בשריפה הוא. יש בכלל אשה ובתה — כלומר אשה ובתה כתיבי בהדיא, כדמפרש בגמרא דהאי אשה ובתה היינו חמותו דשריפה כתיבא בה, כדכתיב (ויקרא כ): (כי יקח איש) את אשה ואת אמה זמה היא באש ישרפו אותו ואתהן. ויש בכללן — כלומר מינייהו ילפינן כולהו הנך בגזירה שוה, כדלקמן בברייתא. בתו — מאנוסתו, דלאו בת אשתו דנחייב עליה משום בת אשתו, דהא אנוסה לאו אשתו היא. בת בתו ובת בנו — שהיה לו מאנוסתו. בת אשתו — בין שהיא בתו בין שהיא חורגתו.

גמרא הבא על האשה שנשא בתה לא קתני — כלומר, מכדי מדקתני סיפא יש בכלל וכו׳ מכלל דהאי אשה ובתה בהנך דכתיבן מיירי, ולאו באשתו ובבת אשתו קאמר, אלא בחמותו — דשריפה כתיב בה, והא הבא על האשה דקתני לאו באשתו הוא — דאם כן הבא על האשה ואמה מבעי ליה למתניה, ואי נמי הך אשה אחמותו קאמר — הוה ליה למתנייה הבא על האשה שנשא בתה דהיינו חמותו, הא לא קתני אלא הבא על אשה ובתה — מכלל דתרוייהו לאיסורא, ולא הוזכרה אשתו לכאן ומאן ניהו — חמותו ואם חמותו, והכי קאמר: הבא על אם חמותו או על בתה דהיינו חמותו, וקתני יש בכלל אשה ובתה כולהו הנך, אלמא הך אשה ובתה כתיבי בהדיא.

NOTES

הַבָּא עַל אִשָּׁה וּבִתָּהּ A man who has intercourse with a woman and her daughter. It may be asked: The Torah mentions the punishment of death by burning in connection with a man who has intercourse with his mother-in-law, as the verse states (Leviticus 20:14): "And if a man takes a woman and her mother, it is wickedness; they shall be burnt with fire, both he and they." Why, then, does the Mishnah not read: "A man who has intercourse with a woman and her *mother*"? *Ran* explains that the Mishnah should be understood in accordance with Rava's explanation in the Gemara: A man who has intercourse with a woman whose daughter he has married, his mother-in-law.

HALAKHAH

וְאֵלּוּ הֵן הַנִּשְׂרָפִין These are those who are burned. "A man who has sexual intercourse with his wife's daughter, granddaughter, mother, or grandmother, or with his own daughter or granddaughter, and the daughter of a priest who commits adultery are liable to death by stoning," following the Mishnah. (*Rambam, Sefer Kedushah, Hilkhot Issurei Bi'ah* 1:5; *Sefer Shofetim, Hilkhot Sanhedrin* 15:11.)

[1]מִכְּלָל דְּתַרְוַיְיהוּ לְאִיסּוּרָא. [2]וּמַאן נִינְהוּ? [3]חֲמוֹתוֹ, וְאֵם חֲמוֹתוֹ. [4]וְקָתָנֵי: "יֵשׁ בִּכְלָל אִשָּׁה וּבִתָּהּ", [5]מִכְּלָל דְּתַרְוַיְיהוּ כְּתִיבִי בְּהֶדְיָא, [6]וְהָנָךְ מִדְּרָשָׁא אָתְיָא. [7]הָנִיחָא לְאַבַּיֵי דְּאָמַר: [8]מַשְׁמָעוּת דּוֹרְשִׁין אִיכָּא בֵּינַיְיהוּ. [9]מַתְנִיתִין מַנִּי? [10]רַבִּי עֲקִיבָא הִיא. [11]אֶלָּא לְרָבָא דְּאָמַר: [12]חֲמוֹתוֹ לְאַחַר מִיתָה אִיכָּא בֵּינַיְיהוּ, [13]מַתְנִיתִין מַנִּי? [14]אָמַר לָךְ רָבָא: [15]תְּנֵי: הַבָּא עַל אִשָּׁה שֶׁנָּשָׂא בִּתָּהּ. [16]"יֵשׁ בִּכְלָל אִשָּׁה וּבִתָּהּ

TRANSLATION AND COMMENTARY

woman and her daughter," [1]**implying that both** women **are forbidden** to him, and that intercourse with either of them is punishable by burning. [2]**And who are** these women? [3]**His mother-in-law and his mother-in-law's mother.** [4]**And** the continuation of the Mishnah **states:** "The penalty of burning that is imposed upon a man who has intercourse with **a woman and her daughter** is extended by a *gezerah shavah* to **include** the following offenders," [5]**implying that** the punishment imposed upon a man who has intercourse with one of **the two** women mentioned in the beginning of the Mishnah — his mother-in-law or his mother-in-law's mother — **is stated explicitly** in the Torah, [6]**and** the punishment imposed upon all **the other** offenders **is derived through interpretation** by a *gezerah shavah*. [7]Now, this interpretation of the Mishnah **is understandable according to Abaye, who said** [8]that the only difference **between** Rabbi Yishmael and Rabbi Akiva (whose views are recorded in the Baraita cited below, 76b) **is their way of interpreting the meaning** of the Biblical text (Leviticus 20:14): "They shall be burnt with fire, both he and they." According to Rabbi Yishmael, the verse itself refers only to the man's mother-in-law, and the punishment of burning that is imposed for intercourse with one's mother-in-law's mother is derived through interpretation by a *gezerah shavah.* Rabbi Akiva disagrees and says that the verse itself refers not only to the man's mother-in-law, but also to his mother-in-law's mother. [9]**In accordance with which** Tanna's view was **our Mishnah** taught? [10]**It was** taught in accordance with the view of **Rabbi Akiva** that the punishment of burning imposed upon a man who had intercourse with his mother-in-law's mother is stated explicitly in the Torah. [11]**But according to Rava, who said** that both Rabbi Yishmael and Rabbi Akiva agree that the punishment of burning that is imposed when a man has intercourse with his mother-in-law's mother is derived by a *gezerah shavah,* [12]and they **disagree** about an entirely different matter (whether or not the punishment of burning is imposed when the man had intercourse with **his mother-in-law after his wife's death**), there is a problem, [13]for **in accordance with which** Tanna's view **was our Mishnah** taught?

אָמַר לָךְ [14]The Gemara responds that **Rava can say to you** that the text of the Mishnah must be slightly emended. [15]**Teach** the Mishnah as follows: **Someone who has** sexual **intercourse with a woman whose daughter he had married.** For all agree that the penalty of burning imposed for that transgression is stated explicitly in the Torah.

יֵשׁ בִּכְלָל [16]We have learned in the Mishnah: "The penalty of burning for having intercourse with **a woman and her daughter** is stated explicitly in the Torah, and is extended by a *gezerah shavah* to **include** intercourse

LITERAL TRANSLATION

[1]implying that both of them are forbidden. [2]And who are they? [3]His mother-in-law, and his mother-in-law's mother. [4]And it teaches: "Included under a woman and her daughter," [5]implying that both of them are written explicitly, [6]and the others are derived through interpretation. [7]This is understandable according to Abaye, who said: [8][The only difference] between them is [their way of] interpreting the meaning [of the Biblical text]. [9]In accordance with whom is our Mishnah? [10]It is Rabbi Akiva. [11]But according to Rava, who said: [12]They disagree about his mother-in-law after [his wife's] death, [13]in accordance with whom is our Mishnah?

[14]Rava can say to you: [15]Teach: Someone who has intercourse with a woman whose daughter he married.

[16]"Included in a woman and her daughter are his mother-in-law,

RASHI

הניחא לאביי דאמר — בפירקין (סנהדרין עו,א) גבי פלוגתא דרבי ישמעאל ורבי עקיבא. משמעות דורשין איכא בינייהו — ומסיק למילתיה דלרבי עקיבא כתיבא בהדיא אם חמותו, מתניתין מני? — רבי עקיבא היא. אלא לרבא דאמר — בין לרבי ישמעאל בין לרבי עקיבא לא כתיבא, אלא בחמותו שבא עליה לאחר מיתת אשתו פליגי — מתניתין מני? אמר לך רבא תני על אשה שנשא בתה — דהיינו חמותו דכתיבא בהדיא "איש כי יקח את אשה" דהיינו אשתו, ואת אמה — דהיינו חמותו. יש בכלל אשה ובתה וכו׳ — קתני נמי חמותו ומילתא דתמיה היא, דההוא לאו מדרשא אתא וקתני בהדייהו.

CONCEPTS

מַשְׁמָעוּת דּוֹרְשִׁין אִיכָּא בֵּינַיְיהוּ **The difference between them is their way of interpreting the meaning of the Biblical text.** This expression has been interpreted in various ways. Some authorities maintain that it means there is really no Halakhic difference between the two interpretations, and that the Sages merely differ concerning the specific Biblical verse which should be taken as the source of this particular Halakhah, with one Sage citing one verse and the other Sage citing a different one.

However, other authorities maintain that although the difference between the two Halakhic Midrashim here may have no explicit effect on the Halakhah at present under discussion, nevertheless there is a potential difference regarding other Halakhot. Since each Sage used a different Biblical verse to prove his point, the verse that he did not cite remains available for further Halakhic Midrash. It is possible that one of these remaining sources may lead the Sages to different conclusions regarding other Halakhot.

NOTES

In the Mishnah, the word "woman" refers to the woman forbidden to the man, and "her daughter" refers to his lawful wife. But in the Torah, the word "woman" refers to his lawful wife, and "her mother" refers to the woman forbidden to him.

[1]חֲמוֹתוֹ וְאֵם חֲמוֹתוֹ, וְאֵם חָמִיו״. [2]לְאַבַּיֵי, אַיְּידֵי דְּקָא בָּעֵי לְמִיתְנָא ״אֵם חָמִיו״ — [3]תָּנֵי נַמִי ״חֲמוֹתוֹ וְאֵם חֲמוֹתוֹ״. [4]לְרָבָא, אַיְּידֵי דְּקָא בָּעֵי לְמִיתְנָא ״אֵם חָמִיו וְאֵם חֲמוֹתוֹ״, [5]תָּנֵי נַמִי ״חֲמוֹתוֹ״. [6]מְנָהָנֵי מִילֵּי? [7]דְּתָנוּ רַבָּנַן: ״׳אִישׁ אֲשֶׁר יִקַּח אֶת אִשָּׁה וְאֶת אִמָּהּ׳. [8]אֵין לִי אֶלָּא אִשָּׁה וְאִמָּהּ. [9]בַּת אִשָּׁה וּבַת בִּתָּהּ וּבַת בְּנָהּ מִנַּיִן? [10]נֶאֱמַר כָּאן: ׳זִמָּה׳, [11]וְנֶאֱמַר לְהַלָּן ׳זִמָּה׳. [12]מַה לְהַלָּן — בִּתָּהּ וּבַת בִּתָּהּ וּבַת בְּנָהּ, [13]אַף כָּאן — בִּתָּהּ וּבַת בִּתָּהּ וּבַת בְּנָהּ. [14]מִנַּיִן לַעֲשׂוֹת זְכָרִים כִּנְקֵבוֹת? [15]נֶאֱמַר כָּאן: ׳זִמָּה׳, [16]וְנֶאֱמַר לְהַלָּן: ׳זִמָּה׳. [17]מַה לְהַלָּן — זְכָרִים כִּנְקֵבוֹת, [18]אַף כָּאן — זְכָרִים כִּנְקֵבוֹת. [19]מִנַּיִן לַעֲשׂוֹת לְמַטָּה כִּלְמַעְלָה? [20]נֶאֱמַר כָּאן:

LITERAL TRANSLATION

[1]his mother-in-law's mother, and his father-in-law's mother." [2]According to Abaye, since it had to teach "his father-in-law's mother," [3]it taught also "his mother-in-law, and his mother-in-law's mother." [4]According to Rava, since it had to teach "his father-in-law's mother, and his mother-in-law's mother," [5]it taught also "his mother-in-law."

[6]From where are these things [derived]? [7]For our Rabbis taught: "'And if a man takes a woman and her mother.' [8]I have only a woman and her mother. [9]From where [do I know about] the woman's daughter, and her daughter's daughter, and her son's daughter? [10]It is stated here: 'Wickedness,' [11]and it is stated below: 'Wickedness.' [12]Just as below — her daughter, and her daughter's daughter, and her son's daughter, [13]so, too, here — her daughter, and her daughter's daughter, and her son's daughter. [14]From where [do I know] to make males like females? [15]It is stated here: 'Wickedness,' [16]and it is stated below: 'Wickedness.' [17]Just as below — males are like females, [18]so, too, here — males are like females. [19]From where [do I know] to make below like above? [20]It is stated here:

RASHI

לאביי – דאמר חמותו ואמה כתיבן בהדיא איידי דתנא בהאי כללא אם חמיו דאתיא מדרשא – נקט אגב ריהטא חמותו ואם חמותו. **אין לי אלא אשה ואמה** – דהיינו חמותו. **נאמר כאן** – בשריפה, ״זמה היא״. **ונאמר** – באזהרת בתה ובת בתה ובת בנה ״שארה הנה זמה היא״. **אף כאן** – לענין עונש שריפה בתה ובת בתה ובת בנה בהאי דינא דהאי קרא. **מנין לעשות זכרים כנקבות** – לקמן מפרש. **מנין לעשות למטה כלמעלה** – לקמן נמי מפרש.

TRANSLATION AND COMMENTARY

with other women, [1]including a man's **mother-in-law, his mother-in-law's mother, and his father-in-law's mother.**" Now, according to Abaye, the punishment of burning for intercourse with a man's mother-in-law or her mother is stated explicitly in the Torah, and according to Rava, the punishment of burning for intercourse with a man's mother-in-law is stated explicitly in the Torah. Why, then, are these women mentioned among the women whose penalty of burning is derived by way of interpretation? [2]**According to Abaye, since** the Mishnah **had to teach "his father-in-law's mother,"** for all agree that the penalty of burning imposed in that case is derived by a *gezerah shavah,* [3]**it taught also "his mother-in-law, and his mother-in-law's mother."** [4]And **according to Rava, since** the Mishnah **had to teach "his father-in-law's mother, and his mother-in-law's mother,"** for Rava maintains that the penalty of burning imposed in those two cases is derived by a *gezerah shavah,* [5]**it taught also "his mother-in-law."**

מְנָהָנֵי מִילֵּי [6]The Gemara asks: **From where are the laws** taught in our Mishnah **derived?** [7]The Gemara answers: As our **Rabbis taught** in a Baraita: "The verse states (Leviticus 20:14): **'And if a man takes a woman and her mother,** it is wickedness; they shall be burnt with fire, both he and they, that there be no wickedness among you.' [8]Had I only this verse, I **would only** know that the penalty of burning is imposed for intercourse with **a woman and her mother.** [9]**From where do I know** that the same punishment is imposed if he takes **the woman's daughter, or her daughter's daughter, or her son's daughter?** This is derived by a *gezerah shavah.* [10]**Here,** regarding the penalty of burning **the verse states:** 'It is **wickedness.**' [11]**And there,** regarding the prohibition against intercourse with one's wife's daughter or granddaughter, **the verse states** (Leviticus 18:17): 'You shall not uncover the nakedness of a woman and her daughter; neither shall you take her son's daughter, or her daughter's daughter, to uncover her nakedness, for they are her near kinswomen; it is **wickedness.**' [12]**Just as there,** the prohibition applies to a woman's **daughter, her daughter's daughter, and her son's daughter,** [13]**so, too, here,** the punishment of burning applies to a woman's **daughter, her daughter's daughter, and her son's daughter.** [14]**From where do I know that I can equate males with females** (as will be explained below)? [15]**Here, the verse states: 'Wickedness,'** [16]**and there, the verse states: 'Wickedness.'** [17]**Just as there, males are equated with females,** [18]**so, too, here, males are equated with females.** [19]**From where do I know to equate below with above?** [20]**Here,**

‏״זִמָּה״, ‏[1]וְנֶאֱמַר לְהַלָּן: ״זִמָּה״. ‏[2]מַה לְּהַלָּן — לְמַטָּה כִּלְמַעְלָה, ‏[3]אַף כָּאן — לְמַטָּה כִּלְמַעְלָה. ‏[4]וּמַה כָּאן — לְמַעְלָה כִּלְמַטָּה, ‏[5]אַף לְהַלָּן — לְמַעְלָה כִּלְמַטָּה.״

‏[6]אָמַר מָר: ״מִנַּיִן לַעֲשׂוֹת זְכָרִים כִּנְקֵבוֹת״? ‏[7]מַאי ״זְכָרִים כִּנְקֵבוֹת״? ‏[8]אִילֵימָא: בַּת בְּנָהּ כְּבַת בִּתָּהּ — ‏[9]בַּהֲדֵי הֲדָדֵי קָאָתְיָאן! ‏[10]אֶלָּא: אֵם חָמִיו כְּאֵם חֲמוֹתוֹ. ‏[11]הַשְׁתָּא, אֵם חֲמוֹתוֹ לֹא קָמָה לָן — ‏[12]אֵם חָמִיו מִיהֲדַר עֲלָהּ?

‏[75B] ‏[13]אָמַר אַבַּיֵי: הָכִי קָאָמַר: ‏[14]מִנַּיִן לַעֲשׂוֹת שְׁאֵר הַבָּא מִמֶּנּוּ כִּשְׁאֵר הַבָּא מִמֶּנָּה? ‏[15]נֶאֱמַר כָּאן: ״זִמָּה״ וְנֶאֱמַר לְהַלָּן ״זִמָּה״ וכו׳.

LITERAL TRANSLATION

'Wickedness,' [1]and it is stated below: 'Wickedness.' [2]Just as below — below is like above, [3]so, too, here — below is like above. [4]And just as below — above is like below, [5]so, too, here — above is like below."

[6]The master said: "From where [do I know] to make males like females?" [7]What is "males like females"? [8]If you say: Her son's daughter is like her daughter's daughter — [9]they are derived together! [10]Rather, his father-in-law's mother is like his mother-in-law's mother. [11]Now, we have not [yet] established his mother-in-law's mother — [12]should we go after his father-in-law's mother?

[75B] [13]Abaye said: He said as follows: [14]From where [do I know] to make relatives coming from him like relatives coming from her? [15]It is stated here: "Wickedness," and it is stated below: "Wickedness," etc.

TRANSLATION AND COMMENTARY

the verse states: 'Wickedness,' [1]**and there the verse states: 'Wickedness.'** [2]**Just as there — below is like above,** [3]**so, too, here — below is like above.** [4]**And just as there — above is like below,** [5]**so, too, here — above is like below."**

אָמַר מָר [6]The Gemara begins to explain this Baraita. **It was stated: "From where do I know to equate males with females?"** [7]The Gemara asks: **What** is the meaning of "equating **males with females**"? [8]**If you say** this means that the law applying to a man who has intercourse with **the daughter** of his wife's **son** (a male) **is equated with** the law applying to a man who has intercourse with **the daughter of her daughter** (a female), there is a difficulty, for the law applying to his wife's son's daughter and the law applying to her daughter's daughter [9]**are derived together** from the same verse by the same *gezerah shavah,* and so there is no need for any additional equation of the two laws. [10]**Rather,** the Baraita must mean that the law applying to a man who has intercourse with **the mother of his father-in-law** (a male) **is equated with** the law applying to someone who has intercourse with **the mother of his mother-in-law** (a female). [11]But this, too, poses a difficulty, for **we have not yet** even clearly **established that** the penalty of burning applies to a man who had intercourse with **his mother-in-law's mother.** [12]**How,** then, can **we go** on to extend that law so that the punishment of burning applies even to a man who had intercourse with **his father-in-law's mother?**

אָמַר אַבַּיֵי [75B] [13]**Abaye said:** When the Baraita speaks of "equating males with females," it refers to man and wife, and **it** means to **say as follows:** [14]**From where do I know to equate his relatives with her relatives,** that is to say, that the law applying to a man who has intercourse with his own daughter or granddaughter born to a woman or the son or daughter of a woman to whom he was not married, is equated with the law applying to a man who has intercourse with his wife's daughter or granddaughter by another man? This is derived by a *gezerah shavah*: [15]**Here the verse states: "Wickedness," and there the verse states: "Wickedness."** Just as a man is liable to the punishment of burning for having intercourse with his wife's daughter or granddaughter, so, too, is he liable to the punishment of burning for having intercourse with his own daughter or granddaughter.

RASHI

ומה כאן למעלה כלמטה אף להלן למעלה כלמטה — לקמן מפרש.
בהדי הדדי אתיין — הא רבינהו לתרוייהו בגזרה שוה דאתיא ״זמה״ ״זמה״. **אלא אם חמיו כאם חמותו** — השתא אם חמותו אכתי לא קמה לן, עדיין לא העמידה על בוריה בשריפה מן התורה, דהא האי תנא לפוס ריהטא שמעינן ליה דהאי אשה דקרא היינו אשתו, ואפילו למאן דאמר אם חמותו כתיבא, לאו ממשמעותא ד״את אשה ואמה״ נפקא ליה, אלא ממשמעותא ד״אותו ואתהן״. **אם חמיו קא מהדר עלה** — מחזר עליה להביאה לתורת אם חמותו דקאמר זכרים כנקבות? הא אכתי לא אשמעינן תנא אם חמותו! **אמר אביי** — האי זכרים ונקבות עליו ועל אשתו קאמר, והכי קאמר: מניין לעשות שאר הבא ממנו, דהיינו בתו ובת בנו ובת בתו מאנוסתו דלאו בכלל אשה ובתה דקרא נינהו, דהתם באשתו על ידי קידושין קאמר דדרשינן לה ביבמות [צו,א] מקראי, דרבה רמי כתיב ״ערות בת בנך או בת בתך וגו׳״ הא בת בנה ובת בתה שלא ילדה ממך — גלה, וכתיב ״ערות אשה ובתה לא תגלה״ משמע בין שילדתו לך בין שילדתו לאיש אחר! — לא קשיא, כאן באנוסין כאן בנישואין. אם אנוסתך או מפותה לך היא אי אתה מוזהר על בתה אלא אם כן ממך היא, ואם אשתך היא — אתה מוזהר אף על בת שילדה לאיש אחר. **בשאר הבא ממנה** — כבת אשתו ובת בתה ובת בנה דרבינן להו לעיל בגזירה שוה. **והא בשאר דידיה לא כתיב זמה** — דמהאי קרא נפקא לן בת בתו ובת בנו מאנוסתו ״ערות בת בנך או בת בתך״ כדפרישית לעיל, ובתו לקמן יליף לה ובההוא קרא זמה לא כתיב.

[1]וְהָא בִּשְׁאֵר דִּידֵיהּ לָא כְּתִיבָא בֵּיהּ ״זִמָּה״! [2]אָמַר רָבָא: אָמַר לִי רַב יִצְחָק בַּר אֲבוּדִימִי: [3]אָתְיָא ״הֵנָּה״ ״הֵנָּה״; [4]אָתְיָא ״זִמָּה״ ״זִמָּה״. [5]אָמַר מַר: ״מִנַּיִן לַעֲשׂוֹת לְמַטָּה כִּלְמַעְלָה״? [6]מַאי ״לְמַטָּה כִּלְמַעְלָה״? [7]אִילֵימָא: בַּת בְּנָהּ וּבַת בִּתָּהּ כְּבִתָּהּ — [8]בַּהֲדֵי הֲדָדֵי קָאָתְיָין! [9]אֶלָּא, אֵם חָמִיו וְאֵם חֲמוֹתוֹ כַּחֲמוֹתוֹ. [10]הַאי ״לְמַטָּה כִּלְמַעְלָה״? [11]״לְמַעְלָה כִּלְמַטָּה״ הֲוַאי! [12]תְּנֵי: ״לְמַעְלָה כִּלְמַטָּה״. [13]אִי הָכִי, ״נֶאֱמַר כָּאן: ׳זִמָּה׳, [14]וְנֶאֱמַר לְהַלָּן ׳זִמָּה׳״. [15]וּמָה הָשְׁתָּא אִינְהִי לָא כְּתִיבָא,

LITERAL TRANSLATION

[1]But surely regarding his relatives, "wickedness" is not written!

[2]Rava said: Rav Yitzhak bar Avudimi said to me: [3]"They" is learned from "they"; [4]"wickedness" is learned from "wickedness."

[5]The master said: "From where [do I know] to make below like above?" [6]What is "below like above"? [7]If you say: Her son's daughter and her daughter's daughter are like her daughter — [8]they are derived together! [9]Rather, his father-in-law's mother and his mother-in-law's mother are like his mother-in-law. [10]Is that "below like above"? [11]It is "above like below"!

[12]Teach: "Above like below."

[13]If so, "It is stated here: 'Wickedness,' [14]and it is stated below: 'Wickedness.'" [15]Now, if they are not written,

TRANSLATION AND COMMENTARY

וְהָא [1]The Gemara objects: **But surely regarding** a man who has intercourse with one of **his** own blood **relatives,** the word **"wickedness" is not used,** for regarding such a man, the verse states (Leviticus 18:10): "The nakedness of your son's daughter, or of your daughter's daughter, their nakedness you shall not uncover; for theirs is your own nakedness"! How, then, can a *gezerah shavah* be drawn between a man's relatives and his wife's relatives?

אָמַר רָבָא [2]**Rava said: Rav Yitzhak bar Avudimi said to me:** The law applying to a woman's relatives is extended to a man's relatives by way of a double *gezerah shavah.* [3]The significance of the word **"theirs** [*henah*]," found in connection with the man's relatives, **is learned from** the word **"they** [*henah*]," found in connection with the woman's relatives. Regarding the man's relatives, the verse states: "For theirs [*henah*] is your own nakedness," and regarding the woman's relatives, the verse states (Leviticus 18:17): "For they [*henah*] are her near kinswomen; it is wickedness." Just as intercourse with one's wife's relatives is called wickedness, so, too, is intercourse with one's own relatives called wickedness. [4]And the significance of the **"wickedness"** relating to a man who has intercourse with his own relatives **is learned from** the word **"wickedness"** found in the verse (Leviticus 20:14): "And if a man takes a woman and her mother, it is wickedness; they shall be burnt with fire, both he and they." Just as there, the wickedness is punished by burning, so, too, here, is the wickedness punished by burning.

אָמַר מַר [5]The Gemara now explains the next clause of the Baraita. **It was stated: "From where do I know to equate below with above?"** [6]The Gemara asks: **What** does the Baraita mean by "equating **below with above"**? [7]**If you say** this means that the law applying to a man who has intercourse with his wife's **son's daughter or her daughter's daughter** (the "lower" generation) **is equated with** the law applying to a man who has intercourse with his wife's **daughter** (the "higher" generation), there is a problem, [8]for the law applying to his wife's granddaughter and the law applying to her daughter **are derived together** from the same verse by the same *gezerah shavah,* and there is no need for any additional equation of the two laws. [9]**Rather,** the Baraita must mean that the law applying to a man who has intercourse with **his father-in-law's mother or his mother-in-law's mother is equated with** the law applying to a man who has intercourse with **his mother-in-law.** [10]But that, too, poses a problem, for **is that** an example of equating **"below with above"?** [11]**Surely, that is** equating **"above"** (the "higher" generation) **with "below"** (the "lower" generation)!

תְּנֵי [12]The Gemara answers that the text of the Mishnah must be slightly emended. **Teach** the Mishnah as follows: "From where do I know to equate **above with below?"**

אִי הָכִי [13]**If so,** there is a problem with the continuation of the Baraita, which states: **"Here the verse states: 'Wickedness,'** [14]**and there the verse states: 'Wickedness.'"** [15]**Now,** the law regarding a man's father-in-law's mother or his mother-in-law's mother **is not written** explicitly in the Torah, neither the prohibition nor

RASHI

אתיא הנה הנה אתיא זמה זמה — מעיקרא מייתינן לה ב״הנה״ ״הנה״ והדר ב״זמה״ ״זמה״. כתיב הכא (ויקרא יח) ״כי ערותך הנה״ וכתיב ״בשאר אשתו״ (שם) שארה הנה — מה להלן זמה עמו אף כאן זמה עמו. ובתר דאייתינן זמה לשאר דידיה, ילפינן בה שריפה ב״זמה״ ״זמה״: נאמר כאן (שם) זמה ונאמר להלן (שם כ) בשריפה, זמה, מה להלן שריפה אף כאן שריפה. **אילימא בת בנה ובת בתה** — שהן דורות תחתונים ואחרונים, כלמעלה, כלומר כבתה שהיא קדמה, והיינו עליונה. **למעלה כלמטה היא** — שהאבות לעולם עליונים נקראו, שהן קדמו. **השתא אינהו לא כתיבן** — אם חמיו ואם חמותו לאזהרתן ולעונשן לא כתיבא.

[1]זִמָּה דִּידְהוּ כְּתִיבָא?

[2]אָמַר אַבַּיֵי: הָכִי קָאָמַר: [3]מִנַּיִן לַעֲשׂוֹת שְׁלֹשָׁה דּוֹרוֹת לְמַעְלָה כִּשְׁלֹשָׁה דּוֹרוֹת לְמַטָּה? [4]נֶאֱמַר לְמַטָּה: "זִמָּה", [5]וְנֶאֱמַר לְמַעְלָה: "זִמָּה". [6]מַה לְמַטָּה שְׁלֹשָׁה דּוֹרוֹת. [7]אַף לְמַעְלָה שְׁלֹשָׁה דּוֹרוֹת. [8]וּמַה בְּעוֹנֶשׁ עָשָׂה לְמַטָּה כִּלְמַעְלָה, [9]אַף בְּאַזְהָרָה נַמִּי עָשָׂה לְמַעְלָה כִּלְמַטָּה.

[10]רַב אַשִׁי אָמַר: לְעוֹלָם, כִּדְקָתָנֵי. [11]וּמַאי "לְמַטָּה"? [12]לְמַטָּה בְּאִיסּוּר.

LITERAL TRANSLATION

[1]their "wickedness" is written?

[2]Abaye said: He said as follows: [3]From where [do I know] to make three generations above like three generations below? [4]Regarding below, it is stated: "Wickedness," [5]and regarding above, it is stated: "Wickedness." [6]Just as below three generations, [7]so, too, above three generations. [8]And just as regarding the punishment it made below like above, [9]so, too, regarding the warning it also made above like below.

[10]Rav Ashi said: In fact, as it is taught. [11]And what is "below"? [12]Inferior in prohibition.

TRANSLATION AND COMMENTARY

the punishment. [1]How, then, can it be that the word **"wickedness" is written** in their regard, so that a *gezerah shavah* can be drawn between them and the man's mother-in-law?

אָמַר אַבַּיֵי [2]**Abaye said:** The Baraita means to **say as follows:** [3]**From where do I know to equate three generations above** a man's wife, that is to say, his wife's father's mother, or his wife's mother's mother, **with three generations below,** that is to say, his wife's son's daughter, or her daughter's daughter? [4]**Regarding** the woman's generations **downward, the verse states** (Leviticus 18:17): "You shall not uncover the nakedness of a woman and her daughter; neither shall you take her son's daughter, or her daughter's daughter, to uncover her nakedness, for they are her near kinswomen; it is **wickedness.**" [5]**And regarding** her generations **upward, the verse states** (Leviticus 20:14): "And if a man takes a woman and her mother, it is **wickedness;** they shall be burnt with fire, both he and they." [6]**Just as downward,** the punishment of burning extends to **the third generation** — to his wife's granddaughter — [7]**so, too, upward,** the punishment of burning extends to **the third generation** — to his father-in-law's mother and his mother-in-law's mother. [8]**And just as regarding the punishment,** the woman's generations **downward** — her daughter and granddaughter, regarding whom the verse does not mention burning — **are equated** by the *gezerah shavah* to her generations **upward** — her mother, regarding whom the verse mentions burning, [9]**so, too, regarding the warning** that such sexual intercourse is forbidden, the woman's generations **upward** — her mother and grandmother, regarding whom there is no explicit warning — **are equated** by the *gezerah shavah* to her generations **downward** — her daughter and granddaughter, regarding whom the prohibition is stated explicitly.

רַב אַשִׁי [10]**Rav Ashi said: In fact,** the Baraita may be understood **as it was taught** without any emendation: "From where do I know to equate below with above?" [11]**And what is** the meaning here of the word **"below"?** [12]**Inferior in prohibition.** Intercourse with one's wife's more distant relative is a "lower" prohibition than intercourse with a closer relative of hers. The Baraita means to say as follows: From where do I know to equate the law applying to a man who has intercourse with his father-in-law's mother or with his mother-in-law's mother (a "lower" prohibition) with the law applying to a man who has intercourse with his mother-in-law (a "higher" prohibition)?

RASHI

זמה דידהו כתיבא — בתמיה דקאמר נאמר כאן זמה. **הכי קאמר** — לעולם אאם חמיו ואאם חמותו מהדר, ובהאי לד נקטיה לדרשה דידיה. **מנין לעשות למעלה** — מאשתו שלשה דורות לאיסור, דהיינו אם חמיו שהוא דור שלישי לאשתו, וכן אם חמותו. **בשלשה דורות למטה** — כמו שמלינו שהוזהר ונענש למטה הימנה שלשה דורות — דהיינו בת בתה וכן בת בנה. **נאמר למטה זמה** — "שארה הנה זמה היא". **ונאמר למעלה זמה** — דכתיב (שם) "כי יקח את אשה ואת אמה זמה היא". **מה למטה שלשה דורות אף למעלה שלשה דורות** — אתרבו בדינא דקרא. הרי למדנו לעונש ועדיין אזהרה לא שמענו בהם דהא זמה למעלה גבי עונש כתיב, והדר יליף מסקנא דברייתא מה בעונש עשה למטה בתה ובת בתה ובת בנה כלמעלה, בחמותו, דהא רבינן להו לעיל שריפה — אף באזהרה עשה למעלה חמותו ואם חמותו ואם חמיו שלא נאמר בהן אזהרה — כלמטה, כבתה ובת בתה ובת בנה, הרי למדנו לעונש (מאזהרה). [ולאזהרה] ולישנא דברייתא הכי קאמר: מנין לעשות למעלה מאשתו כלמטה מאשתו לענין שלשה דורות — נאמר למעלה מאשתו זמה ונאמר למטה מאשתו זמה, ועשה הכתוב למטה כלמעלה, בת בתה כבתה, אף למעלה מאשתו עשה למעלה כלמטה — עשה אם חמותו כחמותו, הרי למדנוס לעונש, ללמדס לאזהרה שאף חמותו עצמה לא — נאמר באזהרה מה בעונש למטה כלמעלה רבינן שאר של מטה הימנה לשריפה כשאר של מעלה ממנה — אף באזהרה עשה שאר של מעלה הימנה כשאר של מטה הימנה, ואף על גב דברייתא איפכא תני, אביי מפיך. **רב אשי אמר לעולם בדקתני** — דלא תצטריך לאפוכה ולמתני מה להלן למטה כלמעלה אף כאן למעלה כלמטה, אלא אף כאן למטה כלמעלה. ומאי למטה דקאמר — למטה באיסור, איסור הקל קרי למטה והחמור קרי למעלה, והכי קאמר: מנין לעשות אם חמיו ואם חמותו שהן רחוקות ואסורין למטה כחמותו שהיא קרובה ואיסורה עליון וחמור — נאמר כאן זמה [כו']. ורב אשי לא קשיא ליה הא דקשיא לן לעיל השתא אינהו לא כתיבי? זמה דידהו כתיבי דהאי נאמר כאן זמה לאו עלייהו קאי. אלא הכי נקט למילתיה:

TRANSLATION AND COMMENTARY

אִי [1]It was stated, above, that we learn by a *gezerah shavah* that the law applying to a man who has intercourse with one of his own blood relatives is equated with the law applying to a man who has intercourse with one of his wife's relatives. The Gemara now asks: Does it not follow from this that, **just as a man's wife's grandmother is forbidden** to him, [2]**so, too, is his** own **grandmother forbidden** to him? If so, then why is a man's grandmother included elsewhere among the incestuous relationships that are forbidden only by Rabbinic decree?

אָמַר אַבַּיֵי [3]**Abaye said:** By Torah law, a man's grandmother is not forbidden to him, for **the verse states** (Leviticus 18:7): "The nakedness of your father, or the nakedness of your mother, you shall not uncover; she is your mother; you shall not uncover her nakedness." The emphasis implied by the words, **"she is your mother,"** [4]teaches that a man **is rendered liable by** having intercourse with **his mother,** [5]**but he is not rendered liable by** having intercourse with **his mother's mother.**

רָבָא אָמַר [6]**Rava said:** Even without the restrictive expression, "she is your mother," we could not learn by a *gezerah shavah* that a man is forbidden by Torah law to have intercourse with his grandmother. [7]**Both according to the** Tanna **who says: "Deduce from it and from it,"** [8]**and according to the** Tanna **who says: "Deduce from it and leave it in its place,"** [9]such a *gezerah shavah* **cannot be learned,** as will now be explained. The Tannaim disagree about the scope of conclusions that can be inferred by a *gezerah shavah*. According to one opinion, the rule is: "Deduce from it and from it," that is to say, deduce a Halakhic point about B from A, and then deduce further from A. Not only is a primary Halakhic point that is stated in the Torah regarding A transferred to B, but other related points are also transferred. According to a second opinion, the rule is: "Deduce from it, and leave it in its place," that is to say, deduce a Halakhic point about B from A, but apply that point only within the context of B. Only the primary Halakhic point is transferred from A to B. But in all other respects, B retains its own Halakhic character. Now, were we to learn by a *gezerah shavah* that a man is forbidden to have intercourse with his grandmother, we would say as follows:

[1]אִי מָה הִיא אֵם אִמָּהּ אֲסוּרָה, [2]אַף הוּא אֵם אִמּוֹ אֲסוּרָה! [3]אָמַר אַבַּיֵי: אָמַר קְרָא: ״אִמְּךָ הִיא״. [4]מִשּׁוּם אִמּוֹ אַתָּה מְחַיְּיבוֹ, [5]וְאִי אַתָּה מְחַיְּיבוֹ מִשּׁוּם אֵם אִמּוֹ. [6]רָבָא אָמַר: [7]בֵּין לְמַאן דְּאָמַר: ״דּוּן מִינָּהּ וּמִינָּהּ״, [8]וּבֵין לְמַאן דְּאָמַר: ״דּוּן מִינָּהּ וְאוֹקֵי בְּאַתְרָהּ״, [9]לָא אָתְיָא.

LITERAL TRANSLATION

[1]Or just as [regarding] her, her mother's mother is forbidden, [2]so, too, [regarding] him, his mother's mother is forbidden!

[3]Abaye said: The verse states: "She is your mother." [4]Because of his mother you make him liable, [5]but you do not make him liable because of his mother's mother.

[6]Rava said: [7]Both according to the one who says: "Deduce from it and from it," [8]and according to the one who says: "Deduce from it and leave it in its place," [9]it is not brought.

RASHI

נאמר כאן בחמותו זמה, ונאמר להלן בבת אשתו זמה, מה להלן למטה באיסור כלמעלה באיסור חייב הכתוב על בת בתה ובת בנה כבתה, אף כאן נעשה אם חמיו ואם חמותו כחמותו והיינו למטה באיסור כלמעלה באיסור. וסיפא דהדר תני מה כאן למטה כלמעלה אף להלן למעלה כלמטה. רב אשי כאביי מפרש לה למילף אזהרה בחמותו ואם חמותו ואם חמיו, והכי קאמר: ומה כאן בעונש רבינן בגזרה שוה שאר של מטה הימנה כשאר של מעלה הימנה לשריפה, אף באזהרה האמורה בשאר של מטה נרבה שאר של מעלה — מאשתו, חמותו, ואם חמותו, כשאר של מטה באזהרה. אי — כיון דאמרת מניין לעשות שאר הבא הימנו כשאר הבא הימנה — נימא מה היא אם אמה אסורה לו אף הוא אם אמו אסורה לו משום ערוה. ואנן גבי שניות מדברי סופרים (תנן) [תניא] לה ביבמות בפרק "כילד" (כא,א). אמך היא — מיעוטא הוא. רבא אמר — לא מבעי ליה קרא למעוטי דלא תיסק אדעתין לאתויי הא בגזירה שוה, דבין למאן דאמר בכל גזירות שוות שבתורה דון מינה ומינה בין למאן דאמר וכו׳, לא אתיא שפיר כדמפרש ואזיל. דון מינה ומינה — לכל דבריה נלמוד ממנה, מאחר שעיקרו של דבר למדתי מחבירו אף לכל דבריה נלמוד ממנה, וכן אם באת ללמוד אם אמו מאם אמה לאיסורא, צריך אתה ללמוד הימנה אף לשריפה שתהא בשריפה. בין למאן דאמרינן דון מינה ואוקי באתרה — דון עיקר הדבר ללמדו מחבירו, אבל לשאר דבריו שאתה מוצא דינו מפורש בו ואתה יכול ללמוד מיניה וביה דבר מדבר ואינך צריך ללמד מחבירו — העמידנו במקומו ואל תשווהו לחבירו, וכאן נמי למוד אם אמו מאם אמה לאיסורא דלא כתיבא בה בהדיא, אבל לענין מיתה תעמידנה במקומה למילף שאר דידיה מיניה וביה דבר מדבר, ולמוד אף אם אמו בסקילה מאמו שהיא בסקילה, דהא גבי דידה נמי אם אמה כאמה הויא לשריפה. ולא אתיא — כדמפרש ואזיל.

NOTES

אֵם אִמּוֹ אֵם אִמָּהּ His mother's mother and her mother's mother. The question has been raised: How is it possible that a man is liable to death by burning if he has sexual intercourse with his wife's grandmother, while at the same time he is permitted to his own grandmother by Torah law, and only forbidden to her by Rabbinic decree? The Rishonim explain that sometimes the Torah imposes a graver prohibition upon a less serious offense, because the opportunity and enticement to sin are greater in the case of the less serious offense than in that of the more serious offense. Because it is extremely unusual for a man to lust after his grandmother, who is so much older than

TERMINOLOGY

אִיכָּא לְמִיפְרַךְ It is possible to refute. An expression used by the Gemara as an introduction to a refutation — in particular of a *kal vaḥomer* or *binyan av*.

TRANSLATION AND COMMENTARY

[1]**According to the** Tanna **who says: "Deduce** a Halakhic point about B **from** A **and** then deduce further **from** A" — [2]we would deduce that, **just as regarding** a man's wife, **her mother's mother is forbidden** to him, [3]**so, too, regarding** the man himself, **is his mother's mother forbidden** to him. [4]**And** we would further deduce **from this** that, **just as** intercourse with **his** wife's grandmother is punishable **by burning,** [5]**so, too,** is intercourse with **his** own grandmother punishable **by burning.** But this *gezerah shavah* must be rejected. [6]**According to the** Tanna **who says** that **burning is** a **more severe** mode of capital punishment than stoning, [7]**it is possible to object** as follows: [8]We understand that a man should be forbidden to have intercourse with **his wife's** grandmother, for the Torah is stringent about intercourse with his wife's relatives, as we know because intercourse with his wife's **mother is** punishable **by burning.** [9]But **will you say** that we should learn from this that intercourse with **his** own grandmother is forbidden, [10]when intercourse with his own **mother is** only punishable by the less severe penalty of **stoning?** [11]**And furthermore, if** intercourse with **his mother is** punishable **by stoning,** [12]**is** it possible that intercourse with **his mother's mother** — a more distant relative — is punishable **by** the more severe penalty of **burning?** [13]**And furthermore,** if we say: "Deduce a Halakhic point about B from A, and then deduce further from A," it should be argued as follows: **Just as regarding his wife's** relatives, **we do not distinguish between her mother and her mother's mother** — intercourse with either one of them being punishable by burning, [14]**so, too, regarding his** own relatives, **we should not distinguish between his mother and his mother's mother,** and so we should say that intercourse with his grandmother is punishable by stoning, just like intercourse with his mother. Since we cannot learn by the *gezerah shavah* that intercourse with one's grandmother is punishable by burning, we cannot even learn that such intercourse is forbidden at all. [15]**And according to the** Tanna **who says** that **stoning is** a **more severe** mode of capital punishment than burning, the first two objections are not valid, [16]but **because of this** third **problem, you cannot deduce** from the prohibition against intercourse with one's wife's grandmother that a man is also forbidden to have intercourse with his own grandmother.

[1]לְמַאן דַּאֲמַר: ״דּוּן מִינָּהּ וּמִינָּהּ״ — [2]מַה הִיא, אֵם אִמָּהּ אֲסוּרָה, [3]אַף הוּא נַמִי, אֵם אִמּוֹ אֲסוּרָה. [4]וּמִינָּהּ, מַה הִיא בִּשְׂרֵיפָה, [5]אַף הוּא נַמִי בִּשְׂרֵיפָה. [6]לְמַאן דַּאֲמַר: ״שְׂרֵיפָה חֲמוּרָה, [7]אִיכָּא לְמִיפְרַךְ: [8]מַה לְהִיא, שֶׁכֵּן אִמָּהּ בִּשְׂרֵיפָה, [9]תֹּאמַר בְּהוּא, [10]שֶׁאִמּוֹ בִּסְקִילָה. [11]וְעוֹד: אִמּוֹ בִּסְקִילָה, [12]אֵם אִמּוֹ בִּשְׂרֵיפָה? [13]וְעוֹד: מַה הִיא לֹא חָלַקְתָּ בָּהּ בֵּין אִמָּהּ לְאֵם אִמָּהּ, [14]אַף הוּא נַמִי, לֹא תַּחֲלוֹק בּוֹ בֵּין אִמּוֹ לְאֵם אִמּוֹ. [15]וּלְמַאן דַּאֲמַר: סְקִילָה חֲמוּרָה, [16]מֵהַאי קוּשְׁיָא לֹא נִידּוֹנָה.

LITERAL TRANSLATION

[1]According to the one who says: "Deduce from it and from it" — [2]just as regarding her, her mother's mother is forbidden, [3]so, too, regarding him, his mother's mother is forbidden. [4]And from it, just as regarding her, by burning, [5]so, too, regarding him, by burning. [6]According to the one who says: Burning is more severe, [7]it is possible to object: [8]If regarding her, whose mother is by burning, [9]will you say regarding him, [10]whose mother is by stoning. [11]And furthermore: [If] his mother is by stoning, [12]is his mother's mother by burning? [13]And furthermore: Just as [regarding] her, you do not distinguish between her mother and her mother's mother, [14]so, too, [regarding] him, you should not distinguish between his mother and his mother's mother. [15]And according to the one who says: Stoning is more severe, [16]because of this difficulty, you cannot deduce it.

RASHI

מה היא בשריפה אף הוא בשריפה — כלומר מה שאר אשתו אם אמו בשריפה היא, אף הוא שאר שלו אם אמו בשריפה. איכא למיפרך — בתחלת הדין דילפת מיניה לאיסורא. מה להיא — לשאר אשתו דין הוא להחמיר ולאסור את אם אמה שכן החמיר הכתוב על אמה לשריפה, ואשכחן בה צד חמור. ועוד אמו בסקילה — שהיא קלה, אם אמו תהא בשריפה חמורה? בתמיהה. ועוד — כיון דאית לן למידן מינה ומינה — מאי חזית דדיינת הכי, דון הכי? מה היא לא חלקת בה בין אמה לאם אמה, אף הוא לא תחלוק וכו׳, הלכך לא אתיא לשריפה. וכיון דלא מצית למילף מינה ומינה, אף תחילת הדין לאיסורא לא תלמוד, ולמאן דאמר נמי סקילה חמורה וליתנהו תרתי פירכי קמאי מיהו משום האי קושיא בתרייתא לא נדונה זה מזה.

NOTES

himself, the Torah did not have to explicitly forbid their union. However, because of the intimate relationship that a boy enjoys with his mother in his early years, it forbade sexual intercourse between mother and son. But since it is possible that a man will be attracted to his wife's grandmother, the Torah forbids their union with a severe prohibition (*Meiri*). *Radbaz* points out that not infrequently a man marries a woman much younger than himself, so that he might even be older than her grandmother.

LITERAL TRANSLATION

[1]And according to the one who says: "Deduce from it [2]and leave it in its place" — [3]just as [regarding] her, her mother's mother is forbidden, [4]so, too, [regarding] him, his mother's mother is forbidden. [5]And leave it in its place — [6]there by burning, [7]but here by stoning, [8]as we find regarding his mother. [9]According to the one who says: Burning is more severe, [10]it is possible to refute: [76A] [11]If, regarding her, whose mother is by burning, [12]will you say regarding him, whose mother is by stoning? [13]And furthermore, [14]he is like her — [15]just as regarding her, you do not distinguish between her daughter and her mother's mother, [16]so, too, regarding him, you should not distinguish between his daughter and his mother's mother. [17]And according to the one who says: Stoning is more severe, [18]because of this difficulty, you cannot deduce it.

[19]Or just as regarding him, his daughter-in-law is forbidden,

[1]וּלְמַאן דַּאֲמַר: "דּוּן מִינָּהּ [2]וְאוֹקֵי בְּאַתְרָהּ" — [3]מַה הִיא אֵם אִמָּהּ אֲסוּרָה, [4]אַף הוּא, נַמִּי אֵם אִמּוֹ אֲסוּרָה. [5]וְאוֹקֵי בְּאַתְרָהּ — [6]הָתָם הוּא דִּבִשְׂרֵיפָה, [7]אֲבָל הָכָא בִּסְקִילָה, [8]כִּדְאַשְׁכַּחַן בְּאִמּוֹ. [9]לְמַאן דַּאֲמַר שְׂרֵיפָה חֲמוּרָה, [10]אִיכָּא לְמִיפְרַךְ: [76A] [11]מַה לְהִיא, שֶׁכֵּן אִמָּהּ בִּשְׂרֵפָה, [12]תֹּאמַר בְּהוּא, שֶׁאִמּוֹ בִּסְקִילָה? [13]וְעוֹד; [14]הוּא כְּהִיא — [15]מַה הִיא, לֹא חָלַקְתָּ בָּהּ בֵּין בִּתָּהּ לְאֵם אִמָּהּ, [16]אַף הוּא, לֹא תַּחֲלוֹק בּוֹ בֵּין בִּתּוֹ לְאֵם אִמּוֹ. [17]וּלְמַאן דַּאֲמַר: סְקִילָה חֲמוּרָה — [18]מֵהַאי קוּשְׁיָא לֹא נִידּוֹנָהּ.

[19]אִי מַה הוּא, כַּלָּתוֹ אֲסוּרָה,

TRANSLATION AND COMMENTARY

וּלְמַאן [1]Rava continues: **And according to the Tanna who says: "Deduce** a Halakhic point about B **from** A, [2]**but apply** that point **within its** own **context**" — [3]we would deduce by a *gezerah shavah* that, **just as regarding** a man's wife, **her mother's mother is forbidden** to him, [4]**so, too, regarding the** man himself, **is his mother's mother forbidden** to him. [5]**But apply** that point **within its own context** — [6]**there,** intercourse with a man's wife's grandmother is punishable **by burning,** [7]**but here,** intercourse with his own grandmother is punishable **by stoning,** [8]**as we find regarding** intercourse with **his** own **mother.** But this *gezerah shavah* must be rejected. [9]**According to the** Tanna **who says** that **burning is** a **more severe** mode of capital punishment than stoning, [10]**it is possible to refute** as follows: [76A] [11]We understand that a man should be forbidden to have intercourse with **his wife's** grandmother. The Torah is stringent about intercourse with a man's wife's relatives, as intercourse with her **mother is** punishable **by burning.** [12]But **will you say** that we should learn from this that intercourse with **his** own grandmother is forbidden, when intercourse with his own **mother is** punishable **by** the less severe penalty of **stoning?** [13]**And furthermore,** if we say: "Deduce a Halakhic point about B from A, but apply that point within its own context," why conclude that a man who has intercourse with his grandmother is liable to death by stoning, just like a man who has intercourse with his mother? It should be argued as follows: [14]Intercourse with **his** relatives should **be** treated **like** intercourse with **his wife's** relatives. [15]**Just as regarding his wife's** relatives, **we do not distinguish between her daughter and her mother's mother** — intercourse with either of them being punishable by burning — [16]**so, too, regarding his** own relatives, **we should not distinguish between his daughter and his mother's mother.** Hence, intercourse with his grandmother ought to be punishable by burning, just like intercourse with his daughter. But this cannot be, for if intercourse with one's mother is punishable by stoning, how can intercourse with one's grandmother — a more distant relative — be punishable by burning? Since we cannot learn by the *gezerah shavah* that intercourse with one's grandmother is punishable by burning, we cannot learn that such intercourse is forbidden at all. [17]**And according to the** Tanna **who says** that **stoning is** a **more severe** mode of capital punishment than burning, the first objection is not valid, [18]but **because of this** second **difficulty, you cannot deduce** from the prohibition against intercourse with one's wife's grandmother that one is also forbidden to have intercourse with one's own grandmother.

אִי [19]It was stated, above, that we learn by a *gezerah shavah* that the law applying to a man who has intercourse with one of his own female relatives is equated with the law applying to a man who has intercourse with one of his wife's female relatives. The Gemara now asks: Does it not follow from this that,

RASHI

איכא למיפרך – על תחילת הדין דקא ילפת לה לאיסורא אם אמו מאם אמה. **מה להיא** – לשאר אשתו דין הוא להחמיר ולאסור את אם אמה שכן מצינו באותו שאר צד חמור – שכן אמה בשריפה. **ועוד מה היא לא חלקת בין בתה לאם אמה אף הוא וכו'** – כלומר, מאי חזית דכי אמרת אוקים באתרה למילף שאר דידיה מיניה וביה, "דבר" מ"דבר" שנאמר דאם אמו היא בסקילה כאמו כי היכי דבשאר דידה אם אמה כאמה, דילמא אוקמא באתרה – ונימא דבשריפה היא כבתו כי היכי דבשאר דידה אם אמה כבתה, והא לא אפשר, כיון דסבירא ליה שריפה חמורה איכא למיפרך: אמו בסקילה ואם אמו בשריפה?!

TRANSLATION AND COMMENTARY

just as a man's daughter-in-law is forbidden to him, as it is stated explicitly in the Torah (Leviticus 18:15): "You shall not uncover the nakedness of your daughter-in-law; she is your son's wife; you shall not uncover her nakedness," [1] **so, too, is his wife's daughter-in-law forbidden** to him?

אָמַר אַבַּיֵי [2] **Abaye said:** A man's wife's daughter-in-law is not forbidden to him by Torah law, for **the verse** regarding a man's daughter-in-law **states: "She is your son's wife;** you shall not uncover her nakedness." [3] The emphasis implied by these words teaches that a man **is liable** to be penalized **for** having intercourse with **his son's wife,** [4] **but he is not liable** to be penalized **for** having intercourse with **the wife of his wife's son.**

רָבָא אָמַר [5] **Rava said:** Even without the restrictive expression, "she is your son's wife," we could not learn by a *gezerah shavah* that a person is forbidden by Torah law to have intercourse with his wife's daughter-in-law. [6] **Both according to the** Tanna **who says: "Deduce** a Halakhic point about B **from** A, **and** then deduce further **from** A," [7] **and according to the** Tanna **who says: "Deduce** a Halakhic point about B **from** A, **but apply** that point **within its own context,"** [8] such a *gezerah shavah* **cannot** be learned, as will now be explained. [9] **According to the** Tanna **who says: "Deduce** a Halakhic point about B **from** A, **and** then deduce further **from** A" — [10] we would deduce that, **just as a man's** own **daughter-in-law is forbidden** to him, [11] **so too is his wife's daughter-in-law forbidden** to him. [12] **And** we would further deduce **from this** that, **just as** intercourse with **his** own daughter-in-law is punishable **by stoning,** [13] **so, too,** is intercourse with **his wife's** daughter-in-law punishable **by stoning.** But this *gezerah shavah* must be rejected. [14] **According to the** Tanna **who says** that **stoning is** a **more severe** mode of capital punishment than burning, [15] **it is possible to object** as follows: We understand that a man should be forbidden to have intercourse with **his** own daughter-in-law, for the Torah is stringent about intercourse with his own relatives, [16] as intercourse with his **mother is** punishable **by stoning.** [17] But **will you say** that we should learn from this that intercourse with **his wife's** daughter-in-law is forbidden, when intercourse with his wife's **mother is** only punishable **by** the less severe penalty of **burning?** [18] **And furthermore, if** intercourse with **his wife's daughter is** punishable **by burning,** [19] **is** it possible that intercourse with **his wife's daughter-in-law** — a more distant relative — is punishable **by** the more severe penalty of **stoning?**

הוּא [20] The Gemara refutes this objection: The laws applying to the relatives of **the man himself prove** that this argument is not valid, [21] **for** intercourse with **his** own **daughter** is punishable **by burning,** [22] **whereas** intercourse with **his daughter-in-law** — a more distant relative — **is** punishable **by** the more severe penalty of **stoning.** We should therefore not be surprised that similar laws apply to his wife's relatives: Intercourse with her daughter is punishable by burning, while intercourse with her daughter-in-law is punishable by stoning.

[1] אַף הִיא, כַּלָּתָה אֲסוּרָה! [2] אָמַר אַבַּיֵי: אָמַר קְרָא: ״אֵשֶׁת בִּנְךָ הִיא״. [3] מִשּׁוּם אֵשֶׁת בִּנְךָ אַתָּה מְחַיְּיבוֹ, [4] וְאִי אַתָּה מְחַיְּיבוֹ מִשּׁוּם אֵשֶׁת בְּנָהּ. [5] רָבָא אָמַר: [6] בֵּין לְמַאן דַּאֲמַר: ״דּוּן מִינָּהּ וּמִינָּהּ״, [7] בֵּין לְמַאן דַּאֲמַר: ״דּוּן מִינָּהּ וְאוֹקֵי בְּאַתְרָהּ״, [8] לָא אָתְיָא. [9] לְמַאן דַּאֲמַר: ״דּוּן מִינָּהּ וּמִינָּהּ״ — [10] מַה הוּא כַּלָּתוֹ אֲסוּרָה, [11] אַף הִיא, נַמִי כַּלָּתָהּ אֲסוּרָה. [12] וּמִינָּהּ, מַה הוּא בִּסְקִילָה, [13] אַף הִיא נַמִי בִּסְקִילָה. [14] לְמַאן דַּאֲמַר: סְקִילָה חֲמוּרָה, [15] אִיכָּא לְמִיפְרַךְ: [16] מַה לְהוּא, שֶׁכֵּן אִמּוֹ בִּסְקִילָה, [17] תֹּאמַר בְּהִיא, שֶׁאִמָּהּ בִּשְׂרֵפָה. [18] וְעוֹד, בִּתָּהּ בִּשְׂרֵפָה, [19] וְכַלָּתָהּ בִּסְקִילָה? [20] הוּא בְּעַצְמוֹ יוֹכִיחַ, [21] דְּבִתּוֹ בִּשְׂרֵפָה, [22] וְכַלָּתוֹ בִּסְקִילָה.

LITERAL TRANSLATION

[1] so, too, her, her daughter-in-law is forbidden! [2] Abaye said: The verse states: "She is your son's wife." [3] Because of your son's wife you make him liable, [4] but you do not make him liable because of her son's wife.

[5] Rava said: [6] Both according to the one who says: "Deduce from it and from it," and [7] according to the one who says: "Deduce from it and leave it in its place," [8] it is not learned. [9] According to the one who says: "Deduce from it and from it" — [10] just as regarding him, his daughter-in-law is forbidden, [11] so, too, regarding her, her daughter-in-law is forbidden. [12] And from it, just as regarding him, by stoning, [13] so, too, regarding her, by stoning. [14] According to the one who says: Stoning is more severe, [15] it is possible to object: [16] If regarding him, whose mother is by stoning, [17] will you say regarding her, whose mother is by burning? [18] And furthermore, [if] her daughter is by burning, [19] is her daughter-in-law by stoning?

[20] He himself will prove it, [21] for his daughter is by burning, [22] and his daughter-in-law is by stoning.

RASHI

אף היא – כלתה אסורה, כיון דרביתה הזכרים כנקבות השוה נמי נקבות לזכרים, שאר אשתו כשארו ויהא אסור אף באשת חורגו ואנן הוא דאמרינן: מותר אדם באשת חורגו. כלתו בסקילה – בפרק "ארבע מיתות" (סנהדרין נג,א). איכא למיפרך – בתחילת הדין

TRANSLATION AND COMMENTARY

אֶלָּא [1]**Rather,** the following objection may be raised against the *gezerah shavah*: Since we say: "Deduce a Halakhic point about B from A, and then deduce further from A," it should be argued as follows: **Just as, regarding the man's** own relatives, **we do not distinguish between his mother and his daughter-in-law** — intercourse with either one of them being punishable by stoning — [2]**so, too, regarding his wife's** relatives, **we should not distinguish between her mother and her daughter-in-law.** Therefore, we should say that intercourse with his wife's daughter-in-law is punishable by burning, just like intercourse with his wife's mother. Since we cannot learn by the *gezerah shavah* that intercourse with his wife's daughter-in-law is punishable by stoning, we cannot learn that such intercourse is forbidden at all. [3]**And according to the** Tanna **who says** that **burning is** a **more severe** mode of capital punishment than stoning, the first objection is not valid, [4]but **because of this** second **difficulty, you cannot deduce** from the prohibition against intercourse with one's own daughter-in-law that one is also forbidden to have intercourse with one's wife's daughter-in-law.

וּלְמַאן דְּאָמַר [5]Rava continues: **And according to the** Tanna **who says: "Deduce** a Halakhic point about A **from** B, [6]**but apply** that point **within its** own **context"** — [7]we would deduce by a *gezerah shavah* that, **just as a man's daughter-in-law is forbidden** to him, [8]**so too is his wife's daughter-in-law forbidden** to him. [9]**But apply** that point **within its own context** — [10]**there,** intercourse with his own daughter-in-law is punishable **by stoning,** [11]**but here,** intercourse with his wife's daughter-in-law is punishable **by burning,** [12]**as we find regarding** intercourse with **his wife's mother.** [13]**According to the** Tanna **who says** that **stoning is** a **more severe** mode of capital punishment than burning, [14]**it is possible to object** as follows: We understand that a man should be forbidden to have intercourse with **his** own daughter-in-law, for the Torah is stringent about intercourse with his own relatives, as intercourse with his own **mother is** punishable **by stoning.** [15]But **will you say** that we should learn from this that intercourse with **his wife's** daughter-in-law is forbidden, when intercourse with his wife's **mother is** only punishable **by** the less severe penalty of **burning?** [16]**And furthermore,** since we say: "Deduce a Halakhic point about B from A, but apply that point within its own context," why conclude that someone who has intercourse with his wife's daughter-in-law is liable to death by burning, just like someone who has intercourse with his wife's mother? It should be argued as follows: [17]**Just as, regarding his** own **relatives, we distinguish between his daughter and his daughter-in-law** — intercourse with his daughter being punishable

[1]אֶלָּא, מַה הוּא לֹא חָלַקְתָּ בּוֹ בֵּין אִמּוֹ לְכַלָּתוֹ, [2]אַף הִיא, לֹא תַּחֲלוֹק בָּהּ בֵּין אִמָּהּ לְכַלָּתָהּ. [3]וּלְמַאן דְּאָמַר: שְׂרֵפָה חֲמוּרָה, [4]מֵהַאי קוּשְׁיָא לֹא נִידּוֹנִין. [5]וּלְמַאן דְּאָמַר: "דּוּן מִינָּהּ [6]וְאוֹקֵי בְּאַתְרָהּ" — [7]מַה הוּא, כַּלָּתוֹ אֲסוּרָה, [8]אַף הִיא, כַּלָּתָהּ אֲסוּרָה. [9]וְאוֹקֵי בְּאַתְרָהּ — [10]הָתָם הוּא דְּבִסְקִילָה, [11]אֲבָל הָכָא בִּשְׂרֵפָה, [12]כִּדְאַשְׁכַּחַן בְּאִמָּהּ. [13]לְמַאן דְּאָמַר: סְקִילָה חֲמוּרָה, [14]אִיכָּא לְמִיפְרַךְ: מַה לְהוּא — שֶׁכֵּן אִמּוֹ בִּסְקִילָה, [15]תֹּאמַר בְּהִיא, שֶׁאִמָּהּ בִּשְׂרֵפָה. [16]וְעוֹד, [17]מַה הוּא חָלַקְתָּ בּוֹ בֵּין

LITERAL TRANSLATION

[1]Rather, just as regarding him, you do not distinguish between his mother and his daughter-in-law, [2]so, too, regarding her, you should not distinguish between her mother and her daughter-in-law. [3]And according to the one who says: Burning is more severe, [4]because of this difficulty, you cannot deduce it.

[5]And according to the one who says: "Deduce from it [6]and leave it in its place" — [7]just as regarding him, his daughter-in-law is forbidden, [8]so, too, regarding her, her daughter-in-law is forbidden. [9]And leave it in its place — [10]there by stoning, [11]but here by burning, [12]as we find regarding her mother. [13]According to the one who says: Stoning is more severe, [14]it is possible to object: If regarding him, whose mother is by stoning, [15]will you say regarding her, whose mother is by burning. [16]And furthermore, [17]just as regarding him, you distinguish between

RASHI

לאוסרה. למאן דאמר שריפה חמורה — ואינה לפירכא קמייתא משום האי קושיא בתרייתא לא נדונה, כלומר לא תילפינהו מהדדי ואפילו לאוסרה דכיון דלא מצית למידן מינה ומינה. הכי גרסינן: אבל הכא בשריפה כדאשכחן באמה — דהיינו אתרה דומיא דידיה דכלתו כאמו. ועוד מה הוא חלקת — כלומר, מאי חזית דכי אוקמת ליה באתרה למילף שאר דידה מיניה וביה שריפה כאמה — דומיא דידיה דכלתו כאמו אוקמת באתרה הכי ולמוד שאר דידיה מיניה וביה, ואימא הכי: כיון דבתה בשריפה צריכין אנו לענוש בכלתה מיתה חמורה מזאת ובסקילה, והיינו מיניה וביה, מבתה שהיא בשריפה אתה למד לכלתה סקילה שצריך אתה לחלוק ולהחמיר בין בתה לכלתה — דמה הוא חלקת בו להחמיר כלתו מבתו אף היא וכו׳, והאי לאו דון מינה ומינה הוא אלא גלויי מילתא בעלמא היא, דכי ילפת שאר דידיה מיניה וביה יש לך להחמיר בכלתה מבתה, ואם באת לומר כן איכא למימר דאין לך ללמוד כן אלא להשוות כלתה לאמה כי היכי דכלתו שוה לאמו, הלכך איכא למימר סקילה ואיכא למימר שרפה — משום הכי לא נדונה.

[1]בִּתּוֹ לְכַלָּתוֹ, [1]אַף הִיא תַּחֲלוֹק בָּהּ בֵּין בִּתָּהּ לְכַלָּתָהּ. [2]וּלְמַאן דְּאָמַר: נַמִי שְׂרֵפָה חֲמוּרָה, [3]מֵהַאי קוּשְׁיָא לֹא נִידוֹנִין. [4]בִּתּוֹ מֵאֲנוּסָתוֹ מִנַּיִן? [5]הָאָמַר אַבַּיֵי: קַל וָחוֹמֶר. [6]עַל בַּת בִּתּוֹ עָנוּשׁ, [7]עַל בִּתּוֹ לֹא כָּל שֶׁכֵּן? [8]וְכִי עוֹנְשִׁין מִן הַדִּין? [9]גִּלּוּיֵי מִילְּתָא בְּעָלְמָא הוּא.

LITERAL TRANSLATION

his daughter and his daughter-in-law, [1]so, too, regarding her, you should distinguish between her daughter and her daughter-in-law. [2]And according to the one who said: Burning is more severe, [3]because of this problem, you cannot deduce it.

[4]From where [do I know about] his daughter from a woman whom he raped?

[5]Surely Abaye said: It is a *kal vaḥomer.* [6]If he is punished for the daughter of his daughter, [7]all the more so for his daughter.

[8]But do we punish on the basis of a *kal vaḥomer*?

[9]It is merely revealing something.

TRANSLATION AND COMMENTARY

by burning, and intercourse with his daughter-in-law being punishable by stoning, [1]**so, too, regarding his wife's** relatives, **we should distinguish between her daughter and her daughter-in-law.** Thus we should say that intercourse with his wife's daughter-in-law is punishable by stoning, even though intercourse with his wife's daughter is punishable by burning. Since we cannot learn by the *gezerah shavah* that intercourse with one's wife's daughter-in-law is punishable by burning, we cannot learn that such intercourse is forbidden at all. [2]**And according to the** Tanna **who says** that **burning is** a **more severe** mode of capital punishment than stoning, the first objection is not valid, [3]but **because of this** second **difficulty, you cannot deduce** from the prohibition against intercourse with one's own daughter-in-law that one is also forbidden to have intercourse with one's wife's daughter-in-law.

בִּתּוֹ [4]We learned in the Mishnah that a man who has intercourse with his daughter, even if he was never married to her mother, is liable to death by burning. The Gemara questions that ruling: **From where do I know** that a man is liable to be punished for having intercourse with **his daughter from a woman he had raped** or seduced, but never married? An explicit prohibition is stated in the Torah regarding a man's granddaughter (Leviticus 18:10): "The nakedness of your son's daughter, or of your daughter's daughter, their nakedness you shall not uncover," and regarding his wife's daughter or granddaughter (Leviticus 18:17): "You shall not uncover the nakedness of a woman and her daughter, neither shall you take her son's daughter, or her daughter's daughter, to uncover their nakedness." Nowhere does the Torah explicitly forbid a man's daughter born to a woman who was not his wife.

הָאָמַר אַבַּיֵי [5]The Gemara responds: **Surely Abaye said:** The punishment imposed upon a man who has intercourse with his daughter **is** derived by **a** *kal vaḥomer* argument. [6]**If** a man **is punished for** having intercourse with **his granddaughter,** [7]should he not be punished **all the more so for** having intercourse with **his daughter?**

וְכִי [8]The Gemara raises an objection: **But** is it possible to **inflict punishment on the basis of** a law that was inferred through **a** *kal vaḥomer* argument, but not explicitly stated in the Torah?

גִּלּוּיֵי מִילְּתָא [9]The Gemara explains: The punishment imposed for having intercourse with one's daughter is not derived by a formal *kal vaḥomer* argument. The punishment for having intercourse with one's granddaughter **merely reveals** that a person is also punished for having intercourse with his daughter.

RASHI

בתו מאנוסתו מניין — בשאר דידיה בקרא ד״ערות בת בנך״ וגו׳ דאוקימנא באונסין לא כתיבא בתו. **גלויי מלתא בעלמא הוא** — ואין זה עונש מן הדין, — דהא בת בתו מקורבת דבתו היא דאתיא, והיכי דמי עונש מן הדין — כגון ״ערות אחותך בת אביך או בת אמך״ — אין לי אלא בת אביו שלא בת אמו ובת אמו שלא בת אביו, ואם באתה להביא בת אביו ובת אמו מקל וחומר — זה עונש מן הדין, דהא לאו מכח קורבה דהא אתיא דזו קורבה מחמת עצמה וזו קורבה מחמת עצמה, אבל הבא על בת בתו אינה קרובה לו אלא משום בתו.

NOTES

גִּלּוּיֵי מִילְּתָא בְּעָלְמָא **It is merely revealing something.** This expression is found in several places in the Talmud regarding various issues. Occasionally, when an objection is raised against the formal validity of a certain Halakhic inference (that the word upon which a *gezerah shavah* is based is not unnecessary in its own context, or that we do

HALAKHAH

בִּתּוֹ מֵאֲנוּסָתוֹ **His daughter from a woman whom he raped.** "If a man has intercourse with an unmarried woman, and a daughter is born from that union, that daughter is forbidden to him. Even though the Torah does not forbid a man's daughter explicitly, since it forbids his granddaughter it did not have to mention his daughter. Therefore, if someone inadvertently has intercourse with his daughter from his wife, he is liable for two sin-offerings, one for

LITERAL TRANSLATION

[1]Rava said: Rabbi Yitzḥak bar Avdimi said to me: [2]"They" is learned from "they"; [3]"wickedness" is learned from "wickedness."

[4]The father of Rabbi Avin taught: [5]"Since we did not learn his daughter from a woman whom he raped, [6]the verse had to say: 'And the daughter of any priest.'"

[7]Just as regarding the daughter of a priest, she is by burning, [8]but her lover is not by burning, [9]so, too, regarding his daughter from a woman whom he raped, she is by burning,

[1]רָבָא אָמַר: אָמַר לִי רַבִּי יִצְחָק בַּר אַבְדִּימִי: [2]אָתְיָא "הֵנָּה", "הֵנָּה", [3]אָתְיָא "זִמָּה", "זִמָּה".

[4]תָּנֵי אֲבוּהּ דְּרַבִּי אָבִין: [5]"לְפִי שֶׁלֹּא לָמַדְנוּ לְבִתּוֹ מֵאֲנוּסָתוֹ, [6]הוּצְרַךְ הַכָּתוּב לוֹמַר: 'וּבַת אִישׁ כֹּהֵן'".

[7]אִי מַה בַּת כֹּהֵן הִיא בִּשְׂרֵפָה [8]וְאֵין בּוֹעֲלָהּ בִּשְׂרֵפָה, [9]אַף בִּתּוֹ מֵאֲנוּסָתוֹ, הִיא בִּשְׂרֵפָה,

RASHI

אתיא הנה הנה לאיסורא — נאמר בשארו הנה ונאמר בשאר אשתו הנה, מה להלן בתה כבת בתה, אף כאן בתו כבת בתו, ומאחר שנתרבית להיות כבת בתו אתיא לשריפה בגזירה שוה ד"זמה" "זמה" כבת בתו כדאמרינן לעיל. **הוצרך הכתוב לומר ובת איש כהן** — דהוה ליה למימר "ובת כהן" וכתוב "איש" — לומר לך בת איש מאנוסתו שאינה בת אשתו "כי תחל לזנות את אביה" כלומר שזנתה מאביה — בשריפה. **אי מה בת כהן** — נשואה שזינתה מאחר היא בשריפה ואין בועלה בשריפה. **אף בתו מאנוסתו היא בשריפה ולא הוא** — דהיא תשרף כתיב ולא הוא.

TRANSLATION AND COMMENTARY

רָבָא אָמַר [1]**Rava said: Rabbi Yitzḥak bar Avdimi said to me:** The punishment imposed for having intercourse with one's daughter is derived by way of a double *gezerah shavah*. [2]The prohibition against intercourse with one's daughter **is learned** by a *gezerah shavah* drawn between the word **"theirs"** found in connection with a man's relatives and the word **"they"** found in connection with his wife's relatives. Regarding a man's relatives, the verse states (Leviticus 18:10): "The nakedness of your son's daughter, or of your daughter's daughter, their nakedness you shall not uncover; for *theirs* [*henah*] is your own nakedness." And regarding his wife's relatives, the verse states (Leviticus 18:17): "You shall not uncover the nakedness of a woman and her daughter; neither shall you take her son's daughter, or her daughter's daughter, to uncover her nakedness, for *they* [*henah*] are her near kinswomen; it is wickedness." A man is forbidden to his wife's daughter just as he is forbidden to her granddaughter, and similarly he is forbidden to his daughter and his granddaughter. Furthermore, just as intercourse with his wife's relatives is called wickedness, so, too, is intercourse with his own relatives called wickedness. [3]The significance of the **"wickedness"** relating to one who has intercourse with his own daughter **is learned from** the word **"wickedness"** found in the verse (Leviticus 20:14): "And if a man take a woman and her mother, it is wickedness; they shall be burnt with fire, both he and they." Just as there, the wickedness is punished by burning, so, too, here, the wickedness is punished by burning.

תָּנֵי [4]**Rabbi Avin's father taught** the following Baraita: [5]**"Since** the Torah **did not** explicitly **teach** the law applying to a man who had intercourse with **his daughter from a woman whom he had raped,** [6]**the verse had to say** (Leviticus 21:9): **"And the daughter of any priest** [וּבַת אִישׁ כֹּהֵן], if she profanes herself by playing the harlot, she profanes her father [אֶת אָבִיהָ]; she shall be burnt with fire." The verse could have read וּבַת כֹּהֵן, "and the daughter of a priest," but instead it reads וּבַת אִישׁ כֹּהֵן, literally, "and the daughter of a man who is a priest." The phrase "the daughter of a man" suggests that the verse refers not only to a priest's daughter who commits adultery, but also to the daughter of a man from a woman whom he raped. The words אֶת אָבִיהָ can also mean "with her father." Thus, the verse teaches that if the daughter of a rape victim has intercourse with her father, she is liable to death by burning.

אִי מַה [7]The Gemara asks: Does it not follow from this that, **just as the daughter of a priest is** liable to death **by burning** for committing adultery, [8]**while her lover is not** liable to death **by burning,** but rather to some other mode of capital punishment (as the verse states: "She shall be burnt with fire" — she, but not he), [9]**so, too, if** a man has intercourse with **his daughter from a woman whom he raped, she should be**

NOTES

not punish on the basis of *kal vaḥomer* argumentation, or that the derivation is from a Prophetic, rather than a Pentateuchal, source), the Gemara explains that the Midrashic explanation of the Biblical verse is not the source of the Halakhah, but merely emphasizes a point that was self-explanatory or known from another source. In our case, the Gemara argues that the punishment for intercourse with one's daughter is not derived by a formal *kal vaḥomer* argument, but rather is implicitly included in the punishment imposed for intercourse with one's granddaughter and merely needs revelation.

HALAKHAH

having intercourse with his daughter, and one for having intercourse with his wife's daughter." (*Rambam, Sefer Kedushah, Hilkhot Issurei Bi'ah* 2:6.)

[1]וְאֵין בּוֹעֲלָהּ בִּשְׂרֵפָה? [2]אָמַר אַבַּיֵי: אָמַר קְרָא: ״אֶת אָבִיהָ הִיא מְחַלֶּלֶת״. [3]מִי שֶׁמְּחַלֶּלֶת אֶת אָבִיהָ, [4]יָצְתָה זוֹ שֶׁאָבִיהָ מְחַלְּלָהּ.

[5]רָבָא אָמַר: [6]בִּשְׁלָמָא הָתָם, אַפִּיקְתֵּיהּ מִדִּינָא דְּבַת כֹּהֵן, [7]וְאוֹקִימְתָּהּ אַדִּינָא דְּבַת יִשְׂרָאֵל? [8]הָכָא, אַדִּינָא דְּמַאן מוֹקְמַת לֵיהּ? [9]אַדִּינָא דִּפְנוּיָה מוֹקְמַת לֵיהּ?

[10]אַזְהָרָה לְבִתּוֹ מֵאֲנוּסָתוֹ מִנַּיִין? [11]בִּשְׁלָמָא לְאַבַּיֵי וְרָבָא — מֵהֵיכָא דְּנָפְקָא לְהוּ עוֹנֶשׁ, [12]מֵהָתָם נָפְקָא לְהוּ אַזְהָרָה. [13]אֶלָּא לִדְתָנֵי אֲבוּהּ דְּרַבִּי אָבִין, [14]מַאי?

[15]אָמַר רַבִּי אִילְעָא: אָמַר קְרָא: [16]״אַל תְּחַלֵּל אֶת בִּתְּךָ לְהַזְנוֹתָהּ״.

[17]מַתְקִיף לָהּ רַבִּי יַעֲקֹב אֲחוּהּ דְּרַב אַחָא בַּר יַעֲקֹב: [18]הַאי ״אַל תְּחַלֵּל אֶת בִּתְּךָ לְהַזְנוֹתָהּ״

LITERAL TRANSLATION

[1]but her lover is not by burning?

[2]Abaye said: The verse states: "She profanes her father." [3]She who profanes her father, [4]to the exclusion of this one whose father profanes her.

[5]Rava said: [6]Granted there, remove him from the law of the daughter of a priest, [7]and apply to him the law of the daughter of an Israelite. [8]Here, whose law will you apply to him? [9]Will you apply to him the law of an unmarried woman?

[10]From where [do I know] a warning regarding his daughter from a woman whom he raped? [11]Granted, according to Abaye and Rava — from where they derived the punishment, [12]from there they can derive the warning. [13]But according to what was taught by the father of Rabbi Avin, [14]what [is there to say]?

[15]Rabbi Il'a said: The verse states: [16]"Do not profane your daughter, to cause her to be a harlot."

[17]Rabbi Ya'akov the brother of Rav Aḥa bar Ya'akov objected: [18]Does "Do not profane your daughter, to cause her to be a harlot"

TRANSLATION AND COMMENTARY

liable to death **by burning,** [1]**but her lover** (her father) **should not be** liable to death **by burning,** but rather to some other mode of capital punishment?

אָמַר אַבַּיֵי [2]**Abaye said:** That distinction does not apply to a man who has intercourse with his daughter from a woman whom he raped, for **the verse states: "She profanes her father."** [3]The emphasis placed on the word "she" teaches that this special law is restricted to a daughter **who profanes her father** by harlotry. [4]This **excludes** a daughter **whose father profanes her** by engaging in intercourse with her.

רָבָא אָמַר [5]**Rava said:** Even without that restrictive expression, the distinction made between the punishment imposed upon the woman and the punishment imposed upon her lover can certainly not be applied to a man who has intercourse with his daughter from a woman whom he raped. [6]**Granted there,** with the daughter of a priest who committed adultery with another man, you can **remove** her lover **from the law relating to the daughter of the priest** — death by burning — [7]**and apply to him the law** relating to a man who committed adultery with **the daughter of an ordinary Jew** — death by strangulation. [8]But **here,** with a man who has intercourse with his daughter from a woman whom he raped, if you remove him from the law applying to his daughter, **whose law can you apply to him?** [9]**Can you apply to him the law relating** to a man who has intercourse with **an unmarried woman,** and exempt him altogether from punishment?

אַזְהָרָה [10]The Gemara asks: **Where** does the Torah issue **a warning** that a man is forbidden to have intercourse with **his daughter from a woman whom he raped** or seduced, and never married? Punishment cannot be imposed unless the Torah issued a warning that the act for which the punishment is to be imposed is forbidden! [11]**Granted according to Abaye and Rava, they derive the punishment** that is imposed for intercourse with one granddaughter [12]**from** the same source as **they derive the warning** that intercourse with one's daughter is forbidden. [13]**But according to** the Baraita **taught by the father of Rabbi Avin,** who ruled that the punishment for intercourse with one's daughter is derived from the punishment imposed upon the daughter of a priest who committed adultery — [14]**what is there to say?** The verse that teaches that punishment does not contain a warning that the act itself is forbidden!

אָמַר רַבִּי אִילְעָא [15]**Rabbi Il'a said:** The warning against intercourse with one's daughter is derived from **the verse** that **states** (Leviticus 19:29): [16]**"Do not profane your daughter, to cause her to be a harlot."**

מַתְקִיף [17]**Rabbi Ya'akov the brother of Rav Aḥa bar Ya'akov objected:** [18]**Does** the verse **"Do not profane your**

RASHI

רבא אמר בשלמא התם — גבי בת כהן בנשואה או בארוסה משמעי קרא, כדילפינן בפרק ארבע מיתות כי אפיקתיה לבועל מדינא דבת כהן. **ואוקמיה אדינא** — דבועל אשת איש, דהא לא נפקא מכלל אשת רעהו, אבל בא על בתו משום קורבא היא בין בפנויה, בין בנשואה, ואי מפקת לאביה מכלל דינא אהי דינא מוקמת ליה? — אדינא דפנויה מוקמת ליה ומפטר אפשר לומר כן?! השתא איהי דלא עבדא מידי מיקטלא, איהו מיפטר?! — והא קיימא לן (בבא קמא טו,ג) השוה הכתוב אשה לאיש לכל עונשין שבתורה! **אל תחלל את בתך** — אל תחללה בזנות.

לְהָכִי הוּא דַּאֲתָא? [1]הַאי מִיבָּעֵי לֵיהּ לְכִדְתַנְיָא: "'אַל תְּחַלֵּל אֶת בִּתְּךָ לְהַזְנוֹתָהּ'. [2]יָכוֹל בְּכֹהֵן הַמַּשִּׂיא אֶת בִּתּוֹ לְלֵוִי וְיִשְׂרָאֵל הַכָּתוּב מְדַבֵּר. [3]תַּלְמוּד לוֹמַר: 'לְהַזְנוֹתָהּ' — [4]בְּחִילּוּל שֶׁבִּזְנוּת הַכָּתוּב מְדַבֵּר, [5]בְּמוֹסֵר אֶת בִּתּוֹ שֶׁלֹּא לְשֵׁם אִישׁוּת".
[6]אִם כֵּן, לֵימָא קְרָא: "אַל תָּחֵל"! [7]מַאי "אַל תְּחַלֵּל"? [8]שְׁמַע מִינָּהּ תַּרְתֵּי.
[9]וְאַבַּיֵי וְרָבָא, הַאי "אַל תְּחַלֵּל אֶת בִּתְּךָ לְהַזְנוֹתָהּ" מַאי עָבְדִי לֵיהּ?
[10]אָמַר רַבִּי מָנִי: זֶה הַמַּשִּׂיא אֶת בִּתּוֹ לְזָקֵן. [11]כִּדְתַנְיָא: "'אַל

LITERAL TRANSLATION

come for this? [1]Surely it is needed for what was taught: "'Do not profane your daughter, to cause her to be a harlot.' [2]I might have thought that the verse is talking about a priest who marries his daughter to a Levite or to an Israelite. [3]The verse states: 'To make her a harlot' — [4]the verse is talking about profanation by harlotry, [5]about someone who delivers his daughter not for the sake of marriage."
[6]If so, let the verse say: *"Al tahel"*! [7]What is *"Al tehalel"*? [8]Infer from this two [things].
[9]And Abaye and Rava, what do they do with this "Do not profane your daughter, to cause her to be a harlot"?
[10]Rabbi Mani said: This is someone who marries his daughter off to an old man. [11]As it was taught: "'Do not

RASHI

יכול בכהן המשיא בתו ללוי ולישראל — שמחללה ופוסלה מתרומה כל זמן היותה תחתיו. **במוסר בתו** — לאדם לבעילת זנות שלא לשם אישות. **תחלל** — שני חלולין משמע. **המשיא בתו לזקן** — ומתוך שאינה מקבלתו מזנה היא עליו.

TRANSLATION AND COMMENTARY

daughter, to cause her to be a harlot" teach us **this** law? [1]**Surely** that verse **is needed for what was taught** in the following Baraita: "The verse states: **'Do not profane your daughter, to cause her to be a harlot.'** Had I only had the first part of the verse, 'Do not profane your daughter,' [2]**I might have thought that the verse was talking about a priest who marries his daughter to a Levite or to an ordinary Jew,** for by marrying her to someone who is not a priest, he profanes her and disallows her to eat terumah. [3]Therefore, **the verse continues: 'To make her a harlot,'** [4]teaching that **the verse is talking about profanation by harlotry,** that is to say, [5]**about someone who delivers his daughter** to another man for sexual intercourse, **not for the sake of marriage,** but for the sake of harlotry."

אִם כֵּן [6]The Gemara answers: If it is **so,** that **the verse** only teaches us that other law, **it should have said:** ***"Al tahel*** [אַל תָּחֵל, 'Do not profane']"! [7]**What is the** meaning of ***"Al tehalel*** [אַל תְּחַלֵּל, 'Do not profane']," with a doubling of the letter *lamed*? [8]**Infer from this** that the verse teaches about **two** profanations — profaning one's daughter by delivering her to another man for sexual intercourse for the sake of harlotry, and profaning one's daughter by having intercourse with her.

וְאַבַּיֵי וְרָבָא [9]The Gemara asks: **What do Abaye and Rava do with this** verse: **"Do not profane your daughter, to cause her to be a harlot,"** for they derive the prohibition against intercourse with one's daughter from another source?

אָמַר רַבִּי מָנִי [10]**Rabbi Mani said: This** verse refers to **someone who marries his daughter to an old man,** for she might not find satisfaction in her marriage, and she will be driven to harlotry. [11]**As it was taught** in

NOTES

מוֹסֵר אֶת בִּתּוֹ שֶׁלֹּא לְשֵׁם אִישׁוּת Someone who delivers his daughter not for the sake of marriage. The interpretation of this statement depends upon whether there is a Torah prohibition against sexual intercourse with an unmarried woman, an issue in dispute between *Rambam* and *Ramban*. *Ran* argues that, while there is no prohibition against sexual intercourse with an unmarried woman, the verse, "do not profane your daughter, to cause her to be a harlot," teaches that a father is forbidden to turn his daughter into a prostitute. Prostitution will result in the birth of children who do not know the identity of their fathers and brothers, a situation that will lead to the proliferation of incest.

הַמַּשִּׂיא אֶת בִּתּוֹ לְזָקֵן Someone who marries his daughter to an old man. This prohibition seems to be limited to a father who marries his daughter to an elderly man. But a woman may indeed agree to marry a much older man on

HALAKHAH

מוֹסֵר אֶת בִּתּוֹ שֶׁלֹּא לְשֵׁם אִישׁוּת Someone who delivers his daughter not for the sake of marriage. "Someone who delivers his daughter for sexual intercourse not for the sake of marriage violates the prohibition, 'do not profane your daughter, to cause her to be a harlot.' If he regularly hands her over for prostitution, both she and her clients violate the prohibition, 'there shall be no prostitute of the daughters of Israel.' Some authorities disagree with this last ruling (*Ramban* and others)." (*Rambam, Sefer Nashim, Hilkhot Na'arah Betulah* 2:17; *Shulhan Arukh, Even HaEzer* 177:5, *Rema*.)

הַמַּשִּׂיא אֶת בִּתּוֹ לְזָקֵן Someone who marries his daughter to an old man. "A young man should not marry an elderly woman, nor should an elderly man marry a young woman, for such unions lead to harlotry." (*Shulhan Arukh, Even HaEzer* 2:9.)

TRANSLATION AND COMMENTARY

the following Baraita: "The verse states: **'Do not profane your daughter, to cause her to be a harlot.'** [1]**Rabbi Eliezer says: This** verse refers to **someone who marries his daughter to an old man.** [2]**Rabbi Akiva says: This** refers to **someone who delays the marriage of his adult daughter,** driving her to harlotry."

אָמַר רַב כָּהֲנָא [3]**Rav Kahana said in the name of Rabbi Akiva: There is no poor man in Israel except for a cunning, wicked man** — a wicked man who tries to conceal his wickedness through cunning and deceit — [4]**and someone who delays the marriage of his adult daughter.**

אִטּוּ [5]The Gemara has difficulty understanding this statement: **Is someone who delays the marriage of his adult daughter not a cunning, wicked man?** Surely he does so in order to take advantage of her services and save the cost of hiring domestic help. This is cunning wickedness, for by delaying his daughter's marriage for his personal gain, the father drives her to harlotry.

אָמַר אַבַּיֵי [6]**Abaye said:** [76B] [7]Rabbi Akiva meant to **say as follows:** There is no poor and cunning wicked man in Israel except for someone who delays the marriage of his adult daughter. [8]**Who is** so **poor** that he turns into **a cunning, wicked man.** [9]**Someone who** lacks domestic help, and therefore **delays the marriage of his adult daughter,** driving her to harlotry.

וְאָמַר רַב כָּהֲנָא [10]The Gemara relates that **Rav Kahana** also **said in the name of Rabbi Akiva:** [11]**Be wary of someone who offers you advice that is advantageous to him,** for he might be blinded by his own interest. This saying explains the motivation of the father, who may persuade himself that he is acting in his daughter's best interests.

אָמַר רַב יְהוּדָה [12]**Rav Yehudah said in the name of Rav: Someone who marries his daughter to an old man,**

תְּחַלֵּל אֶת בִּתְּךָ לְהַזְנוֹתָהּ׳. [1]רַבִּי אֱלִיעֶזֶר אוֹמֵר: זֶה הַמַּשִּׂיא אֶת בִּתּוֹ לְזָקֵן, [2]רַבִּי עֲקִיבָא אוֹמֵר: זֶה הַמַּשְׁהֶא בִּתּוֹ בּוֹגֶרֶת״.

[3]אָמַר רַב כָּהֲנָא מִשּׁוּם רַבִּי עֲקִיבָא: אֵין לְךָ עָנִי בְּיִשְׂרָאֵל אֶלָּא רָשָׁע עָרוּם, [4]וְהַמַּשְׁהֶא בִּתּוֹ בּוֹגֶרֶת.

[5]אִטּוּ הַמַּשְׁהֶא בִּתּוֹ בּוֹגֶרֶת לָאו רָשָׁע עָרוּם הוּא?

[6]אָמַר אַבַּיֵי: [76B] [7]הָכִי קָאָמַר: [8]אֵיזֶהוּ עָנִי רָשָׁע עָרוּם — [9]זֶה הַמַּשְׁהֶא בִּתּוֹ בּוֹגֶרֶת.

[10]וְאָמַר רַב כָּהֲנָא מִשּׁוּם רַבִּי עֲקִיבָא: [11]הֱוֵי זָהִיר מִן הַיּוֹעֶצְךָ לְפִי דַּרְכּוֹ.

[12]אָמַר רַב יְהוּדָה אָמַר רַב: הַמַּשִּׂיא אֶת בִּתּוֹ לְזָקֵן,

LITERAL TRANSLATION

profane your daughter, to cause her to be a harlot.' [1]Rabbi Eliezer says: This is someone who marries his daughter off to an old man. [2]Rabbi Akiva says: This is someone who delays [the marriage of] his adult daughter."

[3]Rav Kahana said in the name of Rabbi Akiva: There is no poor man in Israel except for a cunning, wicked man, [4]and someone who delays [the marriage of] his adult daughter.

[5]Is someone who delays [the marriage of] his adult daughter not a cunning, wicked man?

[6]Abaye said: [76B] [7]He said as follows: [8]Who is poor and a cunning, wicked man? [9]This is someone who delays [the marriage of] his adult daughter.

[10]And Rav Kahana said in the name of Rabbi Akiva: [11]Be wary of someone who advises you for his benefit.

[12]Rav Yehudah said in the name of Rav: Someone who marries his daughter to an old man,

RASHI

זה המשהה בתו בוגרת – שמתאוה להפקירה ומזנה. אין לך עני בישראל – לקמן מפרש לה. משהה בתו בוגרת לאו רשע ערום הוא – שמשהא אותה בשביל מלאכה, וזו היא ערמת רשע שגורם להזנותה בשביל הנאתו, שאין רוצה לקנות שפחה לשמשו. הכי קאמר איזה עני רשע ערום – שבשביל עניות מרשיע, – זה המשהה וכו׳, והכי אתמר אין לך עני רשע ערום בישראל אלא המשהה בתו בוגרת. לפי דרכו – להנאתו.

NOTES

account of his wisdom or other fine qualities. This appears to be the plain meaning of our passage, and is supported by anecdotes reported in the Gemara.

הַמַּשְׁהֶא בִּתּוֹ בּוֹגֶרֶת Someone who delays the marriage of his adult daughter. Some add that the father gave his daughter away in betrothal while she was a minor, and now that she is betrothed, he delays her marriage, thus enjoying the money that he received in exchange for her betrothal, as well as her free services in his household. Such conduct will lead to the daughter's profanation, for should she be seduced during that period, she will be guilty of adultery (*Iyyun Ya'akov*).

הַיּוֹעֶצְךָ לְפִי דַּרְכּוֹ Who advises you for his benefit. This statement might have been placed here as a warning to an adult daughter, that if her father advises her to put off marriage, she should carefully examine his reasoning, and see whether he has his or her best interests at heart. The recipient of advice should always clarify whether or not the person who offers advice has any personal interest at stake (*Rabbenu Yehonatan*).

הַמַּשִּׂיא אֶת בִּתּוֹ לְזָקֵן Someone who marries his daughter to an old man. *Meiri* limits this ruling to an old man who is stricken with disease. Similarly, *Rabbi Ya'akov Emden* restricts this law to an elderly gentleman who is impotent.

TRANSLATION AND COMMENTARY

or takes a mature woman as a **wife for his minor son, or returns a lost object to a non-Jew** — [1]**about him the verses state** (Deuteronomy 29:18-19): **"To add drunkenness to thirst. The Lord will not wish to forgive him."** An old man and a minor who have little sexual desire are considered "drunk, satiated," whereas a woman in her prime who desires sexual relations is considered "thirsty." Her unsatisfied desire may lead her to harlotry. Similarly, a Jew is regarded as being "thirsty" for God's word, whereas a non-Jew is regarded as being "drunk, satiated." Someone who restores lost property to a non-Jew, and thus equates his obligations to a non-Jew with those to his fellow Jew, joins drunkenness to thirst.

מֵיתִיבִי [2]**An objection was raised** against Rav from a Baraita: **"Someone who loves his wife as himself, and honors her** with expensive clothing and jewelry even **more than himself, and guides his sons and daughters in the straight path, and marries them near their period of maturity** — [3]**regarding him the verse states** (Job 5:24): **'And you shall know that your tent is at peace, and you shall visit your habitation, and shall not sin.'"** Thus, we see that it is commendable to marry one's son while he is still a minor, against Rava!

וְהַמַּשִּׂיא אִשָּׁה לִבְנוֹ קָטָן, וְהַמַּחֲזִיר אֲבֵידָה לְנָכְרִי — [1]עָלָיו הַכָּתוּב אוֹמֵר: "לְמַעַן סְפוֹת הָרָוָה אֶת הַצְּמֵאָה לֹא יֹאבֶה ה׳ סְלֹחַ לוֹ".

[2]מֵיתִיבִי: "הָאוֹהֵב אֶת אִשְׁתּוֹ כְּגוּפוֹ, וְהַמְכַבְּדָהּ יוֹתֵר מִגּוּפוֹ, וְהַמַּדְרִיךְ בָּנָיו וּבְנוֹתָיו בְּדֶרֶךְ יְשָׁרָה, וְהַמַּשִּׂיאָן סָמוּךְ לְפִירְקָן — [3]עָלָיו הַכָּתוּב אוֹמֵר: 'וְיָדַעְתָּ כִּי שָׁלוֹם אָהֳלֶךָ וּפָקַדְתָּ נָוְךָ וְלֹא תֶחֱטָא'"!

LITERAL TRANSLATION

and someone who takes a wife for his minor son, and someone who returns a lost object to a non-Jew — [1]about him the verses state: "To add drunkenness to thirst. The Lord will not wish to forgive him."

[2]They raised an objection: "Someone who loves his wife as himself, and honors her more than himself, and guides his sons and daughters in the straight path, and marries them near their time of maturity — [3]regarding him the verse states: 'And you shall know that your tent is at peace, and you shall visit your habitation, and shall not sin.'"

RASHI

למען ספות — לחבור, כמו "ספו שנה על שנה" (ישעיה כט). **רוה את הצמאה** — שבע בדבר עם צמא לדבר, זקן וילדה זאת צמאה לתשמיש וזקן שבע, וכן גדולה לקטן. **והמחזיר אבידה לנכרי** — השוה וחבר נכרי לישראל, ומראה בעצמו שהשבת אבדה אינה חשובה לו מצות בוראו, שאף לנכרי הוא עושה כן שלא נצטווה עליהם. **רוה** — נכרים שבעים ואינן צמאין ליוצרם, **צמאה** — זו כנסת ישראל שצמאה ותאיבה ליראת יוצרה ולקיים מצותיו. **והמכבדה** — בתכשיטין נאין. **סמוך לפירקן** — עדיין קטנים הם.

NOTES

הַמַּחֲזִיר אֲבֵידָה לְנָכְרִי Someone who returns a lost object to a non-Jew. While it is forbidden to deceive a non-Jew, or steal from him, the obligation to restore a lost object to its owner is not included among the self-evident obligations that apply universally to all people (for in many societies, lost property belongs to the government). Restoring lost property is a special act of kindness which a Jew is required to perform for his Jewish brother, but not for a non-Jew, unless the deed will bring about the sanctification of God's Name (see *Meiri*).

סְפוֹת הָרָוָה אֶת הַצְּמֵאָה To add drunkenness to thirst. Some explain that when a father takes a mature woman as a wife for his minor son, he stirs latent sexual desire in his child and thus he causes the "satiated" one to be "thirsty." Similarly, someone who restores lost property to a non-Jew whets the non-Jew's appetite, not only for his own property, but also for Jewish property (*Maharsha*).

הָאוֹהֵב אֶת אִשְׁתּוֹ כְּגוּפוֹ, וְהַמְכַבְּדָהּ יוֹתֵר מִגּוּפוֹ Someone who loves his wife as himself, and honors her more than himself. The Baraita speaks of a husband loving his wife as himself, but honoring her more than himself, because love is a matter of the heart and not measurable, but honor expresses itself materially, so that a man may indeed honor his wife more than himself by providing her with clothing and jewelry that is more expensive than his own (*Ramah*).

סָמוּךְ לְפִירְקָן Near their period of maturity. Some understand that the expression סָמוּךְ לְפִירְקָן is used here in the sense of "near the accepted age for marriage," the age of eighteen (*Meiri*).

HALAKHAH

הַמַּחֲזִיר אֲבֵידָה לְנָכְרִי Someone who returns a lost object to a non-Jew. "If a Jew restores a lost object to a non-Jew in order to sanctify the Name of God, his conduct is praiseworthy. If not returning the lost object will lead to a desecration of God's Name, he is forbidden to keep it, and must return it to the non-Jew." (*Shulḥan Arukh, Ḥoshen Mishpat* 266:1.)

הָאוֹהֵב אֶת אִשְׁתּוֹ כְּגוּפוֹ Someone who loves his wife as himself. "The Sages commanded that a man honor his wife more than himself, and love her as himself." (*Rambam, Sefer Nashim, Hilkhot Ishut* 15:19.)

הַמַּשִּׂיאָן סָמוּךְ לְפִירְקָן Someone who marries them near their period of maturity. "Parents are commanded to marry their sons and daughters soon after they reach puberty, so that they will not engage in forbidden sexual relations or entertain forbidden sexual thoughts. But one should not marry one's son before he reaches the age of thirteen." (*Rambam, Sefer Kedushah, Hilkhot Issurei Bi'ah* 21:25; *Shulḥan Arukh, Even HaEzer* 1:3.)

[1]סָמוּךְ לְפִירְקָן שָׁאנֵי.
[2]תָּנוּ רַבָּנַן: ״הָאוֹהֵב אֶת שְׁכֵינָיו, וְהַמְקָרֵב אֶת קְרוֹבָיו, וְהַנּוֹשֵׂא אֶת בַּת אֲחוֹתוֹ, וְהַמַּלְוֶה סֶלַע לֶעָנִי בִּשְׁעַת דּוֹחֲקוֹ — [3]עָלָיו הַכָּתוּב אוֹמֵר: ׳אָז תִּקְרָא וַה׳ יַעֲנֶה׳״.
[4]תָּנוּ רַבָּנַן: [5]״׳אֹתוֹ וְאֶתְהֶן׳ — [6]אוֹתוֹ וְאֶת אַחַת מֵהֶן: [7]דִּבְרֵי רַבִּי יִשְׁמָעֵאל. [8]רַבִּי עֲקִיבָא אוֹמֵר: אוֹתוֹ וְאֶת שְׁתֵּיהֶן״.
[9]מַאי בֵּינַיְיהוּ?
[10]אָמַר אַבַּיֵי: מַשְׁמָעוּת דּוֹרְשִׁים אִיכָּא בֵּינַיְיהוּ. [11]רַבִּי יִשְׁמָעֵאל סָבַר: ״אֹתוֹ וְאֶתְהֶן״ — [12]אוֹתוֹ

TRANSLATION AND COMMENTARY

סָמוּךְ לְפִירְקָן [1]The Gemara answers. If the boy is already **near his period of maturity**, that is, he is approaching puberty, it **is different.**

תָּנוּ [2]**Our Rabbis taught** a related Baraita: **"Someone who loves his neighbors, and draws his relatives near, and marries his sister's daughter, and lends a sela to a poor man in his time of distress** when nobody else is ready to help him — [3]**regarding him the verses state** (Isaiah 58:7-9): "Is it not to share your bread with the hungry, and that you bring the poor that are cast out to your house; when you see the naked, that you cover him; and that you hide not yourself from your own flesh.... **Then you shall call, and the Lord shall answer.'"**

תָּנוּ רַבָּנַן [4]**Our Rabbis taught** the following Baraita: "The verse states (Leviticus 20:14): 'And if a man takes a woman and her mother, it is wickedness; they shall be burnt with fire, both he and they [אֶתְהֶן].' [5]**'Both he and they' — he** — the man, [6]**and one of them** — his wife's mother; [7]**this is the position of Rabbi Yishmael.** [8]**Rabbi Akiva** disagrees and **says: He** — the man, **and the two of them** (as will be explained below)."

מַאי [9]The Gemara asks: **What is the difference between** the position of Rabbi Yishmael and that of Rabbi Akiva? Surely, Rabbi Akiva does not mean that because a man engaged in forbidden sexual intercourse with his wife's mother, both women are liable to death by burning!

אָמַר אַבַּיֵי [10]**Abaye said:** There is no substantive difference between the position of Rabbi Yishmael and that of Rabbi Akiva. The only difference **between them is** their way of **interpreting the meaning** of the Biblical text. [11]**Rabbi Yishmael maintains** that the words **"Both he and they** [*ethen*]" mean: [12]**He and one of**

LITERAL TRANSLATION

[1]Near to their period of maturity is different.
[2]Our Rabbis taught: "Someone who loves his neighbors, and draws his relatives near, and marries the daughter of his sister, and lends a sela to a poor man in his hour of distress — [3]regarding him the verse states: 'Then you shall call, and the Lord shall answer.'"
[4]Our Rabbis taught: [5]"'Both he and they' — [6]he and one of them; [7][these are] the words of Rabbi Yishmael. [8]Rabbi Akiva says: He and the two of them."
[9]What is [the difference] between them?
[10]Abaye said: [The only difference] between them is [their way of] interpreting the meaning [of the Biblical text]. [11]Rabbi Yishmael maintains: "Both he and they" — [12]he

RASHI

סמוך לפירקן שאני — דלאו היינו קטן כולי האי, דמשום שנה או אלי שנה לא תזנה עליו. **תקרא וה׳ יענה** — לעיל מיניה כתיב ״הלא פרוס לרעב לחמך וגו׳ ומבשרך אל תתעלם״ היינו נושא בת אחותו, ומקרב את קרוביו, ואוהב את שכניו נמי כמקרב את קרוביו, דכתיב (משלי כז) ״טוב שכן קרוב מאח רחוק״, ומלוה סלע לעני בשעת דוחקו בכלל ״פרוס לרעב לחמך״ ״וכי תראה ערום״. **אתהן** — משמע ליה לרבי ישמעאל את האחת מהן, שכן בלשון יוני קורין לאחת הינא, והכי קאמר קרא: ״ואיש אשר יקח את אשה״ זו אשתו, והדר ״את אמה באש ישרפו אותו״ — ואת חמותו. **רבי עקיבא אומר אותו ואת שתיהן** — מפרש ליה התלמוד ואזיל במאי קא מיפלגי, הא ודאי לשרוף את אשתו לא קאמר רבי עקיבא. **משמעות דורשין** — לשון משמעות המקרא דורשין. **לרבי ישמעאל אתהן חדא הוא** — ואחמותו קאי, ואם חמותו מדרשא ד״זמה״ אתיא, כדאמר לעיל מנין לעשות למטה כלמעלה וכו׳.

NOTES

הַנּוֹשֵׂא אֶת בַּת אֲחוֹתוֹ **Someone who marries his sister's daughter.** The Rishonim offer various explanations as to why the Gemara speaks here of someone who marries his sister's daughter, and not his brother's daughter. *Rashi* (*Yevamot* 42b) suggests that a man is closer to his sister than to his brother, and therefore will cherish his sister's daughter as his wife more than he would cherish his brother's daughter. *Tosafot* argues that, as a rule, "children resemble their mother's brother," and so a man prefers to marry his sister's daughter, because his children will resemble himself. The Geonim argue that if a man marries his brother's daughter, and he dies without children, it will not be possible to fulfill the commandment of levirate marriage unless they have other brothers. Some Rishonim maintain that marrying one's son's daughter is also meritorious.

HALAKHAH

הַנּוֹשֵׂא אֶת בַּת אֲחוֹתוֹ **Someone who marries his sister's daughter.** "A man is commanded to marry his sister's daughter. Some say that the same applies to his brother's daughter. (A person should not marry his niece, if there is any concern that such a union will result in diseased children.)" (*Shulḥan Arukh, Even HaEzer* 2:6; *Rema*.)

וְאֶת אַחַת מֵהֶן, [1]שֶׁכֵּן בְּלָשׁוֹן יְוָנִי קוֹרִין לְאַחַת, ״הֵינָא״. [2]וְאֵם חֲמוֹתוֹ מִדְּרָשָׁא אָתְיָא. [3]רַבִּי עֲקִיבָא סָבַר: ״אֹתוֹ וְאֶתְהֶן״ — [4]אוֹתוֹ וְאֶת שְׁתֵּיהֶן. [5]וְאֵם חֲמוֹתוֹ הָכָא כְּתִיבָא.

[6]רָבָא אָמַר: [7]חֲמוֹתוֹ לְאַחַר מִיתָה אִיכָּא בֵּינַיְיהוּ. [8]רַבִּי יִשְׁמָעֵאל סָבַר: חֲמוֹתוֹ לְאַחַר מִיתָה בִּשְׂרֵפָה, [9]וְרַבִּי עֲקִיבָא סָבַר: אִיסּוּרָא בְּעָלְמָא.

משנה [10]וְאֵלּוּ הַנֶּהֱרָגִין: הָרוֹצֵחַ, וְאַנְשֵׁי עִיר הַנִּדַּחַת.

LITERAL TRANSLATION

and one of them, [1]for in the Greek language one is called "hena." [2]And the mother of his mother-in-law is derived through interpretation. [3]Rabbi Akiva maintains: "Both he and they" — [4]he and the two of them. [5]And the mother of his mother-in-law is written here.

[6]Rava said: [7]They disagree about his mother-in-law after [his wife's] death. [8]Rabbi Yishmael maintains: His mother-in-law after [his wife's] death is by burning. [9]And Rabbi Akiva maintains: Merely a prohibition.

MISHNAH [10]And these are the ones who are slain: The murderer, and the inhabitants of a subverted city.

TRANSLATION AND COMMENTARY

them, that is to say, his mother-in-law. [1]Rabbi Yishmael supports this interpretation with the argument that the **Greek** equivalent of the word **"one" is "hena."** Thus, the verse refers only to the man's mother-in-law, [2]**and** the punishment of burning for intercourse with **one's mother-in-law's mother is derived through interpretation** by a *gezerah shavah* (as was explained above, 75b: "From where do I know to make three generations above like three generations below?") [3]**Rabbi Akiva** disagrees and **says** that the words **"both he and they"** mean: [4]**"He and the two of them,"** that is to say, his mother-in-law and his mother-in-law's mother. [5]Thus, the punishment of burning for having intercourse with **one's mother-in-law's mother is written here** explicitly. According to this understanding of the controversy, Rabbi Yishmael and Rabbi Akiva do not disagree about the law itself, but only about whether the penalty of burning that is imposed in the case of a man who has intercourse with his mother-in-law's mother is stated explicitly in the Torah, or whether it is derived by a *gezerah shavah*.

רָבָא אָמַר [6]**Rava said:** Both Rabbi Yishmael and Rabbi Akiva agree that the punishment of burning for having intercourse with one's mother-in-law's mother is derived by a *gezerah shavah*. [7]But, the Tannaim **disagree about** intercourse with **one's mother-in-law after his wife's death.** [8]**Rabbi Yishmael maintains** that someone who has intercourse with **his mother-in-law after his wife's death is** liable to death **by burning,** for the words "both he and they" mean: "He and one of them," teaching that the punishment of burning is imposed even if only his mother-in-law is alive. [9]**Rabbi Akiva** disagrees and **says:** Intercourse with one's mother-in-law after one's wife's death is **merely forbidden,** but it is not punishable by burning, for the words "both he and they" mean: "He and the two of them," teaching that the punishment of burning is only imposed if both of them are alive.

MISHNAH וְאֵלּוּ [10]**These are** the transgressors **who are liable to** the third mode of capital punishment, **slaying** by the sword (decapitation): **A murderer, and the inhabitants of a subverted city** (the majority of whose inhabitants committed idolatry; see Deuteronomy 13:13-19). The punishment imposed for murder is learned from the punishment imposed upon someone who kills his non-Jewish slave, about whom it is stated (Exodus 21:20): "And if a man smites his slave...he shall surely be avenged" — "avenging" referring here to death by the sword, as the verse states elsewhere (Leviticus 26:25): "And I will bring a sword upon you, that shall avenge my covenant." As for the inhabitants of a subverted city, the verse states explicitly (Deuteronomy 13:16): "You shall surely smite the inhabitants of that city with the edge of the sword."

RASHI

לרבי עקיבא אתהן תרתי משמע — חמותו ואם חמותו, והכי קאמר: ״ישרפו אותו ואתהן״ הן שתי אמהות, כגון לקח את אשה ואת אמה ואם אמה. **רבא אמר חמותו שבא עליה חתנה לאחר מיתת בתה איכא בינייהו** — אבל אם חמותו לתרווייהו מדרשא אתיא. **רבי ישמעאל סבר חמותו לאחר מיתה בשריפה** — כמחיים, דהכי קאמר קרא אפילו אין מתקיימת אלא אחת מהן — תשרף, דהא ודאי אאשתו לא קאמר קרא דתשרף. **רבי עקיבא סבר** — אתהן — שתיהן משמע, והכי קאמר: אם אשתו קיימת תשרף חמותו, ואם לאו — אין כאן עונש שריפה אלא איסור ארור שוכב עם חותנתו.

LANGUAGE

הֵינָא ***Hena.*** The Talmud refers to the Greek word, ἕν, *hen*, meaning "one."

HALAKHAH

אִיסּוּרָא בְּעָלְמָא Merely a prohibition. "If someone engages in sexual intercourse with his wife's mother or his wife's daughter after his wife's death, he is liable to excision, but not judicial execution," following Rabbi Akiva against Rabbi Yishmael, and Rava against Abaye. (*Rambam, Sefer Kedushah, Hilkhot Issurei Bi'ah* 2:8.)

וְאֵלּוּ הַנֶּהֱרָגִין: הָרוֹצֵחַ And these are the ones who are slain: The murderer... "If someone intentionally murders another person in the presence of witnesses, he is liable to death by decapitation." (*Rambam, Sefer Nezikin, Hilkhot Rotze'ah* 1:1.)

וְאַנְשֵׁי עִיר הַנִּדַּחַת And the inhabitants of a subverted city. "The inhabitants of a subverted city are put to death by decapitation." (*Rambam, Sefer Mada, Hilkhot Avodah Zarah* 4:1; *Sefer Shofetim, Hilkhot Sanhedrin* 15:12.)

[1] רוֹצֵחַ שֶׁהִכָּה אֶת רֵעֵהוּ בְּאֶבֶן אוֹ בְּבַרְזֶל, [2] וְכָבַשׁ עָלָיו לְתוֹךְ הַמַּיִם אוֹ לְתוֹךְ הָאוּר וְאֵינוֹ יָכוֹל לַעֲלוֹת מִשָּׁם וָמֵת — חַיָּיב. [3] דְּחָפוֹ לְתוֹךְ הַמַּיִם, אוֹ לְתוֹךְ הָאוּר, וְיָכוֹל לַעֲלוֹת מִשָּׁם, וָמֵת — פָּטוּר. [4] שִׁיסָּה בּוֹ אֶת הַכֶּלֶב, שִׁיסָּה בּוֹ אֶת הַנָּחָשׁ — פָּטוּר. [5] הִשִּׁיךְ בּוֹ אֶת הַנָּחָשׁ — [6] רַבִּי יְהוּדָה מְחַיֵּיב, [7] וַחֲכָמִים פּוֹטְרִין.

גמרא [8] אָמַר שְׁמוּאֵל: מִפְּנֵי מַה לֹא נֶאֶמְרָה "יָד" בְּבַרְזֶל?

LITERAL TRANSLATION

[1] A murderer who struck his fellow with a stone or [an] iron [tool], [2] or pushed him into water or into fire, and he was unable to get out from there, and he died, is liable. [3] [If] he pushed him into the water, or into the fire, and he was able to get out from there, and he died, he is exempt.

[4] [If] he set a dog upon him, [or if] he set a snake upon him, he is exempt. [5] [If] he caused the snake to bite him, [6] Rabbi Yehudah says he is liable, [7] but the Sages exempt him.

GEMARA [8] Shmuel said: Why is "hand" not stated regarding [an] iron [tool]?

TRANSLATION AND COMMENTARY

רוֹצֵחַ [1] **A murderer who struck** his victim **with a stone or an iron tool** is liable to the death penalty, as the Torah states (Numbers 35:16-18): "And if he smites him with an instrument of iron, so that he dies, he is a murderer....And if he smites him by hand with a stone, whereby he may die, and he dies, he is a murderer....Or if he smites him with a hand weapon of wood, whereby he may die, and he dies, he is a murderer." [2] If someone **applied** pressure on another person, forcing him to remain **under water or in a fire, and** the victim **was unable to free himself** from the danger, **and he died,** the assailant **is** guilty of murder, and is executed by decapitation. [3] But **if he pushed him into the water, or into the fire, and** the victim **was able free himself** but failed to do so, **and** as a result **he died** in the water or in the fire, the assailant **is exempt** from judicial execution.

שִׁיסָּה [4] **If** someone **set his dog upon** another person, **or if he set his snake upon him,** and the dog or the snake bit the other person, and he died from the bite, the person who set the animal upon the victim **is exempt** from judicial execution, because he did not commit the physical act that killed him. [5] But **if he** held **the snake** against the victim's body, and **caused** it **to bite him,** the Tannaim disagree: [6] **Rabbi Yehudah says he is liable.** [7] But **the Sages say that he is exempt.**

GEMARA אָמַר שְׁמוּאֵל [8] **Shmuel said:** Regarding a stone or wooden murder weapon, the Torah uses the word "hand" (Numbers 35:17-18): "And if he smites him by *hand* with a stone....Or if he smites him with a *hand* weapon of wood." **Why,** then, **regarding an iron tool, is** the word **"hand" not stated,** but only (Numbers 35:16): "And if he smites him with an instrument of iron"? The word "hand" used in connection with a stone or a piece of wood teaches that a killer using such a weapon is only liable to be executed if the instrument is large enough to protrude from his hand. But a smaller instrument is not regarded as deadly.

LANGUAGE (RASHI)

פרמי״ר* is the Old French *premer*, meaning, "to press, push."

RASHI

משנה כבש — *פרמי״ר בלעז, אוחז ראשו של חבירו ותוקפו במים כדי שלא יוכל להרים ראשו, וננער ומת. שיסה = גירה. השיך — שאחז את הנחש בידו והוליכו, והגיע שיני נחש בידו של חבירו, פלוגתא דרבי יהודה ורבנן מפרש בגמרא.

גמרא לא נאמר יד בברזל — כמה שנאמר (במדבר לה) "באבן יד בכלי עץ יד" משמע שיש בה מלא אחיזה, דבעינן שיעורא, אבל בברזל כתיב "ואם בכלי ברזל הכהו".

NOTES

רוֹצֵחַ שֶׁהִכָּה אֶת רֵעֵהוּ **A murderer who struck his fellow.** The Mishnah cites examples of killings which are similar to the four modes of judicial execution: Striking with a stone, which is similar to death by stoning; pushing into a fire, which is similar to death by burning; forcing a person to remain under water, which is similar to strangulation. But nevertheless all those who are guilty of murder are subject to death by decapitation (*Arukh Lener, Rashash*).

HALAKHAH

רוֹצֵחַ שֶׁהִכָּה אֶת רֵעֵהוּ **A murderer who struck another person.** "If someone strikes another person with a stone or a piece of wood that is large enough to deliver a fatal blow, and kills him, he is liable to judicial execution. If someone pushes another person into water or into a fire, and the victim is not able to free himself from the danger, and he dies, the assailant is liable to judicial execution. And similarly, if he applies pressure on the other person, forcing him to remain under water or in the fire, and he dies, he is liable to judicial execution." (*Rambam, Sefer Nezikin, Hilkhot Rotze'aḥ* 3:1,9.)

שִׁיסָּה בּוֹ אֶת הַכֶּלֶב **If he set his dog upon him.** "If someone sets his dog or his snake upon another person, and that person dies from the bite, or even if the assailant holds the snake against the victim's body and causes it to inflict the fatal bite, the assailant is not liable to judicial execution, but he is regarded as a murderer, and is subject to divine retribution." (*Rambam, Sefer Nezikin, Hilkhot Rotze'aḥ* 3:10.)

[1]שֶׁהַבַּרְזֶל מֵמִית בְּכָל שֶׁהוּא. [2]תַּנְיָא נַמִי הָכִי: ״רַבִּי אוֹמֵר: [3]גָּלוּי וְיָדוּעַ לִפְנֵי מִי שֶׁאָמַר וְהָיָה הָעוֹלָם שֶׁהַבַּרְזֶל מֵמִית בְּכָל שֶׁהוּא, [4]לְפִיכָךְ לֹא נָתְנָה תּוֹרָה בּוֹ שִׁיעוּר״.

[5]וְהָנֵי מִילֵּי דִּבְרַזְיֵהּ מִיבְרַז.

[6]״וְכָבַשׁ עָלָיו לְתוֹךְ הַמַּיִם״. [7]רֵישָׁא רְבוּתָא קָא מַשְׁמַע לָן וְסֵיפָא רְבוּתָא קָא מַשְׁמַע לָן. [8]רֵישָׁא רְבוּתָא קָא מַשְׁמַע לָן: [9]אַף עַל גַּב דְּלָאו אִיהוּ דְּחָפוֹ, [10]כֵּיוָן דְּאֵין יָכוֹל לַעֲלוֹת מִשָּׁם וָמֵת, חַיָּיב. [11]סֵיפָא רְבוּתָא קָא מַשְׁמַע לָן: [12]אַף עַל גַּב דִּדְחָפוֹ, כֵּיוָן דְּיָכוֹל לַעֲלוֹת מִשָּׁם וָמֵת, פָּטוּר.

[13]כֶּבֶשׁ מְנָלַן? [14]אָמַר שְׁמוּאֵל: דְּאָמַר קְרָא: ״אוֹ בְאֵיבָה״ — [15]לְרַבּוֹת אֶת הַמְצַמְצֵם.

LITERAL TRANSLATION

[1]Because [an] iron [tool] of any measure kills.

[2]It was also taught thus: "Rabbi says: [3]It is revealed and known to Him who spoke and brought the world into being that [an] iron [tool] of any measure kills. [4]Therefore the Torah did not give a measure regarding it."

[5]And these words apply when he pierced him.

[6]"Or pushed him into water." [7]The first clause teaches us a novel matter, and the last clause teaches us a novel matter. [8]The first clause teaches us a novel matter: [9]Even though he did not push him, [10]since he was unable to get out from there, and he died, he is liable. [11]The last clause teaches us a novel matter: [12]Even though he pushed him, since he was able to get out from there, and he died, he is exempt.

[13]From where do we [know about] forcing down? [14]Shmuel said: For the verse states: "Or in enmity" — [15]to include [someone who forces another person into] confinement.

TRANSLATION AND COMMENTARY

The word "hand" is not used in connection with an iron tool, [1]**because an iron tool of any size can kill** by way of a fatal stab wound.

תַּנְיָא [2]**The same thing was also taught** in the following Baraita: **"Rabbi** Yehudah HaNasi **says:** [3]**It is revealed and known to Him who spoke and brought the world into being that an iron tool of any size can kill.** [4]**Therefore the Torah did not mention a** minimum **size regarding** an iron tool, as it did regarding a stone or a wooden weapon."

וְהָנֵי מִילֵּי [5]The Gemara notes: **The** foregoing **law** only **applies** when the killer **stabbed** his victim with the iron tool. But if he killed his victim with a blow, he is only liable to execution if the instrument was big enough to be considered deadly.

וְכָבַשׁ [6]We have learned in our Mishnah: "If someone **applied pressure on** another person, forcing **him** to remain **under water** or in a fire, and the victim was unable to free himself from the danger, and he died, the assailant is guilty of murder, and is executed by decapitation. But if he pushed him into the water, or into the fire, and the victim was able to save himself but failed to do so, the assailant is exempt from judicial execution." [7]The Gemara remarks: **The first clause teaches us a novel matter, and the second clause teaches us a novel matter.** [8]**The first clause teaches us a novel matter:** [9]**Even though** the assailant **did not push** his victim into the water or into the fire, but rather the victim fell in by himself, [10]**since** the assailant forced him to remain under water or in the fire, and the victim **was unable to** extricate **himself** from the danger, **and** as a result **he died,** the assailant is guilty of murder and is executed by decapitation. [11]**The second clause teaches us a novel matter:** [12]**Even though** the assailant **pushed** his victim into the water or into the fire, **since** the victim **was able to** extricate **himself** from the danger but **died** as a result of his failure to do so, the assailant **is exempt.**

כֶּבֶשׁ מְנָלַן [13]The Gemara asks: **From where do we know** that a person is guilty of murder if **he applied pressure** on his victim, forcing him to remain under water or in a fire? [14]**Shmuel said:** This is derived from **the verse** that **states** (Numbers 35:21): **"Or in enmity** he smites him with his hand, that he dies." [15]The word "or" **includes someone who** causes the death of another person by **forcing him into confinement** where he cannot survive.

RASHI

שהברזל ממית בכל שהוא — על ידי תחיבה, שתוחב לו מחט בושט או בלבו. **דברזיה מיבריז** = *פונש״ט בלע״ז. אבל הכהו לארכו דרך הכאה — שיעורא בעי. **אף על גב דלאו איהו דחפו** — אלא שנפל מעצמו, ובא זה וכבש עליו ולא נתנו להרים ראשו. **שיכול לעלות משם** — אדם אחר כיוצא בזה, ושעה גרמה לו. **פטור** — הדוחף, דלא עביד שיעור מיתה. **או לרבות את המצמצם** — היינו כובש, שאמצאו שם שלא יקום.

LANGUAGE (RASHI)

פונש״ט* should apparently be written פוינ״ט, which is the Old French *poynant*, meaning, "sharp, pointed."

HALAKHAH

הַבַּרְזֶל מֵמִית בְּכָל שֶׁהוּא **Because an iron tool of any measure kills.** "The Torah did not mention a minimum size regarding an iron tool used as a murder weapon. This law applies to an iron tool with a point, and in the case where the killer stabbed his victim. But if the killer delivered a fatal blow with an iron tool, we assess the weapon in order to determine whether or not it can be considered a deadly instrument." (*Rambam, Sefer Nezikin, Hilkhot Rotze'aḥ* 3:4.)

TRANSLATION AND COMMENTARY

הַהוּא גַּבְרָא [1] It was related that **a certain person kept another person's animal in the sun, and the animal died**. The Amoraim disagreed about the case: [2] **Ravina said** that the person who placed the animal in the sun **is liable** to pay damages, as if he had killed the animal with his own two hands. [3] **Rav Aḥa bar Rav said** that **he is exempt,** for he was not the direct cause of the animal's death. [4] **Ravina said** that the person who placed the animal in the sun **is liable** to pay damages, for the following *kal vaḥomer* **argument** may be put forward: [5] **If, regarding a murderer, regarding whom the Torah did not equate someone who acts inadvertently with someone who acts intentionally,** [6] **or someone who acts under compulsion with someone who acts willingly** — for the death penalty is only prescribed for willful and premeditated murder — [7] **it imposed culpability for confinement,** even if the murderer did not commit the physical act that directly caused his victim's death, [77A] then **regarding damages,** [8] concerning **which the Torah equated someone who acts inadvertently with someone who acts intentionally,** [9] **and someone who acts under compulsion with someone who acts willingly,** [10] **is it not right that it should impose** compensation **for confinement,** even if the tortfeasor did not commit the physical act which directly caused the damage?

רַב אַחָא בַּר רַב [11] The Gemara now explains the position of **Rav Aḥa bar Rav,** who **said** that the person who placed the animal in the sun **is exempt** from liability. [12] **Rav Mesharshiya said: What is the reason that my father's father** — Rav Aḥa bar Rav — **said** that the person who placed the animal in the sun **is exempt** from liability? [13] For **the verse states** (Numbers 35:21): "Or in enmity he smites him with his hand, that he dies; ***he* that smote him shall surely be put to death."** The word "he" is used here as a restrictive expression, limiting the culpability that is imposed for confinement. [14] **Regarding a murderer,** the Torah **imposed culpability for confinement,** even though the murderer did not

[1] הַהוּא גַּבְרָא דִּמְצַמְצְמָא לְחֵיוָתָא דְּחַבְרֵיהּ בְּשִׁימְשָׁא, וָמֵתָה, [2] רָבִינָא מְחַיֵּיב, [3] רַב אַחָא בַּר רַב פָּטַר. [4] רָבִינָא מְחַיֵּיב: קַל וָחוֹמֶר, [5] וּמָה רוֹצֵחַ שֶׁלֹּא עָשָׂה בּוֹ שׁוֹגֵג כְּמֵזִיד [6] וְאוֹנֶס כְּרָצוֹן, [7] חִיֵּיב בּוֹ אֶת הַמְּצַמְצֵם, [77A] נְזָקִין, [8] שֶׁעָשָׂה בָּהֶן שׁוֹגֵג כְּמֵזִיד, [9] וְאוֹנֶס כְּרָצוֹן, [10] אֵינוֹ דִּין שֶׁחִיֵּיב בָּהֶן אֶת הַמְּצַמְצֵם?

[11] רַב אַחָא בַּר רַב פּוֹטֵר. [12] אֲמַר רַב מְשָׁרְשִׁיָּא: מַאי טַעְמָא דַּאֲבוּהּ דְּאַבָּא דְּפוֹטֵר? [13] אָמַר קְרָא: "מוֹת יוּמַת הַמַּכֶּה רֹצֵחַ הוּא". [14] בְּרוֹצֵחַ הוּא דְּחַיָּיב לָן

LITERAL TRANSLATION

[1] [There was] a certain person who kept another person's animal in the sun, and it died. [2] Ravina said he is liable, [3] [and] Rav Aḥa bar Rav exempted him. [4] Ravina said he is liable: [There is] a *kal vaḥomer* argument. [5] If, regarding a murderer, concerning whom [the Torah] did not equate someone who acts inadvertently with someone who acts intentionally, [6] or someone who acts under compulsion with someone who acts willingly, [7] it imposed liability for confinement, [77A] when it comes to damages, [8] concerning which [the Torah] equated someone who acts inadvertently with someone who acts intentionally, [9] and someone who acts under compulsion with someone who acts willingly, [10] is it not right that it should impose liability for confinement?

[11] Rav Aḥa bar Rav exempts. [12] Rav Mesharshiya said: What is the reason of my father's father who exempts? [13] The verse states: "He that struck him shall surely be put to death." [14] Regarding a murderer, it imposed liability on us

RASHI

נזקין עשה בו אונס כרצון — היכא דעביד בידים ואפילו ישן, כדיליף בבבא קמא (כו,ב) "פצע תחת פצע" — לחייב על השוגג כמזיד וכו'. רב אחא פוטר — דגרמא בעלמא הוא, דשמשא קטליה. מות יומת המכה וכו' — סיפיה דקרא דלעיל "או באיבה" דרבינן מצמצם, וכתיב "רוצח הוא" מיעוטא למעוטי נזקין.

NOTES

דִּמְצַמְצְמָא לְחֵיוָתָא דְּחַבְרֵיהּ **Who confined another person's animal.** The Rishonim connect this discussion to the general dispute found in various places in the Talmud about whether or not a person is liable for damages that he did not cause directly with his own two hands (see *Ran*).

אֵינוֹ דִּין שֶׁחִיֵּיב בָּהֶן אֶת הַמְּצַמְצֵם? **Is it not right that it should impose liability for confinement?** Even though there is a general rule that we do not inflict punishment on the basis of a *kal vaḥomer* argument, that rule is limited to capital and corporal punishment. But monetary punishments may indeed be imposed on the basis of a *kal vaḥomer* argument (*Arukh Lener*).

בְּרוֹצֵחַ הוּא דְּחַיָּיב **Regarding a murderer, it imposed liability for confinement.** Some of the Aḥaronim ask: Elsewhere

HALAKHAH

דִּמְצַמְצְמָא לְחֵיוָתָא דְּחַבְרֵיהּ **Who kept another person's animal.** "If someone applied pressure on an animal, forcing it to remain under water, or if the animal fell into water, and he prevented it from getting out, or if he kept the animal in the sun, and the animal died, he is liable for damages, following Ravina, and the Gemara's conclusion that a person is liable for the indirect damage that he causes." (*Rambam, Sefer Nezikin, Hilkhot Ḥovel U'Mazik* 6:12.)

מְצַמְצֵם, [1]בִּנְזָקִין, לֹא חִיֵּיב לָן מְצַמְצֵם.
[2]אָמַר רָבָא: כְּפָתוֹ וּמֵת בָּרָעָב, פָּטוּר.
[3]וְאָמַר רָבָא: כְּפָתוֹ בַּחַמָּה וָמֵת, [4]בַּצִּינָּה וָמֵת, חַיָּיב. [5]סוֹף חַמָּה לָבֹא, סוֹף צִינָּה לָבֹא, פָּטוּר.
[6]וְאָמַר רָבָא: כְּפָתוֹ לִפְנֵי אֲרִי,

LITERAL TRANSLATION

for confinement. [1]Regarding damages, it did not impose liability on us for confinement.

[2]Rava said: [If] he tied him up, and he died of starvation, he is exempt.

[3]And Rava said: [If] he tied him up in the sun, and he died, [4][or] in the cold, and he died, he is liable. [5][If] the sun was eventually to shine (lit., "come"), [or] the cold was eventually to come, he is exempt.

[6]And Rava said: [If] he tied him up before a lion,

TRANSLATION AND COMMENTARY

directly cause his victim's death. [1]But **regarding damages,** the Torah **did not impose** compensation **for confinement.**

אָמַר רָבָא [2]**Rava said:** If someone **tied up** another person, and that person later **died of starvation,** the assailant **is exempt** from judicial execution, for he is viewed as being only the indirect cause of his victim's death.

וְאָמַר רָבָא [3]**Rava said:** If someone **tied up** another person and left him out **in the sun, and** that person later **died** of sunstroke, [4]**or** if he tied him up and left him out **in the cold, and** that person later **died** of exposure, the assailant **is liable** to judicial execution, for the conditions that led to his victim's death were already present. [5]But if it was not yet that hot or cold, and only **later did** it become scorching hot **or** extremely **cold,** causing the victim to die of sunstroke or exposure, the one who bound him **is exempt** from judicial execution. He is viewed as only the indirect cause of his victim's death.

וְאָמַר רָבָא [6]**Rava said:** If someone **tied** another person, and set him **before a lion,** and the lion tore the victim to pieces, the assailant **is exempt** from judicial execution, because lions do not necessarily attack

RASHI

כפתו ומת ברעב — דבשעה שכפתו אין כאן דבר הריגה, והרעב בא מאליו והולך וחזק לאחר זמן כל שעה, ולא דמי לנמלס במים ובאור דההורג מזומן. **סוף חמה לבא פטור** — כלומר אם לא היתה שם חמה בשעה שכפתו, אבל סוף לבא כאן, וזה לא יכול לעמוד וסופו למות — פטור, שלא היה ההורג מזומן להריגה וגרמא הוא, ואין דינו מסור לבית דין אלא לשמים. **כפתו לפני ארי פטור** — דאי נמי לא היה כפות לא היה יכול להציל עצמו מן הארי, דכולהו גרסינן אמר רבא.

NOTES

(*Sanhedrin* 15b), the verse, "He that smote him shall surely be put to death," is needed to teach that a person is executed if he murdered another person, but not if his animal killed another person. How, then, can Rav Aḥa bar Rav learn from that same verse that, regarding a murderer, the Torah imposed culpability for confinement, but not regarding a tortfeasor? *Me'lo HaRo'im* suggests that Rav Aḥa bar Rav must learn in a different manner that a person is not executed when his animal kills another person. *Rashash* dismisses the difficulty by citing the reading of *Rosh,* according to whom the law regarding confinement is in fact derived from a different verse.

כְּפָתוֹ וּמֵת בָּרָעָב If he tied him up, and he died of starvation. *Ran* emphasizes that we must be dealing here with a case where the victim was already hungry when he was tied up by his assailant, for if he was not at all hungry, this case would be identical with the case where the assailant tied up his victim, and only later did it become extremely hot or cold, and Rava would not have had to rule on both cases. But nevertheless the assailant is exempt, for this is different from case where the assailant tied up his victim and left him out in the sun or the cold, and he died of sunstroke or exposure. In that case, the assailant is liable, for when he tied up his victim, the heat or the cold was already extreme enough to kill. But in this case, the assailant is exempt from liability, for when he tied up his victim, the victim was not yet so hungry that he was in mortal danger, and only after it later grew in intensity was his hunger fit to kill.

לִפְנֵי אֲרִי וְלִפְנֵי יַתּוּשִׁין Before a lion, before mosquitoes. *Rashi* argues that, if the assailant tied his victim up before a lion, and the lion later tore the victim to pieces, the assailant is exempt from judicial execution, because even had the victim not been tied up, he could not have saved himself from the lion. But if the assailant tied his victim up and exposed him to mosquitoes, and later they bit him until he

HALAKHAH

כְּפָתוֹ וּמֵת בָּרָעָב If he bound him, and he died of starvation. "If someone tied up another person and let him starve to death, he is not liable to judicial execution, but he is regarded as a murderer, and is subject to divine retribution," following Rava. (*Rambam, Sefer Nezikin, Hilkhot Rotze'aḥ* 3:10.)

כְּפָתוֹ בַּחַמָּה וּבַצִּינָּה If he bound him in the sun or in the cold. "If someone tied up another person and left him out in the sun or in the cold, and he died of sunstroke or exposure, the assailant is liable to judicial execution," following Rava. (*Rambam, Sefer Nezikin, Hilkhot Rotze'aḥ* 3:9.)

סוֹף חַמָּה לָבֹא If the sun was eventually to come. "If someone tied up another person and left him in a place that would later become extremely hot or cold, and the victim subsequently died of sunstroke or exposure, the perpetrator is not liable to judicial execution, but he is regarded as a murderer, and is subject to divine retribution." (*Rambam, Sefer Nezikin, Hilkhot Rotze'aḥ* 3:10.)

TRANSLATION AND COMMENTARY

immediately. [1]But if the assailant tied his victim, and **exposed** him to **mosquitoes,** and they bit him until he died, the assailant **is liable** to judicial execution, because mosquitoes always bite immediately.

רַב אַשִׁי [2]**Rav Ashi said: Even** if the assailant exposed his victim to **mosquitoes,** and the victim later died from the bites, the assailant **is exempt** from judicial execution. The mosquitoes that were present when he tied his victim were not the same ones that caused his death. [3]The original mosquitoes **flew off, and** others **came** in their place.

אִיתְּמַר [4]**It was stated** that the Amoraim disagreed about a related matter: **If someone inverted a basin over** another person, and the victim gradually suffocated, [5]**or** if someone **removed the paving** from atop the ceiling of the room where someone was sleeping, and he died from exposure, [6]**Rava and Rabbi Zera disagreed** about the law. [7]**One said** that the perpetrator **is liable** to judicial execution, [8]and the other **one said** that **he is exempt** from that penalty.

תִּסְתַּיֵּים [9]The Gemara now tries to determine which Amora said that the assailant is liable, and which Amora said that he is exempt: **Conclude that it is Rava who said** here that the assailant **is exempt,** [10]**for Rava** himself had **said,** above, that, **if** someone **tied** another person, **and** the victim later **died of starvation,** the assailant **is exempt** from judicial execution.

אַדְּרַבָּה [11]The Gemara counters this argument: **On the contrary, conclude that it is Rabbi Zera who said** that the assailant **is exempt,** [12]**for Rabbi Zera** himself **said: If someone locked another person into an alabaster**

פָּטוּר. [1]לִפְנֵי יַתּוּשִׁין, חַיָּיב. [2]רַב אַשִׁי אָמַר: אֲפִילּוּ לִפְנֵי יַתּוּשִׁין, נַמִי פָּטוּר. [3]הָנֵי אָזְלִי, וְהָנֵי אָתוּ.

[4]אִיתְּמַר: כָּפָה עָלָיו גִּיגִּית [5]וּפָרַע עָלָיו מַעֲזִיבָה, [6]רָבָא וְרַבִּי זֵירָא. [7]חַד אָמַר: חַיָּיב. [8]וְחַד אָמַר: פָּטוּר.

[9]תִּסְתַּיֵּים דְּרָבָא הוּא דְּאָמַר: פָּטוּר, [10]דְּאָמַר רָבָא: כְּפָתוֹ וּמֵת בָּרָעָב, פָּטוּר.

[11]אַדְּרַבָּה, תִּסְתַּיֵּים דְּרַבִּי זֵירָא הוּא דְּאָמַר: פָּטוּר, [12]דְּאָמַר רַבִּי זֵירָא: הַאי מַאן דְּעַיְּילֵיהּ לְחַבְרֵיהּ בְּבֵיתָא דְּשַׁיְשָׁא,

LITERAL TRANSLATION

he is exempt. [1][If he exposes him] to mosquitoes, he is liable.

[2]Rav Ashi said: Even [if he exposes him] to mosquitoes, he is also exempt. [3]These go, and these come.

[4]It was stated: [If] someone inverted a basin over him, [5]or removed the paving above him, [6]Rava and Rabbi Zera [disagreed]. [7]One said: He is liable. [8]One said: He is exempt.

[9]Conclude that it is Rava who said: He is exempt, [10]for Rava said: [If] he tied him up, and he died of starvation, he is exempt.

[11]On the contrary, conclude that it is Rabbi Zera who said: He is exempt, [12]for Rabbi Zera said: [If] someone brought his fellow into an alabaster house,

RASHI

הני אזלי והני אתו – ולא מת על ידי יתושים הראשונים שהיו מוכנים שם, שכמה כתות עברו עליו. **כפה עליו גיגית** – ומת בהבלא. **או שפרע עליו מעזיבה** – וזה היה ישן, ונכנסה שם הצינה – פטור, שההורג בא לאחר זמן. **בביתא דשישא** – שסתום ביותר, ואין הבל האור והנר יכול לצאת ממנו.

NOTES

died, the assailant is liable, for he is viewed as having caused his victim's death, because had he not been tied up, he could have saved himself from the mosquitoes. But our commentary follows *Tosafot* and most Rishonim, who explain that in the case of the lion, the assailant is exempt, because when he set him before the lion, the animal was not yet ready to pounce upon its prey (as is evidenced by the fact that it did not attack while the assailant was tying up his victim), and so this is similar to the case where the assailant tied up his victim and only later did the scorching heat or the fierce cold make itself felt. But in the case of the mosquitoes the assailant is liable, for they were ready to attack the victim as soon as he was set before them.

הָנֵי אָזְלִי, וְהָנֵי אָתוּ **These go, and these come.** According to Rava, the entire swarm of mosquitoes is regarded as a single unit, even if those that bit the victim at the beginning flew off, and others came and finished him off. This is similar to the case where the assailant kept his victim under running water until he drowned, where the water in which the assailant first confined the victim flowed off, and then other water flowed in its place. Rav Ashi distinguishes between the two cases, and says that, whereas all the water adheres together and constitutes a single body of water, each mosquito is a creature unto itself. Thus, the assailant who exposed his victim to mosquitoes is exempt, for the mosquitoes that were present at the time that he tied up his victim are not the same mosquitoes that ultimately caused his death (*Rabbi David Bonfil*).

HALAKHAH

כָּפָה עָלָיו גִּיגִּית וּפָרַע עָלָיו מַעֲזִיבָה **If someone inverted a basin over him, or uncovered the paving above him.** "If someone inverted a basin over another person, causing him to suffocate, or if he removed the paving from the ceiling of the room where another person was sleeping, causing him to die of exposure, he is not liable to judicial execution (see *Kesef Mishneh*)." (*Rambam, Sefer Nezikin, Hilkhot Rotze'aḥ* 3:10.)

הַאי מַאן דְּעַיְּילֵיהּ לְחַבְרֵיהּ בְּבֵיתָא דְּשַׁיְשָׁא **If someone brought another person into an alabaster house.** "If someone locked another person in a sealed house and lit a candle, causing him to suffocate, he is a murderer and liable to judicial execution." (*Rambam, Sefer Nezikin, Hilkhot Rotze'aḥ* 3:9.)

TRANSLATION AND COMMENTARY

house that was totally sealed, [1]**and lit a candle** in the house, **and** the victim **died** from suffocation, the assailant **is liable** to judicial execution. [2]Now, it would seem from this ruling that **the reason** the assailant is liable **is that he lit a candle** in the alabaster house, using up the oxygen. [3]**But had he not lit a candle,** he would **not** be liable to judicial execution, even though the victim would have suffocated eventually in any event.

אָמְרִי [4]The Gemara rejects this argument: The Sages **said** that the two cases are not really comparable. **There,** in the case of the person who locked another person in an alabaster house, **without a candle, the bad air would not start** [77B] to suffocate him **immediately,** for the bad air would be dispersed all over the house. [5]But **here,** if someone inverted a basin over another person, **the bad air would start** to suffocate him **immediately, even without** lighting **a candle.** Thus, even though Rabbi Zera exempts the assailant who locked his victim in an alabaster house without lighting a candle, he might rule that the assailant who inverted a basin over another person's head is liable. Hence, Rava is the one who exempted the assailant in the latter case.

סִימָן [6]The Gemara now offers **a mnemonic device** by which to remember other types of indirect homicide: **Ladder, shield, medicines, at a wall.**

אָמַר רָבָא [7]**Rava said:** If someone **pushed** another person **into a pit, and there was a ladder in the pit and** then **someone else came and removed** the ladder, so the victim died of starvation, the assailant who pushed the victim into the pit is exempt from judicial execution. [8]**Even if** it was the assailant himself **who went ahead and removed** the ladder from the pit, **he is exempt** from judicial execution. [9]He cannot be executed for having pushed the victim into the pit, because **when he cast him into the pit,** his victim **was able** to climb the ladder **to get out.** And he cannot be executed for removing the ladder — that was merely the indirect cause of the victim's death.

וְאָמַר רָבָא [10]**And** similarly, **Rava said:** If someone **shot an arrow** at another person, **and** that other person **had a shield in his hand and** then **someone else came and removed** the shield, and the victim was killed by the arrow, the assailant who shot the arrow is exempt from judicial execution. [11]**Even if** it was the assailant

[1]וְאַדְלִיק לֵיהּ שְׁרָגָא וָמֵת, חַיָּיב. [2]טַעְמָא דְּאַדְלִיק לֵיהּ שְׁרָגָא, [3]הָא לָא אַדְלִיק לֵיהּ שְׁרָגָא, לָא!

[4]אָמְרִי: הָתָם בְּלָא שְׁרָגָא לָא מַתְחִיל הַבְלָא [77B] בְּשַׁעְתֵּיהּ. [5]הָכָא, בְּלָא שְׁרָגָא נַמִי מַתְחִיל הַבְלָא בְּשַׁעְתֵּיהּ.

[6](סִימָן סוּלָ״ם תְּרִי״ס סַמָּנִי״ן בְּכוֹתֶ״ל).

[7]אָמַר רָבָא: דְּחָפוֹ לַבּוֹר, וְסוּלָּם בַּבּוֹר, וּבָא אַחֵר וְסִילְּקוֹ, [8]וַאֲפִילּוּ הוּא קָדַם וְסִילְּקוֹ, פָּטוּר, [9]דִּבְעִידָּנָא דְּשַׁדְיֵיהּ יָכוֹל לַעֲלוֹת הוּא.

[10]וְאָמַר רָבָא: זָרַק חֵץ, וּתְרִיס בְּיָדוֹ, וּבָא אַחֵר וּנְטָלוֹ, [11]וַאֲפִילּוּ

LITERAL TRANSLATION

[1]and lit a candle, and he died, he is liable. [2]The reason is that he lit a candle, [3]but if he did not light a candle, no!

[4]They said. There, without a candle, the bad air does not start [77B] immediately. [5]Here, even without a candle, the bad air starts immediately.

[6](A sign: Ladder, shield, medicines, at a wall.)

[7]Rava said: [If] he pushed him into a pit, and there was a ladder in the pit, and someone else came and removed it, [8]and even if he went ahead and removed it, he is exempt, [9]for when he cast him [into the pit] he was able to get out.

[10]And Rava said: [If] he shot an arrow, and there was a shield in his hand, and someone else came and took it, [11]and even if

RASHI

טעמא דאדליק ליה שרגא — שומן את ההורג. הא לא אדליק ליה שרגא — ומת בהבל פיו, דומיא דכפה עליו גיגית — פטור. בשעתיה — מיד בשעת כפייה מתחיל, ואחר כך הולך וחזק. ואפילו הוא — הדוחף עצמו. קדם וסלקו — קודם נפילתו של זה — פטור. בעידנא דשדייה יכול לעלות הוא — ופטור על הדחייה. ומשום סלוק לא מלית לחיוביה, דגרמא בעלמא הוא. ואפילו הוא קדם — הזורק את החץ ורץ לאחר זריקת החץ קודם שיגיע החץ לחבירו,

LANGUAGE

שְׁרָגָא **Candle.** This word derives from the Persian and is similar to modern Perisan *cira*, which also has a cognate in Arabic.

תְּרִיס **Shield.** This is derived from the Greek θυρέος, *thyreos*, among the meanings of which is "shield."

BACKGROUND

תְּרִיס **Shield.**

A Roman soldier standing with a large shield.

HALAKHAH

דְּחָפוֹ לַבּוֹר, וְסוּלָּם בַּבּוֹר **If he pushed him into a pit, and there was a ladder in the pit.** "If someone pushed another person into a pit, and there was a ladder in the pit so the victim could climb out, and someone else (or even the assailant himself) removed the ladder, and the victim died of starvation, or if someone shot an arrow at another person, and that other person had a shield in his hand to block the arrow, and someone else (or even the assailant himself) came and removed the shield from his hand, and the arrow struck the victim and he died — in both cases the assailant is exempt from judicial execution, but he is nevertheless accountable to Heaven." (*Rambam, Sefer Nezikin, Hilkhot Rotze'aḥ* 3:11.)

הוּא קָדַם וּנְטָלוֹ, פָּטוּר, [1]דִּבְעִידָּנָא דְּשַׁדְיֵיהּ בֵּיהּ — מִיפְסַק פִּיסְקֵיהּ גִּירֵיהּ.

[2]וְאָמַר רָבָא: זָרַק בּוֹ חֵץ וְסַמָּנִין בְּיָדוֹ, [3]וּבָא אַחֵר וּפִיזְּרָן, [4]וַאֲפִילּוּ הוּא קָדַם וּפִיזְּרָן, פָּטוּר, [5]דִּבְעִידָּנָא דִּשְׁדָא בֵּיהּ יָכוֹל לְהִתְרַפְּאוֹת הֲוָה.

[6]אָמַר רַב אַשִׁי: [7]הִלְכָּךְ, אֲפִילּוּ סַמָּנִין בַּשּׁוּק.

[8]אָמַר לֵיהּ רַב אַחָא בְּרֵיהּ דְּרָבָא לְרַב אַשִׁי: נִזְדַּמְּנוּ לוֹ סַמָּנִין, [9]מַהוּ?

[10]אֲמַר לֵיהּ: הֲרֵי יָצָא מִבֵּית דִּין זַכַּאי.

[11]וְאָמַר רָבָא: זָרַק צְרוֹר בַּכּוֹתֶל וְחָזְרָה לַאֲחוֹרֶיהָ וְהָרְגָה, חַיָּיב.

LITERAL TRANSLATION

he went ahead and took it, he is exempt, [1]for when he shot it at him, his arrow was separated [from him].

[2]And Rava said: [If] he shot an arrow at him, and he had medicines in his hand, [3]and someone else came and scattered them, [4]and even if he went ahead and scattered them, he is exempt, [5]for when he shot it at him, he was able to cure himself.

[6]Rav Ashi said: [7]Therefore, even if there were medicines in the market.

[8]Rav Aḥa the son of Rava said to Rav Ashi: [If] he happened upon medicines, [9]what [is the law]?

[10]He said to him: He leaves the court vindicated.

[11]And Rava said: [If] he threw a stone at a wall, and it rebounded, and killed, he is liable.

TRANSLATION AND COMMENTARY

himself **who ran ahead and removed** the shield from his victim's hand before the arrow hit him, **he is exempt** from judicial execution. [1]**For when he shot it at his** victim, **his arrow was separated from him** by the shield. Nor can he be executed for removing the shield, for that was merely the indirect cause of the victim's death.

וְאָמַר רָבָא [2]**And** similarly, **Rava said: If** someone **shot an arrow at** another person, **and** that person **had medicines in his hand** to treat an arrow wound, [3]**and** then **someone else came and scattered** those medicines, leaving him without a cure, and he died, the assailant who shot the arrow is exempt from judicial execution. [4]**Even if** it was the assailant himself **who went ahead and scattered** the medicines, **he is exempt** from judicial execution. He cannot be executed for shooting the arrow, [5]**for when he shot it at his** victim, his victim **would have been able to treat himself.** And he cannot be executed for having scattered the medicines, for that was merely the indirect cause of his victim's death.

אָמַר רַב אַשִׁי [6]**Rav Ashi said:** Since the assailant is exempt from judicial execution if the victim had medicines to treat his wound when he was shot, [7]the assailant is **therefore** exempt **even if** such **medicines were** only available **in the market.**

אָמַר לֵיהּ [8]**Rav Aḥa the son of Rava said to Rav Ashi: If** such medicines were not available at the time of the shooting, but later the victim **happened upon** those **medicines,** [9]**what is the law** if the victim failed to buy them and consequently died from his wound?

אָמַר לֵיהּ [10]Rav Ashi **said to** Rav Aḥa the son of Rava: The assailant **leaves the court vindicated,** since the victim could have acquired the necessary medicines.

וְאָמַר רָבָא [11]**And Rava said: If** someone **threw a stone** with the intention of killing another person, and the stone hit **a wall and rebounded** and killed the intended victim, the assailant **is liable** to execution.

RASHI

ונטל התריס הימנו. סמנין — הרפואין לרפאותו. בידו — של הרוג. הלכך — כיון דאם יש שם סמנין הרפואין לרפאותו בידו פטרת ליה, אפילו אינם בידו אלא שמצויין בשוק לקנות בשעת זריקה הרי אלו כאלו הן בידו ופטור, ואפילו לא נמצאו לאחר מכאן. נזדמנו לו סמנין — למוכה אחר המכה ולא קנאן ולא ריפא עצמו. מהו — מי אמרינן הרי היה יכול להתרפאות, או דילמא כיון דבשעת זריקה לא הוי סמנין, מיחייב, דהא מכת מות הוא. הרי יצא מבית דין זכאי — כלומר הואיל וקודם עמדו בדין מצאו לו זכות אין לנו לחייבו. זרק צרור בכותל — ונתכוין להרוג את חבירו, וזרק צרור והכה בכותל בכח וחזרה מכחו לאחוריה והרגו — חייב, דהא נמי כחו הוא.

NOTES

אֲפִילּוּ הוּא קָדַם וּנְטָלוֹ **Even if he removed it before anyone else.** *Meiri* suggests that the assailant was holding a rope that was attached to his victim's shield. As soon as he shot the arrow, he pulled the rope, removing the shield from his victim's hand.

HALAKHAH

זָרַק צְרוֹר בַּכּוֹתֶל **If he threw a stone at a wall.** "If someone threw a stone at a wall, and it rebounded and killed another person, he is responsible for the victim's death. If people were playing with a ball, throwing it against a wall, and they were warned that the ball might bounce off and kill someone, and the ball struck someone standing within four cubits of the wall, they are exempt. But if the ball struck someone standing beyond four cubits from the wall, they are liable, provided that the ball was capable of killing a person." (*Rambam, Sefer Nezikin, Hilkhot Rotze'aḥ* 3:12.)

TRANSLATION AND COMMENTARY

וְתַנָּא תּוּנָא [1]The Gemara notes that **a Tanna taught** the same law in the following Baraita: [2]"Regarding **those playing with a ball,** which **killed** another person as it rebounded off a wall — if they killed the other person **intentionally, they are** liable to death by **slaying** with the sword; [3]and if they acted **inadvertently, they are sent into exile** to a city of refuge."

בְּשׁוֹגֵג גּוֹלִין [4]The Gemara comments: The Baraita states that if the ballplayers acted **inadvertently, they are sent into exile** to a city of refuge. [5]But surely **this is obvious!** Why did it have to be said?

בְּמֵזִיד [6]The Gemara answers: Indeed, **it was** only **necessary to teach** the first half of the Baraita, which states that if the ballplayers killed the other person **intentionally, they are** liable to death by **slaying** with the sword. [7]Otherwise **you might have said** that the killers should be exempt from this penalty, because in order to be liable to punishment, one must receive a formal warning prior to committing an offense, stating that the act is forbidden. [8]The warning that can be given here **is** only **a doubtful warning** — which does not suffice for the administration of punishment — for **who says that** the ball **will rebound** and strike the intended victim? [9]**Therefore,** the Baraita **teaches us** that the ballplayers are indeed liable if they killed the other person intentionally. Since they are skilled players, they know that the ball will rebound and strike the intended victim.

תָּנֵי [10]**Rav Taḥlifa bar Ma'arva taught** the following Baraita **before Rabbi Abbahu:** [11]"Regarding **those playing with a ball,** which **killed** another person as it rebounded off a wall — if the victim was standing **within four cubits** of the wall when the ball hit him, the one who threw the ball at the wall **is exempt.** [12]But if the victim was standing **beyond four cubits** from the wall, the one who threw the ball at the wall **is liable."**

אֲמַר לֵיהּ [13]**Ravina said to Rav Ashi: How do you visualize the case?** [14]**If** the person who threw the ball **wanted** the ball to rebound as it did, then **even** if it only returned **a small distance** — less than four cubits — he should **also** be liable. [15]And **if** the person who threw the ball **did not want** the ball to rebound as it did, then **even** if it returned **a great distance** — more than four cubits — he should **not** be liable.

אֲמַר לֵיהּ [16]Rav Ashi **said to** Ravina: **As a rule** with **those who play with a ball, the further that** the ball **goes**

[1]וְתַנָּא תּוּנָא: [2]"כְּגוֹן אֵלּוּ הַמְשַׂחֲקִין בְּכַדּוּר שֶׁהָרְגוּ, בְּמֵזִיד — נֶהֱרָגִין, [3]בְּשׁוֹגֵג — גּוֹלִין".

[4]"בְּשׁוֹגֵג גּוֹלִין" [5]פְּשִׁיטָא!

[6]"בְּמֵזִיד נֶהֱרָגִין" אִיצְטְרִיךְ לֵיהּ. [7]מַהוּ דְּתֵימָא: [8]הַתְרָאַת סָפֵק הִיא — מִי יֵימַר דְּהָדְרָה? [9]קָא מַשְׁמַע לָן.

[10]תָּנֵי רַב תַּחְלִיפָא בַּר מַעַרְבָא קַמֵּיהּ דְּרַבִּי אַבָּהוּ: [11]"כְּגוֹן אֵלּוּ הַמְשַׂחֲקִין בְּכַדּוּר שֶׁהָרְגוּ — תּוֹךְ אַרְבַּע אַמּוֹת, פָּטוּר; [12]חוּץ לְאַרְבַּע אַמּוֹת, חַיָּיב".

[13]אֲמַר לֵיהּ רָבִינָא לְרַב אַשִׁי: הֵיכִי דָּמֵי? [14]אִי דְּקָא נִיחָא לֵיהּ, אֲפִילּוּ פּוּרְתָּא נַמִי. [15]אִי דְּלָא נִיחָא לֵיהּ, אֲפִילּוּ טוּבָא נַמִי, לָא!

[16]אֲמַר לֵיהּ: סְתָם מְשַׂחֲקִין

LITERAL TRANSLATION

[1]And a Tanna taught it: "[2]Like those playing with a ball, who killed — intentionally, they are slain; [3]inadvertently, they are exiled."

[4]"Inadvertently, they are exiled." [5]This is obvious!

[6]It was necessary [to teach]: "Intentionally, they are slain." [7]Lest you say: [8]It is a doubtful warning — who says that it will rebound? [9][Therefore] it teaches us.

[10]Rav Taḥlifa bar Ma'arva taught before Rabbi Abbahu: [11]"Those playing with a ball, which killed — within four cubits, he is exempt; [12]outside four cubits, he is liable."

[13]Ravina said to Rav Ashi: How do you visualize the case? [14]If it is pleasing to him, even a little also. [15]If it is not pleasing to him, even a lot, not!

[16]He said to him: As a rule, those who play

RASHI

כגון אלו המשחקין בכדור שהרגו — רגילין תינוקות להכות הכדור בכותל בכח כדי שתחזור לאחוריה הרבה, ולאחר שזורק הוא רץ וחבירו אוחז את הכדור ומכה אותו בה אם יכול לכוון ההוא דזרק בכותל, אשמעינן תנא דאם נתכוין שתהרוג את חבירו בחזרתה לאחוריה ויש בו כדי להמית — חייב. **כגון אלו המשחקין בכדור שהרגו תוך ארבע אמות פטורין** — אם היה המוכה עומד בתוך ארבע אמות של כותל ולא הספיקה לחזור ארבע אמות עד שמלאתו והרגתו פטור הזורק מגלות. **חוץ לארבע אמות חייב** — גלות. **אי דניחא ליה** — (שלא) שתחזור יותר. **אפילו פורתא נמי** — ליחייב גלות, דהא הרג בשוגג וטעמא ליכא למיפטריה. **ואי לא ניחא ליה** — שתחזור כל כך. **אפילו טובא נמי** — יותר מארבע אמות ליפטר, דלא נתקיימת מחשבתו דאמר מר (מכות ז,ב): "ואשר לא צדה" — פרט למתכוין לזרוק שתים וזרק ארבע, אלמא כיון דלא ניחא ליה דניזיל — לא. **סתם משחקין**

BACKGROUND

מְשַׂחֲקִים בְּכַדּוּר Playing with a ball.

Women playing ball, from a Roman painting of the Mishnaic period.

Various ball games were played in the Mishnaic and Talmudic periods. From the context here it appears that the game in question involved throwing a rather heavy ball against a wall, and the ball was supposed to bounce back a certain distance at a determined angle.

NOTES

תּוֹךְ אַרְבַּע אַמּוֹת, פָּטוּר Within four cubits, he is exempt. *Meiri* explains that if the ball rebounded less than four cubits, the person who threw it is exempt, for had the ball accidentally struck the wall, it would have rebounded that small distance. Thus the rebounding is not a continuation of the thrower's physical act. But if the ball rebounded more than four cubits, the person who threw it is liable, for surely it traveled by way of the thrower's agency.

בְּכַדּוּר, כַּמָּה דְּעַיְּילִי טְפֵי מֵינָח נִיחָא לֵיהּ.
[1] לְמֵימְרָא דִּכְהַאי גַּוְונָא כֹּחוֹ הוּא? [2] וּרְמִינְהוּ: [3] ״הַמְקַדֵּשׁ, וְנָפַל קִידּוּשׁ עַל יָדוֹ אוֹ עַל הַצַּד, וְאַחַר כָּךְ נָפַל לַשּׁוֹקֶת, פָּסוּל״!
[4] הָכָא בְּמַאי עָסְקִינַן בְּשׁוֹתֵת.
[5] תָּא שְׁמַע: [6] ״מַחַט שֶׁהָיָה נְתוּנָה עַל הַחֶרֶס, וְהִזָּה עָלֶיהָ, סָפֵק עַל הַמַּחַט הִזָּה, סָפֵק עַל

LITERAL TRANSLATION

with a ball, the more they come in, the more it is pleasing to them.

[1] Is this to say that in this way it is his agency? [2] They cast together: [3] "[If] someone was putting ashes [into the purification waters], and the sanctified ashes fell on his hand or on the side, and afterward they fell into the container, it is disqualified."

[4] What we are dealing with here is where it fell gently.

[5] Come [and] hear: [6] "If a needle was resting on a sherd, and he sprinkled on it, and it is in doubt whether he sprinkled on the needle or he sprinkled on

TRANSLATION AND COMMENTARY

from the wall, **the more they are pleased** by where it went. Thus, we assume that the person who threw the ball wanted it to rebound at least four cubits, and so if it hit someone standing within four cubits of the wall, he is exempt, and if it hit someone standing beyond four cubits from the wall, he is liable.

לְמֵימְרָא [1] The Gemara asks: **Is this to say that,** in **such** a case, rebounding **is** considered **a continuation of** the thrower's **physical act?** [2] The Gemara points to **a contradiction** between this conclusion and what we have learned elsewhere in the Mishnah regarding the ashes of a red heifer. In order to remove the ritual impurity resulting from contact with a human corpse, purification by means of water mixed with the ashes of a red heifer is necessary. Naturally flowing water is directed into a container, and some ashes from the red heifer are added. The resulting mixture is sprinkled on the people or objects to be purified. The ashes must be added to the water by a direct physical act performed by the person preparing the purification waters. The Mishnah (*Parah* 6:1) states: [3] **"If someone was putting** the **ashes** of the red heifer **into the** water that was to become purification water, **and the sanctified ashes fell** first **on his hand, or on the side** of the container, **and** only **afterward** did they fall **into the container** containing the water, the water **is** rendered **unfit,** because the ashes were not added to the water by a direct physical act performed by the person preparing the purification waters." Now, if the rebounding of a ball thrown against a wall is considered a continuation of the thrower's physical act, why are the ashes that fell onto the person's hand or the side of the container, and then rebounded into the container, not regarded as having landed in the container as the result of his direct physical act?

הָכָא [4] The Gemara answers: **Here,** in the Mishnah, we are not dealing with a case where the ashes bounced off the person's hand or off the side of the container, and fell into the water by the force of his original act, but rather **we are dealing with** a case **where** the ashes landed on the person's hand or the side of the container, and later **fell gently** into the water. In such a case, the ashes are not viewed as having landed in the container by way of the person's direct physical act.

תָּא שְׁמַע [5] The Gemara points to a contradiction between the Baraita cited above and another Mishnah. **Come and hear** what we have learned in the following Mishnah (*Parah* 12:2): [6] **"If a** ritually impure **needle was resting on a sherd, and someone sprinkled** purification water **on** the needle, **but it is in doubt whether he sprinkled** the water directly **on the needle or he sprinkled** it **on the sherd, and** from there **it splashed**

RASHI

בכדור כמה דעיילי — ומקרבי לכותל בשעה שזורקין מינח ניחא ליה, כדי שתחזור הרבה, הלכך בציר מארבע אמות לא ניחא ליה דתיזיל, אית דמפרשי האי חייבין ופטורין — ממיתה, וכגון שהתרו בו. **דבי האי גוונא** — שחזרה לאחוריה מכח זריקתו, חשיב להו כחו. **המקדש** — מי חטאת באפר, נתינת אפר על המים קרי קידוש, כדתנן במסכת פרה (פרק ו משנה ב): (הרי קודש) לף על המים. **ואחר כך נפל לשוקת** — אבן חלולה שהמים נכנסין בו מן המעין דרך נקב שפופרת, דכתיב (במדבר יט) ״מים חיים אל כלי״ שתהא חיותן בכלי. וקא סלקא דעתך דהאי נפל דקתני כגון שנפל על ידו בכח, או על הצד, כלומר על צד הכלי ומשם ניתז בכח לשוקת וקתני דפסול. **בשותת** — לא ניתז מכח נפילה ראשונה, אלא מעצמו חזר ושתת מידו לשוקת שותת כמו (ברכות כב,ב) מים שותתין על ברכיו = *קולי״ר בלע״ז, שאינו ניתז למרחוק אלא נופל ויורד כנגדו. **והזה עליה** — ונתכוון להזות עליה לטהרה מטמא מת, וההזיה נראית עליה, אבל ספק על המחט נפל ההזיה כשיוצאת מידו ספק על החרס הזה תחלה.

LANGUAGE (RASHI)

*קולי״ר Old French *coler,* meaning "to rinse, to fall."

HALAKHAH

הַמְקַדֵּשׁ, וְנָפַל קִידּוּשׁ עַל יָדוֹ **If someone was putting ashes into the purification waters, and the sanctified ashes fell on his hand.** "The person preparing the purification waters must put the ashes of the red heifer into the water on purpose and with his own hand. If the ashes fell first on his hand or on the side of the water container, and then into the water, the water cannot be used in the purification process," following the Gemara. (*Rambam, Sefer Taharah, Hilkhot Parah Adumah* 9:2.)

מַחַט שֶׁהָיָה נְתוּנָה עַל הַחֶרֶס **If a needle was resting on a sherd.** "If a ritually impure needle was resting on a sherd, and someone sprinkled purification water on the needle, but it is in doubt whether he sprinkled the water directly on the needle, or he sprinkled it on the sherd and from there it splashed onto the needle, his sprinkling is disqualified." (*Rambam, Sefer Taharah, Hilkhot Parah Adumah* 12:3.)

TRANSLATION AND COMMENTARY

onto the needle, [1]**his sprinkling is disqualified,** and the needle remains ritually impure." Purification is only effective if the water is sprinkled directly on the impure object. But if the rebounding of a ball thrown against a wall is considered a continuation of the thrower's physical act, as is implied by the Baraita, how is it different from water which fell on the sherd and then splashed onto the needle?

אֲמַר [2]**Rav Ḥinana bar Yehudah said in the name of Rav:** The text of the Mishnah should be slightly emended. The Mishnah should not read: "And it splashed [מִיצָּה] onto it," [3]but rather **it should read: "And he found [מָצָא] it on it."** The needle was found wet, and we do not know whether or not the water was sprinkled directly on it. But bouncing a ball from a wall is indeed a continuation of the thrower's physical act.

אָמַר רַב פַּפָּא [4]**Rav Pappa said: If someone tied up another person** along a river bank, **and** then **directed a burst of water upon him,** and he drowned, the water **is** considered as the assailant's **arrows, and he is** therefore **responsible** for his killing. [5]**This ruling applies** when the water fell upon the victim **by** the assailant's **direct agency.** [6]But if the water only fell upon the victim **by** the assailant's **indirect agency,** as when the assailant tied the victim up some distance away, and the water flowed along the ground for a while before drowning the victim, the assailant is exempt from liability for his victim's death, [7]for the drowning **is merely** the result of his indirect **causation.**

וְאָמַר רַב פַּפָּא [8]**Rav Pappa said: If someone threw a stone up** into the air, **and** instead of coming straight down, [9]the stone veered **to the side and killed** another person as it landed, the stone-thrower **is liable.**

הַחֶרֶס הִזָּה וּמִיצָּה עָלֶיהָ, [1]הַזָּאָתוֹ פָּסוּל״.
[2]אֲמַר רַב חִינָּנָא בַּר יְהוּדָה מִשְּׁמֵיהּ דְּרַב: [3]״מָצָא״ אִיתְּמַר.
[4]אָמַר רַב פַּפָּא: הַאי מַאן דִּכְפַתֵּיהּ לְחַבְרֵיהּ וְאַשְׁקֵיל עֲלֵיהּ בִּידְקָא דְמַיָּא, גִּירֵי דִּידֵיהּ הוּא, וּמִיחַיַּיב. [5]הָנֵי מִילֵּי — בְּכֹחַ רִאשׁוֹן, [6]אֲבָל בְּכֹחַ שֵׁנִי, [7]גְּרָמָא בְּעָלְמָא הוּא.
[8]וְאָמַר רַב פַּפָּא: זָרַק צְרוֹר לְמַעְלָה, [9]וְהָלְכָה לַצְּדָדִין וְהָרְגָה, חַיָּיב.

LITERAL TRANSLATION

the sherd, and it splashed onto it, [1]his sprinkling is disqualified."

[2]Rav Ḥinana bar Yehudah said in the name of Rav: [3]It is stated: "He found [it on it]."

[4]Rav Pappa said: Someone who tied up another person and directed a burst of water upon him, they are his arrows, and he is liable. [5]These words — with direct agency; [6]but with secondary agency, [7]it is mere causation.

[8]And Rav Pappa said: [If] someone threw a stone up, [9]and it went to the side and killed, he is liable.

RASHI

ומיצה עליה — כלומר ומן החרס חזרה ונתזה עליה, וקתני פסולה, אלמא לאו כחו היא. **מצא אתמר** — לאו לשון מלוי דהוה התזה קתני, אלא לשון מציאה, כלומר ההזאה נמצאת עליה ואין ידוע אם בתחלה הזה עליה או חזר מכח היתוז. או שמא לא זה ולא זה אלא על החרס הזה, והיה מדרון והלכה ההזאה על המחט דליכא כחו כלל. **דכפתיה** — קשר ידיו ורגליו על שפת הים. **ואשקיל עליה בידקא דמיא** — הפנה את מרוצת המים עליו. **גיריה דידיה הוא** — הן הן חציו, והרי הוא כזורק בו חץ וכדמפרש ואזיל שהמים באים בכח ראשון עליו מיד, כגון שהניחו סמוך לשפת הים והשפה מדרון. **בכח ראשון** — כשפינה להם דרך לגד זה מיד נפלו עליו דהוי כחו. **אבל בכח שני** — שהניחו רחוק קצת ולא נפלו המים מיד בצאתו מגדרותיהן עליו, אלא לאחר מכאן הלכו על המקום שהוא שם, גרמא הוא ולא מכחו. **והלכה לצדדין** — דרך נפילתה שלא נפלה כנגדו אלא כשהיא חוזרת לארץ היתה מתרחקת לצדדין, אבל אם נפלה נוכחה והרגה — פטור, דלאו כחו הוא אלא היא חוזרת לארץ מאליה.

NOTES

מָצָא — מִיצָּה **And it splashed — he found it.** According to *Ramah,* the Gemara's initial reading of the Mishnah was מָצָא, and the emended reading is מִיצָּה (the reverse of what is found in the standard edition). The Gemara first thought that the Mishnah is referring to a case where the water was found on the needle, and it is in doubt whether the water landed directly on it, or landed on the sherd and then splashed onto the needle, thus suggesting that the rebounding of a ball thrown against a wall is not a continuation of the sprinkler's physical act. According to the Gemara's emendation of the Mishnah, the water ran down the sherd until it reached the needle, rather than wetting the needle as a result of the sprinkler's physical act. It would appear from *Rambam* and *Meiri* that the Gemara emended the Mishnah from מִיצָּה to נִמְצָה — from "it splashed" (by the force of the sprinkler's physical act) to "it dripped" (see *Rashash*).

כֹּחַ רִאשׁוֹן **Direct agency.** *Ramah* understands that when the Gemara speaks of water that fell upon the victim by

HALAKHAH

בִּידְקָא דְמַיָּא **A burst of water.** "If someone tied up another person so that he could not run away, and he then flooded the area and the victim drowned, the assailant is liable, provided that the victim died as a result of the assailant's direct agency." (*Rambam, Sefer Nezikin, Hilkhot Rotze'aḥ* 3:13.)

זָרַק צְרוֹר לְמַעְלָה **If someone threw a stone up.** "If someone threw a stone into the air, and it landed to the side, killing another person, he is liable," following Rav Pappa. (*Rambam, Sefer Nezikin, Hilkhot Rotze'aḥ* 3:13.)

TRANSLATION AND COMMENTARY

אָמַר לֵיהּ [1]**Mar bar Rav Ashi said to Rav Pappa: Why** is the stone-thrower liable? [2]Surely, because the stone struck the victim as a consequence of the stone-thrower's direct **agency. Otherwise** the stone-thrower should be exempt. [3]But this is difficult, for if the stone was moving through the air **by** the thrower's **agency,** then **it should have** continued to **go up.**

[78A] וְאִי לָאו [4]Rav Pappa answered: **If** the stone **was not** moving through the air by the thrower's **agency,** [5]then **it should have come** straight **down**, not to the side! [6]**Rather, it** must be that the stone was moving through the air by way of **his weakened agency,** and that suffices to make him responsible for his victim's death.

תָּנוּ רַבָּנַן [7]**Our Rabbis taught** the following Baraita: **"If ten people struck** someone **with ten clubs, and** that person **died** from the beating, [8]**whether** the ten struck their victim **all at once or one after the other,** all ten **are exempt** from culpability for murder, for no one person is solely responsible for the victim's death. [9]**Rabbi Yehudah ben Betera says:** If the ten people struck their victim all at once, they are all exempt. [10]But if the ten struck their victim **one after the other, the last one** to inflict a blow **is** guilty of murder, **for he hastened his death** with that final blow."

אָמַר רַבִּי יוֹחָנָן [11]**Rabbi Yoḥanan said: Both of them** — the Rabbis and Rabbi Yehudah ben Betera — **expounded the same verse,** for it is stated (Leviticus 24:17): [12]**"If a man strikes any human soul,** he shall surely be put to death." [13]**The Rabbis maintain** that the words **"any soul"** imply that a murderer is not liable **unless** he killed **an entire soul** and he alone was responsible for his victim's death. But if a number of

[1]אָמַר לֵיהּ מָר בַּר רַב אַשִׁי לְרַב פַּפָּא: מַאי טַעְמָא? [2]מִשּׁוּם דְּכֹחוֹ הוּא. [3]אִי כֹּחוֹ, תֵּיזֵיל לְעֵיל!

[78A] [4]וְאִי לָאו כֹּחוֹ הוּא, [5]תֵּיזֵיל לְתַחַת!

[6]אֶלָּא: כֹּחַ כָּחוּשׁ הוּא.

[7]תָּנוּ רַבָּנַן: "הִכּוּהוּ עֲשָׂרָה בְּנֵי אָדָם בַּעֲשָׂרָה מַקְלוֹת וָמֵת, [8]בֵּין בְּבַת אַחַת בֵּין בָּזֶה אַחַר זֶה, פְּטוּרִין. [9]רַבִּי יְהוּדָה בֶּן בְּתֵירָא אוֹמֵר: [10]בָּזֶה אַחַר זֶה — הָאַחֲרוֹן חַיָּיב, מִפְּנֵי שֶׁקֵּירֵב אֶת מִיתָתוֹ".

[11]אָמַר רַבִּי יוֹחָנָן: וּשְׁנֵיהֶם מִקְרָא אֶחָד דָּרְשׁוּ: [12]"וְאִישׁ כִּי יַכֶּה כָּל נֶפֶשׁ אָדָם". [13]רַבָּנַן סָבְרִי: "כָּל נֶפֶשׁ" — עַד דְּאִיכָּא

LITERAL TRANSLATION

[1]Mar bar Rav Ashi said to Rav Pappa: What is the reason? [2]Because it is his agency. [3]If it is his agency, let it go up!

[78A] [4]If it is not his agency, [5]let it go down!

[6]Rather, it is his weakened agency.

[7]Our Rabbis taught: "If ten people struck him with ten clubs, and he died, [8]whether all at once, or one after the other, they are exempt. [9]Rabbi Yehudah ben Betera says: [10]One after the other, the last one is liable, for he hastened his death."

[11]Rabbi Yoḥanan said: And the two of them expounded the same verse: [12]"If a man strikes any human soul." [13]The Rabbis maintain: "Any soul" — until there is

RASHI

תיזיל לעיל — דהא כלפי מעלה זרקה כנגדו, ולא לצדדין. **אי לאו כחו תיזיל לתחת** — תפול מיד כנגדה ולא לצדדין. **אלא כח כחוש הוא** — אינו כחו חזק, אלא קצת כחו יש כאן, והאי דלא אזלה לעיל משום שכלה כח חוזק הזריקה והאבן חוזרת לארץ, אבל עדיין הולכת היא ממקצת כחו. **הכי גרסינן** — **רבי יהודה בן בתירא אומר בזה אחר זה האחרון חייב וכו׳. עד דאיכא כל נפש** — וכיון דמתחילה סייעו הראשונים בהריגתו — ליכא

NOTES

the assailant's direct agency, it means that the victim drowned in water that had been standing immediately adjacent to a partition that the assailant removed; and that when the Gemara speaks of water that fell upon the victim by the assailant's indirect agency, it means that the victim drowned in water that flowed from further away. Alternatively, when the Gemara speaks of water that fell upon the victim by the assailant's direct agency, it means that the water fell upon the victim without having been stopped at all between the time when the assailant removed the partition and the time when it inundated him. When the Gemara speaks of water that fell upon the victim by indirect agency, it means that the water was first blocked by some obstacle, and then surmounted the obstacle.

כָּל נֶפֶשׁ **An entire soul.** The Rishonim ask: How can the very same expression serve as the source for two contradictory positions? Some suggest that the Tannaim do not disagree about the meaning of the word *kol,* but rather about the word *nefesh,* whether or not it can be applied even to some minimal life force. Others argue that we find the word *kol* used in the sense of "entire, every," as in (Deuteronomy 14:11): "All [*kol*] clean birds you may eat," and we also find that the word is used in the sense of "any," as in (Deuteronomy 20:16): "You shall not save alive any [*kol*] life." Thus, there is room to disagree about the meaning of the expression *kol nefesh* regarding murder (*Rabbi David Bonfils*).

HALAKHAH

הִכּוּהוּ עֲשָׂרָה בְּנֵי אָדָם **If ten people struck him.** "If ten people struck another person with ten clubs, and he died, whether the ten struck their victim all at once or one after the other, they are all exempt from judicial execution. A person is only guilty of murder if he killed another person by himself," following the anonymous first Tanna of the Baraita. (*Rambam, Sefer Nezikin, Hilkhot Rotze'aḥ* 4:6.)

TRANSLATION AND COMMENTARY

people inflicted a series of blows upon the victim, the person who inflicted the final blow is exempt, because he did not kill an entire soul. [1]**And Rabbi Yehudah ben Betera maintains** that the words **"any soul"** imply that a murderer is liable if he killed **any part of a soul** — that is to say, even if he inflicted the last of a series of fatal blows.

אָמַר רָבָא [2]**Rava said: All agree** — both the Rabbis and Rabbi Yehudah ben Betera — **that** if **someone kills a person** who was suffering from **a** clearly visible **fatal injury**, he **is exempt,** for such a person is regarded as a dead man. [3]And all also agree that if **someone kills a person** who was already **dying** of a disease sent **by God, he is liable** for having hastened his death. [4]The Tannaim **only disagree about someone who kills a person** who was already **dying** from a blow inflicted **by** another **man.** [5]**The one Sage** — the Rabbis — **compares** the victim in such a case **to a person** who was suffering from **a** clearly visible **fatal wound,** [6]**and the other Sage** — Rabbi Yehudah ben Betera — **compares** the victim **to a person** who was already **dying** of a disease sent **by God.**

מַאן דִּמְדַמֵּי לֵיהּ [7]The Gemara asks: As for the Rabbis **who compare** a person who was already dying from a blow inflicted by another man **to a person** who was suffering from **a** clearly visible **fatal wound** — [8]**what is the reason that they do not compare him to a person** who was **dying** of a disease sent **by God?** [9]The Gemara explains: Regarding **a person** who was already **dying** of a disease sent **by God,** [10]**a physical act was not perpetrated against him** by another person. But regarding a person who was already dying from a blow inflicted by another person, [11]**a physical act was perpetrated against him** by another person.

כָּל נֶפֶשׁ. [1]וְרַבִּי יְהוּדָה בֶּן בְּתֵירָא סָבַר: "כָּל נֶפֶשׁ" — כָּל דְּהוּא נֶפֶשׁ.

[2]אָמַר רָבָא: הַכֹּל מוֹדִים בְּהוֹרֵג אֶת הַטְּרֵיפָה שֶׁהוּא פָּטוּר. [3]בְּגוֹסֵס בִּידֵי שָׁמַיִם — שֶׁהוּא חַיָּיב. [4]לֹא נֶחְלְקוּ אֶלָּא בְּגוֹסֵס בִּידֵי אָדָם. [5]מָר מְדַמֵּי לֵיהּ לִטְרֵיפָה, [6]וּמָר מְדַמֵּי לֵיהּ לְגוֹסֵס בִּידֵי שָׁמַיִם.

[7]מַאן דִּמְדַמֵּי לֵיהּ לִטְרֵיפָה — [8]מַאי טַעְמָא לָא מְדַמֵּי לֵיהּ לְגוֹסֵס בִּידֵי שָׁמַיִם? [9]גּוֹסֵס בִּידֵי שָׁמַיִם — [10]לָא אִיתְעֲבֵיד בֵּיהּ מַעֲשֶׂה, [11]הַאי אִיתְעֲבֵיד בֵּיהּ מַעֲשֶׂה.

LITERAL TRANSLATION

an entire soul. [1]And Rabbi Yehudah ben Betera maintains: "Any soul" — any part of a soul.

[2]Rava said: All agree that someone who kills a person with a fatal injury is exempt, [3][and that someone who kills] a person dying at the hands of Heaven is liable. [4]They only disagree about [someone who kills] a person dying at human hands. [5]One Sage compares him to a person with a fatal injury, [6]and the other Sage compares him to a person dying at the hands of Heaven.

[7]He who compares him to a person with a fatal injury — [8]what is the reason that he does not compare him to a person dying at the hands of Heaven? [9]A person dying at the hands of Heaven — [10]a [physical] act was not carried out against him. [11]This one — a [physical] act was carried out against him.

RASHI

כולה נפש במכת האחרון. כל דהוא נפש — אפילו מקצתה. ומיהו היכא דהכהו בבת אחת לא קטלינן לכלהו, ד"איש כי יכה" אמר רחמנא ולא שנים שהכוהו. הכל מודים בהורג את אדם טריפה — כגון נקב הוושט או קרום המוח. שהוא פטור — מדלא אפליגו ביה שמע מינה כיון דניכרים חתיכת סימנין חיותו — גברא קטילא חשיב ליה. בגוסס בידי שמים — ובא אחר והרגו — הכל מודים שחייב, דלא איתעביד ביה מעשה ברישא והרי הוא כחי. בגוסס בידי אדם — כגון זה שקרוב למות מחמת המכות, אלא לא עשאוהו הראשונים טריפה.

NOTES

טְרֵיפָה **A person with a fatal injury.** The concept of *terefah* stems from the verse (Exodus 22:30): "Neither shall you eat any meat that is torn of beasts [*terefah*] in the field." But in the Talmud, the term refers not only to an animal that was torn to pieces by beasts of the field, but to any animal suffering from a fatal injury or illness. So, too, regarding a human being, the term *terefah* refers to a person afflicted with a severe organic disease, congenital defect, or injury that will cause him to die within twelve months. It is clear from the Gemara that here we are dealing with a person suffering from a clearly visible external injury, and not an internal defect.

הַהוֹרֵג אֶת הַטְּרֵיפָה **Someone who kills a person with a fatal injury.** It may be stated: We find that King David executed the Amalekite who killed Saul, even though Saul

HALAKHAH

הַהוֹרֵג אֶת הַטְּרֵיפָה **Someone who kills a person with a fatal injury.** "If someone killed a person who was suffering from an injury which doctors said would surely kill him — even if at the time of his death the victim was eating, drinking, and going about his business — the assailant is exempt from judicial execution." (*Rambam, Sefer Nezikin, Hilkhot Rotze'aḥ* 2:8.)

גּוֹסֵס בִּידֵי שָׁמַיִם, בִּידֵי אָדָם **A person dying of an act of God, and a person dying of an act of man.** "Someone who killed a person who was already dying of a disease sent by God is liable to judicial execution. But someone who killed a person who was dying of a blow inflicted by another man is exempt from judicial execution." (*Rambam, Sefer Nezikin, Hilkhot Rotze'aḥ* 2:7.)

[1]וּמַאן דִּמְדַמֵּי לֵיהּ לְגוֹסֵס בִּידֵי שָׁמַיִם — [2]מַאי טַעְמָא לָא מְדַמֵּי לֵיהּ לִטְרֵיפָה? [3]טְרֵיפָה — מְחַתְּכִי סִימָנִים. [4]הָא — לָא מְחַתְּכִי סִימָנִים.
[5]תָּנֵי תַּנָּא קַמֵּיהּ דְּרַב שֵׁשֶׁת: "וְאִישׁ כִּי יַכֶּה כָּל נֶפֶשׁ אָדָם", — [6]לְהָבִיא הַמַּכֶּה אֶת חֲבֵירוֹ וְאֵין בּוֹ כְּדֵי לְהָמִית, [7]וּבָא אַחֵר וֶהֱמִיתוֹ שֶׁהוּא חַיָּיב.
[8]אֵין בּוֹ כְּדֵי לְהָמִית — פְּשִׁיטָא! [9]אֶלָּא: "יֵשׁ בּוֹ כְּדֵי לְהָמִית, [10]וּבָא אַחֵר וֶהֱמִיתוֹ, שֶׁהוּא חַיָּיב". [11]וּסְתָמָא כְּרַבִּי יְהוּדָה בֶּן בְּתֵירָא.
[12]אָמַר רָבָא: הַהוֹרֵג אֶת הַטְּרֵיפָה — פָּטוּר. [13]וּטְרֵיפָה שֶׁהָרַג, בִּפְנֵי בֵּית דִּין — חַיָּיב,

LITERAL TRANSLATION

[1]And he who compares him to a person dying at the hands of Heaven — [2]what is the reason that he does not compare him to a person with a fatal injury? [3]A person with a fatal injury — his vital organs are cut. [4]This one — his vital organs are not cut.

[5]A Sage taught [a Baraita] before Rav Sheshet: "'If a man strikes any human soul' — [6]to include someone who strikes another person, and [the blow] is not sufficient to kill, [7]and someone else comes and kills him, he is liable."

[8]If it is not sufficient to kill — it is obvious!

[9]Rather: "It is able to kill, [10]and someone else comes and kills him, [then] he is liable." [11]And the anonymous Baraita is like Rabbi Yehudah ben Betera.

[12]Rava said: [If] someone kills a person with a fatal injury, he is exempt. [13][If] a person with a fatal injury kills [another person] before a court, he is liable.

TRANSLATION AND COMMENTARY

וּמַאן דִּמְדַמֵּי לֵיהּ [1]The Gemara asks: **And** as for Rabbi Yehudah ben Betera, **who compares** a person who was already dying from a blow inflicted by another man **to a person** who was **dying** of a disease sent **by God** — [2]**what is the reason that he does not compare him to a person** who was suffering from **a** clearly visible **fatal injury?** [3]The Gemara explains: With **a person** who was suffering from **a** clearly visible **fatal injury,** one of **his vital organs was** clearly **injured,** and it was obvious that he was soon to die. But with a person who was dying from a blow inflicted by another person, [4]**his vital organs were not** obviously **injured,** so it was not clearly evident that he was dying, but rather he appeared like any other sick person.

תָּנֵי [5]The Gemara continues: **A Sage taught** the following Baraita **before Rav Sheshet:** "The verse that states (Leviticus 24:17): **'And he that kills any man** shall surely be put to death,' [6]comes **to teach that** if **someone struck another person,** inflicting **a non-lethal blow,** [7]**and** then **someone else came and killed** the victim, it is the second assailant who **is liable** for his murder."

אֵין בּוֹ כְּדֵי [8]The Gemara responds: **If** the first assailant inflicted **a non-lethal blow** upon the victim, surely **it is obvious** that the second assailant is liable for the murder!

אֶלָּא [9]**Rather,** the Baraita should read as follows: "The verse that states: 'And he that kills any man shall surely be put to death,' teaches that if someone struck another person, inflicting **a lethal blow,** [10]**and** then **someone else came and killed him,** the second assailant **is liable."** [11]**And** this **anonymous Baraita follows** the view of **Rabbi Yehudah ben Betera,** who maintains that if several assailants struck another person one after the other, the last one is liable for his murder.

אָמַר רָבָא [12]**Rava said: If someone kills a person** who was already suffering from **a fatal injury, he is exempt,** for such a person is regarded as a dead man. [13]**If a person** who was suffering from **a fatal injury killed another person before a court** that was authorized to judge capital cases, so that a ruling could be issued even without

RASHI

מחתכי סמנין — סימן חיותא. כל נפש להביא וכו׳ — דמשמע כל דהוא נפש. שהוא חייב — האחרון.

NOTES

was at the time surely suffering from a clearly visible fatal injury after stabbing himself with his own spear (see II Samuel 1)! *Rabbi Ya'akov Emden* suggests that, since Saul was the king, the Amalekite had no right to kill him, even if he was suffering from a fatal injury. Moreover, David's ruling was an emergency decision, and therefore cannot serve as a precedent for later generations.

בִּפְנֵי בֵּית דִּין — חַיָּיב Before a court. The Rishonim ask: Elsewhere (*Rosh HaShanah* 26a), we learned that, according to Rabbi Akiva, a court which witnessed a murder may not sit in judgment of the murderer, for it will not be able to seek arguments in his favor. How, then, can we say here that if a person suffering from a fatal injury killed another person before a court, that very court can sentence him to

HALAKHAH

טְרֵיפָה שֶׁהָרַג If a person with a fatal injury killed. "If a person suffering from a fatal injury killed another person before a court, he is liable to judicial execution, for the verse states, 'And you shall put away the evil from the midst of you.' But if he killed the other person outside of court, he cannot become liable to judicial execution on the basis of the testimony of witnesses, for their testimony is not subject to allegations of perjury." (*Rambam, Sefer Nezikin, Hilkhot Rotze'aḥ* 2:9.)

TRANSLATION AND COMMENTARY

the presentation of testimony, the killer **is liable** for murder. [1]But if he did **not** commit his offense **before a court, he is exempt** from punishment.

בְּפְנֵי בֵּית דִּין [2]The Gemara explains: If the murder is committed **before a court, what is the reason that he is liable?** [3]**Because the verse states** (Deuteronomy 13:6): **"And you shall put away the evil from the midst of you."** The court witnessed an evil offense which it is obligated to wipe out. [4]But if the murder was **not** committed **before a court,** the assailant **is exempt,** [5]**because** he can only be convicted on the basis of the testimony of witnesses who saw him kill another person, and **the testimony** they offer **is not subject to refutation.** [6]**And** there is a general rule that **any testimony that is not subject to refutation is not** valid **testimony.** "Refutation" here means that the testimony given by two witnesses was invalidated by a second set of witnesses, who testified that the first witnesses were not present when the incident allegedly transpired. The first pair of witnesses are then subject to the penalty that they had sought to inflict on the defendant. If witnesses testify that a person who was suffering **from** a fatal injury killed another person, and their testimony is refuted by a second set of witnesses, the first witnesses do not become subject to the penalty that they had sought to inflict because the defendant was already suffering from a fatal wound, and someone who kills another person who was already suffering from a fatal injury is exempt. Since the witnesses' testimony is not subject to punishment for perjury, their testimony is not valid.

וְאָמַר רָבָא [7]**And** similarly **Rava said: If someone committed sodomy with a person** who was suffering from **a fatal injury, he is liable** to the death penalty for homosexual intercourse. [8]**If a person** who was suffering from **a fatal injury committed sodomy with another person before a court** that was authorized to judge capital cases, so that a ruling could be issued even without the presentation of testimony, the offender **is liable** to the death penalty. [9]But if he did **not** commit his offense **before a court, he is exempt** from punishment.

בְּפְנֵי בֵּית דִּין [10]As in the previous example, if the man suffering from a fatal injury committed sodomy **before a court, he is liable** to the death penalty **because the verse states** (Deuteronomy 13:6): **"And you shall put away the evil from the midst of you."** The court witnessed an evil offense which it is obligated to wipe out. [11]But if he did **not** commit sodomy **before a court, he is exempt** from punishment, [12]**because** he can

[1]שֶׁלֹּא בִּפְנֵי בֵּית דִּין — פָּטוּר. [2]בִּפְנֵי בֵּית דִּין, מַאי טַעְמָא חַיָּיב? [3]דִּכְתִיב ״וּבִעַרְתָּ הָרָע מִקִּרְבֶּךָ״. [4]שֶׁלֹּא בִּפְנֵי בֵּית דִּין פָּטוּר, [5]דְּהָוְיָא לָהּ עֵדוּת שֶׁאִי אַתָּה יָכוֹל לַהֲזִימָּהּ. [6]וְכָל עֵדוּת שֶׁאִי אַתָּה יָכוֹל לַהֲזִימָּהּ לֹא שְׁמָהּ עֵדוּת.

[7]וְאָמַר רָבָא: הָרוֹבֵעַ אֶת הַטְּרֵיפָה, חַיָּיב. [8]טְרֵיפָה שֶׁרָבַע, בִּפְנֵי בֵּית דִּין, חַיָּיב, [9]שֶׁלֹּא בִּפְנֵי בֵּית דִּין, פָּטוּר.

[10]בִּפְנֵי בֵּית דִּין חַיָּיב, דִּכְתִיב: ״וּבִעַרְתָּ הָרָע מִקִּרְבֶּךָ״. [11]שֶׁלֹּא בִּפְנֵי בֵּית דִּין פָּטוּר, [12]דְּהָוְיָא

LITERAL TRANSLATION

[1]Not before a court, he is exempt.

[2]Before a court, what is the reason that he is liable? [3]Because it is written: "And you shall put away the evil from the midst of you." [4]Not before a court, he is exempt, [5]because it is testimony that you cannot refute. [6]And any testimony that you cannot refute is not called testimony.

[7]And Rava said: [If] someone committed sodomy with a person with a fatal injury, he is liable. [8][If] a person with a fatal injury committed sodomy [with another person] before a court, he is liable. [9]Not before a court, he is exempt.

[10]Before a court, he is liable, because it is written: "And you shall put away the evil from the midst of you." [11]Not before a court, he is exempt, [12]because

RASHI

ובערת הרע — והרי ראוהו רואה. שלא בפני בית דין — ואתה בא לחייבו על פי עדים — פטור, דאין עדותן עדות, דהויא עדות שאי אתה יכול להזימה לקיים בה דין הזמה, שאם הוזמו אין נהרגין, דגברא קטילא בעו למיקטל. את הטריפה — אדם טריפה ורבעו חבירו במשכב זכור. חייב — דהא איכא הנאה.

NOTES

death? Some suggest that, since it is impossible to try the killer before another court, he may be tried by the court that witnessed the killing, in fulfillment of the obligation to "put away the evil from the midst of you" (*Talmidei Rabbenu Peretz, Ḥamre Veḥaye*). Others argue that, since the killer is suffering from a fatal injury, we are not concerned that the court will be unable to seek arguments in his favor, for even if they find him guilty, they are merely hastening the death of a dying person (*Meiri,* and see *Tzofnat Pa'ane'aḥ*).

HALAKHAH

הָרוֹבֵעַ אֶת הַטְּרֵיפָה If someone committed sodomy with a person with a fatal injury. "If someone had sexual intercourse with a woman with a fatal injury who was forbidden to him, or if he committed sodomy with a man suffering from a fatal injury, or if he committed bestiality with an animal suffering from a fatal injury, he is liable to judicial execution." (*Rambam, Sefer Kedushah, Hilkhot Issurei Bi'ah* 1:12; *Tur, Even HaEzer* 20.)

TRANSLATION AND COMMENTARY

only be convicted on the basis of the testimony of witnesses who saw him commit his offense, and **the testimony** they offer is not valid, because it **is not subject to refutation.**

הָא [1]The Gemara questions the necessity of this second set of rulings: **Why do I also need** to be taught the laws governing a person with a fatal injury in the case of homosexual intercourse? [2]Surely **those** laws **are the same as** the laws governing such a person in the case of murder!

הָרוֹבֵעַ [3]The Gemara answers: **It was necessary to teach** the law governing **someone who committed sodomy with a person** suffering from **a fatal injury.** [4]For had Rava not taught that law, **you might have said** that, since a person with a fatal injury is regarded as if he were a dead man, someone who committed sodomy with him **should be considered like someone who engaged in intercourse with a dead man, and** thus he **should be exempt** from all punishment. [5]**Therefore,** Rava had to **teach us that** a person who commits sodomy is liable to be punished **on account of the pleasure,** [6]**and this one** who committed sodomy with the person suffering from a fatal injury also **derived pleasure** from his sexual act, and so he, too, is liable to the death penalty.

וְאָמַר רָבָא [7]**And** similarly **Rava said:** [8]**If** a set of **witnesses testified against a person** suffering from **a fatal injury,** claiming that he was guilty of a capital offense, **and** later **they were refuted** by a second set of witnesses who testified that the first set of witnesses were elsewhere when the incident allegedly transpired, the first set of witnesses **are not executed,** for they had conspired to bring about the execution of someone who was already regarded as a dead man. [9]But **if witnesses** suffering from **fatal injuries** testified against another person, claiming that he was guilty of a capital offense, and later they **were refuted** and shown to be false conspiring witnesses, **they are executed,** for the verse (Deuteronomy 13:6) states: "And you shall put away the evil from the midst of you." They committed a crime that the court is obligated to wipe out.

רַב אַשִׁי [10]**Rav Ashi** disagreed with Rava and **said: Even witnesses** suffering from **fatal injuries who** testified in a capital case, and **were** later **refuted** and shown to be false conspiring witnesses **are not executed,** [11]**for** their testimony **is not subject to the law regarding the refuters of refuters.** Ordinarily, if a second set of witnesses came and refuted the first set of witnesses who had come to convict the defendant of a capital offense, and then later a third set of witnesses came and refuted the second set of witnesses, the second set of witnesses are declared false, conspiring witnesses, and they are subject to the penalty that they had

לָהּ עֵדוּת שֶׁאִי אַתָּה יָכוֹל לַהֲזִימָּהּ.

[1]הָא תּוּ לָמָּה לִי? [2]הַיְינוּ הָךְ!

[3]הָרוֹבֵעַ אֶת הַטְּרֵיפָה אִיצְטְרִיכָא לֵיהּ. [4]מַהוּ דְּתֵימָא: לֶיהֱוֵי כְּמַאן דִּמְשַׁמֵּשׁ מֵת, וְלִיפָּטַר, [5]קָא מַשְׁמַע לָן דְּמִשּׁוּם הֲנָאָה הוּא, [6]וְהָא אִית לֵיהּ הֲנָאָה.

[7]וְאָמַר רָבָא: [8]עֵדִים שֶׁהֵעִידוּ בִּטְרֵיפָה וְהוּזְמוּ, אֵין נֶהֱרָגִין, [9]עֵדֵי טְרֵיפָה שֶׁהוּזְמוּ, נֶהֱרָגִין.

[10]רַב אַשִׁי אָמַר: אֲפִילּוּ עֵדֵי טְרֵיפָה שֶׁהוּזְמוּ אֵין נֶהֱרָגִין, [11]לְפִי שֶׁאֵינָן בְּזוֹמְמֵי

LITERAL TRANSLATION

it is testimony that you cannot refute.

[1]Why do I need this also? [2]This is that!

[3]It was necessary [to teach about] someone who committed sodomy with a person with a fatal injury. [4]You might have said: He should be [considered] like someone who has intercourse with a dead man, and is exempt. [5][Therefore,] it teaches us that it is on account of the pleasure, [6]and this one has pleasure.

[7]And Rava said: [8][If] witnesses testified against a person with a fatal injury, and they were refuted, they are not executed. [9]If witnesses with fatal injuries were refuted, they are executed.

[10]Rav Ashi said: Even witnesses with fatal injuries who were refuted are not executed, [11]because they are not subject to [the law regarding] refuters

RASHI

כמאן דמשמש מת – רובע את המת. **והא אית ליה הנאה** – אבל רובע את המת ליכא הנאה, שעבר חמימותו ולחלוחותו ונצטנן. **עדי טריפה** – שהן עצמן טריפה. **שהוזמו נהרגין** – דכתיב "ובערת הרע מקרבך". **לפי שאינן בזוממי זוממין** – בדין זוממי זוממין, אותם שהזימום ואמרו להם "באותה שעה עמנו הייתם" אם היו באין שנים אחרים ומזימין אותם לומר "היאך אתם מזימין את אלו, והרי אתם עמנו הייתם במקום פלוני" – אין הזוממין שנמצאו עכשיו זוממין נהרגין, משום דגברא קטילא בעי למיקטל. הלכך כי לא אתזמו נמי לא מקטלי הנך טריפה אפומייהו, דהוה ליה עדות שאי אתה יכול להזימה ולא מקטלי. ולרבא, כיון דעדות זוממין חדוש הוא אף על גב דהוי עדות שאי אתה יכול להזימה – מקטלי. **זוממי זוממין** – המזימין את הראשונים

HALAKHAH

עֵדִים שֶׁהֵעִידוּ בִּטְרֵיפָה, וְעֵדֵי טְרֵיפָה Witnesses who testified against a person with a fatal injury, and witnesses with fatal injuries. "If witnesses testified against a person with a fatal injury, and were refuted, they are not executed. Similarly, if witnesses suffering from fatal injuries testified against another person, and were refuted, they are not executed," following Rav Ashi. (*Rambam, Sefer Shofetim, Hilkhot Edut* 20:7.)

TRANSLATION AND COMMENTARY

sought to inflict by their testimony on the first set of witnesses. But if witnesses suffering from fatal injuries testified against a defendant in a capital case, and then a second set of witnesses came and refuted them, and then a third set of witnesses came and refuted the second set of witnesses, the second set of witnesses do not become subject to the penalty that they had sought to inflict on the first set of witnesses. For they wished to impose the death penalty upon the first set of witnesses (the penalty that the first set of witnesses had sought to impose on the defendant), but the death penalty cannot be imposed upon them, for they had wished to kill people who were already suffering from fatal injuries, and someone who kills a person who is already suffering from a fatal injury is exempt. Since the second set of witnesses are not subject to the death penalty even if they are refuted, the first set of witnesses are also not subject to the death penalty even if they are refuted, for the testimony needed to convict them is not subject to allegations of perjury.

וְאָמַר רָבָא [1]And similarly **Rava said: If an ox** suffering from **a fatal injury killed** a person, **it is liable** to be put to death, just like any other animal which killed a person. [2]**But if an ox belonging to a man with a fatal injury killed** a person, **it is exempt** from the death penalty.

מַאי טַעְמָא [3]The Gemara asks: **Why** is an ox belonging to a man with a fatal injury which killed a person not liable to be put to death? [4]The Gemara explains: **The verse states** (Exodus 21:29): "But if the ox was wont to gore with his horn in time past...and it killed a man or a woman, **the ox shall be stoned, and its owner also shall be put to death."** Earlier in the tractate we learned that this verse teaches that the laws that apply to the execution of the owner apply also to the execution of the ox. [5]Thus, **wherever we can apply: "And its owner also shall be put to death,"** [6]**we apply: "The ox shall be stoned."** [7]**And wherever we cannot apply: "And its owner also shall be put to death,"** [8]**we do not apply: "The ox shall be stoned."** If a person who was already suffering from a fatal injury killed another person outside the courtroom, he is exempt from punishment, as was established above. Thus, his ox is also not liable to be put to death if it killed a person.

רַב אַשִׁי [9]**Rav Ashi said: Even an ox with a fatal injury that killed** a person **is exempt** from execution.

מַאי טַעְמָא [10]The Gemara asks: **Why** is such an animal exempt? [11]The Gemara explains: **If the owner of the animal had** a fatal injury, and he killed another person, **he would be exempt.** [12]**So, too,** then, is **an ox** with a fatal injury that killed a person **exempt,** for as we said above, the laws that apply to the execution of the owner apply also to the execution of the ox.

זוֹמְמִין.

[1]וְאָמַר רָבָא: שׁוֹר טְרֵיפָה שֶׁהָרַג, חַיָּיב. [2]וְשׁוֹר שֶׁל אָדָם טְרֵיפָה שֶׁהָרַג, פָּטוּר.

[3]מַאי טַעְמָא? [4]אָמַר קְרָא: ״הַשּׁוֹר יִסָּקֵל וְגַם בְּעָלָיו יוּמָת״. [5]כָּל הֵיכָא דְּקָרֵינָא בֵּיהּ ״וְגַם בְּעָלָיו יוּמָת״ — [6]קָרֵינַן בֵּיהּ ״הַשּׁוֹר יִסָּקֵל״. [7]וְכָל הֵיכָא דְּלָא קָרֵינַן בֵּיהּ ״וְגַם בְּעָלָיו יוּמָת״, [8]לָא קָרֵינַן בֵּיהּ ״הַשּׁוֹר יִסָּקֵל״.

[9]רַב אַשִׁי אָמַר: אֲפִילּוּ שׁוֹר טְרֵיפָה נַמִי שֶׁהָרַג פָּטוּר.

[10]מַאי טַעְמָא? [11]כֵּיוָן דְּאִילּוּ בְּעָלִים הָווּ פְּטִירִי, [12]שׁוֹר נַמִי פָּטוּר.

LITERAL TRANSLATION

of refuters.

[1]And Rava said: [If] an ox with a fatal injury killed, it is liable. [2]But [if] an ox belonging to a man with a fatal injury killed, it is exempt.

[3]What is the reason? [4]The verse states: "The ox shall be stoned, and its owner shall also be put to death." [5]Wherever we can apply: "And its owner also shall be put to death," [6]we apply: "The ox shall be stoned." [7]And wherever we cannot apply: "And its owner also shall be put to death," [8]we do not apply: "The ox shall be stoned."

[9]Rav Ashi said: Even an ox with a fatal injury that killed is exempt.

[10]What is the reason? [11]Since, if the owner had [a fatal injury], [12]he would be exempt, the ox, too, is exempt.

RASHI

כשהן נעשו זוממין הוו להו זוממין של זוממין קמאי. כל עדות זומם קרו זוממי של נדון, כדאמרינן זוממי בת כהן באלו הן הנחנקין (סנהדרין פד,ב). **וגם בעליו יומת** — כלומר כמיתת בעלים (בסנהדרין ב,א) כך מיתת השור. ולהא מילתא נמי מקשינן להו דכיון דאילו קטיל מריה שלא בבית דין לא מקטיל על פי עדים כדאמרינן לעיל, שורו נמי לא מקטיל. **כיון דאילו הוו בעלים טריפה** — דכוותיה לא הוי מקטלי, שור טריפה נמי לא מקטיל, דהא למיתת בעלים הוקש.

HALAKHAH

שׁוֹר טְרֵיפָה, וְשׁוֹר שֶׁל אָדָם טְרֵיפָה **An ox with a fatal injury, and an ox belonging to a man with a fatal injury.** "If an ox suffering from a fatal injury or an ox belonging to a person with a fatal injury killed someone, it is not subject to stoning, following Rav Ashi. According to *Ra'avad,* if the ox killed the person before a court, it is subject to stoning, as is a person suffering from a fatal injury who killed another person." (*Rambam, Sefer Nezikin, Hilkhot Nizkei Mamon* 10:7.)

BACKGROUND

אֶרֶס נָחָשׁ Snake's venom. The source of a snake's venom is in special venom glands which release it into the fangs. Some venomous snakes have slits in their fangs to convey the poison, while others have hollow fangs. Regarding the latter, it may be said that the venom is in their teeth. However, the difference of opinion here regards the issue of whether a snake secretes venom intentionally, or whether the secretion is a reflex occurring as soon as the snake makes contact with human flesh.

TRANSLATION AND COMMENTARY

שִׁיסָּה בּוֹ [1]We have learned in our Mishnah: "If someone **set his dog** or his snake **upon** another person, and the dog or the snake bit the other person, and he died from the bite, the person who set the animal upon the victim is exempt from judicial execution. He is regarded as having caused his victim's death, but not as having committed the physical act that actually killed him. But if he held the snake against the victim's body, and caused it to bite him, the Tannaim disagree: Rabbi Yehudah says he is liable to be judicially executed, for he is regarded as if he had killed his victim with his own two hands. But the Sages say that he is exempt, for even in that case the assailant is regarded as having caused his victim's death, but not as having committed the physical act that actually killed him." [2]**Rav Aḥa bar Ya'akov said: When you analyze the matter** carefully, [3]**you will find that, according to Rabbi Yehudah, a snake's venom is stored between its teeth,** and once the snake bites a person, its venom can kill without any further action on the snake's part. [4]**Therefore,** if **someone** held a snake against another person's body, and **caused** it **to bite** him, and the victim died from the bite, the assailant is liable to death **by decapitation** like any other murderer. [5]**The snake** itself **is exempt** from execution, for it did not commit the physical act that killed the victim. [6]**According to the Sages,** even when someone holds a snake against another person's body and causes it to bite him, **the snake spits its venom of its own accord,** and is responsible for the victim's death. [7]**Therefore, the snake** is put to death **by stoning,** like any other animal that killed a person, [8]**and the** assailant **who** held the snake and **caused it to bite the other person is exempt.** He is regarded as having caused his victim's death, but not as having committed the physical act that actually killed him.

MISHNAH הַמַּכֶּה [9]**If someone struck another person, whether with a stone or** with his **fist,** [10]**and** the court **assessed** that the victim **would die** from the blow, **and** his condition **improved** so that the court reassessed the situation and predicted that he would in fact live, [11]**but** then **afterwards** his condition **worsened, and** he did in fact **die,** the assailant **is liable** to execution, just like any other murderer. [12]**Rabbi Neḥemyah** disagrees and **says:**

[1]״שִׁיסָּה בּוֹ אֶת הַכֶּלֶב וכו׳״. [2]אָמַר רַב אַחָא בַּר יַעֲקֹב: כְּשֶׁתִּמְצָא לוֹמַר, [3]לְדִבְרֵי רַבִּי יְהוּדָה — אֶרֶס נָחָשׁ בֵּין שִׁינָּיו הוּא עוֹמֵד. [4]לְפִיכָךְ: מַכִּישׁ — בְּסַיִיף, [5]וְנָחָשׁ פָּטוּר. [6]לְדִבְרֵי חֲכָמִים, אֶרֶס נָחָשׁ מֵעַצְמוֹ הוּא מֵקִיא. [7]לְפִיכָךְ: נָחָשׁ — בִּסְקִילָה, [8]וְהַמַּכִּישׁ — פָּטוּר.

משנה [9]הַמַּכֶּה אֶת חֲבֵירוֹ, בֵּין בְּאֶבֶן בֵּין בָּאֶגְרוֹף, [10]וַאֲמָדוּהוּ לְמִיתָה וְהֵיקֵל מִמַּה שֶּׁהָיָה, [11]וּלְאַחַר מִכָּאן הִכְבִּיד וָמֵת, חַיָּיב. [12]רַבִּי נְחֶמְיָה

LITERAL TRANSLATION

[1]"[If] he set his dog upon him, etc." [2]Rav Aḥa bar Ya'akov said: When you succeed in analyzing [the matter, [3]you will find that,] according to Rabbi Yehudah, a snake's venom is stored between its teeth. [4]Therefore, the one who caused [his snake] to bite [the other person] — by the sword, [5]and the snake is exempt. [6]According to the Sages, a snake's venom, it spits of its own will. [7]Therefore, the snake — by stoning, [8]and the one who caused [the snake] to bite [the other person] is exempt.

MISHNAH [9][If] someone struck another person, whether with a stone or a fist, [10]and they predicted [that he would] die, and [his condition] improved from what it was, [11]and afterwards he got worse and died, he is liable. [12]Rabbi Neḥemyah

RASHI

שיסה = גירה. השיך — שאחז הנחש והוליכו והשיך הנחש בבשרו. בין שיניו עומד — והרי הוא כתוקע סכין בבטנו, דלאו גרמא הוא שהרי כלי משחיתו בידו. מכיש בסייף — כדין רוצח. מעצמו מקיא — בנשיכתו, וכשהשיכו זה עדיין אין בו כדי להמית לפיכך גרמא בעלמא הוא, אף על פי שיודע שסופו להקיא מיהו לאו מכחו מיית. לפיכך נחש בסקילה — כדין שור שהמית, דכל בהמה וחיה כשור הן, אלא שדבר הכתוב בהוה.

משנה ואמדוהו למיתה — בית דין. אבל אמדוהו תחילה לחיים, אפילו לרבנן פטור, כדלקמן. והיקל ממה שהיה — וחזרו ואמדוהו לחיים.

HALAKHAH

אֶרֶס נָחָשׁ מֵעַצְמוֹ הוּא מֵקִיא A snake's venom, it spits of its own accord. "A snake spits its venom of its own accord. Therefore, if a person holds a snake against somebody else's body, and causes it to bite him, the snake is put to death, and the person is exempt from judicial execution." (*Rambam, Sefer Nezikin, Hilkhot Nizkei Mamon* 10:8.)

אֲמָדוּהוּ לְמִיתָה וְהֵיקֵל מִמַּה שֶּׁהָיָה, וּלְאַחַר מִכָּאן הִכְבִּיד וָמֵת **They predicted that he would die, and his condition improved from what it was, and afterward he got worse and died.** "If someone struck another person, and the victim was considered about to die, and then his condition improved, but then later it worsened again, and he died, the assailant is liable to execution," following the anonymous Tanna of the Mishnah. (*Rambam, Sefer Nezikin, Hilkhot Rotze'aḥ* 4:5.)

TRANSLATION AND COMMENTARY

The assailant **is exempt, for there is reason** to believe that the victim did not die from the blow that he received from his assailant, for his condition had improved in the meantime, but rather he died from some other cause.

GEMARA תָּנוּ רַבָּנַן [1]**Our Rabbis taught** a related Baraita: **"Rabbi Neḥemyah expounded** the following verses (Exodus 21:18-19): [2]'And if men strive together, and one strikes another with a stone, or with his fist, and he does not die, but stays in bed. **If he rises again, and walks abroad** [78B] **upon his staff, then shall he that struck him be acquitted;** only he shall pay for the loss of his time, and shall cause him to be thoroughly healed.' If the words, 'If he rises again, and walks abroad upon his staff,' mean that the victim enjoyed a full recovery, why did the verse have to state: 'Then shall he that struck him be acquitted'? [3]**Would it enter your mind that** if the victim survived the attack and is **walking** about **in the marketplace,** the assailant **should be put to death?** [4]**Rather,** the verse is referring to **someone whom** the court first **assessed would die** from the blow received from his assailant, **and** his condition **improved** so that he walked about on his staff, and the court reassessed the situation and predicted that he would live, [5]**but afterwards** his condition **worsened, and** he in fact **died.** Regarding such a situation, the verse states: [6]'Then shall he that struck him be acquitted,' teaching that the assailant **is exempt."**

וְרַבָּנַן [7]The Gemara asks: **How do the Rabbis** who disagree with Rabbi Neḥemyah **interpret this** verse: **"Then shall he that struck him be acquitted"?**

אוֹמֵר: פָּטוּר, שֶׁרַגְלַיִם לַדָּבָר.

גמרא [1]תָּנוּ רַבָּנַן: "אֶת זוֹ דָּרַשׁ רַבִּי נְחֶמְיָה [2]'אִם יָקוּם וְהִתְהַלֵּךְ בַּחוּץ [78B] עַל מִשְׁעַנְתּוֹ, וְנִקָּה הַמַּכֶּה, [3]וְכִי תַּעֲלֶה עַל דַּעְתְּךָ שֶׁזֶּה מְהַלֵּךְ בַּשּׁוּק וְזֶה נֶהֱרָג? [4]אֶלָּא, זֶה שֶׁאֲמָדוּהוּ לְמִיתָה וְהֵקֵל מִמַּה שֶּׁהָיָה, [5]וּלְאַחַר כָּךְ הִכְבִּיד וָמֵת, [6]שֶׁהוּא פָּטוּר".

[7]וְרַבָּנַן הַאי "וְנִקָּה הַמַּכֶּה" מַאי דָּרְשֵׁי בֵּיהּ?

LITERAL TRANSLATION

says: He is exempt, for there is reason.

GEMARA [1]Our Rabbis taught: "This Rabbi Neḥemyah expounded: [2]'If he rise again, and walk abroad [78B] upon his staff, then shall he that struck him be acquitted.' [3]Would it enter your mind that this one walks in the marketplace and this one is put to death? [4]Rather, [regarding] someone whom they estimated would die, and his condition improved, [5]but afterwards he got worse and died, [6]he is exempt."

[7]And the Rabbis, this: "Then shall he that struck him be acquitted"— how do they interpret it?

RASHI

שרגלים לדבר — שלא מת מחמת מכה זו, שהרי היקל.

גמרא על משענתו — מתרגמינן "על בורייה" שנתרפא לגמרי ונשען על כחו. **וכי תעלה על דעתך** — למה לי למימר "ונקה המכה" ממיתה. **אלא זה שאמדוהו** — מתחילה למיתה, ובא הכתוב ללמדך שאם יקום מן המשכב והתהלך בחוץ ואמדוהו למשענת חיים — "ונקה המכה" ואפילו מת לאחר מכן, שחזר והכביד. **ורבנן האי ונקה המכה מלמד שחובשין אותו** — אם אמדוהו למיתה חובשין את המכה שלא יברח עד שנראה אם ימות אם לאו. להכי אתי "ונקה המכה" דמשמע לכשיקום "ונקה", מכלל דעד השתא חבוש הוא.

NOTES

שֶׁרַגְלַיִם לַדָּבָר **For there is reason.** According to some, the words, "for there is a reason," refer to the position of the anonymous first Tanna of the Mishnah, that the assailant is liable, for there is reason to say that the victim died of the blow that he had received from his assailant (see Jerusalem Talmud, *Nazir* 9:4 and *Rambam's* Commentary to our Mishnah). Others argue that these words refer both to the position of the anonymous first Tanna and that of Rabbi Neḥemyah (*Rabbenu Yehonatan*).

עַל מִשְׁעַנְתּוֹ **Upon his staff.** According to *Ramah,* Rabbi Neḥemyah and the Rabbis disagree about the meaning of the words עַל מִשְׁעַנְתּוֹ, "upon his staff." The Rabbis interpret those words as did Onkelos, to mean "restored completely to his former health." In such a case all agree that the assailant is exempt from execution, even if the victim later dies, for he can surely not be subject to liability. Rabbi Neḥemyah, on the other hand, interprets those words to mean that the victim's condition improved slightly, and he was able to walk about but only "upon his staff." Thus, he understands that if the victim's condition improved slightly, then even if it once again worsens, and he dies, the assailant is exempt from execution.

HALAKHAH

אֲמָדוּהוּ **If they assessed.** "If someone struck another person, the court assesses the condition of the victim. If he is expected to live, the assailant makes restitution for the five categories of harm caused (damages, pain, humiliation, medical costs, and loss of livelihood). Even if the victim's condition worsens, and he dies, the assailant is exempt. If the victim is expected to die, the assailant is imprisoned. If the victim does die, the assailant is executed, but if the victim enjoys a full recovery and is able to walk about like any other healthy person, the assailant makes restitution for the five categories of damages, and is exempt from execution." (*Rambam, Sefer Nezikin, Hilkhot Rotze'aḥ* 4:3.)

TRANSLATION AND COMMENTARY

מְלַמֵּד [1]According to the Rabbis, **this** verse **teaches that** if the victim was expected to die, his assailant **is incarcerated** until the victim either dies or recovers. The verse that states: "If he rises again...then shall he that struck him be acquitted," implies that the assailant is incarcerated until the victim's condition is clear.

וְרַבִּי נְחֶמְיָה [2]The Gemara asks: **From where does Rabbi Neḥemyah derive** the ruling that the assailant is **incarcerated** until his victim's fate is determined?

יָלֵיף [3]The Gemara explains: Rabbi Neḥemyah **learns** that the assailant is incarcerated **from** what the Torah says about **the man who** profaned the Sabbath in the days of Moses by **gathering** sticks (Numbers 15:34): "And they put him in custody, because it was not declared what should be done to him."

וְרַבָּנַן [4]The Gemara challenges this use of that verse: **Let the Rabbis also learn**, then, that the assailant is incarcerated **from** what the Torah says about **the** stick-**gatherer!**

מְקוֹשֵׁשׁ [5]The Gemara answers: In fact, the law regarding the assailant cannot be inferred from the law regarding the stick-gatherer. It was obvious to Moses that **the** stick-**gatherer was liable** to death by **execution,** for the verse states (Exodus 31:14): "Everyone who profanes it shall surely be put to death." [6]**But he did not know by which means his execution should be carried out.** Therefore the Sabbath-desecrator was put in custody until the matter was clarified. [7]But it does **not** follow that the law of incarceration should **be extended** to an assailant whose victim has not yet expired, **when we do not know** yet **whether or not** the assailant **is** even **liable** to death by **execution.**

וְרַבִּי נְחֶמְיָה [8]The Gemara asks: **And** how does **Rabbi Neḥemyah** counter this argument?

יָלֵיף [9]The Gemara answers: He **learns** that the assailant is incarcerated, not from the case of the stick-gatherer, but **from** that of **the blasphemer,** [10]**for** Moses **did not know whether** or not **he was liable** to death by **execution, and** nevertheless **he was incarcerated,** as the verse states (Leviticus 24:12): "And they put him in custody, that the mind of the Lord might be shown them."

וְרַבָּנַן [11]The Gemara asks: **And** what do **the Rabbis** say about this?

מְגַדֵּף [12]The Gemara explains: They maintain that the law regarding the incarceration of **the blasphemer was a temporary ruling,** and so we cannot learn other laws from it.

[1]מְלַמֵּד שֶׁחוֹבְשִׁין אוֹתוֹ.
[2]וְרַבִּי נְחֶמְיָה, חֲבִישָׁה מְנָא לֵיהּ?
[3]יָלֵיף מִמְּקוֹשֵׁשׁ.
[4]וְרַבָּנַן נַמִי, לִילְפֵי מִמְּקוֹשֵׁשׁ!
[5]מְקוֹשֵׁשׁ בַּר קְטָלָא הוּא, [6]וּמֹשֶׁה לָא הֲוָה יָדַע קַטְלֵיהּ בְּמַאי. [7]לְאַפּוּקֵי הַאי, דְּלָא יָדְעִינַן אִי בַּר קְטָלָא הוּא, אִי לָאו בַּר קְטָלָא הוּא.
[8]וְרַבִּי נְחֶמְיָה?
[9]יָלֵיף מִמְּגַדֵּף, [10]דְּלָא הֲוָה יָדַע אִי בַּר קְטָלָא הוּא, וַחֲבָשׁוּהוּ.
[11]וְרַבָּנַן?
[12]מְגַדֵּף הוֹרָאַת שָׁעָה הָיְתָה.

LITERAL TRANSLATION

[1]This teaches that they incarcerate him.
[2]And Rabbi Neḥemyah, from where does he [derive] incarceration?
[3]He learns it from the gatherer.
[4]And the Rabbis also, let them learn from the gatherer!
[5]The gatherer was liable [to death by] execution, [6]but Moses did not know by which means his execution [should be carried out]. [7]To the exclusion of this one, that we do not know whether he is liable [to death by] execution, or he is not liable [to death by] execution.
[8]And Rabbi Neḥemyah?
[9]He learns it from the blasphemer, [10]for he did not know whether he was liable [to death by] execution, and they incarcerated him.
[11]And the Rabbis?
[12]The [incarceration of the] blasphemer was a temporary ruling.

RASHI

ילִיף ממקושש – דכתיב (במדבר טו) "ויניחו אותו במשמר". **מקושש בר קטלא הוא** – פשיטא ליה למשה דבר קטלא הוא, כדאייתי לקמן בברייתא יודע היה משה רבינו שהמקושש במיתה שהרי כבר נאמר בתורה "מחלליה מות יומת" אבל לא היה יודע באיזו מיתה יומת. רבנן סבירא להו כמאן דאמר לא בעינן שיודיעוהו בהתראתו באיזה מיתה נהרג. **דלא היה יודע אי בר קטלא הוא אי לא** – כדמפרש לקמן, אבל מגדף לא נאמר בו אלא לפרש וכו׳. **הוראת שעה היתה** – אי לא כתב, חבישה דהכא מחבישה דהתם לא הוה גמרינן דהוראת שעה היתה – שהרי לא נצטוו מתחילה על אותה חבישה ומעלמם עשו, דכיון דלא נאמר בו מיתה מתחילה מה ספק היה להם להטיל עליו ספק מיתה ולחובשו.

NOTES

הוֹרָאַת שָׁעָה הָיְתָה It was a temporary ruling. Our commentary follows *Rashi* and others who understand that the law regarding the incarceration of the blasphemer was a temporary ruling, for it was not yet known whether or not he was liable to execution. Others explain that the entire law regarding the blasphemer was a temporary ruling, since he was executed even though he had not received a warning. Hence nothing at all can be learned from that incident for later generations.

[1]כִּדְתַנְיָא: ״יוֹדֵעַ הָיָה מֹשֶׁה רַבֵּינוּ שֶׁהַמְקוֹשֵׁשׁ בְּמִיתָה, [2]שֶׁנֶּאֱמַר: ׳מְחַלְלֶיהָ מוֹת יוּמָת׳. [3]אֶלָּא לֹא הָיָה יוֹדֵעַ בְּאֵיזוֹ מִיתָה נֶהֱרָג, [4]שֶׁנֶּאֱמַר: ׳כִּי לֹא פֹרַשׁ וגו׳׳. [5]אֲבָל מְגַדֵּף, לֹא נֶאֱמַר בּוֹ אֶלָּא: ׳לִפְרֹשׁ לָהֶם עַל פִּי ה׳׳, [6]שֶׁלֹּא הָיָה מֹשֶׁה יוֹדֵעַ אִם הוּא בֶּן מִיתָה כָּל עִיקָּר, אִם לָאו״.

[7]בִּשְׁלָמָא לְרַבִּי נְחֶמְיָה, [8]הַיְינוּ דִּכְתִיבִי תְּרֵי אוּמְדָּנֵי, [9]חַד אֲמָדוּהוּ לְמִיתָה וְחָיָה, [10]וְחַד אֲמָדוּהוּ לְמִיתָה וְהֵקֵל מִמַּה שֶּׁהָיָה. [11]אֶלָּא לְרַבָּנַן, תְּרֵי

LITERAL TRANSLATION

[1]As it was taught: "Moses our master knew that the gatherer was liable [to death by] execution, [2]for it is stated: 'Those who profane it shall surely be put to death.' [3]But he did not know by which mode of execution he should be put to death, [4]as it is stated: 'Because it was not declared, etc.' [5]But [regarding] the blasphemer, it was only stated: 'That the mind of the Lord might be shown them,' [6]for Moses did not know whether he was at all liable [to death by] execution, or not."

[7]Granted, according to Rabbi Neḥemyah, [8]this is why two assessments are written, [9]one [when] they estimated [that he] would die, and he lived, [10]and one [when] they estimated [that he] would die, and he improved from what he was. [11]But according to the Sages, why

TRANSLATION AND COMMENTARY

כִּדְתַנְיָא [1]The Gemara corroborates earlier statements by citing another Baraita. **It was taught: "Moses our master knew that the** stick-gatherer **was liable** to death by **execution,** [2]**for the verse states** (Exodus 31:14): 'And you shall keep the Sabbath, for it is holy to you; **whoever profanes it shall surely be put to death.'** [3]**But he did not know by which mode of execution he should be put to death,** [4]**as the verse states** (Numbers 15:34): 'And they put him in custody, **because it was not declared** what should be done to him.' [5]**But regarding the blasphemer, the verse only states** (Leviticus 24:12): 'And they put him in custody, so **that the mind of the Lord might be shown them,'** [6]**for Moses did not know whether or not** the blasphemer **was at all liable** to be **executed."**

בִּשְׁלָמָא [7]We have been discussing the following verse (Exodus 21:18-19): "And if men strive together, and one strikes another with a stone, or with his fist, and he does not die, but keeps his bed. If he rises again, and walks abroad upon his staff, then shall he that struck him be acquitted; only he shall pay for the loss of his time, and shall cause him to be thoroughly healed." The expressions, "and he does not die," and "if he rises again, and walks abroad upon his staff," are extraneous. If these verses teach us only that someone who causes another person bodily injury must compensate him for his medical costs and loss of livelihood, it should have stated: "And if men strive together, and one strikes another with a stone, or with his fist, and he keeps his bed, he shall pay for the loss of his time, and shall cause him to be thoroughly healed." **Granted, according to Rabbi Neḥemyah,** who maintains that if the victim was first expected to die, and then his condition improved, and he was expected to live, and then his condition deteriorated, and he died, the assailant is exempt — [8]**this is why two** extraneous clauses **were written** to teach about two **assessments.** [9]**One** extraneous clause, "and he does not die," teaches about the victim who **was** first thought likely **to die, but** then **he** recovered and **lived.** For you might have thought that in such a case, the assailant is liable to death by execution because his victim was expected to die. Therefore, the Torah says, "and he does not die," teaching that if someone strikes another person, and the person does not die as he is expected to do, but recovers instead, he is liable to pay monetary compensation but not to be executed. [10]**And the other** extraneous clause, "if he rises again, and walks abroad upon his staff," teaches about a victim who **was** first thought likely **to die,** but then his condition **improved,** so that he walked about on his staff, and the court reassessed the situation and predicted that he would live, but afterward his condition deteriorated, and he died. Regarding such a case, the verse states: "Then shall he that struck him be acquitted." [11]**But according to the Sages, why do I need** two extraneous clauses to teach me about **two** different **assessments?** The verse should have merely stated, "And he does not die,

RASHI

כדתניא — סייעתא להא דאמר לעיל מקושש לא נסתפקו עליו אלא באיזה מיתה יומת, אבל מגדף לא היו יודעין שהיה חייב מיתה. **מה יעשה לו** — משמע בר עשייה הוא אבל לא היו יודעין מהו. **לפרוש להם** — ולא כתוב מה יעשה. משמע, כל דינו היו צריכין לפרש להם. **בשלמא לרבי נחמיה** — דאמר "ונקה המכה" — לאמדוהו למיתה והקל וחזר והכביד אתא, היינו דכתיבי תרי קראי יתירא, לאומדנא. דאם בא ללמדנו שהחובל בחבירו חייב בריפוי ושבת כדמסיק "שבתו יתן וגו׳" נכתוב "והכה את רעהו באבן או באגרוף ונפל למשכב, שבתו יתן ורפא ירפא", "ולא ימות" יתירא הוא למדרש, וכן "אם יקום והתהלך בחוץ". **חד אמדוהו למיתה וחיה** — דלא תימא הואיל ויצא מבית דין חייב — נקטליה דהא דהדר חיי הס רחמנא עליה להכי אתא "ולא ימות" כלומר "והכה איש וגו׳" "ולא ימות" כמה שאמדוהו אלא נפל למשכב — "שבתו יתן", ממון ולא מיתה. או "אם יקום והתהלך בחוץ" לאחר שאמדוהו למיתה — "ונקה המכה" אפילו חזר והכביד ומת. **אלא לרבנן** — דאמרי לחבישה אתא, תרי אומדני למה לי? — לכתוב "ולא ימות ונפל למשכב ונקה המכה שבתו יתן", ושמעינן מינה אמדוהו למיתה וחיה — ממון יתן

אוּמְדָּנֵי לָמָּה לִי?
[1]חַד אֲמָדוּהוּ לְמִיתָה וְחָיָה,
[2]וְחַד אֲמָדוּהוּ לְחַיִּים וָמֵת.
[3]וְרַבִּי נְחֶמְיָה? [4]אֲמָדוּהוּ לְחַיִּים, וָמֵת, לֹא צָרִיךְ קְרָא — [5]שֶׁהֲרֵי יָצָא מִבֵּית דִּין זַכַּאי.
[6]תָּנוּ רַבָּנַן: ״הַמַּכֶּה אֶת חֲבֵירוֹ וַאֲמָדוּהוּ לְמִיתָה וְחָיָה, פּוֹטְרִין אוֹתוֹ. [7]אֲמָדוּהוּ לְמִיתָה וְהֵקֵל מִמַּה שֶּׁהָיָה, [8]אוֹמְדִין אוֹתוֹ אוֹמֶד שֵׁנִי לְמָמוֹן. [9]וְאִם לְאַחַר כֵּן הִכְבִּיד וָמֵת, [10]הַלֵּךְ אַחַר אוֹמֶד הָאֶמְצָעִי. [11]דִּבְרֵי רַבִּי נְחֶמְיָה. [12]וַחֲכָמִים אוֹמְרִים: אֵין אוֹמֶד אַחַר אוֹמֶד״.

LITERAL TRANSLATION

do I need two assessments?

[1]One [when] they estimated [that he] would die, and he lived, [2]and one [when] they estimated [that he] would live, and he died.

[3]And Rabbi Neḥemyah? [4]For [when] they estimated [that he] would live, and he died, there is no need for a verse, [5]for he left the court exonerated.

[6]Our Rabbis taught: "[If] someone struck another person, and they estimated [that he] would die, and he lived, we exempt him. [7][If] they estimated [that he] would die, and he got better, [8]they make a second assessment for compensation. [9]And if afterward he got worse and died, [10]go after the middle assessment. [11][These are] the words of Rabbi Neḥemyah. [12]And the Sages say: There is no assessment after assessment."

TRANSLATION AND COMMENTARY

but keeps his bed. Then shall he that struck him be acquitted; only he shall pay for the loss of his time." The words, "and he does not die," would teach that if the victim was first expected to die, but then recovered and lived, the assailant is to pay monetary compensation, and not to be executed. And the words, "then shall he that struck him be acquitted," would teach that if the victim was expected to die, his assailant is incarcerated until the victim expires or recovers.

חַד [1]The Gemara explains: According to the Sages, **one** extraneous clause, "if he rises again, and walks about on his staff," teaches about a victim who **was** first expected about **to die, but** then recovered and **lived** — that in such a case the assailant is liable to pay monetary compensation, as the passage continues, "only he shall pay for his loss of time," but he is not executed. [2]**And the other** extraneous clause, "and he does not die," teaches about a victim who **was** first expected **to live** ("and he does not die"), **but** then his condition worsened and **he died.** In such a case, as well, the assailant is liable to pay monetary compensation, and not to be executed. But if the victim was first expected to die, and then his condition improved and the court reassessed the situation and predicted that he would live, but afterward his condition worsened, and he died, the assailant is indeed liable to death by execution.

וְרַבִּי נְחֶמְיָה [3]The Gemara asks: **And** from where does **Rabbi Neḥemyah** learn that if the victim was first expected to live, but then his condition deteriorated and he died, that the assailant is exempt from execution? [4]The Gemara explains: Regarding a victim who **was** first expected **to live, but** then **died, there is no need for a verse** to teach me that the assailant is only liable to pay monetary compensation, [5]**for he** already **left the court exonerated.** When the court expected the victim to live, it exempted the assailant from capital punishment. And there is a general rule that, once a defendant has been acquitted, he cannot be brought back to court to be condemned.

תָּנוּ רַבָּנַן [6]**Our Rabbis taught** a related Baraita: **"If** a person **struck** someone, **and** the victim **was** expected **to die, but** then recovered and **lived, we exempt** the assailant from execution, but obligate him to pay monetary compensation for the damage he caused the victim. [7]**If** the victim **was** expected **to die, but** then his condition **improved,** [8]**a second assessment is made** to determine the amount of monetary **compensation** that the assailant must pay the victim. [9]**If afterward** the victim's condition deteriorated, **and he died,** [10]**we follow the second assessment,** that the victim would live, and exempt the assailant from execution. [11]**This is the position of Rabbi Neḥemyah.** [12]**The Sages** disagree and **say: There is no assessment after assessment** to free the assailant from liability should the victim's condition once again deteriorate and lead to his death. In such a case, the assailant is liable."

RASHI

ולא מיתה. ומונקה המכה יתירא שמעינן דכשיבורר לנו שלא ימות הוא — "ונקה המכה", מכלל דעד השתא חבוש הוא. **חד אמדוהו למיתה וחיה וחד אמדוהו לחיים ומת** — ואיפכא דרש להו, "ולא ימות" דרשי ליה לאמדוהו לחיים ומת, והכי משמע "ולא ימות" אם אמדוהו תחלה שלא ימות אפילו מת לאחר מכאן, "שבתו יתן ורפא ירפא", יתן האומד שאמדוהו לכמה חליו עולה ושבתו ורפואתו שכך היו אומדין אותו כשהיה נאמד לחיים. ואם אמדוהו למיתה ואחר כך "יקום והתהלך בחוץ" — שלא מת "שבתו יתן". אבל אמדוהו מתחילה למיתה ויצא מבית דין — חייב. וסוף דבר, מת אף על פי שהקל באמצע לא פטריה רחמנא. **שהרי יצא מבית דין זכאי** — והא נפקא לן מ"צדיק אל תהרוג" בפרק "אחד דיני ממונות" (סנהדרין לג,ב): מנין ליוצא מבית דין זכאי ואמר אחד יש לי ללמד עליו חובה, שאין מחזירין אותו, שנאמר "וצדיק אל תהרוג". **פוטרין אותו** — ממיתה, ונותן חמשה דברים. **אומד שני לממון** — כמה ראוי לשכב מחולי זה, ולכמה יעלה שבתו ורפואתו. **אומד האמצעי** — היינו אומד שני. **אין אומד אחר אומד** — לחשב כיוצא מבית דין זכאי

TRANSLATION AND COMMENTARY

תַּנְיָא אִידָךְ [1]**It was taught** also **in a different Baraita: "If** someone struck another person, and the victim **was** initially expected **to die,** and his condition improved, so that he is now expected **to live,** the assailant is exempt from execution. [2]But if the victim was expected **to live,** and his condition deteriorated and he died, we do **not** say that the first prognosis was erroneous, and the victim should have been expected **to die.** Rather the assailant leaves the court vindicated by the first assessment. [3]**If** the victim **was expected to die, but** then his condition **improved,** [4]**a second assessment is made** to determine the amount of monetary **compensation** he must pay the victim. [5]**If afterward** the victim's condition deteriorated **and he died,** we follow the second assessment, and exempt the assailant from execution, [6]but obligate him to **pay damages and** compensation for the victim's **pain** as well as compensation for his medical costs and loss of livelihood, and for humiliation **to** the victim's **heirs.** [7]**From what point do** we determine the damages that the assailant must **pay?** [8]**From the time that** the assailant **struck him."**

וּסְתָמָא [9]The Gemara notes that this **anonymous Baraita follows** the position of **Rabbi Neḥemyah,** for it exempts the assailant from execution if the victim was expected to die, but then his condition improved, even though he later died.

MISHNAH נִתְכַּוֵּין [10]**If someone intended to kill an animal, but** by accident **killed the person** who was standing next to the animal; [11]or if he intended to kill **a non-Jew,** for whose death a Jew is not liable to be judicially executed, **but** by accident **killed a Jew;** [12]or if he intended to kill **a nonviable infant,** whose murder does not carry the death penalty, **but** by accident **killed a viable infant** — in all these cases, the killer **is exempt** from judicial execution, for he did not intend to kill a person for whose death he would be liable to capital punishment.

[1]תַּנְיָא אִידָךְ: ״אֲמָדוּהוּ לְמִיתָה אוֹמְדִין אוֹתוֹ לְחַיִּים. [2]לְחַיִּים, אֵין אוֹמְדִין אוֹתוֹ לְמִיתָה. [3]אֲמָדוּהוּ לְמִיתָה וְהֵקֵל מִמַּה שֶּׁהָיָה — [4]אוֹמְדִין אוֹתוֹ אוֹמֶד שֵׁנִי לְמָמוֹן, [5]וְאִם לְאַחַר כֵּן הִכְבִּיד וָמֵת, [6]מְשַׁלֵּם נֶזֶק וְצַעַר לַיּוֹרְשִׁים. [7]מֵאֵימָתַי מְשַׁלֵּם? [8]מִשָּׁעָה שֶׁהִכָּהוּ״.

[9]וּסְתָמָא כְּרַבִּי נְחֶמְיָה.

משנה [10]נִתְכַּוֵּין לַהֲרוֹג אֶת הַבְּהֵמָה וְהָרַג אֶת הָאָדָם; [11]לְנָכְרִי וְהָרַג אֶת יִשְׂרָאֵל; [12]לִנְפָלִים וְהָרַג אֶת בֶּן קַיָּימָא, פָּטוּר.

LITERAL TRANSLATION

[1]It was taught in a different [Baraita]: "[If] they assessed [that he] would die, they may still assess [that he] will live. [2]To live, they do not assess [that he] will die. [3][If] they assessed [that he] would die, and he improved from what he was, [4]they make a second assessment for compensation. [5]And if afterward he got worse and died, [6]he pays damages and [compensation for] pain to the heirs. [7]From when does he pay? [8]From the time that he struck him."

[9]And the anonymous Baraita is in accordance with Rabbi Neḥemyah.

MISHNAH [10][If] he intended to kill an animal, and he killed a person; [11]a non-Jew, and he killed a Jew; [12]a nonviable infant, and he killed a viable infant, he is exempt.

RASHI

ולהפטר אם לאחר מכאן הכביד ומת, אלא בתר מעשה דהשתא אזלינן, דהואיל והכביד ומת חייב המכה מיתה. **אמדוהו למיתה אומדין אותו לחיים** — אם ראינו שהקל ולא אמרינן הואיל ויצא מבית דין חייב הרי זה יהרג. **לחיים אין אומדין אותו למיתה** — לומר טעינו באומד ראשון ולחייבו לזה, שהרי יצא מבית דין זכאי, ואמרינן: מחמת חולי אחר שבא עליו הכבידה המכה. **נותן נזק וצער ליורשין** — והוא הדין לרפוי ושבת ובשת, דהא בתר אומד האמצעי אזלינן ולכולהו אמדוהו, אלא לאו אורחיה דתנא למחשב כרוכלא. **אימתי משלם** — [כלומר] מאיזו שעה אומדין אותו כשהקל. **משעה שהכהו** — אומדין כמה היה יפה קודם הכאה, וכמה היה יפה אחר הכאה. ולא אמרינן הואיל ועד השתא לא אמדינן [ליה] אלא למיתה והשתא הוא דאמדינן ליה לממון נאמדיה כדקאי השתא והרי הוקל, ומפסדינן ליה לניזק. **וסתמא כרבי נחמיה** — והך סתמא כרבי נחמיה מוכחא דפטר ליה ממיתה אף על פי שהכביד ומת.

משנה נתכוין להרוג את הבהמה — היה עומד אדם אצל בהמה ונתכוין להרוג בהמה והרג אדם — פטור, משום דכי אתרו ביה התראת ספק הוא, אף על פי שקבל עליו התראה שאומר להם ״יודע אני שהוא בן ברית ועל מנת כן אני עושה שאם אהרגנו אני אתחייב מיתה״ — פטור, דשמא לא יהרגנו. **אנפלים לא מיחייב** — דכמו דקטיל דמו.

NOTES

נֶזֶק וְצַעַר לַיּוֹרְשִׁים **Damages and pain to the heirs.** Our commentary follows *Rashi,* who says that the assailant must pay the victim's heirs not only damages and compensation for the victim's pain, but also compensation for his medical costs, loss of livelihood, and humiliation. *Ramah* disagrees and says that the victim's medical costs are not paid to his heirs. Regarding medical costs, the verse says: "He shall cause him to be thoroughly healed," implying that the obligation applies only while the victim can be healed. But regarding compensation for loss of livelihood, the verse states, "he shall pay only for the loss of his time," implying that the assailant must pay for the victim's loss of livelihood in any case, even to the victim's heirs.

נִתְכַּוֵּין לַהֲרוֹג אֶת הַבְּהֵמָה וְהָרַג אֶת הָאָדָם **If he intended to kill an animal, and he killed a person.** According to *Rashi,* the assailant is exempt because the warning that he received was given in circumstances of doubt, since the person who issued the warning did not know that the assailant would strike the person standing next to the animal. But others understand that the assailant is exempt because he did not intend to strike the person, and so his action with regard to the person was inadvertent (see *Meiri*).

TRANSLATION AND COMMENTARY

נִתְכַּוֵּין [1]**If someone intended to strike** another person **in his loins, and** the blow **would not have killed him** had it actually struck **his loins,** [2]**but** by accident the blow struck the victim's **heart, where it was likely to prove fatal, and** the victim in fact **died,** the killer **is exempt** from judicial execution, for he did not intend to inflict a fatal wound upon his victim. [3]**If someone intended to strike** another person **in his heart,** [79A] [4]**and** the blow **would have been capable of killing him** had it actually struck him **in his heart,** [5]**but** instead it struck the victim's **loins, and** such a blow **would not** ordinarily **have been able to kill him,** [6]**but** nevertheless the victim **died,** the killer **is exempt** from judicial execution, although he did strike him with a deadly blow.

נִתְכַּוֵּון [7]**If someone intended to strike an adult, and** the blow **would not have been fatal** had it actually struck **an adult,** [8]**but** the blow **fell on a minor, and** such a blow **was** sufficient **to kill a minor, and he** in fact **died,** the killer **is exempt** from judicial execution, for he did not intend to inflict a fatal wound. [9]**If someone intended to strike a minor, and** the blow **would have been fatal** had it actually struck **a minor,** [10]**but** the blow **fell on an adult, and** such a blow **would not** ordinarily **have been** sufficient **to kill an adult,** [11]**but** nevertheless the victim **died,** the killer **is exempt** from judicial execution, for he did not strike him with a normally deadly blow.

אֲבָל [12]**But if someone intended to strike** another person in **his loins, and** the blow **would have been fatal** had it actually struck him **in the loins,** [13]**but** the blow struck the victim's **heart,** where it was certainly sufficient to kill him, **and** the victim **died,** the killer **is liable** to judicial execution, for he intended to kill his victim, and he struck him with a deadly blow. [14]Similarly, **if someone intended to strike an adult, and** the blow **would have been fatal** had it actually struck **an adult,** [15]**but** the blow instead struck **a minor,** whom it certainly could be expected to kill, **and** the victim in fact **died,** the killer **is liable** to judicial execution.

[1]נִתְכַּוֵּין לְהַכּוֹתוֹ עַל מָתְנָיו, וְלֹא הָיָה בָּהּ כְּדֵי לַהֲמִיתוֹ עַל מָתְנָיו, [2]וְהָלְכָה לָהּ עַל לִבּוֹ, וְהָיָה בָּהּ כְּדֵי לַהֲמִיתוֹ עַל לִבּוֹ וָמֵת, פָּטוּר. [3]נִתְכַּוֵּין לְהַכּוֹתוֹ עַל לִבּוֹ [79A] [4]וְהָיָה בָּהּ כְּדֵי לְהָמִית עַל לִבּוֹ, [5]וְהָלְכָה לָהּ עַל מָתְנָיו וְלֹא הָיָה בָּהּ כְּדֵי לְהָמִית עַל מָתְנָיו, [6]וָמֵת, פָּטוּר.

[7]נִתְכַּוֵּון לְהַכּוֹת אֶת הַגָּדוֹל וְלֹא הָיָה בָּהּ כְּדֵי לְהָמִית הַגָּדוֹל, [8]וְהָלְכָה לָהּ עַל הַקָּטָן וְהָיָה בָּהּ כְּדֵי לְהָמִית אֶת הַקָּטָן וָמֵת, פָּטוּר. [9]נִתְכַּוֵּן לְהַכּוֹת אֶת הַקָּטָן, וְהָיָה בָּהּ כְּדֵי לְהָמִית אֶת הַקָּטָן, [10]וְהָלְכָה לָהּ עַל הַגָּדוֹל וְלֹא הָיָה בָּהּ כְּדֵי לְהָמִית אֶת הַגָּדוֹל [11]וָמֵת, פָּטוּר.

[12]אֲבָל נִתְכַּוֵּון לְהַכּוֹת עַל מָתְנָיו וְהָיָה בָּהּ כְּדֵי לְהָמִית עַל מָתְנָיו, [13]וְהָלְכָה לָהּ עַל לִבּוֹ וָמֵת, חַיָּיב. [14]נִתְכַּוֵּון לְהַכּוֹת אֶת הַגָּדוֹל וְהָיָה בָּהּ כְּדֵי לְהָמִית אֶת הַגָּדוֹל, [15]וְהָלְכָה לָהּ עַל הַקָּטָן וָמֵת, חַיָּיב.

LITERAL TRANSLATION

[1][If] he intended to strike him in his loins, and it [the blow] was not able to kill him in his loins, [2]but it went to his heart, and it was able to kill him in his heart, and he died, he is exempt. [3][If] he intended to strike him in his heart, [79A] [4]and it was able to kill him in his heart, [5]but it went to his loins, and it was not able to kill him in his loins, [6]and he died, he is exempt.

[7][If] he intended to strike an adult, and it was not able to kill an adult, [8]but it went to a minor, and it was able to kill a minor, and he died, he is exempt. [9][If] he intended to strike a minor, and it was able to kill a minor, [10]but it went to an adult, and it was not able to kill an adult, [11]and he died, he is exempt.

[12]But if he intended to strike his loins, and it was able to kill him in his loins, [13]but it went to his heart, and he died, he is liable. [14][If] he intended to strike an adult, and it was able to kill an adult, [15]but it went to a minor, and he died, he is liable.

RASHI

והיה בה כדי להמית על לבו — האבן הזאת אם תכה על לב ראויה להרוג, אבל על המתנים אין בה כדי להמית — פטור, דתרתי בעינן, שיהא מתכוין למכת מיתה ושיכנו מכת מיתה, דאם לא נתכוין למכת מיתה התראת ספק היא דהתרו בו אל תזרוק דשמא תלך על לבו.

HALAKHAH

נִתְכַּוֵּין לְהַכּוֹתוֹ עַל מָתְנָיו וְהָלְכָה לָהּ עַל לִבּוֹ If he intended to strike him in his loins, but it went to his heart. "If someone intended to strike another person in his loins, and the blow would not have been sufficient to kill him had it actually struck there, but by accident the blow struck the victim's heart, and it was sufficient to kill him there, and the victim died, the killer is exempt from judicial execution. Similarly, if someone intended to strike another person in his heart, and the blow would have been sufficient to kill him had it actually struck him there, but the blow struck the victim's loins, and such a blow would not ordinarily have been sufficient to kill him there, but nevertheless the victim died, the killer is exempt from judicial execution. But if he intended to strike him in his loins, and the blow would have been sufficient to kill him had it actually struck him there, but by accident the blow struck the victim's heart, and the victim died, the killer is liable to execution. (*Rambam, Sefer Nezikin, Hilkhot Rotze'aḥ* 4:2.)

LITERAL TRANSLATION

[1]Rabbi Shimon says: Even if he intended to kill this one and he killed that one, he is exempt.

GEMARA [2]Rabbi Shimon — on what? [3]If you say the last clause, [4]it should have said: "Rabbi Shimon exempts." [5]Rather, the first clause: "[If] he intended to kill an animal, and he killed a person; [6]a non-Jew, and he killed a Jew; [7]a nonviable infant, and he killed a viable infant, [8]he is exempt." [9]But if he intended to kill this one, and he killed that one, [10]he is liable. [11]"Rabbi Shimon says: Even if he intended to kill this one and he killed that one, he is exempt."

[12]It is obvious [that if] Reuven and Shimon were standing, [13]and he said: "I intend [to kill] Reuven,

[1]רַבִּי שִׁמְעוֹן אוֹמֵר: אֲפִילּוּ נִתְכַּוֵּון לַהֲרוֹג אֶת זֶה וְהָרַג אֶת זֶה, פָּטוּר.

גמרא [2]רַבִּי שִׁמְעוֹן אַהַיָּיא? [3]אִילֵימָא אַסֵּיפָא, [4]"רַבִּי שִׁמְעוֹן פּוֹטֵר" מִיבָּעֵי לֵיהּ! [5]אֶלָּא אַרֵישָׁא: "נִתְכַּוֵּון לַהֲרוֹג אֶת הַבְּהֵמָה וְהָרַג אֶת הָאָדָם; [6]לְנָכְרִי וְהָרַג אֶת יִשְׂרָאֵל; [7]לִנְפָלִים וְהָרַג אֶת בֶּן קַיָּימָא, [8]פָּטוּר". [9]הָא נִתְכַּוֵּון לַהֲרוֹג אֶת זֶה וְהָרַג אֶת זֶה, [10]חַיָּיב. [11]"רַבִּי שִׁמְעוֹן אוֹמֵר: אֲפִילּוּ נִתְכַּוֵּין לַהֲרוֹג אֶת זֶה וְהָרַג אֶת זֶה פָּטוּר".

[12]פְּשִׁיטָא, קָאֵי רְאוּבֵן וְשִׁמְעוֹן, [13]וְאָמַר: "אֲנָא לִרְאוּבֵן קָא

RASHI

גמרא **אי נימי אסיפא** — דקאמר תנא קמא נתכוון להכות את הגדול והלכה לה על הקטן ומת — חייב, אלמא נתכוון להרוג את זה והרג את זה חייב. **רבי שמעון פוטר מיבעי ליה** — דהא בהדיא קאמר לה תנא קמא, ולמה ליה לרבי שמעון למהדר פרושא, ומאי "אפילו". **הא נתכוון להרוג את זה** — והתרו בו עליו דהתראה ודאי הוא, והרג את זה — חייב, דאיכא התראה על בן ברית והרי מתכוון לבן בריתו והרגו, ורבי שמעון אומר וכו', והאי דשביק רבי שמעון לסיפא בהדיא ומהדר אדוקיא דרישא — דלא תימא רבי שמעון פוטר אכולהו ואפילו נתכוון על מתניו והלכה לו על לבו.

TRANSLATION AND COMMENTARY

רַבִּי שִׁמְעוֹן [1]**Rabbi Shimon** disagrees and **says: Even if someone intended to kill** a certain person, **but** as it turned out **he killed** someone else, **he is exempt** from judicial execution, even though the murder of either one of them carries the death penalty, for a killer is only culpable for killing a person whom he intended to kill.

GEMARA רַבִּי שִׁמְעוֹן [2]The Gemara asks: **To which** part of the Mishnah do the words of **Rabbi Shimon** relate? [3]**If you say** that they refer to **the last clause** of the Mishnah, where the anonymous first Tanna rules that a person is liable if he intended to strike an adult with a deadly blow, but hit a minor instead and killed him, why does the Mishnah continue: "Rabbi Shimon says: Even if he intended to kill this one and he killed that one, he is exempt"? Why the repetition, and why say "even"? [4]The Mishnah **should** simply **have stated: "Rabbi Shimon exempts."** [5]**Rather,** Rabbi Shimon's words relate to **the first clause** of the Mishnah, which reads: **"If someone intended to kill an animal, but** by accident **killed a person;** [6]or if he intended to kill **a non-Jew, but** by accident **killed a Jew;** [7]or if he intended to kill **a nonviable infant, but** by accident **killed a viable infant** — [8]in all these cases, the killer **is exempt** from judicial execution, for he did not intend to kill a person for whose death would render him liable to capital punishment." [9]**But** it follows from here that **if** someone had **intended to kill** a certain person, for whose murder he would be liable to judicial execution, **but** as it turned out **he killed** another person, whose murder also carries the death penalty, [10]the killer **is** in fact **liable** to be executed. [11]Therefore the Mishnah continues: **"Rabbi Shimon** disagrees and **says: Even if someone intended to kill** a certain person, **but** as it turned out **he killed** another person, **he is exempt** from judicial execution, for a killer is only culpable for killing a person whom he intended to kill."

פְּשִׁיטָא [12]The Gemara wishes to clarify the limits of this Tannaitic dispute: **It is obvious that if Reuven and Shimon were standing** together, **and** before the killer cast his stone or shot his arrow, [13]**he said: "I intend**

NOTES

אֲפִילּוּ נִתְכַּוֵּון לַהֲרוֹג אֶת זֶה **Even if he intended to kill this one.** It has been noted that Rabbi Shimon's position is based on the principle that, in fixing a criminal's punishment, we consider not only his actions, but also his intentions. Regarding culpability for the violation of the laws of Shabbat, everybody agrees that if someone intended to carry out a particular type of labor but did something else instead, he is exempt. Regarding Shabbat violations, liability is only imposed for intentional work. Rabbi Shimon extends this principle to other areas of Halakhah.

HALAKHAH

נִתְכַּוֵּון לַהֲרוֹג אֶת זֶה וְהָרַג אֶת זֶה **If he intended to kill this one, and he killed that one.** "If someone intended to kill a certain person, but in fact killed another person, he is exempt from judicial execution and from having to pay monetary compensation." (*Rambam* apparently rules in accordance with the School of Ḥizkiyah, whose position is discussed below; see *Ra'avad* and *Kesef Mishneh*.) (*Rambam, Sefer Nezikin, Hilkhot Rotze'aḥ* 4:1.)

TERMINOLOGY

אַהַיָּיא **To what does this refer?** (Lit., "on what?"). Sometimes, when a concluding sentence in a Mishnah, Baraita or Amoraic statement refers to or differs from an earlier statement in the same source, and it is not clear to which of the previous statements it is referring, the Talmud may ask: "To which statement does this sentence refer?"

SAGES

רַבִּי שִׁמְעוֹן **Rabbi Shimon.** Where the name Rabbi Shimon occurs without a patronymic in Tannaitic literature, it usually refers to Rabbi Shimon bar Yoḥai, one of the greatest Tannaim of the generation preceding the completion of the Mishnah. Rabbi Shimon was a close disciple of Rabbi Akiva, and regarded himself as following in his teacher's path. Rabbi Akiva thought very highly of his disciple, saying of him: "It is sufficient for you that I and your Creator know your power."

Rabbi Shimon was a master of both Halakhah and Aggadah, and his teachings are quoted frequently throughout the Talmud. Although the Halakhah does not always follow his rulings (especially against Rabbi Yose and Rabbi Yehudah), nevertheless in many important areas of Halakhah his opinion prevails. Rabbi Shimon used a particular method of Halakhic Midrash called "seeking the reason for the verse" — drawing Halakhic conclusions from the Bible on the basis of the spirit and intent of particular passages.

Rabbi Shimon was sent to Rome as an emissary of the Jews, though he was deeply hostile to the Romans. Because he did not conceal his feelings about them, he was sentenced to death and forced to remain in hiding for many years.

His character was ascetic, and he tended to be stringent in his rulings. He was famous in his generation as a righteous man and as a miracle worker, and there are many famous stories about the numerous wonders he performed.

Sifrei — a collection of Halakhic Midrashim on Numbers and Deuteronomy — was produced in his academy. He

TRANSLATION AND COMMENTARY

to kill Reuven, and not Shimon," but he killed Shimon by mistake, [1] **this is** the basic case that is **in dispute** between the anonymous Rabbis of the Mishnah and Rabbi Shimon. According to the Rabbis, he is liable to judicial execution, and according to Rabbi Shimon, he is exempt. [2] But **what is the law,** according to Rabbi Shimon, **if the killer said,** "I intend to kill **one of them,"** and does so. Is he considered as having killed the person whom he intended to kill, or not? [3] **And also, what is the law,** according to Rabbi Shimon, **if the killer mistook** the identity of his victim and **thought that** he was killing **Reuven, but it turned out** that he killed **Shimon?** Is he considered as having killed the person whom he had intended to kill, or not?

תָּא שְׁמַע [4] **Come and hear** a resolution to these questions, **for it was taught** in a Baraita: [5] **"Rabbi Shimon** disagrees with the anonymous first Tanna of the Mishnah and **says:** A killer is not liable to judicial execution, **unless he said: 'I intend to kill So-and-so,'** and then killed him." But if he merely said: "I intend to kill one of the two," without specifically designating his victim, or if he mistook the identity of his victim, he is exempt from the death penalty.

מַאי טַעְמָא [6] The Gemara asks: **What is the reasoning of Rabbi Shimon?** The Gemara explains: [7] **The verse states** (Deuteronomy 19:11): "But if any man hates his neighbor, **and lies in wait** for him, **and rises up against him,** and strikes him mortally so that he dies." [8] This implies that the murderer is not liable **unless he intended to kill** a specific victim.

וְרַבָּנַן [9] The Gemara asks: **And** how do **the Rabbis** who disagree with Rabbi Shimon interpret this verse?

אָמְרִי [10] They explain it as they did in the School of Rabbi Yannai, for **they said in the School of Rabbi Yannai:** The verse cited above **excludes** from capital punishment **someone who threw a stone at a group of people,** consisting of Jews and non-Jews, killing one of the Jews. In such a case the killer is exempt from the death penalty. But if someone intended to kill a certain Jew but killed a different one, he would indeed be liable to judicial execution.

הֵיכִי דָמֵי [11] The Gemara comments: It is obvious that the murderer is only liable if he intended to kill a person for whose murder he would be liable. **How,** then, according to the Rabbis, **do** we regard **the case** referred to in the verse? [12] **If you say** that **there was** a group of **nine non-Jews, and one Jew** was **with**

LITERAL TRANSLATION

[and] I do not intend [to kill] Shimon" — [1] this is their dispute. [2] [If] he said: "One of them," what [is the law]? [3] And also, if he thought it was Reuven, and it turned out to be Shimon, what [is the law]?

[4] Come [and] hear, for it was taught: [5] "Rabbi Shimon says: Until he says: 'I intend [to kill] So-and-so.'"

[6] What is the reason[ing] of Rabbi Shimon? [7] The verse states: "And lie in wait for him, and rise up against him" — [8] [implying that he is not liable] unless he intended [to kill] him. [9] And the Rabbis?

[10] They said in the School of Rabbi Yannai: To exclude someone who throws a stone into [a group of people]. [11] How do we visualize the case (lit., "how it is like")? [12] If you say [that] there are nine non-Jews and one Jew

מִיכַּוַּונָא, לְשִׁמְעוֹן לָא קָא מִיכַּוַּונָא" — [1] הַיְינוּ פְּלוּגְתַּיְיהוּ. [2] אָמַר "לְחַד מִינַּיְיהוּ", מַאי? [3] אִי נַמִי, כִּסְבוּר רְאוּבֵן וְנִמְצָא שִׁמְעוֹן, מַאי?

[4] תָּא שְׁמַע, דְּתַנְיָא: [5] רַבִּי שִׁמְעוֹן אוֹמֵר: 'עַד שֶׁיֹּאמַר לִפְלוֹנִי אֲנִי מִתְכַּוֵּון' ".

[6] מַאי טַעְמָא דְּרַבִּי שִׁמְעוֹן? [7] אָמַר קְרָא: "וְאָרַב לוֹ וְקָם עָלָיו" — [8] עַד שֶׁיִּתְכַּוֵּון לוֹ. [9] וְרַבָּנַן?

[10] אָמְרִי דְּבֵי רַבִּי יַנַּאי: פְּרָט לְזוֹרֵק אֶבֶן לְגוֹ. [11] הֵיכִי דָּמֵי? [12] אִילֵּימָא דְּאִיכָּא תִּשְׁעָה נָכְרִים וְאֶחָד יִשְׂרָאֵל

RASHI

אמר לחד מינייהו — קָא מִיכַּוֵּינָא וְלֹא אִיכְפַת לְהִי לְהִי מִינַּיְיהוּ. **מאי** — לְרַבִּי שִׁמְעוֹן מִקְרֵי לֵיהּ מִיתְכַּוֵּון לוֹ, וּמִיחַיֵּיב, אוֹ דִילְמָא כֵּיוָן דְּאִי אָזְלָא אֲחִידָךְ וְשַׁבְקָהּ לֵיהּ לְהַאי הַוָה נַמִי נִיחָא לֵיהּ לָאו מִתְכַּוֵּון הוּא. **אי נמי** — לְהַכּוֹת אֶת הַגּוּף הַזֶּה, אֲבָל כִּסְבוּר הוּא שֶׁהוּא רְאוּבֵן וְנִמְצָא שִׁמְעוֹן, מִי אָמְרִינַן כֵּיוָן דְּלְהַאי גּוּפָא אִיתְכַּוֵּון מִתְכַּוֵּון הוּא נָן, אוֹ דִילְמָא כֵּיוָן דְּלְהַאי גַּבְרָא לֹא אִיכַּוֵּון פָּטַר לֵיהּ רַבִּי שִׁמְעוֹן. **עד שיאמר לפלוני אני מתכוין** — וְאוֹתוֹ פְּלוֹנִי הָרַג, וְכִי אָמַר "לְחַד מִינַּיְיהוּ" לֹא יְיַחֵד אוֹתוֹ, וְכֵן כִּסְבוּר רְאוּבֵן וְנִמְצָא שִׁמְעוֹן — לֹא זֶהוּ פְּלוֹנִי שֶׁנִּתְכַּוֵּון לוֹ. **וארב לו** — קְרָא יְתֵירָא הוּא כְּתוּב "כִּי יִהְיֶה אִישׁ שׂוֹנֵא לְרֵעֵהוּ וְקָם עָלָיו". **ורבנן** — דְּפְלִיגִי עֲלֵיהּ דְּרַבִּי שִׁמְעוֹן מַאי דְרְשִׁי בֵּיהּ. אָמְרֵי דְּבֵי רַבִּי יַנַּאי פְּרָט לְזוֹרֵק **אבן לגו** — לְתוֹךְ חֲבוּרָה שֶׁל בְּנֵי אָדָם נָכְרִים וְיִשְׂרְאֵלִים, אֲבָל נִתְכַּוֵּון לְיִשְׂרָאֵל זֶה וְהָרַג אֶת חֲבֵירוֹ לֹא אָתָא קְרָא לְמַעוּטֵי.

HALAKHAH

זוֹרֵק אֶבֶן לְגוֹ **If he throws a stone at a group of people.** "If someone throws a stone at a group of Jews, and kills one of them, he is exempt from judicial execution," following the Rabbis (see *Kesef Mishneh*). (*Rambam, Sefer Nezikin, Hilkhot Rotze'aḥ* 4:1.)

is also the central figure in the principal book of Kabbalah, the *Zohar,* and was regarded with extraordinary veneration in his own time and in following generations. Among his major students was Rabbi Yehudah HaNasi, the editor of the Mishnah. Rabbi Shimon's son, Rabbi Elazar, was also a famous Sage.

רַבִּי יַנַּאי **Rabbi Yannai.** A Palestinian Amora of the first generation, Rabbi Yannai was a disciple of Rabbi Yehudah HaNasi and Rabbi Ḥiyya. He lived near Safed in Upper Galilee, and founded a yeshivah there that bore his name: בֵּי רַבִּי יַנַּאי — "the School of Rabbi Yannai." His best-known disciples were Rabbi Yoḥanan and Resh Lakish.

בֵּינֵיהֶן, [1]תֵּיפּוֹק לֵיהּ דְּרוּבָּא נָכְרִים נִינְהוּ. [2]אִי נַמִי פַּלְגָּא וּפַלְגָּא — [3]סָפֵק נְפָשׁוֹת לְהָקֵל! [4]לָא צְרִיכָא, דְּאִיכָּא תִּשְׁעָה יִשְׂרָאֵל וְנָכְרִי אֶחָד בֵּינֵיהֶן, [5]דַּהֲוָה לֵיהּ נָכְרִי קָבוּעַ, [6]וְכָל קָבוּעַ כְּמֶחֱצָה עַל מֶחֱצָה דָּמֵי. [7]בִּשְׁלָמָא לְרַבָּנַן, דְּאָמְרִי: נִתְכַּוֵּון לַהֲרוֹג אֶת זֶה וְהָרַג אֶת זֶה, חַיָּיב, [8]דִּכְתִיב: ״וְכִי יִנָּצוּ אֲנָשִׁים וְנָגְפוּ אִשָּׁה הָרָה״. [9]וְאָמַר רַבִּי אֶלְעָזָר: בְּמַצּוּת שֶׁבְּמִיתָה הַכָּתוּב מְדַבֵּר,

LITERAL TRANSLATION

among them, [1]then let him derive it from [the fact that] the majority are non-Jews. [2]Or even half and half — [3][when there is] a doubt concerning capital cases, [we rule] leniently.

[4]No. It is necessary where there are nine Jews and one non-Jew among them, [5]so that the non-Jew is fixed, [6]and all that is fixed is considered as half and half.

[7]Granted, according to the Rabbis, who say: [If] he intended to kill this one and he killed that one, he is liable, [8]for it is written: "If men strive, and hurt a pregnant woman." [9]And Rabbi Elazar said: Scripture refers to striving with [the intention] of killing,

TRANSLATION AND COMMENTARY

them, and the murderer threw a stone at the group and killed the Jew, why do we need a special verse to teach us that the murderer is exempt from capital punishment? [1]**Let them deduce** this law **from the fact that the majority** of the group **were non-Jews!** It is obvious that we should follow the majority and assume that he had intended to kill a non-Jew, and he should be exempt from capital punishment if he mistakenly killed the one Jew. [2]**And even** if you say that **half** the group were non-Jews **and half** Jews, there should still be no need to teach us that the murderer is exempt from capital punishment. Since the group is mixed, the killer's intention is unclear, [3]and **when there is a doubt concerning a capital crime, we rule leniently.** Concerning what case, then, was it necessary for the verse to teach us that the murderer is exempt from capital punishment?

לָא צְרִיכָא [4]The Gemara answers: The verse was **only necessary** regarding a group of **nine Jews and one non-Jew.** [5]The man who threw a stone at such a group is exempt from capital punishment **because the non-Jew** who constitutes the minority **was fixed** in his place, [6]and any doubt concerning something or someone **while it is fixed** in its place **is considered as an evenly balanced doubt.** Hence we follow the general principle that, where there is doubt concerning a capital crime, we rule leniently.

בִּשְׁלָמָא [7]The Gemara raises a related question: **Granted, according to the Rabbis who** disagree with Rabbi Shimon and **say** that **if** the murderer **intended to kill** a certain person, **but killed** another person, **he is liable** to the death penalty, [8]we understand **the verse** that **states** (Exodus 21:22): **"If men strive, and hurt a pregnant woman,** so that her fruit departs from her, and yet no further harm ensues; he shall surely be punished, according as the woman's husband may exact from him, and he shall give as the judges determine." [9]**And Rabbi Elazar said: Scripture refers** here **to** men **striving with the intention of killing** one

RASHI

תיפוק ליה וכו׳ — ולמה לי קרא. **אי נמי פלגא ופלגא** — למה לי קרא למפטריה? — הא כיון דמצי למימר לנכרים קא מתכווינא אית לך למפטריה משום דספק נפשות להקל מ״והצילו העדה״ (יומא פד,ב). **לא צריכא וכו׳** — ואשמעינן קרא דפטור משום דהוה ליה נכרי קבוע ביניהם, וילפינן מהאי קרא דכל קבוע לא פחות מלהיות נדון כמחצה על מחצה והוי ספק נפשות להקל, ומהכא נפקא לן בכל דוכתי דכל קבוע כמחצה על מחצה דמי. והא ליכא למילף מיניה כרובא דמי, דהא מהיכא תיתי לן, דילמא האי דפטר ליה להאי משום דספק נפשות להקל, ולא משום דחשבינן ליה כרובא. אבל מחצה על מחצה ילפינן מיניה — דאי לאו כמחצה על מחצה דמי לא הוה ליה ספק נפשות להקל ואמאי פטור? הא רובא דישראל נינהו! ורבנן אית להו נתכוון לזה והרג את זה חייב. **במצות שבמיתה הכתוב מדבר** — שהיה מתכוון להרוג את חבירו.

NOTES

וְכָל קָבוּעַ כְּמֶחֱצָה עַל מֶחֱצָה **And all that is fixed is considered as half and half.** In most areas of Halakhah, we follow the majority, whether we are dealing with a majority of opinions or a statistical majority. But regarding this second type of majority, when we make assumptions based on probability and not on any direct connection between the various factors taken into consideration (as in the case of someone who throws a stone at a group of people, where there is no direct connection between the throwing of the stone and the person whom it hit, but only a statistical probability), we must consider the notion of a "fixed object." The laws of a statistical majority apply only to a random sample, but when there is a fixed object, so that the sample is selective, the laws of probability are not legally relevant and we say that the possibilities one way or the other are considered equal.

וְכָל קָבוּעַ כְּמֶחֱצָה עַל מֶחֱצָה **And all that is fixed is considered as half and half.** Both *Rashi* and *Tosafot* note that this ruling is the source of the principle that, with respect to a fixed object, the possibilities one way or the other are considered to be equal. The question has been raised: How can we extend a law that we find regarding capital cases (about which we rule leniently in cases of doubt) to other areas of the law? It has been suggested that since the principle that we follow the majority is based on what the Torah says about judges (Exodus 23:2): "After a multitude to incline," and we see that we do not always follow the majority, but rather we take other factors into account, it follows that these factors apply to other areas of Halakhah as well (*Talmidei Rabbenu Peretz*).

LITERAL TRANSLATION

[1]for it is written: "But if any harm ensue, then you shall give life for life." [2]But according to Rabbi Shimon, [3]what does he do with this: "Then you shall give life for life"?

[4]Money, like that of Rabbi, [5]for it was taught: "Rabbi says: [6]'Then you shall give life for life' — [7]money. [8]You say money, [9]but might it not be an actual life? [10]Giving is mentioned below, [11]and giving is mentioned [79B] above. [12]Just as there, money, [13]so, too, here, money.

[14]Rava said: That which was taught [by a Sage] of the School of Ḥizkiyah [15]is excluded from Rabbi and excluded from the Rabbis, [16]for it was taught [by a Sage] of the School of Ḥizkiyah: [17]"[Regarding] someone who strikes a person and someone who strikes an animal, [18]just

[1]דִּכְתִיב: "אִם אָסוֹן יִהְיֶה וְנָתַתָּה נֶפֶשׁ תַּחַת נָפֶשׁ". [2]אֶלָּא לְרַבִּי שִׁמְעוֹן, [3]הַאי "וְנָתַתָּה נֶפֶשׁ תַּחַת נָפֶשׁ" מַאי עָבֵיד לֵיהּ?

[4]מָמוֹן, וְכִדְרַבִּי, [5]דְּתַנְיָא: "רַבִּי אוֹמֵר: [6]'וְנָתַתָּה נֶפֶשׁ תַּחַת נָפֶשׁ' — [7]מָמוֹן. [8]אַתָּה אוֹמֵר מָמוֹן, [9]אוֹ אֵינוֹ אֶלָּא נֶפֶשׁ מַמָּשׁ? [10]נֶאֶמְרָה נְתִינָה לְמַטָּה, [11]וְנֶאֶמְרָה [79B] נְתִינָה לְמַעְלָה. [12]מַה לְּהַלָּן, מָמוֹן, [13]אַף כָּאן מָמוֹן.

[14]אָמַר רָבָא: הַאי דְּתָנָא דְּבֵי חִזְקִיָּה [15]מַפְּקָא מִדְּרַבִּי, וּמַפְּקָא מִדְּרַבָּנַן, [16]דְּתָנָא דְּבֵי חִזְקִיָּה: [17]"מַכֵּה אָדָם וּמַכֵּה בְהֵמָה, [18]מַה

TRANSLATION AND COMMENTARY

another, [1]**for the** next **verse states** (Exodus 21:23): **"But if any harm ensues, then you shall give life for life."** Rabbi Elazar understands that this second verse teaches that, if the woman dies, the one who struck her must pay with his life. Now, in this case, the killer must have fought with the other man with the intent to kill him, for had he not intended to kill anybody, he would not be liable to capital punishment. The killer is liable to the death penalty, even though he intended to kill the other man but killed the pregnant woman. [2]**But** a problem arises **according to Rabbi Shimon,** [3]for **what does he do with this** verse: **"Then you shall give life for life"?** Surely, according to Rabbi Shimon, such a killer is exempt from the death penalty!

מָמוֹן [4]The Gemara answers: According to Rabbi Shimon, the verse does not refer to judicial execution, but to **monetary compensation,** which the killer must pay to the woman's heirs, **as Rabbi** Yehudah HaNasi **said,** [5]**for it was taught** in a Baraita: **"Rabbi** Yehudah HaNasi **says:** The verse that states: [6]**'Then you shall give life for life,'** [7]refers to **monetary compensation.** [8]**You say** that the verse refers to **monetary compensation,** [9]**but might it not** refer **actually** to the taking of the killer's **life?** [10]The term **'giving' is mentioned below** (verse 23) — [11]'Then you shall give life for life, **and** the term **'giving' is mentioned** [79B] **above** (verse 22) — 'And he shall give as the judges determine.' [12]**Just as there,** the verse refers to **monetary compensation** for the loss of the unborn fetus, [13]**so, too, here,** the verse refers to **monetary compensation** for the loss of the woman."

אָמַר רָבָא [14]**Rava said:** The position that **was taught by a Sage of the School of Ḥizkiyah,** regarding someone who intended to kill one person but killed someone else, [15]**is different from** that of **Rabbi** Yehudah HaNasi **and different from** that of **the Rabbis** who disagree with him. According to the Rabbis, the murderer is liable to judicial execution; according to Rabbi Yehudah HaNasi he is exempt from judicial execution, but liable to pay monetary compensation; but according to the Sage of the School of Ḥizkiyah, he is exempt from both judicial execution and monetary compensation. [16]**For a Sage of the School of Ḥizkiyah taught** a Baraita commenting on the verse (Leviticus 24:21): "And he that strikes an animal shall pay for it, and he that strikes a man shall be put to death." The Baraita states: [17]"The verse places the law **regarding someone who strikes a person** in juxtaposition with the law regarding **someone who strikes an animal.** According to traditional hermeneutic principles, the Torah juxtaposes two different laws in this way to teach us that they are subject to the same rules. Hence, in determining the penalty, we apply the same rules to someone who kills an animal as to someone who kills another human being, and we say: [18]**In the case of someone who strikes an**

RASHI

כדכתיב "ואם אסון יהיה ונתתה נפש תחת נפש" — ואי לא נתכוון להרוג היאך מקטיל, וכי איתכוון מיהא חייב אף על גב דלא נתכוון אלא לחבירו, דהא כתיב "וכי ינצו אנשים וגו'". **ממון** — דמי האשה יתן ליורשיה. **נתינה למעלה** — גבי "לא יהיה אסון ונתן בפלילים" (שמות כא) דמי ולדות. **והא דתנא דבי חזקיה מפקא מדרבי ורבנן** — דרבנן מחייבי ליה מיתה לנתכוין להרוג את זה והרג את זה, ורבי מחייב ליה ממון, ואילו לתנא דבי חזקיה לא מיחייב ממון ולא מיתה. **מכה אדם ומכה בהמה** — לכך הוקשו בהאי קרא "מכה בהמה ישלמנה ומכה אדם יומת" ומשמע בבהמה חייב ממון ובאדם פטור

SAGES

חִזְקִיָּה Ḥizkiyah. The son of Rabbi Ḥiyya, Ḥizkiyah was a first-generation Amora. He and his twin brother Yehudah immigrated to Eretz Israel from Babylonia while they were still young. In Eretz Israel they studied with Rabbi Yehudah HaNasi, even though they were already considered important scholars in their own right. Rabbi Yehudah HaNasi held Rabbi Ḥiyya and his sons in high esteem, and maintained a warm relationship with them because of his high regard for their learning and piety.

Ḥizkiyah's brother, Yehudah, died young. Ḥizkiyah edited collections of Baraitot (as his father Rabbi Ḥiyya had done before him), and these are often cited by the Gemara as "the teachings of Ḥizkiyah's school" (תְּנָא דְּבֵי חִזְקִיָּה). Ḥizkiyah engaged in Halakhic discussions with other leading disciples of Rabbi Yehudah HaNasi. His own students included the noted Sage Rabbi Yoḥanan, as well as other Amoraim of that generation. Ḥizkiyah and his brother apparently earned their livelihood from commerce, and from their extensive real-estate holdings. Ḥizkiyah lived in Tiberias and was buried there, near his father's grave.

NOTES

תְּנָא דְּבֵי חִזְקִיָּה A Sage of the School of Ḥizkiyah. According to the Tanna of the School of Ḥizkiyah, whenever a person commits a capital offense, whether or not he commits it in such a manner that capital punishment can in fact be administered, he is automatically exempt from paying monetary compensation — either a ransom or a damage payment.

TRANSLATION AND COMMENTARY

animal, we make no distinction between what **was done inadvertently and** what was done **deliberately.** A human being is liable for all direct damage, even if accidental. [1]Similarly, we make no distinction **between 'intentionally'** and **'unintentionally,' between** an animal that was killed **while** the man was **'going down'** (when the blow was such that if it had killed a human being accidentally, the killer would be sent into exile) **and** an animal killed **while** the man was **'going up'** (when an accidental homicide would not be subject to atonement through exile). [2]**Just as** in all these cases we do not **exempt** the man **from paying money** for the animal, even if he was not at fault, **and we oblige him to pay money** in all cases, [3]**so too if someone strikes a person, we should make no distinction between** what **was done inadvertently** and that which was done **deliberately**. [4]Nor should we make a distinction **between** a person who struck **intentionally** and one who struck **unintentionally**. [5]Moreover, we should make no distinction **between** a person who was killed **while** his killer was **'going down,'** in which case he is sent into exile for his negligence, **and** a person who was killed **while** his killer was **'going up,'** when the killer was not even negligent and is not required to go into exile. In all these cases the killer is not **obliged to pay** any sort of **monetary compensation,** either ransom or a damage payment, [6]**and we must exempt him from paying money.**" [7]Now, **what** does the Baraita mean when it speaks of someone who killed another person **"unintentionally"**? [8]**If you say that** the killer **did**

מַכֶּה בְּהֵמָה, לֹא חָלַקְתָּ בָּהּ בֵּין שׁוֹגֵג לְמֵזִיד, [1]בֵּין מִתְכַּוֵּין לְשֶׁאֵינוֹ מִתְכַּוֵּין, בֵּין דֶּרֶךְ יְרִידָה לְדֶרֶךְ עֲלִיָּיה [2]לְפוֹטְרוֹ מָמוֹן, אֶלָּא לְחַיְּיבוֹ מָמוֹן, [3]אַף מַכֶּה אָדָם לֹא תַּחֲלוֹק בּוֹ בֵּין שׁוֹגֵג לְמֵזִיד, [4]בֵּין מִתְכַּוֵּין לְשֶׁאֵין מִתְכַּוֵּין, [5]בֵּין דֶּרֶךְ יְרִידָה לְדֶרֶךְ עֲלִיָּיה לְחַיְּיבוֹ מָמוֹן, [6]אֶלָּא לְפוֹטְרוֹ מָמוֹן״. [7]מַאי ״שֶׁאֵין מִתְכַּוֵּין״? [8]אִילֵימָא שֶׁאֵין מִתְכַּוֵּין כְּלָל, הַיְינוּ שׁוֹגֵג.

LITERAL TRANSLATION

as [when] someone strikes an animal, you made no distinction between [doing it] inadvertently and deliberately, between [doing it] intentionally and unintentionally, [1]between [doing it] while going down and while going up, [2]in order to exempt him [from paying] money, but to oblige him [to pay] money, [3]so too [when] someone strikes a person you should make no distinction between [doing it] inadvertently and deliberately, [4]between [doing it] intentionally and unintentionally, [5]between [doing it] while going down and while going up, in order to oblige him [to pay] money, [6]but to exempt him [from paying] money." [7]What is "[doing it] unintentionally"? [8]If you say that he does not intend [it] at all, that is [doing it] inadvertently.

RASHI

ממון. דכתיב ״בהמה ישלמנה״ ולא אדם, והקיש לך הכתוב פטור תשלומין של אדם לחיוב תשלומין של בהמה — מה להלן לא חלקת בין מתכוין, לקמן מפרש ואזיל מאי היא. דרך עלייה — לא שייך למתני גבי בהמה, אלא משום דבאדם אשכחן ביה חילוק בהורג בשוגג דרך ירידה חייב גלות אבל דרך עלייה בהרימו את ידו פטור מגלות דכתיב (במדבר לה) ״ויפל עליו וימת״ דרך נפילה בעינן. לפוטרו ממון — כלומר לא חלקת בו שום צד להפטר מן תשלומין, אלא בכל צדדין הוא דמחייב, דרבינן כל נזקין בבבא קמא (כו,ב) מ״פצע תחת פצע״ — לחייב על השוגג כמזיד, ועל האונס כרצון. ומכה בהמה נזק הוא. אף מכה אדם — אין דין פטור תשלומין הכתוב בו חלוק לשום צד שיתחייב ממון, אלא כל שעה פטור מממון בין בשוגג ואין נתכון דפטור ממיתה, בין במזיד ונתכוון דחייב מיתה.

NOTES

לֹא תַּחֲלוֹק בּוֹ בֵּין שׁוֹגֵג לְמֵזִיד You made no distinction between doing it inadvertently and deliberately. It may be asked: If the Tanna of the School of Ḥizkiyah maintains that someone who intended to kill one person but in fact killed another is neither liable to judicial execution, nor to pay monetary compensation, how, then, does he understand the verses (Exodus 21:22-23): "If men strive, and hurt a pregnant woman....But if any harm ensues, then you shall give life for life"? We must say that he disagrees with Rabbi Elazar, who says that the verse refers to men striving with the intent to kill one another. Rather the verse refers to men who had no intention of killing anybody, and so the man who killed the woman is indeed liable to pay monetary compensation (*Rabbi David Bonfils*).

דֶּרֶךְ יְרִידָה לְדֶרֶךְ עֲלִיָּיה While going down and while going up. Regarding someone who kills another person inadvertently, the Halakhah distinguishes between a killer who struck his victim while going down, meaning that something fell from the killer's hand and struck the victim, in which case the killer is sent into exile for his negligence,

HALAKHAH

מַכֶּה בְּהֵמָה, לֹא חָלַקְתָּ בָּהּ בֵּין שׁוֹגֵג לְמֵזִיד Regarding someone who strikes an animal, you made no distinction between doing it inadvertently and deliberately. "Someone who damaged another person's property is liable to pay for the damage, whether he caused it deliberately or inadvertently, or even if it occurred through no fault of his own (but not if the damage arose through circumstances totally beyond his control; *Rema*)." (*Shulḥan Arukh, Ḥoshen Mishpat* 378:1.)

מַכֶּה אָדָם לֹא תַּחֲלוֹק בּוֹ Regarding someone who strikes a person you should make no distinction. "If someone struck a pregnant woman, and she miscarried and died, even if he killed her unintentionally he is exempt from paying damages," following the School of Ḥizkiyah. (*Shulḥan Arukh, Ḥoshen Mishpat* 423:4.)

[1]אֶלָּא, פְּשִׁיטָא שֶׁאֵין מִתְכַּוֵּין לָזֶה אֶלָּא לָזֶה. [2]וְקָתָנֵי: "לְחַיְּיבוֹ מָמוֹן אֶלָּא לְפוֹטְרוֹ מָמוֹן". [3]וְאִי בַּר קְטָלָא הוּא, מַאי אִיצְטְרִיךְ לְמִיפְטְרֵיהּ מָמוֹן?

[4]אֶלָּא, לָאו שְׁמַע מִינָּהּ, [5]לָאו בַּר קְטָלָא הוּא, וְלָאו בַּר מָמוֹנָא הוּא.

מִשְׁנָה [6]רוֹצֵחַ שֶׁנִּתְעָרֵב בַּאֲחֵרִים — כּוּלָּן פְּטוּרִין. [7]רַבִּי יְהוּדָה אוֹמֵר: כּוֹנְסִין אוֹתָן לַכִּיפָּה.

[8]כָּל חַיָּיבֵי מִיתוֹת שֶׁנִּתְעָרְבוּ זֶה בָּזֶה [9]נִידּוֹנִין בַּקַּלָּה.

LITERAL TRANSLATION

[1]Rather, it is obvious that he does not intend [to kill] this one, but rather that one. [2]And it states: "To oblige him [to pay] money, but to exempt him [from paying] money." [3]And if he is liable to execution, why was it necessary to exempt him [from paying] money?

[4]Rather, infer from this [5][that] he is not liable to be executed, nor to pay monetary [compensation].

MISHNAH [6]A murderer who was intermingled with others — all are exempt. [7]Rabbi Yehudah says: They put them in a chamber.

[8]All who are liable to execution [and] who were mingled with each other [9]are punished with the more lenient [mode of execution].

TRANSLATION AND COMMENTARY

not at all intend to kill anybody, **that is** the same as killing **inadvertently.** [1]**Rather, it is obvious that** the killer **did not intend to kill** the person whom he actually killed, **but rather** some **other person.** [2]**And the Baraita states:** "The killer should not be **obliged to pay** any sort of **monetary compensation, and we must exempt him from paying money.**" Thus, we see that someone who intended to kill a certain person, but killed another person by mistake, is exempt from paying monetary compensation. Such a person is certainly exempt from judicial execution, [3]for **were he liable to** judicial **execution, why would it have been necessary to exempt him from paying money?** A person cannot become liable to the death penalty and to monetary compensation for the same offense!

אֶלָּא [4]The Gemara concludes: **Rather, infer from this** Baraita that, according to the Sage of the School of Ḥizkiyah, someone who intended to kill a certain person, [5]but in fact killed another person, **is liable neither to** judicial **execution nor** to **monetary compensation,** against the opinions of both Rabbi Yehudah HaNasi and the Rabbis who disagree with him.

MISHNAH רוֹצֵחַ [6]If **a murderer became intermingled with others,** so that we do not know who committed the crime, **all are exempt,** for we cannot identify the guilty party. [7]**Rabbi Yehudah says: They are** all **put into a** narrow, vaulted prison-**chamber** where they are left to die of hunger (as will be explained in the Gemara).

כָּל חַיָּיבֵי מִיתוֹת [8]If criminals **who are liable to death** by modes of **execution** of varying degrees of severity intermixed **with each other** so that we no longer know which offender is subject to which mode of execution, [9]they **are all put to death by the most lenient mode of execution** to which any one of them was subject.

RASHI

אלא לפטרו — אלמא פטור מממון לתנא דבי חזקיה, וממיתה נמי שמע מינה דפטר ליה, מדאצטריך למפטריה מתשלומין, כדמפרש ואזיל, ואי בר קטלא מי אצטריך למפטר.

משנה שנתערב באחרים — בגמרא מפרש הנך אחרים מאן נינהו. **כונסין אותן לכיפה** — ושם מאכילין אותן שעורים עד שתבקע כריסן, כדתני לקמן בפירקין (פא,ב). **נדונין בקלה** — מאחר שנתערבו ואי אתה מכיר מי המחויב את החמורה ומי המחויב את הקלה — אי אתה רשאי להחמיר עליו למושכו למיתה חמורה שלא נתחייב בה אלא ידונו בקלה שישנה בכלל החמורה.

NOTES

and a killer who struck his victim while going up, meaning that he threw something into the air and it accidentally struck the victim on the way up, in which case the killer is not subject to exile.

רוֹצֵחַ שֶׁנִּתְעָרֵב בַּאֲחֵרִים A murderer who was mixed with others. The question arises: Why does the Mishnah refer here to a murderer who was placed with others, when the same law applies to any capital offender who was placed with others? *Torat Ḥayyim* suggests that the Mishnah speaks of a murderer here, because Rabbi Yehudah says the prisoners are all put into a prison-chamber where they are left to die, the same penalty which, according to the Mishnah (below, 81b), is imposed upon a murderer who cannot be executed for technical reasons.

HALAKHAH

רוֹצֵחַ שֶׁנִּתְעָרֵב בַּאֲחֵרִים A murderer who became intermingled with others. "If a murderer whose verdict has been issued became mixed with innocent people, so that we cannot identify the murderer," all of them are exempt from punishment. (*Rambam, Sefer Nezikin, Hilkhot Rotze'aḥ* 4:7; *Sefer Shofetim, Hilkhot Sanhedrin* 14:7.)

כָּל חַיָּיבֵי מִיתוֹת שֶׁנִּתְעָרְבוּ זֶה בָּזֶה All who are liable to execution who were placed with each other. "If criminals liable to different modes of execution became mixed with each other, they are all put to death by the most lenient mode of execution for which any of them was liable," following the Mishnah. (*Rambam, Sefer Shofetim, Hilkhot Sanhedrin* 14:6.)

[1]הַנִּסְקָלִין בַּנִּשְׂרָפִין, [2]רַבִּי שִׁמְעוֹן אוֹמֵר: נִידּוֹנִין בִּסְקִילָה, [3]שֶׁהַשְּׂרֵיפָה חֲמוּרָה. [4]וַחֲכָמִים אוֹמְרִים: נִידּוֹנִין בִּשְׂרֵיפָה, [5]שֶׁהַסְּקִילָה חֲמוּרָה. [6]אָמַר לָהֶן רַבִּי שִׁמְעוֹן: אִילּוּ לֹא הָיְתָה שְׂרֵיפָה חֲמוּרָה לֹא נִתְּנָה לְבַת כֹּהֵן שֶׁזִּנְּתָה! [7]אָמְרוּ לוֹ: אִילּוּ לֹא הָיְתָה סְקִילָה חֲמוּרָה, [8]לֹא נִתְּנָה לַמְגַדֵּף וְלָעוֹבֵד עֲבוֹדָה זָרָה.

[9]הַנֶּהֱרָגִין בַּנֶּחֱנָקִין. [10]רַבִּי שִׁמְעוֹן אוֹמֵר: בַּסַּיִיף. [11]וַחֲכָמִים אוֹמְרִים: בַּחֶנֶק.

גמרא [12]מַאן אֲחֵרִים? [13]אִילֵימָא אֲחֵרִים כְּשֵׁרִים — [14]פְּשִׁיטָא! [15]וְתוּ, בְּהָא לֵימָא רַבִּי יְהוּדָה: [16]כּוֹנְסִין אוֹתָן לַכִּיפָּה?

[17](סִימָן בשר"ק).

LITERAL TRANSLATION

[1]Those liable to [be executed by] stoning with those liable to [be executed by] burning, [2]Rabbi Shimon says. They are punished by stoning, [3]for burning is more severe. [4]And the Sages say: They are punished with burning, [5]for stoning is more severe. [6]Rabbi Shimon said to them: Were burning not more severe, it would not have been imposed on to the daughter of a priest who committed adultery. [7]They said to him: Were stoning not more severe, [8]it would not have been given to a blasphemer and an idol worshipper.

[9]Those liable to [be executed by] slaying with those liable to [be executed by] strangulation. [10]Rabbi Shimon says: By the sword. [11]And the Sages say: By strangulation.

GEMARA [12]Who are the others? [13]If you say others who are fit — [14]that is obvious! [15]And furthermore, about them Rabbi Yehudah would say: [16]They put them in a chamber? [17](A sign: Bshr"k.)

TRANSLATION AND COMMENTARY

הַנִּסְקָלִין [1]If criminals **liable to execution by stoning** intermixed **with** criminals **liable to execution by burning,** the Tannaim disagree about which mode of execution is imposed. [2]**Rabbi Shimon says: They are** all **put to death by stoning,** [3]**for** death by **burning is** a more **severe** mode of execution. [4]**The Sages** disagree and **say:** They are all **put to death by burning,** [5]**for** death by **stoning is** a more **severe** mode of execution. [6]**Rabbi Shimon said to** the Sages: **Were** death by **burning not more severe** than death by stoning, the Torah **would not have** designated burning as the mode of execution **imposed upon the daughter of a priest who committed adultery.** The betrothed daughter of an ordinary Jew who committed adultery is liable to death by stoning, whereas the betrothed daughter of a priest who committed adultery is liable to death by burning, and surely the Torah imposed the more severe punishment upon the daughter of the priest. [7]The Rabbis **said to** Rabbi Shimon: On the contrary, **were** death by **stoning not more severe** than death by burning, [8]the Torah **would not have** designated stoning as the mode of execution **imposed upon a blasphemer and an idol worshipper,** criminals guilty of the most heinous offenses.

הַנֶּהֱרָגִין [9]If criminals **liable to slaying** by the sword — decapitation — became mixed **with** criminals **liable to death by strangulation,** the Tannaim disagree about which mode of execution is imposed. [10]**Rabbi Shimon says:** They are all put to death **by the sword,** for strangulation is a more severe mode of execution. [11]**The Sages** disagree and **say:** They are all put to death **by** way of **strangulation,** for decapitation is a more severe mode of execution.

GEMARA מַאן אֲחֵרִים [12]The Gemara comments: The first clause of the Mishnah speaks of a murderer who was intermingled with others. **Who are these "others"?** [13]**If you say** that the Mishnah refers to **innocent people,** there is a difficulty, [14]for **it is obvious** that we would not punish the entire lot for the sin of a single individual. [15]**And furthermore,** could **Rabbi Yehudah** possibly **have said about them:** [16]**"They are** all **put into a** narrow, vaulted prison-**chamber** where they are left to die of hunger"?

סִימָן [17]Before clarifying the issue, the Gemara offers **a mnemonic device** to help the student remember the names of the Sages whose positions are about to be mentioned: **Bshr"k** (Rabbi *Ab*bahu in the name of *Sh*muel, *R*ava, Resh La*k*ish).

RASHI

הנסקלין בנשרפין – אף על גב דרובא דהני נשרפין כדקתני נסקלין בנשרפין, משמע חד נסקל שנתערב בנשרפין טובא – אפילו הכי לרבי שמעון ידונו כולן בסקילה מפני שהשריפה חמורה. **לא נתנה למגדף ולעובד עבודה זרה** – שפושטין ידן בעיקר. **לא ניתנה לבת כהן שזנתה** – שעבירתה חמורה שמחללת את אביה, כדאמר ב"ארבע מיתות" (סנהדרין נב,א) שנוהגין בו חול. **בסייף** – שחנק חמור. **וחכמים אומרים בחנק** – שסייף חמור, וטעמא מפרש ב"ארבע מיתות".

HALAKHAH

הַנִּסְקָלִין בַּנִּשְׂרָפִין Those liable to stoning with those liable to burning. "Stoning is a more severe mode of execution than burning, and burning is a more severe mode of execution than decapitation, and decapitation is a more severe mode of execution than strangulation. If criminals liable to different modes of execution became intermixed with each other, they are all put to death by the most lenient mode of execution to which any of them was liable." (*Rambam, Sefer Shofetim, Hilkhot Sanhedrin* 14:4,6.)

TRANSLATION AND COMMENTARY

אָמַר [1] **Rabbi Abbahu said in the name of Shmuel: Here,** in the Mishnah, **we are dealing with a murderer whose verdict had not** yet **been issued** and **who** was intermixed with **other murderers whose verdicts had** already **been issued,** so that we cannot identify the murderer whose trial has not been concluded. [2] **The Rabbis maintain** that the defendant's **verdict can only be issued in his presence.** Since we cannot identify the murderer who is now on trial, we cannot issue a verdict in his case. Because one of the murderers cannot be put to death, [3] **all** the murderers **are exempt** from punishment. [4] **Rabbi Yehudah** disagrees and **maintains: To grant them** all **absolute exemptions,** we **also cannot** do, [5] **for** surely **they are** all **murderers.** [6] **Therefore, they are** all **put in a** narrow, vaulted prison-**chamber** where they are left to die of hunger.

רֵישׁ לָקִישׁ [7] **Resh Lakish said: Regarding a human** murderer who became intermixed with other murderers, **all** — both Rabbi Yehudah and the Rabbis — agree **that they are** all **exempt** from punishment. [8] **But here,** in the Mishnah, the Tannaim **disagree about a** killer **ox whose verdict has not been issued,** [9] **which became intermingled with other** killer **oxen whose verdicts have been issued.** [10] **The Rabbis maintain** that the laws that apply to **the execution of the owner** apply **also to the execution of the ox,** [11] **and** consequently **an ox's verdict can only be issued in its presence.** We cannot identify the ox whose fate is now to be determined, so we cannot issue a verdict in its case. [12] Since one of the oxen cannot be put to death, **all** the oxen **are exempt** from execution. [13] **Rabbi Yehudah** disagrees and **maintains: They are** all **put in an enclosure** where they are left to die of hunger.

[1] אָמַר רַבִּי אַבָּהוּ אָמַר שְׁמוּאֵל: הָכָא בְּרוֹצֵחַ שֶׁלֹּא נִגְמַר דִּינוֹ, שֶׁנִּתְעָרֵב בְּרוֹצְחִים אֲחֵרִים שֶׁנִּגְמַר דִּינָן עָסְקִינַן. [2] רַבָּנַן סָבְרִי: אֵין גּוֹמְרִין דִּינוֹ שֶׁל אָדָם אֶלָּא בְּפָנָיו. [3] הִלְכָּךְ כּוּלָּן פְּטוּרִין. [4] וְרַבִּי יְהוּדָה: מִיפְטְרִינְהוּ לְגַמְרֵי נַמִי לֹא, [5] כֵּיוָן דְּרוֹצְחִין נִינְהוּ. [6] הִלְכָּךְ, כּוֹנְסִין אוֹתָן לַכִּיפָּה.

[7] רֵישׁ לָקִישׁ אָמַר: בְּאָדָם דְּכוּלֵּי עָלְמָא לָא פְּלִיגִי דִּפְטִירִי. [8] אֲבָל הָכָא בְּשׁוֹר שֶׁלֹּא נִגְמַר דִּינוֹ [9] שֶׁנִּתְעָרֵב בִּשְׁוָרִים אֲחֵרִים שֶׁנִּגְמַר דִּינָן קָמִיפַּלְגִי. [10] רַבָּנַן סָבְרִי: כְּמִיתַת בְּעָלִים כָּךְ מִיתַת הַשּׁוֹר, [11] וְאֵין גּוֹמְרִין דִּינוֹ שֶׁל שׁוֹר אֶלָּא בְּפָנָיו. [12] הִלְכָּךְ, כּוּלָּן פְּטוּרִין. [13] וְרַבִּי יְהוּדָה סָבַר: כּוֹנְסִין אוֹתָן לַכִּיפָּה.

LITERAL TRANSLATION

[1] Rabbi Abbahu said in the name of Shmuel: Here we are dealing with a murderer whose judgment was still pending who was intermixed with other murderers whose judgments were finished. [2] The Rabbis maintain: They only finish a man's judgment in his presence. [3] Therefore all are exempt. [4] And Rabbi Yehudah [maintains]: To exempt them absolutely also not, [5] for they are murderers. [6] Therefore they put them in a chamber.

[7] Resh Lakish said: Regarding a person all agree (lit., "the entire world does not disagree") that they are exempt. [8] But here they disagree about an ox whose judgment was not finished [9] that was intermingled with other oxen whose judgments were finished. [10] The Rabbis maintain: Like the death of the owner, so is the death of the ox, [11] and they only finish an ox's judgment in its presence. [12] Therefore they are all exempt. [13] And Rabbi Yehudah maintains: They put them in a chamber.

RASHI

גמרא אלא בפניו — כיון דאין מכירין אותו לא הויא בפניו. וכיון דרוצח הוא — שהרי קבלו העדיות ונשאו ונתנו בדבר. דפטירי — הואיל ואיכא חד דלא נגמר דינו אין לך ראיה לזכות גדולה מזו, ורחמנא אמר "והצילו העדה" (במדבר לה).

NOTES

נִתְעָרֵב בְּרוֹצְחִים אֲחֵרִים שֶׁנִּגְמַר דִּינָן **A murderer who was intermixed with other murderers whose judgments were finished.** *Tzofnat Pa'ane'aḥ* argues that the Mishnah's ruling is limited to a murderer whose verdict has not been issued and who became intermixed with other murderers whose verdicts had been issued. But if the murderer becomes intermixed with other murderers whose verdicts have also not been issued, the verdicts of all the murderers can be issued simultaneously, even though we cannot say for sure which criminal is guilty of which particular crime.

שׁוֹר שֶׁנִּתְעָרֵב בִּשְׁוָרִים אֲחֵרִים **An ox whose judgment was not finished that was mingled with other oxen.** The Gemara says that when a killer ox whose verdict has not been issued became mingled with other killer oxen whose

HALAKHAH

רוֹצֵחַ שֶׁנִּתְעָרֵב בְּרוֹצְחִים אֲחֵרִים **A murderer who was intermixed with other murderers.** "If a murderer whose verdict has not been issued becomes intermixed with other murderers whose verdicts have been issued, all of them are exempt from judicial execution, for a verdict can be issued only in the defendant's presence," following the Sages. But they are all incarcerated. (*Rambam, Sefer Nezikin, Hilkhot Rotze'aḥ* 4:7; *Sefer Shofetim, Hilkhot Sanhedrin* 14:7.)

שׁוֹר שֶׁנִּתְעָרֵב בִּשְׁוָרִים אֲחֵרִים **An ox that was mingled with other oxen.** "If a killer ox whose verdict has not been issued becomes mingled with oxen whose verdicts have been issued, all of them are exempt from execution, for an ox's verdict can only be issued in its presence," following the Sages according to Resh Lakish. (*Rambam, Sefer Nezikin, Hilkhot Nizkei Mamon* 11:10.)

TRANSLATION AND COMMENTARY

אָמַר רָבָא [1]Rava said: [80A] [2]If it is so, that the Mishnah refers to the case where a murderer whose verdict was not yet issued was placed with other murderers whose verdicts had already been issued, as was argued by Shmuel, or that the Mishnah refers to a killer ox whose verdict was not yet issued and who was mingled with other killer oxen whose verdicts were issued, as was argued by Resh Lakish — then how can we understand the Baraita that **was taught in reference to** the Mishnah, stating: "If a murderer was intermixed with others, all are exempt. [3]**Rabbi Yose said: Even if** my own father, the wise and righteous **Abba Ḥalafta, was among them,** they are all exempt"? This statement makes no sense, given that understanding of the Mishnah, for Rabbi Yose would not have included his father in a group of murderers, and his father would certainly be irrelevant to a case of mingled oxen!

אֶלָּא [4]**Rather, Rava said:** The Mishnah meant to **say as follows:** [5]**If two** people **were standing** together, **and an arrow** was **shot out from among them,** but we do not know which of the two shot the arrow, **and** the arrow **killed** someone, [6]**both of them are exempt,** for we do not know who committed the crime. [7]**And Rabbi Yose added: Even if one of the** two **was** a righteous person like my father **Abba Ḥalafta,** who could not possibly have committed the offense, we cannot convict the other person unless two witnesses clearly saw him shooting the fatal arrow. Regarding this point, Rabbi Yehudah agrees with the anonymous Rabbis. He only disagrees with them about a second ruling of theirs which was omitted from the Mishnah, [8]for the Rabbis say that if **a** killer **ox whose verdict** of execution **had** already **been issued was mingled with other fit oxen** which had not killed anyone, [9]**we stone** all of **them.** It is forbidden to derive any benefit from an ox that has been sentenced to stoning, and if such

[1]אָמַר רָבָא: [80A] [2]אִי הָכִי, הַיְינוּ דְּקָתָנֵי עֲלָהּ: [3]״אָמַר רַבִּי יוֹסֵי: אֲפִילּוּ אַבָּא חֲלַפְתָּא בֵּינֵיהֶן״?!

[4]אֶלָּא, אָמַר רָבָא: הָכִי קָאָמַר: [5]שְׁנַיִם שֶׁהָיוּ עוֹמְדִין וְיָצָא חֵץ מִבֵּינֵיהֶם וְהָרַג, [6]שְׁנֵיהֶם פְּטוּרִין. [7]וְאָמַר רַבִּי יוֹסֵי: אֲפִילּוּ אַבָּא חֲלַפְתָּא בֵּינֵיהֶן. [8]וְשׁוֹר שֶׁנִּגְמַר דִּינוֹ שֶׁנִּתְעָרֵב בִּשְׁוָורִין אֲחֵרִים מַעַלְיָיא, [9]סוֹקְלִין אוֹתָן.

LITERAL TRANSLATION

[1]Rava said: [80A] [2]If so, that which was taught in reference to it: [3]"Rabbi Yose said: Even if Abba Ḥalafta was among them"!?

[4]Rather, Rava said: Thus he said: [5][If] two were standing, and an arrow was shot (lit., "went") out from among them, and killed, [6]the two of them are exempt. [7]And Rabbi Yose said: Even if Abba Ḥalafta was among them. [8]And an ox whose judgment was finished that was mingled with other fit oxen, [9]they stone them.

SAGES

אַבָּא חֲלַפְתָּא **Abba Ḥalafta.** Rabbi Ḥalafta of Sepphoris lived during Second Temple times and debated with Rabban Gamliel the Elder. He continued to live long after the destruction of the Temple and was prominent in his native city of Sepphoris, determining customs and laws there.

He discussed issues of Halakhah with Rabbi Yoḥanan ben Nuri, but most of his Halakhic teachings were transmitted by his son, Rabbi Yose ben Ḥalafta, who is always referred to simply as Rabbi Yose. He revered his father and often presented him as an example of a righteous and saintly man.

Rabbi Ḥalafta dealt in leather, and it is thought that in addition to his famous son, Rabbi Yose, he had another son, Rabbi Shimon ben Ḥalafta, though some authorities believe that Rabbi Shimon was the great-grandson of Rabbi Ḥalafta.

RASHI

אי הכי הא דתני עלה וכו׳ – בין לריש לקיש בין לשמואל קא מותיב, אי הכי דהני אחרים דמתניתין דרוצחים קאמר. והאי רוצח שנתערב בהוכר ולבסוף נתערב קאמר, הא דתני עלה בברייתא הכי: רוצח שנתערב באחרים – כולן פטורין, אמר רבי יוסי אפילו אבא חלפתא ביניהן כולן פטורין?! מאי אפילו דקאמר רבי יוסי. אלא אמר רבא – בשלא הוכר לבית דין קאמר, כגון שנים עומדין ויצא חץ מביניהם ואין יודעין אי זה מהן זרקו – שניהם פטורין, אמר רבי יוסי: אפילו אבא חלפתא ביניהם. שהכל יודעין שהוא חסיד ולא זרקו לא מחייבינן לאידך משום האי חזקה. ובהא אפילו רבי יהודה מודה. ורבי יהודה דאמר כונסין אותן לכיפה לא עלה קאי אלא הכי קאמר תנא קמא וחסורי מחסרא מתניתין והכי קתני: ושור שנגמר דינו וכו׳ סוקלין אותו, דהא על כרחיך כולהו אסירי בהנאה ואין הפסד לבעלים בסקילה הלכך סוקלין אותם כדי שתתקיים מצות סקילה – במחויב בה.

NOTES

verdicts had been issued, the Rabbis say that all the oxen are exempt. Some Rishonim argue that this means that all the oxen are exempt from execution, but they are nevertheless all forbidden for benefit (*Rabbi David Bonfils, Meir,* thus resolving the difficulty raised by *Tosafot,* s.v., *beshor*).

אֲפִילּוּ אַבָּא חֲלַפְתָּא בֵּינֵיהֶן **Even if Abba Ḥalafta was among them.** It may be asked: Why should we not rely on Abba Ḥalafta's presumption of fitness, just as we rely on other presumptions even in capital cases? For example, a son is executed for striking or cursing his father, even though we only presume that the person known to be the son's father is indeed his father. Why, then, do we not rely on Abba Ḥalafta's presumption of fitness, and conclude that the fatal arrow must have been shot by the other person? *Arukh Lener* explains that the other person, even if he is not known to be a particularly pious person, is also presumed to be fit, and his presumption of fitness is not cancelled by Abba Ḥalafta's presumption of fitness.

יָצָא חֵץ מִבֵּינֵיהֶם **An arrow was shot out from among them.** *Rambam* appears to have understood the Gemara differently — that it refers to two people who shot an arrow together. Their exemption is based on the rule that two

HALAKHAH

יָצָא חֵץ מִבֵּינֵיהֶם **An arrow was shot out from among them.** "If a group of people were sitting together, and an arrow shot out from among them and killed somebody, all of them are exempt from liability," following Rava. (*Rambam, Sefer Nezikin, Hilkhot Rotze'aḥ* 4:6.)

שׁוֹר שֶׁנִּגְמַר דִּינוֹ שֶׁנִּתְעָרֵב **An ox whose judgment was finished that was mingled.** "If a killer ox whose verdict of execution was issued became mingled with other oxen, even a thousand in number, they are all stoned to death and buried, and it is forbidden to derive any benefit from any of them, in accordance with the law pertaining to a killer ox." (*Rambam, Sefer Nezikin, Hilkhot Nizkei Mamon* 11:10.)

TRANSLATION AND COMMENTARY

an ox was mingled with other oxen, it is forbidden to derive benefit from any one of them. [1]**Rabbi Yehudah** disagrees and **says:** Rather than stone the oxen, they **are put into an enclosure** and left to starve to death.

וְהָתַנְיָא [2]The Gemara notes: **And similarly it was taught** in the following Baraita: **"If a cow killed** a man, **and afterward calved,** the following distinction applies: [3]**If** it **calved before the verdict** of stoning **was issued, her offspring is permitted** for benefit (as will be explained below). [4]But **if she calved** only **after the verdict** of stoning **was issued, her offspring is forbidden** (as will also be explained below). [5]**If** the cow **was mingled with other cows,** so that we can no longer identify the animal that had killed the man and must now be stoned, **and those other** animals were then mingled **with** yet **other** animals, [6]all the animals **are put into an enclosure** where they are left to starve to death. [7]**Rabbi Elazar the son of Rabbi Shimon** disagrees and **says:** All the animals **are brought to court, and stoned** to death." Thus, Rabbi Yehudah of our Mishnah follows the position of the anonymous first Tanna of the Baraita.

אָמַר מַר [8]**It was stated above** in the Baraita: **"If** the cow that gored **calved before its verdict** of stoning **was issued, her offspring is permitted** for benefit." [9]The Gemara asks: Does this mean that the offspring is permitted for benefit **even if** the mother **was pregnant when it gored** the person? [10]**But surely Rava said: The offspring of an animal that gored is forbidden** to be

[1]רַבִּי יְהוּדָה אוֹמֵר: כּוֹנְסִין אוֹתָן לַכִּיפָּה.

[2]וְהָתַנְיָא: "פָּרָה שֶׁהֵמִיתָה וְאַחַר כָּךְ יָלְדָה — [3]אִם עַד שֶׁלֹּא נִגְמַר דִּינָהּ יָלְדָה, וְוַלָדָהּ מוּתָּר; [4]אִם מִשֶּׁנִּגְמַר דִּינָהּ יָלְדָה, וְוַלָדָהּ אָסוּר. [5]נִתְעָרֵב בַּאֲחֵרִים, וַאֲחֵרִים בַּאֲחֵרִים, [6]כּוֹנְסִין אוֹתָן לַכִּיפָּה. [7]רַבִּי אֶלְעָזָר בְּרַבִּי שִׁמְעוֹן אוֹמֵר: מְבִיאִין אוֹתָן לְבֵית דִּין וְסוֹקְלִין אוֹתָן".

[8]אָמַר מַר: "אִם עַד שֶׁלֹּא נִגְמַר דִּינָהּ יָלְדָה, וְוַלָדָהּ מוּתֶּרֶת". [9]וְאַף עַל גַּב דְּכִי נָגְחָה הֲוַת מִיעַבְּרָה? [10]וְהָאָמַר רָבָא: וְלַד

LITERAL TRANSLATION

[1]Rabbi Yehudah says: They put them in a chamber. [2]And so it was taught: "[If] a cow killed, and afterwards calved — [3]if it calved before its judgment was finished, its offspring is permitted; [4]if it calved after its judgment was finished, its offspring is forbidden. [5]If it was mingled with others, and [those] others with others, [6]they put them in a chamber. [7]Rabbi Elazar the son of Rabbi Shimon says: They bring them to court, and stone them."

[8]The master said: "If it calved before its judgment was finished, its offspring is permitted." [9]Even if when it gored it was pregnant? [10]But surely Rava said: The offspring

RASHI

כונסין אותן לכיפה — שאין צריך לסוקלן, שלא להטריח בית דין, אלא כונסין אותן בחדר והם מתים ברעב. **והתניא** — בניחותא. **ולדה מותר** — לקמן מפרש לה. **ולדה אסור** — דעובר ירך אמו הוא, וגם הוא נאסר בגמר דין אמו. **והאמר רבא ולד הנוגחת אסור** — בהקרבה, כגון שנגחה על פי עד אחד או על פי הבעלים דמתסרא לגבוה ולא להדיוט. הלכך על כרחיך שמעינן מדרבא דהיכא דאית עדים אסור אף להדיוט, וצריך לגמור דין שניהם. והא ליכא למימר טעמא דתנא קמא דתני וולדה מותר משום דלא נגמר דינו עמה, דאי בשלא בא לבית דין מאי איריא

NOTES

people who jointly committed a transgression are exempt from punishment (*Tzofnat Pa'ane'aḥ*).

כּוֹנְסִין אוֹתָן לַכִּיפָּה **They put them in an enclosure.** Some argue that this ruling is limited to a killer ox that was mingled with other oxen. Only in such a case does Rabbi Yehudah say that all the animals are put into an enclosure to starve to death, for there is an obligation to "put away the evil from the midst of you." But if an animal with which someone had committed bestiality mingled with other oxen, they are not put into such an enclosure, for the obligation to "put away the evil" does not apply in such a case (*Tzofnat Pa'ane'aḥ*).

וְהָתַנְיָא **And so it was taught.** The expression וְהָתַנְיָא usually introduces an objection based on a Baraita: "But surely it has been taught differently in the following Baraita!" Occasionally, however, this term introduces a Baraita in support of the previous statement. When it is used in this sense, *Rashi* usually observes in his commentary that this expression is to be interpreted בְּנִיחוּתָא — "non-interrogatively," "calmly" — or as a סַיְיעָתָא, "help," not an objection. The meaning of the expression can only be determined from the context.

HALAKHAH

פָּרָה שֶׁהֵמִיתָה וְאַחַר כָּךְ יָלְדָה **If a cow killed, and afterward calved.** "If a cow gored an animal and killed it, and then conceived, the following distinction applies: If the cow gave birth before its verdict of stoning was issued, its offspring is permitted, But if it gave birth after its verdict of stoning was issued, its offspring is forbidden just like the cow itself, for a fetus is regarded as a limb of its mother. If that offspring was mingled with others, all the animals are put into an enclosure where they are left to die," following the Baraita, and the Gemara, below. (*Rambam, Sefer Nezikin, Hilkhot Nizkei Mamon* 11:12.)

TRANSLATION AND COMMENTARY

offered on the altar as a sacrifice, just like its mother, [1]for we say that both the parent **itself and its offspring gored** the person to death. [2]And similarly **the offspring of an animal that was the object of bestiality is forbidden** to be offered on the altar as a sacrifice, just like its mother, [3]for we say that both the mother **itself and her offspring were the objects of bestiality,** and thus the two became forbidden.

אֵימָא [4]The Gemara explains: According to Rava, if the mother was pregnant when she gored the person, her offspring is indeed forbidden, even if it was born before the mother's verdict of stoning was delivered, for both the mother and her offspring gored the person to death. And the Baraita is not difficult, for Rava can **say** that the Baraita should be understood as follows: **If** a cow that gored a person to death **conceived and calved** after it killed the person but **before its verdict** of stoning **was issued,** [5]**its offspring is permitted** for benefit, for the young was not part of its mother at the time of the killing, nor at the time of the verdict, and it was not born to an animal that was forbidden for benefit. [6]But **if** the cow that gored **conceived and calved after its verdict** of stoning was **issued, its offspring is forbidden.** The offspring born to an animal that is already forbidden for benefit is also forbidden for benefit.

הָנִיחָא [7]The Gemara comments: **Granted, according to the** authority **who says** that **the product of combined causes is forbidden,** we understand the second ruling of the Baraita. Elsewhere, the authorities disagree about the product of combined causes, one permitted and one forbidden. For example, if a dam is forbidden and a sire is permitted, is the offspring permitted or forbidden? According to the authority who says that the product of such a union is forbidden, we understand why the offspring of a murderous cow that conceived and calved after its verdict of stoning was issued is forbidden. That offspring is the product of combined causes, a mother that is forbidden for benefit, and a father that is permitted for benefit. [80B] [8]**But according to the** authority **who says** that **the product of combined causes is permitted, what is there to say?**

הַנּוֹגַחַת אָסוּר, [1]הִיא וּוְלָדָהּ נָגְחוּ. [2]וְלַד הַנִּרְבַּעַת אָסוּר, [3]הִיא וּוְלָדָהּ נִרְבְּעוּ!

[4]אֵימָא: אִם עַד שֶׁלֹּא נִגְמַר דִּינָהּ עִיבְּרָהּ וְיָלְדָה, [5]וּוְלָדָהּ מוּתָּר. [6]אִם מִשֶּׁנִּגְמַר דִּינָהּ עִיבְּרָהּ וְיָלְדָה, וּוְלָדָהּ אָסוּר.

[7]הָנִיחָא לְמַאן דַּאֲמַר: זֶה וָזֶה גּוֹרֵם, אָסוּר. [80B] [8]אֶלָּא לְמַאן דַּאֲמַר: זֶה וָזֶה גּוֹרֵם, מוּתָּר, מַאי אִיכָּא לְמֵימַר?

LITERAL TRANSLATION

of an animal that gored is forbidden, [1]she and her offspring gored. [2]The offspring of an animal that was the object of bestiality is forbidden, [3]she and her offspring were the object of bestiality.

[4]Say: If she conceived and calved before her judgment was finished, [5]her offspring is permitted. [6]If she conceived and gave birth after her judgment was finished, her offspring is forbidden.

[7]Granted, according to the one who says: [If] this and that caused, it is forbidden. [80A] [8]But according to the one who says: [If] this and that caused, it is permitted, what is there to say?

RASHI

ולדה — אפילו אמו נמי אם לא נגמר דינה לא מיתסרא. וכי איצטריך תנא למיתני מותר — הכי אשמעינן, דאין זקוק להביאה לבית דין קאמר, ותיובתא דרבא. אימא אם עד שלא נגמר דינה עיברה וילדה — דהיינו בין נגיחה לגמר דין, דלא הוה ולד לא בשעת נגיחה ולא בשעת גמר דין ולא נולד מן האיסור דאכתי אימיה הות שריא — ולדה מותר. אם משנגמר דינה עיברה וילדה — דנולד מן האיסור — אסור, אף על גב דלא הוה בשעת נגיחה ולא בשעת גמר דין. הניחא למאן דאמר — פלוגתא הוא בתמורה (ל,א). מאי איכא למימר — דהא כשנולד לאחר גמר דין לאו איהו לחודיה גרמא ליה, שאף מן הזכר הוא בא, דהיתר ואיסור גרמו לו שיבא.

NOTES

הִיא וּוְלָדָהּ נָגְחוּ She and her offspring gored. This rationale differs from what is found below (80b): "A fetus is considered the thigh of its mother." There, we say that the offspring is forbidden for benefit, not because it was responsible for the goring, but because it is part of its mother, which was responsible for the goring. Here, we say that the offspring is forbidden for benefit, because it is viewed as an independent entity which shares the responsibility for the goring with its mother (see *Rabbi David Bonfil, Ran*).

HALAKHAH

הִיא וּוְלָדָהּ נָגְחוּ She and her offspring gored. "If a pregnant cow gored a person to death, or if it served as the object of bestiality, its offspring is treated like its mother, so that it, too, is subject to stoning. Similarly, if a pregnant cow gored a person to death, or if it was the object of bestiality, its offspring is forbidden to be offered on the altar as a sacrifice, just like its mother. This law applies only if the cow gored the person or was the object of bestiality while it was pregnant. But if the cow conceived after it gored the person or served as the object of bestiality, its offspring is fit to be sacrificed on the altar." (*Rambam, Sefer Nezikin, Hilkhot Nizkei Mamon* 11:11; *Sefer Korbanot, Hilkhot Issurei Mizbe'aḥ* 3:12-13.)

זֶהוָזֶהגּוֹרֵם This and that caused. "Any product of combined causes, one permitted and one forbidden, is permitted." (*Shulḥan Arukh, Yoreh De'ah* 142:11.)

[1]אֶלָּא, אָמַר רָבִינָא: [2]אֵימָא: אִם עַד שֶׁלֹּא נִגְמַר דִּינָהּ עִיבְּרָהּ וְיָלְדָה, וְלָדָהּ מוּתָּר. [3]וְאִם עַד שֶׁלֹּא נִגְמַר דִּינָהּ עִיבְּרָהּ, וּמִשֶּׁנִּגְמַר דִּינָה יָלְדָה — וְלָדָהּ אָסוּר, [4]עוּבָּר יֶרֶךְ אִמּוֹ הוּא.

[5]״כָּל חַיָּיבֵי מִיתוֹת״. [6]שְׁמַע מִינָּהּ: מוּתְרֶה לְדָבָר חָמוּר הָוֵי מוּתְרֶה לְדָבָר קַל.

[7]אָמַר רַבִּי יִרְמְיָה: הָכָא בְּמַאי עָסְקִינַן? [8]כְּגוֹן שֶׁהִתְרוּ בּוֹ סְתָם. [9]וְהַאי תַּנָּא הוּא, [10]דְּתַנְיָא: ״וּשְׁאָר חַיָּיבֵי מִיתוֹת שֶׁבְּתוֹרָה

LITERAL TRANSLATION

[1]Rather, Ravina said: Say: [2]If it conceived and calved before its judgment was finished, its offspring is permitted. [3]And if it conceived before its judgment was finished, and calved after its judgment was finished, its offspring is forbidden. [4]A fetus is [like] the thigh of its mother.

[5]"All who are liable to execution." [6]Infer from this: Someone who is warned regarding a severe matter is [considered] warned regarding a lenient matter.

[7]Rabbi Yirmeyah said: What are we dealing with here? [8]Such as if they warned him without specifying. [9]And it is this Tanna, [10]for it was taught: "And the rest of those who are liable to capital punishment in the Torah

TRANSLATION AND COMMENTARY

אֶלָּא [1]**Rather, Ravina said:** If the murderous cow conceived and calved only after its verdict of stoning was issued, its offspring is in fact permitted, for the product of combined causes is permitted. [2]And the Baraita is not difficult, for we can **say** that it should be understood as follows: **If** the cow that gored a person to death **conceived and calved** after it killed the person, but **before its verdict** of stoning **was issued, its offspring is permitted** for benefit, for the young was not part of its mother, either at the time of the killing or at the time of the verdict. [3]But **if** the cow that gored **conceived** after it killed the person but **before its verdict** of stoning **was issued, and** it **calved** only **after the verdict** of stoning **was delivered, its offspring is forbidden** for benefit, [4]for **a fetus is considered like a limb of its mother.**

כָּל חַיָּיבֵי מִיתוֹת [5]We have learned in our Mishnah: "If criminals **who are liable to execution** in different ways are mixed with each other, so that we no longer know which offender is liable to which mode of execution, they are all put to death by the most lenient mode of execution for which any one of them was liable." [6]The Gemara notes: **Infer from this** ruling that if **someone was warned** that the action he was about to take was subject to **a severe penalty**, he **is considered** as having also been **warned** that the action is subject to a more **lenient penalty.** Otherwise, why would criminals liable to stoning who were subsequently mixed with criminals liable to decapitation be put to death by the more lenient mode of execution? Surely, they were warned that their actions were subject to stoning, but they were not warned that their actions were subject to decapitation!

אָמַר רַבִּי יִרְמְיָה [7]**Rabbi Yirmeyah** rejected this argument, **saying: Here,** in the Mishnah, **what are we dealing with?** [8]The witnesses warned the offender that his action was forbidden, and that if he violated the prohibition he would be liable to the death penalty, but they **did not specify** the mode of execution to which he would be liable. [9]**And** the Mishnah follows the position of **the Tanna** who maintains that it is not necessary to specify the mode of execution in the warning. [10]**For it was taught** in the following Baraita: "**And** as for **the rest of those who are liable to capital punishment by Torah law, the death sentence may**

RASHI

ואם עד שלא נגמר דינה הוכר עוברה — דהיינו בין נגיחה לגמר דין. **ומשנגמר דינה ילדה ולדה אסור** — אף על גב דלא הוה בשעת נגיחה, כיון דהוה בשעת גמר דין נאסר בגמר דין עם אמו, דעובר ירך אמו הוא. **שמע מינה** — מדקתני ידונו בסקילה מותרה למיתה חמורה הוי מותרה למיתה קלה, משום דקלה בכלל חמורה. דאי לא הוי מותרה למיתה קלה — הנך דנתחייבו חמורה היאך נתחייבו בסקילה, הא לא אסרו בהם מיתה זו, ונפטריה לגמרי! — אלא נילף מהכא דהוי מותרה. **אמר רבי ירמיה** — מהכא ליכא למילף — הכא בהתרו בהם מיתה סתם — ולפיכך קלה וחמורה במשמע. **והאי תנא הוא** — דקאמר לא בעינן להזכיר שם אותה מיתה. **ושאר חייבי מיתות** — חוץ ממסית שאינו צריך התראה, דרחמנא אמר ״לא תחמול ולא תכסה עליו״.

NOTES

מוּתְרֶה לְדָבָר חָמוּר **Someone who is warned regarding a severe matter.** Regarding a capital offender who cannot be executed in the manner to which he is liable, the Rishonim disagree as to whether or not it is permissible to kill him in some other manner. According to *Rambam*, any capital offender may be put to death by any means of execution if it is impossible to put him to death by the mode of execution to which he is liable, whereas according to others, that law is restricted to a murderer and the inhabitants of a condemned city. According to *Ramban*, the Gemara is difficult, for even if we say that someone who was warned that the action that he was about to take was subject to a severe penalty is not considered as having also been warned that the action is subject to a more lenient penalty — since we cannot administer the mode of execution to which he is liable, it should be possible to administer another mode of execution. But according to the other Rishonim, we understand why the Gemara had to offer a separate explanation for the law recorded in the Mishnah, that if criminals who are liable to modes of execution of varying degrees of severity become

אֵין מְמִיתִין אוֹתָן אֶלָּא בְּעֵדָה וְעֵדִים וְהַתְרָאָה, [1]וְעַד שֶׁיּוֹדִיעוּהוּ שֶׁהוּא חַיָּיב מִיתַת בֵּית דִּין. [2]רַבִּי יְהוּדָה אוֹמֵר: עַד שֶׁיּוֹדִיעוּהוּ בְּאֵיזֶה מִיתָה הוּא נֶהֱרָג״.

[3]תַּנָּא קַמָּא יָלֵיף מִמְּקוֹשֵׁשׁ. [4]וְרַבִּי יְהוּדָה אוֹמֵר: מְקוֹשֵׁשׁ הוֹרָאַת שָׁעָה הָיְתָה.

[5]״הַנִּסְקָלִין בַּנִּשְׂרָפִין״. [6]מַתְנֵי לֵיהּ רַב יְחֶזְקֵאל לְרָמִי בְּרֵיהּ: ״הַנִּשְׂרָפִין בַּנִּסְקָלִין. [7]רַבִּי שִׁמְעוֹן אוֹמֵר: יִדּוֹנוּ בִּסְקִילָה, שֶׁהַשְּׂרֵיפָה חֲמוּרָה״.

LITERAL TRANSLATION

we do not execute them without a congregation, and witnesses, and a warning, [1]and unless they inform him that he is liable to judicial execution. [2]Rabbi Yehudah says: Unless they inform him by which [mode of] execution he will be executed."

[3]The first Tanna learns from the gatherer. [4]And Rabbi Yehudah says: The gatherer['s] was a temporary ruling.

[5]"Those liable to [execution by] stoning with those liable to [execution by] burning." [6]Rav Yeḥezkel taught Rami, his son: "Those liable to [execution by] burning with those liable to [execution by] stoning. [7]Rabbi Shimon says: They are punished with stoning, for burning is more severe."

TRANSLATION AND COMMENTARY

not be imposed unless the defendant has been judged by a court consisting of **a congregation** of twenty-three judges, unless testimony concerning the offense was submitted by two qualified **witnesses,** unless **a warning** was given to the defendant immediately prior to his transgression that the act he was about to commit was unlawful, [1]**and unless** the witnesses **informed** the defendant at the time **that he would be liable to judicial execution.** [2]**Rabbi Yehudah says:** The death sentence may not be imposed **unless** the witnesses **had** also **informed** the defendant prior to his transgression **by which mode of execution he would be executed** if found guilty."

תַּנָּא קַמָּא [3]The Gemara notes that **the** anonymous **first Tanna** of the Baraita **learns** that the death sentence may be imposed upon the defendant without specifying the mode of execution, from the warning concerning **the** stick-**gatherer** who profaned the Sabbath in the days of Moses (see Numbers 15:32-36). The stick-gatherer was put to death, even though the witnesses could not have specified the mode of execution to which he would be subject. The penalty was unknown until God told Moses that the Sabbath-desecrator was to be stoned. [4]**And Rabbi Yehudah says** that the penalty imposed upon **the** stick-**gatherer was a temporary ruling** based on the direct word of God, and so it cannot serve as a precedent teaching that it is not necessary to tell the offender by which mode of execution he would be put to death should he commit his crime.

הַנִּסְקָלִין בַּנִּשְׂרָפִין [5]We have learned in our Mishnah: "If criminals **liable to stoning** became intermixed **with** criminals **liable to burning,** Rabbi Shimon and the Sages disagree about which mode of execution is imposed." [6]**Rav Yeḥezkel taught** the Mishnah to **his son Rami** with a slight difference in formulation: "If criminals **liable to burning** became intermixed with **those liable to stoning,** [7]**Rabbi Shimon says: They are** all **put to death by stoning, for** death by **burning is** a **more severe** mode of execution than death by stoning."

RASHI

עדה ועדים – לאו דוקא, דמסית נמי עדים ועדה קא בעי, והא דנקט ״ושאר״ משום התראה נקט לה. **יליף ממקושש** – שהמוצאים אותו לא התרו בו שם מיתתו, דלא הוו ידעי לה אלא מיתה סתם. **הוראת שעה היתה** – ועל פי הדבור מחייב ולא גמרינן מינה לדורות, הואיל ונפקא לן התראה מ״יומת המת״ – שיתיר עצמו למיתה, אותה מיתה משמע. **הנשרפין בנסקלין** – משמע כגון דהוו נסקלין רובא ואיערבא בהו מיעוטא נשרפין.

SAGES

רַב יְחֶזְקֵאל **Rav Yeḥezkel.** A Babylonian Amora of the first generation, Rav Yeḥezkel was a contemporary of the great Amora Shmuel. Two of his sons were famous Sages — his elder son Rav Yehudah, and his younger son, Rami (Rav Ammi). Though Rav Yehudah was a greater Sage than his father, Shmuel instructed Rav Yehudah, his disciple, to give particular honor to his father, and Shmuel himself often honored him as a "master of deeds," a charitable and pious man.

NOTES

mixed with each other, they are all put to death by the most lenient mode of execution for which any one of them was liable.

בְּעֵדָה וְעֵדִים וְהַתְרָאָה **A congregation, and witnesses, and a warning.** To be precise, it should be noted that a warning is not always necessary, for a rebellious elder and false, conspiring witnesses may be executed without a warning, as can a blasphemer, according to *Rambam*.

הוֹרָאַת שָׁעָה הָיְתָה **A temporary ruling.** Some explain the Gemara as follows: The warning that the witnesses gave the stick-gatherer was indeed a valid warning at the time, since no one knew what the penalty would be. The Tannaim disagree about whether that warning can serve as a precedent for future generations, or whether we say that once we know the mode of execution for each capital offense, a warning that does not specify the mode of execution is not valid (*Ramah*).

מְקוֹשֵׁשׁ הוֹרָאַת שָׁעָה הָיְתָה **The rule concerning the gatherer was a temporary one.** It has been argued that the court of Moses was permitted to judge on the basis of a prophetic spirit (because the entire Torah had not yet been given); hence it could know that even had the stick-gatherer received a warning which specified the mode of execution to which he would be subject, he would still have committed his transgression (see *Margoliyot HaYam*).

HALAKHAH

עַד שֶׁיּוֹדִיעוּהוּ שֶׁהוּא חַיָּיב מִיתַת בֵּית דִּין **Unless they inform him that he is liable to execution.** "In order for a capital offender to be liable to punishment, he must be given the following warning: Know that the act that you are about to perform is forbidden and punishable by judicial execution. (But it is not necessary to specify the mode of execution to which he is liable, following the Sages; *Kesef Mishneh*.)" (*Rambam, Sefer Shofetim, Hilkhot Sanhedrin* 12:2.)

LANGUAGE

שִׁינָּנָא Sharp-witted one. This appellation for Rav Yehudah, which is found in several places in the Talmud, is understood by many commentators as meaning "sharp" or "acute," based on the analogy with the Hebrew word שָׁנַן, which has that meaning. However, the Geonim wrote that they were sure the term referred to a person with large teeth, based on the Aramaic and Hebrew word שֵׁן, meaning "tooth."

LITERAL TRANSLATION

[1]Rav Yehudah said to him: [2]"Father, do not teach him that way! [3]Why mention that burning is more severe? [4]Derive it [from the fact] that the majority are liable to stoning!"

[5]"Rather how should I teach him?"

[6]"Those liable to stoning with those liable to burning, [7]Rabbi Shimon says: They are punished with stoning, for burning is more severe."

[8]"If so, consider the last clause: [9]'And the Sages say: They are punished with burning, for stoning is more severe.' [10]Derive it [from the fact] that the majority are liable to burning!"

[11]"There, the Rabbis said to Rabbi Shimon: [12]According to you, who said [that] burning is more severe — [13]no, stoning is more severe."

[14]Shmuel said to Rav Yehudah: "Sharp-witted one! [81A] [15]Do not speak that way to your father,

[1]אָמַר לֵיהּ רַב יְהוּדָה: [2]"אַבָּא, לָא תִיתְנְיֵיה הָכִי! [3]מַאי אִירְיָא דִּשְׂרֵיפָה חֲמוּרָה? [4]תֵּיפּוֹק לֵיהּ דְּרוּבָּה נִסְקָלִין נִינְהוּ"!

[5]"אֶלָּא הֵיכִי אַתְנְיֵיהּ"?

[6]"הַנִּסְקָלִין בַּנִּשְׂרָפִין, [7]רַבִּי שִׁמְעוֹן אוֹמֵר: יִדּוֹנוּ בִּסְקִילָה שֶׁהַשְּׂרֵיפָה חֲמוּרָה".

[8]"אִי הָכִי אֵימָא סֵיפָא: [9]'וַחֲכָמִים אוֹמְרִים: יִדּוֹנוּ בִּשְׂרֵיפָה, שֶׁהַסְּקִילָה חֲמוּרָה'. [10]תֵּיפּוֹק לֵיהּ דְּרוּבָּה נִשְׂרָפִין נִינְהוּ"!

[11]"הָתָם רַבָּנַן הוּא דְּקָאָמְרוּ לֵיהּ לְרַבִּי שִׁמְעוֹן: [12]לְדִידָךְ דְּאָמְרַתְּ שְׂרֵיפָה חֲמוּרָה — [13]לֹא, סְקִילָה חֲמוּרָה".

[14]אֲמַר לֵיהּ שְׁמוּאֵל לְרַב יְהוּדָה: "שִׁינָּנָא! [81A] [15]לָא תֵּימָא לֵיהּ לַאֲבוּךְ הָכִי,

TRANSLATION AND COMMENTARY

אָמַר לֵיהּ [1]Rav Yeḥezkel's other son, **Rav Yehudah, said to him:** [2]**"Father, do not teach** the Mishnah **that way.** [3]**Why** was it necessary for Rabbi Shimon to **mention that burning is** a **more severe** mode of execution than death by stoning? The formulation, "If criminals liable to burning became intermixed with those liable to stoning," implies that a smaller number of criminals liable to burning were mixed with a larger number of criminals liable to stoning. [4]Rabbi Shimon **should** therefore **have derived** the law that they are all put to death by stoning **from the fact that the majority** of offenders **are liable to stoning,** following the general principle that we follow the majority!"

אֶלָּא [5]Rav Yeḥezkel said to Rav Yehudah: **"How, then, should I teach** the Mishnah?"

הַנִּסְקָלִין בַּנִּשְׂרָפִין [6]Rav Yehudah said to his father: "You should teach the Mishnah as follows: 'If criminals **liable to stoning** became intermixed **with** criminals **liable to burning,** [7]**Rabbi Shimon says: They are** all **put to death by stoning, for** death by **burning is** a **more severe** mode of execution than death by stoning.' This formulation implies that a smaller number of criminals liable to stoning became intermixed with a larger number of criminals liable to burning. Rabbi Shimon teaches that even though a majority of the offenders are liable to death by burning, they are all put to death by way of stoning, because death by burning is a more severe mode of execution than death by stoning."

אִי הָכִי [8]Rav Yeḥezkel said to his son: **"If so, consider the next clause** of the Mishnah: [9]**'The Sages** disagree with Rabbi Shimon and **say: They are** all **put to death by burning, for** death by **stoning is** a **more severe** mode of execution.' Now, if a smaller number of criminals liable to stoning became intermixed with a larger number of criminals liable to burning, why was it necessary for the Sages to mention that stoning is a more severe mode of execution than death by burning? [10]They **should have derived** the law that they are all put to death by way of burning **from the fact that the majority** of offenders **are liable to burning,** in keeping with the general principle that we follow the majority!"

הָתָם רַבָּנַן [11]Rav Yehudah answered: **"There, the Sages said to Rabbi Shimon** as follows: If a smaller number of criminals liable to stoning became intermixed with a larger number of criminals liable to burning, they are all put to death by way of burning, because the majority of offenders are liable to burning. [12]**As for what you have said, that burning is** a **more severe** mode of execution than stoning, and therefore we cannot impose death by burning upon any of the offenders because of those who are only liable to stoning — [13]know that this is **not** true, for **stoning is** in fact a **more severe** mode of execution than burning."

אֲמַר לֵיהּ [14]When **Shmuel** heard about this exchange between Rav Yehudah and Rav Yeḥezkel, he **said to Rav Yehudah: "You sharp-witted man!** [81A] [15]**You should not have spoken that way to your father,** embarrassing

RASHI

תיפוק ליה דרובא נסקלין נינהו — היכי נקט טעמא משום דאי אתה רשאי למושכו למיתה חמורה בלאו הכי נדייניהו בסקילה, (הוה) בתר רובא. **אלא היכי איתנייהו** — אבוה מהדר ליה אלא היכי אלמדנו. **אמר ליה רב יהודה הנסקלין בנשרפין** — דאף על גב דנשרפין רובא מדתני לרבי שמעון בסקילה מפני שהשריפה חמורה. **התם** — הוא דקא מסיימי רבנן שהסקילה חמורה לאו למיתב טעמא למילתייהו מסיימי הכי, אלא הכי קאמרי: ידונו בשריפה כדינייהו בתר רובא, ודקאמרת למיזל בתר מיעוטא משום דשריפה חמורה ואין אנו רשאין למשוך את הקלים — לאו חמורה היא אלא קלה היא. **לא תימא ליה לאבוך הכי** — להודיעו בהדיא שהוא טועה,

TRANSLATION AND COMMENTARY

him by telling him directly that he had made an error, [1]**for it was taught** in a Baraita: **'If** someone sees that **his father is violating the words of the Torah,** [2]**he should not say to him: Father, you have violated the words of the Torah.** [3]**Rather,** the son **should say to** his father: **Father, is it written thus in the Torah?'"**

סוֹף סוֹף [4]The Gemara objects: **In the end,** speaking to one's father in **this** manner **is** no different from speaking to him in **that** other manner, for either way the son embarrasses his father by questioning the way he acted!

אֶלָּא [5]The Gemara explains: The Baraita should be understood as follows: **Rather,** the son **should say to** his father: [6]**"Father, the verse written in the Torah is as follows,"** without making direct reference to what the father has done.

MISHNAH מִי שֶׁנִּתְחַיֵּיב [7]If **someone** committed two capital offenses, so that he **became liable to two** different **modes of judicial execution,** he **is sentenced to the more severe** mode of execution.

עָבַר עֲבֵירָה [8]**If someone committed a** single **transgression for which he is liable to two modes of judicial execution,** for example by having sexual intercourse with his mother-in-law who was also a married woman, so that he became liable to both burning and strangulation, **he is sentenced to the more severe** mode of execution. [9]**Rabbi Yose** disagrees and **says: He is sentenced** for violating **the prohibition that applied to him first.**

[1]דְּתַנְיָא: ׳הֲרֵי שֶׁהָיָה אָבִיו עוֹבֵר עַל דִּבְרֵי תוֹרָה, [2]לֹא יֹאמַר לוֹ: ״אַבָּא! עָבַרְתָּ עַל דִּבְרֵי תוֹרָה״. [3]אֶלָּא אוֹמֵר לוֹ: ״אַבָּא, כָּךְ כְּתִיב בַּתּוֹרָה״׳״?
[4]סוֹף סוֹף, הַיְינוּ הָךְ!
[5]אֶלָּא, אוֹמֵר לוֹ: [6]״אַבָּא, מִקְרָא כָּתוּב בַּתּוֹרָה כָּךְ הוּא״.

משנה [7]מִי שֶׁנִּתְחַיֵּיב בִּשְׁתֵּי מִיתוֹת בֵּית דִּין, נִידּוֹן בַּחֲמוּרָה. [8]עָבַר עֲבֵירָה שֶׁנִּתְחַיֵּיב שְׁתֵּי מִיתוֹת, נִידּוֹן בַּחֲמוּרָה. [9]רַבִּי יוֹסֵי אוֹמֵר: נִידּוֹן בַּזִּיקָה הָרִאשׁוֹנָה שֶׁבָּאָה עָלָיו.

LITERAL TRANSLATION

[1]for it was taught: 'If someone's father was violating the words of the Torah, [2]he should not say to him: "Father, you have violated the words of the Torah." [3]Rather, he should say to him: "Father, is it written thus in the Torah?"'"

[4]In the end, this is that!

[5]Rather, he should say to him: [6]"Father, the verse written in the Torah is as follows."

MISHNAH [7]He who is liable to two [modes of] judicial execution is sentenced to the more severe one.

[8][If] he committed a transgression for which he is liable to two [modes of] judicial execution, he is sentenced to the more severe one. [9]Rabbi Yose says: He is sentenced for the first obligation that applied to him.

RASHI

אלא אומר לו אבא כך כתוב בתורה – קא סלקא דעתך בתמיהה קאמר: וכי כך כתיב בתורה? **סוף סוף היינו הך** – דמביישו ואומר וכי יפה אתה עושה. **אלא** – בניחותא אומר לו מקרא האמור בתורה, ואומר לו: אבי, מקרא כך וכך כתוב בתורה. והוא עצמו ישים על לבו על מה זה מזכירו, והכי נמי אין לך לומר לאביך ״לא תתנייה הכי״.

משנה עבר עבירה שיש בה שתי מיתות – כגון חמותו והיא אשת איש. **בזיקה הראשונה** – בגמרא מפרש לה.

NOTES

הָיָה אָבִיו עוֹבֵר עַל דִּבְרֵי תוֹרָה **If someone's father was violating the words of the Torah.** According to some authorities, a son may not point out his father's violation directly if the father has already violated a Torah prohibition or committed some other Halakhic error. But if the father has not yet sinned, but is about to do so, his son may prevent him from transgressing, by telling him directly that what he is about to do is in violation of Torah law (*Rishon Letzion*).

מִקְרָא כָּתוּב בַּתּוֹרָה כָּךְ הוּא **The verse written in the Torah is as follows.** *Rambam* appears to have understood this passage in the opposite manner: If a person sees his father violating a Torah prohibition, he should not tell him categorically that it is written otherwise in the Torah. Rather he should ask: Is it written thus in the Torah? (See also *Meiri.*)

HALAKHAH

הָיָה אָבִיו עוֹבֵר עַל דִּבְרֵי תוֹרָה **If someone's father was violating the words of the Torah.** "If someone saw his father violating a Torah prohibition, he should not say to him directly: Father, you have sinned. But rather he should say to him in the form of a question: Father, is it stated thus in the Torah?" (following *Rambam*'s interpretation of our Gemara). (*Rambam, Sefer Shofetim, Hilkhot Mamrim* 6:11; *Shulḥan Arukh, Yoreh De'ah* 240:11.)

מִי שֶׁנִּתְחַיֵּיב בִּשְׁתֵּי מִיתוֹת בֵּית דִּין **He who is liable to two modes of judicial execution.** "If someone is liable to two different modes of judicial execution, he is sentenced to the more severe mode, whether he committed two different transgressions one after the other, or a single transgression for which he became liable to two modes of execution. Even if he was sentenced to the more lenient mode of execution and later committed the second transgression for which he became liable to the more severe mode of execution, he is sentenced to the more severe mode of execution," following the Mishnah. (*Rambam, Sefer Shofetim, Hilkhot Sanhedrin* 14:4.)

גמרא [1]פְּשִׁיטָא! [2]אֶלָּא אִיתַּגּוּרֵי אִיתַּגּוּר?

[3]אָמַר רָבָא: [4]הָכִי בְּמַאי עָסְקִינַן? כְּגוֹן שֶׁעָבַר עֲבֵירָה קַלָּה, [5]וְנִגְמַר דִּינוֹ עַל עֲבֵירָה קַלָּה, וְחָזַר וְעָבַר עֲבֵירָה חֲמוּרָה. [6]סָלְקָא דַּעְתָּךְ אָמִינָא: כֵּיוָן דְּנִגְמַר דִּינוֹ לַעֲבֵירָה קַלָּה, [7]הַאי גַּבְרָא קְטִילָא הוּא. [8]קָא מַשְׁמַע לָן.

[9]בְּעָא מִנֵּיהּ אֲבוּהּ דְּרַב יוֹסֵף בַּר חָמָא מֵרַבָּה בַּר נָתָן: [10]מְנָא הָא מִילְּתָא דַּאֲמוּר רַבָּנַן: מִי שֶׁנִּתְחַיֵּיב שְׁתֵּי מִיתוֹת בֵּית דִּין נִידּוֹן בַּחֲמוּרָה?

[11]דִּכְתִיב: ״וְהוֹלִיד בֵּן פָּרִיץ שֹׁפֵךְ דָּם [וגו׳] אֶל הֶהָרִים אָכַל, וְאֶת אֵשֶׁת רֵעֵהוּ טִמֵּא...וְאֶל הַגִּלּוּלִים נָשָׂא עֵינָיו״. [12]״וְהוֹלִיד בֵּן פָּרִיץ שֹׁפֵךְ דָּם״ — בְּסַיִיף, [13]״אֶת אֵשֶׁת רֵעֵהוּ טִמֵּא״ — זוֹ אֵשֶׁת אִישׁ, בְּחֶנֶק. [14]״וְאֶל הַגִּלּוּלִים נָשָׂא עֵינָיו״ — זוֹ עֲבוֹדָה זָרָה, בִּסְקִילָה. [15]וּכְתִיב:

LITERAL TRANSLATION

GEMARA [1]It is obvious! [2]Should he benefit?

[3]Rava said: [4]What are we dealing with here? As when he committed a lenient transgression, [5]and his judgment was finished regarding the lenient transgression, and then he committed a severe transgression. [6]It might have entered your mind to say: Since his judgment was finished regarding the lenient transgression, [7]he is a dead man. [8][Therefore], it teaches us.

[9]The father of Rav Yosef bar Ḥama asked Rabbah bar Natan: [10]From where [do we know] this matter that the Rabbis said: He who is liable to two [modes of] judicial execution is sentenced to the more severe one?

[11]For it is written: "If he has begotten a son who is a robber, a shedder of blood...has eaten on the mountains, and defiled his neighbor's wife... and has lifted up his eyes to the idols." [12]"If he has begotten a son who is a robber, a shedder of blood" — by the sword; [13]"and defiled his neighbor's wife" — this is a married woman, by strangulation; [14]"and has lifted up his eyes to the idols" — this is idolatry, by stoning. [15]And it is written:

TRANSLATION AND COMMENTARY

GEMARA פְּשִׁיטָא [1]We learned in the Mishnah: "If someone committed two capital offenses, so that he became liable to two different modes of judicial execution, he is sentenced to the more severe mode of execution." The Gemara objects: Surely **it is obvious** that a person guilty of two capital crimes is sentenced to the more severe mode of execution! [2]**Should he benefit** by violating two prohibitions and be sentenced to the more lenient punishment?

אָמַר רָבָא [3]**Rava said**: Indeed, it is obvious that if the offender had committed both transgressions before being tried for either offense, he is sentenced to the more severe mode of punishment. [4]But **here** in the Mishnah **we are dealing with** an offender who first [5]**committed the** more **lenient** capital **transgression,** and was brought to trial for that offense. **A verdict was issued regarding that** more **lenient transgression, and** only **then did he commit the** more **severe transgression.** [6]In such a case **you might have thought of saying** that, **since a verdict has been issued regarding the** more **lenient transgression,** and the offender has been sentenced to death, [7]**he is** already regarded as **a dead man,** so that he cannot become liable for subsequent transgressions. [8]**Therefore,** the Mishnah **teaches us** that this is not so, for he can still become liable to a more severe mode of execution if he commits a more severe transgression.

בְּעָא מִנֵּיהּ [9]**Rav Yosef bar Ḥama's father asked Rabbah bar Natan:** [10]**From where do we know what the Rabbis taught** in our Mishnah, that if someone committed two capital offenses, so that **he became liable to two** different **modes of judicial execution,** he **is sentenced to the more severe** mode of execution?

דִּכְתִיב [11]Rabbah bar Natan answered: This is derived from **the verses** that **state** (Ezekiel 18:10-12): **"If he has begotten a son** who **is a robber, a shedder of blood,** and who has done the like of any one of these things, though he has not done any of these, yet the other **has eaten on the mountains, and defiled his neighbor's wife,** has oppressed the poor and needy, has committed robbery, has not restored a pledge, **and has lifted up his eyes to the idols,** he has committed abomination." [12]**"If he has begotten a son** who **is a robber, a shedder of blood"** means that he murdered someone and became liable to death **by decapitation;** [13]**"and defiled his neighbor's wife"** means that he had sexual intercourse with **a married woman** and became liable to death **by strangulation;** [14]**"and has lifted up his eyes to the idols"** means that he committed **idolatry** and became liable to death **by stoning.** [15]**And** regarding such a person who committed all these offenses, **the**

RASHI

גמרא פשיטא — דבחמורה נדון, שהרי אף בה נתחייב דהיכי סליק אדעתן לידון בקלה? — וכי אתגורי אתגר במה שעבר שתי עבירות? אילו לא עבר אלא על החמורה היה נדון בה, ועכשיו שהוסיף לעבור עמה עבירה אחרת נדון בקלה?! **אמר רבא** — ודאי אי מקמי דאתא לקמן עבדינהו לתרוייהו לא איצטריך לאשמועינן, כי איצטריך לאתנייה כגון דנגמר דינו תחלה לקלה סלקא דעתך אמינא וכו׳. **מנא הא מילתא וכו׳** — ואף על גב דנגמר דינו לקלה.

TRANSLATION AND COMMENTARY

next **verse states** (verse 13): **"He shall surely die; his blood shall be upon him."** We learned earlier in the tractate that the expression "his blood shall be upon him" alludes to death **by stoning,** which is more severe than decapitation or strangulation. Thus, we see that if someone committed a number of capital offenses which are punishable by different modes of judicial execution, he is sentenced to the most severe mode of execution among them.

מַתְקִיף לָהּ [1]**Rav Naḥman bar Yitzḥak strongly objected:** Why not **say that all** the transgressions alluded to in these verses **are** punishable **by stoning?** How so? [2]**"If he has begotten a son** who **is a robber, a shedder of blood"** refers to **a stubborn and rebellious son, who is** liable to death **by stoning;** [3]**"and defiled his neighbor's wife"** means that he engaged in sexual intercourse with **a betrothed girl,** a crime punishable **by stoning;** [4]**"and has lifted up his eyes to the idols"** means that he committed **idolatry,** another crime punishable **by stoning."**

אִם כֵּן [5]The Gemara asks: Granted, according to the first explanation of these verses, the Prophet Ezekiel comes to teach us that if someone committed a number of capital offenses which are punishable by different modes of judicial execution, he is sentenced to the most severe mode of execution among them. But **if** it is **so,** that these verses allude to transgressions all of which are punishable by stoning, **what does Ezekiel** come to **teach us?** Surely it is obvious that such a person is put to death by stoning!

דִּלְמָא [6]The Gemara answers: **Perhaps** Ezekiel did not mean to teach anything new, but merely to **repeat what had been stated in the Torah,** and admonish the people to observe God's commandments.

אִם כֵּן [7]The Gemara rejects this argument: **If so,** Ezekiel **should have repeated** what is stated in the Torah, using the same formulations **as our master Moses used.** The wording of Ezekiel's admonitions proves that he was teaching a new law, that if someone committed several offenses that are punishable by modes of execution of varying degrees of severity, he is sentenced to the most severe mode of execution among them.

דָּרַשׁ [8]The Gemara now turns to the verses that immediately precede these in Ezekiel. **Rav Aḥa the son of Rabbi Ḥanina expounded: What is** meant by the verses that **state** (Ezekiel 18:5-9): "But if a man is righteous, and does that which is lawful and right, and has not eaten upon the mountains, nor lifted up his eyes to the idols of the house of Israel, nor defiled his neighbor's wife, nor come near to a menstruating woman...he is righteous; he shall surely live, says the Lord God"? Surely, these verses cannot be understood according to their plain sense, for a person who only refrains from violating the prohibitions referred to in

"מוֹת יוּמָת דָּמָיו בּוֹ יִהְיֶה" — בִּסְקִילָה.

[1]מַתְקִיף לָהּ רַב נַחְמָן בַּר יִצְחָק: אֵימָא כּוּלְּהוּ בִּסְקִילָה: [2]"וְהוֹלִיד בֵּן פָּרִיץ שֹׁפֵךְ דָּם" — זֶה בֵּן סוֹרֵר וּמוֹרֶה, דִּבִסְקִילָה. [3]"אֵשֶׁת רֵעֵהוּ טִמֵּא" — זוֹ נַעֲרָה הַמְאוֹרָסָה, דִּבִסְקִילָה. [4]"וְאֶל הַגִּלּוּלִים נָשָׂא עֵינָיו" — זוֹ עֲבוֹדָה זָרָה, דִּבִסְקִילָה.

[5]אִם כֵּן, מַאי קָא מַשְׁמַע לָן יְחֶזְקֵאל?

[6]דִּלְמָא, תּוֹרָה קָא מְהַדֵּר?

[7]אִם כֵּן אִיבָּעֵי לֵיהּ לְאַהְדּוֹרָהּ כִּי הֵיכִי דְּאַהַדְרָהּ מֹשֶׁה רַבֵּינוּ.

[8]דָּרַשׁ רַב אַחָא בְּרַבִּי חֲנִינָא:

LITERAL TRANSLATION

"He shall surely die; his blood shall be upon him" — by stoning.

[1]Rav Naḥman bar Yitzḥak strongly objected: Say that they are all [punishable] by stoning: [2]"If he has begotten a son who is a robber, a shedder of blood" — this is a stubborn and rebellious son, who is [punished] by stoning; [3]"and defiled his neighbor's wife" — this is a betrothed girl, which is [punished] by stoning; [4]"And has lifted up his eyes to the idols" — this is idolatry, which is [punished] by stoning."

[5]If so, what does Ezekiel teach us?

[6]Perhaps he repeats [what is stated in] the Torah.

[7]If so, he should have repeated it as Moses our master repeated it.

[8]Rav Aḥa the son of Rabbi Ḥanina expounded:

RASHI

בסקילה — דכל "דמיהם בם" בסקילה דהיא חמורה, ואי דלא נגמר דינו קודם לכן לא איצטריך קרא לאשמועינן. **בן סורר ומורה** — וקרי ליה שופך דם על שם שסופו לשפוך, כדאמרינן (עב,א) שעומד בפרשת דרכים וכו׳. **דאהדריה משה** — במשנה תורה.

SAGES

רַב נַחְמָן בַּר יִצְחָק Rav Naḥman bar Yitzḥak. One of the leading Babylonian Amoraim of the fourth generation, Rav Naḥman bar Yitzḥak was born in Sura. His mother was the sister of Rav Aḥa bar Yosef. His principal teacher was Rav Naḥman bar Ya'akov, but he also studied under Rav Ḥisda. After the death of Rava, Rav Naḥman bar Yitzḥak was appointed head of the Pumbedita Yeshivah.

NOTES

שֹׁפֵךְ דָּם — זֶה בֵּן סוֹרֵר וּמוֹרֶה A shedder of blood — this is a stubborn and rebellious son. *Rashi* explains that a stubborn and rebellious son is referred to here as "a shedder of blood," because of what he would do were he allowed to live, since his present conduct shows that he will eventually bring his parents to ruin, and become a robber and a murderer (see *Sanhedrin* 72a). *Rashash* suggests that he is called "a shedder of blood" because he causes his own blood to be shed as a result of his wicked behavior.

לְאַהְדּוֹרָהּ כְּמֹשֶׁה As Moses repeated it. Some understand the Gemara's argument as follows: Had Ezekiel really intended to repeat what had already been stated in the Torah, then he should have reviewed the entire Torah, as Moses did in the Book of Deuteronomy (*Ramah*).

מַאי דִּכְתִיב: [1] ״אֶל הֶהָרִים לֹא אָכָל״ — שֶׁלֹּא אָכַל בִּזְכוּת אֲבוֹתָיו. [2] ״וְעֵינָיו לֹא נָשָׂא אֶל גִּלּוּלֵי בֵּית יִשְׂרָאֵל״ — [3] שֶׁלֹּא הָלַךְ בְּקוֹמָה זְקוּפָה. [4] ״וְאֶת אֵשֶׁת רֵעֵהוּ לֹא טִמֵּא״ — שֶׁלֹּא יָרַד לְאוּמָּנוּת חֲבֵירוֹ. [5] ״וְאֶל אִשָּׁה נִדָּה לֹא קִירֵב״ — שֶׁלֹּא נֶהֱנָה מִקּוּפָּה שֶׁל צְדָקָה, [6] וּכְתִיב: ״צַדִּיק הוּא חָיֹה יִחְיֶה״. [7] כְּשֶׁהָיָה רַבָּן גַּמְלִיאֵל מַגִּיעַ לַמִּקְרָא הַזֶּה הָיָה בּוֹכֶה, וְאָמַר: [8] ״מַאן דְּעָבֵיד לְכוּלְּהוּ — הוּא דְּחַיֵּי, [9] בְּחֲדָא מִינַּיְיהוּ, לָא״. [10] אָמַר לֵיהּ רַבִּי עֲקִיבָא: ״אֶלָּא מֵעַתָּה ׳אַל תִּטַּמְּאוּ בְּכָל אֵלֶּה׳

LITERAL TRANSLATION

What is that which is written: [1] "And has not eaten upon the mountains" — who has not eaten by the virtue of his forefathers; [2] "Nor lifted up his eyes to the idols of the house of Israel" — [3] who has not walked with proud bearing; [4] "Nor defiled his neighbor's wife" — who has not trespassed upon someone else's occupation; [5] "Nor come near to a menstruating woman" — who has not benefited from the charity chest. [6] And it is written: "He is righteous; he shall surely live."

[7] When Rabban Gamliel reached this verse, he wept and said: [8] "Someone who performs all of these, he will live, [9] [but] one of them, not." [10] Rabbi Akiva said to him: "But now, 'Defile not yourselves in all of these things'

TRANSLATION AND COMMENTARY

these verses can hardly be called "righteous"! Rather, the words, [1] **"and has not eaten upon the mountains,"** intimate that the verse refers here to someone **who has not had to rely on the virtues of his** righteous **forefathers** (metaphorically referred to here as "mountains"), for he himself is a pious and righteous man; and the words, [2] **"nor lifted up his eyes to the idols of the house of Israel,"** intimate that he has distanced himself from anything resembling idol worship, [3] and so **he has not walked with a proud bearing,** for a proud and arrogant man is regarded as an idolator; and the words, [4] **"nor defiled his neighbor's wife,"** intimate that **he has not trespassed upon someone else's occupation,** stealing his business from him; and the words, [5] **"nor come near to a menstruating woman,"** intimate that **he has not benefited from the charity chest,** even in his time of need. [6] Regarding such a person, **the verse states: "He is righteous; he shall surely live."**

כְּשֶׁהָיָה [7] The Gemara continues with the following anecdote: **When Rabban Gamliel reached the verse** at the end of this passage in Ezekiel (verse 19), "And has kept all [כָּל] my statutes, and has done them, he shall surely live," **he wept, and said:** [8] "This verse implies that only **someone who performs all of** the good deeds mentioned here **will enjoy** eternal **life,** [9] **but** someone who performs only **one of them** will **not** enjoy eternal life. What will happen to all those who are unable to perform all of the commandments?" [10] **Rabbi Akiva said to** Rabban Gamliel in consolation: **"But now** that you understand the implications of this verse in this manner, regarding the verse that concludes the Torah passage relating to incest (Leviticus 18:24), **'Defile not yourselves in all [כָּל] of these things,'**

RASHI

אל ההרים לא אכל — סיפיה דקרא ״צדיק הוא חיה יחיה״, לומר, זה צדיק גמור ועל כרחך משום דלא עביד הני לאו צדיק הוא אם עבר עבירות אחרות, אלא לאו כמשמעותיה מדריש. **אל ההרים לא אכל** — שלא נצטרך לזכות אבותיו מתוך שהוא חסיד. **שלא נהנה מקופה של צדקה** — שהוא דבר גנאי לאדם הגון.

NOTES

שֶׁלֹּא יָרַד לְאוּמָּנוּת חֲבֵירוֹ Who has not trespassed upon someone else's occupation. This exposition of the verse is based on what the Gemara says elsewhere (*Kiddushin* 30b) about the verse (Ecclesiastes 9:9): "Live joyfully with the wife whom you love," that "the wife whom you love" refers to a vocation. Thus, a person who trespasses upon someone else's occupation can be seen as having defiled his neighbor's wife.

וְאֶל אִשָּׁה נִדָּה לֹא קִירֵב Nor come near to a menstruating woman. Taking from a charity chest is compared here to having intercourse with a woman who is menstruating, for when a person who is not in need takes from the charity chest, he receives undue benefit, just like someone who has intercourse with his wife while she is menstruating (*Ramah*). Alternatively, just as a woman is only temporarily forbidden to her husband while she is menstruating, and will eventually become permitted to him, so, too, is charity forbidden only to those who are not needy (*Ḥayyim Shenayim Yeshalem*). Or else we have here a play on the word נִדָּה, "menstruating woman," which is understood in this context as נֵדֶה, "gift" (Ezekiel 16:33), and therefore a fitting designation of a charity chest (*Rabbi M. Arak*).

שֶׁלֹּא נֶהֱנָה מִקּוּפָּה שֶׁל צְדָקָה Who has not benefited from the charity chest. Some understand that the Gemara refers here to a person who did not take from the charity chest when he was not actually in need (*Ramah, Meiri*). *Rashi* suggests that a distinguished person should not take from the charity chest, even if he is in real need, but rather should trust that God will provide for him. Some suggest that we are dealing here with a charity collector who is forbidden to take even a small amount of money from the charity chest for his own personal concerns, even if he plans to return the money afterwards (*Meiri*).

כָּל אֵלֶּה All of these. Some suggest that the discussion here is related to the Tannaitic dispute (see above, 78a) regarding the verse (Leviticus 24:17): "And he that kills *kol nefesh*," whether the words *kol nefesh* mean "an entire soul" or "any part of a soul" (*Torat Ḥayyim*).

— [1]הָכִי נַמִי, בְּכוּלְּהוּ, אִין, [2]בַּחֲדָא מִינַּיְיהוּ לָא? [3]אֶלָּא, בְּאַחַת מִכָּל אֵלֶּה; [4]הָכִי נַמִי, בְּאַחַת מִכֹּל אֵלֶּה״.
[5]״עָבַר עֲבֵירָה״. [6]תַּנְיָא: ״כֵּיצַד אָמַר רַבִּי יוֹסֵי: [7]נִידּוֹן בְּזִיקָּה רִאשׁוֹנָה הַבָּאָה עָלָיו? [8]חֲמוֹתוֹ וְנַעֲשֵׂית אֵשֶׁת אִישׁ, [9]נִידּוֹן בַּחֲמוֹתוֹ. [10]אֵשֶׁת אִישׁ וְנַעֲשֵׂית חֲמוֹתוֹ, [11]נִידּוֹן בְּאֵשֶׁת אִישׁ״.
[12]אָמַר לֵיהּ רַב אַדָּא בַּר אַהֲבָה לְרָבָא: ״חֲמוֹתוֹ וְנַעֲשֵׂית אֵשֶׁת אִישׁ, [13]נִידּוֹן בַּחֲמוֹתוֹ״? [14]לִידּוֹן נַמִי אַאִיסּוּר אֵשֶׁת אִישׁ, [15]דְּהָא אָמַר רַבִּי אַבָּהוּ: מוֹדֶה רַבִּי

LITERAL TRANSLATION

— [1]thus also, all of them, yes, [2][but] one of them, not? [3]Rather, in one of all these; [4]so, too, one of all those."

[5]"[If] he committed a transgression." [6]It was taught: "How did Rabbi Yose say: [7]He is sentenced for the first obligation that applied to him? [8]His mother-in-law, who became a married woman, [9]he is sentenced for his mother-in-law. [10]A married woman who became his mother-in-law, [11]he is sentenced for a married woman."

[12]Rav Adda bar Aḥavah said to Rava: "His mother-in-law who became a married woman, [13]he is sentenced for his mother-in-law." [14]Let him be sentenced also for the prohibition regarding a married woman, [15]for surely Rabbi Abbahu said: Rabbi

TRANSLATION AND COMMENTARY

[1]would you say that **here, too,** only someone who defiles himself by violating **all of** the prohibitions regarding incest will **indeed** be punished, [2]**but** someone who defiles himself by violating only **one of** the prohibitions will **not** be punished? Surely this is not the intent of that verse! [3]**Rather,** the verse means to say: Defile not yourselves by violating **one of these** prohibitions. [4]**So, too,** the verse in Ezekiel means to say that someone who has kept **one of those** statutes will enjoy eternal life."

עָבַר עֲבֵירָה [5]We have learned in the Mishnah: **"If someone committed a** single **transgression** for which he is liable to two modes of judicial execution, he is sentenced to the more severe mode of execution. Rabbi Yose disagrees and says: He is sentenced for violating the prohibition that applied to him first." [6]**It was taught** in a related Baraita: **"What did Rabbi Yose** mean when he **said:** [7]**He is sentenced for violating the prohibition that applied to him first?** [8]If someone married the daughter of a widow or a divorcee, so that her mother became forbidden to him as **his mother-in-law,** and then the mother remarried, so that she was now also forbidden to him as **a married woman,** and then he had sexual intercourse with her, [9]**he is sentenced** to death by burning for having intercourse with **his mother-in-law,** which is the prohibition that applied to him first. [10]If someone was forbidden to a certain woman as **a married woman,** and he then married her daughter, so that now the woman was also forbidden to him as **his mother-in-law,** and then he had sexual intercourse with the mother, [11]**he is sentenced** to death by strangulation for having intercourse with **a married woman,** even though the second prohibition carries the more severe punishment of death by burning. The prohibition against having intercourse with a married woman applied to him first, and a second violation cannot take effect where another transgression already exists."

אָמַר לֵיהּ [12]**Rav Adda bar Aḥavah said to Rava:** It was taught in the Baraita: "If someone married the daughter of a widow or a divorcee, so that her mother became forbidden to him as **his mother-in-law,** and then the mother married, so that she was now also forbidden to him as **a married woman,** and then he had sexual intercourse with her, [13]**he is sentenced** to death by burning for having intercourse with **his mother-in-law,** for that prohibition had applied to him first." [14]But **let** the man **be sentenced also for** violating **the prohibition** against intercourse with **a married woman,** [15]**for surely Rabbi Abbahu said: Rabbi Yose agrees about a prohibition that adds!** Rabbi Yose maintains that a general rule applies to the Torah's prohibitions: Once an object or action is prohibited, additional prohibitions cannot apply to it. But even he agrees that an exception is made when the second prohibition is extended to additional individuals, or for a longer period of time, or with greater severity than the first. Thus, in our case the prohibition against intercourse with a married woman should take effect even though the woman is already forbidden as the transgressors's mother-in-law. Before the woman married, she was forbidden only to her son-in-law, but when she married, she became forbidden to all men except her husband. Since the second prohibition

RASHI

בזיקה הראשונה — באותו איסור שהוזקק זה תחלה להזהר בו ולפרוש ממנו הוא נדון, אבל לא באיסור הבא עליו אחרון אף על פי שהוא חמור, דקסבר רבי יוסי אין איסור חל על איסור ואפילו חמור על הקל — הלכך אין כאן שתי מיתות. **חמותו ונעשית אשת איש** — כגון נשא בת אלמנה ונאסרה אמה משום חמותו. ואחר כך נשאת ונאסרה עליו משום אשת איש — נדון בחמורה, בשריפה, דהיא קדמה. אבל אם היתה אשת איש ונעשית חמותו — הואיל כשנשא בתה כבר היתה זו אסורה עליו משום אשת איש — תו לא חייל אסור חמותו אאסור אשת איש, ואינו נדון אלא בחנק. **דאמר רבי אבהו** — ביבמות בפרק ״ארבעה אחין״. מודה רבי

LANGUAGE

כִּיפָּה Chamber. This term apparently derives from כְּפִיָּה, "coercion," and כְּפִפָה, "subjection," and it means a place where a person is imprisoned by force. In Targum Yonatan to Jeremiah (20,2), the Hebrew מַהְפֶּכֶת, "prison," is rendered in Aramaic as כיפתא, "vault."

TRANSLATION AND COMMENTARY

applies to all men, it should also apply to the man to whom she was already forbidden — her son-in-law! [81B] [1]Rava **said to** Rav Adda bar Ahavah: **Adda, my son, can you execute** a person **by way of two modes of execution?** Rabbi Yose agrees that the prohibition against intercourse with a married woman applies also to a man to whom the woman was already forbidden — her son-in-law. Consequently, if someone inadvertently engaged in sexual intercourse with his mother-in-law after she remarried, he is liable for two guilt-offerings. But here the man intentionally engaged in sexual intercourse with the woman, violating both prohibitions. Therefore he is sentenced to the more severe punishment of death by burning for having intercourse with his mother-in-law. Obviously, he cannot also be sentenced to death by strangulation for having intercourse with a married woman.

MISHNAH מִי שֶׁלָּקָה [2]**If someone** sinned and **was flogged, and then** he repeated his offense, and was flogged **a second time**, and then he committed that same offense a third time, [3]**the court puts him in a** narrow, vaulted prison-**chamber,** [4]**and feeds him barley until his stomach bursts** and he dies.

GEMARA מִשּׁוּם [5]The Gemara asks in astonishment: Is it possible that, just **because** a person **was flogged** for some relatively minor offense, **and then** he repeated that offense and was flogged **a second time,** [6]**the court puts him in a** narrow, vaulted prison-**chamber** for a third offense and allows him to die there?

יוֹסֵי בְּאִיסּוּר מוֹסִיף! [81B]
[1]אֲמַר לֵיהּ: אַדָּא בְּרִי, בִּתְרֵי קָטְלֵי קָטְלַתְּ לֵיהּ?
מִשְׁנָה [2]מִי שֶׁלָּקָה וְשָׁנָה, [3]בֵּית דִּין מַכְנִיסִין אוֹתוֹ לַכִּיפָּה, [4]וּמַאֲכִילִין אוֹתוֹ שְׂעוֹרִין, עַד שֶׁכְּרֵיסוֹ מִתְבַּקַּעַת.
גְּמָרָא [5]מִשּׁוּם דְּלָקָה וְשָׁנָה, [6]בֵּית דִּין כּוֹנְסִין אוֹתוֹ לַכִּיפָּה?

LITERAL TRANSLATION

Yose agrees about a prohibition that adds! [81B] [1]He said to him: Adda, my son, do you execute him with two [modes of] execution?

MISHNAH [2][If] someone was flogged and then again a second time, [3]the court puts him in a chamber, [4]and feeds him barley, until his stomach bursts.

GEMARA [5]Because he was flogged and then again a second time, [6]the court puts him in a chamber?

RASHI

יוסי באסור מוסיף – ומחדש דבר על האשה הזאת לאסור בה דבר חדש (או) לאסרה על מי שלא היתה אסורה עליו מתחלה, כגון הכא כשהיתה אלמנה והיא חמותו היתה אסורה לו משום חמותו ומותרת לכל אדם. וכשנעשית אשת איש הוסיף בה השם הזה איסור שאסרה לכל העולם, וכי האי גוונא מודה רבי יוסי דאסור חל על אסור, מגו דחייל אכולא עלמא שהיתה מותרת להם עד עכשיו – חייל נמי אהאי ואף על פי שאסורה לו ועומדת. **אמר ליה אדא ברי בתרי קטלי קטלת ליה?** בתמיה, אמת שחלו שתיהן עליו, ועבירה שיש בה שתי מיתות – הוא נדון בחמורה, והילך אתה בא לדונו אף באשת איש, וכי תהרגנו שתי פעמים?! וכי חייל אשת איש אחמותו לרבי יוסי לענין שוגג הוא, ולהתחייב שתי חטאות.

משנה מי שלקה ושנה – שלקה שתי פעמים על שתי עבירות.

NOTES

אִיסּוּר מוֹסִיף A prohibition that adds. The Tannaim disagree about whether additional prohibitions can apply to a prohibited object or an action. Even those who say that, as a rule, one prohibition cannot be added to another, concede that there are certain exceptions: (1) If two prohibitions come into effect at the same time, a person transgressing them is liable on both counts. For example, when a man marries a woman, she becomes forbidden to his brother, both because of the prohibition against relations with a married woman, and because of the prohibition against relations with one's brother's wife, for they come into effect at the same time. (2) The second prohibition takes effect if is is more comprehensive than the first. For example, if a man marries his brother's wife's sister, his brother's wife is now forbidden to him not only because of the prohibition against relations with one's brother's wife, but also because of the prohibition against relations with one's wife's sister, which is more comprehensive than the first prohibition because it applies also to his wife's other sisters. (3) The second prohibition takes effect if it also applies to additional individuals, or for a longer period of time, or with greater severity than the first. For example, if a man's sister marries, she is forbidden to him not only because of the prohibition against relations with one's sister, but also because of the prohibition against relations with a married woman, which adds to the first prohibition because it applies not only to her brother, but to all men.

מַכְנִיסִין אוֹתוֹ לַכִּיפָּה They put him in a chamber. The Rishonim discuss at length the source of the law permitting the court to incarcerate an offender and allow him to die in prison. They ask whether the law was given to Moses at Sinai or whether it is a Rabbinic enactment designed to protect society from criminals who had escaped punishment by Torah law. Concern to protect society from known criminals is particularly evident in the case of murder. Starving a murderer to death also fulfills the Biblical injunctions of Numbers 35:33: "And the land cannot be cleansed of the blood that is shed therein, but by the blood of him that shed it," and Deuteronomy 13:6: "And you shall put the evil away from the midst of you" (see *Rabbi David Bonfils, Ran,* and *Tzofnat Pa'ane'aḥ*).

HALAKHAH

מַכְנִיסִין אוֹתוֹ לַכִּיפָּה They put him in a chamber. "If someone was flogged for violating a prohibition punishable by excision, and then he was flogged again for violating that prohibition a second time, and then he violated it again, he is not subject to additional lashes. Rather, he is thrown into a prison-chamber," following the Mishnah and the Gemara, and against the position of Abba Shaul. (*Rambam, Sefer Shofetim, Hilkhot Sanhedrin* 18:4.)

[1]אָמַר רַבִּי יִרְמְיָה אָמַר רַבִּי שִׁמְעוֹן בֶּן לָקִישׁ: [2]הָכָא בְּמַלְקִיּוֹת שֶׁל כְּרִיתוּת עָסְקִינַן, [3]דְּגַבְרָא בַּר קְטָלָא הוּא, וְקָרוֹבֵי הוּא דְּלָא מִיקְרַב קְטָלֵיהּ. [4]וְכֵיוָן דְּקָא מְוַתֵּר לָהּ נַפְשֵׁיהּ, [5]מְקָרְבִינַן לֵיהּ לִקְטָלֵיהּ עִילָוֵיהּ.

[6]אָמַר לֵיהּ רַבִּי יַעֲקֹב לְרַבִּי יִרְמְיָה בַּר תַּחֲלִיפָא: תָּא אַסְבְּרָא לָךְ: [7]בְּמַלְקִיּוֹת שֶׁל כָּרֵת אַחַת. [8]אֲבָל שֶׁל שְׁתַּיִם וְשֶׁל שָׁלֹשׁ כְּרִיתוּת — [9]אִיסּוּרֵי הוּא דְּקָא טָעֵים, [10]וְלֹא מְוַתֵּר כּוּלֵּי הַאי.

[11]״מִי שֶׁלָּקָה וְשָׁנָה״. [12]שָׁנָה, אַף עַל גַּב דְּלֹא שִׁילֵּשׁ. [13]לֵימָא מַתְנִיתִין דְּלָא כְּרַבָּן שִׁמְעוֹן בֶּן גַּמְלִיאֵל, [14]דְּאִי רַבָּן שִׁמְעוֹן בֶּן גַּמְלִיאֵל, [15]הָא אָמַר: עַד תְּלָת זִימְנֵי לָא הָוְיָא חֲזָקָה!

[16]אָמַר רָבִינָא: אֲפִילּוּ תֵּימָא

LITERAL TRANSLATION

[1]Rabbi Yirmeyah said in the name of Rabbi Shimon ben Lakish: [2]Here we are dealing with lashes for [violating a prohibition punishable by] excision, [3]when the person is liable to death, but his death is not yet near. [4]Since he forfeits his life, [5]we bring his death closer.

[6]Rabbi Ya'akov said to Rabbi Yirmeyah bar Taḥlifa: Come, I will explain [it] to you: [7]With lashes for a single [violated prohibition punishable by] excision. [8]But two or three [violated prohibitions punishable by] excision — [9]he is tasting forbidden things, [10]but does not forfeit that much.

[11]"[If] someone was flogged and then again a second time." [12][If he was flogged] a second time, even if not a third time. [13]Shall we say [that] our Mishnah is not like Rabban Shimon ben Gamliel, [14]for if it is Rabban Shimon ben Gamliel, [15]surely he said: Without three occurrences, there is no presumption!

[16]Ravina said: You can even say

TRANSLATION AND COMMENTARY

אָמַר רַבִּי יִרְמְיָה [1]**Rabbi Yirmeyah said in the name of Rabbi Shimon ben Lakish:** If a person repeatedly violated an ordinary negative precept that is subject to the penalty of lashes, he is indeed flogged for each offense, and not thrown into a prison-chamber, even if he committed the crime 100 times. [2]But **here,** in the Mishnah, **we are dealing with** someone who received **lashes for** violating **a prohibition punishable by excision** (someone who does this is subject to lashes if he was warned about lashes before committing his offense). [3]Such **a person is liable to** premature or sudden **death** at the hand of Heaven, **but** he is still alive because the time appointed by God for **his death** has **not yet** come. [4]**Since he** himself **forfeits his life** by repeatedly violating a prohibition that is punishable by excision, [5]**we may hasten his death.**

אָמַר לֵיהּ [6]**Rabbi Ya'akov said to Rabbi Yirmeyah bar Taḥlifa: Come, I will explain to you** the details regarding this law: [7]Here, in the Mishnah, we are dealing **with** someone who has received **lashes** twice **for** violating **the same prohibition that is punishable by excision.** If he committed that same offense a third time, he is thrown into prison and allowed to die. [8]**But** if someone has been flogged for **two or three** different **prohibitions** which **are punishable by excision,** he is not locked up in a prison-chamber for his next offense, for his actions show that he committed those offenses [9]because **he** wished to **taste** various **forbidden things,** [10]**and not** because he was ready to **forfeit** his life.

מִי שֶׁלָּקָה [11]We have learned in our Mishnah: **"If someone** sinned and **was flogged, and then** repeated his offense and was flogged **a second time,** and then he committed that same offense again, the court locks him up in a narrow, vaulted prison-chamber and feeds him barley until his stomach bursts and he dies." [12]A careful reading of the Mishnah teaches that, **if** the chronic offender was flogged **a second time,** he is thrown into the prison-chamber, **even if** he was **not** flogged **a third time.** [13]The Gemara now asks: **Shall we say that our Mishnah** — which maintains that a person can be established as a chronic offender after only two floggings — **does not follow** the position of **Rabban Shimon ben Gamliel,** [14]**for if** our Mishnah **follows** the position of **Rabban Shimon ben Gamliel,** there is a difficulty. [15]**Surely he said** elsewhere, with regard to the prohibition against marrying a woman who has been widowed a number of times, that **until the same thing happens on three** separate **occasions, a presumption** that it will happen again **is not established.** In his view, two offenses do not make a chronic offender.

אָמַר רָבִינָא [16]The Gemara rejects this argument: **Ravina said: You can even say** that our Mishnah follows

RASHI

גמרא של כריתות — לאו שיש בו כרת והתרו בו למלקות. דגברא בר קטלא הוא — בידי שמים יכרתוהו. וקרובי הוא דלא מקרב קטלא — עדיין לא נתקרבה מיתתו. דמוותר נפשיה — דמפקיר עצמו לעבירות. של כרת אחת — שעבר אותה עבירה עצמה שלש פעמים — על השתים לוקה, ובשלישית יכנסוהו לכיפה. דרבן שמעון — ביבמות, נשאת לראשון — ומת, לשני — ומת, לשלישי תנשא, לרביעי לא תנשא. דעד תלתא זימנין לא הויה מוחזקת לקבור את בעליה. לימא מתניתין — דבשתי מלקיות מחזקת ליה רשע ובעי כיפה, דלא כרבן שמעון בן גמליאל.

TRANSLATION AND COMMENTARY

the position of **Rabban Shimon ben Gamliel.** [1]The Tanna of our Mishnah **maintains** that it is the offender's **transgressions** — and not the punishments that he receives — that **establish the presumption** he is a chronic offender. After transgressing twice and being flogged twice, he committed the same offense again, establishing the presumption that he is a chronic offender, and so he is thrown into prison and allowed to die.

מֵיתִיבִי [2]**An objection was raised** against Ravina from the following Baraita: **"If someone committed a transgression that is subject to lashes the first and the second time, they flog him.** [3]If he committed that same transgression **a third time, they put him in a** narrow, vaulted prison-**chamber,** where he is allowed to die. [4]**Abba Shaul** disagrees and **says: Even** if he committed that same transgression **a third time, they flog him.** [5]Only if he committed that transgression **a fourth time, do they put him in a** prison-**chamber,** where he is allowed to die." About what issue do the Tannaim disagree? [6]**Is it not that all** the Tannaim — the anonymous first Tanna of the Baraita and Abba Shaul — [7]**maintain that** it is the **lashes** the offender receives — and not his transgressions — that **establish the presumption** that he is a chronic offender, [8]**and** that **they disagree about the matter in dispute between Rabbi** Yehudah HaNasi **and Rabban Shimon ben Gamliel** regarding the number of times the same thing must occur before a presumption is established that it will happen again. The anonymous first Tanna, who says that the offender is thrown into the prison-chamber after two floggings, agrees with Rabbi Yehudah HaNasi, who said that if the same thing happens twice, a presumption is established that it will happen again. And Abba Shaul, who says that the offender is only thrown into the prison-chamber if he was flogged three times, agrees with Rabban Shimon ben Gamliel that a presumption is only established after three repetitions. Since the position of our Mishnah corresponds to that of the anonymous first Tanna of the Baraita, it cannot follow the view of Rabban Shimon ben Gamliel, against Ravina!

לָא [9]However, the issue as to whether the transgression or the lashes establish the presumption has not been laid to rest. **No, all** the Tannaim whose views are recorded in the Baraita **accept** the position of **Rabban Shimon ben Gamliel** that three violations are necessary to establish a presumption that it will happen again. [10]**And here** the Tannaim **disagree about** the following matter: [11]**One Sage** — the anonymous first Tanna of the Baraita — **maintains** that the offender's **transgressions establish the presumption** that he is a chronic offender, so he is thrown into the prison-chamber after committing the same transgression a third time. [12]**And the other Sage** — Abba Shaul — **maintains** that **lashes establish the presumption** that he is a chronic offender. Thus the offender is only thrown into the prison-chamber the fourth time that he commits the same transgression, after having already received three floggings.

רַבָּן שִׁמְעוֹן בֶּן גַּמְלִיאֵל, [1]קָסָבַר: עֲבֵירוֹת מַחֲזִיקוֹת. [2]מֵיתִיבִי: "עָבַר עֲבֵירָה שֶׁיֵּשׁ בָּהּ מַלְקוּת פַּעַם רִאשׁוֹנָה וּשְׁנִיָּה, מַלְקִין אוֹתוֹ. [3]וּשְׁלִישִׁית כּוֹנְסִין אוֹתוֹ לַכִּיפָּה. [4]אַבָּא שָׁאוּל אוֹמֵר: אַף בַּשְּׁלִישִׁית מַלְקִין אוֹתוֹ. [5]בָּרְבִיעִית כּוֹנְסִין אוֹתוֹ לַכִּיפָּה". [6]מַאי לָאו, [7]דְּכוּלֵּי עָלְמָא מַלְקֻיּוֹת מַחֲזִיקוֹת, [8]וּבִפְלוּגְתָּא דְּרַבִּי וְרַבָּן שִׁמְעוֹן בֶּן גַּמְלִיאֵל קָמִיפַּלְגִי! [9]לָא, דְּכוּלֵּי עָלְמָא אִית לְהוּ דְּרַבָּן שִׁמְעוֹן בֶּן גַּמְלִיאֵל, [10]וְהָכָא בְּהָא קָא מִיפַּלְגִי, [11]דְּמָר סָבַר: עֲבֵירוֹת מַחֲזִיקוֹת, [12]וּמָר סָבַר: מַלְקֻיּוֹת מַחֲזִיקוֹת.

LITERAL TRANSLATION

Rabban Shimon ben Gamliel. [1]He maintains: Transgressions establish the presumption.

[2]They raised an objection: "[If] he committed a transgression that is subject to lashes the first and [the] second time, they flog him. [3]The third time they put him in a chamber. [4]Abba Shaul says: Also the third time they flog him. [5]The fourth time they put him in a chamber." [6]Is it not [7]that they all maintain [that] lashes establish the presumption, [8]and they disagree about the [matter in] dispute between Rabbi and Rabban Shimon ben Gamliel? [9]No, everyone (lit., "the entire world") has Rabban Shimon ben Gamliel, [10]and here they disagree about this. [11]One Sage maintains: Transgressions establish the presumption. [12]And the other Sage maintains: Lashes establish the presumption.

RASHI

עבירות מחזיקות — אותו בחזקת רשע הוא, וההתראה ולא מלקות, הלכך בשלישי כונסין אותו לכיפה דהא איתחזק ליה בשלש עבירות. **מיתיבי** — לרבינא דמהדר לאוקומה למתניתין כרבן שמעון בן גמליאל, מדפליג אבא שאול ואמר כרבן שמעון בן גמליאל — מכלל דתנא קמא לאו כרבן שמעון בן גמליאל. **ומר סבר לא הוחזק עד שילקה שלש מלקיות** — וכיון דלקי על השלישית אף על גב דאיתחזק השתא רשע לא מעיילינן ליה לכיפה, דבתרי דיני לא דיינינן ליה.

TRANSLATION AND COMMENTARY

וְהָדְתַנְיָא [1]The Gemara questions this interpretation of the Tannaitic dispute: **But surely it was taught** in another Baraita: **"If** witnesses **warned** the offender regarding lashes, **and he remained silent,** appearing to acknowledge the warning tacitly, [2]**or they warned him** regarding lashes, **and he bowed his head,** nodding his assent, but not stating it explicitly, such warnings do not suffice to make the offender subject to lashes. However, they do help establish the presumption that he is a chronic offender. [3]Thus, **the first and the second time** that he commits the offense after being warned, **they** merely **warn him** again and set him free. [4]But **the third time** that he commits the offense, **they put him in a** prison-**chamber,** and leave him to die. [5]**Abba Shaul** disagrees and **says:** Even if he commits the same transgression **a third time, they** merely **warn him** against future wrongdoing. [6]Only if he commits that transgression **a fourth time, do they put him in a** prison-**chamber** where he is allowed to die." [7]**Now** in this example **there are no lashes** at all, for the offender did not explicitly acknowledge the warning. Surely then all must agree that transgressions and not the lashes establish the presumption! [8]**About what,** then, **do they disagree?** Why does Abba Shaul say that the offender is only put in the prison-chamber after committing the transgression a fourth time?

אָמַר רָבִינָא [9]**Ravina said:** Both the anonymous first Tanna of the Baraita and Abba Shaul maintain that the offender's transgressions — following warnings regarding lashes, whether acknowledged explicitly or implicitly — establish the presumption that he is a chronic offender. And they both accept the position of Rabban Shimon ben Gamliel that a presumption is only established after three occurrences. [10]The Tannaim **disagree about whether a warning is required** before the offender is thrown into the prison-**chamber.** According to the anonymous first Tanna, the third time the sinner violates the prohibition he is established as a chronic offender, and so he is thrown into the prison-chamber because a warning about that penalty is not necessary. Abba Shaul disagrees and says that, even after the sinner is established as a chronic offender, he cannot be thrown into the prison-chamber until he violates the prohibition a fourth time, before which he must be warned that, if he sins again, he will suffer that punishment.

וּמַאי כִּיפָה [11]The Gemara asks: **What is** the nature of the prison-**chamber** mentioned in our Mishnah? [12]**Rav Yehudah said:** This prison-chamber is a narrow, vaulted room the **height of a man.**

LITERAL TRANSLATION

[1]But that which was taught: "[If] they warned him, and he was silent, [2][or] they warned him, and he bowed his head — [3]the first and the second time, they warn him, [4]the third time, they put him in a chamber. [5]Abba Shaul says: Also the third time they warn him; [6]the fourth time they put him in a chamber." [7]And there are no lashes. [8]About what do they disagree?
[9]Ravina said: [10]They disagree about whether a chamber requires a warning.
[11]And what is a chamber? [12]Rav Yehudah said: His full height.

וְהָדְתַנְיָא: "הִתְרוּ בּוֹ וְשָׁתַק,
²הִתְרוּ בּוֹ וְהִרְכִּין רֹאשׁוֹ, ³פַּעַם
רִאשׁוֹנָה וּשְׁנִיָּה מַתְרִין בּוֹ;
⁴שְׁלִישִׁית, כּוֹנְסִין אוֹתוֹ לַכִּיפָה. ⁵אַבָּא שָׁאוּל אוֹמֵר: אַף
בַּשְּׁלִישִׁית מַתְרִין בּוֹ;
⁶בָּרְבִיעִית כּוֹנְסִין אוֹתוֹ
לַכִּיפָה". ⁷וְהָתָם מַלְקוּת לֵיכָּא.
⁸בְּמַאי קָמִיפַּלְגִי?
⁹אָמַר רָבִינָא: ¹⁰בְּכִיפָּה צְרִיכָה
הַתְרָאָה קָמִיפַּלְגִי.
¹¹וּמַאי כִּיפָּה? ¹²אָמַר רַב
יְהוּדָה: מְלֹא קוֹמָתוֹ.

RASHI

הִתְרוּ בּוֹ וְשָׁתַק — שֶׁהַרְאָה בְּעַצְמוֹ כִּמְקַבֵּל הַתְרָאָה, וּמֵיהוּ לֹא הִתִּיר עַצְמוֹ לְמַלְקוּת בְּהֶדְיָא, וְכֵן בְּהִרְכִּין בְּרֹאשׁוֹ וְרָמַז שֶׁהוּא מְקַבְּלָהּ. אַף עַל פִּי דְּלֹא לָקֵי בְּהַתְרָאוֹת כִּי הַנֵּי דְּלֹא הִתִּיר עַצְמוֹ לְמַלְקוּת — מִכָּל מָקוֹם הַתְרָאוֹת נִינְהוּ לְהַחְזִיקוֹ רָשָׁע. וּפַעַם רִאשׁוֹנָה מַתְרִין בֵּיהּ וְשָׁבְקִין לֵיהּ, וְכֵן בַּעֲבֵירָה שְׁנִיָּה שָׁבְקִין לֵיהּ, וּבַשְּׁלִישִׁית מַתְרִין בֵּיהּ לְמַלְקוּת וְכוֹנְסִין אוֹתוֹ לְכִיפָה עָלֶיהָ, שֶׁהֲרֵי הוּחְזַק רָשָׁע בְּשָׁלֹשׁ עֲבֵירוֹת שֶׁל הַתְרָאַת מַלְקוּת. אַבָּא שָׁאוּל אוֹמֵר וְכוּ' — וְהָא הָכָא מַלְקוּת לֵיכָּא דְּלֹא הִתִּיר עַצְמוֹ לְמַלְקוּת שֶׁהֲרֵי שָׁתַק, דְּנֵימָא טַעֲמָא דְּאַבָּא שָׁאוּל מִשּׁוּם דְּמַלְקִיּוֹת מְחֻזָּקוֹת וְלֹא הוּחְזַק עַד שִׁילְקָה, וְכֵיוָן דְּלָקָה עַל הַשְּׁלִישִׁית לֹא עָיֵיל לֵיהּ לְכִיפָה. בְּמַאי קָא מִיפְלְגִי — וְהָא לֹא לְרָבִינָא מוֹתִיב דְּהָא לְדִידֵן נַמִּי קַשְׁיָא, — דְּבִפְלוּגְתָּא דְּרַבִּי שִׁמְעוֹן וְרַבָּן שִׁמְעוֹן בֶּן גַּמְלִיאֵל לֹא מַלֵּינוּ לְאוֹקוּמָהּ, דְּהָא עַל כָּרְחָךְ עֲבֵירוֹת מַחֲזִיקוֹת סְבִירָא לְהוּ, דְּהָא אֵין כָּאן מַלְקוּת! וּמַאי אָמְרִי בֵּי אַבָּא שָׁאוּל רְבִיעִית? אָמַר רָבִינָא — בֵּין הַכָּא בֵּין בְּמַתְנִיתִין קַמַּיְיתָא בְּכִיפָה צְרִיכָה הַתְרָאָה קָא מִיפְלְגִי, וּדְכוּלֵי עָלְמָא כְּרַבָּן שִׁמְעוֹן בֶּן גַּמְלִיאֵל וְלֹא הוּחְזַק עַד שָׁלֹשׁ עֲבֵירוֹת שֶׁל הַתְרָאַת מַלְקוּת מְקוּבָלוֹת אוֹ בְּפִיו, אוֹ בִּשְׁתִיקָה, אוֹ בְּהַרְכָּנַת רֹאשׁ. וְקָמִיפְלְגִי בְּכִיפָה אִי צְרִיכָה הַתְרָאָה. — תַּנָא קַמָּא סָבַר כֵּיוָן שֶׁהוּחְזַק רָשָׁע עַל שָׁלֹשׁ הַתְרָאוֹת שֶׁל מַלְקוּת כּוֹנְסִין אוֹתוֹ לְכִיפָה, וְאַף עַל פִּי שֶׁלֹּא הוּתְרָה עַל כָּךְ. וְאַבָּא שָׁאוּל סָבַר — עַל שָׁלֹשׁ הַתְרָאוֹת שֶׁל מַלְקוּת הוּחְזַק רָשָׁע, וְלֹא עַל הַשְּׁתִיס, וּמִשְׁתַּמֵּא בְּעֵינָן עֲבֵירָה רְבִיעִית לְהַתְרוֹת בּוֹ: אִם תַּעֲבוֹר — מַכְנֵס לְכִיפָה. מְלֹא קוֹמָתוֹ — גּוּבַהּ.

HALAKHAH

הִתְרוּ בּוֹ וְשָׁתַק **If they warned him, and he was silent.** "If someone violated a prohibition punishable by excision or judicial execution, and when he was forewarned, he remained silent or bowed his head, but did not explicitly accept the warning, he is not liable to execution or lashes. If this happened again, he is still not liable to execution or lashes. If this happened yet again, he is put into a prison-chamber and kept there until he dies. In those cases where the offender did not explicitly accept the warning, he is liable to lashes by Rabbinic decree." (Rambam, Sefer Shofetim, Hilkhot Sanhedrin 18:5.)

LANGUAGE (RASHI)

אמ״ו* Should apparently read אי״ם, the Old French *aim*, meaning "a hook."

TRANSLATION AND COMMENTARY

וְהֵיכָא רְמִיזָא [1]The Gemara asks: **Where is there an allusion** in the Bible to such a punishment? [2]**Resh Lakish said:** This penalty is alluded to in the verse (Psalms 34:22): **"Evil shall slay the wicked,"** meaning that a chronically wicked man ought to die.

וְאָמַר רֵישׁ לָקִישׁ [3]Having cited this homiletical remark by Resh Lakish, the Gemara now cites another: **Resh Lakish said: What is** meant by the verse that **states** (Ecclesiastes 9:12): **"For man also knows not his time; like the fish that are taken in an evil net"?** [4]**What is** meant here by **"an evil net"?** [5]**Resh Lakish said:** This refers to **a fishhook,** which, though small, can catch big fish.

MISHNAH הַהוֹרֵג נֶפֶשׁ [6]**If** it is clear to the court that **someone killed** another **person,** but for technical reasons he cannot be executed, as when there were **no** valid **witnesses** to the crime, [7]**they put him in a** narrow, vaulted prison-**chamber,** [8]**and feed him** what the Prophet called (Isaiah 30:20) **"bread of adversity and water of affliction"** until he dies.

GEMARA מְנָא יָדְעִינַן [9]The Gemara asks: If there were no witnesses to the crime, then **how do we know** that the defendant is guilty?

אָמַר רַב [10]**Rav said:** In this case the two witnesses saw the crime **separately.** One witness viewed the event from one window, and the other saw it from another window, and they did not see each other. Such testimony is accepted as the truth, but for technical reasons is insufficient for judicial execution. In such a case, the court may throw the defendant into a narrow prison-chamber where he is left to die.

וּשְׁמוּאֵל אָמַר [11]**Shmuel said:** Here in the Mishnah there were two witnesses to the crime, but they did **not** formally **warn** the defendant that he was about to commit a capital offense. He cannot be executed without such a warning, but he may be thrown into prison and kept there until he dies.

[1]וְהֵיכָא רְמִיזָא? [2]אָמַר רֵישׁ לָקִישׁ: ״תְּמוֹתֵת רָשָׁע רָעָה״. [3]וְאָמַר רֵישׁ לָקִישׁ: מַאי דִּכְתִיב: ״כִּי [גַם] לֹא יֵדַע הָאָדָם אֶת עִתּוֹ כַּדָּגִים שֶׁנֶּאֱחָזִים בִּמְצוֹדָה רָעָה?״ [4]מַאי ״מְצוֹדָה רָעָה״? [5]אָמַר רֵישׁ לָקִישׁ: חַכָּה.

משנה [6]הַהוֹרֵג נֶפֶשׁ שֶׁלֹּא בְעֵדִים, [7]מַכְנִיסִין אוֹתוֹ לַכִּיפָּה, [8]וּמַאֲכִילִין אוֹתוֹ לֶחֶם צַר וּמַיִם לַחַץ.

גמרא [9]מְנָא יָדְעִינַן? [10]אָמַר רַב: בְּעֵדוּת מְיוּחֶדֶת. [11]וּשְׁמוּאֵל אָמַר: שֶׁלֹּא בְּהַתְרָאָה.

LITERAL TRANSLATION

[1]And where is there an allusion? [2]Resh Lakish said: "Evil shall slay the wicked."

[3]And Resh Lakish said: What is that which is written: "For man also knows not his time; like the fish that are taken in an evil net"? [4]What is "an evil net"? [5]Resh Lakish said: A fishhook.

MISHNAH [6][If] someone killed a person without witnesses, [7]they put him in a chamber, [8]and feed him bread of adversity and water of affliction.

GEMARA [9]From where do we know?

[10]Rav said: With separated evidence.

[11]And Shmuel said: Without a warning.

RASHI

והיכא רמיזא — ודאי הלכה למשה מסיני היא הך עונש דכיפה, ומיהו היכא רמיזא מקרא. **תמותת רשע רעה** — מי שהוחזק רשע — תמיתתו רעתו. אלמא, מוחזק רשע — בר מיתה הוא. **במצודה רעה** — איידי דאיירי הכא ריש לקיש בהאי קרא, מייתינן לאידך דרשא דריש לקיש. **מאי מצודה רעה חכה** = *אמ״ו בלעז, שהוא רע וחלש וקטן ואוחז בו דגים גדולים פתאום ואינו רואה. ואינו דומה לנאחז ברשתות על ידי מארב ותחבולות.

משנה שלא בעדים — שלא ניתן לבית דין להרגו. **לחם צר** — לקמן בעי מאי שנא בכיפה קמייתא.

גמרא מנא ידעינן — הואיל וליכא עדות. **בעדות מיוחדת** — דשנים מעידין עליו ועדותן אמת, אלא שאין מיתתו מסורה לבית דין כגון שנים רואין אותו אחד מחלון זה ואחד מחלון זה, דאמר במסכת מכות (ו,ב) דלא מיקטל עליה. ומיהו הכא תנינן דעייל לכיפה. אבל על פי עד אחד מוציא דבה בעלמא הוא.

NOTES

בִּמְצוֹדָה רָעָה **In an evil net.** A fishhook is referred to as an "evil net," because it causes the fish great pain, even before it is removed from the water. Hence, there is a certain connection between a fishhook and the prison-chamber in which a chronic offender is left to die. There, too, the criminal's death is preceded by a great amount of suffering (*Ramah*).

בְּעֵדוּת מְיוּחֶדֶת **With separate testimony.** It would appear from the Gemara that if a murderer confessed to his crime on his own, we do not accept his confession, and he may not even be put in a prison-chamber and left to die (*R. M. Arak*).

HALAKHAH

הַהוֹרֵג נֶפֶשׁ שֶׁלֹּא בְּעֵדִים **If someone killed a person without witnesses.** "If someone killed another person, but the two witnesses did not see the crime together, or they did not warn him, or they contradicted each other concerning a circumstantial matter during the interrogation — in all these cases the killer is thrown into a prison-chamber until he dies." (*Rambam, Sefer Nezikin, Hilkhot Rotze'aḥ* 4:8.)

TRANSLATION AND COMMENTARY

וְרַב חִסְדָּא [1]**Rav Ḥisda said in the name of Avimi:** [2]We are dealing here with a case **where** the two witnesses who testified against the defendant **contradicted each other** during the **interrogation** — on questions not relating to the substance of the facts at issue, but to accompanying and surrounding circumstances — [3]**but they did not contradict each other during** the **inquiries** — concerning the seven fundamental questions relating to the time and place of the event. Witnesses are interrogated about the accompanying circumstances of the crime, [4]**as we have learned** in the Mishnah (*Sanhedrin* 40a): **"It once happened that Ben Zakkai interrogated** witnesses **about the stems of figs.** Witnesses testified that the defendant murdered someone under a fig tree, and Ben Zakkai asked them about the color and shape of the stems of the figs that connected the fruit to the tree." Now, while it is true that any contradiction between the two witnesses, either circumstantial or substantial, disqualifies the testimony, so that the defendant cannot be executed on the basis of that testimony, if the witnesses only contradicted each other on the circumstances, their testimony is still accepted as the truth, and so the defendant may be thrown into the prison-chamber, where he is left to die.

LITERAL TRANSLATION

[1]And Rav Ḥisda said in the name of Avimi: [2]As when they contradicted each other during interrogation, [3]but they did not contradict each other during inquiries, [4]as we have learned: "It once happened that Ben Zakkai interrogated [witnesses] about the stems of figs."

[5]"And they feed him bread of adversity and water of affliction." [6]What is the difference that here it states: "They give him bread of adversity and water of affliction," [7]and there it states: "They feed him barley, until his stomach bursts"?

[8]Rav Sheshet said: This and that — [9]they give him bread of adversity and water of affliction until his bowels shrink, [10]and then they feed him barley until his stomach bursts.

MISHNAH [11][If] someone steals the *kasvah*, or curses [God] with [the name of] a false god, or has intercourse with

[1]וְרַב חִסְדָּא אָמַר אֲבִימִי: [2]כְּגוֹן דְּאִיתְכַּחוּשׁ בִּבְדִיקוֹת, [3]וְלָא אִיתְכַּחוּשׁ בַּחֲקִירוֹת. [4]כִּדְתְנַן: "מַעֲשֶׂה וּבָדַק בֶּן זַכַּאי בְּעוּקְצֵי תְאֵנִים".

[5]"וּמַאֲכִילִין אוֹתוֹ לֶחֶם צַר וּמַיִם לַחַץ". [6]מַאי שְׁנָא הָכָא דְּקָתָנֵי: "נוֹתְנִין לוֹ לֶחֶם צַר וּמַיִם לַחַץ", [7]וּמַאי שְׁנָא הָתָם דְּקָתָנֵי: "מַאֲכִילִין אוֹתוֹ שְׂעוֹרִין עַד שֶׁכְּרֵיסוֹ מִתְבַּקַּעַת"?

[8]אָמַר רַב שֵׁשֶׁת: אִידִי וְאִידִי — [9]נוֹתְנִין לוֹ לֶחֶם צַר וּמַיִם לַחַץ עַד שֶׁיּוּקְטַן מַעְיָינוֹ, [10]וַהֲדַר מַאֲכִילִין אוֹתוֹ שְׂעוֹרִין עַד שֶׁכְּרֵיסוֹ מִתְבַּקַּעַת.

מִשְׁנָה [11]הַגּוֹנֵב אֶת הַקַּסְוָה, וְהַמְקַלֵּל בַּקּוֹסֵם, וְהַבּוֹעֵל

RASHI

בעוקצי תאנים — בדיקות יתירא הוא, ונהי דבן זכאי פטר ליה בההוא הכחשה מקטלא, מיהו עדות אמת הוא ועייל לכיפה. **מעייניה** — בני מעיו. **והדר מאכילין אותו שעורין** — שנופחין בתוך מעיו, ומתוך שהוקטן מעיינו הוא נבקע.

משנה הקסוה — מפרש בגמרא.

וּמַאֲכִילִין [5]We learned in our Mishnah: "They put him in a narrow, vaulted prison-chamber, **and feed him bread and water** until he dies." [6]**What is the difference that, here,** our Mishnah **states: "They give him bread and water** until he dies," [7]**and there,** the previous Mishnah **states: "They feed him barley, until his stomach bursts** and he dies"?

אָמַר רַב שֵׁשֶׁת [8]**Rav Sheshet said:** Both **here and there** the same procedure is followed. The court puts the criminal in a narrow, vaulted prison-chamber. [9]There, **he is given bread and water** to eat **until his bowels shrink,** [10]**and then he is fed barley,** which expands inside his body and causes **his stomach** to **burst.**

MISHNAH הַגּוֹנֵב [11]**If someone steals the *kasvah*** (which will be explained in the Gemara), **or curses God** by using **the name of a false god, or has intercourse with a non-Jewish woman,** he is not subject to judicial

HALAKHAH

נוֹתְנִין לוֹ לֶחֶם צַר **They feed him the bread of adversity.** "The prison-chamber about which the Mishnah speaks is a chamber as high as the criminal, and so narrow that he cannot lie down. The criminal was fed bread and water until his bowels shrunk, and then he was fed barley until his stomach burst. This punishment was imposed both upon known killers who could not be executed because of legal technicalities, and also upon a person who three times committed a sin punishable by excision," following Rav Sheshet. (*Rambam, Sefer Nezikin, Hilkhot Rotze'aḥ* 4:8; *Sefer Shofetim, Hilkhot Sanhedrin* 18:4.)

הַגּוֹנֵב אֶת הַקַּסְוָה, וְהַמְקַלֵּל בַּקּוֹסֵם **If someone steals the *kasvah*, or curses God with the name of a false god.** "If someone steals a sacred utensil from the Temple, or curses God by using the name of a false god, the court does not punish him, but a zealous person may strike him dead while he is doing his deed. Whoever kills him is worthy of merit." (*Rambam, Sefer Shofetim, Hilkhot Sanhedrin* 18:6.)

הַבּוֹעֵל אֲרַמִּית **If he has intercourse with a non-Jewish woman.** "If someone has intercourse with a non-Jewish woman in the presence of ten Jews, a zealous person who strikes him dead is worthy of praise." (*Rambam, Sefer*

[1]אֲרָמִית — קַנָּאִין פּוֹגְעִין בּוֹ. [2]כֹּהֵן שֶׁשִּׁמֵּשׁ בְּטוּמְאָה, [3]אֵין אֶחָיו הַכֹּהֲנִים מְבִיאִין אוֹתוֹ לְבֵית דִּין. [4]אֶלָּא פִּרְחֵי כְהוּנָּה מוֹצִיאִין אוֹתוֹ חוּץ לָעֲזָרָה וּמַפְצִיעִין אֶת מוֹחוֹ בְּגִזִירִין. [5]זָר שֶׁשִּׁמֵּשׁ בַּמִּקְדָּשׁ, [6]רַבִּי עֲקִיבָא אוֹמֵר: בְּחֶנֶק. [7]וַחֲכָמִים אוֹמְרִים: בִּידֵי שָׁמַיִם.

גמרא [8]מַאי קַסְוָה? [9]אָמַר רַב יְהוּדָה: כְּלִי שָׁרֵת, [10]וְכֵן הוּא אוֹמֵר: "וְאֵת קְשׂוֹת הַנָּסֶךְ". [11]וְהֵיכָא רְמִיזָא? [12]"וְלֹא יָבֹאוּ לִרְאוֹת כְּבַלַּע אֶת הַקֹּדֶשׁ וָמֵתוּ".

LITERAL TRANSLATION

a non-Jewish (lit.,"Aramean") woman, [1]the zealous may strike him.

[2][If] a priest served while ritually impure, [3]his priestly brethren do not bring him before a court. [4]But rather the young priests remove him from the Temple Courtyard and smash his brains with clubs.

[5][If] a non-priest served in the Temple, [6]Rabbi Akiva says: By strangulation. [7]And the Sages say: By the hands of Heaven.

GEMARA [8]What is a *kasvah*? [9]Rav Yehudah said: A sacred utensil. [10]And similarly it says: "And the utensils [*keshot*] for pouring out." [11]And where is there an allusion? [12]"But they shall not go in to see when the holy things are covered, lest they die."

TRANSLATION AND COMMENTARY

execution, for the Torah does not declare these offenses to be capital crimes. [1]Nevertheless, **a zealous person** who apprehends an individual while he is committing one of these transgressions **may strike him** dead.

כֹּהֵן [2]**If a priest served** in the Temple **while ritually impure,** so that his service is disqualified and he is liable to be put to death at the hand of Heaven, [3]**his priestly brethren do not bring him before an** earthly **court** for flogging (a crime punishable by death at the hand of Heaven is also subject to lashes). [4]**Rather the young priests remove** the offending priest **from the Temple courtyard,** so as not to defile the Temple, **and** then **smash his brains with clubs.**

זָר [5]**If** an ordinary Jew who was **not a priest** descending from Aaron **served in the Temple,** [6]**Rabbi Akiva says:** He is liable to death **by strangulation.** [7]**The Sages** disagree and **say:** He is liable to death **at the hand of Heaven.**

GEMARA מַאי קַסְוָה [8]The Gemara asks: **What is the** ***kasvah*** mentioned in our Mishnah?

אָמַר [9]**Rav Yehudah said:** That term refers to **a sacred utensil** used in the Temple service. [10]**And similarly** the verse (Numbers 4:7) **states: "And the utensils [*keshot*] for pouring out."** [11]The Gemara asks: **Where is there an allusion** in the Bible to someone who steals a sacred utensil being fit to die? [12]The Gemara explains: This is learned from the verse (Numbers 4:20) that states: **"But they shall not go in to see when the holy things are covered, lest they die."** The words כְּבַלַּע אֶת הַקֹּדֶשׁ, translated here as "when the holy things are covered," can also be understood here as "when the holy things are swallowed up," meaning stolen. Thus, the verse intimates that someone who steals a sacred utensil is fit to die.

RASHI

ארמית — בת נכרי. **קנאין פוגעין בו** — בני אדם כשרין המתקנאין קנאתו של מקום פוגעין בו בשעה שרואין את המעשה אבל לאחר מיכן אין מיתתו מסורה לבית דין, והלכה למשה מסיני הוא. פוגעין = ממיתין, כמו "לך ופגע בו" (מלכים א׳ ב). גזירין = פקעין, *אשעל"ש בלעז.

גמרא והיכא רמיזא — דשייכא בה מיתה. **כבלע את הקדש** — לשון גנב שמבליעין ומחביאין, ורמז בעלמא הוא ולא מקרא נפיק. דעיקר קרא בלוים כתוב שהוזהרו שלא לראות בסלוק מסעות

LANGUAGE (RASHI)

אשעל"ש* Should apparently read אשטייל"ש, Old French *asteles*, meaning "scraps, torn pieces."

NOTES

מַפְצִיעִין אֶת מוֹחוֹ בְּגִזִירִין They smash his brains with clubs. According to some authorities, this, too, is a law given to Moses at Sinai (*Ran*): The zealous are permitted to kill a priest who served in the Temple while ritually impure. Such an offender is handed over to his priestly brethren for punishment so that that they themselves may "put away the evil in their midst" (see *Tzofnat Pa'ane'aḥ*). Others suggest that, since the offender is liable to death at the hand of Heaven, zealous people who kill him are regarded as having killed a dying person, which in this case was permitted with full approval for the sake of the honor of the priesthood (*She'elot u'Teshuvot HaRadbaz*).

מַאי קַסְוָה? What is the *kasvah*? The Mishnah singled out the *kasvah* because a *kasvah* is a sacred utensil of relatively little value. The Mishnah ruled that, if someone stole a *kasvah*, a zealous person may strike him dead, and all the more so if he stole a sacred utensil of greater value (*Rabbenu Yonatan*). Alternatively, the Mishnah chose this example, because a *kasvah* is small and relatively easy to steal (*Meiri*).

כְּבַלַּע אֶת הַקֹּדֶשׁ When the holy things are covered. We find the term בַּלַּע used in connection with stealing, as in

HALAKHAH

Shofetim, Hilkhot Sanhedrin 18:6; *Sefer Kedushah, Hilkhot Issurei Bi'ah* 12:4; *Shulḥan Arukh, Ḥoshen Mishpat* 425:4, *Rema*.)

כֹּהֵן שֶׁשִּׁמֵּשׁ בְּטוּמְאָה If a priest served while ritually impure. "If a priest served in the Temple while ritually impure, he was liable to lashes. But the other priests would not bring such an offender to court for flogging. Rather they removed him from the Temple Courtyard, and smashed his brains with clubs, and the Sages did not object." (*Rambam, Sefer Shofetim, Hilkhot Sanhedrin* 18:6; *Sefer Avodah, Hilkhot Bi'at Mikdash* 4:2.)

זָר שֶׁשִּׁמֵּשׁ בַּמִּקְדָּשׁ If an ordinary Jew served in the Temple. "If an ordinary Jew served in the Temple, his service is disqualified, and he is liable to death at the hand of

TRANSLATION AND COMMENTARY

וְהַמְקַלֵּל [1]We learned in the Mishnah: "If someone **curses God with the name of a false god,** a zealous person may strike him dead." [2]**Rav Yosef taught a related Baraita:** "We are dealing here with someone who curses God with the name of a false god, saying: **'May the false god strike his false god,'** referring to God as a false god."

רַבָּנַן [3]**The Rabbis said (and some say** that it was **Rabbah bar Mari** who said): We are dealing here with someone who curses another person saying: [4]**"May the false god strike him** [the other person] **and his master and provider** [God]."

וְהַבּוֹעֵל [5]We learned in the Mishnah: "If someone **has intercourse with a non-Jewish woman,** a zealous person may strike him dead." [6]**Rav Kahana asked Rav:** [82A] [7]**"If** someone had intercourse with a non-Jewish woman, and **a zealous person did not strike him** dead, **what is his punishment?"** [8]**Rav** was unable to answer Rav Kahana, for he **forgot the tradition** that he had received from his teachers. [9]That night **Rav Kahana had a dream** in which the following verse (Malachi 2:11) **was read** to him: **"Judah has dealt treacherously, and an abominable thing has been done in Israel and in Jerusalem; for Judah has profaned the holiness of the Lord whom he loves, and has married the daughter of a strange god."** [10]Rav Kahana **went** to Rav **and said to him: "The following** verse **was read to me** last night in a dream." [11]**Rav** then **remembered** that he had indeed received **a** pertinent **tradition** based on that verse: **"Judah has dealt treacherously"** — **this** refers to **idol worship.** [12]**And similarly** the verse (Jeremiah 3:20) **says:** "Surely as a wife treacherously departs from her husband, **so you have dealt treacherously with me, O house of Israel, says the Lord."** [13]**"And an abominable thing has been done in Israel and in Jerusalem"** — **this** refers to **homosexual intercourse.** [14]**And similarly** the verse (Leviticus 18:22) **says: "You shall not lie with a man after the manner of a woman; it is abomination."** [15]**"For Judah has profaned**

[1]"וְהַמְקַלֵּל בְּקוֹסֵם". [2]תָּנֵי רַב יוֹסֵף: "יַכֶּה קוֹסֵם אֶת קוֹסְמוֹ". [3]רַבָּנַן, וְאִיתֵּימָא רַבָּה בַּר מָרִי, אָמְרִי: [4]"יַכֵּהוּ קוֹסֵם לוֹ וּלְקוֹנוֹ וּלְמַקְנוֹ".

[5]"וְהַבּוֹעֵל אֲרַמִּית". [6]בְּעָא מִינֵּיהּ רַב כָּהֲנָא מֵרַב: [82A] [7]"לֹא פָּגְעוּ בּוֹ קַנָּאִין מַהוּ"? [8]אִינְשְׁיֵיהּ רַב לִגְמָרֵיהּ. [9]אַקְרְיוּהוּ לְרַב כָּהֲנָא בְּחֶלְמֵיהּ: "בָּגְדָה יְהוּדָה וְתוֹעֵבָה נֶעֶשְׂתָה בְיִשְׂרָאֵל וּבִירוּשָׁלָיִם כִּי חִלֵּל יְהוּדָה קֹדֶשׁ ה' אֲשֶׁר אָהֵב וּבָעַל בַּת אֵל נֵכָר". [10]אֲתָא אֲמַר לֵיהּ: "הָכִי אַקְרְיוּן". [11]אַדְכְּרֵיהּ רַב לִגְמָרֵיהּ: "בָּגְדָה יְהוּדָה" — זוֹ עֲבוֹדָה זָרָה. [12]וְכֵן הוּא אוֹמֵר: "[כֵּן] בְּגַדְתֶּם בִּי בֵּית יִשְׂרָאֵל נְאֻם ה'". [13]"וְתוֹעֵבָה נֶעֶשְׂתָה בְיִשְׂרָאֵל וּבִירוּשָׁלָיִם" — זֶה מִשְׁכַּב זָכוּר. [14]וְכֵן הוּא אוֹמֵר: "וְאֶת זָכָר לֹא תִשְׁכַּב מִשְׁכְּבֵי אִשָּׁה תּוֹעֵבָה הִיא". [15]"כִּי חִלֵּל

LITERAL TRANSLATION

[1]"Or curses [God] with [the name of] a false god." [2]Rav Yosef taught: "May the false god strike his false god." [3]The Rabbis (and some say, Rabbah bar Mari) said: [4]"May the false god strike him, and his master, and his provider."

[5]"Or has intercourse with a non-Jewish woman." [6]Rav Kahana asked Rav: [82A] [7]"[If] the zealous did not strike him, what [is his punishment]?" [8]Rav forgot his tradition. [9]They read to Rav Kahana in his dream: "Judah has dealt treacherously, and an abominable thing has been done in Israel and in Jerusalem; for Judah has profaned the holiness of the Lord whom he loves, and has married the daughter of a strange god." [10]He came [and] said to him: "Thus they read to me." [11]Rav remembered his tradition: "Judah has dealt treacherously" — this is idol worship. [12]And similarly it says: "So you have dealt treacherously with me, O house of Israel, says the Lord." [13]"And an abominable thing has been done in Israel and in Jerusalem" — this is homosexual intercourse. [14]And similarly it says: "You shall not lie with a man after the manner of a woman; it is abomination." [15]"For

RASHI

בשעת הכנסת כלים לנרתק שלהן, שהיו אהרן ובניו מכסין הארון והמזבחות כמו שכתוב שם, "ובא אהרן בנסעם והורידו". יכה קוסם את קוסמו — שמקלל כלפי מעלה בקוסם, יכה הקוסם זה את קוסמו היינו כלפי מעלה שנותן קסמים האלו בלבו. (קסבר המקלל דקא מחשב ליה) האי קוסם בעיניו שהוא ראוי ויש בו כח לקלל בו. יכהו קוסם — מקלל את חבירו ואומר יכהו הקוסם הזה. לו ולקונו ולמקנו — דהיינו כלפי מעלה, שהוא קונה את העולם ומקנה לבריותיו את טובו. לא פגעו בו קנאין מהו — מה עונש בדבר. אנשייה רב לגמריה — שכח מה שגמר מרבו בדבר זה, ולא ידע להשיבו. וכן הוא אומר ואת זכר וגו' — סיפיה דקרא "תועבה היא".

NOTES

(Job 20:15): "He has swallowed down [בָּלַע] riches, and he shall vomit them up again" (*Rabbenu Yonatan, Ramban* in his *Commentary to the Torah*).

HALAKHAH

Heaven," following the Sages. (*Rambam, Sefer Avodah, Hilkhot Bi'at Mikdash* 9:1.)

TRANSLATION AND COMMENTARY

the holiness [קֹדֶשׁ] **of the Lord" — this is a prostitute.** [1]**And similarly** the verse (Deuteronomy 23:18) **says: "There shall be no female prostitute** [קְדֵשָׁה] **of the daughters of Israel,** nor a male prostitute of the sons of Israel." [2]**"And has married the daughter of a strange god" — this** refers to **someone who has intercourse with a non-Jewish woman.** [3]**And the next verse** (Malachi 2:12) **states** regarding all those guilty of such offenses: **"The Lord will cut off from the man** who **does this all living offspring from the tents of Jacob, or any to present an offering to the Lord of hosts."** [4]**If he is a Torah scholar, he will not have** a son who is sufficiently sharp and **alert** to hold his own in a Halakhic discussion **among the Sages, or** a son **who can answer** questions among **the disciples.** [5]And **if he is a priest, he will not have a son who will present an offering** in the Temple **to the Lord of hosts.**

אָמַר [6]**Rabbi Ḥiyya bar Avuyah said: Whoever has intercourse with a non-Jewish woman is considered as if he has married an idol,** [7]**for the** verse (Malachi 2:11) **states: "And has married the daughter of a strange god."** [8]It may be asked: **Does a strange god have a daughter?** [9]**Rather,** this verse refers to **someone who has intercourse with a non-Jewish woman** who cleaves to a strange god.

וְאָמַר [10]Having mentioned one teaching of Rabbi Ḥiyya bar Avuyah, the Gemara presents another. **Rabbi Ḥiyya bar Avuyah said:** The following words **were inscribed on** King **Jehoiakim's skull:** [11]**"This, and yet another,"** meaning that Jehoiakim has already received this punishment — he was denied an honorable burial — and has yet to receive another one. [12]It was related that **Rabbi Perida's grandfather** — Rabbi Ḥiyya bar Avuyah — once **found a skull that had been**

יְהוּדָה קֹדֶשׁ ה׳ — זוֹ זוֹנָה. [1]וְכֵן הוּא אוֹמֵר: "לֹא (יִהְיֶה קָדֵשׁ) [תִהְיֶה קְדֵשָׁה מִבְּנוֹת יִשְׂרָאֵל]". [2]"וּבָעַל בַּת אֵל נֵכָר" — זֶה הַבָּא עַל הַנָּכְרִית, [3]וּכְתִיב בַּתְרֵיהּ: "יַכְרֵת ה׳ לָאִישׁ אֲשֶׁר יַעֲשֶׂנָּה עֵר וְעֹנֶה (מֵאֱלֹהֵי) [מֵאָהֳלֵי] יַעֲקֹב וּמַגִּישׁ מִנְחָה לַה׳ צְבָאוֹת". [4]אִם תַּלְמִיד חָכָם הוּא, לֹא יִהְיֶה לוֹ עֵר בַּחֲכָמִים, וְעוֹנֶה בַּתַּלְמִידִים. [5]אִם כֹּהֵן הוּא, לֹא יִהְיֶה לוֹ בֵּן מַגִּישׁ מִנְחָה לַה׳ צְבָאוֹת.

[6]אָמַר רַבִּי חִיָּיא בַּר אֲבוּיָה: כָּל הַבָּא עַל הַנָּכְרִית כְּאִילּוּ מִתְחַתֵּן בַּעֲבוֹדָה זָרָה, [7]דִּכְתִיב: "וּבָעַל בַּת אֵל נֵכָר". [8]וְכִי בַּת יֵשׁ לוֹ לְאֵל נֵכָר? [9]אֶלָּא, זֶה הַבָּא עַל הַנָּכְרִית.

[10]וְאָמַר רַבִּי חִיָּיא בַּר אֲבוּיָה: כָּתוּב עַל גֻּלְגָּלְתּוֹ שֶׁל יְהוֹיָקִים: [11]"זֹאת וְעוֹד אַחֶרֶת". [12]זְקֵינוֹ דְּרַבִּי פְּרִידָא אַשְׁכַּח הַהוּא גּוּלְגָּלְתָּא דַּהֲוַת שַׁדְיָא בְּשַׁעֲרֵי יְרוּשָׁלַיִם, וַהֲוָה כָּתוּב עִילָּוֵיהּ:

LITERAL TRANSLATION

Judah has profaned the holiness of the Lord" — this is a prostitute. [1]And similarly it says: "There shall be no female prostitute of the daughters of Israel." [2]"And has married the daughter of a strange god" — this is someone who has intercourse with a non-Jewish woman. [3]And afterwards it is written: "The Lord will cut off from the man that does this all living offspring from the tents of Jacob, or any to present an offering to the Lord of hosts." [4]If he is a Torah scholar, he will not have someone alert among the Sages, or someone who can answer among the disciples. [5]If he is a priest, he will not have a son who will present an offering to the Lord of hosts.

[6]Rabbi Ḥiyya bar Avuyah said: Whoever has intercourse with a non-Jewish woman is considered as if he has married an idol, [7]for it is written: "And has married the daughter of a strange god." [8]Does a strange god have a daughter? [9]Rather, this is someone who has intercourse with a non-Jewish woman.

[10]And Rabbi Ḥiyya bar Avuyah said: It was written on Jehoiakim's skull: [11]"This, and yet another." [12]Rabbi Perida's grandfather found a skull that had been cast aside at the gates of Jerusalem, and it was written on it:

RASHI

זונה — מופקרת ואפילו ישראלית. קדש — מפקיר קדושתו והולך לרדוף זונות, "קדשה" — מחללת קדושתה וכן "קדש" — מחלל קדושתו. כתוב על גלגלתו של יהויקים — משום רבי חייא בר אבויה נקט לה. זאת ועוד אחרת — נקמה נעשית בה כבר, ועוד אחרת תעשה בה. זקינו דרבי פרידא — הוא רבי חייא בר אבויה, והכי אמרינן ב"חלק".

NOTES

אִם תַּלְמִיד חָכָם הוּא **If he is a Torah scholar.** It is not clear from here what will happen to someone who has intercourse with a non-Jewish woman, if he is neither a Torah scholar nor a priest, but it would appear from the verse that he is subject to excision ("The Lord will cut off"). The Aharonim discuss whether there is such a thing as excision by Rabbinic decree.

HALAKHAH

הַבָּא עַל הַנָּכְרִית **Someone who has intercourse with a non-Jewish woman.** "If someone had intercourse with a non-Jewish woman, and he was not struck down by a zealous person, nor given lashes, he is liable to excision, as is stated explicitly in the words of the Prophets." (*Shulḥan Arukh, Even HaEzer* 16:2.)

[1] ״זֹאת וְעוֹד אַחֶרֶת״. [2] קְבָרָהּ,
וַהֲדַר נַבוֹג; [3] קְבָרָהּ וַהֲדַר נַבוֹג.
[4] אָמַר: הַאי גּוּלְגָלְתָּא שֶׁל
יְהוֹיָקִים, דִּכְתִיב בֵּיהּ: [5] ״קְבוּרַת
חֲמוֹר יִקָּבֵר סָחוֹב וְהַשְׁלֵךְ
מֵהָלְאָה לְשַׁעֲרֵי יְרוּשָׁלָיִם״.
[6] אָמַר: מַלְכָּא הוּא, וְלָאו אוֹרַח
אַרְעָא לְבַזּוּיֵי. [7] שְׁקַלָהּ, כְּרָכָהּ
בְּשִׁירָאֵי, וְאוֹתְבֵיהּ בְּסִיפְטָא.
[8] אֲתַאי דְּבֵיתְהוּ חֲזֵיתָהּ. [9] נָפְקַתְ
אֲמַרָה לְהוּ לְשִׁיבַבְתָהָא.
[10] אָמְרִי לָהּ: הַאי דְּאִיתְּתָא
קַמָּיְיתָא הִיא, דְּלָא קָא מַנְשֵׁי
לָהּ. [11] שְׁגַרְתָּא לְתַנּוּרָא, וּקְלָתָהּ.
[12] כִּי אֲתָא אֲמַר: הַיְינוּ דִּכְתִיב
עִילָּוֵיהּ: [13] ״זֹאת וְעוֹד אַחֶרֶת״.
[14] כִּי אֲתָא רַב דִּימִי, אֲמַר: בֵּית
דִּינוֹ שֶׁל חַשְׁמוֹנַאי גָּזְרוּ: [15] הַבָּא
עַל הַנָּכְרִית חַיָּיב עָלֶיהָ מִשּׁוּם
נִדָּה, שִׁפְחָה, גּוֹיָּה, אֵשֶׁת אִישׁ.
[16] כִּי אֲתָא רָבִין, אֲמַר: מִשּׁוּם

LITERAL TRANSLATION

[1] "This, and yet another." [2] He buried it, but it rose again; [3] he buried it, but it rose again. [4] He said: This is the skull of Jehoiakim, about which it is written: [5] "He shall be buried with the burial of an ass, drawn and cast forth beyond the gates of Jerusalem." [6] He said: He was the king, and it is not proper conduct to degrade him. [7] He took it, wrapped it in silk, and placed it in a cupboard. [8] His wife came and saw it. [9] She went out, and told her neighbors. [10] They said to her: That is from his first wife, whom he cannot forget. [11] She heated the oven and burned it. [12] When he came, he said: That is what was written on it: [13] "This, and yet another."

[14] When Rav Dimi came, he said: The court of the Hasmoneans decreed: [15] Someone who has intercourse with a non-Jewish woman is liable on account of a menstruating woman, a maidservant, a non-Jewish woman, [and] a married woman.

[16] When Ravin came, he said: On account of

TRANSLATION AND COMMENTARY

cast aside by the gates of Jerusalem, and on it was inscribed: [1] **"This, and another one."** [2] Out of respect for the dead, **he buried** the skull, **but it** immediately **rose again** from the grave. [3] **He** tried again to **bury** the skull, **but again it rose** from the grave. [4] Rabbi Ḥiyya bar Avuyah then **said** to himself: **This must be the skull of** King **Jehoiakim, about whom the verse states** (Jeremiah 22:19): [5] **"He shall be buried with the burial of an ass, drawn and cast forth beyond the gates of Jerusalem."** [6] **He said:** As evil as he may have been, Jehoiakim **was** nevertheless **the king** of Judah, **and it is not proper that he should be degraded** in this manner. [7] So **he took** the skull home with him, **wrapped it in silk, and placed it in a cupboard.** [8] **His wife came and saw** the skull. [9] **She went out, and told her neighbors** about the skull. [10] They **said to her:** Surely, it **must belong to** your husband's **first wife, whom he cannot forget.** [11] She **heated the oven** and **burned** the skull. [12] **When** Rabbi Ḥiyya bar Avuyah **came** home and saw what his wife had done, **he said:** Thus was fulfilled **that which had been inscribed on** the skull: [13] **"This, and yet another,"** for not only was Jehoiakim's skull cast out of his grave, but now it has been consumed by fire.

כִּי [14] **When Rav Dimi came** to Babylonia from Eretz Israel, **he said: The court of the Hasmoneans decreed:** [15] If **someone has intercourse with a non-Jewish woman** outside of marriage, he **is liable** by Rabbinic decree **for** having had intercourse with **a menstruating woman, a maidservant, a non-Jewish woman, and a married woman.** By Torah law, the menstrual blood of a non-Jewish woman does not impart ritual impurity, but by decree of the Hasmonean court a Jew may not have intercourse with a menstruating non-Jewish woman, because this might lead him to have intercourse with a menstruating Jewish woman. Similarly, the Rabbis decreed that a Jew may not have intercourse with a non-Jewish woman, because this might lead him to have intercourse with a non-Jewish maidservant, who is forbidden to him by Torah law. By Torah law, a Jew is also forbidden to marry a non-Jewish woman. Therefore, by Rabbinic decree, a Jew may not have intercourse with a non-Jewish woman even outside of marriage, because this might lead him to marry her. Moreover, even though by Torah law a non-Jewish woman is not bound to her husband by a marital bond that would forbid her to a Jew, the Rabbis decreed that a Jew is forbidden to have intercourse with a married non-Jewish woman because this might lead him to have intercourse with a married Jewish woman.

כִּי [16] **When Ravin came** to Babylonia from Eretz Israel, **he said:** If someone has intercourse with a non-Jewish woman outside of marriage, he is liable by Rabbinic decree **on account of** *nashgaz* — an acronym

RASHI

נבוג — בצבצה ויצאה מקבורתה. קבורת חמור — מושלך ברחובות. בסיפטא — ארגז. לשיבבתהא — לשכנותיה. דלא קא מנשי לה — אינה נשכחת מלבו. שגרתה לתנורא — הסיקה את התנור. חייב עליה — כלומר נענש בה משום כל אלו. נדה — אף על פי שדם כותית כדם בהמה — מכל מקום מיאוס וחילול לקדושת השם הוא. שפחה — שהיא כשפחה אצלו, שכנסת ישראל גבירה נקראת. גויה — ״לא תתחתן בם כי יסיר וגו׳״ כל המסירות את הלב במשמע. ומיהו לאו דלא תתחתן ליכא דאורייתא, דדרך חתנות משמע, ובית דינו של חשמונאי גזרו דלפרוש מינה משום כל הני. אשת איש — ולאו ממש, דקדושין לית להו, ומיהו לאשת איש דמיא וחייב לפרוש הימנה שלא יהא רגיל באשת איש.

LANGUAGE

נְבוֹג It rose. The root of this word is נבג in Syrian, which is cognate with **pi** in Arabic, meaning "to emerge, to come out."

שִׁירָאֵי Silk. This word derives from the Greek σηρικον, *syrikon*, meaning "silk," from the place name Σηρ (Syr) in India, from which silk was brought to the West.

סִיפְּטָא Cupboard. This word apparently derives from the Persian *sapad*, meaning "a basket." Its ancient meaning was a place to store objects, and a similar word is used in related languages to refer to a strongbox covered in copper embossed with iron.

LITERAL TRANSLATION

nashgaz — a menstruating woman, a maidservant, a non-Jewish woman, [and] a prostitute. [1]But on account of marriage — they do not have.

[2]And the other one? [3]They surely do not give their wives up [to prostitution].

[4]Rav Ḥisda said: Someone who comes for advice — they do not instruct him.

[5]It was also stated: Rabbah bar bar Hannah said in the name of Rabbi Yoḥanan: Someone who comes for advice — they do not instruct him. [6]And moreover, had Zimri withdrawn, and Phinehas slain him, he would have been executed because of him. [7]Had Zimri turned around and slain Phinehas, he would not have been executed because of him, [8]for he was a pursuer.

[9]"And Moses said to the judges of Israel, etc." [10]The tribe of

נשג״ז נִדָּה, שִׁפְחָה, גּוֹיָה, זוֹנָה. [1]אֲבָל מִשּׁוּם אִישׁוּת — לֵית לְהוּ.

[2]וְאִידָךְ? [3]נְשָׁיְיהוּ וַדַּאי לָא מִיפְקְרֵי.

[4]אָמַר רַב חִסְדָּא: הַבָּא לִימָּלֵךְ, אֵין מוֹרִין לוֹ.

[5]אִיתְּמַר נַמִי, אָמַר רַבָּה בַּר בַּר חָנָה אָמַר רַבִּי יוֹחָנָן: הַבָּא לִימָּלֵךְ, אֵין מוֹרִין לוֹ. [6]וְלֹא עוֹד אֶלָּא, שֶׁאִם פֵּירֵשׁ זִמְרִי וַהֲרָגוֹ פִּנְחָס, נֶהֱרַג עָלָיו. [7]נֶהְפַּךְ זִמְרִי וַהֲרָגוֹ לְפִנְחָס, אֵין נֶהֱרַג עָלָיו, [8]שֶׁהֲרֵי רוֹדֵף הוּא.

[9]״וַיֹּאמֶר מֹשֶׁה אֶל שֹׁפְטֵי יִשְׂרָאֵל וגו׳״. [10]הָלַךְ שִׁבְטוֹ שֶׁל

RASHI

אבל אישות אין להם — שסתם גויה מופקרת ואינה מיוחדת לבעלה, ולא דמיא לאשת איש. אמר רב חסדא — קנאי הבא לימלך בבית דין ובשעת מעשה אם יפגע בו — אין מורים לו, שלא נאמרה אלא למקנא מעצמו ואינו נמלך. ולא עוד — אלא שאם פירש זמרי — מן האשה והרגו פנחס אחר כן — נהרג עליו, שלא נאמרה הלכה דא אלא בשעת מעשה. זמרי — הוא שלומיאל.

TRANSLATION AND COMMENTARY

for **a menstruating woman** (*niddah*), **a maidservant** (*shifḥah*), **a non-Jewish woman** (*goyah*), **and a prostitute** (*zonah*). [1]**But** he is not liable **for** having had intercourse with **a married woman,** for non-Jews **do not have** the institution of a stable marriage, comparable to that of a Jewish marriage.

וְאִידָךְ [2]The Gemara asks: How does **the other** Amora — Rav Dimi — counter this argument? [3]The Gemara explains: He maintains that non-Jewish men are **surely not** ready to **give up their wives to prostitution.** Thus, there is indeed a similarity between a married non-Jewish woman and a married Jewish woman, and so there was room for the Rabbis to decree that a Jew is forbidden to have intercourse with a married non-Jewish woman, lest he come to have intercourse with a married Jewish woman.

אָמַר רַב חִסְדָּא [4]**Rav Ḥisda said:** If **someone** witnessed an act for which a zealous person may kill the transgressor, and he **came** before a court **for advice** as to how he should act, the court **may not permit him** to slay the transgressor.

אִיתְּמַר נַמִי [5]**It was also stated** that **Rabbah bar bar Ḥannah said in the name of Rabbi Yoḥanan:** If **someone** witnessed such an offense, and he **came** before a court **for advice,** the court **may not tell him** that he is permitted to slay the transgressor. [6]**Moreover, had Zimri** ben Salu already **withdrawn** from the Midianite woman with whom he was engaging in sexual relations (see Numbers 25), **and** only then **did Phinehas slay him, he** — Phinehas — **would have been liable to execution.** [7]Furthermore, **had Zimri turned around, and slain Phinehas** in self-defense, **he would not have been liable to execution,** [8]**for** Phinehas **was pursuing** him with the manifest intention of killing him.

וַיֹּאמֶר מֹשֶׁה [9]The Gemara now considers the Torah passage dealing with Zimri and Phinehas: The Torah (Numbers 25:5) states: **"And Moses said to the judges of Israel,** Slay every one his men who have attached themselves to Baal Peor." [10]Members of **the tribe of Simeon went to Zimri ben Salu,** their chief, and **said to**

NOTES

אִישׁוּת — לֵית לְהוּ **Marriage they do not have.** *Rabbenu Yonatan* suggests that, since non-Jews can end their marital bond through the declaration of one of the parties of his or her desire to end the marriage, it therefore follows that if a Jew had intercourse with a non-Jewish woman, we should assume that she had wanted to be divorced from her husband, and so there is no room to find him liable for having had intercourse with a married woman.

אֵין מוֹרִין לוֹ **They do not instruct him.** The Jerusalem Talmud cites an opinion according to which a zealous person who strikes a criminal dead does so to the displeasure of the Sages. Moreover, had not God Himself approved of Phinehas' actions by saying (Numbers 25:13), "And he shall have it, and his seed after him, the covenant of an everlasting priesthood," the Sages would have placed Phinehas under a ban.

HALAKHAH

הַבָּא לִימָּלֵךְ **Someone who comes for advice.** "If someone is engaging in sexual intercourse with a non-Jewish woman in public in the sight of ten other Jews, a zealous person may kill him. He may only kill the offender while he is actually committing the transgression, but if the offender has already withdrawn from the woman, he may no longer kill him. The zealous person may only kill the offender after having properly warned him against committing the transgression. If the zealous person comes before a court for advice, the court may not tell him that he is permitted

שִׁמְעוֹן אֵצֶל זִמְרִי בֶּן סָלוּא, אָמְרוּ לוֹ: ״הֵן דָּנִין דִּינֵי נְפָשׁוֹת, וְאַתָּה יוֹשֵׁב וְשׁוֹתֵק״? [1]מֶה עָשָׂה? [2]עָמַד וְקִיבֵּץ עֶשְׂרִים וְאַרְבָּעָה אֶלֶף מִיִּשְׂרָאֵל, וְהָלַךְ אֵצֶל כָּזְבִּי, [3]אָמַר לָהּ: ״הַשְׁמִיעִי לִי״! [4]אָמְרָה לוֹ: ״בַּת מֶלֶךְ אֲנִי, וְכֵן צִוָּה לִי אָבִי: [5]׳לֹא תִּשְׁמְעִי אֶלָּא לַגָּדוֹל שֶׁבָּהֶם׳״. [6]אָמַר לָהּ: ״אַף הוּא נְשִׂיא שֵׁבֶט הוּא, [7]וְלֹא עוֹד אֶלָּא שֶׁהוּא גָּדוֹל מִמֶּנּוּ, שֶׁהוּא שֵׁנִי לַבֶּטֶן וְהוּא שְׁלִישִׁי לַבֶּטֶן״. [8]תְּפָשָׂהּ בִּבְלוֹרִיתָהּ, וֶהֱבִיאָהּ אֵצֶל מֹשֶׁה. [9]אָמַר לוֹ: ״בֶּן עַמְרָם! [10]זוֹ אֲסוּרָה אוֹ מוּתֶּרֶת? [11]וְאִם תֹּאמַר אֲסוּרָה, בַּת יִתְרוֹ מִי הִתִּירָהּ לְךָ״? [12]נִתְעַלְּמָה מִמֶּנּוּ הֲלָכָה, [13]גָּעוּ כּוּלָּם בִּבְכִיָּה, וְהַיְינוּ דִּכְתִיב: [14]״וְהֵמָּה בֹכִים פֶּתַח אֹהֶל מוֹעֵד״. [15]וּכְתִיב: ״וַיַּרְא פִּינְחָס בֶּן אֶלְעָזָר״. [16]מָה רָאָה? [17]אָמַר רַב: רָאָה מַעֲשֶׂה, וְנִזְכַּר הֲלָכָה.

LITERAL TRANSLATION

Simeon went to Zimri ben Salu. They said to him: "They are judging capital cases, and you sit and remain silent?" [1]What did he do? [2]He stood up and gathered twenty-four thousand people of Israel, and went to Kozbi. [3]He said to her: "Listen to me." [4]She said to him: "I am the daughter of a king, and thus my father instructed me: [5]'Only listen to the greatest among them.'" [6]He said to her: "He, too, is the chief of a tribe. [7]Moreover, he is greater than him, for he is the second from the womb, and he is the third from the womb." [8]He seized her by her locks, and brought her to Moses. [9]He said to him: "Son of Amram! [10]Is this one forbidden or permitted? [11]And if you say she is forbidden, who permitted the daughter of Jethro to you?" [12]The law escaped him. [13]They all burst into weeping. And this is what is written: [14]"Who were weeping before the Tent of Meeting." [15]And it is written: "And when Phinehas, the son of Elazar, saw it." [16]What did he see? [17]Rav said: He saw the incident, and remembered the law.

TRANSLATION AND COMMENTARY

him: "They have begun to **judge capital cases,** and slay people, **and you sit** still **and remain silent?"** [1]**What did** Zimri **do?** [2]**He stood up and gathered twenty-four thousand people of Israel, and went to** the Midianite princess, **Kozbi,** the daughter of Zur. [3]**He said to her: "Listen to me,"** meaning, have intercourse with me.

אָמְרָה לוֹ [4]The Midianite princess **answered** Zimri: **"I am the daughter of a king, and my father instructed me** as follows: [5]**'Only agree** to have intercourse **with the greatest among them.'"** [6]Zimri **said to her: "I, too, am the chief of** my **tribe,** the tribe of Simeon. [7]**Moreover, I am** even **greater than** Moses, the leader of all Israel, **for I am** a member of the tribe of Simeon, **the second** son **born** to the Patriarch Jacob, **while he,** Moses, **is** only a member of the tribe of Levi, Jacob's **third-born** son." [8]Zimri then **seized** Kozbi **by her locks, and brought her before Moses.** [9]Openly challenging Moses' authority, Zimri **said to him: "Son of Amram!** [10]**Is this** woman **forbidden** to a member of Israel **or permitted** to him? [11]**If you say she is forbidden, who,** then, **permitted you** to marry Zipporah, **the daughter of Jethro,** a woman of similar Midianite origin?" (This was, of course, not a sin, for Moses had taken Zipporah as his wife before the Torah was given at Sinai.) [12]Moses did not know what to do, for **the law** allowing a zealous person to kill someone having intercourse with a non-Jewish person **escaped him.** [13]The judges of Israel **all burst into tears,** as **the verse** (Numbers 25:6) **states:** "And behold, one of the children of Israel came and brought to his brethren a Midianite woman in the sight of Moses, and in the sight of the congregation of the children of Israel, [14]**who were weeping before the Tent of Meeting."** [15]**And the** following **verse** (Numbers 25:7) **states: "And when Phinehas, the son of Elazar,** the son of Aaron the priest, **saw it,** he rose up from among the congregation, and took a spear in his hand." [16]**What did** Phinehas **see** that stirred him into action? [17]**Rav said:** Phinehas **saw the incident and remembered the law** that Moses had once taught

RASHI

נשיא שבט — שמעון, כדלקמן. **שמעון** — שני לבטן, לוי, שלישי לבטן. **בת יתרו מי התירה לך** — משה קודם מתן תורה נשא, וכשנתנה תורה כולן בני נח היו ונכנסו לכלל מצות והיא עמהם, וגרים רבים של ערב רב. **ונתעלמה ממנו הלכה** — שנאמר לו בסיני הבועל נכרית וכו׳.

NOTES

בַּת יִתְרוֹ מִי הִתִּירָהּ לְךָ? Who permitted the daughter of Jethro to you? The verse does not state explicitly that Zimri had intercourse with the Midianite woman, but only (Numbers 25:6): "And he brought to his brethren a Midianite woman in the sight of Moses." Thus, the verse alludes to Zimri's conversation with Moses in which he mentioned Moses' Midianite wife.

HALAKHAH

to slay the transgressor. If the transgressor killed the zealous person in self-defense, he is not liable for his death." (*Rambam, Sefer Kedushah, Hilkhot Issurei Biah* 12:5; *Shulḥan Arukh, Ḥoshen Mishpat* 425:5, *Rema*.)

[1]אָמַר לוֹ: ״אֲחִי אֲבִי אַבָּא, לֹא כָּךְ לִימַּדְתַּנִי בְּרִדְתְּךָ מֵהַר סִינַי: [2]הַבּוֹעֵל אֶת הַנׇּכְרִית קַנָּאִין פּוֹגְעִין בּוֹ״! [3]אָמַר לוֹ: ״קַרְיָינָא דְּאִיגַּרְתָּא אִיהוּ לֶיהֱוֵי פַּרְוָונְקָא״. [4]וּשְׁמוּאֵל אָמַר: רָאָה שֶׁ״אֵין חָכְמָה וְאֵין תְּבוּנָה וְאֵין עֵצָה לְנֶגֶד ה׳״ — [5]כׇּל מָקוֹם שֶׁיֵּשׁ חִילּוּל הַשֵּׁם, אֵין חוֹלְקִין כָּבוֹד לָרַב.

[6]רַבִּי יִצְחָק אָמַר רַבִּי אֱלִיעֶזֶר: רָאָה שֶׁבָּא מַלְאָךְ וְהִשְׁחִית בָּעָם.

[7]״וַיָּקׇם מִתּוֹךְ הָעֵדָה וַיִּקַּח רֹמַח בְּיָדוֹ״. [8]מִיכָּן שֶׁאֵין נִכְנָסִין בִּכְלֵי זַיִין לְבֵית הַמִּדְרָשׁ.

[9]שָׁלַף שְׁנָנָהּ, וְהִנִּיחָהּ בְּאוּנְקְלוֹ, וְהָיָה [82B] נִשְׁעָן וְהוֹלֵךְ עַל מַקְלוֹ, [10]וְכֵיוָן שֶׁהִגִּיעַ אֵצֶל שִׁבְטוֹ שֶׁל שִׁמְעוֹן אָמַר: ״הֵיכָן

LITERAL TRANSLATION

[1]He said to him: "O brother of my father's father, did you not teach me thus when you came down from Mount Sinai: [2]'[If] someone has intercourse with a non-Jewish woman, the zealous may strike him'?" [3]He said to him: "Let the one who reads the letter be the messenger."

[4]And Shmuel said: He saw: "There is no wisdom or understanding or counsel against the Lord" — [5]wherever there is a profanation of God's name, honor is not shown to the master.

[6]Rabbi Yitzḥak said in the name of Rabbi Eliezer: He saw that an angel came, and smote the people.

[7]"He rose up from among the congregation, and took a spear in his hand." [8]From here, that one may not enter the study hall with weapons.

[9]He removed the point, and placed it inside his garment, and [82B] walked, leaning on his stick. [10]When he reached the tribe of Simeon, he said: "Where

TRANSLATION AND COMMENTARY

him. [1]He turned to Moses and **said to him: "O brother of my father's father** [Moses was the brother of Aaron, Phinehas' grandfather], **when you came down from Mount Sinai, did you not teach me as follows:** [2]**'If someone has** sexual **intercourse with a non-Jewish woman, a zealous** person who catches him in the act **may strike him** dead'?" [3]Moses **said** to Phinehas: "Indeed, you are right. And as people say, **let the person who reads the letter aloud be the carrier.** Go now, and carry out the law that you have so well remembered."

וּשְׁמוּאֵל אָמַר [4]**Shmuel said:** What did Phinehas see? **He saw** before his eyes the verse (Proverbs 21:30) that states: **"There is no wisdom or understanding or counsel against the Lord"** — [5]**wherever there is a profanation of God's name, one need not show honor to** one's **master.** Thus, Phinehas did not consult with Moses before taking action. Rather he killed Zimri on his own, lest people think that fornicating with non-Jewish women is permitted, and God's name be desecrated.

רַבִּי יִצְחָק [6]**Rabbi Yitzḥak said in the name of Rabbi Eliezer:** What did Phinehas see? **He saw that an angel had come, and** began to **smite the people** for Zimri's transgression, and he understood that it was time for him to take immediate action in order to prevent the plague from spreading further.

וַיָּקׇם [7]The verse (Numbers 25:7) continues: **"He rose up from among the congregation, and took a spear in his hand."** [8]**From** the fact that the verse states **here** that Phinehas took the spear in his hand only after he rose up from the congregation, meaning the court that had convened to judge those who had joined themselves to Baal Peor, we learn **that one may not enter the study hall with weapons** in hand.

שָׁלַף [9]The Gemara explains: Phinehas **removed the point** from the end of his spear, **and placed it under his garment,** so that his spear appeared like an ordinary walking stick. [82B] He then began to **walk** about, **leaning on his stick,** so that people would not suspect that he was armed. [10]**When he reached the tribe of Simeon,**

RASHI

אחי אבי אבא — היינו משה, שהיה אחי אבי אביו אהרן. **פרוונקא** = שליח. **שמואל אמר מאי וירא ראה שאין חכמה** — כלומר: נזכר פסוק "אין חכמה ואין תבונה נגד ה'" שכל מקום שיש חילול השם אין חולקין כבוד לרב. לפיכך הורה פנחס הלכה בפני רבו, ולא המתין ליטול רשות ממשה, שלא יראו הרואים וילמדו להתיר את הנכרית. **ויקם ויקח** — מכלל דעד השתא לאו בידו הוה. **העדה** — סנהדרין, שהיו יושבים ודנין, כדכתיב, "קח את כל ראשי" ואמרינן בפרק רביעי (לה,א): חלק להם בתי דינין לדונם דיני נפשות על עון פעור. **שלף שננה** — שלף הברזל שבראש העץ של רומח. **אונקלי** = מלבוש. **נשען והולך על מקלו** — על העץ לבדו בלי הברזל, שלא יהיו מכירים בו בני שבטו שלהרוג הוא בא.

LANGUAGE

פַּרְוָונְקָא **Messenger.** This word is of Iranian origin, probably from the Middle Persian *parvanak*, meaning "a guide" and also "a general." Hence in Arabic and Medean, which is related to Persian, it means "an emissary, especially a postman."

אוּנְקְלוֹ **Garment.** This word apparently derives from the Greek ἀνάκωλος, *anakolos*, meaning "short, cut off," and it refers to a short tunic coming to the knees.

NOTES

אָמַר לוֹ: קַרְיָינָא דְּאִיגַּרְתָּא **He said to him: Let the one who reads the letter.** It may be asked: If so, then Moses told Phinehas to go out and kill Zimri, in contradiction to what we said above, that if the zealous person comes before a court for advice, the court may not tell him that he is permitted to slay the offender! It may be suggested that Moses did not actually tell Phinehas to kill Zimri. Rather he agreed with him that that was the law. Or else, because of the special circumstances and the plague, Moses did in fact encourage Phinehas to kill Zimri and halt the plague (*Rabbi David Bonfils*).

TRANSLATION AND COMMENTARY

he said: "Where do we find an allusion **that the tribe of Levi is greater than that of Simeon?** If you may chase after the daughters of Moab, then so may I." [1]The people of the tribe of Simeon **said** to one another: **"Allow him** to enter the chamber where Zimri is fornicating with Kozbi, for **he, too,** wishes to **enter** the chamber in order **to satisfy his** sexual **desires.** [2]Let us rejoice, for surely **the saintly** (among whom Phinehas is counted) must have **permitted the matter."** Then Phinehas entered Zimri's chamber, and killed the couple.

אָמַר רַבִּי יוֹחָנָן [3]**Rabbi Yoḥanan said: Six miracles were performed for Phinehas** when he killed Zimri: [4]**First, Zimri could have withdrawn** from the Midianite woman with whom he was having sexual relations, in which case Phinehas would have been forbidden to kill him, **but** Zimri **did not withdraw** from her. [5]**Second,** Zimri **could have shouted** for help, and his fellow tribesmen would have rushed to his aid, **but he did not shout** out for help. [6]**Third,** Phinehas successfully aimed his spear so that **it struck** Zimri and Kozbi **precisely in their genitals,** so it was evident to all why he killed them. [7]**Fourth,** Zimri and Kozbi **did not slip away from the spear** until after everybody had seen that he had killed them when a zealous person was permitted to do so. [8]**Fifth, an angel came and raised the lintel** of the entranceway to the chamber, and thus it was possible to remove them from the room with the spear remaining in place. [9]**And sixth, an angel came and smote the people** standing outside the chamber, creating a panic to keep them from killing Phinehas.

בָּא [10]The Gemara continues: Phinehas **threw** Zimri and Kozbi **down** to the ground **before God,** [11]and **said to Him: "Master of the universe,** was it **because of these** two that **twenty-four thousand** people **of Israel fell?"** [12]**For the verse** (Numbers 25:9) **states: "And those who died in the plague were twenty-four**

מָצִינוּ שֶׁשִּׁבְטוֹ שֶׁל לֵוִי גָּדוֹל מִשֶּׁל שִׁמְעוֹן״? [1]אָמְרוּ: ״הַנִּיחוּ לוֹ, אַף הוּא לַעֲשׂוֹת צְרָכָיו נִכְנָס. [2]הִתִּירוּ פְּרוּשִׁין אֶת הַדָּבָר״.

[3]אָמַר רַבִּי יוֹחָנָן: שִׁשָּׁה נִסִּים נַעֲשׂוּ לוֹ לְפִנְחָס: [4]אֶחָד — שֶׁהָיָה לוֹ לְזִמְרִי לִפְרוֹשׁ וְלֹא פֵּירֵשׁ, [5]וְאֶחָד — שֶׁהָיָה לוֹ לְדַבֵּר וְלֹא דִּבֵּר, [6]וְאֶחָד — שֶׁכִּוֵּון בְּזַכְרוּתוֹ שֶׁל אִישׁ וּבְנַקְבוּתָהּ שֶׁל אִשָּׁה, [7]וְאֶחָד — שֶׁלֹּא נִשְׁמְטוּ מִן הָרוֹמַח, [8]וְאֶחָד — שֶׁבָּא מַלְאָךְ וְהִגְבִּיהַּ אֶת הַמַּשְׁקוֹף, [9]וְאֶחָד — שֶׁבָּא מַלְאָךְ וְהִשְׁחִית בָּעָם.

[10]בָּא וַחֲבָטָן לִפְנֵי הַמָּקוֹם. [11]אָמַר לְפָנָיו: ״רִבּוֹנוֹ שֶׁל עוֹלָם, עַל אֵלּוּ יִפְּלוּ עֶשְׂרִים וְאַרְבָּעָה אֶלֶף מִיִּשְׂרָאֵל״? [12]שֶׁנֶּאֱמַר: ״וַיִּהְיוּ הַמֵּתִים

LITERAL TRANSLATION

do we find that the tribe of Levi is greater than that of Simeon?" [1]They said: "Leave him be. He, too, enters to take care of his needs. [2]The saintly permitted the matter."

[3]Rabbi Yoḥanan said: Six miracles were performed for Phinehas: [4]One, for Zimri should have withdrawn, but he did not withdraw. [5]And another, for he should have spoken, but he did not speak. [6]And another, that he struck precisely the male genitals of the man and the female genitals of the woman. [7]And another, that they did not slip away from the spear. [8]And another, that an angel came and raised the lintel. [9]And one, that an angel came and smote the people.

[10]He came and threw them down before God. [11]He said before Him: "Master of the universe, because of these, twenty-four thousand of Israel fell?" [12]For it is stated: "And those who died

RASHI

היכן מצינו כו׳ — כלומר אתם מפקירים עצמכם אחר בנות מואב: אני למה לא אעשה כמותכם? וכי שבט שלי גדול משלכם שאהיה פרוש וטהור יותר מכולכם? כיון ששמעו כן אמרו: הניחו לו ליכנס לקובה, שאף הוא רוצה כמותינו. **צרכיו** — תשמיש. **התירו פרושין את הדבר** — ״ודאי מותר לעשות כן שהרי פנחס עשה כמותינו״, כך אמרו העומדים שם כשראו שנכנס. **שהיה לו לפרוש** — מן האשה, ושוב אין ניתן להורגו. **לדבר** — לזעוק לאנשי שבטו לסייעו. **שכוון בזכרותו ובנקבותה** — וראו אותם דבוקים זה בזה, וידעו שניתן רשות לקנאי לפגוע בו ולא יאמרו שנאה היתה בלבו עליו. **שלא נשמטו** — לפרוש זה מזה, עד שראו שהרגם בדין. **והגביה את המשקוף** — והוציאן נדבקים ולא הוצרך להשפיל הרומח וישמטו. **ואחד שבא מלאך והשחית** — והוטרדו בני שבטו ולא הרגו לפנחס.

NOTES

שִׁשָּׁה נִסִּים נַעֲשׂוּ לוֹ לְפִנְחָס **Six miracles were performed for Phinehas.** According to the Aramaic translation of the Torah attributed to Yonatan ben Uziel, twelve miracles were performed for Phinehas. Different counts of these miracles are found in the various Midrashic sources.

שֶׁהָיָה לוֹ לְזִמְרִי לִפְרוֹשׁ **For Zimri should have withdrawn.** Zimri should have withdrawn from the Midianite woman and stood up to resist Phinehas. Alternatively, he should have withdrawn from the woman on account of his stab wound, but he remained attached to her, so that all would see that Phinehas had been justified in killing him (*Ramah*).

בְּמַגֵּפָה אַרְבָּעָה וְעֶשְׂרִים אָלֶף״. [1]וְהַיְינוּ דִּכְתִיב: ״וַיַּעֲמֹד פִּינְחָס וַיְפַלֵּל״. [2]אָמַר רַבִּי אֶלְעָזָר: ״וַיִּתְפַּלֵּל״ לֹא נֶאֱמַר, [3]אֶלָּא ״וַיְפַלֵּל״. [4]מְלַמֵּד כִּבְיָכוֹל שֶׁעָשָׂה פְּלִילוּת עִם קוֹנוֹ. [5]בִּקְשׁוּ מַלְאֲכֵי הַשָּׁרֵת לְדָחֳפוֹ, [6]אָמַר לָהֶן: ״הַנִּיחוּ לוֹ, קַנַּאי בֶּן קַנַּאי הוּא, [7]מֵשִׁיב חֵימָה בֶּן מֵשִׁיב חֵימָה הוּא״. [8]הִתְחִילוּ שְׁבָטִים מְבַזִּין אוֹתוֹ: ״רְאִיתֶם בֶּן פּוּטִי זֶה, שֶׁפִּיטֵּם אֲבִי אִמּוֹ עֲגָלִים לַעֲבוֹדָה זָרָה, וְהָרַג נְשִׂיא שֵׁבֶט מִיִּשְׂרָאֵל״? [9]בָּא הַכָּתוּב וְיִחֲסוֹ: ״פִּנְחָס בֶּן אֶלְעָזָר בֶּן אַהֲרֹן הַכֹּהֵן״. [10]אָמַר לוֹ הַקָּדוֹשׁ בָּרוּךְ הוּא לְמֹשֶׁה: ״הַקְדֵּם לוֹ שָׁלוֹם״, [11]שֶׁנֶּאֱמַר: ״לָכֵן אֱמֹר הִנְנִי נוֹתֵן לוֹ אֶת בְּרִיתִי שָׁלוֹם״. [12]וּרְאוּיָה כַּפָּרָה זוֹ שֶׁתְּהֵא מְכַפֶּרֶת וְהוֹלֶכֶת לְעוֹלָם.

LITERAL TRANSLATION

in the plague were twenty-four thousand." [1]And this is what is written: "And Phinehas stood up, and executed judgment." [2]Rabbi Elazar said: It is not stated: "And he prayed," [3]but rather: "And he executed judgment." [4]This teaches that he entered into a judgment, as it were, with his Maker. [5]The ministering angels wished to push him away. [6]He said to them: "Leave him be. He is a zealot, the son of a zealot. [7]He is one who deflects wrath, the son of one who deflects wrath." [8]The tribes began to scorn him: "Do you see that son of Puti whose mother's father fattened calves for idol worship, and he killed a chief of a tribe of Israel?" [9]Scripture comes and records his genealogy: "Phinehas, the son of Elazar, the son of Aaron the priest." [10]The Holy One, blessed is He, said to Moses: "Greet him." [11]As it is stated: "Wherefore say, Behold, I give to him my covenant of peace." [12]And this atonement is fit to atone forever.

TRANSLATION AND COMMENTARY

thousand." [1]**And this is** the meaning of **the verse** that **states** (Psalm 106:30): **"And Phinehas stood up, and executed judgment,** and so the plague was stayed." [2]Regarding this verse, **Rabbi Elazar said: The verse does not state: "And he prayed** [וַיִּתְפַּלֵּל]," [3]**but rather** it states: **"And he executed judgment** [וַיְפַלֵּל]." [4]**This teaches that** Phinehas **entered into a judgment, as it were, with his Maker,** arguing with Him about the punishment meted out to Israel. [5]**The ministering angels wished to push him away** for speaking to God with such impudence. [6]But God **said to them: "Let him be,** for **he is a zealot, the son of a zealot.** This refers to Levi, who had acted zealously on behalf of his sister Dinah, as the verse states (Genesis 34:25): 'Two of Jacob's sons, Simeon and Levi, Dinah's brethren, took each man his sword, and came upon the city unresisted, and slew all the males.' [7]Moreover, **he is someone who turns away wrath the son of someone who turned away wrath.** This refers to Aaron, who halted the plague that broke out following the rebellion of Korah, as the verse states (Numbers 17:12): 'And he put on incense, and made atonement for the people.'" [8]Then **the** other **tribes began to scorn** Phinehas, saying: **"Do you see that son of Puti whose mother's father fattened calves for idol worship, and he** had the audacity to **kill a chief of a tribe of Israel** without even a trial?" Phinehas' father, Elazar, married one of the daughters of Putiel, as the verse states (Exodus 6:25): "And Elazar Aaron's son took him one of the daughters of Putiel to wife; and she bore him Phinehas." According to the Midrash, this Putiel may be identified with Jethro, who had fattened (*pitem*, in Hebrew) calves for idol worship. Following Phinehas' act of zealotry, the other tribes began to scorn him by reminding him of his maternal grandfather. [9]Therefore, **Scripture came and recorded** Phinehas' **genealogy** on his father's side, stating (Numbers 25:11): **"Phinehas, the son of Elazar, the son of Aaron the priest,** has turned my wrath away from the children of Israel." [10]**The Holy One, blessed is He, said to Moses:** "Go out and **greet him** before the entire people," [11]**as the verse states** (Numbers 25:12): **"Wherefore say, Behold, I give to him my covenant of peace."** And the verse continues (Numbers 25:13): "And he shall have it, and his seed after him, the covenant of an everlasting priesthood; because he was zealous for his God, and made atonement for the children of Israel," [12]teaching that **this atonement** which Phinehas achieved through his act of zealotry **is fit to atone** for the sins of Israel **forever.**

RASHI

פלילות = ריב. **בן קנאי** — משבט לוי שקינא במעשה דינה דכתיב (בראשית לד) ״הכזונה יעשה את אחותנו״. **בן משיב חמה** — אהרן במעשה דקרח דכתיב ״כי יצא הקצף״ וכתיב ״ויתן את הקטורת״. **אבי אמו** — יתרו, דאלעזר אבי פנחס לקח מבנות יתרו דכתיב ״ואלעזר בן אהרן לקח לו מבנות פוטיאל לו לאשה״, ומפרש באגדה: פוטיאל זה יתרו שפיטם עגלים לעבודה זרה. ואמרו בסוטה פוטיאל זה בנו של יוסף שפטפט ביצרו. ומשנינן: אי אבוה דאמיה מיתרו — אמיה דאימיה מיוסף, אי אבוה דאימיה מיוסף — אימיה דאימיה מיתרו, דיקא נמי דכתיב ״פוטיאל״ ולא ״פוטאל״. **וראויה כפרה זו** — שעשה פנחס. **שתהא מכפרת לעולם** — דכתיב (במדבר כה) ״לברית כהונת עולם תחת אשר קנא לאלהיו ויכפר״.

TRANSLATION AND COMMENTARY

אָמַר רַב נַחְמָן [1]The Gemara presents further Midrashic comments about Zimri and Kozbi. **Rav Naḥman said in the name of Rav: What is** meant by **the verse that states** (Proverbs 30:31): [2]**"A greyhound** [זַרְזִיר מָתְנַיִם]; **a he-goat also** [תָּיִשׁ]; **and a king against whom there is no rising up** [מֶלֶךְ אַלְקוּם עִמּוֹ]"? [3]Rav Naḥman interprets this verse homiletically as referring to Zimri and Phinehas. **On that day that wicked man** Zimri **engaged in four-hundred-and-twenty-four acts of** illicit **intercourse** (the numerical value of the Hebrew term זַרְזִיר is four-hundred-and-twenty-four), [4]**and Phinehas waited for him** (the Hebrew term מָתְנַיִם is interpreted here in the sense of הַמְתָּנָה, "waiting") **until he grew weak** (the Hebrew term תָּיִשׁ is interpreted here in the sense of תָּשַׁשׁ, "grew weak"), **not knowing that** it was unnecessary for him to wait that long, for God, **the king against whom there is no rising up, was with him.**

בְּמַתְנִיתָא תָּנָא [5]A slightly different tradition regarding Zimri's transgression **was taught in the** following **Baraita:** "On that day Zimri engaged in **sixty** acts of illicit intercourse with Kozbi, **until** his semen **became** weak and murky **like an infertile egg,** [6]**and she became** saturated with his semen **like a garden-bed full of water."**

אָמַר רַב כָּהֲנָא [7]In order to emphasize Kozbi's depravity and licentiousness, **Rav Kahana said** in exaggeration: Kozbi's **bottom was a** *bet se'ah*, the area required in order to sow a seah of produce. [8]And similarly **Rav Yosef taught** a Baraita stating: "Kozbi's **uterus was a cubit** in size."

אָמַר רַב שֵׁשֶׁת [9]**Rav Sheshet said:** The Midianite woman's **name was not** really **Kozbi, but rather her name was Shevilnai the daughter of Zur.** [10]**Why,** then, **was she called Kozbi** (כָּזְבִּי)? [11]**Because she was false** (כִּזְּבָה) **to her father,** disobeying his instructions not to have intercourse with anybody but the leader of all Israel. [12]**Another**

[1]אָמַר רַב נַחְמָן אָמַר רַב: מַאי דִּכְתִיב: [2]"זַרְזִיר מָתְנַיִם אוֹ תָיִשׁ וּמֶלֶךְ אַלְקוּם עִמּוֹ", [3]אַרְבַּע מֵאוֹת וְעֶשְׂרִים וְאַרְבַּע בְּעִילוֹת בָּעַל אוֹתוֹ רָשָׁע אוֹתוֹ הַיּוֹם. [4]וְהִמְתִּין לוֹ פִּנְחָס עַד שֶׁתָּשַׁשׁ כֹּחוֹ, וְהוּא אֵינוֹ יוֹדֵעַ שֶׁמֶּלֶךְ אַלְקוּם עִמּוֹ.

[5]בְּמַתְנִיתָא תָּנָא: "שִׁשִּׁים, עַד שֶׁנַּעֲשָׂה כַּבֵּיצָה הַמּוּזֶרֶת, [6]וְהִיא הָיְתָה כַּעֲרוּגָה מְלֵיאָה מַיִם". [7]אָמַר רַב כָּהֲנָא: וּמוֹשָׁבָהּ בֵּית סְאָה. [8]תָּנֵי רַב יוֹסֵף: קֶבֶר שֶׁלָּהּ אַמָּה.

[9]אָמַר רַב שֵׁשֶׁת: לֹא כָּזְבִּי שְׁמָהּ, אֶלָּא שְׁוִילְנָאי בַּת צוּר שְׁמָהּ. [10]וְלָמָּה נִקְרָא שְׁמָהּ כָּזְבִּי? [11]שֶׁכִּזְּבָה בְּאָבִיהָ. [12]דָּבָר

LITERAL TRANSLATION

[1]Rav Naḥman said in the name of Rav: What is that which is written: [2]"A greyhound; a he-goat also; and a king against whom there is no rising up"? [3]On that day that wicked man engaged in four-hundred-and-twenty-four acts of intercourse, [4]and Phinehas waited for him until his power grew weak, not knowing that the king against whom there is no rising up was with him.

[5]It was taught in a Baraita: "Sixty, until he became like an infertile egg, [6]and she became like a garden-bed full of water." [7]Rav Kahana said: And her bottom was a *bet se'ah.* [8]Rav Yosef taught: "Her uterus (lit., 'tomb') was a cubit."

[9]Rav Sheshet said: Her name was not Kozbi, but rather her name was Shevilnai the daughter of Zur. [10]And why was her name called Kozbi? [11]Because she was false to her father. [12]Another explanation:

RASHI

ארבע מאות וכו' — זרזיר בגימטריא הכי הוו. **מתנים** — לשון המתנה. **או תיש** — עד שתשש כחו. **אלקום עמו** — שכל הקומות שלו. ופנחס לא היה יודע — שהקדוש ברוך הוא, ששמו מלך אלקום, — עמו, שלא היה צריך להמתין שיתשש כחו, ונראה בעיני שהתיבה הזאת לשון ערבי שכל פתיחת תיבותיהן "אל". **ששים** — ואין לדבר רמז במקרא. **שנעשה** — ביצים שלו כביצים מוזרות, שהוקלש ונתבלבל שכבת זרע שבתוכו מרוב בעילות. **והיא נתמלאה** — שכבת זרע כערוגה מלאה מים. **מושבה** — מקום מושבה, שהיתה רחבה ביותר. **וקבר שלה** — פתיחת רחמה. **שכזבה באביה** — שלוה אליה אל תשמעי אלא לגדול שבהם.

BACKGROUND

כַּבֵּיצָה הַמּוּזֶרֶת **Like an infertile egg.** Because of the frequency of conjugal relations, the sperm in the testicles becomes scarce, and the semen is thinner, like an egg that was unfertilized but was incubated for some time.

NOTES

מֶלֶךְ אַלְקוּם עִמּוֹ **A king against whom there is no rising up.** It has been suggested that these words allude to the evil inclination (which is likened to a king in several Biblical passages). Phinehas did not know that it was because of the strength of Zimri's evil inclination that he could think about nothing else (*R. A. M. Horowitz*).

מוֹשָׁבָהּ בֵּית סְאָה **Her bottom was a** ***bet se'ah.*** It would appear from the *Arukh* and the Geonim (who had a slightly different reading of the text) that, because of the many acts of sexual intercourse in which Kozbi engaged, the whole surrounding area (referred to here in an exaggerated manner as a *bet se'ah*) was saturated with bodily fluids.

קֶבֶר שֶׁלָּהּ אַמָּה **Her uterus was a cubit.** The term *kever* is used here as an allusion to Kozbi's licentious behavior. Alternatively, it refers to Kozbi's grave, the literal meaning of the term. Even though she was a noble woman during her lifetime, she was buried in ignominy and stuffed into a tiny grave one cubit long.

שְׁוִילְנָאי **Shevilnai.** During the Amoraic period, Shevilnai was a popular name adopted by prostitutes. The Amoraim had a tradition that Kozbi's real name was Shevilnai, and that prostitutes of later generations took the name from her. As for the expression גַּפְּתָה לְאִמָּהּ, some understand that Kozbi engaged in prostitution in the presence of her mother, and it had no more importance to her than the skin of a reed (קְלִפֵּי דְּקָנֵי) (*Geonim*).

LANGUAGE (RASHI)

אשטוינ״א* It should be אושייר״ש, from the Old French *osiers*, meaning "willow branches."

TRANSLATION AND COMMENTARY

explanation: The woman was called **Kozbi because she said to her father: "Slaughter this people through me** [כּוֹס בִּי]." And because Kozbi was really named Shevilnai, that name became associated with all prostitutes, which explains [1]**what people say: "What has Shevilnai to do** in a secluded place **between the reeds and the bulrushes** other than prostitution?" [2]Or else: **"What has Shevilnai to do among the reeds?** Surely she has gone there to engage in prostitution." [3]Or else: "Shevilnai **has tarnished her mother's** reputation with the allegation of **prostitution,** for everybody refers to the daughter as a prostitute who is the daughter of a prostitute."

אָמַר רַבִּי יוֹחָנָן [4]**Rabbi Yoḥanan said:** Zimri **had** the following **five names:** [5]**Zimri** (Numbers 25:14), **the son of Salu** (Numbers 25:14), **Saul** (Genesis 46:10), **the son of the Canaanite woman** (Genesis 46:10), **and Shelumiel ben Tzurishadai** (Numbers 7:36). [6]**Zimri** (זִמְרִי), **because** his semen **became** weak and murky **like an infertile** (מוּזֶרֶת) **egg.** [7]**The son of Salu** (סָלוּא), **because** his wicked behavior **caused the sins of his family to be remembered** (הִסְלִיא). [8]**Saul** (שָׁאוּל), **because he lent himself out** (הִשְׁאִיל) **for a sin.** [9]**The son of a Canaanite woman, because he acted in the manner of** the people of **Canaan.** [10]**And what was his** real **name?** His real **name was Shelumiel ben Tzurishadai.**

כֹּהֵן שֶׁשִּׁימֵּשׁ [11]We learn in the next clause of our Mishnah: **"If a priest served** in the Temple **while ritually impure,** his priestly brethren do not bring him before an earthly court for flogging, but rather the young priests kill him." [12]**Rav Aḥa bar Huna asked Rav Sheshet: If a priest served** in the Temple **while ritually impure, is he liable to death at the hand of Heaven or is he not liable to death at the hand of Heaven?**

אָמַר לֵיהּ [13]Rav Sheshet **said to** Rav Aḥa bar Huna: **You have** already **learned** the Mishnah that gives the answer to your question: [14]**"If a priest served** in the Temple **while ritually impure, his priestly brethren**

אַחֵר: כָּזְבִּי — שֶׁאָמְרָה לְאָבִיהָ: "כּוֹס בִּי עַם זֶה". [1]וְהַיְינוּ דְּאָמְרִי אֱינָשֵׁי: "בֵּין קָנֵי לְאוּרְבָנֵי שְׁוִילְנָאי מַאי בָּעְיָא?" [2]"בַּהֲדֵי קַלְפֵּי דְקָנֵי שְׁוִילְנָאי מַאי בָּעְיָא?" [3]"גַּפְתָּהּ לְאִמָּהּ". [4]אָמַר רַבִּי יוֹחָנָן: חֲמִשָּׁה שֵׁמוֹת יֵשׁ לוֹ. [5]זִמְרִי, וּבֶן סָלוּא, וְשָׁאוּל, וּבֶן הַכְּנַעֲנִית, וּשְׁלוּמִיאֵל בֶּן צוּרִי שַׁדַּי. [6]זִמְרִי — עַל שֶׁנַּעֲשָׂה כְּבֵיצָה הַמּוּזֶרֶת, [7]בֶּן סָלוּא — עַל שֶׁהִסְלִיא עֲוֹנוֹת שֶׁל מִשְׁפַּחְתּוֹ, [8]שָׁאוּל — עַל שֶׁהִשְׁאִיל עַצְמוֹ לִדְבַר עֲבֵירָה, [9]בֶּן הַכְּנַעֲנִית — עַל שֶׁעָשָׂה מַעֲשֵׂה כְּנַעַן — [10]וּמַה שְּׁמוֹ? שְׁלוּמִיאֵל בֶּן צוּרִי שַׁדַּי שְׁמוֹ.

[11]"כֹּהֵן שֶׁשִּׁימֵּשׁ בְּטוּמְאָה". [12]בְּעָא מִינֵּיהּ רַב אַחָא בַּר הוּנָא מֵרַב שֵׁשֶׁת: כֹּהֵן שֶׁשִּׁימֵּשׁ בְּטוּמְאָה חַיָּיב מִיתָה בִּידֵי שָׁמַיִם אוֹ אֵין חַיָּיב מִיתָה בִּידֵי שָׁמַיִם? [13]אָמַר לֵיהּ; תְּנִיתוּהָ: [14]"כֹּהֵן שֶׁשִּׁימֵּשׁ בְּטוּמְאָה אֵין אֶחָיו

LITERAL TRANSLATION

Kozbi — for she said to her father: "Slaughter this people through me." [1]And this is what people say: "What has Shevilnai to do between the reeds and the bulrushes?" [2]"What has Shevilnai to do among the skins of reeds?" [3]"She tarnished her mother with prostitution."

[4]Rabbi Yoḥanan said: He had five names: [5]Zimri, the son of Salu, and Saul, and the son of the Canaanite woman, and Shelumiel ben Tzurishadai. [6]Zimri, because he became like an infertile egg. [7]The son of Salu, because he caused the sins of his family to be remembered. [8]Saul, because he lent himself out for a sin. [9]The son of a Canaanite woman, because he did an act of Canaan. [10]And what was his name? Shelumiel ben Tzurishadai was his name.

[11]"[If] a priest served while ritually impure." [12]Rav Aḥa bar Huna asked Rav Sheshet: [If] a priest served while ritually impure, is he liable to death at the hand of Heaven or is he not liable to death at the hand of Heaven?

[13]He said to him: You have learned it: [14]"[If] a priest served while ritually impure, his

RASHI

כוס בי עם זה — שחוט אותם על ידי. **והיינו דאמרי אינשי** — על שם כזבי אומרים דבר זה. **בין קני לאורבני** — מקום יחוד. **אורבני** — ערבה דקה הגדלה בין האגמים *אשטוינ״א בלעז. **מאי בעי?** — ודאי משום זנות הלכה לשם. **בהדי קלפי דקני** — קליפות הקנים. **שוילנאי מאי בעיא?** — ודאי משום זנות הלכה שם. **גפתה לאמה** — הנאיפה אמה, כלומר הוציאה שם גפייתה על אמה, שכיון שזינתה קורין אותה זונה בת זונה. **הסליא** — גרם שיזכרו ויספרו, לשון "לא תסולה" (איוב כח) "המסולאים בפז" (איכה ד), שהיו מעריכין עצמן בפז, ואת זה ואת משפחתו סלו בניאופים, לישנא אחרינא: גרס לחפש ולדקדק אחר עונש לשון "מסלסל בשערו" (נזיר ג,א). **מעשה כנען** — זמה, כדאמרינן ב"ערבי פסחים" (קיג, ב): חמשה דברים צוה כנען את בניו, ואהבו את הזמה.

NOTES

הִסְלִיא עֲוֹנוֹת **He caused the sins to be remembered.** Some understand that the word הִסְלִיא means "he lifted, he raised" — in other words, that he lifted the sins of his family and showed them to all (*Arukh*).

TRANSLATION AND COMMENTARY

do not bring him before an earthly **court.** [1]**Rather the young priests remove** the offending priest **from the Temple Courtyard,** so as not to defile the Temple, **and** then **smash his brains with clubs."** [2]**Now if you think that** a priest who participated in the Temple service while ritually impure **is liable to death at the hand of Heaven,** [3]then surely the young priests **should leave** the offending priest alone, **so that he can be killed at the hand of Heaven!**

אֶלָּא מַאי [4]Rav Aḥa bar Huna rejected this argument: **Rather, what** is the law, that such a person **is not liable** to death at the hand of Heaven? If so, how can his young colleagues club him to death? [5]**Is there any** offender **whom the Torah** totally **exempts** from the death penalty, both judicial execution and death at the hand of Heaven, but **we kill him** nonetheless?

וְלָא [6]Rav Sheshet said to him: Do we **not** find such a case? [7]**But surely we have learned** in the Mishnah, above (81b): **"If someone** sinned and **was flogged, and then** he repeated his offense, and was flogged **a second time,** and then he committed that same offense a third time, **the court puts him in a** prison-**chamber** and allows him to die there." There, too, you should argue: [8]If **the Torah exempts** the offender from the death penalty, how can **we kill him?**

הָאָמַר [9]Rav Aḥa bar Huna countered: **Surely Rabbi Yirmeyah said in the name of Resh Lakish:** [10]There, in the Mishnah, **we are dealing with** someone who had twice received **lashes for** violating **a prohibition** which is **punishable by excision.** [11]Such **a person is** indeed **liable to** premature or sudden **death** at the hand of Heaven.

וְהָא גּוֹנֵב הַקַּסְוָה [12]Rav Sheshet argued further: **But** we have learned in our Mishnah that if **someone steals the *kasvah*,** a zealous person may strike him dead. There, too, you should argue: If the Torah exempts the offender from the death penalty, how can we kill him?

הָאָמַר רַב יְהוּדָה [13]Rav Aḥa bar Huna countered: **Surely Rav Yehudah said:** Here, in the Mishnah, **we are dealing with** someone who steals **a sacred utensil,** [14]**and** the death penalty he deserves **is alluded to by** the verse (Numbers 4:20): **"But they shall not go in to see when the holy things are covered, lest they die."**

הַכֹּהֲנִים מְבִיאִין אוֹתוֹ לְבֵית דִּין. [1]אֶלָּא פִּירְחֵי כְהוּנָּה מוֹצִיאִין אוֹתוֹ חוּץ לָעֲזָרָה וּפוֹצְעִין אֶת מוֹחוֹ בִּגְיזְרִין״. [2]וְאִי סָלְקָא דַעְתָּךְ מִחַיַּיב בִּידֵי שָׁמַיִם, [3]לִישְׁבְּקֵיהּ דְּלִיקְטוֹל בִּידֵי שָׁמַיִם.

[4]אֶלָּא מַאי — אֵינוֹ חַיָּיב? [5]מִי אִיכָּא מִידֵּי דְּרַחֲמָנָא פַּטְרֵיהּ וַאֲנַן נֵיקוּם וְנִיקְטוֹל לֵיהּ?

[6]וְלָא? [7]וְהָתְנַן: ״מִי שֶׁלָּקָה וְשָׁנָה בֵּית דִּין מַכְנִיסִין אוֹתוֹ לַכִּיפָּה״. [8]רַחֲמָנָא פַּטְרֵיהּ וַאֲנַן קָטְלִינַן לֵיהּ!

[9]הָאָמַר רַבִּי יִרְמְיָה אָמַר רֵישׁ לָקִישׁ: [10]בְּמַלְקוּת שֶׁל כְּרֵיתוֹת עָסְקִינַן, [11]דְּגַבְרָא בַּר קְטָלָא הוּא.

[12]וְהָא גּוֹנֵב הַקַּסְוָה!

[13]הָאָמַר רַב יְהוּדָה: בִּכְלֵי שָׁרֵת עָסְקִינַן, [14]וּרְמִיזָא: ״לֹא יָבֹאוּ לִרְאוֹת כְּבַלַּע אֶת הַקֹּדֶשׁ וָמֵתוּ״.

LITERAL TRANSLATION

priestly brethren do not bring him before a court. [1]Rather the young priests remove him from the Temple Courtyard and smash his brains with clubs." [2]And if it enters your mind that he is liable [to death] at the hand of Heaven, [3]let them leave him so that he can be killed at the hand of Heaven!

[4]Rather, what — he is not liable? [5]Is there anything regarding which the Torah (lit., "the Merciful") exempts him, and we rise and kill him?

[6]And not? [7]But surely we have learned: "[If] someone was flogged and then again a second time, the court puts him in a chamber." [8]The Torah exempts him, but we kill him!

[9]Surely Rabbi Yirmiyah said in the name of Resh Lakish: [10]We are dealing with lashes for [a prohibition punishable by] excision, [11]where the person is liable to death.

[12]But [there is] someone who steals the *kasvah*!

[13]Surely Rav Yehudah said: We are dealing with a sacred utensil, [14]and it is alluded to by: "But they shall not go in to see when the holy things are covered, [lest] they die."

NOTES

לִישְׁבְּקֵיהּ דְּלִיקְטוֹל בִּידֵי שָׁמַיִם **Let them leave him so that he can be killed at the hand of Heaven.** We find in various places that if a criminal who is liable to a certain punishment at the hand of man goes unpunished, he is liable to a more severe penalty at the hand of God. Thus, it follows that if a person committed a serious transgression, and the Torah did not obligate the court to save his soul by taking his life, it is preferable to allow him to be killed at the hand of Heaven, and thus allow for the fulfillment of the verse (Psalms 34:22): "Evil shall slay the wicked" (see *Margoliyot HaYam*).

[1]וְהָא הַמְקַלֵּל אֶת הַקּוֹסֵם!
[2]הָא תָּנֵי רַב יוֹסֵף: ״יַכֶּה קוֹסֵם אֶת קוֹסְמוֹ״, [3]דְּמִיחֲזֵי כִּמְבָרֵךְ אֶת הַשֵּׁם.
[4]וְהָא בּוֹעֵל אֲרַמָּאִית!
[5]הָא אַקְרִיוּהּ לְרַב כָּהֲנָא בְּחֶלְמֵיהּ, [6]וְאַדְכְּרֵיהּ רַב לִגְמָרֵיהּ.
[7]אֵיתִיבֵיהּ: [8]״הַיּוֹצֵק וְהַבּוֹלֵל וְהַפּוֹתֵת, הַמּוֹלֵחַ, [9]הַמֵּנִיף, הַמַּגִּישׁ, וְהַמְסַדֵּר אֶת הַשּׁוּלְחָן, [10]הַמֵּטִיב אֶת הַנֵּרוֹת, וְהַקּוֹמֵץ, וְהַמְקַבֵּל דָּמִים בַּחוּץ — [11]פָּטוּר. [12]וְאֵין חַיָּבִין עֲלֵיהֶן

LITERAL TRANSLATION

[1]But [there is] someone who curses [God] with [the name of] a false god!

[2]Surely Rav Yosef taught: "May the false god strike his false god," [3]for he appears like someone who blasphemes (lit., "blesses") God.

[4]But [there is] someone who has intercourse with a non-Jewish woman!

[5]Surely they read to Rav Kahana in his dream, [6]and Rav remembered his tradition.

[7]They raised an objection: [8]"Someone who pours, or mixes, or crumbles, or salts, [9]or waves, or brings near, or arranges the table, [10]or prepares the candles, or scoops out a handful, or receives blood outside — [11]is exempt. [12]And one is not liable on account of them

TRANSLATION AND COMMENTARY

וְהָא הַמְקַלֵּל [1]Rav Sheshet continued: **But** we have learned in our Mishnah that if **someone curses God by** using **the name of a false god,** a zealous person may strike him dead. Now, such a person is exempt from judicial execution, so how can we kill him?

הָא תָּנֵי רַב יוֹסֵף [2]Rav Aḥa bar Huna answered: **Surely Rav Yosef taught** that we are dealing here with someone who curses God with the name of a false god, saying: **"May the false god strike his false god,"** meaning God, to whom he refers by the name of the false god. [3]Such a person **appears** to be **blaspheming God,** and so he is fit to die.

וְהָא בּוֹעֵל [4]Rav Sheshet puts forward one more case: **But** we have learned in our Mishnah that if **someone has** sexual **intercourse with a non-Jewish woman,** a zealous person may strike him dead, even though the offender is not liable to judicial execution.

הָא אַקְרִיוּהּ [5]Rav Aḥa bar Huna answered: **Surely Rav Kahana had a dream** in which the verse in Malachi **was read to him,** and when he reported the dream to Rav, [6]**Rav remembered** that he had received **a tradition** that someone who has intercourse with a non-Jewish woman is in fact liable to excision.

אֵיתִיבֵיהּ [7]**An objection was raised** against Rav Sheshet from a Mishnah (*Zevaḥim* 112a) dealing with the prohibition against offering sacrifices outside the Temple Courtyard: [8]"If **someone pours** oil on a meal-offering, **or mixes** the flour with the oil, **or breaks** the meal-offering into pieces after it is baked, **or salts** the handful of flour from the meal-offering or the meat of a sacrifice that is to be burned on the altar, [9]**or waves** the meal-offering, **or brings** the meal-offering **near** to the altar, **or arranges** the shewbread on **the** sacred **table,** [10]**or prepares the candles** in the candelabrum for lighting, **or scoops out a handful** of flour from the meal-offering, **or receives** sacrificial **blood,** and performed any one of these tasks **outside** the Temple Courtyard, [11]he **is exempt** from the penalty of excision. A person is only liable to excision if he performed the last stage of a particular service outside the Temple. For example, if he sprinkled the blood of a sacrificial animal (the final task involving sacrificial blood), or he burned sacrificial meat (the final task involving such meat) outside the Temple, he has committed a transgression punishable by excision. But all the tasks listed here are followed by additional tasks which complete the service. [12]**And** similarly, if a non-priest performed one of these tasks inside the Temple, **he is not liable** to death at the hand of Heaven

RASHI

הא אקריוה לרב כהנא בחלמיה — ״יכרת וגו׳״ אלמא בר כרת הוא. **היוצק** — שמן על מנחה. **והבולל** — בשמן. **והפותת** — פתים לאחר אפייתה כגון מנחת מחבת ומרחשת, ומאפה תנור, שהן באות אפויות. **והמניפה והמגישה** — בקרן מערבית דרומית כנגד חודה של קרן, כדאמרינן בסוטה בפרק שני (יב,ב), והמסדר שלחן (ולחם) הפנים. **בחוץ** — אם עשה אחת מאלו בחוץ. **פטור** — דלא חייב כרת אלא שוחט דכתיב (ויקרא יז) ״אשר ישחט וגו׳״, ומעלה דכתיב (שם) ״אשר יעלה עולה״. וזורק דאתרבי מ״דם שפך״ בפרק רביעי (לד,ב), וכל הני דיש אחריה עבודה אמעיט בפרק בתרא דזבחים (קטו, ב): מה העלאה מיוחדת שהוא גמר עבודה — אף כל שהוא גמר עבודה.

HALAKHAH

הַיּוֹצֵק וְהַבּוֹלֵל **Someone who pours, or mixes.** "If someone pours oil on a meal offering, or mixes the flour with the oil, or breaks the meal-offering into pieces after it is baked, or salts the handful of flour from the meal-offering or the meat of a sacrifice that is to be burned on the altar, or waves the meal-offering, or brings the meal-offering near the altar, or arranges the shewbread on the sacred table, or prepares the candles in the candelabrum for lighting, or scoops out a handful of flour from the meal-offering, or receives sacrificial blood, and performs any one of these tasks outside the Temple Courtyard — he is exempt from the penalty of excision. A person is only liable if he performed the final stage of a particular service outside the Temple, and all the aforementioned tasks are followed by the additional tasks that are required to complete the service." (*Rambam, Sefer Avodah, Hilkhot Ma'aseh HaKorbanot* 19:6.)

[83A] [1]לֹא מִשּׁוּם זָרוּת, [2]וְלֹא מִשּׁוּם טוּמְאָה, [3]וְלֹא מִשּׁוּם מְחוּסַּר בְּגָדִים, [4]וְלֹא מִשּׁוּם רְחוּץ יָדַיִם וְרַגְלַיִם״. [5]הָא מְקַטֵּר חַיָּיב. [6]מַאי, לָאו — מִיתָה!
[7]לֹא, בְּאַזְהָרָה.
[8]אֶלָּא זָר נַמִי לְאַזְהָרָה?

LITERAL TRANSLATION

[83A] [1]for [the prohibition concerning] non-priests, [2]nor for [the prohibition concerning] ritual impurity, [3]nor for [the prohibition concerning someone who is] lacking garments, [4]nor for [the prohibition concerning] the washing of hands and feet." [5]But if he burned [a sacrifice on the altar] he is liable. [6]What, is it not death?

[7]No, a prohibition (lit., "warning").

[8]But a non-priest also for a prohibition?

TRANSLATION AND COMMENTARY

[83A] [1]**for** violating the prohibition against **non-priests** performing the divine service, for that penalty, too, applies only to tasks that constitute the last stage of a particular service. Similarly, if a priest performed one of these tasks inside the Temple but while ritually impure, [2]he is **not** liable for violating the prohibition against performing the Temple service while in a state of **ritual impurity.** Further, if a priest performed one of these tasks without wearing all the priestly garments, [3]he is **not** liable for violating the prohibition against performing the Temple service **lacking** one of the priestly **garments.** Finally, if a priest performed one of these tasks without first washing his hands and feet, [4]he is **not** guilty of violating the prohibition against serving in the Temple without first **washing** his **hands and feet.** Liability is only imputed if he concluded a particular service." [5]**However, if he burned** sacrificial meat on the altar — the final task involving such meat — in a disqualified state **he** would indeed **be liable.** [6]To what punishment would he be liable? **Is it not** that he would be liable to **death** at the hand of Heaven? Thus, we see that a priest who served in the Temple while ritually impure is in fact liable to death at the hand of Heaven, against the position of Rav Sheshet!

לֹא [7]The Gemara rejects this argument: **No,** in such a case he would liable for violating **an** ordinary **prohibition,** and therefore he would be subject to lashes.

אֶלָּא [8]The Gemara asks: **But** then it should follow that **a non-priest** who burned sacrificial meat on the altar is **also** only liable to lashes **for** violating **an** ordinary **prohibition.** The law regarding a non-priest who served in the Temple is mentioned together with the law regarding a priest who participated in the service while ritually impure, implying that they

RASHI

לא משום זרות — זר שעשה אחת מהם בפנים אינו חייב מיתה, דנפקא לן בסדר יומא (כד,א) מועבדתם עבודת מתנה ודרשינן: עבודה תמה ולא עבודה שיש אחריה עבודה, וכל הני יש אחריה עבודה, יולק ובולל ושאר עבודות דמנחה יש אחריה עבודה דהקטרת הקומץ אחר כולן. מסדר השולחן עבודה אחרונה של לחם הפנים היינו סילוק בזיכין והקטרתן, המטיב את הנרות המדשנס שחרית יש אחריה הדלקת ערבית, מקבל דמים יש אחריו זריקה. **ולא משום טומאה** — כהן טמא ששימש, דזרות ושמוש בטומאה מחד קרא נפקי אזהרה דידהו בפרק "כל הזבחים" תנינא בשחיטת קדשים (זבחים טו,ב) "וינזרו מקדשי בני ישראל ולא יחללו" — דהיינו טומאה, כדכתיב בתריה "אמור אליהם לדורותיכם וגו'" וזר נמי מיניה דרשינן מדאיצטריך קרא למיכתב בני ישראל למעוטי מאי — אי למעוטי קדשי נכרים וקדשי נשים, וכי בטומאה קרבי? והא אמרינן התם דלא! — אלא הכי קאמר: בני ישראל נמי שהם זרים לא יעבדו שלא יחללו. וכיון דזרות וטומאה מחד קרא נפקי מאן דמחייב אזרות מחייב נמי אטומאה. **ולא משום מחוסר בגדים** — דאינהו נמי מזרות אתרבאי בפרק שני דזבחים (יז,ב) דכתיב "וחגרת אותם אבנט וגו'" בזמן שבגדיהם עליהם כהונתם עליהם, אין בגדיהם וכו' והוו להו זרים. **ולא משום שלא רחוץ ידים ורגלים** — ד"חוקה" "חוקה" ממחוסר בגדים גמר לה התם לענין אחולי עבודה, והאי תנא נמי יליף מינה דאמר מה מחוסר בגדים לא מיחייב אלא אגמר עבודה — האי נמי לא מיחייב אלא אעבודה שהוא גמר. **הא מקטיר** — דהויא עבודה תמה שאין אחריה עבודה — חייב משום טומאה, ומאי חייב, לאו מיתה! **לא, לאו** — הוא דמחייב, דכתיב "ולא יחללו". **ופרכינן אלא זר נמי** — הא דדייקינן הא מקטיר לענין זרות תימא נמי דלאו הוא דמחייב, והא מיתה בהדיא כתיב "והזר הקרב וגו'".

HALAKHAH

לֹא מִשּׁוּם זָרוּת **Not for the prohibition concerning non-priests.** "If a non-priest pours oil on a meal-offering, or mixes the flour with the oil, or breaks the meal-offering into pieces after it is baked, or salts the handful of flour from the meal-offering, or the meat of a sacrifice that is to be burned on the altar, or waves the meal-offering, or brings the meal-offering near to the altar, or arranges the shewbread on the sacred table, or prepares the candles in the candelabrum for lighting, or lights a fire on the altar, or scoops out a handful of flour from the meal-offering, or receives sacrificial blood — even though he is liable to lashes, he is exempt from the penalty of death at the hand of Heaven, for a non-priest is only liable to death at the hand of Heaven if he performed a task which is the final stage of a particular service, and all the aforementioned tasks are followed by the additional tasks that are required to complete the service." (*Rambam, Sefer Avodah, Hilkhot Bi'at HaMikdash* 9:5.)

וְלֹא מִשּׁוּם טוּמְאָה, וְלֹא מִשּׁוּם מְחוּסַּר בְּגָדִים, וְלֹא מִשּׁוּם רְחוּץ יָדַיִם וְרַגְלַיִם **Nor for the prohibition concerning ritual impurity, nor for the prohibition concerning someone who is lacking garments, nor for the prohibition concerning the washing of hands and feet.** "If a ritually impure priest, or a priest with a physical defect, or a priest who did not wash his hands or feet served in the Temple, he is only liable if he performed a task for which a non-priest would be liable to death at the hand of Heaven. (A priest who served in the Temple without wearing all of

TERMINOLOGY

קְרָא אַסְמַכְתָּא בְּעָלְמָא The verse is mere support. This expression is found in various places in the Talmud, and is used frequently by the Tosafists and other Rishonim. It means that the Biblical verse cited as the basis for a law is merely an allusion to the law rather than its actual source. Thus, the law does not have the authority of a Biblical injunction, but is merely a Rabbinic decree, with the Biblical text serving simply as a sort of mnemonic device for remembering the law. The Aḥaronim discuss the possibility of identifying markers which can determine whether a particular verse is cited as the actual source of a law or as a mere support (see *Yad Malakhi*).

[1] וְהָכְתִיב: ״וְהַזָּר הַקָּרֵב יוּמָת״! [2] הָא כִּדְאִיתָא, וְהָא כִּדְאִיתָא. [3] מִכְּלָל דְּיוֹצֵק וּבוֹלֵל לָאו נַמִי לָא? [4] וְהָתַנְיָא: ״אַזְהָרָה לְיוֹצֵק וּבוֹלֵל מִנַּיִין? [5] תַּלְמוּד לוֹמַר: ׳קְדֹשִׁים יִהְיוּ...וְלֹא יְחַלְּלוּ׳״! [6] מִדְּרַבָּנַן, וּקְרָא אַסְמַכְתָּא בְּעָלְמָא. [7] מֵיתִיבִי: ״וְאֵלּוּ הֵן שֶׁבְּמִיתָה: טָמֵא שֶׁשִּׁימֵּשׁ״! [8] תְּיוּבְתָּא. [9] גּוּפָא: ״וְאֵלּוּ שֶׁבְּמִיתָה: [10] הָאוֹכֵל אֶת הַטֶּבֶל, [11] וְכֹהֵן טָמֵא שֶׁאָכַל תְּרוּמָה טְהוֹרָה,

LITERAL TRANSLATION

[1] But surely it is written: "And the stranger that comes near shall be put to death"!

[2] This as it is, and this as it is.

[3] This implies that [regarding] someone who pours or mixes, there is also no [prohibition]. [4] But surely it was taught: "From where [do we derive] a warning regarding someone who pours or mixes? [5] The verse states: 'They shall be holy...and not profane!'"

[6] By Rabbinic decree, and the verse is mere support.

[7] They raised an objection: "And these are [liable] to death: A ritually impure [priest] who served!"

[8] A refutation.

[9] The thing itself: "And these are [liable] to death: [10] Someone who eats *tevel*, [11] and a ritually impure priest who ate ritually pure *terumah*,

TRANSLATION AND COMMENTARY

are the same. [1] **But surely** this is not so, for there is an explicit **verse** which **states** (Numbers 18:7): **"And the stranger that comes near shall be put to death,"** meaning at the hand of Heaven!

הָא כִּדְאִיתָא [2] The Gemara responds: This is not difficult, for **one case** stands **as it is, and the other case** stands **as it is,** and no inference may be drawn from their juxtaposition.

מִכְּלָל [3] The Gemara raises another difficulty: If it is true that a priest who burned sacrificial meat on the altar while he was ritually impure is only guilty of violating an ordinary prohibition, and therefore only subject to lashes, then **it follows that** a priest **who poured** oil on a meal-offering **or mixed** the flour with the oil while in a state of ritual impurity **is not even** liable for violating **a prohibition.** [4] **But surely it was taught** otherwise in the following Baraita: **"From where do we derive a prohibition** in the case of a priest **who pours** oil on a meal-offering **or mixes** the flour with the oil while he is ritually impure? [5] This is derived from **the verse** that **states** (Leviticus 21:6): **'They shall be holy** to their God, **and not profane** the name of their God; for the offerings of the Lord made by fire, the bread of their God, do they offer.'"

מִדְּרַבָּנַן [6] The Gemara answers: Pouring oil on a meal offering or mixing flour with the oil while in a state of ritual impurity is in fact only forbidden **by Rabbinic decree, and the verse** cited in the Baraita **is merely an allusion** to the law, rather than its actual source.

מֵיתִיבִי [7] **An objection was raised** against Rav Sheshet from a Baraita: "The following offenders **are liable to death** at the hand of Heaven, including **a ritually impure priest who served** in the Temple." Thus, the Baraita states explicitly that a priest who served in the Temple while in a state of ritual impurity is liable to death at the hand of Heaven, against Rav Sheshet!

תְּיוּבְתָּא [8] The Gemara concludes this discussion: This Baraita is indeed **a** conclusive **refutation** of the position of Rav Sheshet.

גּוּפָא [9] The Gemara now returns to the Baraita it had cited earlier. **It was stated** there: "The following offenders **are liable to death** at the hand of Heaven: [10] **Someone who eats *tevel*** (produce from which the priestly dues have not yet been separated); [11] **a ritually impure priest who ate ritually pure *terumah*** (the portion of

RASHI

הא כדאיתא וכו׳ — בזרות דייקינן הא מקטר חייב מיתה, ולענין טומאה לאו. מכלל דיוצק ובולל — מדקאמר מקטר לאו בעלמא הוא דאית ביה, ומההוא חיובא ממעיט ליוצק ובולל אלמא אפילו לאו לא מיחייב משום טומאה. אזהרה ליוצק ובולל — לטומאת הגוף מנין. קדושים יהיו ולא יחללו — אם אינו ענין לעבודה תמה דהא כתיב ״וינזרו ולא יחללו״ — תנהו ענין לעבודה שיש אחריה עבודה. ואלו שבמיתה — ברייתא היא וחשיב נמי טובא, ותני נמי טמא ששימש. האוכל את הטבל וכו׳ — כולה מתניתין יליף לה מקראי לקמן.

NOTES

וְאֵלּוּ שֶׁבְּמִיתָה And these are liable to death. It has already been noted that the Baraita does not list all the offenses that render the offender subject to death at the hand of Heaven, and so we must say, as the Gemara states

HALAKHAH

his priestly garments is treated like a non-priest who served in the Temple; *Kesef Mishneh*.)" (*Rambam, Sefer Avodah, Hilkhot Bi'at HaMikdash* 9:10.)

הָאוֹכֵל אֶת הַטֶּבֶל Someone who eats *tevel*. "If someone eats produce the size of an olive from which *terumah* and tithe-*terumah* have not yet been set aside, he is liable to death at the hand of Heaven. (*Rambam, Sefer Kedushah, Ma'akhalot Asurot* 10:19.)

כֹּהֵן טָמֵא שֶׁאָכַל תְּרוּמָה טְהוֹרָה A ritually impure priest who ate ritually pure *terumah*. "A ritually impure priest is

TRANSLATION AND COMMENTARY

produce that is set aside and given to a priest); [1]**a non-priest who ate** ***terumah;*** [2]**a non-priest who served in the Temple,** [3]**a ritually impure priest who served** in the Temple; [4]a priest **who served** in the Temple after **immersing himself** in a ritual bath **during the day** in order to rid himself of ritual impurity, but before his purification process was completed at nightfall; [5]a priest who performed the Temple service **without** wearing all the priestly **garments;** a priest who served in the Temple after being cured of gonorrhea or leprosy, but before bringing the sacrifices that are required to complete his purification process, [6]so that he is still **lacking atonement;** [7]a priest who served in the Temple **without having washed his hands and feet** beforehand; [8]a priest who performed the Temple service while **intoxicated with wine;** [9]**and** a priest who participated in the Temple service **with** long **hair** that had not been cut for thirty days. [10]**But an uncircumcised** priest

[1]וְזָר שֶׁאָכַל אֶת הַתְּרוּמָה, [2]וְזָר שֶׁשִּׁימֵּשׁ, [3]וְטָמֵא שֶׁשִּׁימֵּשׁ, [4]וּטְבוּל יוֹם שֶׁשִּׁימֵּשׁ, [5]וּמְחוּסַּר בְּגָדִים, [6]וּמְחוּסַּר כַּפָּרָה, [7]וְשֶׁלֹּא רָחַץ יָדַיִם וְרַגְלַיִם, [8]וּשְׁתוּיֵי יַיִן, [9]וּפְרוּעֵי רֹאשׁ. [10]אֲבָל

LITERAL TRANSLATION

[1]and a non-priest who ate *terumah,* [2]and a non-priest who served [in the Temple], [3]and a ritually impure [priest] who served, [4]and someone who immersed himself during the day and [then] served, [5]and someone lacking garments, [6]and someone lacking atonement, [7]and someone who did not wash his hands and feet, [8]and those intoxicated with wine, [9]and those with wild hair. [10]But

RASHI

ופרועי ראש – ששימשו פרועי ראש, שעברו עליהם יותר משלשים יום שלא גלחו ראשם.

NOTES

elsewhere, that the Baraita taught certain cases, and left other cases to be added (*Ramban* in his critique of *Rambam's Sefer HaMitzvot*).

טָמֵא שֶׁשִּׁימֵּשׁ A ritually impure priest who served. The Rishonim ask: How can it be that a priest who served in the Temple while ritually impure is liable to death at the hand of Heaven, if he was already liable to excision (a more severe penalty) from the time that he entered the Temple in his ritually impure state? *Ra'avad* suggests that the priest was standing outside the Temple and participating in the Temple service with a long utensil. *Tosafot* and *Rabbi David Bonfils* propose that the Gemara is referring here to a priest who contracted ritual impurity inside the Temple. Others argue that the priest inadvertently entered the Temple in a state of ritual impurity and learned of his impurity only after the fact. Alternatively, he entered into the Temple by the roof, in such a manner that he did not become liable for doing so (*Meiri, Mishneh LeMelekh*).

HALAKHAH

forbidden to eat *terumah,* whether ritually pure or impure. If he ate ritually pure *terumah,* he is liable to death at the hand of Heaven." (*Rambam, Sefer Zeraim, Hilkhot Terumah* 7:1.)

זָר שֶׁאָכַל אֶת הַתְּרוּמָה A non-priest who ate *terumah.* "If a non-priest ate *terumah,* whether he was ritually pure or impure, and whether the *terumah* was ritually pure or impure, he is liable to death at the hand of Heaven." (*Rambam, Sefer Zeraim, Hilkhot Terumah* 6:6.)

זָר שֶׁשִּׁימֵּשׁ A non-priest who served in the Temple. "If a non-priest served in the Temple, his service is disqualified, and he is liable to death at the hand of Heaven. (*Rambam, Sefer Avodah, Hilkhot Bi'at HaMikdash* 9:1.)

טָמֵא שֶׁשִּׁימֵּשׁ A ritually impure priest who served. "If a ritually impure priest served in the Temple, his service is disqualified, and he is liable to death at the hand of Heaven." (*Rambam, Sefer Avodah, Hilkhot Bi'at HaMikdash* 4:1.)

טְבוּל יוֹם שֶׁשִּׁימֵּשׁ Someone who immersed himself during the day. "If a priest who was ritually impure immersed himself in a ritual bath, and then participated in the Temple service before nightfall, his service is disqualified, and he is liable to death at the hand of Heaven." (*Rambam, Sefer Avodah, Hilkhot Bi'at HaMikdash* 4:4.)

מְחוּסַּר בְּגָדִים Someone lacking garments. "If an ordinary priest served in the Temple without wearing all four of his priestly garments, of if the High Priest served in the Temple without wearing all eight of his priestly garments, his service is disqualified, and he is liable to death at the hand of Heaven." (*Rambam, Sefer Avodah, Hilkhot Kelei HaMikdash* 10:4.)

מְחוּסַּר כַּפָּרָה Someone lacking atonement. "According to *Rambam,* if a priest served in the Temple before bringing the sacrifices that are required to complete his purification, his service is disqualified, but he is not liable to death at the hand of Heaven. According to *Ra'avad,* he is indeed liable to death at the hand of Heaven. (*Kesef Mishneh* tries to reconcile the position of *Rambam.*) (*Rambam, Sefer Avodah, Hilkhot Bi'at HaMikdash* 4:4.)

שֶׁלֹּא רָחַץ יָדַיִם וְרַגְלַיִם Someone who did not wash his hands and feet. "If a priest served in the Temple without washing his hands and feet beforehand, his service is disqualified, and he is liable to death at the hand of Heaven." (*Rambam, Sefer Avodah, Hilkhot Bi'at HaMikdash* 5:1.)

שְׁתוּיֵי יַיִן Those intoxicated with wine. "A priest who drank wine, even if he is otherwise fit for service, may not enter the Temple compound past the altar. If he entered and performed the service, his service is disqualified, and he is liable to death at the hand of Heaven." (*Rambam, Sefer Avodah, Hilkhot Bi'at HaMikdash* 1:1.)

פְּרוּעֵי רֹאשׁ Those with wild hair. "A priest with long hair may not enter the Temple compound past the altar. If he entered and performed the service, his service is disqualified, and he is liable to death at the hand of Heaven." (*Rambam, Sefer Avodah, Hilkhot Bi'at HaMikdash* 1:8.)

TRANSLATION AND COMMENTARY

who served in the Temple, **or** a priest who took part in the Temple service while **in acute mourning** on the day of death of a close relative, **or** a priest who performed the Temple service while **seated, is not liable to death** at the hand of Heaven, [1]**but rather** he has merely violated **a prohibition.** [2]The Tannaim disagree about a priest **with a physical defect** who served in the Temple. [3]**Rabbi** Yehudah HaNasi **says:** He is liable **to death** at the hand of Heaven. [4]**And the Sages say:** He has merely violated **a prohibition.** The Tannaim also disagree about someone who **committed intentional trespass,** making unlawful use of consecrated property. Someone who unintentionally benefits from consecrated property or damages it through use must repay the Temple for the loss he caused or the benefit he gained, plus a fine of one-fifth of the value of that loss or benefit, and he must bring a special offering. If he committed the offense intentionally, [5]**Rabbi** Yehudah HaNasi **says:** He is liable **to death** at the hand of Heaven. [6]**And the Sages say:** He has merely violated **a prohibition."**

הָאוֹכֵל [7]The Gemara now seeks the Biblical source for each of the laws taught in the Baraita. It was taught in the Baraita: **"Someone who eats** ***tevel*** is liable to death at the hand of Heaven." **From where do we know this** law? [8]The Gemara explains: **As Shmuel said in the name of Rabbi Eliezer: From where do we know that someone who eats** ***tevel*** **is liable to death** at the hand of Heaven? [9]**For the verse states** (Leviticus 22:15): **"And they shall not profane the holy things of the children of Israel, which they will set aside to the Lord."** The future form of the verb יָרִימוּ, "they will set aside," [10]teaches that **Scripture speaks** here **about** *tevel* from which ***terumah*** **will be set aside in the future.** And the verse states "And they shall not profane," teaching that one is forbidden to eat such produce as long as those priestly dues have not been removed. [11]**We** may **learn** the penalty for violating this prohibition by a *gezerah shavah* drawn between this instance of the word **"profanation"** and another instance of the word **"profanation"** mentioned **with regard to** a ritually impure priest who ate ritually pure ***terumah.*** [12]**Just as, there,** the offender is liable

עָרֵל וְאוֹנֵן וְיוֹשֵׁב — אֵינָן בְּמִיתָה, [1]אֶלָּא בְּאַזְהָרָה. [2]בַּעַל מוּם, [3]רַבִּי אוֹמֵר: בְּמִיתָה. [4]וַחֲכָמִים אוֹמְרִים: בְּאַזְהָרָה. הֵזִיד בִּמְעִילָה, [5]רַבִּי אוֹמֵר: בְּמִיתָה. [6]וַחֲכָמִים אוֹמְרִים בְּאַזְהָרָה״.

[7]״הָאוֹכֵל אֶת הַטֶּבֶל״. מְנָלַן? [8]דְּאָמַר שְׁמוּאֵל מִשּׁוּם רַבִּי אֱלִיעֶזֶר: מִנַּיִין לְאוֹכֵל אֶת הַטֶּבֶל שֶׁהוּא בְּמִיתָה? [9]דִּכְתִיב: ״וְלֹא יְחַלְּלוּ אֶת קָדְשֵׁי בְּנֵי יִשְׂרָאֵל [אֵת] אֲשֶׁר יָרִימוּ לַה׳״. [10]בַּעֲתִידִים לִתְרוֹם הַכָּתוּב מְדַבֵּר, [11]וְיָלֵיף ״חִילּוּל״ ״חִילּוּל״ מִתְּרוּמָה. [12]מַה לְהַלָּן

LITERAL TRANSLATION

an uncircumcised man, or someone in acute mourning, or someone seated is not [liable] to death, [1]but rather [is liable for violating] a prohibition. [2]Someone with a physical defect, [3]Rabbi says: To death. [4]And the Sages say: For a prohibition. [If] he committed intentional trespass, [5]Rabbi says: To death. [6]And the Sages say: For a prohibition."

[7]"Someone who eats *tevel.*" From where do we [know this]? [8]As Shmuel said in the name of Rabbi Eliezer: From where [do we know that] someone who eats *tevel* is liable to death? [9]For it is written: "And they shall not profane the holy things of the Children of Israel, which they will set aside to the Lord." [10]Scripture speaks about those who will set aside [*terumah*] in the future. [11]And he learns "profanation" "profanation" from *terumah.* [12]Just as there

RASHI

אבל ערל — שמתו אחיו מחמת מילה, וכן אונן ששימש, וכן מי ששימש מיושב דכל הני כולהו קים להו בהוא דמחלי עבודה בפרק שני דזבחים (טו, ב), אפילו הכי ליתנהו במיתה אלא באזהרה, ולקמן מפרש לה. **בעל מום** — כהן בעל מום ששימש. **רבי אומר במיתה** — לקמן מפרש פלוגתייהו. **הזיד במעילה** — נהנה מן הקדש שיש בו מעילה במזיד. **אשר ירימו** — שעתידין לתרום וקאמר דלא יחללום שאסור לאכלם בטבלם. **מתרומה** — שאכלה בטומאה דכתיב ״ומתו בו כי יחללוהו״.

HALAKHAH

עָרֵל **An uncircumcised person.** "If an uncircumcised priest served in the Temple, he is subject to lashes, but he is not liable to death at the hand of Heaven." (*Rambam, Sefer Avodah, Hilkhot Bi'at HaMikdash* 6:8.)

אוֹנֵן **Someone in acute mourning.** "A priest who is in acute mourning (on the day of death of a close relative) is forbidden to serve in the Temple. But if he participated in the service, he is not subject to lashes." (*Rambam, Sefer Avodah, Hilkhot Bi'at HaMikdash* 2:8.)

יוֹשֵׁב **Someone seated.** "If a priest performed the Temple service while seated, his service is disqualified, but he is not subject to lashes, for he has violated a prohibition that stems from a positive commandment." (*Rambam, Sefer Avodah, Hilkhot Bi'at HaMikdash* 5:17.)

בַּעַל מוּם **Someone with a physical defect.** "If a priest with a physical defect served in the Temple, his service is disqualified, and he is subject to lashes (following the Sages; *Kesef Mishneh*)." (*Rambam, Sefer Avodah, Hilkhot Bi'at HaMikdash* 6:6.)

הֵזִיד בִּמְעִילָה **If he committed intentional trespass.** "Whoever commits intentional trespass is liable to lashes," following the Sages, and against the position of Rabbi Yehudah HaNasi. (*Rambam, Sefer Avodah, Hilkhot Meilah* 1:3.)

בְּמִיתָה, [1]אַף כָּאן בְּמִיתָה.
[2]וְנֵילוּף "חִילּוּל" "חִילּוּל" מִנּוֹתָר. [3]מַה לְּהַלָּן בְּכָרֵת, [4]אַף כָּאן בְּכָרֵת!
[5]מִסְתַּבְּרָא, מִתְּרוּמָה הֲוָה לֵיהּ לְמֵילַף, [6]שֶׁכֵּן: תְּרוּמָה, [7]חוּצָה לָאָרֶץ, [8]הוּתְּרָה, [9]בְּרַבִּים, [10]פֵּירוֹת, [11]פִּיגּוּל, [12]וְנוֹתָר.
[13]אַדְּרַבָּה, מִנּוֹתָר הֲוָה לֵיהּ לְמֵילַף, [14]שֶׁכֵּן: פְּסוּל אוֹכֶל, [15]אֵין לוֹ הֶיתֵּר בְּמִקְוֶה.
[16]הָנָךְ נְפִישָׁן.

LITERAL TRANSLATION

by death, [1]so, too, here by death.

[2]But let him learn "profanation" "profanation" from a leftover sacrifice. [3]Just as there by excision, [4]so, too, here by excision!

[5]It stands to reason that he should learn from *terumah*, [6]for indeed: *Terumah*, [7]outside the land, [8]it is permitted, [9]in the plural, [10]produce, [11]an offering disqualified by improper intention, [12]and a leftover sacrifice.

[13]On the contrary, he should have learned from a leftover sacrifice, [14]for indeed: Disqualified food, [15]it is not permitted by a ritual bath!

[16]Those are many.

TRANSLATION AND COMMENTARY

to death at the hand of Heaven, as the verse states (Leviticus 22: 9): "They shall therefore keep my charge, lest they bear sin for it, and die for it, if they profane it," [1]**so, too, here,** the offender is liable **to death** at the hand of Heaven.

וְנֵילוּף [2]The Gemara comments: **But let us learn** the penalty for eating *tevel* by a different *gezerah shavah* drawn between this instance of the word **"profanation"** and another instance of the word **"profanation"** regarding someone who eats part of a **sacrifice left over** after the time permitted for it to be eaten; of such a person the verse states (Leviticus 19:8): "Therefore everyone who eats of it shall bear his iniquity, because he has profaned the hallowed thing of the Lord." [3]**Just as, there,** the offender is liable to the penalty of **excision,** as the aforementioned verse continues, "And that soul shall be cut off from among his people," [4]**so, too, here,** the offender should be liable to the penalty of **excision.**

מִסְתַּבְּרָא [5]The Gemara continues: **It stands to reason that we should learn** the penalty for eating *tevel* **from** the penalty for eating ***terumah*** while in a state of ritual impurity, [6]**for** there are **indeed** numerous similarities between *terumah* and *tevel,* as distinct from eating a leftover sacrifice. (1) Both are ***terumah,*** the one being outright *terumah,* and the other being a mixture of *terumah* and ordinary produce. [7](2) Neither applies **outside the Land** of Israel, for *terumah* is only set aside from produce that grew in the Land of Israel, [8](3) There **is a way to permit** ritually pure *terumah* to a ritually impure priest, and *tevel* to all people. The former is accomplished by having the priest immerse himself in a ritual bath and rid himself of his ritual impurity, and the latter is done by setting aside the necessary *terumah;* but there is no way to permit a person to eat a leftover sacrifice. [9](4) The word "profanation" regarding a ritually impure priest who eats ritually pure *terumah* (יְחַלְּלֻהוּ) and the word "profanation" regarding someone who eats *tevel* (יְחַלְּלוּ) are both formulated **in the plural,** whereas the word "profanation" regarding someone who eats a leftover sacrifice (חלל) is formulated in the singular. [10](5) Both *terumah* and *tevel* apply to **produce,** and not meat, whereas the prohibition against eating a leftover sacrifice applies to meat. [11](6) Neither *terumah* nor *tevel* is governed by the law regarding **an offering disqualified by improper intention.** [12](7) Neither *terumah* nor *tevel* is governed by the law regarding a **leftover** sacrifice.

אַדְּרַבָּה [13]The Gemara counters: **On the contrary, we should have learned** the penalty for eating *tevel* **from** the penalty for eating a **leftover sacrifice,** [14]**for** there are **indeed** similarities between the two prohibitions: (1) Both *tevel* and leftover sacrifices are themselves **disqualified foods,** whereas when a priest eats ritually pure *terumah* while in a state of ritual impurity, the *terumah* itself is not disqualified, but the ritually impure priest is disqualified from eating it; [15](2) there is **no way to permit** *tevel* or a leftover sacrifice **by** immersion in **a ritual bath,** whereas a ritually impure priest is permitted to eat ritually pure *terumah* after immersing himself in such a bath.

הָנָךְ נְפִישָׁן [16]The Gemara continues: We should nevertheless learn the penalty for eating *tevel* from the penalty for eating *terumah* while in a state of ritual impurity, for the similarities between *terumah* and *tevel* **are many,** whereas the similarities between *tevel* and leftover sacrifices are few.

RASHI

מנותר — "כי את קדש ה׳ חלל".

תרומה חוצה לארץ וכו׳ — סימן הוא, זה תרומה וזה תרומה מעורבת בו ואין נוהגין בחוצה לארץ, אבל נותר נוהג במדבר ובשעת היתר הבמות בכל מקום, ויש היתר לאיסורו. — זה יש היתר לאיסורו בהפרשה וזה יש היתר לאיסורו דטביל ומותר בתרומה, אבל נותר אין היתר לאיסורו. זה נאמר בו חלול בלשון רבים "ולא יחללו" וזה בלשון רבים "כי יחללוהו", אבל נותר לשון יחיד "קדש ה׳ חלל". **פגול ונותר** — אין נוהג לא בטבל ולא בתרומה אלא בקדשים. **שכן פסול אוכלין** — נותר וטבל שניהם פסול המאכל, אבל תרומה פסול הגוף הוא, ד"כי יחללוהו" בטומאת הגוף כתיב, טבל ונותר אין להם טהרה במקוה, אבל טמא בתרומה יש לו טהרה במקוה.

[1] רָבִינָא אָמַר: [2] ״חִילּוּל״ דְּרַבִּים מֵ״חִילּוּל״ דְּרַבִּים עָדִיף.
[3] ״וְכֹהֵן טָמֵא שֶׁאָכַל תְּרוּמָה טְהוֹרָה״, מְנָלַן? [4] דְּאָמַר שְׁמוּאֵל: מִנַּיִין לְכֹהֵן טָמֵא שֶׁאָכַל תְּרוּמָה טְהוֹרָה שֶׁהוּא בְּמִיתָה בִּידֵי שָׁמַיִם? [5] דִּכְתִיב: ״וְשָׁמְרוּ אֶת מִשְׁמַרְתִּי וְלֹא יִשְׂאוּ עָלָיו חֵטְא וגו׳״. [6] טְהוֹרָה — אִין; [7] טְמֵאָה — לָא. [8] דְּאָמַר שְׁמוּאֵל אָמַר רַבִּי אֱלִיעֶזֶר: מִנַּיִין לְכֹהֵן טָמֵא שֶׁאָכַל תְּרוּמָה טְמֵאָה שֶׁאֵינוֹ בְּמִיתָה? [9] שֶׁנֶּאֱמַר: ״וּמֵתוּ בוֹ כִּי יְחַלְּלֻהוּ״ — [83B] פְּרָט לָזוֹ שֶׁמְחוּלֶּלֶת וְעוֹמֶדֶת.
[10] ״וְזָר שֶׁאָכַל אֶת הַתְּרוּמָה״. [11] אָמַר רַב: זָר שֶׁאָכַל אֶת הַתְּרוּמָה לוֹקֶה.
[12] אָמְרִי לֵיהּ רַב כָּהֲנָא וְרַב אַסִּי לְרַב: לֵימָא מָר בְּמִיתָה, [13] דִּכְתִיב: ״וְכָל זָר לֹא יֹאכַל קֹדֶשׁ״!

LITERAL TRANSLATION

[1] Ravina said: [2] "Profanation" in the plural from "profanation" in the plural is preferable.
[3] "And a ritually impure priest who ate ritually pure *terumah*." From where do we [know this]? [4] As Shmuel said: From where [do we know that] a ritually impure priest who ate ritually pure *terumah* is liable to death at the hand of Heaven? [5] For it is written: "They shall therefore keep my charge, lest they bear sin for it, etc." [6] Ritually pure — yes; [7] ritually impure — no. [8] For Shmuel said in the name of Rabbi Eliezer: From where [do we know that] a ritually impure priest who ate ritually impure *terumah* is not liable to death? [9] For it is written: "And die for it, if they profane it" — [83B] to the exclusion of that which is already profaned.
[10] "And a non-priest who ate *terumah*." [11] Rav said: A non-priest who ate *terumah* is flogged.
[12] Rav Kahana and Rav Assi said to Rav: Let the master say: [13] [He is liable] to death, for it is written: "No stranger shall eat of the holy thing!"

TRANSLATION AND COMMENTARY

רָבִינָא אָמַר [1] **Ravina said:** Even without this argument we should learn the penalty for eating *tevel* from the penalty for eating ritually pure *terumah* while in a state of ritual impurity, [2] for **it is preferable** to draw the *gezerah shavah* between one instance of the word **"profanation"** formulated **in the plural** and another instance of the word **"profanation"** formulated **in the plural.**

וְכֹהֵן טָמֵא [3] It was taught in the Baraita: **"A ritually impure priest who ate ritually pure *terumah*** is liable to death at the hand of Heaven." The Gemara asks: **From where do we know this** law? [4] **As Shmuel said: From where do we know that a ritually impure priest who ate ritually pure *terumah* is liable to death at the hand of Heaven?** [5] **For the verse states** (Leviticus 22:9): **"They shall therefore keep my charge, lest they bear sin for it,** and die for it, if they profane it." [6] The Gemara adds: When the Baraita stated that a ritually impure priest who ate ritually pure *terumah* is liable to death at the hand of Heaven, it was being precise. A ritually impure priest who ate **ritually pure** *terumah* is **indeed** liable to death at the hand of Heaven, [7] but a ritually impure priest who ate **ritually impure** *terumah* is **not** liable to death at the hand of Heaven. [8] **For Shmuel said in the name of Rabbi Eliezer: From where do we know that a ritually impure priest who ate ritually impure *terumah* is not liable to death?** [9] **For the verse states:** "They shall therefore keep my charge, lest they bear sin for it, **and die for it, if they profane it."** If the *terumah* is already ritually impure, the impure priest did not profane it. [83B] This **excludes** the case of a ritually impure priest who ate ritually impure *terumah* **which is already profaned** because of its impurity, for in such a case, the offender is not liable to death at the hand of Heaven.

וְזָר [10] The Gemara continues to clarify the Biblical sources of the laws taught in the Baraita. It was taught: **"A non-priest who ate *terumah*** is liable to death at the hand of Heaven." [11] **Rav said: A non-priest who ate *terumah* is liable to flogging.**

אָמְרִי לֵיהּ [12] **Rav Kahana and Rav Assi said to Rav: The master should have said** that a non-priest who ate *terumah* is liable **to death** at the hand of Heaven, [13] **for it is stated** (Leviticus 22:9-10): "They shall keep my charge, lest they bear sin for it, and die for it, if they profane it; I the Lord do sanctify them. **No stranger shall eat of the holy thing."** Now, the first verse deals with a ritually impure priest who ate ritually pure *terumah*, and it teaches that he is liable to death at the hand of Heaven. The second verse deals with a

BACKGROUND

מִיתָה בִּידֵי שָׁמַיִם **Death at the hand of Heaven.** The expression, "death at the hand of Heaven," does not appear in the Bible, but we do find the expressions, "he shall die [וּמֵת]," or "they shall die [וּמֵתוּ]," which are understood as referring to death at the hand of Heaven, unless they refer to judicial execution (regarding which the Torah usually uses the expression, "he shall surely die [מוֹת יוּמַת]." Death at the hand of Heaven is similar to the punishment of excision, but slightly less severe. The punishment of a person who is subject to excision only begins with his death, for it extends to his descendants, or to his soul in the afterlife. In contrast, the punishment of a person who is subject to death at the hand of Heaven is his death itself. The punishment of death at the hand of Heaven is ascribed for the most part to people who sinned by desecrating or defiling holy things (see *Meiri, Tosafot Yom Tov*).

RASHI

שנאמר ושמרו את משמרתי וגו׳ — לכהנים טמאים דבר הכתוב, בפרשת ״אמור״: ״איש איש מזרע אהרן״. **טהורה אין** — מילתא באפי נפשה היא, וקאי אדשמואל דאמר טמא שאכל תרומה טהורה קאמר: טהורה דווקא, אבל טמאה — לאו במיתה, אם אכלה בטומאת הגוף. **לימא מר במיתה** — דכתיב בתריה ״ומתו בו כי

HALAKHAH

כֹּהֵן טָמֵא שֶׁאָכַל תְּרוּמָה טְמֵאָה **A ritually impure priest who ate ritually impure *terumah*.** If a ritually impure priest ate ritually impure *terumah*, even though he violated a prohibition, he is not liable to lashes or death at the hand of Heaven." (*Rambam, Sefer Zeraim, Hilkhot Terumah* 7:1.)

TRANSLATION AND COMMENTARY

non-priest who ate *terumah,* but it does not specify the penalty to which he is liable. But surely the juxtaposition of the two verses imply that the two offenders are subject to the same punishment, and so it follows that a non-priest who ate *terumah* is liable to death at the hand of Heaven!

אֲנִי [1]Rav answered: The words, **"I the Lord do sanctify them,"** [2]**interrupt** between "and die for it, if they profane it," and "no stranger shall eat." Therefore the juxtaposition of the two verses teaches us nothing about the penalty that is imposed upon a non-priest who ate *terumah*.

מֵיתִיבֵי [3]**An objection was raised** against Rav's ruling from the Baraita: "The following offenders **are liable to death** at the hand of Heaven, [4]included among whom is **a non-priest who ate *terumah*."** How, then, can Rav maintain that he is only subject to lashes?

מַתְנִיתָא [5]The Gemara refutes this objection: Do **you seek to contradict** a ruling of **Rav** on the basis of **a Baraita?** [6]**Rav** himself **is a Tanna, and** he has the authority to **disagree** with rulings found in a Baraita.

וְזָר [7]It was taught in the next clause of the Baraita: **"A non-priest who served in the Temple** is liable to death at the hand of Heaven." [8]The Gemara explains: This law is derived from **the verse** that **states** (Numbers 18:7): "Therefore you and your sons with you shall keep your priest's office for everything that concerns the altar...**and the stranger that comes near shall be put to death."**

וְטָמֵא [9]The Baraita continues: **"A ritually impure priest who served** in the Temple is liable to death at the hand of Heaven." [10]As for the source of this law, the Gemara explains that it is **as Rav Ḥiyya bar Avin asked Rav Yosef: From where do we know that a ritually impure priest who served** in the Temple **is liable to death** at the hand of Heaven? Rav Yosef answered: [11]This law is derived from **the verse** that **states** (Leviticus 22:2): **"Speak to Aaron and to his sons, that they separate themselves from the holy things of the children of Israel** which they hallow to me, **and they profane not my holy name,** I am the Lord," which teaches that a ritually impure priest may not serve in the Temple. [12]**And we** may **learn** the penalty for violating this

[1]"אֲנִי ה׳ מְקַדְּשָׁם", [2]הִפְסִיק הָעִנְיָן.
[3]מֵיתִיבִי: "וְאֵלּוּ הֵן שֶׁבְּמִיתָה:
[4]זָר הָאוֹכֵל אֶת הַתְּרוּמָה"!
[5]מַתְנִיתָא אַדְּרַב קָא רָמֵית?
[6]רַב תַּנָּא הוּא, וּפָלֵיג.
[7]"וְזָר שֶׁשִּׁימֵּשׁ". [8]דִּכְתִיב: "וְהַזָּר הַקָּרֵב יוּמָת".
[9]"וְטָמֵא שֶׁשִּׁימֵּשׁ". [10]כְּדִבְעָא מִינֵּיהּ רַב חִיָּיא בַּר אָבִין מֵרַב יוֹסֵף: מִנַּיִן לְטָמֵא שֶׁשִּׁימֵּשׁ שֶׁהוּא בְּמִיתָה? [11]דִּכְתִיב: "דַּבֵּר אֶל אַהֲרֹן וְאֶל בָּנָיו וְיִנָּזְרוּ מִקָּדְשֵׁי בְנֵי יִשְׂרָאֵל וְלֹא יְחַלְּלוּ אֶת שֵׁם קָדְשִׁי". [12]וְיָלֵיף

LITERAL TRANSLATION

[1]"I the Lord do sanctify them" [2]interrupts the matter.
[3]They raised an objection: "And these are [liable] to death: [4]A non-priest who eats *terumah*"!
[5]You raise (lit., "cast") a contradiction [from] a Baraita against Rav? [6]Rav is a Tanna, and disagrees.
[7]"And a non-priest who served [in the Temple]." [8]As it is written: "And the stranger that comes near shall be put to death."
[9]"And a ritually impure [priest] who served." [10]As Rav Ḥiyya bar Avin asked Rav Yosef: From where [do we know that] a ritually impure [priest] who served is liable to death? [11]For it is written: "Speak to Aaron and to his sons, that they separate themselves from the holy things of the Children of Israel, and they profane not my holy name." [12]And he learns

RASHI

יחללוהו וכל זר לא יאכל קדש" וכל פרשתא בתרומה קאי דכתיב (ויקרא כב) "ובא השמש וטהר ואחר יאכל מן הקדשים" — שאין כפרתו מעכבתו, ואילו קדשים לא אכיל עד שיביא כפרה. הפסיק — בין "ומתו בו ובין כל זר" ומשמע דלא כתיב מיתה אלא לגבי כהנים ומשום טומאה. וינזרו — ויבדלו מלעבוד.

NOTES

רַב תַּנָּא הוּא, וּפָלֵיג Rav is a Tanna, and disagrees. This argument is found in several places in the Talmud (a similar argument is also made with respect to Rav Ḥiyya). The early authorities disagree about the meaning of this argument. Some understand that Rav's authority is equal to that of the Tannaim, although he was actually an Amora in Babylonia, and so he is permitted to disagree with them. The Geonim claim a tradition according to which there are three Talmudic passages where Rav's position is presented in a Baraita (there he is referred to by name as Rabbi Abba), and so Rav was himself a Tanna. In any event, this argument is only used when there is no other way to reconcile the difficulty raised by the Gemara (see *Yad Malakhi*).

וְהַזָּר הַקָּרֵב יוּמָת And the stranger that comes near shall be put to death. It has been asked regarding the Torah's ruling: "And the stranger that comes near shall be put to death," why do we not say that it refers to judicial execution? Perhaps because we do not find that the violation of any of the prohibitions relating to the desecration of the Temple or sacrifices is subject to judicial execution (*Sefer Yere'im*).

TRANSLATION AND COMMENTARY

prohibition by a *gezerah shavah* drawn between this instance of the word **"profanation"** and another use of the word **"profanation" pertaining to** a ritually impure priest who ate ritually pure ***terumah.*** [1]**Just as, there,** the offender is liable **to death** at the hand of Heaven, as the verse states (Leviticus 22: 9): "They shall therefore keep my charge, lest they bear sin for it, and die for it, if they profane it," [2]**so, too, here,** the offender is liable **to death** at the hand of Heaven.

וְנֵילַף [3]The Gemara adds: **But let us learn** the penalty imposed upon a ritually impure priest who served in the Temple by a different *gezerah shavah* drawn between this use of the word **"profanation"** and another use of the word **"profanation,"** pertaining to someone who eats part of a **sacrifice left over** after the time permitted for it to be eaten (Leviticus 19:8): "Therefore everyone who eats of it shall bear his iniquity, because he has profaned the hallowed thing of the Lord." [4]**Just as, there,** the offender is liable to the penalty of **excision,** as the aforementioned verse continues, "And that soul shall be cut off from among his people," [5]**so, too, here,** the offender should be liable **to** the penalty of **excision.**

מִסְתַּבְּרָא [6]The Gemara continues: **It stands to reason that we should learn** the penalty for serving in the Temple while ritually impure **from** the penalty for eating *terumah* while in that state, [7]**for** there are **indeed** numerous similarities between the two prohibitions: (1) In both cases, it is the **person** himself who is disqualified, either from eating *terumah* or from serving in the Temple, whereas regarding a leftover sacrifice, it is the meat that is prohibited; [8](2) in both cases, the prohibition arises from the **ritual impurity** of the priest, which is not the case regarding a leftover sacrifice; [9](3) in both cases, the prohibition is removed once the priest immerses himself in a **ritual bath** and rids himself of his impurity, but there is no way of permitting a leftover sacrifice; and [10](4) the word "profanation" regarding a ritually impure priest who eats ritually pure *terumah* (יְחַלְּלֻהוּ) and the word "profanation" regarding a ritually impure priest who serves in the Temple (יְחַלְּלוּ) are both formulated **in the plural,** whereas the word "profanation" regarding someone who eats of a leftover sacrifice (חִלֵּל) is formulated in the singular.

אַדְּרַבָּה [11]The Gemara counters: **On the contrary, we should have learned** the penalty for serving in the Temple while ritually impure **from** the penalty for eating **a leftover sacrifice,** [12]**for** there are **indeed** several similarities between the two prohibitions: (1) Both relate to sacrifices which are **holy things,** as opposed to *terumah* which does not share the same level of sanctity; [13](2) both relate to the sacrificial service that is performed **inside** the Temple, whereas *terumah* is not related to the Temple; [14](3) both relate to sacrifices which are governed by the law regarding **an offering disqualified by improper intention; and** [15](4) both relate to sacrifices which are governed by the law regarding **a leftover sacrifice!**

חִילּוּל [16]The Gemara continues: Even though the two sets of similarities are equal in number, we should still learn the penalty for serving in the Temple while in a state of ritual impurity from the penalty for eating *terumah* in that state, for **it is preferable** to draw the *gezerah shavah* between one instance of the word **"profanation"** formulated **in the plural** and another instance of the word **"profanation"** formulated **in the plural.**

טְבוּל יוֹם [17]It was taught in the next clause of the Baraita: "A priest **who served** in the Temple after **immersing himself** in a ritual bath **during the day** to rid himself of ritual impurity, but before his purification process was completed at nightfall, is liable to death at the hand of Heaven." [18]The Gemara asks: **From**

"חִילּוּל" "חִילּוּל" מִתְּרוּמָה. [1]מַה לְהַלָּן בְּמִיתָה, [2]אַף כָּאן בְּמִיתָה.

[3]וְנֵילַף "חִילּוּל" "חִילּוּל" מִנּוֹתָר. [4]מַה לְהַלָּן כָּרֵת, [5]אַף כָּאן כָּרֵת!

[6]מִסְתַּבְּרָא מִתְּרוּמָה הֲוָה לֵיהּ לְמֵילַף, [7]שֶׁכֵּן: גּוּף, [8]טָמֵא, [9]מִקְוֶה, [10]בְּרַבִּים.

[11]אַדְּרַבָּה, מִנּוֹתָר הֲוָה לֵיהּ לְמֵילַף, [12]שֶׁכֵּן: קֹדֶשׁ, [13]פְּנִים, [14]פִּיגּוּל, [15]וְנוֹתָר!

[16]"חִילּוּל" דְּרַבִּים מֵ"חִילּוּל" דְּרַבִּים עָדִיף.

[17]"טְבוּל יוֹם שֶׁשִּׁימֵּשׁ". [18]מְנָלַן?

LITERAL TRANSLATION

"profanation" "profanation" from *terumah.* [1]Just as there by death, [2]so, too, here by death.

[3]But let him learn "profanation" "profanation" from a leftover sacrifice. [4]Just as there by excision, [5]so, too, here by excision!

[6]It stands to reason that he should learn from *terumah,* [7]for indeed: Person, [8]ritually impure, [9]ritual bath, [10]in the plural.

[11]On the contrary, he should have learned from a leftover sacrifice, [12]for indeed: Holy thing, [13]inside, [14]an offering disqualified by improper intention, [15]and a leftover sacrifice!

[16]"Profanation" in the plural from "profanation" in the plural is preferable.

[17]"Someone who immersed himself during the day and [then] served." [18]From where

RASHI

גוף טמא מקוה ברבים – טמא ששימש, וטמא שאכל תרומה – שניהם פסולי הגוף ושניהם פסולי טומאה, ויש להם היתר במקוה, וחלולו בלשון רבים. שכן קדש – טמא ששימש ועסק בקדשים ונותר קדש ושניהם בפנים, מה שאין כן בתרומה.

TRANSLATION AND COMMENTARY

where do we know this law? [1]The Gemara explains: **As it was taught** in a Baraita: **"Rabbi Simai says:** [2]**Where is there a** Scriptural **allusion that if** a priest **served** in the Temple after **immersing himself** in a ritual bath **during the day** to rid himself of ritual impurity, but before his purification process was completed at nightfall, his service **is disqualified?** [3]This is learned from **the** verse that **states** (Leviticus 21:6): **'They shall be holy to their God, and not profane** the name of their God.' [4]**If** that verse **does not refer to a ritually impure priest who served** in the Temple, [5]**for that** prohibition is **derived from** the verse (Leviticus 22:2): 'Speak to Aaron and to his sons, **that they separate themselves** from the holy things of the children of Israel which they hallow to me, and they profane not my holy name, I am the Lord' — [6]**it refers to** a priest **who served** in the Temple after **immersing himself** in a ritual bath **during the day** to rid himself of ritual impurity, but before his purification process was completed at nightfall." [7]**And we learn** the penalty for violating this prohibition by a *gezerah shavah* drawn between this use of the word **"profanation"** and another use of the word **"profanation" pertaining to** a ritually impure priest who ate ritually pure *terumah.* [8]**Just as, there,** the offender is liable **to death** at the hand of Heaven, [9]**so, too, here,** the offender is liable **to death** at the hand of Heaven.

ומחוסר [10]The Baraita continues: "A priest who performed the Temple service **without** wearing all the priestly **garments** is liable to death at the hand of Heaven." The Gemara asks: **From where do we know this** law? [11]**Rabbi Abbahu said in the name of Rabbi Yoḥanan, and they cited** an even earlier scholar as the source of this statement and reported it **in the name of Rabbi Elazar the son of Rabbi Shimon:** [12]This is derived from the verse that states (Exodus 29:9): **"And you shall gird them with girdles,** Aaron and his sons, and put the turbans on them; and the priest's office shall be theirs for a perpetual statute." [13]This verse teaches us that **when the** priestly **garments are upon** the priests, **their priesthood is upon them,** [14]but **when their** priestly **garments are not upon them, their priesthood is not upon them.** [15]Thus, without their special garments, **they are** considered **like non-priests,** [16]**and it was** already **said,** above, that **a non-priest who served** in the Temple **is liable to death** at the hand of Heaven.

[1]דְּתַנְיָא: ״רַבִּי סִימַאי אוֹמֵר: [2]רֶמֶז לִטְבוּל יוֹם שֶׁאִם עָבַד חִילֵּל מִנַּיִין? [3]תַּלְמוּד לוֹמַר: ׳קְדֹשִׁים יִהְיוּ לֵאלֹהֵיהֶם וְלֹא יְחַלְּלוּ׳. [4]אִם אֵינוֹ עִנְיָן לְטָמֵא שֶׁשִּׁימֵּשׁ, [5]דְּנָפְקָא לַן מ ׳וְיִנָּזְרוּ׳ [6]תְּנֵיהוּ עִנְיָן לִטְבוּל יוֹם שֶׁשִּׁימֵּשׁ״. [7]וְיָלֵיף ״חִילּוּל״ ״חִילּוּל״ מִתְּרוּמָה. [8]מָה לְהַלָּן בְּמִיתָה, [9]אַף כָּאן בְּמִיתָה.

[10]וּמְחוּסַּר בְּגָדִים מְנָלַן? [11]אָמַר רַבִּי אַבָּהוּ אָמַר רַבִּי יוֹחָנָן, וּמָטוּ בָּהּ מִשְּׁמֵיהּ דְּרַבִּי אֶלְעָזָר בְּרַבִּי שִׁמְעוֹן: [12]״וְחָגַרְתָּ אֹתָם אַבְנֵט״ — [13]בִּזְמַן שֶׁבִּגְדֵיהֶם עֲלֵיהֶם, כְּהוּנָּתָם עֲלֵיהֶם; [14]אֵין בִּגְדֵיהֶם עֲלֵיהֶם, אֵין כְּהוּנָּתָם עֲלֵיהֶם, [15]וְהָווּ לְהוּ זָרִים, [16]וְאָמַר מָר: זָר שֶׁשִּׁימֵּשׁ בְּמִיתָה.

LITERAL TRANSLATION

do we [know this]? [1]As it was taught: "Rabbi Simai says: [2]Where is there an allusion that if someone who had immersed himself during the day served, he disqualified [the service]? [3]The verse states: 'They shall be holy to their God, and not profane.' [4]If it does not refer to a ritually impure [priest] who served, [5]for we derive [that] from 'that they separate themselves,' [6]it refers to someone who immersed himself during the day and [then] served." [7]And he learns "profanation" "profanation" from *terumah.* [8]Just as there by death, [9]so, too, here by death.

[10]"And someone lacking garments." From where do we [know this]? [11]Rabbi Abahu said in the name of Rabbi Yoḥanan, and they cited (lit., "reached up to") in the name of Rabbi Elazar the son of Rabbi Shimon: [12]"And you shall gird them with girdles" — [13]when their garments are upon them, their priesthood is upon them; [14]when their garments are not upon them, their priesthood is not upon them, [15]and they are [like] non-priests, [16]and the master said: A non-priest who served is [liable] to death.

RASHI

וחגרת אותם אבנט וגו׳ — ״והיתה להם כהונה״, משמע שעל ידי בגדים הויא כהונה.

TERMINOLOGY

מָטוּ בָּהּ They reached up to.... When a statement is reported as having been handed down orally from one scholar to another, the list of scholars may close with the remark: "They reached up to an even earlier scholar as the source of this statement and reported it in his name."

NOTES

מְחוּסַּר בְּגָדִים מְנָלַן? And someone lacking garments. From where do we know this? The Rishonim ask: Surely the Torah states explicitly (Exodus 28:43): "And they [the priestly garments] shall be upon Aaron, and his sons...that they bear not iniquity, and die"! Why, then, does the Gemara not use this verse to prove that a priest who performed the Temple service without wearing all the priestly garments is liable to death at the hand of Heaven? *Tosafot* and *Rabbi David Bonfils* in the name of *Ramban* answer that, according to its plain sense, the verse refers only to the priestly trousers, and teach nothing about the other priestly garments. Others suggest that the verse

TRANSLATION AND COMMENTARY

וּמְחוּסַּר [1]It was taught in the next clause of the Baraita: "A priest who served in the Temple after being cured of gonorrhea or leprosy, but before bringing the sacrifices required to complete his purification process, so that he is still **lacking atonement,** is liable to death at the hand of Heaven." The Gemara asks: **From where do we know this** law? [2]**Rav Huna said:** This is derived from a verse dealing with a woman who gave birth and now must offer a purification sacrifice in the Temple. [3]**The verse states** (Leviticus 12:8): **"And the priest shall make atonement for her, and she shall be clean,"** [4]**implying** that until she brings the sacrifice and the priest makes atonement for her, **she is** still **ritually impure.** The same law applies to other people who must bring sacrifices to complete their purification process, such as a man healed after suffering from gonorrhea, or a healed leper. [5]**And it was stated,** above, that **a ritually impure priest who served** in the Temple **is liable to death** at the hand of Heaven.

וְשֶׁלֹּא [6]The Baraita continues: "A priest who served in the Temple **without washing his hands and feet** is liable to death at the hand of Heaven." The Gemara asks: **From where do we know this** law? [7]The Gemara answers: This is derived from **the verse** that **states** (Exodus 30:20): **"When they go into the Tent of Meeting, they shall wash with water, that they die not."**

וּשְׁתוּיֵי יַיִן [8]It was taught in the next clause of the Baraita: "A priest who performed the Temple service while **intoxicated with wine** is liable to death at the hand of Heaven." From where do we know this law? [9]The Gemara explains: This is derived from **the verse** that **states** (Leviticus 10:9): **"Do not drink wine or strong drink,** you, nor your sons with you, when you enter the Tent of Meeting, lest you die."

וּפְרוּעֵי רֹאשׁ [10]The Baraita continues: "A priest who served in the Temple **with overgrown hair** that has not been cut for thirty days is liable to death at the hand of Heaven." From where do we learn this law? [11]The Gemara explains: This is derived from **the verse** dealing with the priests, which **states** (Ezekiel 44:20): **"Nor shall they shave their heads, nor suffer their locks to grow long,"** [12]**and the** very **next verse,** which **states** (Ezekiel 44:21): **"Nor shall any priest drink wine,** when they enter into the inner court." [13]The juxtaposition of these two verses teaches that the law applying to a priest **with long hair may be compared to** the law applying to a priest who is **intoxicated with wine.** [14]**Just as** a priest who served in the Temple while **intoxicated with**

[1]״וּמְחוּסַּר כַּפָּרָה״. מְנָלַן? [2]אָמַר רַב הוּנָא: [3]דְּאָמַר קְרָא: ״וְכִפֶּר עָלֶיהָ הַכֹּהֵן וְטָהֵרָה״ — [4]טָהֳרָה מִכְּלָל שֶׁהִיא טְמֵאָה. [5]וְאָמַר מָר: טָמֵא שֶׁשִּׁימֵּשׁ בְּמִיתָה.

[6]״וְשֶׁלֹּא רְחוּץ יָדַיִם וְרַגְלַיִם״. מְנָלַן? [7]דִּכְתִיב: ״בְּבֹאָם אֶל אֹהֶל מוֹעֵד יִרְחֲצוּ מַיִם וְלֹא יָמוּתוּ״.

[8]״וּשְׁתוּיֵי יַיִן״ [9]דִּכְתִיב: ״יַיִן וְשֵׁכָר אַל תֵּשְׁתְּ וגו׳״.

[10]״וּפְרוּעֵי רֹאשׁ״. [11]דִּכְתִיב: ״רֹאשָׁם לֹא יְגַלֵּחוּ וּפֶרַע לֹא יְשַׁלֵּחוּ״, [12]וּכְתִיב: ״בַּתְרֵיהּ וְיַיִן לֹא יִשְׁתּוּ״. [13]אִיתְקַשׁ פְּרוּעַ רֹאשׁ לִשְׁתוּיֵי יַיִן. [14]מָה שְׁתוּיֵי יַיִן

LITERAL TRANSLATION

[1]"And someone lacking atonement." From where do we [know this]? [2]Rav Huna said: [3]For the verse states: "And the priest shall make atonement for her, and she shall be clean" — [4]which implies that she is ritually impure. [5]And the master said: A ritually impure [priest] who served is [liable] to death.

[6]"And someone who did not wash his hands and feet." From where do we [know this]? [7]For it is written: "When they go into the Tent of Meeting, they shall wash with water, that they die not."

[8]"And those intoxicated with wine." [9]For it is written: "Do not drink wine or strong drink, etc."

[10]"And those with wild hair." [11]For it is written: "Nor shall they shave their heads, nor suffer their locks to grow long," [12]and it is written afterward: "Nor shall [any priest] drink wine." [13]Someone with wild hair is compared to those intoxicated with wine. [14]Just as those intoxicated with wine

RASHI

מכלל שהיא טמאה — קודם כפרה.

NOTES

would not suffice to teach us about a High Priest who served in the Temple without wearing all eight of his priestly garments (*Riva* on the Torah). *Ramah* argues that this verse does not contain an explicit prohibition against serving in the Temple without wearing all the priestly garments, but only a prohibition inferred from a positive commandment: "And they shall be upon Aaron." Moreover, according to the plain sense of the text, the verse does not teach that a priest who serves without wearing all his priestly garments is subject to death at the hand of Heaven, but rather that the penalty for desecrating the service is administered even if the priest was wearing his garments.

פְּרוּעֵי רֹאשׁ Those with wild hair. The Rishonim ask: Why does the Gemara not bring a proof-text from the Torah passage (Leviticus 10:6): "Let the hair of your heads not grow long, neither rend your clothes." *Rabbi Meir* answers

TRANSLATION AND COMMENTARY

wine is liable to death at the hand of Heaven, [1]**so, too, is** a priest who served in the Temple **with overgrown hair liable to death** at the hand of Heaven.

אֲבָל עָרֵל [2]It was taught in the next clause of the Baraita: "**But an uncircumcised** priest who served in the Temple, **or** a priest who took part in the Temple service while **in acute mourning, or** a priest who **performed** the Temple service while **seated,** rather than in a standing position, is not liable to death at the hand of Heaven, but rather he has merely violated **a prohibition.**" [3]The Gemara asks: **From where do we know that an uncircumcised** priest is forbidden to perform the Temple service? [4]**Rav Ḥisda said: We did not learn this matter from the Torah** that we received **from our master, Moses,** [5]and we did not know it **until** the Prophet **Ezekiel ben Buzi came and taught us** (Ezekiel 44:9): "**No stranger, uncircumcised in heart,** [84A] **nor uncircumcised in flesh, shall enter into my sanctuary.**"

אוֹנֵן [6]The Gemara asks: **From where do we know** that a priest **in acute mourning** is forbidden to perform the Temple service? [7]**For the verse** relating to a High Priest whose mother or father died **states** (Leviticus 21:12): "**Neither shall he go out of the sanctuary, nor profane the sanctuary of his God,**" teaching that even if the High Priest's mother or father died, he must not leave the sanctuary, for if he remains in the sanctuary and serves, he does not profane the service. [8]**But** it follows from this that if **someone else** — not the High Priest, but an ordinary priest — **does not leave** the sanctuary when he is in acute mourning, he does in fact **profane** the service, for performing the Temple service while in acute mourning is forbidden to him.

אֲמַר לֵיהּ [9]**Rav Adda said to Rava: But** then **we should learn** the penalty for violating this prohibition by a *gezerah shavah* drawn between this instance of the word **"profanation"** and another instance of the word **"profanation"** mentioned **with regard to** a ritually impure priest who ate ritually pure ***terumah.*** [10]**Just as, there,** the offender is liable **to death** at the hand of Heaven, **so, too, here,** the offender should be liable **to death** at the hand of Heaven!

מִי כְּתִיב [11]Rava answered: **Is** the word "profanation" **written with regard** to the ordinary priest **himself?**

[1]בְּמִיתָה, אַף פְּרוּעֵי רֹאשׁ בְּמִיתָה.

[2]״אֲבָל עָרֵל, אוֹנֵן, יוֹשֵׁב — בְּאַזְהָרָה״. [3]עָרֵל מְנָלַן? [4]אָמַר רַב חִסְדָּא: דָּבָר זֶה מִתּוֹרַת מֹשֶׁה רַבֵּינוּ לֹא לָמַדְנוּ, [5]עַד שֶׁבָּא יְחֶזְקֵאל בֶּן בּוּזִי וְלִמְּדָנוּ: ״כָּל בֶּן נֵכָר עָרֵל לֵב [84A] וְעֶרֶל בָּשָׂר לֹא יָבוֹא אֶל מִקְדָּשִׁי (לְשָׁרְתֵנִי)״.

[6]אוֹנֵן מְנָלַן? [7]דִּכְתִיב: ״וּמִן הַמִּקְדָּשׁ לֹא יֵצֵא וְלֹא יְחַלֵּל אֵת מִקְדַּשׁ אֱלֹהָיו״. [8]הָא אַחֵר שֶׁלֹּא יָצָא — חִילֵּל.

[9]אֲמַר לֵיהּ רַב אַדָּא לְרָבָא: וְנֵילַף ״חִילּוּל״ ״חִילּוּל״ מִתְּרוּמָה. [10]מַה לְהַלָּן בְּמִיתָה, אַף כָּאן בְּמִיתָה!

[11]מִי כְּתִיב בֵּיהּ בְּגוּפֵיהּ?

LITERAL TRANSLATION

are [liable] to death, [1]so, too, those with wild hair are [liable] to death.

[2]"But an uncircumcised man, or someone in acute mourning, or someone seated — [he is liable for] violating a prohibition." [3]An uncircumcised man — from where do we [know this]? [4]Rav Ḥisda said: This matter we did not learn from the Torah of Moses our master, [5]until Ezekiel ben Buzi came and taught us: "No stranger, uncircumcised in heart, [84A] nor uncircumcised in flesh, shall enter into my sanctuary [to serve me]."

[6]Someone in acute mourning — from where do we [know this]? [7]For it is written: "Neither shall he go out of the sanctuary, nor profane the sanctuary of his God." [8]But someone else who does not go out profanes.

[9]Rav Adda said to Rava: But let him learn "profanation" "profanation" from *terumah.* [10]Just as there by death, so, too, here by death!

[11]Is it written regarding him himself?

RASHI

בן נכר – כהן מומר לעבודת כוכבים, שהוא ערל לב, ונתנכרו מעשיו לאביו שבשמים. וערל בשר – שמתו אחיו מחמת מילה. לא יבא – והיינו אזהרה מדברי קבלה בעלמא, ולא לקי עלה. ומן המקדש לא יצא וגו׳ – כלומר אף על פי שמתו אביו ואמו אין צריך לצאת מן המקדש, שאם יעבוד לא יחלל, הא כהן אחר שלא יצא – חלל. מי כתיב בגופיה – מי כתיב בכהן הדיוט גופיה חילול, מכלל דמכהן גדול דכתיב ביה אונן ואינו מחלל הוא דקא אתי.

NOTES

that this verse does not teach that there is a prohibition against serving in the Temple with overgrown hair, but only that Aaron and his sons were not required to grow their hair long following the death of Nadab and Abihu. Alternatively, that verse only proves that a priest is forbidden to grow his hair long during bereavement, as was the case under discussion (*Maharsha*). Or else, we might have thought that that prohibition applied only at that particular time, and so an additional verse was required to teach that the prohibition applies in all generations (*Imrei Tzvi*).

[1]מִכְּלָלָא קָאָתֵי. [2]הָוֵי דָּבָר הַבָּא מִן הַכְּלָל, [3]וְכָל דָּבָר הַבָּא מִן הַכְּלָל, אֵין דָּנִין אוֹתוֹ בִּגְזֵרָה שָׁוָה.
[4]יוֹשֵׁב מְנָלַן? [5]אָמַר רָבָא אָמַר רַב נַחְמָן: אָמַר קְרָא: ״כִּי בוֹ בָּחַר ה׳ אֱלֹהֶיךָ מִכָּל שְׁבָטֶיךָ לַעֲמֹד לְשָׁרֵת״ — [6]לַעֲמִידָה בְּחַרְתִּיו וְלֹא לִישִׁיבָה.
[7]״בַּעַל מוּם, רַבִּי אוֹמֵר: בְּמִיתָה. [8]וַחֲכָמִים אוֹמְרִים: בְּאַזְהָרָה״. [9]מַאי טַעְמָא דְּרַבִּי? [10]דִּכְתִיב: ״אַךְ אֶל הַפָּרֹכֶת לֹא יָבֹא וגו׳״. [11]וְיָלֵיף ״חִילּוּל״ ״חִילּוּל״ מִתְּרוּמָה. [12]מַה לְהַלָּן בְּמִיתָה, [13]אַף כָּאן בְּמִיתָה.
[14]וְנֵילַף ״חִילּוּל״ ״חִילּוּל״ מִנּוֹתָר. [15]מַה לְהַלָּן בְּכָרֵת, [16]אַף כָּאן בְּכָרֵת!

LITERAL TRANSLATION

[1]It is derived by implication. [2]It is a matter derived by implication, [3]and any matter derived by implication, we do not apply to it a *gezerah shavah.*
[4]Someone seated — from where do we [know this]? [5]Rava said in the name of Rav Naḥman: The verse states: "For the Lord your God has chosen him out of all your tribes, to stand to minister" — [6]I have chosen him for standing, and not for sitting.
[7]"Someone with a physical defect — Rabbi says: For death. [8]And the Sages say: For a prohibition." [9]What is the reason of Rabbi? [10]For it is written: "Only he shall not go in unto the curtain, etc." [11]And he learns "profanation" "profanation" from *terumah.* [12]Just as there by death, [13]so, too, here by death.
[14]But let him learn "profanation" "profanation" from a leftover sacrifice. [15]Just as there by excision, [16]so, too, here by excision!

TRANSLATION AND COMMENTARY

[1]As was argued above, the law regarding an ordinary priest **is derived by implication** from the law regarding the High Priest that is stated explicitly in the Torah. [2]Thus, **it is a matter** which is only **derived by implication,** [3]**and** there is a rule that **any matter** which is only **derived by implication is not subject to** inferences drawn by **a** ***gezerah shavah.***

יוֹשֵׁב מְנָלַן [4]The Gemara continues: **From where do we know** that a priest is forbidden to perform the Temple service while he is in a **seated** position? [5]**Rava said in the name of Rav Naḥman:** This is derived from **the verse** that **states** (Deuteronomy 18:5): **"For the Lord your God has chosen him out of all your tribes, to stand to minister** in the name of the Lord, him and his sons for ever," [6]teaching that God **chose** Aaron and his sons to minister in his name **while standing, and not while sitting.**

בַּעַל מוּם [7]It was taught in the next clause of the Baraita: "Regarding a priest **with a physical defect** who served in the Temple, **Rabbi** Yehudah HaNasi **says:** He is liable **to death** at the hand of Heaven. [8]**The Sages** disagree and **say:** He has merely violated **a prohibition.**" [9]The Gemara asks: **What is the reasoning of Rabbi** Yehudah HaNasi? [10]The Gemara explains: **For the verse states** (Leviticus 21:23): **"Only he shall not go in unto the curtain,** nor come near to the altar, because he has a blemish; that he profane not My holy places." [11]**And we learn** the penalty for violating this prohibition by a *gezerah shavah* drawn between this instance of the word **"profanation"** and another instance of the word **"profanation"** mentioned **with regard to** a ritually impure priest who ate ritually pure ***terumah.*** [12]**Just, as, there,** the offender is liable **to death** at the hand of Heaven, [13]**so, too, here,** the offender is liable **to death** at the hand of Heaven.

וְנֵילַף [14]The Gemara continues: **But let us learn** the penalty for serving in the Temple while suffering from a physical defect through a different *gezerah shavah* drawn between this instance of the word **"profanation"** and another instance of the word **"profanation"** referring to someone who eats part of a **sacrifice leftover** after the time permitted for it to be eaten. [15]**Just, as, there,** the offender is liable to the penalty of **excision,** [16]**so, too, here,** the offender should be liable to the penalty of **excision!**

RASHI

ולא לישיבה — דכיון דלא נבחר הוה ליה כזר. ובפרק שני דזבחים (כג,ב) רמינן: מכדי יושב כזר דמי ומיחל עבודה, — אימא: במיתה הוא כזר, אלמה תניא אינו במיתה?! והתם מפרק לה: משום דהוי זר, ושלא רחץ ידים ורגלים, ושתויי יין, שלשה כתובים הבאים כאחד דכתיב בהו מיתה — ואין מלמדין.

NOTES

יוֹשֵׁב מְנָלַן **Someone seated — from where do we know this.** *Rashi* understands that, since God chose Aaron and his sons to minister in His name while standing, a priest who serves while sitting is treated as a non-priest. According to this, the question arises: Why, then, is a priest who performed the Temple service in a seated position not liable to death at the hand of Heaven, just like a non-priest who served in the Temple? *Rashi* understands that this is the question raised and answered by the Talmud itself in *Zevaḥim* 23b. *Ramah* understands our Gemara differently: The verse, "For the Lord your God has chosen him...to stand to minister," does not teach that a priest who served while seated is regarded as not having been chosen, i.e., as being a non-priest, but only that his service is not chosen, i.e., his service is not valid. *Ramah* also understands the Gemara in *Zevaḥim* in a slightly different

CONCEPTS

דָּבָר הַבָּא מִן הַכְּלָל **A matter derived by implication.** This principle is meant to restrict the use of the hermeneutic principles through which the Torah is interpreted. There is a certain similarity between this rule and the rule that a *kal vaḥomer* argument cannot be applied to a law given to Moses at Sinai but not recorded in the Torah. The fact that a certain law was not stated in the Torah (or not stated explicitly) does not detract from its authority as a Biblical law, but because it was not written explicitly in the Torah, it is not subject to the hermeneutic principles through which the Torah is interpreted.

TRANSLATION AND COMMENTARY

מִסְתַּבְּרָא [1]It stands to reason that we should learn the penalty for serving in the Temple while afflicted with a physical defect from the penalty for eating *terumah* while ritually impure, [2]for in that way we learn about a prohibition stemming from a disqualification of the person from another prohibition stemming from a disqualification of the person. Regarding both prohibitions, the priest himself is disqualified, either from serving in the Temple because of his physical defect or from eating *terumah* because of his ritual impurity, whereas regarding a leftover sacrifice, it is the meat that may not be eaten.

אַדְּרַבָּה [3]The Gemara counters: On the contrary, we should have learned the penalty for serving in the Temple while suffering from a physical defect from the penalty for eating a leftover sacrifice, [4]for there are indeed several similarities between the two prohibitions: (1) Both relate to sacrifices which are holy things, as opposed to *terumah* which does not share the same level of sanctity; (2) [5]both relate to the sacrificial service which is performed inside the Temple, whereas *terumah* is not related in any way to the Temple; (3) [6]both relate to sacrifices which are governed by the law regarding an offering disqualified by improper intention; and (4) [7]both relate to sacrifices that are governed by the law regarding a leftover sacrifice!

אֶלָּא [8]The Gemara now retracts its previous explanation and explains the reasoning of Rabbi Yehudah HaNasi differently: Rather, we learn the penalty for serving in the Temple while afflicted with a physical defect through a *gezerah shavah* from the penalty imposed upon a ritually impure priest who served in the Temple. Just as, there, the offender is liable to death at the hand of Heaven, so, too, here the offender is liable to death at the hand of Heaven. [9]In that way we learn about a prohibition stemming from a disqualification of the person from another prohibition stemming from a disqualification of the person. [10]And in that way we learn about a prohibition relating to a sacrifice which is a holy thing, offered inside the Temple, [11]and governed by the law regarding an offering disqualified by improper intention and the law regarding a leftover sacrifice, [12]from another prohibition relating to a sacrifice which is a holy thing, offered inside the Temple, [13]and governed by the law regarding an offering disqualified by improper intention and the law regarding a leftover sacrifice.

וְרַבָּנַן [14]The Gemara asks: What is the reasoning of the Sages who disagree with Rabbi Yehudah HaNasi and say that a priest with a physical defect who served in the Temple is not liable to death at the hand of Heaven? The Gemara explains: They learn this from the verse regarding a ritually impure priest who ate ritually pure *terumah*, which states (Leviticus 22:9): "They shall therefore keep my charge, lest they bear sin for it, and die for it, if they profane it." The words "for it" constitute a restrictive expression, teaching that a priest who ate *terumah* while in a state of ritual impurity is liable to death at the hand of Heaven, [15]but not a priest with a physical defect who served in the Temple.

הֵזִיד בִּמְעִילָה [16]The Baraita concludes: "Regarding someone who committed intentional trespass, Rabbi Yehudah HaNasi says: He is liable to death at the hand of Heaven. [17]The Sages disagree and say: He has

[1]מִסְתַּבְּרָא מִתְּרוּמָה הֲוָה לֵיהּ לְמֵילַף, [2]שֶׁכֵּן: פְּסוּל הַגּוּף מִפְּסוּל הַגּוּף.
[3]אַדְּרַבָּה, מִנּוֹתָר הֲוָה לֵיהּ לְמֵילַף, [4]שֶׁכֵּן: קוֹדֶשׁ, [5]פְּנִים, [6]פִּיגּוּל, [7]וְנוֹתָר!
[8]אֶלָּא: מִטָּמֵא שֶׁשִּׁימֵּשׁ גָּמַר: [9]פְּסוּל הַגּוּף מִפְּסוּל הַגּוּף, [10]קוֹדֶשׁ, פְּנִים, [11]פִּיגּוּל וְנוֹתָר, [12]מִקּוֹדֶשׁ פְּנִים [13]פִּיגּוּל וְנוֹתָר.
[14]וְרַבָּנַן? אָמַר קְרָא: "בּוֹ" — [15]וְלֹא בְּבַעַל מוּם.
[16]"הֵזִיד בִּמְעִילָה, רַבִּי אוֹמֵר: בְּמִיתָה. [17]וַחֲכָמִים אוֹמְרִים:

LITERAL TRANSLATION

[1]It stands to reason that he should learn from *terumah*, [2]for indeed: A disqualification of the person from a disqualification of the person.

[3]On the contrary, he should have learned from a leftover sacrifice, [4]for indeed: Holy things, [5]inside, [6]an offering disqualified by improper intention, [7]and a leftover sacrifice!

[8]Rather, he learns from a ritually impure [priest] who served: [9]A disqualification of the person from a disqualification of the person; [10]a holy thing, inside, [11]an offering disqualified by improper intention, and a leftover sacrifice [12]from a holy thing, inside, [13]an offering disqualified by improper intention, and a leftover sacrifice.

[14]And the Rabbis? The verse states: "For it" — [15]and not someone with a physical defect.

[16]"[If] he committed intentional trespass, Rabbi says: For death. [17]And the Sages say:

RASHI

אמר קרא בו — בתרומה במיתה, דכולהו נמי מיניה גמרי ואתא "בו" למיעוטא ולא בעל מום. ומסתברא בעל מום הוא דקא ממעט ולא טמא וטבול יום שהן פסול טומאתן במיתה.

NOTES

manner: If a seated priest invalidates his service just as a non-priest invalidates his service, why not learn by way of analogy that a seated priest who served in the Temple is also liable to death at the hand of heaven, just like a non-priest who participated in the divine service?

TRANSLATION AND COMMENTARY

merely violated **a prohibition."** [1]The Gemara asks: **What is the reasoning of Rabbi** Yehudah HaNasi? [2]**Rabbi Abbahu said: We learn** the penalty for intentional trespass from a *gezerah shavah* drawn between the word **"sin"** mentioned with respect to trespass and the word **"sin"** in reference to a ritually impure priest who ate ***terumah.*** Regarding trespass, the verse states (Leviticus 5:15): "If a person commits a trespass, and sin," and regarding eating *terumah* in a state of ritual impurity, the verse states (Leviticus 22: 9): "Lest they bear sin for it, and die for it." [3]**Just as, there,** the offender is liable **to death** at the hand of Heaven, **so, too, here,** the offender is liable **to death** at the hand of Heaven.

וְרַבָּנַן [4]The Gemara asks: What is the reasoning of **the Sages** who disagree with Rabbi Yehudah HaNasi and say that a person who committed intentional trespass is not liable to death at the hand of Heaven? [5]The Gemara explains: They learn this from **that same verse** regarding a ritually impure priest who ate ritually pure *terumah,* which **states** (Leviticus 22:9): "They shall therefore keep my charge, lest they bear sin for it, and die **for it,** if they profane it." The words "for it" constitute a restrictive expression, teaching that eating *terumah* in a state of ritual impurity is subject to the penalty of death at the hand of Heaven, [6]**but not** intentional **trespass.**

זָר [7]The Gemara now reconsiders what was taught in the Baraita: **"A non-priest who served in the Temple** is liable to death at the hand of Heaven." [8]**It was taught** in a related Baraita that this ruling is the subject of a Tannaitic dispute: [9]**"Rabbi Yishmael says: It is stated, here,** regarding a non-priest who serves in the Temple (Numbers 18:7): 'Therefore, you and your sons with you shall keep your priest's office for everything that concerns the altar ... **and the stranger that comes near shall be put to death.'** [10]**And it is stated elsewhere** regarding the death of Koraḥ's company (Numbers 17:28): **'Every one who comes at all near the tabernacle of the Lord will die.'** [11]**Just as, there,** the sinful followers of Koraḥ died **at the hand of Heaven,** as the verse states (Numbers 16:35): 'And there came out a fire from the Lord, and consumed the two hundred and fifty men that offered the incense,' [12]**so, too, here** the non-priest who serves in the Temple is liable to death **at the hand of Heaven.** [13]**Rabbi Akiva says: It is stated, here,** regarding a non-priest who serves in the Temple (Numbers 18:7): **'And the stranger who comes near shall be put to death,' and it is stated, elsewhere,** regarding a Prophet who incites others to commit idolatry (Deuteronomy 13:6): **'And that prophet, or that dreamer of dreams, shall be put to death.'** [14]**Just as, there,** the offender is liable to death **by stoning, so, too, here,** the offender is liable to death **by stoning.** [15]**Rabbi Yoḥanan ben Nuri says: Just as, there,** the offender is liable to death **by strangulation, so, too, here,** the offender is liable to death **by strangulation."**

בְּאַזְהָרָה״. [1]מַאי טַעְמָא דְּרַבִּי? [2]אָמַר רַבִּי אַבָּהוּ גָּמַר ״חֵטְא״ ״חֵטְא״, מִתְּרוּמָה. [3]מַה לְּהַלָּן בְּמִיתָה, אַף כָּאן בְּמִיתָה.

[4]וְרַבָּנַן אָמְרִי: [5]אָמַר קְרָא: ״בּוֹ״ — [6]בּוֹ וְלֹא בִּמְעִילָה.

[7]״זָר שֶׁשִּׁימֵּשׁ בַּמִּקְדָּשׁ״. [8]תַּנְיָא: [9]״רַבִּי יִשְׁמָעֵאל אוֹמֵר: נֶאֱמַר כָּאן: ׳וְהַזָּר הַקָּרֵב יוּמָת׳, [10]וְנֶאֱמַר לְהַלָּן: ׳כָּל הַקָּרֵב הַקָּרֵב אֶל מִשְׁכַּן ה׳ יָמוּת׳. [11]מַה לְּהַלָּן בִּידֵי שָׁמַיִם, [12]אַף כָּאן בִּידֵי שָׁמַיִם. [13]רַבִּי עֲקִיבָא אוֹמֵר: נֶאֱמַר כָּאן: ׳וְהַזָּר הַקָּרֵב יוּמָת׳, וְנֶאֱמַר לְהַלָּן: ׳וְהַנָּבִיא הַהוּא אוֹ חֹלֵם הַחֲלוֹם הַהוּא יוּמָת׳. [14]מַה לְהַלָּן בִּסְקִילָה, אַף כָּאן בִּסְקִילָה. [15]רַבִּי יוֹחָנָן בֶּן נוּרִי אוֹמֵר: מַה לְהַלָּן בְּחֶנֶק אַף כָּאן בְּחֶנֶק״.

LITERAL TRANSLATION

For a prohibition." [1]What is the reason of Rabbi? [2]Rabbi Abbahu said: He learns "sin" "sin" from *terumah.* [3]Just as there by death, so, too, here by death.

[4]And the Rabbis say: [5]The verse states: "For it" — [6]and not for trespass.

[7]"A non-priest who served [in the Temple]." [8]It was taught: [9]"Rabbi Yishmael says: It is stated here: 'And the stranger who comes near shall be put to death,' [10]and it is stated below: 'Everyone who comes at all near the tabernacle of the Lord will die.' [11]Just as below at the hand of Heaven, [12]so, too, here at the hand of Heaven. [13]Rabbi Akiva says: It is stated here: 'And the stranger who comes near shall be put to death,' and it is stated below: 'And that prophet, or that dreamer of dreams, shall be put to death.' [14]Just as there by stoning, so, too, here by stoning. [15]Rabbi Yoḥanan ben Nuri says: Just as there by strangulation, so, too, here by strangulation."

RASHI

גמר חטא חטא מתרומה — מעילה כתיב בה ״וחטאה בשגגה״ והכא כתיב ״ולא ישאו עליו חטא ומתו״. **בו ולא במעילה** — וממיתה לחודה הוא דאמעיט, דגבי מיתה הוא דכתיב ״בו״, אבל אזהרה מגמרא גמר להזיד במעילה בגזרה שוה ד״חטא״ ״חטא״ מתרומה. **מה להלן בידי שמים** — דבמאתים וחמשים איש דקרח בשרופים כתיב (במדבר יז). **רבי יוחנן בן נורי וכו׳** — דסבירא ליה נביא שהדיח את הרבים — בחנק, ולקמן מפרש במאי פליגי.

[1]בְּמַאי קָמִיפַּלְגִי רַבִּי יִשְׁמָעֵאל וְרַבִּי עֲקִיבָא? [2]רַבִּי עֲקִיבָא סָבַר: דָּנִין ״יוּמָת״ מִ״יּוּמָת״ [3]וְאֵין דָּנִין ״יוּמָת״ מִ״יָּמוּת״. [4]וְרַבִּי יִשְׁמָעֵאל סָבַר: דָּנִין הֶדְיוֹט מֵהֶדְיוֹט, [5]וְאֵין דָּנִין הֶדְיוֹט מִנָּבִיא.

[6]וְרַבִּי עֲקִיבָא? [7]כֵּיוָן שֶׁהִדִּיחַ, אֵין לְךָ הֶדְיוֹט גָּדוֹל מִזֶּה.

[8]בְּמַאי קָמִיפַּלְגִי רַבִּי עֲקִיבָא וְרַבִּי יוֹחָנָן בֶּן נוּרִי? [9]בִּפְלוּגְתָּא דְּרַבִּי שִׁמְעוֹן וְרַבָּנַן. [10]דְּתַנְיָא: ״נָבִיא שֶׁהִדִּיחַ, בִּסְקִילָה. [11]רַבִּי שִׁמְעוֹן אוֹמֵר: בְּחֶנֶק״.

[12]הָא אֲנַן תְּנַן: [13]״רַבִּי עֲקִיבָא אוֹמֵר: בְּחֶנֶק״!

LITERAL TRANSLATION

[1]About what do Rabbi Yishmael and Rabbi Akiva disagree? [2]Rabbi Akiva maintains: We learn "he shall be put to death" from "he shall be put to death," [3]and we do not learn "he shall be put to death" from "he shall die." [4]And Rabbi Yishmael maintains: We learn an ordinary person from an ordinary person, [5]and we do not learn an ordinary person from a prophet.

[6]And Rabbi Akiva? [7]Since he incited, you do not have an ordinary person greater than that.

[8]About what do Rabbi Akiva and Rabbi Yohanan ben Nuri disagree? [9][They disagree about the matter] in dispute between Rabbi Shimon and the Rabbis. [10]For it was taught: "A prophet who incited, by stoning. [11]Rabbi Shimon says: By strangulation."

[12]Surely we have learned: [13]"Rabbi Akiva says: By strangulation!"

TRANSLATION AND COMMENTARY

בְּמַאי קָמִיפַּלְגִי [1]**About what** theoretical issue **do Rabbi Yishmael and Rabbi Akiva disagree?** [2]The Gemara explains: **Rabbi Akiva maintains:** It is preferable that **we learn** the meaning of the expression **"he shall be put to death"** (regarding a non-priest who served in the Temple) through a *gezerah shavah* **from** another instance of that same expression, **"he shall be put to death"** (regarding a Prophet who incited others to idolatry), [3]**and** that **we not learn** the meaning of the expression, **"he shall be put to death"** (regarding a non-priest who served in the Temple) through a *gezerah shavah* **from** a slightly different expression, **"he will die"** (regarding the members of Korah's company). [4]**And Rabbi Yishmael maintains:** Even though there is a slight difference between the two expressions, it is preferable that **we learn** the law applying to **an ordinary person** (who served in the Temple) through a *gezerah shavah* **from** another law applying to **an ordinary person** (the members of Koraḥ's company), [5]**and** that **we not learn** the law applying to **an ordinary person** (a non-priest who served in the Temple) through a *gezerah shavah* **from** the law applying to **a Prophet** (a Prophet who incited others to idolatry).

וְרַבִּי עֲקִיבָא [6]The Gemara asks: How does **Rabbi Akiva** counter Rabbi Yishmael's argument? [7]The Gemara explains: **Once** a Prophet **incites** others to commit idolatry, **there is no person more ordinary than that.** Hence the law regarding a non-priest who served in the Temple may be derived from the law regarding a Prophet who incited others to idolatry.

בְּמַאי קָמִיפַּלְגִי [8]The Gemara now asks: **About what** issue **do Rabbi Akiva and Rabbi Yoḥanan ben Nuri disagree?** [9]The Gemara explains: Rabbi Akiva and Rabbi Yoḥanan **disagree about the matter in dispute between Rabbi Shimon and the Rabbis.** [10]**For it was taught** in a Baraita: **"A Prophet who incited** others to idolatry is liable to death **by stoning.** [11]**Rabbi Shimon says:** He is liable to death **by strangulation."**

הָא אֲנַן תְּנַן [12]The Gemara comments: But **surely we have learned** in the Mishnah (above, 81a): "If a non-priest served in the Temple, [13]**Rabbi Akiva says:** He is liable to death **by strangulation."** This contradicts the Baraita which states that, according to Rabbi Akiva, a non-priest who served in the Temple is liable to death by stoning!

RASHI

פלוגתא דרבי שמעון ורבנן – ב״אלו הן הנחנקין״, ויליף טעמא מקרא. והא תנן – זר ששימש, רבי עקיבא אומר: בחנק, ובברייתא קתני: לרבי עקיבא בסקילה.

NOTES

הֶדְיוֹט מִנָּבִיא **An ordinary person from a Prophet.** *Rashash* argues that when the Gemara speaks here of a *hedyot*, it does not use the term in its usual sense as referring to an ordinary person, as opposed to a person of distinction. Rather, it refers to someone who does something that he is not authorized to do. An ordinary person who performs the Temple service surely falls under the heading of *hedyot* according to this definition, for only priests are authorized to serve in the Temple. Rabbi Yishmael and Rabbi Akiva disagree about a Prophet who incites others to idolatry. According to Rabbi Yishmael, such a person is not regarded as a *hedyot*, because he is authorized to prophesy. Rabbi Akiva argues that, since he incites others to commit idolatry, he is certainly a *hedyot* who is not authorized to speak in the name of God.

TRANSLATION AND COMMENTARY

תְּרֵי תַּנָּאֵי [1]The Gemara continues: **Two** later **Tannaim** reported the view of **Rabbi Akiva** differently. [2]**The Mishnah** reflects the position of **Rabbi Shimon,** who reported the view of his teacher, **Rabbi Akiva,** for, according to Rabbi Shimon, a Prophet who incited others to idolatry is liable to death by strangulation, and the penalty imposed upon a non-priest who served in the Temple is learned from the penalty imposed upon a Prophet who incited others to idolatry, so that he, too, is liable to death by strangulation. [3]**The Baraita** reflects the position of **the Rabbis** who disagree with Rabbi Shimon, and who reported the view of **Rabbi Akiva** differently, for, according to the Rabbis, a Prophet who incited others to idolatry is liable to death by stoning, and the penalty imposed upon a non-priest who served in the Temple is learned from the penalty imposed upon a Prophet who incited others to idolatry, so that he, too, is liable to death by stoning.

[1]תְּרֵי תַּנָּאֵי וְאַלִּיבָּא דְּרַבִּי עֲקִיבָא. [2]מַתְנִיתִין רַבִּי שִׁמְעוֹן וְאַלִּיבָּא דְּרַבִּי עֲקִיבָא. [3]בָּרַיְיתָא רַבָּנַן וְאַלִּיבָּא דְּרַבִּי עֲקִיבָא.

הדרן עלך אלו הן הנשרפין

LITERAL TRANSLATION

[1]Two Tannaim, according to Rabbi Akiva. [2]Our Mishnah [follows] Rabbi Shimon, and according to Rabbi Akiva. [3]The Baraita [follows] the Rabbis, and according to Rabbi Akiva.

RASHI

מתניתין רבי שמעון — דאמר נביא שהדיח בחנק, וזר ששימש מיניה גמר. ורבי שמעון תלמידו של רבי עקיבא הוא, ואמר לרבי עקיבא זר ששימש בחנק נביא שהדיח בחנק. **ובברייתא רבנן** — בני מחלוקתו של רבי שמעון, ואף הם תלמידי רבי עקיבא הוו, ואמרי משמו סקילה בתרוייהו.

הדרן עלך אלו הן הנשרפין

Conclusion to Chapter Nine

This chapter clarifies some of the Halakhic Midrashim dealing with transgressions punishable by burning, but it mainly deals with laws governing murder, and the other punishments imposed by a court to maintain its authority over the people.

In the Halakhot governing murder, several definitions were stated that greatly restrict and limit the instances in which a person may be found guilty as a murderer subject to capital punishment by the court. The first definition is that one is not a murderer unless one does a deed that causes death with one's own force. If an act only indirectly causes death, or if death is not a direct outcome of the killer's deed, it is not regarded as murder. Second, the killer is only liable if, at the time of the action, he intended to murder a specific person. Third, the killer is not liable unless, under reasonable circumstances, his action was sufficient to kill someone. Fourth, only someone who acted singly and by himself is found guilty of murder. Fifth, the killer is not liable unless, at the time of the act, the victim had no way of being saved from the results of the act.

So long as these conditions are not fulfilled, the killer is not subject to capital punishment, though according to Divine law he is guilty of taking a human life, and there can be no atonement for that, not even in exile in a refuge city.

Regarding transgressions which are particularly despicable, although they may not be subject to capital punishment by a court of law, zealous people were given the right to strike the transgressor and kill him at the moment he was caught committing the crime, and this is by virtue of the general injunction to extirpate evil from the Jewish people.

List of Sources

Aḥaronim, lit., "the last," meaning Rabbinic authorities from the time of the publication of Rabbi Yosef Caro's code of Halakhah, *Shulḥan Arukh* (1555).

Arba'ah Turim, code of Halakhah by Rabbi Ya'akov ben Asher, b. Germany, active in Spain (c. 1270-1343).

Arukh, Talmudic dictionary, by Rabbi Natan of Rome, 11th century.

Arukh LeNer, novellae on the Talmud by Rabbi Ben Tzion Ya'akov Etlinger, Germany (1798-1871).

Baḥ (Bayit Ḥadash), commentary on *Arba'ah Turim*, by Rabbi Yoel Sirkes, Poland (1561-1640).

Be'er HaGolah, commentary on unusual Aggadic passages in the Talmud by Rabbi Yehudah Loew ben Betzalel of Prague (1525-1609).

Bereshit Rabbah, Midrash on the Book of Genesis.

Bertinoro, Ovadyah, 15th century commentator on the Mishnah.

Bet Yosef, Halakhic commentary on *Arba'ah Turim* by Rabbi Yosef Caro (1488-1575), which is the basis of his authoritative Halakhic code, *Shulḥan Arukh.*

Birkei Yosef, novellae on *Shulḥan Arukh* by Rabbi Ḥayyim Yosef David Azulai, Israel and Italy (1724-1807).

Darkhei Moshe, commentary on *Tur* by Rabbi Moshe ben Isserles, Poland (1525-1572).

Ein Ya'akov, collection of Aggadot from the Babylonian Talmud by Rabbi Ya'akov ben Shlomo Ḥabib, Spain and Salonika (c. 1445-1515).

Even HaEzer, section of *Shulḥan Arukh* dealing with marriage, divorce, and related topics.

Geonim, heads of the academies of Sura and Pumbedita in Babylonia from the late 6th century to the mid-11th century.

Hagahot Maimoniyot, commentary on *Mishneh Torah,* by Rabbi Meir HaKohen, Germany, 14th century.

Hagahot Ram Arak, novellae on the Talmud by Rabbi Meir Arak, Poland, early 20th century.

Hagahot Ri Pik Berlin, Rabbi Yeshayahu Pik Berlin, Talmudic scholar, Breslau (1725-1799).

Halakhot Gedolot, a code of Halakhic decisions written in the Geonic period. This work has been ascribed to Sherira Gaon, Rav Hai Gaon, Rav Yehudah Gaon and Rabbi Shimon Kayyara.

Ḥamra Veḥaye, novellae on tractate *Sanhedrin,* by Rabbi Ḥayyim Benevisti, Turkey, 17th century.

Hayyim Shenayim Yeshalem, novellae on *Sanhedrin,* by Rabbi Shmuel Vital.

Ḥokhmat Manoaḥ, commentary on the Talmud by Rabbi Manoaḥ ben Shemaryah, Poland, 16th century.

Ḥoshen Mishpat, section of *Shulḥan Arukh* dealing with civil and criminal law.

Imrei Tzvi, novellae of the Talmud by Rabbi Tzvi Kohen, Vilna, 19th century.

Iyyun Ya'akov, commentary on *Ein Ya'akov*, by Rabbi Ya'akov bar Yosef Riesher, Prague, Poland, and France (d. 1733).

Keli Yakar, commentary on the Torah by Rabbi Shlomo Efrayim of Luntshitz, Poland (d. 1619)

Keneset HaGedolah (see *Shayarei Keneset HaGedolah*).

Kesef Mishneh, commentary on *Mishneh Torah,* by Rabbi Yosef Caro, author of *Shulḥan Arukh.*

Keset HaSofer, laws regarding the writing of Torah scrolls and mezuzahs, by Rabbi Shlomo Ganzfried, Hungary (19th century).

Ketzot HaḤoshen, novellae on *Shulḥan Arukh, Ḥoshen Mishpat,* by Rabbi Aryeh Leib Heller, Galicia (1754?-183).

Kos Yeshuot, novellae on the Talmud by Rabbi Shmuel HaKohen Shatin, Germany (d. 1719).

Leḥem Mishneh, commentary on the *Mishneh Torah,* by Rabbi Avraham di Boton, Salonica (1560-1609).

Lekaḥ Tov, Midrashim and commentary on the Torah by Rabbi Tuvyah the son of Rabbi Eliezer, Bulgaria (11th century).

Levush, abbreviation of *Levush Mordekhai,* Halakhic code by Rabbi Mordekhai Yaffe, Poland (1530-1612).

Magen Avraham, commentary on *Shulḥan Arukh, Oraḥ Hayyim,* by Rabbi Avraham HaLevi Gombiner, Poland (d. 1683).

Maggid Mishneh, commentary on *Mishneh Torah,* by Rabbi Vidal de Tolosa, Spain, 14th century.

Maharal, Rabbi Yehudah Loew ben Betzalel of Prague (1525-1631). Novellae on the Talmud.

Maharam Schiff, novellae on the Talmud by Rabbi Meir ben Ya'akov HaKohen Schiff (1605-1641), Frankfurt, Germany.

Maharik, Rabbi Yosef Kolon, France and Italy (c. 1420-1480). Responsa literature.

Maharsha, Rabbi Shmuel Eliezer ben Yehudah HaLevi Edels, Poland (1555-1631). Novellae on the Talmud.

Maharshal, Rabbi Shlomo ben Yeḥiel Luria, Poland (1510-1573). Novellae on the Talmud.

Maharshashakh, Rabbi Shmuel Shotten, Germany (17th century). Novellae on the Talmud.

Margoliyot HaYam, novellae on tractate *Sanhedrin* by Rabbi Reuben Margoliyot, Poland, 20th century.

Megaleh Amukot, Kabbalistic commentary on the Torah by Rabbi Natan Shapiro, Poland (1585-1633).

Meir Einei Soferim, laws regarding the writing of Torah scrolls, mezuzahs, and bills of divorce, by Rabbi David Krosik.

Meiri, commentary on the Talmud (called *Bet HaBeḥirah*), by Rabbi Menaḥem ben Shlomo, Provence (1249-1316).

Mekhilta, Halakhic Midrash on the Book of Exodus.

Melekhet Shlomo, commentary on the Mishnah by Rabbi Shlomo Adeni, Yemen and Israel (1567-1626).

Melo HaRo'im, commentary on the Talmud by Rabbi Ya'akov Tzvi Yolles, Poland (c. 1778-1825).

Menorat HaMa'or, Anthology of Midrashim, by Rabbi Yitzḥak Abohav (15th century).

Midrash Shir HaShirim Rabbah, Midrash on the Song of Songs.

Midrash Tanḥuma, see *Tanḥuma.*

Mishneh LeMelekh, commentary on *Mishneh Torah* by Rabbi Yehudah ben Shmuel Rosanes, Turkey (1657-1727).

Mishnah Berurah, commentary on *Shulḥan Arukh, Oraḥ Ḥayyim,* by Rabbi Yisrael Meir HaKohen, Poland (1837-1933).

Mitzpeh Eitan, glosses on the Talmud by Rabbi Avraham Maskileison, Byelorussia (1788-1848).

Nimmukei Yosef, commentary on *Hilkhot HaRif,* by Rabbi Yosef Ḥaviva, Spain, early 15th century.

Oraḥ Ḥayyim, section of *Shulḥan Arukh* dealing with daily religious observances, prayers, and the laws of the Sabbath and Festivals.

Pirkei DeRabbi Eliezer, Aggadic Midrash on the Torah.

Pitḥei Teshuvah, compilation of responsa literature on *Shulḥan Arukh* by Rabbi Avraham Tzvi Eisenstadt, Russia (1812-1868).

Ra'avad, Rabbi Avraham ben David, commentator and Halakhic authority. Wrote comments on *Mishneh Torah.* Provence (c. 1125-1198?).

Rabbenu Ḥananel (ben Ḥushiel), commentator on the Talmud, North Africa (990-1055).

Rabbenu Meshulam, French Tosafist, 12th century.

Rabbenu Sa'adya Gaon, scholar and author, Egypt and Sura, Babylonia (882-942).

Rabbenu Shimshon of Sens, Tosafist, France and Eretz Israel (late 12th-early 13th century).

Rabbenu Tam, commentator on the Talmud, Tosafist, France (1100-1171).

Rabbenu Yehonatan of Lunel, Yehonatan ben David HaKohen of Lunel, Provence, Talmudic scholar (c.1135-after 1210).

Rabbenu Yonah, see *Talmidei Rabbenu Yonah.*

Rabbenu Zeraḥyah HaLevi, author of *HaMa'or,* commentary on *Hilkhot HaRif.* Spain, 12th century.

Rabbi David Bonfil (Bonfied), commentary on tractate *Sanhedrin* by Rabbi David Bonfil (Bonfied), France, 11th century.

Rabbi David Pardo, novellae on the Talmud, Italy, 18th century.

Rabbi E. M. Horowitz, Rabbi Elazar Moshe Horowitz, novellae on the Talmud, Pinsk (19th century).

Rabbi Issac Ḥaver, novellae on the Talmud by Rabbi Issac Ḥaver, Poland, 18th century.

Rabbi Tzvi Ḥayyot (Chajes), Galician Rabbi, 19th century.

Rabbi Ya'akov Emden, Talmudist and Halakhic authority, Germany (1697-1776).

Rabbi Yehudah Almandri, author of commentary on *Rif,* tractate *Sanhedrin,* Syria, 13th century.

Rabbi Yeshayahu Pik Berlin, Talmudic scholar, Breslau (1725-1799).

Rabbi Yitzḥak Ibn Giyyat, Halakhist, Bible commentator and liturgical poet, Spain (1038-1089).

Rabbi Yosef of Jerusalem, French Tosafist of the twelfth and thirteenth centuries, France and Eretz Israel.

Rabbi Yoshiyah Pinto, Eretz Israel and Syria (1565-1648). Commentary on *Ein Ya'akov.*

Rabbi Zeraḥyah ben Yitzḥak HaLevi, Spain, 12th century. Author of *HaMa'or,* Halakhic commentary on *Hilkhot HaRif.*

Radak, Rabbi David Kimḥi, grammarian and Bible commentator, Narbonne, Provence (1160?-1235?).

Radbaz, Rabbi David ben Shlomo Avi Zimra, Spain, Egypt, Eretz Israel, and North Africa (1479-1574). Commentary on *Mishneh Torah.*

Raḥ, Rabbenu Ḥananel (ben Ḥushiel), commentator on the Talmud, North Africa (990-1055).

Ramah, novellae on the Talmud by Rabbi Meir ben Todros HaLevi Abulafiya, Spain (c. 1170-1244). See *Yad Ramah.*

Rambam, Rabbi Moshe ben Maimon, Rabbi and philosopher, known also as Maimonides. Author of *Mishneh Torah,* Spain and Egypt (1135-1204).

Ramban, Rabbi Moshe ben Naḥman, commentator on Bible and Talmud, known also as Naḥmanides, Spain and Eretz Israel (1194-1270).

Ran, Rabbi Nissim ben Reuven Gerondi, Spanish Talmudist (1310?-1375?).

Rash, Rabbi Shimshon ben Avraham, Tosafist, commentator on the Mishnah, Sens (late 12th- early 13th century).

Rashash, Rabbi Shmuel ben Yosef Shtrashun, Lithuanian Talmud scholar (1794-1872).

Rashba, Rabbi Shlomo ben Avraham Adret, Spanish Rabbi famous for his commentaries on the Talmud and his responsa (c. 1235-c.1314).

Rashbam, Rabbi Shmuel ben Meir, commentator on the Talmud, France (1085-1158).

Rashi, Rabbi Shlomo ben Yitzḥak, the paramount commentator on the Bible and the Talmud, France (1040-1105).

Rav Aha of Sabha, author of *She'iltot,* Babylonia, 8th century.

Rav Hai Gaon, Babylonian Rabbi, head of Pumbedita Yeshivah, 10th century.

Rav Natronai Gaon, of the Sura Yeshivah, 9th century.

Rav Sherira Gaon, of the Pumbedita Yeshivah, 10th century.

Rav Tzemaḥ Gaon, Tzemaḥ ben Ḥayyim, Gaon of Sura (889-895).

Rema, Rabbi Moshe ben Yisrael Isserles, Halakhic authority, Poland (1525-1572).

Responsa of Ḥatam Sofer, responsa literature by Rabbi Moshe Sofer (Schreiber), Pressburg (1763-1839).

Ri, Rabbi Yitzḥak ben Shmuel of Dampierre, Tosafist, France (died c. 1185).

Ri Almandri, Rabbi Yehudah Almandri. Author of commentary on *Rif,* tractate *Sanhedrin,* Syria, 13th century.

Ri Migash, Rabbi Yosef Ibn Migash, commentator on the Talmud, Spain (1077-1141).

Ri Yolles, Rabbi Ya'akov Tzvi Yolles, Talmudic scholar, Poland (c. 1778-1825).

Rif, Rabbi Yitzḥak Alfasi, Halakhist, author of *Hilkhot HaRif,* North Africa (1013-1103).

Rishonim, lit., "the first," meaning Rabbinic authorities active between the end of the Geonic period (mid-11th century) and the publication of *Shulḥan Arukh* (1555).

Ritva, novellae and commentary on the Talmud by Rabbi Yom Tov ben Avraham Ishbili, Spain (c. 1250-1330).

Riva, Rabbenu Yitzḥak ben Asher, Tosafist, novellae on tractate *Sanhedrin.*

Rosh, Rabbi Asher ben Yeḥiel, also known as Asheri, commentator and Halakhist, German and Spain (c. 1250-1327).

Sanhedrei Ketanah, novellae on tractate *Sanhedrin* by Rabbi Avraham Yehoshua Bornstein, Russia, 19th century.

Sefer Meir Einayim, see *Sma.*

Shakh (Siftei Kohen), commentary on the *Shulḥan Arukh* by Rabbi Shabbetai ben Meir HaKohen, Lithuania (1621-1662).

Shayarei Keneset HaGedolah, a Halakhic work by Rabbi Ḥayyim Benevisti, Turkey, 17th century.

Shelah (Shenei Luḥot HaBrit), an extensive work on Halakhah, ethics and Kabbalah by Rabbi Yeshayahu ben Avraham HaLevi Horowitz. Prague, Poland and Eretz Israel (c. 1565-1630).

She'eilot U'Teshuvot HaMibit, Responsa literature of Rabbi Moshe of Tirani, Sefad (1500-1580).

Shemot Rabbah, Midrash on the Book of Exodus.

Shulḥan Arukh, code of Halakhah by Rabbi Yosef Caro, b. Spain, active in Eretz Israel (1488-1575).

Sifrei, Halakhic Midrash on the Books of Numbers and Deuteronomy.

Sma, (Sefer Meirat Einaim), commentary on *Shulḥan Arukh, Ḥoshen Mishpat,* by Rabbi Yehoshua Falk Katz, Poland (c.1550-1614).

Smag, (Sefer Mitzvot Gedolot), an extensive work on the positive and negative commandments by Rabbi Moshe ben Ya'akov of Coucy, 13th century.

Talmid Rabbenu Peretz, commentary on the Talmud by the school of Rabbi Peretz of Corbiel, France (13th century)

Talmidei Rabbenu Yonah, commentary on *Hilkhot HaRif* by the school of Rabbi Yonah of Gerondi, Spain (1190-1263).

Tanḥuma, Midrash on the Five Books of Moses.

Tashbatz, Respona literature of Rabbi Shimon ben Tzemaḥ Duran, Spain and Algeria (1361-1444).

Taz, abbreviation for *Turei Zahav.* See *Turei Zahav.*

Tiferet Yisrael, commentary on the Mishnah, by Rabbi Yisrael Lipshitz, Germany (1782-1860).

Torat Ḥayyim, novellae on the Talmud by Rabbi Avraham Ḥayyim Shor, Galicia (d.1632).

Tosafot, collection of commentaries and novellae on the Talmud, expanding on Rashi's commentary, by the French-German Tosafists (12th and 13th centuries).

Tosafot Ḥadashim, commentary on the Mishnah by Rabbi Shimshon Bloch, Hamburg, Germany (d. 1737).

Tosefot Hokhmei Angli'a, collection of novellae on the Talmud by English Tosafists (13th century).

Tosefot Rabbenu Peretz, Tosefot of the school of Rabbi Peretz ben Eliyahu of Corbeil (d. 1295).

Tosefot Rosh, an edition based on *Tosefot Sens* by the *Rosh,* Rabbi Asher ben Yeḥiel, Germany and Spain (c. 1250-1327).

Tosefot Yom Tov, commentary on the Mishnah by Rabbi Yom Tov Lipman HaLevi Heller, Prague and Poland (1579-1654).

Tur, abbreviation of *Arba'ah Turim,* Halakhic code by Rabbi Ya'akov ben Asher, b. Germany, active in Spain (c. 1270-1343).

Tzofnat Pa'ane'aḥ, novellae and commentaries by Rabbi Yosef Rozin, Lithuania (1858-1936).

Yad Malakhi, a work on Talmudic and Halakhic methodology, by Rabbi Malakhi ben Ya'akov HaKohen, Italy (died c. 1785).

Yafeh Mar'eh, commentary on the Midrash by Rabbi Shmuel Yaffe, Turkey, 16th century.

Yalkut (see *Yalkut Shimoni*).

Yalkut Shimoni, Aggadic Midrash on the Bible.

Yefeh Enayim, cross-references and notes to the Jerusalem Talmud, by Rabbi Yeshayahu Pik Berlin, Breslau (1725-1799).

Yoreh De'ah, section of *Shulḥan Arukh* dealing mainly with dietary laws, interest, ritual purity, and mourning.

About the Type

This book was set in Leawood, a contemporary typeface designed by Leslie Usherwood. His staff completed the design upon Usherwood's death in 1984. It is a friendly, inviting face that goes particularly well with sans serif type.